THE UNITED NATIONS SERIES

ROBERT J. KERNER, GENERAL EDITOR

SATHER PROFESSOR OF HISTORY IN THE
UNIVERSITY OF CALIFORNIA

CZECHOSLOVAKIA
EDITED BY ROBERT J. KERNER

THE NETHERLANDS
EDITED BY BARTHOLOMEW LANDHEER

POLAND
EDITED BY BERNADOTTE E. SCHMITT

BELGIUM
EDITED BY JAN-ALBERT GORIS

CHINA
EDITED BY HARLEY FARNSWORTH MACNAIR

NEW ZEALAND
EDITED BY HORACE BELSHAW

BRAZIL
EDITED BY LAWRENCE F. HILL

AUSTRALIA
EDITED BY C. HARTLEY GRATTAN

YUGOSLAVIA
EDITED BY ROBERT J. KERNER

CANADA
EDITED BY GEORGE W. BROWN

CANADA

CANADA

Chapters by Edgar McInnis, James Wreford Watson, Gustave Lanctot, A. L. Burt, D. G. Creighton, C. P. Stacey, H. A. Innis, W. T. Easterbrook, A. W. Currie, Vernon C. Fowke, Benjamin H. Higgins, Arthur Lermer, R. MacGregor Dawson, Hugh McD. Clokie, K. Grant Crawford, Frank H. Underhill, Alexander Brady, Samuel Delbert Clark, Elizabeth S. L. Govan, Walter Herbert, Watson Kirkconnell, Arthur R. M. Lower, George P. de T. Glazebrook, John Bartlet Brebner, Frank A. Knox, F. H. Soward

Edited by GEORGE W. BROWN

Professor of History in the University of Toronto

UNIVERSITY OF CALIFORNIA PRESS
BERKELEY AND LOS ANGELES · 1950
CAMBRIDGE UNIVERSITY PRESS, LONDON

UNIVERSITY OF CALIFORNIA PRESS
BERKELEY AND LOS ANGELES
CALIFORNIA

CAMBRIDGE UNIVERSITY PRESS
LONDON, ENGLAND

PRINTED IN THE UNITED STATES OF AMERICA
BY THE VAIL-BALLOU PRESS, INC., BINGHAMTON, N.Y.

The United Nations Series

THE UNITED NATIONS SERIES *is dedicated to the task of mutual understanding among the Allies of the Second World War and to the achievement of successful coöperation in the peace. The University of California offered the first volumes of this series as a part of its contribution to the war effort of this state and nation and of the nations united in the greatest conflict known to history; it offers the later volumes, of which this is one, to the peace effort; and it heartily thanks the editors of the respective volumes and their collaborators for their devoted service and for their efforts to present an honest, sincere, and objective appraisal of the United Nations.*

ROBERT J. KERNER
General Editor

Contents

PAGE

CHAPTER VI

The Twentieth Century 124

By C. P. Stacey, O.B.E., B.A. (Toronto, Oxon.), Ph.D. (Princeton)

Colonel and Director, Historical Section, General Staff, Army Headquarters, Ottawa; Department of History, Princeton University, 1935–1940; author of *Canada and the British Army, 1846–1871* (1936); *The Military Problems of Canada* (1940); *Canada's Battle in Normandy* (1946); *The Canadian Army, 1939–1945: An Official Historical Summary* (1948); and of other works.

PART THREE: THE ECONOMY

CHAPTER VII

Fundamental and Historic Elements . . . 155

By H. A. Innis, M.A. (McMaster), Ph.D. (Chicago), F.R.S.C.

Professor of Political Economy, and Dean, School of Graduate Studies, University of Toronto; member of Royal Commission, Economic Enquiry, Nova Scotia, 1934; past president, Royal Society of Canada, Canadian Political Science Association, and Economic History Society; co-editor (with A. F. W. Plumptre), *The Canadian Economy and Its Problems* (1934); author of *A History of the Canadian Pacific Railway* (1923); *The Fur Trade in Canada* (1930); *The Cod Fisheries* (1940); and of other volumes.

and W. T. Easterbrook, B.A. (Manitoba), Ph.D. (Toronto)

Associate Professor of Economics, University of Toronto; formerly Lecturer in Economics, University of Manitoba; author of *Farm Credit in Canada* (1938); *Economic History of the North Pacific* (in preparation).

CHAPTER VIII

Eastern Canada 165

By A. W. Currie, B. Com. (Queen's), D. Com. Sc. (Harvard)

Associate Professor of Political Economy, University of Toronto; Associate Professor of Commerce, University of British Columbia, 1938–1945; Assistant to Director-General of Economic Research,

PART FOUR: POLITICAL AND CONSTITUTIONAL SCENE

PAGE

CHAPTER XI

The Federal Constitution 281

By R. MacGregor Dawson, M.A. (Dalhousie), D. Sc. (London), F.R.S.C.

Professor of Political Economy, University of Toronto; Royal Commissioner on Provincial Development, Nova Scotia, 1943–1945; past president, Canadian Political Science Association; on editorial committee, *Canadian Journal of Economics and Political Science,* 1936–1944; author of *The Principle of Official Independence* (1922); *The Development of Dominion Status, 1900–1936* (1937); *The Civil Service of Canada* (1939); *The Government of Canada* (1947); and of other works.

CHAPTER XII

The Machinery of Government 297

By Hugh McD. Clokie, M.A. (Oxon.)

Professor of Government, and head of Department of Political Science, University of Manitoba; author of *The Origin and Nature of Constitutional Government* (1936); *Canadian Government and Politics* (1944); and of numerous articles and pamphlets on international affairs and comparative government.

CHAPTER XIII

Local Government 314

By K. Grant Crawford, M.A. (Western Ontario)

Associate Professor, and Director of Institute of Local Government, Queen's University, Ontario; secretary-treasurer, Ontario Municipal Association, and Municipal Clerks and Finance Officers' Association of Ontario; City Clerk, London, Ontario, 1934–1944.

CHAPTER XIV

Political Parties and Ideas 331

By Frank H. Underhill, B.A. (Toronto), M.A. (Oxon.), F.R.S.C.

Professor of History, University of Toronto; Professor of History, University of Saskatchewan, 1914–1927; past president, Canadian

PART SIX: EXTERNAL RELATIONS

List of Illustrations

PLATES

(Following page 316)

MAPS IN TEXT

A POLITICAL MAP OF CANADA

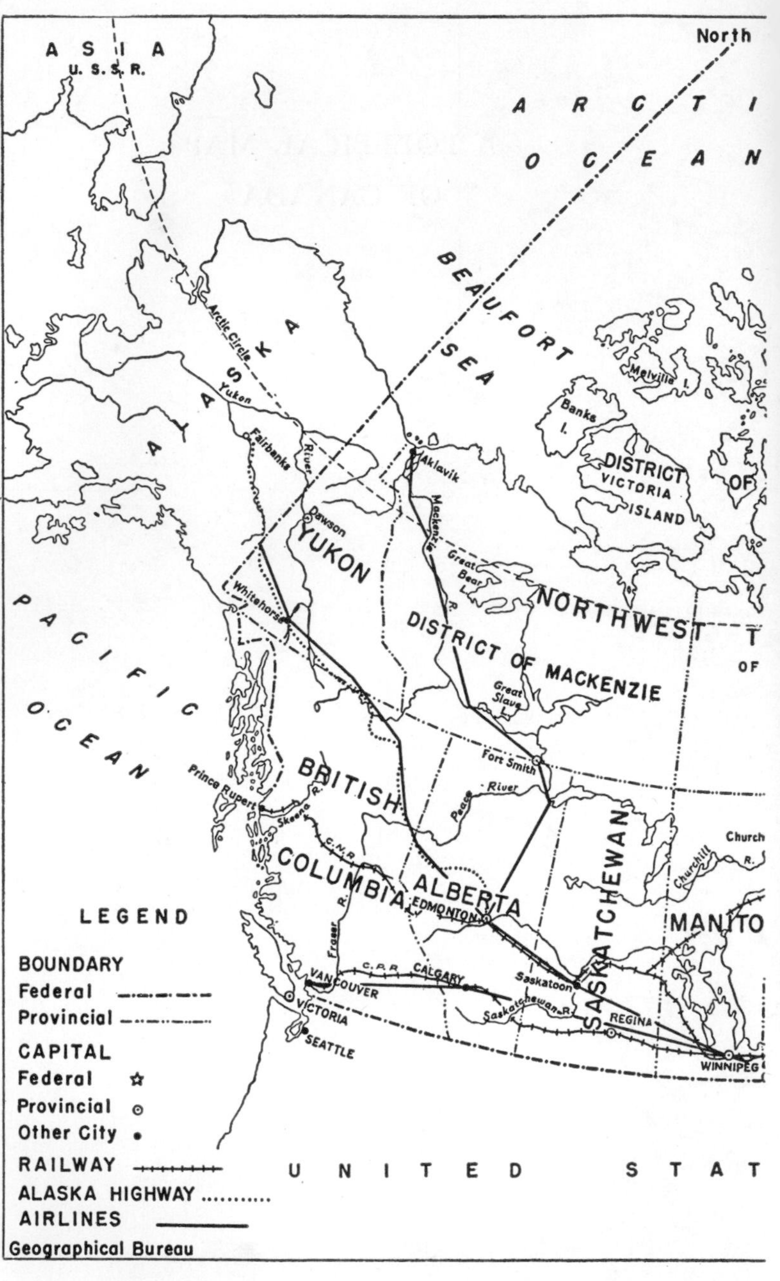
ASIA
U. S. S. R.
North
ARCTIC OCEAN
BEAUFORT SEA
ALASKA
Arctic Circle
Yukon River
Fairbanks
Aklavik
Mackenzie R.
Banks I.
Melville I.
DISTRICT OF
VICTORIA ISLAND
Dawson
YUKON
Great Bear
NORTHWEST T
Whitehorse
DISTRICT OF MACKENZIE
OF
PACIFIC OCEAN
Great Slave
Fort Smith
Peace River
Prince Rupert
Skeena R.
C.N.R.
BRITISH COLUMBIA
ALBERTA
EDMONTON
SASKATCHEWAN
Church
Churchill R.
MANITO
Fraser R.
C.P.R.
CALGARY
VANCOUVER
VICTORIA
SEATTLE
Saskatoon
Saskatchewan R.
REGINA
WINNIPEG
LEGEND
BOUNDARY
Federal
Provincial
CAPITAL
Federal
Provincial
Other City
RAILWAY
ALASKA HIGHWAY
AIRLINES
Geographical Bureau
UNITED STAT

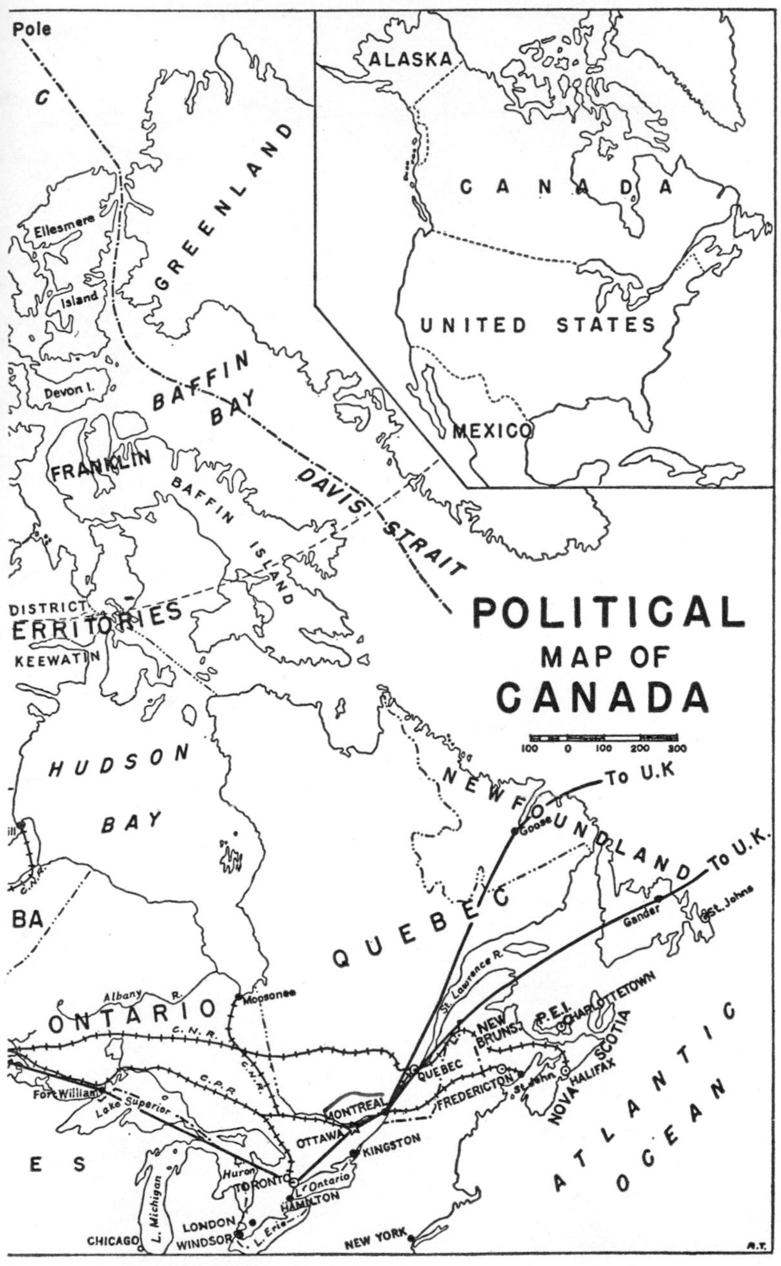
POLITICAL
MAP OF
CANADA
100 0 100 200 300
Pole
GREENLAND
Ellesmere
Island
Devon I.
BAFFIN
BAY
FRANKLIN
BAFFIN
ISLAND
DAVIS STRAIT
DISTRICT
ERRITORIES
KEEWATIN
HUDSON
BAY
NEWFOUNDLAND
Goose
To U.K
To U.K.
Gander
St. Johns
QUEBEC
St. Lawrence R.
ONTARIO
Albany R.
Moosonee
C.N.R.
C.P.R.
Fort William
Lake Superior
MONTREAL
QUEBEC
OTTAWA
KINGSTON
Huron
TORONTO
L. Ontario
HAMILTON
L. Michigan
LONDON
WINDSOR
L. Erie
CHICAGO
NEW YORK
FREDERICTON
St. John
NEW BRUNS.
P.E.I.
CHARLOTTETOWN
NOVA SCOTIA
HALIFAX
ATLANTIC
OCEAN
BA
ES
ALASKA
CANADA
UNITED STATES
MEXICO
R.T.

INTRODUCTION

Introduction

CANADA has achieved nationhood by processes at many points typically American, at others so sharply different from those of her neighbours that they mark her off as unique among the nations of the American hemisphere. On the one hand, like every American nation she has felt the full impact of the New World environment. To America, men and women brought not only their material possessions, but their habits, attitudes, and ambitions, and under the relentless pressure of geography and circumstance moulded them into new patterns of thought and action. So were formed all the varied societies of the New World, and Canada has shared fully in this typical American experience, evolving from her background of European and American origins her own institutions and ways of life and thought.

In her political development, on the other hand, Canada has diverged sharply from the American pattern. Alone among American nations she did not share in the revolutions which, in the fifty years following the Declaration of Independence, created over a score of American republics north and south. No difference in political thinking marked off Canada so sharply from her American neighbours, through the nineteenth century and indeed to our own day, as did this absence of the revolutionary tradition. To them, revolution and the assertion at one stroke of national sovereignty were the essential prerequisites of political growth, and the development of self-government without the revolutionary tradition was well-nigh incomprehensible. In sharp contrast, the changing British Empire of the nineteenth century was for Canada a framework within which the forces for nationalism were able to work towards fruition. Without that framework it is difficult to see how those forces, strong as they were, could have succeeded against obstacles of geography, cultural division, and local patriotism. The Confederation agreement itself, which in 1867 for the first time brought four provinces together into a national union, was carried through by an Imperial Act, which the "Fathers of Confederation," using a technique that was unprecedented, were themselves able to frame for submission to the British Parliament. Moreover, the full weight of British policy was thrown not only behind the acceptance of the Confederation agreement, but behind that remarkable series of decisions and accomplishments which within a generation carried the bounds of the new nation west and north to the Pacific and the Arctic. While this is by no means the whole story, it is scarcely too much to say that Canada gained self-government and an empire because she was herself part of an empire.

This revolution—for it was nothing less—by which Canada moved from colonialism to nationhood spanned a century. Writing in 1838, Lord Durham, in his famous *Report on the Affairs of British North America,* urged the possibility of creating a nation in the northern half of the continent. "These small and unimportant communities"—Upper and Lower Canada, Nova Scotia, New Brunswick, the Islands of Prince Edward and Newfoundland, to which he had been appointed as Governor General Extraordinary—could, he believed, be elevated "into a society having some objects of a national importance." In the perspective of a hundred years one wonders whether to be more surprised at the boldness or at the accuracy of Durham's judgement. Certainly there seemed little basis for it in 1838. Strung for over a thousand miles along a hostile frontier, divided by geographical barriers of sea and land, with thin and patchy strips of settlement, many of them scarcely beyond the pioneer stage, these scattered and isolated colonies had neither the common contacts nor the common experiences for national union. Two of them had just been torn by rebellions which were in fact little civil wars, and in one of these —Lower Canada—strife had flared up out of a bitter conflict of two apparently irreconcilable cultures, French and English. True, there were, as Durham pointed out, some common loyalties and political practices, and a common repulsion against absorption in the rapidly expanding continental empire of the United States. But all this was certainly little on which to base any hope of a strong and distinctive national development.

Durham's political solution for the problem of British North America was as simple as it was revolutionary. Urged on him first by a Canadian, Robert Baldwin, it was the application to the colonies of the system of Cabinet, or "responsible," government on the British model—the logical and complete extension of the parliamentary principle overseas which had begun more than two hundred years earlier in the first elected assembly of colonial Virginia.

Simple as it was in principle, Durham's proposal of responsible government was anything but simple in practice. In fact, it was incapable of defence by any system of legalistic logic. How could final authority be divided between the King's ministers in London and the ministers of the Crown in an overseas colony? Durham himself suggested that imperial interests in the colonies be hedged about and set apart. Within the Cabinet system, however, lay the seeds of full self-government. Once established, as it was in the 1840's, responsible government, given favourable circumstances, was bound to work itself out to completion. The process by which Canada moved towards nationhood and complete self-government was thus not theoretical or legalistic but pragmatic and intuitive. To Canadians themselves it is perhaps not surprising that Canada has always been more concerned with the substance of self-government than with the technicalities or even the symbols of national sovereignty. Step by step the evolution towards national sovereignty took place, and now that it is in fact complete it is difficult to say when it was accomplished. Vestigial remnants of apparent colonialism lingered on paradoxically into the time when Canada was accepted as a "middle power" among the nations of the world. This growth of responsible government with all its implications is a commonplace of Canadian history, but it is little wonder that it has remained a mystery to those who have had no practical knowledge of it.

Even Canadians themselves have not, however, usually realized how important was Canada's part in the transformation of the British Empire. That transformation from the mercantilism of the early nineteenth century to the free association of nations in the British Commonwealth has been one of the central facts in the history of the modern world, and at every stage of it Canada's influence has been a powerful, sometimes a decisive, factor. Responsible government, once accepted for British North America in the 1840's, was of necessity extended elsewhere, and worked itself out in varying degrees and ways not only in Canada but in Australia, New Zealand, South Africa, India, and other parts of the Empire. By the early years of the twentieth century the Empire was already becoming in embryo a kind of international system within the larger framework of world affairs, thus foreshadowing the merging of the British Commonwealth into the international organizations which emerged from the First and Second World Wars. Canada's experience in this evolutionary process and her traditional emphasis on the substance of autonomy rather than on the technicalities of sovereignty has perhaps made it easier for her than for some others to adjust herself to a world in which national sovereignty in its old sense has become an anachronism and new concepts and practices are being hammered out by the pressure of relentless forces and events.

In Canada's internal development no pattern has been more persistent and important than the survival of two cultures, French and English—one of them, the French, being particularly associated with a province, Quebec. The results of these bi-cultural relations pervade in greater or less degree every aspect of Canadian life, and give a character to Canadian affairs that is sharply different, for instance, from that in the United States, where nationalism and democracy, in spite of an emphasis on individualism, are marked by concepts of uniformity and standardization that are impossible in a bi-cultural nation. It is true that the union of French-speaking and English-speaking Canada is and always has been a marriage of convenience rather than one of romantic attachment, but it is none the less valid and has withstood repeated and severe strains. The marriage is, indeed, not merely one of convenience. English Canada, not less than French Canada, has had the determination to survive, the will to resist absorption, and only through this union could each achieve its purpose.

Canada's experience in bi-cultural relations is not unique. It is but the Canadian version of a problem which forces itself increasingly on the modern world: the problem of harmonizing the particular and the general, of finding means for the preservation of special loyalties and interests within the framework of wider coöperation. Signs are not lacking that there is a deeper appreciation of such considerations in the relations of French-speaking and English-speaking Canadians than there has been at many points in the past.

Canada is thus the product of the delicate balancing of diverse forces and problems. She has had to meet at one and the same time the baffling difficulties of geography and sectionalism, the necessity of developing and harmonizing two types of culture, and the problem of reaching political maturity within a complex and rapidly changing network of external relations. Few countries have had to face a more tangled pattern within so brief a space of time. It is not surprising that Canada's most distinctive accomplishments have thus far been in her material and institutional development—in the creation of a Canadian economy with the transportation systems and other agencies necessary to support it, and in the evolution of her political, religious, educational, and other institutions. There have, however, been other achievements and, especially during the past generation, signs of a maturing cultural development.

It is too much to expect that a single volume will touch adequately on every point worthy of note, but it is the hope of its authors that it will present a picture of mid-twentieth-century Canada that is understandable and in spots even illuminating. While, however, the picture has a contemporary interest, and in places the factual material has a relation to the moment of writing, the attempt has been made to emphasize fundamental and historic tendencies, and to make clear the persistent characteristics which mark the course of Canadian development.

On his own behalf the editor wishes to express his warm appreciation to those who have been associated with him: to Professor Kerner, the General Editor of the United Nations Series, for his unflagging patience and encouragement; to the contributors for their coöperation in the face of a vigorously wielded editorial pencil; to the staff of the Toronto Public Libraries for bibliographical information; and to the Department of External Relations and the Geographical Bureau of the Department of Mines and Resources for assistance in connexion with illustrations and maps.

George W. Brown

Toronto, Canada
January, 1950

Part One

THE SETTING

CHAPTER I

The People

BY EDGAR MCINNIS

IN THE BASIC PATTERN of Canadian life, one of the most pervasive factors is the racial dualism which colours almost every phase of national activity. It is a factor which stems inescapably from the very fact of Canada's existence as an independent community. Geography and history have combined to produce a situation in which the two paramount stocks, British and French, have had no other choice than to live side by side as distinct peoples within a single state. Neither of them has proved strong enough to absorb, or even to impose its outlook and standards and policies on, the other. The price of political unity has been the acceptance of ethnic and cultural diversity, with all that that implies in the way of concessions and compromise.

This situation, so striking to even the casual observer, has frequently obscured the fact that the population of Canada is multi-racial rather than merely bi-racial in its origins. Slightly less than half of her 13,500,000 people are of British stock. The French account for another 30 per cent. The remainder—one-fifth of the whole—is made up of people drawn from all the diverse races of Europe, with a sprinkling from those of Asia as well.

Looked at from this aspect, the fundamental dualism of the Dominion can be seen to lie in cultural rather than in purely racial divergences. Ethnic differences gain their real significance when they are joined to differences in language and religion, in social customs and historical traditions, which combine to produce differing concepts of the type of society towards which the community should strive. None the less, there is a very real sense in which these divisions follow racial lines. In the history of the Dominion the contrast has been between the English concept of liberty and progress and the French emphasis on authority and stability. Whatever variants have been introduced by other racial elements—and many of them have made their own distinctive contribution to Canadian life—have still been of secondary significance. Apart from a few special groups, even those who have preserved their own folk-ways have been drawn into an allegiance, tacit or overt, to one of the two dominant cultures, and most frequently to that of the English-speaking population.

The present population structure of the Dominion is of relatively recent date. Even the balance between English and French, viewed in historical perspective, is a comparatively modern development. It is easy to forget that the growth of an English-speaking community in central Canada has taken place during the span of two reasonably long lifetimes. The major part of the settlement in the West has occurred within the past half-century. The foundations of urban industrial development were laid during the nineteenth century, but the transformation of Canada into an important industrial state dates from little more than a generation. In the course of this evolution, old balances have shifted and new elements have been injected, and it is only within the past twenty years that a measure of stability—perhaps even now a purely temporary one—has been evident in the ethnic composition of the Dominion.

On the eve of the American Revolution the nucleus of what is now Canada lay in two diverse and widely separated regions.[1] On the east coast the province of Nova Scotia had recently undergone an upheaval as a result of political and strategic pressures. The first roots of English settlement were planted in 1749 with the founding of Halifax. Efforts to draw Protestant settlers from continental Europe brought Germans to Lunenburg and other coastal towns. The expulsion of the Acadians, which began in 1755, uprooted the greater part of the old French population; but a remnant evaded deportation, and some of the exiles drifted back in later years. Meanwhile, however, the vacant Acadian farms were seized by New Englanders, who speedily became the

[1] For notes to chapter i see page 571.

leading element in the population. A migration of Scotch-Irish from Ulster took place in the 'sixties. Highlanders from Scotland planted settlements during the next decade in Prince Edward Island and along the Gulf shore of Nova Scotia. Within a quarter of a century the region of the Maritime Provinces was transformed from a purely French community to one that was multi-racial in its composition.

In contrast, the settled area along the St. Lawrence remained almost wholly French. A few hundred British merchants settled in Quebec and Montreal after the Conquest. A few discharged soldiers took up farms or adopted the congenial occupation of tavern-keepers. Numerically these new arrivals formed a tiny minority in the midst of a solidly French community—a community which already had a long tradition and a sense of its distinctive character. Emigration from France virtually ceased in 1672, yet by 1765 the population had increased more than tenfold to approximately 70,000, and almost every habitant could trace his Canadian ancestry for several generations. Long residence in a new land had created an embryo nation whose sense of an identity separate from the mother country was already full-blown. The *Canadiens* were French in origin and heritage, yet vigorously Canadian in interests and outlook.

This whole balance was drastically changed by the outcome of the American Revolution. The Loyalists who flooded into Nova Scotia brought changes which were perhaps more significant for the political temper than for the racial balance of that region. The new influx was American in origin; but, in contrast to the sense of kinship which the earlier arrivals retained with New England, the new refugees were divided by bitterness and hostility from their former compatriots, and even seemed inclined to extend those sentiments to the inhabitants of Yankee stock who were already planted in Nova Scotia. Within a short time the Loyalist tradition and attitude were established as basic elements in the outlook of the Maritime Provinces, modified by the practical considerations arising from the continued trade connexions between that region and New England. The racial composition of the province was affected chiefly by being weighted still further on the Anglo-American side, thus increasing the existing tendency to absorb the other European racial stocks, although the Acadians still clung stubbornly to the position of a separate minority with their own language and customs.

In the St. Lawrence region a wholly different situation arose. The effect of the new influx was not so much to alter the character of the existing French community as to change its position by creating an English-speaking community alongside it. The French population retained its compactness and its distinctive character. The new arrivals, with relatively few exceptions, planted themselves in regions which were almost untouched by French settlement—the north bank of Lake Ontario and the upper St. Lawrence, the Niagara peninsula, the fringe along the American border that was to evolve into the Eastern Townships of Quebec. Racial dualism became an established fact with the failure of old inhabitants and new arrivals to find a common basis which would weld them into a single cohesive community.

The years that followed brought other contrasts between the Maritime Provinces and the St. Lawrence region. In the former the arrival of the Loyalists was, for all practical purposes, the end of immigration from what was now the United States. From then on, such immigration as took place came almost entirely from the British Isles. In the period before 1815 the chief source was the Highlands of Scotland, where an agricultural revolution had been driving distressed crofters to lands overseas. During this same period, however, a steady stream of American settlers was flowing into the Ontario peninsula—the northern fringe of the migration that was spreading beyond the Alleghenies to populate the American Middle West. Loyalists were followed by land-seekers who strengthened and extended the Anglo-American character of the new settlements in Upper Canada.

The American Revolution had thus a decisive influence on the lines of Canadian development. The War of 1812 marked another significant though less drastic change in pattern. The tide of immigration from the United States ebbed after 1815; the real immigration from the British Isles began. The effects of the Industrial Revolution, accentuated by the dislocation that followed the Napoleonic Wars, brought unemployment and distress to large sections of the British population. For a full generation, economic pressure at home sent hundreds of thousands annually to start a new life abroad, and Canada received a share of the migration that was flowing still more strongly to the United States. Starving hand-loom weavers and unemployed artisans, discharged soldiers and retired naval officers, English farmers and Irish paupers, all contributed to the stream. The former trickle from England was greatly augmented, and to the Scottish immigration which was already under way there was now added a growing volume of Catholic Irish fleeing from rack-rents and starvation. Small numbers of settlers from the countries of north-west Europe added an element of diversity, but the overwhelming majority of new settlers were of British stock. The first census of the Dominion in 1871 showed that over nine-tenths of the population was of either British or French origin; and in spite of the influx of the previous half-century, four-fifths of the inhabitants were Canadian by birth.

Confederation in 1867 was followed by Canada's acquisition of the prairie West, and it was the West that first attracted any substantial body of settlers from the European continent. The final quarter of the nineteenth century saw a new wave of transatlantic migration which for the first time drew heavily on the countries of eastern and south-eastern Europe. Economic unrest, racial oppression, and religious persecution contributed to the movement. To most of the migrants the United States appeared as the promised land; but Canada lay on the fringe of this as of earlier migrations, and the appearance of Icelanders and Scandinavians and German-speaking Mennonites from the Volga as pioneers on the Canadian prairies foreshadowed an increasing racial diversity.

It was, however, the closing years of the century that inaugurated a new stage in the growth of Canada's population. The virtual disappearance of free land in the United States swung the tide of settlement north to the Canadian prairies. The development of new mining areas, the expansion of forest industries, and the new outburst of railway construction brought a rapid increase in Canada's industrial production. The search for settlers, for construction labourers, for workers in factories and mines, was actively pursued by public authorities as well as by private interests. The majority of the immigrants were still akin to the existing stocks. The wave of American pioneer settlement flowed north across the border into the last remaining segment of the fertile western plains, bringing with it many returning Canadians who had gained pioneering experience in the American West. Across the Atlantic, the British Isles and the countries of north-west Europe remained preferred sources of immigrants. None the less, the influx contained a significant proportion of racial groups, many of which were completely new to Canada. The subject races of western and southern Russia, the Hungarians and the various Slavic groups of the old polyglot Habsburg Empire, the diverse nationalities of the Balkans and the eastern Mediterranean, all had a share in the settlement of the prairies and the growth of Canada's industrial and commercial centres.

In 1900 there were 41,000 immigrants to Canada; in 1913 the new arrivals numbered over 400,000. This was the climax of a decade during which nearly 2,500,000 people—a figure equal to nearly half the population of Canada at the beginning of the century—came to the Dominion. The outbreak of war in 1914 caused a drastic decline in the number of entrants; and, although immigration was resumed in the 'twenties, it never again reached its pre-war proportions. The depression of the 'thirties, accompanied as it was by new and stringent regulations, reduced the influx to a mere trickle, and marked the end of a major phase in Canada's population growth.

The effect of these fluctuations on the racial balance can be seen in the census figures since the beginning of the century. Canada's population grew from 5,371,315 in 1901 to 11,506,655 in 1941. At the beginning of the period the two major groups, British and French, constituted 88 per cent of the population. Forty years later their proportion, in spite of the fact that their numbers had doubled, had declined to 80 per cent. During the same period the percentage of native-born declined from 87 per cent to a low point of 77.75 per cent in 1921, remained virtually stable for the next decade, and then reflected the decline of immigration in a rise to 82.46 per cent in 1941. Not least significant, the proportion of those born abroad in lands other than the British Isles and the United States, which had been negligible in 1871 and stood at 2.80 per cent in 1901, had reached 7.50 per cent in 1931, and even the decline during the subsequent decade when immigration was negligible still left it at 6.10 per cent.

Simultaneously, other important changes were taking place in the pattern of Canadian life. Even while the settlement of the prairie farming region was lifting Canada into the ranks of the major wheat-producing countries of the world, she was also being

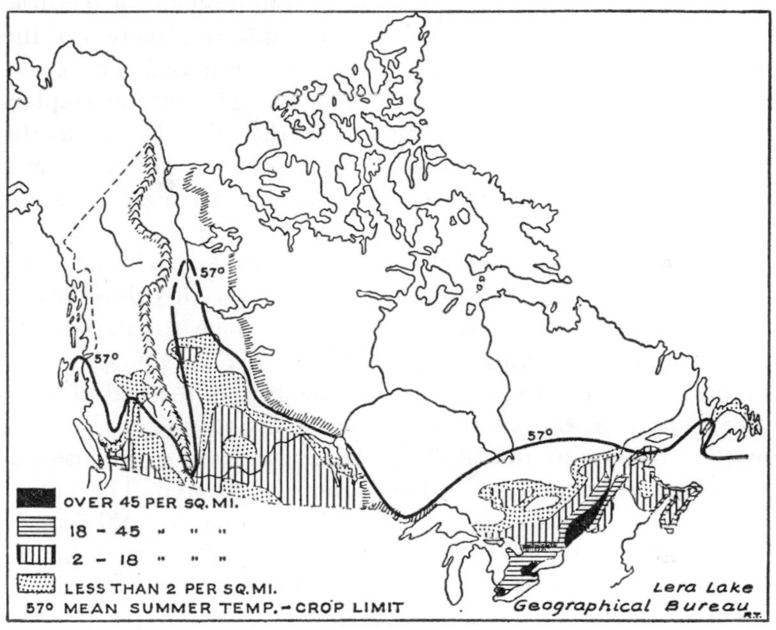

POPULATION OF CANADA

transformed from a rural to a predominantly urban nation. The growth of agriculture carried with it a stimulus to commerce, to manufacturing, to finance and transportation. The production demands of the First World War accentuated the trend. In the early 1920's the urban population reached a figure in excess of the rural, and during the subsequent decade the towns and cities absorbed three-quarters of the increase in Canada's population. In 1901 only Toronto and Montreal had more than 100,000 inhabitants. By 1931 there were seven cities in this class, Montreal had a population of over 800,000, and Toronto had tripled in size to reach 630,000.

It is significant that this trend continued steadily throughout the period between wars in spite of the fact that employment in agriculture, manufacturing, and trade showed relatively little change. Two factors in particular contributed to this result. On the one hand was the increasing mechanization of agriculture, which, like technological advances in industry, increased the productive capacity of the individual and decreased the need—and to a considerable extent the opportunity—for the employment of more people on the farms. On the other hand was the growth of the service occupations as a feature of urban life and their absorption of a large part of the urban increase during this period.

Then came the impact of the Second World War, with demands on Canada's productive resources that far exceeded those of the earlier conflict. War industry provided a new urban magnet. Employment in manufacturing, which stood at 543,000 at the outbreak of war, had risen to over 1,200,000 by the end of 1945. The movement of population from farms to cities, already a marked feature in the older provinces of eastern and central Canada, now became noticeable in the West as well. The Prairie Provinces began to lose population to the cities of central Canada and British Columbia; the drain on the older rural areas was accentuated at the same time. "Far more than the total natural increase of the farm areas," it was stated, "moved to urban places. For the first time in the history of Canada the total population of farm counties seems to be falling."[2] The situation was initially the product of extraordinary war conditions; but the permanent effect of the war on the balance between agriculture and industry, while it cannot yet be estimated conclusively, is likely to be shown in a continuation of the urbanizing process as part of the new phase into which the war has thrust the Canadian economy.

The first half of the twentieth century thus saw the introduction of new and significant factors into Canada's economic and cultural structure. The consequences were not merely an increase in racial diversification and a shift in the urban-rural balance. The changes also held important implications which affected the relative positions of the two major races in the Dominion and the prospects for a modification of the cultural cleavage by which they were divided.

The solidarity of French Canada is one of the basic themes in Canadian history. It rests not merely on race but on a distinctive set of institutions and traditions. Putting it again in the form of a rough generalization, it might be said that while the British element places the chief emphasis on progress, the French are more concerned with stability. There has been no lack of individual initiative in French Canada from the days of the *coureurs de bois* to the present time. Yet such a feature as the strength of the Catholic Church, with its insistence on authority and discipline, is symbolic of the spirit pervading the community. On the one hand its influence has inculcated and preserved these qualities; on the other, the devotion of the French-Canadian population to the Church shows how well that institution expresses the temper and outlook of the people. In particular, the importance of the family as an institution is an article of faith which finds the teaching of the Church in perfect harmony with the traditional social structure, and gives to this feature a significance different in the scope of its implications from that which attaches to it in most of the other sections of Canada.

Not only are the French traditions those of a long-established community whose essential composition has been little changed during three centuries. They are also the expression of a community that was primarily rural in its structure. The farm and the village as the bases of social and economic life, the family and the parish as basic social institutions, were determining factors in the French-Canadian outlook. Other groups in Canada also had a rural outlook and attached importance to the ties of family and religion, but the close interaction of all these factors in French Canada produced a type of culture which was distinct from that of the rest of the continent. And as the French felt themselves increasingly a minority in North America, they became increasingly concerned to defend their peculiar way of life against the inroads of the alien civilization that was pressing upon them. Race and religion became each the handmaid of the other in maintaining solidarity, and language was made the main instrument of a determined separatism from the Anglo-Saxon world and its influences.[3]

These divergences had important manifestations in the economic sphere. Indeed, one of the virtues which is frequently attributed to the French Canadian is his indifference to material wealth. This view needs some qualification before acceptance. Many of the habitants spring from Norman peasant stock—a race whose proverbial frugality sometimes borders on avarice. Yet here, too, the desire for stability and security tempers the worldly ambition of many French Canadians. The family farm is the basis of the rural economy; the small family business is characteristic of commercial life in the towns and villages. A recent observer quotes a *curé* as admonishing his flock: "The patriotic way for the true French Canadian to live is to save and become a small proprietor. English methods are not ours. The French became great by small savings and small business."[4] In the professions as well as in commerce, much the same outlook is to be found—an outlook not too remote from that of the middle-class *rentier* in France itself.

As a result, large-scale enterprise is almost entirely in the hands of the English-speaking element. It is they who have control of or access to substantial amounts of capital and credit, and who are willing, as most of the French are not, to accept the risks attached to large-scale ventures. Thus, while French enterprise remains chiefly local, the British control those enterprises that are national in their scope—the chief manufacturing concerns, the main establishments in trade and transportation, the large units in the forest and mining industries.[5] Quebec markets are served largely by the goods of non-French manufacturers; Quebec's resources in timber and minerals and water-power have been exploited by non-French capital; Quebec workers find employment in firms the ownership and management of which are looked upon as alien. The consequences of cultural separatism extend beyond exclusion from ownership and control of the leading business enterprises. A system of higher education centring around the classical college offers limited opportunities for training in science and engineering. It is the older traditional professions such as law and medicine that attract the educated French Canadians. They have left almost entirely to their English-speaking compatriots the field for trained technicians that is so important in the modern industrial world, as well as the newer field for administrative specialists which the expanding sphere of government action makes increasingly significant.

This situation has a direct bearing on the relations of the newer stocks to the two older races. Strictly from the cultural point of view, there is no reason why many immigrant groups from Europe should not gravitate to the French rather than to the British community. Catholic groups such as the Poles, and still more the Italians, have far more natural affinities with the French than with an Anglo-Saxon Protestant culture. When such groups find opportunities for residence and livelihood within a French district, their absorption takes place with relative ease.[6]

These qualifications, however, go to the root of the matter. For most of the new comers the road of opportunity leads to English-speaking Canada. The majority of the French-Canadian population is concentrated in the single geographic area of Quebec and the adjacent districts in Ontario and New Brunswick. That region provides relatively few opportunities for new settlers. Some may find employment in the mines or the forest industries, but the number is almost negligible. Out of 112,000 Italians in Canada in 1941, for instance, only 28,000 were in the Province of Quebec, and nearly 24,000 of these were in the city of Montreal, which is a leading centre of English business interests.[7] For Jews, the largest minority group in the metropolis, the figures were 170,000 for all Canada, 66,000 for Quebec Province, and 51,000 for Montreal; for them, far more than for the Italians, the tendency has been to form links with the English rather than the French element in the bi-racial metropolis.[8] In the Maritime Provinces and the West, though scattered French-Canadian communities exist, they are seldom large enough to compete in absorptive power with the English-speaking population that surrounds them.

Thus the fact of geographical solidarity, which has been of great value to the French in their effort to maintain a separate identity, serves as an obstacle to any significant recruitment of strength from among the newer immigrants. This could be achieved only by the development of some strong counter-attraction to the Anglo-Saxon environment in which most of the newer arrivals find themselves. As things stand, the pull is almost wholly in the other direction. French cultural attraction is not strong enough to offset the overwhelming economic attraction of the English-speaking community. The great majority of the new comers settled in the Western Provinces. Most of the remainder went to the cities of central Canada. For both, English was the language of communication with their neighbours, the essential medium for business dealings, the necessary foundation for advancement in every important field of action, and often for the securing of any sort of employment. It is significant that of those groups which acquire or already possess a knowledge of the French language, as do many of the Italians and Belgians, nearly all learn English as well.

This phenomenon is even more striking among the French themselves. Over a million out of three and a half million French are bilingual; less than a quarter of a million out of nearly six million British can speak both French and English. This is not purely the result of a greater adeptness on the part of the French Canadians or of a misguided resistance to the use of any language other than English on the part of those of British stock. Both these factors exist, but they are not the determinants. The British have little opportunity to use French in ordinary daily intercourse, and even less incentive. Large numbers of the French have both, and the need has increased with the growing urbanization and industrialization of Quebec. "For many of the French, in short, English is a necessity, either in dealing with their superiors at work or with customers and clients. The English in industry are so placed that they need not speak French to please or satisfy anyone."[9]

Such factors, important as they are, have not eliminated cultural and racial diversity. French Canada has maintained her sense of cohesion and distinctiveness throughout a century of Canada's growth as a commercial and industrial nation. Finns and Ukrainians do not at once lose their separate racial identities in their new cultural and linguistic environment. None the less, the barriers are unavoidably weakened by these developments. The use of a common language, the competition (and still more, where it exists, the coöperation) within a common economic structure, inevitably create cultural bridges which blur the lines of division. In the modern industrial cities it is more difficult for a minority group to maintain its self-contained character through successive generations than it is in the older type of rural communities; and even these communities are far more open to outside influences through such media as the press and radio and automobile than they were at the beginning of the century.

Internal factors arising from the evolution of the Canadian economy have thus resulted in trends which, potentially at least, are influences on the side of a greater national coherence. External factors have also played their part, and chief among them is the constant and pervasive influence of the United States. The proximity of that country, with its much larger population and more advanced economic structure, has been one of the determining elements in Canadian history. Here, too, the influence has been changed in both nature and degree by the increased urbanization of the Dominion and the growth of modern facilities for the exchange of both products and ideas.

The fact that Canada is a North American country would by itself account for many similarities in the conditions on either side of the international boundary. The advance of pioneer settlement, the exploitation of the chief natural resources, the construction of a transportation system across the breadth of the continent—these and similar tasks confronted both nations and favoured the development of similar techniques. Not only did Canadians borrow freely from American experience; much of that experience was carried directly to Canada by migrating Americans. Successive waves of settlers, from the New Englanders who helped to colonize Nova Scotia to the experienced pioneer farmers who contributed to the settlement of the Canadian prairies, brought to the Canadian community a vitally important element that did much to shape the outlook and methods and living habits of the Canadian people.

Hardly less important was the flow of Canadians into the United States. For more than a century Canada has been a land of simultaneous immigration and emigration to an extent that is unique among modern states. While new comers were pouring in from the British Isles and the continent of Europe—some of them to pause only briefly before resuming their migration southward—many native-born Canadians were seeking new opportunities in the larger and more diversified community across the border. This movement too had its influence on Canadian life. Large numbers of Canadians—probably the great majority of them—had ties of blood with relatives in the United States. Interest in conditions there—conditions which in many aspects had a vital bearing on Canada's own prospect—was heightened by the sense of personal connexion, and perhaps even more by the knowledge that the United States offered alternative opportunities to those which Canadians might find at home. In spite of political separation, factors such as these kept alive an underlying sense of the essential unity of the continent, and encouraged the maintenance of a basic similarity in the social and economic structure of the two countries.[10]

The greater production facilities and more advanced techniques which at an early stage made the United States important as a source of manufactured goods for the Canadian market extended also to the cultural and intellectual sphere. The media of mass entertainment and information that developed in the United States were on a scale which Canada could not match. With no language barrier and few cultural obstacles, it was natural for English-speaking Canada to be receptive towards these as towards other types of American products. American news services, American books and periodicals, American stage productions, attained a predominance that was only slightly restricted by contributions from Canadian and British sources. With the coming of the motion picture and the radio, American influences became even more wide-spread and pervasive, reaching not only the mass population of the chief cities but small towns and many rural areas as well.

The impact has been felt by both racial groups, though in different degrees. To the French, clinging to their distinctive culture, American influences have seemed not only alien but dangerous in a way that has little real parallel for English-speaking Canada. The deliberate effort to strengthen the barrier of language against outside influences has been all the more determined because of the fear of Americanization and the sense of the strong and constant pressure to which French Canada, a small racial and cultural island in the predominantly Anglo-Saxon society of North America, is inevitably subjected. French resistance has been only partially successful. American goods, American fashions, and American popular periodicals (often of the cheapest and least edifying type) exert their attractions over French Canadians; American motion pictures and radio programmes reach wide audiences in spite of the encouragement of French films and the existence of a French-language network of radio stations. Bilingualism in French Canada opens the door still wider to these influences, and even the French Canadian who knows no English may still be entertained by American films and illustrated magazines, or insensibly influenced by French-Canadian newspapers, the contents of which, from news dispatches to advertisements, are often American in character and even in origin. Here, too, the growing urbanization of French Canada has facilitated the spread of new influences which are at variance with older traditions and which further contribute to the blurring of the lines of division between the two major races in the Dominion.

In the face of the internal divisions and external pressures which have marked the progress of the Dominion towards nationhood, the development of a distinct Canadian community is no small achievement. The very fact that this aim has been consciously pursued and successfully realized testifies to an underlying unity of purpose that has proved stronger than any racial divergences.

The initial basis of the Canadian community has unquestionably been a determination to remain independent of the United States. The many similarities in the structure of the two communities, the closeness of their economic relations, the strong cultural influences from the American side—all these have served to strengthen rather than weaken resistance to political absorption. Canadians as individuals have felt no insuperable objections to becoming residents and citizens of the United States; Canadians as a body have stoutly resisted the incorporation of their country into the American union, whether by peaceful amalgamation or by force of arms. The threat of forcible conquest has long since abated, and with it the sense of an urgent need to subordinate internal differences to a united stand against external danger. Even the possibility of peaceful absorption, however, has kept alive an apprehension sufficiently strong and persistent to serve as a national bond. Undoubtedly the emotion has operated more strongly on the French than on the British side. Canadians of British stock, closer to Americans in language and general outlook, have on occasion felt that their special interests might possibly be served best by a union with their more powerful neighbour. But the periodic emergence of annexationist sentiments has never been wide-spread or sustained enough to hold much prospect of realization. For British and French alike, the desire for political independence has been the prime factor compelling them to join in the pursuit of a common destiny.

This factor has operated in relation not only to the United States but also to Great Britain. In the latter, the motives have been less urgent and the manifestations less vigorous. Many of the French have been restrained by the feeling that the British connexion has in more than one respect operated as a safeguard to their cultural autonomy. On the Anglo-Canadian side, sentiment has been added to interest as a deterrent to drastic action. None the less, the steady evolution towards full national stature has been an expression of a common desire on the part of the majority of Canadians to secure unhampered control of their own affairs. They might differ on the extent to which some formal ties with Britain should be retained. They might find it difficult to agree on the kind of nation they wanted to build when they were free to make their own decisions. Yet the difficulties arising from internal division have not prevented the steady growth of a determination that whatever decision may be taken, it shall be taken by Canadians themselves.

The fact is that a sense of common Canadianism does not depend for its strength on a concept of national uniformity. Indeed, its effectiveness is all the more remarkable in the light of the limitations imposed on its application by racial and sectional diversities. Yet there is obviously a point beyond which these differences could not be multiplied or extended without stultifying the sense of a common national purpose. The broader the area of common outlook and agreement between British and

French, and the closer the identity of the newer racial groups with this common ground, the fewer will be the internal strains on the Canadian structure.

In the latter respect the record of the older provinces is of hopeful augury. Their racially composite character has presented few permanent barriers to social homogeneity. It is sometimes overlooked that even the British people come from divergent racial stocks and that the divergences were reflected among the immigrants to Canada. The Irish who fled the repression of an English government and the grinding exploitation of English landlords had relatively little in common with the emigrants from England during the early nineteenth century, even though these also might be escaping from economic distress and political repression. The Highlanders who came to the Maritime Provinces and Ontario formed communities which were distinct in language and customs and even in religion from the adjacent settlements. The successive waves of American settlers came from a country where the population was already racially mixed. At the time of Confederation the Irish were second only to the French in numbers, and the Germans—many of them originally part of the movement from the United States—ranked next in size to the British and French groups. All these groups have retained a consciousness of ancestry and even certain distinctive racial characteristics through succeeding generations, without detriment to their amalgamation into a solid cultural unity.

Time is an essential part of this process, and time has not yet worked to full effect on the new races which established themselves in Canada during the twentieth century. Moreover, many of them are more widely different from the original population in origin and background than were the immigrants of the nineteenth century. The chief obstacle to assimilation, however, is not any single factor, but a combination of linguistic and religious differences, especially when reinforced by group settlement in a compact community. These are the factors which make for the strength of French cultural separatism. Their significance is evident in such special sects as the Mennonites and the Doukhobors. The familiar tendency of racial groups to congregate, whether in rural areas or mining settlements or industrial cities, frequently retards their absorption. But unless there is the bond of some peculiar creed or ideology to strengthen linguistic or geographic isolation, the influences of environment operate with increasing strength on each successive generation. A wide variety of forces, from newspapers and moving pictures to trade unions and farm organizations, contribute to the leavening process. Possibly most important of all, the public-school system provides a relatively uniform framework of education throughout English-speaking Canada, and exerts a formative influence in the direction of cultural unity.

Canada thus presents the picture of a nation which retains a strong sense of kinship with the wider English-speaking community, modified, however, in significant respects by circumstances peculiar to itself. Not only does the French section of the population give its allegiance to a different culture; but also even the English-speaking portion, which includes various groups that are not British by racial origin, is itself conscious of qualities which set it apart from the United States or the other member nations of the British Commonwealth and which seem to Canadians to justify their aspirations towards the development of a distinct national entity.

The nature of this specifically Canadian character is not easy to define with accuracy. Try to do it in terms of the characteristics of the average individual Canadian and it will elude your grasp. The qualities common to the fisherman of the Maritime Provinces, the French-Canadian farmer or lumber-man, the Ontario dairyman and the prairie wheat-grower, or business men from different cities with different roles in the national economy are not to be discerned at first glance. Set them down in an American community and it would be hard for the ordinary observer to distinguish many of these Canadians from those about them. Yet in their community aspect they do exhibit certain characteristics which find expression in community action and which arise out of the fundamental factors in Canada's structure and development.

For one thing, Canada is a relatively small nation, with all the inescapable sense of limitations which must be felt by any small nation in the modern world. Her peculiarly intimate relations with two Great Powers have the effect of emphasizing rather than diminishing this aspect. Time and again she has been forced to recognize that her destiny is not completely in her own hands, but is subject to the operation of forces over which she has little or no control. Such a position demands not only an awareness of external conditions in their bearing on the national interest but also a sense of the limits within which national policies must operate and an adaptability in making the most of the possibilities presented by existing circumstances. Her record of achievement since the Dominion came into being, and not least her contribution during two world wars, has imbued Canadians with confidence in the ability of their country to pursue a course that combines progress with stability and to make an effective contribution to world order. Yet the inescapable fact remains that without the initiative of some more powerful nation, an initiative by Canada can lead to only limited accomplishments either in world affairs or in the advancement of her own security and prosperity.

There are comparable limitations in internal matters. In many respects Canada is richly endowed and fortunately situated. Her natural resources hold promises of wealth the full extent of which has yet to be ascertained. Her North American position reduces her need to stand guard against predatory aggressors. Yet the very extent of the land, with the relatively small proportion that has hitherto proved hospitable to settlement, presents serious problems. The physical and financial effort involved in developing a national system of transportation, in exploiting the mineral resources of the northern wilderness, and in realizing Canada's potential wealth in hydro-electric power is heavy in proportion to the population and national wealth of the Dominion. The dependence on the export of natural staples or manufactured goods in order to pay for the wide range of needed imports introduces further complications. The achievement of Canada's full possibilities calls for bold and imaginative policies. The limitations of her available assets frequently mean that patience and tenacity are needed to carry such policies into execution.

One consequence is that individual initiative in Canada tends to operate on a somewhat different pattern from the same spirit in the United States, in spite of the many similarities between the two countries. For one thing, there are certain differences in the attitude towards public authority. Canadians are prone to contrast the strength of the tradition of British justice in their own country with the somewhat anarchic outlook which marks certain aspects of American life. Yet both countries inherited the system of British law; it is the lines of development that have diverged as a result of different circumstances. American expansion was marked by the repeated spread of settlement beyond the range of constituted authority and the need for frontier communities to develop their own modes of action outside the bounds of formal law. No such situation developed in Canada; and if one consequence has been a somewhat less vigorous stress on unrestrained individualism, this has perhaps been balanced by a greater willingness to subordinate the impulses of individuals or communities to the due operation of the law.

A comparable manifestation—though one that springs from different causes—can be seen in the economic sphere. Freedom of enterprise was a concept widely accepted in Canada as in other capitalist countries, perhaps all the more so because of the element of pioneering that entered into nearly every aspect of the country's economic expansion. Yet it became clear at a very early stage that this expansion would be retarded, if not actually frustrated, if it were left entirely to private interests. Their resources were too limited for a task of such magnitude. They needed government coöperation, not only in the form of laws which would aid commerce and regulations which would protect infant industries, but also in the raising of capital and the construction of canals and railways and hydro-electric plants. Canadian governments had to get actively into business if Canadian business was to prosper. Moreover, many of the basic activities called for large-scale organization if they were to be carried on effectively. The fur trade was an early example; civil aviation is one of the most recent; transportation and finance and a number of key industries provide further instances. Even in agricultural staples such as wheat, the marketing problem has called either for direct government action or for the type of large-scale coöperation exemplified in the western wheat pools. And however much business might dislike government regulation, the intimate connexion between public and private enterprise has meant a steady growth of regulation and supervision in economic affairs. The intermingling of public and private interest is evident in a wide variety of fields, from the railways and the banking system to radio and scientific research. Canadians are accustomed to corporate action on a national scale when private initiative seems inadequate, and to a positive role by government in the operation of the national economy.

One can, in fact, discern in Canadian life a strong strain of ambition tempered by realism. The circumstances of Canada's evolution lent special weight to the combination of such qualities as energy and tenacity, moderation and adaptability. There are observers who feel that certain Scottish traits are particularly evident in the Canadian character. Such a view naturally seems most obvious to Scotsmen, who can point with legitimate pride to the colourful and constructive role which their countrymen have played in the growth of the Dominion—in the fur trade during its greatest days, in early agricultural settlement, in business and education and public life for well over a century. Yet it is no disparagement to suggest that it is inescapable necessity which has developed in Canadians a certain attitude of canniness in harmony with the Scottish temperament rather than borrowed from it. A shrewd sense of the possible has been essential to Canada's growth and even to her survival. Undue caution in policy might mean the loss of vital opportunities; undue rashness might lead to disaster. The margin of risk was often perilously slim in political as in economic affairs. Externally there were distinct limits to which she could push her independence of action in view of her dependence on good relations with both Britain and the United States. Internally she had to keep continually in mind the existence of two major races and the impossibility of pursuing policies which outraged the vital interests of either one. This national training in restraint has at times had its disadvantages, but at others has possibly saved the nation from courses that would have been calamitous.

It may be that this aspect will stand out with greater clarity as the nation grows in maturity. In the past there has been a tendency, natural in a small state, for Canada to emulate her larger and wealthier neighbour and to lag behind in certain respects through failure to develop initiative. Examples of this are so obvious that they have tended to obscure the extent to which, in the past, Canada has tackled her own problems in her own way, borrowing from the experience of other countries, yet adapting this to her own purpose, and evolving new methods and approaches when adaptation failed to serve her needs. As her problems become more distinct from those of other countries, the tendency to strike out along her own line of policy will necessarily increase.

The crisis of the Second World War presented just such a situation, and Canada showed her ability to organize methods of direction and control on her own initiative and in the interests of the maximum use of her resources in the cause of victory. The need to harmonize her efforts with those of her allies and associates remained a conditioning factor. The desire to continue that harmony is still a paramount consideration in the post-war world. Yet new circumstances have arisen and new difficulties have developed which may call for bolder and more drastic courses, and may impose a test of unprecedented severity on Canada's ability to chart a successful course as an independent nation, and on the qualities which her people have developed in their evolution as a distinct community.

CHAPTER II

The Geography

BY JAMES WREFORD WATSON

CANADA, once on the frontiers of civilization, today occupies a strategic position. She is among powerful neighbours—the United States of America to the south, Soviet Russia to the north, Great Britain on the east, and Japan on the west. The northward trend of political and economic power has created a world-girdling ring of states which looks in upon a northern centre of its own, the Arctic Ocean, the Mediterranean of the future. These states, which include Canada and the Scandinavian countries, already touch in Korea, the Sea of Japan, the Bering Sea, Germany, and the Baltic Sea. As modern methods of communication and development subjugate the northern *tundras,* the frozen islands, and the ice-filled waters, this ring of states will be drawn closer, whether for peace or for war, and the strategic importance of a weaker state among strong neighbours is likely to increase proportionately.

In such an alignment, with only 13,500,000 inhabitants, surrounded by more powerful and more populous nations, Canada's area of 3,845,000 square miles, the second largest of any country in the world, is a questionable asset. The problem of development is acute in face of the general land-hunger and the exhaustion of many resources in the United States and western Europe. The problem of defence has also become acute with the emphasis of modern warfare on defence-in-depth. If Canada cannot fully develop or defend her vast areas, the temptation for other nations to assist in their use and protection will grow. Thus Canada has everything to gain from world unity and everything to lose by a division into power blocs.[1]

The shape and structure of Canada strengthen the pattern of external contacts. The natural divisions of the North American continent are north-south rather than east-west. The southern, western, and eastern borders of Canada are closely integrated with American sea approaches and inland water-ways, and Canadian territory thrusts deep into the industrial heart of the United States. In the west, Canada continues the trend of the Pacific states into Alaska, all being part of the circum-Pacific *vallum* of young mountains that sweeps through the Andes and Rockies, and around the Aleutians, Japan, and New Zealand. In the east, with Newfoundland and Labrador, Canada continues the older Appalachian trends. These are linked, beyond the shortest Atlantic crossing, with Great Britain, Norway, and Spitzbergen. Canada is also part of a vast Arctic Shield which extends across the Archipelago to Greenland, and which has its counterpart in the Russian and Siberian shields in the opposite hemisphere.

This continuity of structure has not encouraged cultural and economic ties with nations separated from Canada by great stretches of ocean, but the nearness of the United States, combined with structural continuity, has given the two countries a sense of likeness. The ways of life in the valleys of the western mountains, on the ranches and wheat-lands of the western plains, on the shores of the Great Lakes or of Fundy, and in the towns and cities are so similar north and south of the frontier that it is impossible to question their underlying unity.[2]

How then, it may be asked, has Canada escaped political assimilation? The answer lies in minor features of relief and drainage, following a latitudinal trend, which lent themselves to westward explorations and pioneer drives from European bases on the Atlantic Coast, and have been emphasized by later historical developments. The arcuate front of the Canadian Shield, and of the great ice-sheet that advanced and retreated over it, formed the huge arc of Lake Winnipeg, Lake of the Woods, the Rainy River, the Great Lakes, the St. Lawrence River, and the Gulf of St. Lawrence, which has been the fundamental basis of Canada's

[1] For notes to chapter ii see pages 571–572.

east-west alignment. This is supported by a second arc, more broken but none the less important, of the English River, the Great Clay Belt, and the Ottawa Valley.

Westward along these arcs of rivers, lakes, and connecting portages moved the French fur-traders and missionaries. When the American War of Independence finally broke the north-

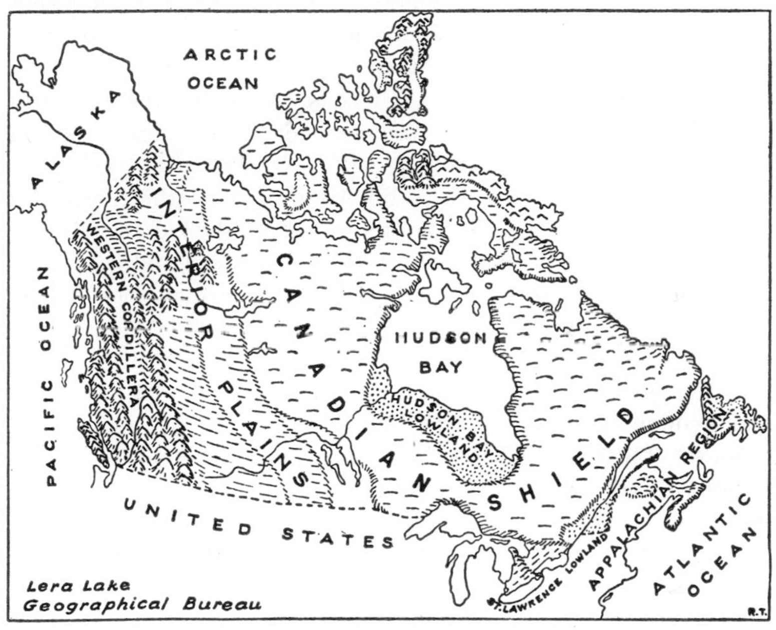

PHYSIOGRAPHIC DIVISIONS OF CANADA

south connexion which the French had sought to establish between New Orleans and Quebec by way of the Mississippi, the Ohio, the Great Lakes, and the St. Lawrence, the westward lines of trading-posts beyond the Great Lakes increased in number and importance. The fur-traders' canoe routes were succeeded by river and lake ports, and later by a network of railways. Connecting systems tied in the Maritime Provinces and the prairies and British Columbia by way of the lateral rivers thrown off in both directions by the Appalachian and Rocky Mountain divides. Later and more direct rail connexion took advantage of the

Matapedia and Temiscouata and Megantic gaps in the east and the Crowsnest and Kicking Horse and Yellowhead passes in the west. Thus, politically and economically, Canada, like the United States, has grown up about an east-west axis;[3] and, in spite of the pulls north and south, her east-west lines of communication have become the very warp of national unity and identity.

If unity for Canada was made possible by festoons of rivers, diversity was enforced by climate and soils. Lying between 42° and 83° North Latitude, the country is dominated by polar air masses, varying according to their relation to the coastal oceans and modified in summer by invasions of the tropical Gulf air mass from the south.

In the far north, including the Arctic, the northern parts of the Shield, and the Hudson Bay plain, occurs the *tundra* climate, dominated by the polar continental mass. It is dry and cold, with long, dark winters and short summers. The warmest month does not average above 50° F. Winter temperatures are from —10° to —30° F. Vegetation is limited to mosses, lichens, stunted willows, and juniper bushes. The land has a bleak, open appearance and is commonly referred to as "The Barrens."

South of this the sub-arctic climate prevails from Alaska to Labrador, including the middle and upper Mackenzie River and the southern part of the Canadian Shield. It is a climate of extremes, with very bitter winters and short but surprisingly warm summers. Temperatures range from a record low of —79° F. to a record high of 103° F. The long winter, under the dry, clear air of the polar continental mass, freezes rivers, lakes, and soil. In the short summer, lasting up to 90 days, with long periods of sunshine, temperatures rise to an average of over 60° F. following the invasion of tropical Gulf air; the soil thaws out; there is much soil moisture and considerable rain. The rapid growth of small hardwoods and conifers, with berry bushes and undergrowth, generally forms a heavy forest, interspersed with innumerable lakes and rivers, marshy tracts, and large areas of muskeg. The heavily leached, greyish podsols are acid and infertile, but can be cultivated when they are drained and limed.

The northern prairies, the southern fringe of the Shield, the St. Lawrence Lowlands, and the Maritime Provinces have a cool, temperate, humid climate. Winters are severe, with subfreezing temperatures, but polar airs yield to warmer airs from the south for a period of 90 to 150 days. The July average of 60° to 70° F. and the longer days stimulate mixed forest growth, for which heavy winter snow-fall, spring-melt waters, and summer rains give ample water-supply. The podsolized grey soil is often weak in the melanization so important for agriculture, and must be artificially stimulated by drainage and fertilization; the short growing season is also a handicap. On the south slopes of the Shield, in the Ottawa Valley and parts of the St. Lawrence, and in the Maritime Provinces the brown podsolic soil is tolerably useful.

In southern peninsular Ontario and the Montreal plain a warmer climate prevails, with a July average of over 70° F., and with 150 to 170 days free from frost. This warm-summer phase of the humid microthermal climate, which is due to the strong effect of the tropical Gulf air mass advancing up the Ohio, accounts for the hardwood forests of maple mixed with oak, chestnut, and hickory. The grey-brown podsolic soil, the melanization usually very strong, is agriculturally the best in eastern Canada.

The middle-latitude southern prairies are subject in winter to the very dry mass of polar continental air, with dry, cold air-currents sent out by local high pressures over the mountains, and in spring and summer to the hot, dry Chinooks blowing down from the same quarter, bringing rapid changes in temperature. In summer, tropical Gulf air brings the chief rains of the year, but they are partly spent by the time they reach the interior, and the average annual precipitation is but 15 to 20 inches, with less in the south-west.[4] The low rainfall and high evaporation discourage tree growth. Tall-grass prairies, fringing the northern forest front, give way to short-grass prairies farther south, and eventually to short grass with a light, semi-desert growth. The soils follow a well-marked zoning: black soils on the tall prairies, chestnut on the semi-arid, brown on the areas of least rainfall. The black and chestnut soils, rich in organic matter and fairly rich in minerals, are among Canada's most fertile, but the short growing season and the extreme variability of the weather, with periodic droughts, are serious handicaps.

British Columbia's intermontane upland and the valleys between the Coast Range and the Selkirks are also dry, shut off by the mountains from rain-bearing winds. However, snow-fed rivers and numerous lakes make irrigation practicable and successful. The mountain climate is humid and sub-arctic to polar, the subarctic slopes bearing dense forests of western hemlock, pine, and spruce. Farther north, in the Yukon, the climate is more severe.

The Fraser delta and the west coast, including Vancouver Island and the Queen Charlottes, have a west-maritime, humid, equable climate, dominated by the polar Pacific air mass, which is mild and wet in winter, cool and moist in summer. Westerly winds from the ocean keep average temperatures between 40° F. (January) and 64° F. (July). The annual rainfall is from 30 to 100 inches, with a marked winter maximum. The resultant dense forest of very tall cedars, Douglas fir, western hemlock, and Sitka spruce offers some of the finest stands of timber on the continent. The summers are too cool for the best yields of cereal crops, however, and the high rainfall leaches many plant nutrients from the forest brown soils.

Although the Canadian climate is associated with severe frost hazards throughout most of the country and with drought hazards in the arid interior, it is adequate for productivity, and with its varied conditions and great number of cyclonic storms is undoubtedly very stimulating. It has been said that the most favourable climate for life is that with a July average of 68° and a January average of 42° F. The most thickly-settled parts of Canada are close to these averages, but much the greater part of the total area lies on the poleward margin of these conditions, with cooler summers and colder winters, and thus is at some disadvantage in comparison with the northern United States. However, history shows that a challenge too severe for one time or people may stimulate the finest achievement of another. Life in Canada is perhaps still in too experimental a stage, with extensive scientific development of the Arctic an imminent possibility, to permit final judgement on optimum conditions.

The climate and soils of Canada are well suited to forest growth. Nearly two-fifths of the total land area is under forest, and an area about seven times the size of Britain is considered suitable for cutting, of which over half is economically accessible at present. The Canadian Shield is the greatest source of supply.

Quebec and Ontario have nearly two-thirds of the timber at present accessible, and the softwoods of the southern Shield are particularly important for pulp- and paper-making. Since the forest comes to the margin of the Great Lakes and the St. Lawrence, and can also be reached by large tributaries such as the Nipigon, the Ottawa, and the St. Maurice, it is cheap to harvest. The huge power developments of the lakes and rivers facilitate processing. Paper-mills can readily obtain machinery and chemicals from the industrialized areas near by, and finished products have easy access to the chief consuming centres in the Canadian and American industrial belts and to export points for shipment overseas. Labour and capital are readily available. Thus the two provinces produce about 76 per cent of Canada's annual 5,000,000 tons of pulp and about 80 per cent of its 3,330,000 tons of newsprint. The pulp and paper industries were for a decade Canada's highest in gross value, being replaced in 1935 by metal industries. "In world trade, pulp and paper are Canada's main commodities except gold; greater than wheat and far greater than nickel. Newsprint alone over a considerable period brought more export dollars than wheat."[5]

British Columbia is Canada's chief source of sawn lumber, producing about 44 per cent. The taller, harder trees are better suited for construction purposes than for pulp- and paper-making, and the opening of the Panama Canal has provided a relatively cheap all-water route to the eastern United States and Britain, the principal markets.

In the Prairie and Maritime Provinces the forest industries are on a smaller scale. The Prairie forests are far to the north and rather inaccessible, but they are being swiftly invaded. Much is cut for firewood. The total Maritime cut is not great, but it bulks large in the economy of the region, and in New Brunswick amounts to nearly one-third by value of all products. In Newfoundland there is a considerable forest reserve and lumbering is important in the provincial economy.

The forests are likely to retain their importance in Canadian production and trade. Government departments have made considerable progress in the development of scientific forestry, in the prevention of fire and disease, and in the control of logging operations. Many mills employ trained foresters to direct their forest operations, and the lengthening of leases is expected to make logging companies more efficient in their methods and more careful of their reserves. It is maintained that the average annual rate of growth is about twice that needed to replace loss by normal depletion.[6] This should leave a margin for increased cutting to meet rising export opportunities. Canada, rich in woods, is surrounded by wood-hungry lands. The United States has depleted much of its forest wealth, and imports great quantities of news-print and lumber from Canada. Mexico and the Caribbean lands, with scarcely any softwood forest, and western Europe and the Far East are additional markets. At the same time, Canadian consumption is not high in proportion to production. There is thus a good margin for export. Since 1913 Canada has been the world's chief exporter of news-print, and in the period immediately preceding the Second World War was contributing nearly two-thirds of the international trade.

Associated with the forests, and originally largely dependent on them, is Canada's fur trade. First linked with London and Paris,[7] the trade now supplies wider markets with fox, beaver, musk-rat, mink, squirrel, marten, otter, ermine, badger, wolf, and other pelts. The beaver has become the national emblem and has appeared on Canadian stamps and coinage; the selection of a mink coat as a wedding present from the Dominion to H.R.H. Princess Elizabeth indicates the outstanding quality associated with this Canadian industry. To maintain production, conservation of fur-bearing animals is practised, and fur farms have been established throughout Canada. Prince Edward Island makes a specialty of them. Fox, mink, raccoon, and rabbit farms are common. The Dominion Department of Agriculture introduced a system of fur-grading in 1939, so that foreign buyers need not examine skins personally but can purchase them by grade. This, and the conservation measures, should do much to maintain the output and traditions of the Canadian fur trade.

Though it is younger than the activities connected with the forest, agriculture has long been an industry of basic importance.

As might be expected from limitations of topography and climate, the occupied farm and ranch lands are relatively limited, being only about 12 per cent of the total area of the country. They lie in a comparatively narrow, interrupted strip along the southern border, with northern extensions into the Skeena, Peace, Abitibi, and Saguenay valleys. In so large a country, however, even this narrow strip is very considerable, amounting to 175,000,000 acres, of which some 92,000,000 are improved. A trend towards rural depopulation and abandonment of farms began as early as about 1870 in the Maritime Provinces and spread to Ontario, Quebec, and eventually the Western Provinces. The tendency is to let submarginal land go back to forest or prairie, and to make more economical use of better land, either by intensive cultivation or by larger-scale mechanized farming. Agriculture still accounts for over 30 per cent of the gainfully employed males, and during the Second World War an all-time high in production was achieved, thanks largely to better methods and more machines.

In the adjustment of agricultural practice to local geography and overseas markets, four major regions have emerged, of which the first—eastern, settled Canada—consists of the Maritime Provinces, the St. Lawrence plains, the Ottawa Valley, and peninsular Ontario. Its southern fringe, with longer summers and July temperatures averaging above 70° F., produces a variety of specialized crops. The chief fruit belts of this section are those of Owen Sound, Leamington, Niagara, and Prince Edward County—all in Ontario, —parts of the Eastern Townships of Quebec, and the Annapolis Valley in Nova Scotia. Hops, sugar-beets, and seed-corn are associated with the Windsor district in western Ontario; tobacco, with the Lake Erie townships and the Montreal plain. Canning and truck crops are grown extensively throughout this southern part of the belt. Farther north in this eastern farming district, the greater hazard of frost results in an emphasis on live-stock, bacon, cheese, and eggs.

The settled prairies lie south-west of a line drawn roughly from Winnipeg, through Prince Albert, to Edmonton. Three broad climatic and soil zones, in concentric arcs, control the uses of land.[8] The northern, sub-humid, dark-soil arc supports dairying and mixed farming. Wheat, though important, occupies less than half of the field-crop area. The growing season is rather too short for concentration on wheat, the danger of frost somewhat too great.

In the semi-arid chestnut-soil arc, where there is relatively little danger from frost or drought, almost 80 per cent of the field-crop area is under wheat. Though the Second World War, with its emphasis on protective foods, raised dairying to first place in Canada, rising grain prices may restore wheat to its pre-war pre-eminence. The yield per acre is low in comparison with countries like Britain, where plentiful labour and investment capital, high land values, and a good home market encourage intensive cultivation. On the other hand, Canada has the space and machines for large-scale farming, which is profitable with a lower margin of production, and has for some years been the world's chief exporter of wheat and flour.

In the light-brown soil zone of the south-west, the climate is not only semi-arid but extremely variable, the extremes of rainfall at Medicine Hat being 146 per cent of the average. In wetter-than-usual years, the zone is well suited to wheat, but several critical droughts, particularly that coinciding with the depression of 1931–1934, have led to the abandonment of farms, and it is now conceded that the zone is better left to cattle and sheep except where irrigation is possible or soils are heavy. Existing and projected areas of irrigated farming amount to some 3,500,000 acres, mostly between Lethbridge, Medicine Hat, and the international boundary.

The Cordilleran region has all the variety of agriculture expected of a mountainous district. On the well-watered fields of Vancouver Island and the Fraser delta the equable climate encourages concentration on vegetables and dairy products, with highly-specialized methods of production. In the intermontane upland and interior valleys, semi-desert conditions prevail. North of Kamloops, cattle and sheep predominate. Southward, irrigation permits orchard cultivation, and the apples and peaches of British Columbia are famous throughout the country and in overseas markets.

Across northern Canada runs the pioneer farm belt, including scattered communities in the Skeena and Peace River districts, the

Great Clay Belt, and the Lac Saint-Jean district. In the aggregate these districts must total 200,000,000 acres; the Great Clay Belt alone covers 70,000,000. The development of this huge area is limited, thus far, to a comparatively negligible 5,000,000 or so acres. In the Peace country, which comprises 3,500,000 acres of this, a small percentage of high-grade soils forms little "prairies" of grass-covered black earth in the midst of the forested podsols, so that settlements are isolated. Though land is cheap, transportation costs are still high, and commercial development is limited. Moreover, the growing season is only 100 days long. Few varieties of wheat can flourish at present, and much of the crop, together with all the coarse grains, is fed to hogs and cattle, "in order to give a product better able to stand the high transportation charges to market."[9] The Great Clay Belt has even less good soil and a shorter growing season, and it is a sad commentary on the high hopes once entertained for this region that it cannot yet feed itself, let alone export food; many farms have already been abandoned. It is possible that this will remain primarily a lumber region and that efforts will be concentrated on replenishing the forest rather than cutting it off, except where people are satisfied with subsistence farming.[10]

Until the Second World War brought its great industrial expansion, Canada was considered to be preëminently an agricultural country with, by the 'forties, a total production valued at $2,700,000,000, of which $1,000,000,000 worth was for export. Ontario and Saskatchewan, representing *par excellence* the dairy and wheat interests, accounted between them for over half of this, with Alberta, Quebec, and Manitoba following in that order.

The limits of productivity are not strictly fixed, owing to the use of irrigation in overcoming drought and the use of frost-resistant grains such as Marquis wheat, which has extended the northern frontier. Doubtless other means will be developed for extending the frontier still farther. Yet a great expansion of Canada's agricultural area, though physically possible, seems at present to be economically unlikely. With two-thirds of the production for export, the keen competition normally found in world markets does not encourage the immediate exploitation of the less profitable areas. Recent population trends show an increasing migration from rural areas, and it is doubtful if Canadian agriculture could at present absorb even a few hundred thousand immigrants, much less the hundred million or so sometimes mooted.

The oldest resources to be developed by Canada—which first brought Europeans regularly to her shores—are the fisheries, among the most prolific in the world. The Banks, lying off the Maritime Provinces, and including the Grand Bank of Newfoundland, cover 70,000 square miles. The shallow water, stirred by the mixing of the Labrador Current and the Gulf Stream, supplies abundant food. The drowned shores of Newfoundland, lower Quebec, and the Maritime Provinces afford many harbours. Dense forests supply lumber for boats. The fish-eating nations of the Mediterranean, the Caribbean, and South America offer excellent, accessible overseas markets. For three decades the Atlantic Banks "have yielded, annually, more than eleven hundred million pounds of cod alone, and here undoubtedly is to be found the greatest cod and haddock fishery in the world."[11] The inshore fisheries on the Bay of Fundy and the Gulf of St. Lawrence provide important catches of sardines, lobsters, and oysters. Many small fishing-ports on the Great Lakes bring in a large catch of whitefish. The salmon fisheries of British Columbia are concentrated at the mouths of the rivers, all along the deeply-indented coast, which the fish ascend to spawn, and are probably the largest of their kind in the world. There are also important halibut fisheries around the islands off the coast.

Canada's position in minerals and fuels is one of growing importance. The Dominion is already the world's leading producer of nickel and platinum; the third in copper, gold, and silver; the fourth in lead and zinc; the fourteenth in iron. Europe has exhausted many of its supplies. The United States has also reached a point where it consumes more than it produces; it is short of oil, iron, copper, and zinc; buys more gold than it produces; and has long looked to Canada for nickel and asbestos. Canada's mining products will thus increase in importance, and the supply of radium and uranium, probably the second in the world, may be specially significant.

The Canadian Shield, core of the continent, covering 1,825,000 square miles, or more than half the area of Canada, is of an age and structure which are heavily mineralized. This area has played a great role in metal production.[12] It is predominantly igneous, with bands of Precambrian sediment squeezed between great bosses of granite. Most of the rocks are highly metamorphosed. They were folded up into mountain ranges, but in later geological ages have been planed down. The old folded areas, the metamorphosed sediments, and the crystalline bosses are seamed with

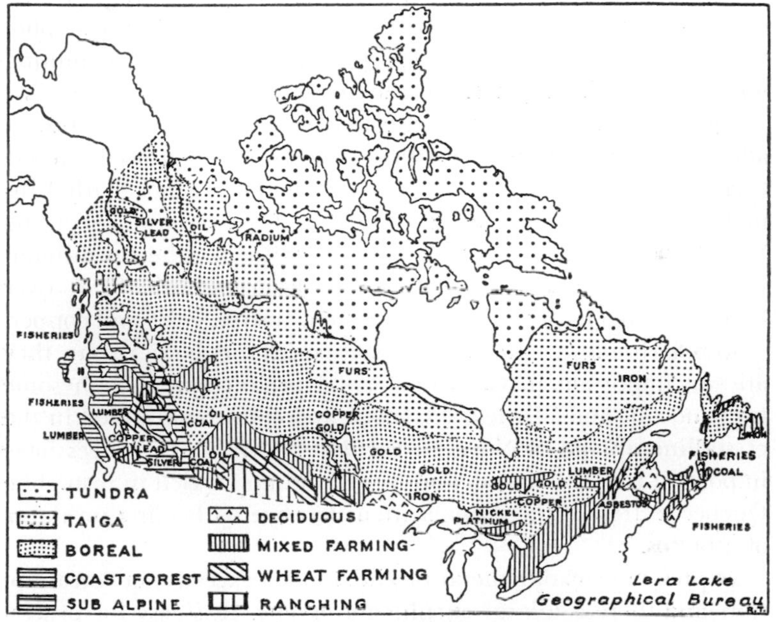

ECONOMIC GEOGRAPHY OF CANADA

deposits of precious and base metals. Yet the greater part of the wealth of the Shield remains unprospected. Much of it is remote from railways and settlement. The terrain is difficult, with few practicable water-ways. The climate is too severe for food to be grown locally. Consequently the chief developments have been along the southern margin.

Sudbury has nickel, copper, and zinc; Porcupine and Kirkland Lake, gold and silver; Flin Flon and Sheridan, gold, silver, zinc, and copper; Great Bear Lake, radium and uranium. There is gold also near Athabaska and Great Slave lakes. Comparatively small deposits of iron are worked at Steep Rock and Algoma, and now that the high-grade ores south of Lake Superior are nearing exhaustion, the less easily mined Canadian fields are likely to be further developed, particularly such a field as Ruth Lake, one of the largest on the continent, lying on the borders of Quebec and Labrador. Indeed, Canada, with the inclusion of Newfoundland and Labrador, may yet become the chief source of iron for American industry. In recent years the use of aircraft in aerial photography and geophysical prospecting has revolutionized mining methods and life in general in the north.

The western Cordillera is also rich in metals and contains, in addition, important sources of fuel. Veins of metal occur in the Coast Range and the Selkirks where giant igneous batholiths make contact with surrounding rocks. The importance of the Yukon Valley and its tributaries is well known. The Cordilleran provinces produce most of Canada's lead and zinc, and over half of her silver, together with tungsten, arsenic, gold, and copper.

Appalachian structures also have small ore-bodies, but they are not important in Canadian metal production, though some lead and zinc and a little gold, silver, and copper are mined in the crystalline upland of Nova Scotia. The Maritime Provinces have important reserves of coal, and Newfoundland is rich in iron. The Quebec section of the Appalachians has been a leading producer of asbestos.

At present Canada's metal production far exceeds her consumption, and there is a large surplus for export. It is easy for processors to buy the tin and bauxite which the country lacks, and the iron and ferro-alloys which it cannot yet provide as cheaply as the United States can. Bauxite comes in from British Guiana, North Africa, and France, and cryolite from Greenland; immense hydro-electric reserves permit smelting at such reasonable rates that Canada has become the world's fourth largest producer of aluminium.

Canada, indeed, has a higher potential supply of power than any other nation but Russia. The generally humid climate, with low evaporation; the vast forest cover; the marginal mountains and Shield; the large glacial lakes and long and serviceable rivers

—all contribute. Moreover, the proximity of the central plateau to populous areas, from Tadoussac through Ottawa and Sudbury and Algoma to Winnipeg, makes the power readily available to the chief centres of consumption, while Calgary and Vancouver tap Cordilleran sources and the Eastern Townships of Quebec those of the Appalachians. Considerable power reserves exist in Newfoundland and Labrador.

The chief industrial belt lies between Quebec's line of power-sites along the Laurentian and Appalachian rivers and the St. Lawrence rapids, and Ontario's along the string of falls over the south edge of the Shield, with the great developments at Niagara Falls and Queenston. Power from the Winnipeg River is used in Winnipeg and neighbouring municipalities. The Bow River, flowing from the Rockies, supplies western Alberta from Calgary to Edmonton. British Columbia ranks second to Quebec in power resources, but has the greater part still to develop. Even in the Maritime Provinces, the short rivers afford much local power for pulp- and paper-mills, fish-packing plants, creameries, and so on. "It is estimated that Canada's presently recorded water-power provides for an installation of more than 52,000,000 horse-power. Of this, the present development represents only 25 per cent."[13] In addition to its wide-spread use in homes and agricultural industries, this power provides for important demands in pulp and paper manufacturing, metal-refining, and electro-metallurgical and electro-chemical industries.

The fuel situation in Canada is a strange one. Besides the fields already in production, Canada is known to have the world's largest remaining source of crude oil, locked up in the Mackenzie tar-sands, requiring only the contrivance of satisfactory methods of extraction. She has also one of the world's largest coal-fields, in Alberta, with others in the Maritime Provinces and British Columbia. Nevertheless, the country imports most of its coal and all but about 15 per cent of its oil. The chief fuel-consuming provinces, Ontario and Quebec, are very remote from the coal-fields of Alberta and other western fields. They are distant even from the Nova Scotia fields, particularly when winter closes the St. Lawrence route. These large industrial and domestic markets can thus satisfy themselves more easily and cheaply from the United

States. The north-south lines of geographical continuity have proved more effective here than the east-west lines of national development, though the situation may change as United States supplies, particularly of oil, diminish, and demand in both countries increases.

With her great natural wealth, Canada was long content to be a producer of primary goods. Industry developed chiefly to extract and process them. Export of the greater part enabled Canada to buy iron and steel goods, textiles, and other consumer products. The basis of trade and development was typically colonial and, indeed, at first discouraged manufacturing.

Local manufacturing arose from difficulties in distribution. Through the vast and rather unorganized area, small flour- and grist-mills, tanneries, woollen-mills, paper-mills, and iron-foundries sprang up in the wake of settlement. Canals and railways facilitated larger-scale undertakings. British capital investment began to flow into the country. Soon after the federal union of 1867, Sir John A. Macdonald proposed his "National Policy," and duties imposed on imported pig-iron and finished products provided a stimulus to industrialization. Rapid increase in population after 1896 provided more labour and a larger and more varied home market. It was difficult to keep pace with the demand for railways, telegraph lines, farm machinery, and machinery for mining and lumbering. The First World War increased tremendously the demand in western Europe for metals, wood products, and farm goods, and decreased its supply of consumer goods for export. Simultaneously, all kinds of military equipment and war supplies were required. Canadian towns became industrial rather than primarily commercial, and capital investment more than doubled.

Thus within sixty years after Confederation the country seemed to have acquired the chief prerequisites of a great industrial nation. There was an extensive transportation system. Raw materials were accessible and labour forces adequate. There were considerable capital investments, an incipient industrial tradition, a substantial home market, and an increasing foreign market. Lack of readily available fuel was partly offset by abundant hydroelectric power, but many industrial skills were lacking, and the basic iron and steel, tooling, and machine industries were still insufficiently developed. The great dependence on foreign markets also presented a grave problem, and Canadian production was affected very severely by the general regression in the 'thirties.

The extraordinary demands of the Second World War enabled Canada to turn to account the mass-production methods introduced in the interests of greater efficiency, and to become one of the world's leading industrial nations. The manufacture of consumer goods expanded rapidly, but the extraction and processing of raw materials and the production of munitions and war supplies outstripped it. Thus, while vegetable products increased by 24.6 per cent, animal products by 40.4 per cent, and miscellaneous industries by 68 per cent, non-ferrous metal products increased by 129.9 per cent, iron products by 222.2 per cent, and chemical and allied products by 262.5 per cent. This development of the metal and chemical industries marks a real change. In 1922 the three principal industries, flour-milling, pulp- and paper-making, and slaughtering and meat-packing, reflected the continued importance of primary production. At that time non-ferrous metal-smelting and -refining, chemical production and ship-building, secondary processing of iron and steel, and aircraft manufacture did not rank among the forty leading industries; twenty-five years later they stood first, second, fourth, fifth, and eighth, respectively. Electrical apparatus had climbed from seventeenth to ninth place, and primary iron and steel from twentieth to tenth. Flour-milling had fallen from first to twelfth. Automobiles were still in sixth place.

Industries needing large capital, extensive plants, plentiful labour, great stocks of fuel and raw materials, and a ramified transportation system tend to concentrate where these conditions are met. They are followed by others which feed or are fed by them. Consequently, a distinct manufacturing belt has grown up from Quebec to Windsor, along the shores of the St. Lawrence and the Lower Lakes. Of Canada's ten leading cities, producing about four billion dollars' worth of the country's gross production valued at nine billion dollars, seven are in Quebec and Ontario. This is not surprising in view of the geographical advantages of these provinces and their early start towards industrialization. They command one of the continent's chief trade-routes, destined to grow still greater as the St. Lawrence Seaway. They lie between the Canadian Shield, one of the continent's chief sources of metals, wood, and water-power, and the Appalachians, its chief source of coal. Thus they have ample raw material, fuel, and power. Their fertile plains supply large amounts of food, particularly the dairy and truck products that urban populations require. Both have surplus farm population and straddle the chief immigration route, and Quebec has the largest rate of natural increase; the result is a plentiful and varied supply of labour. Quebec is the most urbanized province, with 63 per cent of its people living in manufacturing centres. The figures for Ontario are similar: 61.7 per cent urban and 38.3 per cent rural.[14] An early start gave them the industrial "know-how" and the accumulation of capital to use their several advantages to the full. British Columbia is the third most important manufacturing province, with its own rich capital of water-power and raw materials. Ship-building plants, saw-mills, pulp and paper-mills, fish-curing and -canning establishments, and petroleum-refining depots relate to distinctive products and oceanic connexions, and are concentrated chiefly in or near Vancouver.

Canada has an important place in world trade as a result of her extensive resources, large-scale production, well-developed transportation system, and large surpluses for export. Indeed, during the Second World War the country became the world's third largest external trader. The value of visible exports is twice that of visible imports, and thus Canada has a favourable balance of trade, though difficulties arose after the Second World War, when the post-war dollar shortage confronted Canada with the necessity of cutting down imports from the United States or increasing exports.[15]

In future, Canada will probably manufacture more of the goods previously imported and bring to a finish many of the goods she now sells in semi-manufactured condition. This trend has been growing. In the 'thirties "the proportion of raw materials to total exports gradually declined, with many products hitherto exported as raw materials undergoing some form of processing. In 1939 fully manufactured goods comprised 43.7

per cent of total exports. By 1944 this proportion had risen to 63.3 per cent despite the fact that 1944 exports of raw materials and partly manufactured goods were nearly two and a half times as great as in 1939."[16] The continuation of this trend, which fell off slightly in the years immediately following the war, would tend to bring Canada's trade more nearly into equilibrium.

Although the United States has had a slight edge on Great Britain as Canada's chief customer, the Dominion exports more to the Commonwealth and the Empire, as a whole, than to the United States and Central and South America. The European market is also important, and normal trade with Italy *or* with France is worth more than that with Mexico *and* the principal South American states put together. But the dollar exchange situation seems likely to alter sharply the traditional lines of Canadian trade.

Over half of Canada's imports normally come from the United States, the rest chiefly from the Empire and western Europe. Tin from Malaya and bauxite from British Guiana fill important gaps in Canada's metal production. Indeed, from her trade connexions, Canada's role, economically as well as historically, would seem to be that of a linchpin in British-American relations.

Although Canada is the world's second largest country and the third largest trader, she ranks only twenty-eighth in population. Her importance rests on vast natural resources and high per capita production rather than on man-power. The relatively small and scattered population increases the cost of goods and services and puts industry to the risk of having to depend too much on foreign trade. Consequently there is much to be said for increasing population by encouraging a higher birth-rate and by admitting large-scale immigration. Increases in population in the 'fifties and 'sixties of the last century, and in the first two decades of this, were followed by a flow of capital into the country, rapid expansion of railways and of commerce or industry, and the spirit of enterprise and self-reliance which culminated in federation in 1867 and the growth of national responsibility during the present century. At the same time, the problem of assimilating mass immigration is increased by the present regional and racial diversities (see chap. i). It has been argued also, in view of the receding agricultural frontier, the dependence of industrial expansion on foreign trade, and the recent excess of emigrants over immigrants, that the absorptive capacity of Canada is not high for the size of the country. Estimates based on current trends in fertility and mortality suggest a population of 25,000,000 by the end of the century. Immigration might fairly be planned to increase the total; with changes in science, technology, and organization, a considerably greater population might be supported.[17]

This brief survey of the geography of Canada has shown us a country in a strategic international location, with ample space, considerable resources, high per capita production, and a growing population. Canada faces great problems in a heterogeneous population, rather narrow habitable limits, the need for efficient use of space and resources with a population small as yet, and great dependence on international trade. The history of colonization and the geography of its development link Canada almost equally with Great Britain and the United States. But Canada has fundamental economic interests throughout the Commonwealth and the Empire, and important connexions with Central and South America. Of necessity, also, her geographical position must give her important relations with Russia and the Orient. Thus, while Canada has preserved her identity through stressing the east-west features of her geography, and has developed an oceanic integration with Britain and a continental solidarity with the United States which have made her a linchpin of the Atlantic world, she now finds that the demands of her location and experience require her to play a wider role, for no nation is more anxious to do whatever is possible to maintain the unity of the world as a whole.

Part Two

HISTORICAL BACKGROUND

CHAPTER III

The Founding of French Canada

BY GUSTAVE LANCTOT

CANADA, despite her size and geological age, never had an indigenous population. The first inhabitants, of a Mongoloid race, with swarthy faces, prominent cheek-bones, and straight black hair, came over from Asia by the Bering Strait, thousands of years before the Christian Era. From the Pacific Coast they slowly penetrated, in the course of the centuries, right to the Atlantic Seaboard. They used the skins of animals for clothing, and lived chiefly on fish and game, though some of the eastern stocks, such as the Iroquois and Hurons in the region of the St. Lawrence, practised a rudimentary agriculture, cultivating corn, squashes, and tobacco. The tribes at large had no knowledge of the use of iron, salt, the wheel, or domestic animals. Armed with bows and arrows, tomahawks, and spears, they travelled by canoes, snow-shoes, or toboggan and travois with dogs. Their total number probably did not exceed 220,000 when the Europeans arrived.[1]

In the year 1000, daring Icelanders appeared on the future Canadian coasts in their one-sail *dakkars,* but their places of landing and subsequent settlement remain unidentified. They abandoned them in a few years, being chased out by the fierce natives of the country, but subsequent expeditions returned from time to time. In 1121 Bishop Eric of Greenland went in search of Vineland. In 1347 a small ship bound from Greenland to Markland was driven back to Iceland. In 1472, probably on a voyage

[1] For notes to chapter iii see pages 572–573.

to Greenland, John Scolp[2] sailed along a coast that was doubtless the present Labrador.

Meanwhile, adventurous fishermen from Brittany and Normandy were crossing the Atlantic in small boats to fish for cod on the Banks of Newfoundland; and, although these obscure voyages remained officially unknown, there must have been tales to tell on *quai* or in tavern to stir the imaginations of merchants and even of courtiers. Similarly, in England's westward-looking seaport of Bristol, a decade or two before Columbus reached his "West Indies," merchants were ready to finance voyages in search of Brazil (the O'Brasil and Hy-Brazil of legend) and the Seven Cities, as a step to Cathay, Cipangu, and the Spice Islands.[3]

In 1497 the Italian, John Cabot, sailing from Bristol harbour under the English flag, made a rapid examination of the coast from Newfoundland to Cape Breton. Next year he found his way farther south, past the coasts of what is today Nova Scotia. Some voyages were made by Portuguese mariners also, under the auspices of Bristol merchants. In 1500 and 1501 Gaspar and Miguel Corte-Real explored the Newfoundland coast up to Labrador for Portugal, and Portuguese fishermen followed those of France and England on the Banks. In 1504 fishermen from Normandy joined the Bretons in greater number and made their way to Newfoundland itself, using ports north and west of those claimed by the Portuguese; and in 1506 Jean Denis, of Honfleur, mapped the Atlantic seashore.[4] Fourteen years later the Portuguese Fagundez explored the coast of Cape Breton Island from south to north, and tried without success to found a settlement. In 1524–1525 Spanish ships scanned the coast of Nova Scotia and discovered the Bay of Fundy; and Verrazzano's French expedition explored from Florida as far north as the land "that in times past was discovered by the Britons, which is in fiftie degrees,"[5] naming the country New France. In the spring of 1527 the *Mary Guildford,* from London, searching in vain along Labrador for a rift in the continental seashore, found, in "a good Haven, called St. John," eleven Norman vessels, one Breton, and two Portuguese, "all a fishing."[6]

Still seeking the fabled north-west passage to the spice lands of the Pacific, the great economic object of the period, and aiming also at the discovery of islands rich with gold, Jacques Cartier, in 1534, was the first to succeed in crossing the continental frontier. By way of the Strait of Belle Isle, he entered the Gulf of St. Lawrence and, on the twenty-fourth of July, erected at Gaspé a cross bearing the arms of France; he returned to St. Malo with two captured Indians aboard. These natives having asserted the existence of a land of Saguenay, rich with "great quantities of gold and copper,"[7] the French king ordered a second expedition the next year.

This time Cartier, with three ships, ascended the St. Lawrence as far as Stadacona, the future site of Quebec, where he established his base. From there he pushed on to the village of Hochelaga, today Montreal, at which point he was stopped by the Lachine Rapids. In the course of the winter, scurvy decimated his crews. Forced to return to France, he found the country at war. It was not until 1541 that he was sent out again with a flotilla to pave the way for settlement under Roberval. The enterprise failed when the gold and the "diamonds" brought back were found to be worthless, except to provide the French with a parallel to the later Yankee expression, "Not worth a continental" —*"Voilà un diamant de Canada!"* Thenceforth for a time only fishermen continued to frequent the Canadian coasts, and it was not until the possibilities of the fur trade became known that there were further attempts at settlement.

With the end of the century and a temporary cessation in the struggles and persecutions attendant upon the Reformation, men's minds returned with more zest to the possibilities of the New World, but the first efforts of the French to establish permanent settlements in Acadia[8] were, like those of the English farther south, unsuccessful and sometimes tragic. The little post founded on Sable Island in 1598 to control the fur trade was soon ruined by a revolt of the colonists, a group of undesirable beggars who had been deported by royal command. An attempt in 1600 to establish a settlement at Tadoussac on the lower St. Lawrence failed likewise.

Chastes' company, which next took over the monopoly, is notable chiefly because its preliminary reconnaissance brought to Canada in 1603 the man generally regarded as the father of the country, Samuel Champlain. In the following year Champlain returned as geographer and historian to the energetic Calvinist Monts, who obtained the fur monopoly in return for a promise to colonize and to propagate the Roman Catholic faith. The first permanent European settlement on the mainland[9] of what was to become the Dominion of Canada dug itself in at Port Royal (Annapolis, Nova Scotia) in 1605. From this centre Champlain continued his explorations, finding time, between-whiles, to organize the Order of Good Times to keep up the spirits of his fellows during the long, hungry winter. Doubtless he chatted with Louis Hébert on the agricultural possibilities of the country, while the wild bees hummed through the summer sunshine over the little herb garden of his apothecary friend.

Champlain was a man of wide vision and indefatigable energy. He approached the problems of colonization as a true artist, with whom everything else had to be subordinated to the necessities of creation—even the comfort or the security of the creator. When Monts' charter expired in 1607, Champlain persuaded him to seek a year's extension and start afresh in the St. Lawrence Valley, which supplied a greater abundance of furs and an avenue of exploration for gold, or perhaps for a passage towards the Orient, though it is doubtful if Champlain was deeply interested in any of these things except as means of attracting aristocratic sponsorship and securing the needful financial backing from merchants.

It was Champlain who in 1608 founded Quebec, the oldest capital north of the Rio Grande, and it was Champlain, under a series of absentee viceroys and associated merchant backers—sometimes almost in defiance of them,—who planted Normandy and Brittany, Gascony and Navarre, ineradicably in the soil of Canada. It was in the interests of trade that Champlain formed his famous and ill-starred alliance with the Hurons and Algonquins against the stronger and more warlike Iroquois; but it was not because of trade that he alone remembered the company's missionary undertakings, bringing back with him after a personal visit to France in 1615 the Récollets, who in their turn sent for the Jesuits. He may have been looking for the northwest passage when he explored the upper St. Lawrence and its great tributaries, but he was also constantly seeking new settlers and was on the watch for means of maintaining them. He planted fields near Quebec, and induced Louis Hébert, his old friend of Port Royal days, to return to Canada and become the country's first farmer.

When all Champlain's efforts proved vain, when Quebec, twenty years after its founding, still had less than a hundred residents, he appealed to Richelieu, who formed the new and powerful Company of New France, called the Hundred Associates. This association guaranteed to people the country with Roman Catholics, settle them on the land with proper safeguards, and provide for their religious education and that of their savage neighbours. Two contingents of colonists set off in 1628 with food and materials. Unfortunately, war broke out and they were captured by English ships, which forced the starving little group at Quebec also to capitulate in July, 1629. Five families, including the Héberts, stayed in New France; the rest were evacuated by the English.

Meanwhile, what of Acadia? Port Royal had languished after the departure of Champlain, although a successor had brought a few more colonists. An independent community, founded by the Jesuits in 1613 after a quarrel with the main settlement, was immediately destroyed by adventurers from Virginia, who captured and devastated Port Royal itself in the following year. Thereafter the English were a constant menace. In 1621, disregarding French claims, James I conceded the whole region, under the name of Nova Scotia, to a Scottish nobleman who sent out a few colonists in 1627. The new comers took possession of Port Royal; the remaining French found refuge in forts at Cape Sable and the St. John River until the Treaty of St. Germain-en-Laye returned both Acadia and Canada to France.

That same year, with the support of Richelieu, Lieutenant General Isaac de Razilly, a man of parts, arrived in Acadia with three hundred colonists from Touraine and Brittany, whom he established at La Hève, on the Atlantic Coast. His work scarcely begun, he died in 1635. Rival fur-traders now carried on open warfare like feudal barons, complicated by English raids and alliances, gallant ladies, deaths by drowning, power marriages, and a seizure of the colony for debt. The conflict of forces made the Gulf of St. Lawrence a focal point of national and international rivalries. In 1654, in the midst of peace, an English expedition captured Port Royal and Fort Saint-Jean (on the St. John River). The country, where a few French farmers still remained, passed by British grant into the hands of William Crowne and Sir William Temple until 1667, when the Treaty of Breda restored it to France.

At the other end of the St. Lawrence region, on the departure of the English, Champlain had reëntered Quebec in 1633 with a group of colonists. He established a post at Three Rivers in 1634, and was active in promoting settlement and cultivation until his death in 1635. He had started the movement, and the Company, under a governor chosen by its directors but appointed by the king, conceded vast tracts of land in fiefs and seigneuries, on conditions of fealty and homage with occasional modest fees. The proprietors, called "seigneurs," allotted long, narrow tracts of land to colonists (*censitaires*) who paid a modest yearly ground-rent (*cens et rentes*) and had their grain ground at the seigneurial mill. Under this fresh impulse, new immigrants, mostly from Le Perche and Normandy, settled around Quebec and Three Rivers. This progress was reinforced in 1642, when Maisonneuve, accompanied by the nurse Jeanne Mance, founded Ville-Marie (Montreal) with the object of making it a centre of Indian evangelization.

With some three hundred souls, strong men and courageous women, New France took root. It had for its clergy and educators the Jesuits; for its nurses, the Hospital Nuns of St. Joseph; and for its school-mistresses, the Ursulines, to whom were soon added, at Montreal, the Sulpicians, the *Hôtel-Dieu,* and Marguerite Bourgeoys' school. Each year brought new colonists; and soon a judicial system of seigneurial and royal courts was organized, with appeal to the governor.

In 1645 the Company of the Hundred Associates, ruined by the capture of its first fleet, ceded its commercial monopoly to the Community of New France (*Les Habitants*) on condition of their financing the colony's budget, which had reached almost 40,000 *livres* a year. From this was born the most surprising institution of the period: a council comprising the governor general, the governor of Montreal, and the highest ecclesiastic in the country, with the power to regulate commerce and finances. At first, three elected syndics represented Quebec, Montreal, and Three Rivers, respectively, as consultants; but after modifications the council, in 1657, was composed of the governor and four councillors elected by the colony. It is an extraordinary fact that under the absolute monarchy the colony enjoyed, for a time, within this rudimentary framework of a first Canadian Parliament, popular suffrage and representative government a century and a half before France herself.

In that period, in spite of the culture which progressed with the arrival of new colonists, New France existed solely by trading furs, which came mainly from the western territories. Consequently, by the nature of their occupation, fur-traders became explorers. The missionaries, enduring countless privations and difficulties, travelling in canoes or on snow-shoes to preach the gospel to the Abenaquis of the east, the Montagnais of the north, and the Hurons of the west, also opened new territories. As early as 1634 Jean Nicolet visited the Lake Michigan district; the Jesuits opened Huron missions on Georgian Bay; and between 1654 and 1660 or thereabouts Radisson and Groseilliers reached Lake Superior and the upper Mississippi region and pushed towards Hudson Bay.

This progress along the St. Lawrence and the activities branching from it were endangered by the war with the Iroquois, which started in 1643 and increased to the point of paralysing the whole country. These barbarians held a grudge against the French, who were allied with the Hurons, for suppressing their profitable role as intermediaries between the interior tribes, and suppliers of furs, and the Dutch of New Amsterdam, the future New York, who furnished arms and merchandise. After destroying the Huron villages (1648–1650) and massacring their missionaries, Daniel, Brébeuf, and Lalemant, the Iroquois carried on a blood-thirsty guerrilla warfare against the colony. In small groups, they lay in ambush near the settlements, slaying by bullet or tomahawk the ploughman in his field or the wood-cutter in the forest. They tortured their prisoners and scalped the dead. The colonists had to sow and reap in groups, muskets slung on their shoulders. The western Indians rarely dared to descend the Ottawa River with their furs. The fur trade fell off: no more beaver, no more money. The colony parleyed with New England with a view to forming an alliance against the Iroquois, but Boston was interested only in a commercial treaty (1650–1652). Despite the cruel war and continual ambushes, the colonists, both men and women, refused to give up. They held their own throughout and repulsed a strong attack on Montreal. This led the Iroquois to sue for peace (1653), which lasted four years.

New colonists arrived from France to take up land in the seigneuries, and hasty marriages resulted in a high birth-rate. But the Iroquois war soon broke out again with violence, and the death of Dollard des Ormeaux and his sixteen companions, killed to the last man at the Long Sault by an army of seven hundred warriors which threatened to invade the country, has become a legend of Canadian heroism. To this war, which bathed the colony in blood and paralysed agriculture and trade, was added a politico-religious quarrel over the sale of liquor to the Indians, who when drunk gave way to all kinds of excesses. Bishop Laval forbade it under penalty of excommunication, despite the opposition of successive governors.

The year 1663 marked the end of the first phase of the history of New France: that of its discovery and its exploitation by trading companies. In the task of colonizing the country the latter had failed miserably. On their suppression the country was in a crisis: the Iroquois war, the interruption of trade, the bankruptcy of the Company of the Hundred Associates, the failure of the Community of New France and discord between the governor and the bishop. The colony still had to import flour to keep alive, and its population numbered scarcely 2,500 souls. On the other hand, the seigneurs and colonists had shown initiative, endurance, and courage. In this country, with its rigorous climate, dense forests, and savage natives, they had explored wide territories, cleared the ground, established an important trade, and founded three centres, Quebec, Montreal, and Three Rivers, with a complete organization, civil, religious, and military. In 1663

New France was well established, but it trembled on the brink of ruin.

In this extremity, when there was even talk of abandoning the country, Louis XIV intervened on the advice of Colbert: in 1663 he cancelled the charter of the Hundred Associates and restored to the royal domain all New France, Canada, and Acadia. The colony became simply a French province in America. The King named a royal governor, who held supreme authority. To assist him, he created a Sovereign Council, on which sat the bishop and five councillors. Functioning essentially as a court of appeal, it acted also as a legislative body, regulating through ordinances the public affairs of the country. But in 1665, as a result of differences between the governor and the bishop, an intendant was sent to Canada, charged exclusively with the administration of finance, justice, and police. As a result, the bishop soon dropped out of the political scene, while the Council retained simply its original function as high court of appeal, acting as a legislative body only occasionally and in the presence or with the authorization of the intendant.

In 1664 Louis XIV conceded the trading monopoly of the colony to the West Indies Company. Fortunately, during this régime, which lasted only ten years, the King continued to administer and people the country. His first task was to suppress the Iroquois menace. Lieutenant General M. de Tracy landed in 1665 with a detachment of regular troops, of which the Carignan Regiment comprised the main body. He built forts which closed the invasion route, the Richelieu; then carried an attack into Iroquois territory, destroying several of their villages. This forced the enemy into signing, in 1667, a peace which was to last for eighteen years.

The next royal objective was to reinforce the colony through an increase of its feeble population. The task was entrusted to the Intendant, Jean Talon, a man of initiative and energy, with far-reaching purposes. Under Colbert's direction a systematic immigration policy was organized. Nearly every year convoys of immigrants, recruited in Normandy, Anjou, Poitou, and other western provinces, landed at Quebec. Released by peace, four hundred soldiers of the Carignan Regiment became colonists. For the bachelors, brides chosen with discrimination were brought to Canada—"daughters of the King"—who, on marriage, received a dowry of fifty *livres* in provisions and household articles. In this way 1,800 French entered the country in eight years. The young people married early, the boys before twenty and the girls before sixteen. To the latter the King made a present of twenty *livres*. He gave allowances to families of ten or more children, and deprived bachelors of the right to hunt or trade.

To settle these colonists Talon conceded large additional tracts of land for seigneuries, measuring on the average one league in frontage by several leagues in depth, on the banks of the St. Lawrence, as the river was the only route in this country of forests. The seigneurs, in turn, busied themselves in finding *censitaires*. Everywhere, trees fell under the axe, and in the clearings rose the modest homes of colonists—here and there a few manors, as well as unpretentious churches—while the wings of windmills revolved high above new harvests.

To increase the live-stock and extend cultivation, Talon imported from France domestic animals: horses, cows, pigs, sheep, and fowl; and the usual grains: oats, barley, wheat, hemp, and flax; as well as fruits, kitchen vegetables, and herbs. In the three towns, Quebec, Montreal, and Three Rivers, he installed craftsmen of the essential trades: bakers, carpenters, shoe-makers, masons, bricklayers, blacksmiths, and weavers. He opened a shipyard at Quebec, established fisheries along the St. Lawrence, and sought to create an export trade in lumber and grain with the West Indies. In a few years the colony produced enough to feed and clothe itself. Its modest population of 3,000 in 1665 was more than doubled by 1673, and its three little towns possessed the essential industries, hospitals, and educational institutions.

Unfortunately, in 1672 Talon left Canada, and Louis XIV, having declared war against Holland, put an end to official emigration. The demographic progression continued only by virtue of the remarkable fecundity of the people. In 1679 the country numbered 9,400 inhabitants, with 22,000 acres of land under cultivation, and 8,000 head of cattle. In all his programme Colbert encountered only one failure: the Frenchifying of the Indians.

The Jesuits had succeeded in converting only a small number of them; the Indian children avoided the schools and the adults preferred their nomadic life to a sedentary existence. The King's grant in favour of marriage between Frenchmen and Indians was fruitless: the colonists refused to intermarry.

In 1674 the bankruptcy of the West Indies Company restored all rights in the country—this time for good—to the Crown; and the administration assumed the form which it retained until the end. At its head, with residence in Quebec, the capital, stood the governor, who represented the King, commanded the troops, watched over the well-being of the colony, and governed relations with the Indians. Next to him was the intendant, who administered justice, finances, and police—really managing the whole civil economy of the country. Nevertheless, from Versailles the King and his ministers supervised every move of the two colonial chiefs. A Sovereign Council, more and more rarely consulted, formed the high court of appeal, whose judgements were revocable by the King's Council.

The judicial administration comprised royal courts at Quebec, Montreal, and Three Rivers. In five or six of the seigneuries, lower seigneurial courts were held for suits involving small amounts. Above all, a protection for the common people, free of charge, was to be found in the jurisdiction of the intendant, who could judge any civil or criminal affair, especially the disputes between seigneurs and their tenants. Unable to attend to all this, he was continually naming sub-delegates, thus extending this benefit throughout the colony.

There was no municipal organization, however; the intendant, through ordinances, attended to the policing of towns and country places. In the towns the royal judge administered municipal regulations, and the road engineer looked after the country roads. In rural districts the captain of the militia in each parish carried out the military and civil ordinances of both the governor and the intendant. In matters of policy, when it was necessary to consult public opinion, the governor called a meeting of the prominent people. The people at large could get permission from the authorities to hold a meeting in the presence of an official representative. The governors of Montreal and Three Rivers were merely military men, commanding the town garrisons and maintaining order in the districts.

Landholding was based mainly on the feudal law embodied in the *Coutume de Paris,* but adapted to local conditions. In the restricted economy of the colony the abuses which characterized the decay of the feudal system in Europe were not apparent, but, revitalized under New World conditions, the system proved very advantageous for colonization. The colonist's only obligations were to perform some small statute labour, to serve in the militia, and to mark out the roads in winter.

Agriculture was the basic occupation of over two-thirds of the population. To the settler, who paid neither taxes nor duty, the soil gave its wheat, fruits, and vegetables; the forest provided him with wood for his house, his furniture, and his fuel; and at his door there was abundant hunting and fishing. Indeed, he lived more happily than many who were considered in France to be prosperous farmers. As early as 1688 a rural population of about 8,000 had 28,000 *arpents* of land under cultivation, with a harvest of 100,000 bushels of wheat, and each farm had its cattle, pigs, sheep, and poultry.

The only important industry was fur-trading. At first the Indians themselves brought beaver skins to the towns; after 1667, with free trading, began the rush of *coureurs de bois* to pick up skins in the Indian villages at better prices. It was a hard life travelling by birch-bark canoe, loaded with arms, blankets, provisions, utensils, and merchandise, running dangerous rapids and making numberless portages. But the profits were great and adventure lurked at every Indian village.

Every year from three to four hundred *coureurs de bois* left the colony—a damaging exodus, since it represented about an eighth of the male population. To stamp out this desertion the King tried several remedies: fines, whippings, the galleys, even execution. But to no avail. Too many people—employees, merchants, silent partners, officers—profited by this trade. Besides, many ways were found of cheating the law. Then there was the danger that the *coureurs de bois* might take their furs to the English colonies. Louis XIV had to grant an amnesty to the culprits; and he established a system of twenty-five annual trading permits, to be distributed by the governor. This was necessary: the fur trade provided the colony with its greatest revenue, the best agents of its Indian alliances, and the indispensable companions of its explorers.

Through these years explorations continued, with the joint objective of furthering the fur trade and missions, especially during the first long governorship of Frontenac, the Indians' "Great Onontio," and the first real military organizer of the colony. Between 1669 and 1681 explorers visited the Lake Ontario and Lake Erie districts, ascended the Saguenay, penetrated west of Lake Superior, and explored the upper Mississippi. Two surpassed all the others. Louis Jolliet in 1673 descended the Mississippi as far as Arkansas and, in front of the site of Chicago, foresaw the possibility of a canal joining Lake Michigan to the Mississippi. Cavalier de la Salle, who in 1679 launched on Lake Erie the first ship built on the Great Lakes, explored the Illinois country in 1681, and in the following year descended the Mississippi to the Gulf of Mexico, giving Louisiana its name.

North of the vast region thus opened to the French, English fur-traders were already active, and in 1670 "The Governor and Company of Adventurers of England trading into Hudson's Bay"[10] received a royal charter. Although the French also claimed this region, the English were left in undisturbed possession until one of their forts on the Nelson River was seized in 1682, on behalf of the "Compagnie Française de la Baie du Nord de Canada." Thereafter clashes occurred periodically and governors of Canada were warned to check encroachments from this quarter.

The activities of the English colonies of New York and Massachusetts had also, and for some time, been restricted by the existence of New France. English and Dutch merchants, as well as their allies, the Iroquois, sought to capture the fur trade of the West. The English could offer merchandise at lower prices than the French, but they had difficulty in competing with an adversary who bartered in the wigwams of the Indians and won their friendship. When the Iroquois attacked the Ottawas and the Miamis, friends and customers of the French, the French came to their allies' defence and started a campaign; but, without engaging the enemy, signed a humiliating peace in 1684. Three years later, by treachery, they seized forty Iroquois chiefs and sent them to the galleys. Hostilities continued, aggravated by the Anglo-French War of 1688, and in 1689 the Iroquois burned the village of Lachine[11] and massacred all its inhabitants.

Frontenac, hastily reappointed to Canada, fortified the country and protected it by sudden destructive attacks on three villages in the American colonies. These colonies countered by invading Canada in 1690. But their land-army coming down Lake Champlain was crippled by disease, and their fleet was repulsed before Quebec by Frontenac. The Iroquois continued their raids and ambuscades. The colonists had to carry arms at work. Madeleine de Verchères, at fourteen,[12] defended her father's fort against a band of Indians. Frontenac invaded Iroquois territory, destroying several villages. In the mean time, Pierre Le Moyne d'Iberville, of a very old Canadian family, captured Fort Nelson, on Hudson Bay (1694), took Pemaquid on the Massachusetts coast, as well as several posts in Newfoundland (1696), and finally, with one ship, the *Pélican,* defeated three English vessels in Hudson Bay (1697). In the same year the Treaty of Ryswick ended the war with the English, restoring all conquests; and four years later the Iroquois signed a peace which lasted almost half a century.

Unfortunately, a new Anglo-French war broke out: the War of the Spanish Succession (1702). Colonial detachments harassed the frontiers of the English colonies. In revenge the English launched two expeditions against Canada, but the fleet, ascending the St. Lawrence, encountered a storm which broke up ten of its ships, whereupon the land-army, coming north by way of Lake Champlain, beat a retreat.

Meanwhile, things had gone differently in Acadia. After the Treaty of Breda in 1667, the Atlantic colony, with Port Royal its only little town and stronghold, had been neglected by the mother country, whose main effort was devoted to Canada. Although Acadia was important to France as the first line of defence in America, as a key to the sea-route to Quebec, and as a refuge for French fishing vessels and war-ships, it received for years only a few colonists. To expand, it had to depend on the high birth-rate of its small population of 500 souls: it achieved this miracle of multiplying and creating new settlements at Grand Pré, at

Beaubassin, and even on the north bank of the Bay of Fundy, at Fort Saint-Jean. In 1710 the population had risen to 2,000.

It was Acadia's misfortune to lie athwart the route of the Boston merchants to the fishing-grounds and commerce of Newfoundland, and to be the supply base of the Abenaquis, the sworn enemies of the English. When the War of 1688 had broken out, Massachusetts had invaded Acadia, and the English fleet had captured Port Royal. The taking of Pemaquid by Iberville had aggravated the enemy, who returned to ravage Beaubassin and the surrounding district. Again, during the War of the Spanish Succession, the Canadians and Abenaquis devastated the Massachusetts frontiers. In retaliation, the Acadian coast was laid waste, though later the English were repulsed before Port Royal. Finally, attacked in force in 1710, the little Acadian capital had to capitulate. Three years later, defeated by Marlborough on the European fields, Louis XIV had to sign the Treaty of Utrecht, which left New France untouched, but ceded definitively to Great Britain peninsular Acadia (the Nova Scotia mainland) and the Hudson's Bay Company Territories.

The next half-century was a dark period in Acadian history. The inhabitants refused to take the oath of allegiance to England, and offered passive but inflexible resistance to attempts at Anglicization. Many escaped to new French colonies on Île Royale (Cape Breton) and Île Saint-Jean (Prince Edward Island), but there are said to have been still 10,000 people in 1755, when some 7,000 were deported on grounds of military necessity under circumstances which aroused great sympathy then and since.[13]

After the Treaty of Utrecht, New France, which in a century had experienced fifty years of hostilities, was to enjoy at last a long period of peace. Versailles' first move, however, was to prepare for war. In order to close the breach opened by the loss of Acadia, the new colony on Île Royale was developed around the fortress of Louisbourg, a bastion guarding the gateway to Canada and a port of call for war-ships and fishing vessels in the North Atlantic.

In the Laurentian colony the great weakness was the small population of 18,000 in territory extending from Labrador to Lake Superior. After the signing of peace a few hundred demobilized soldiers turned settlers, and every year about thirty others got married and took up land. A few immigrants still arrived from overseas, as well as a small number of workers which every ship had to bring from France to the colonies. Thanks to these additions, and above all to the high birth-rate, the population showed an increase at each census and reached 24,000 in 1720. But already the Canadians had begun to spread out: a number had settled at Detroit and others were strung along the Mississippi as far as New Orleans.

This growing population turned in greater numbers towards agriculture, the more so as a superabundance of beaver had caused a drop in the price of furs. What the forest lost in *coureurs de bois* the farming communities gained in workers. The seigneuries were invaded by new colonists. The land under cultivation jumped from 43,000 *arpents*[14] in 1706 to 71,000 in 1719, and wheat rose from 160,000 bushels to 234,000. Production of oats, corn, barley, and peas also increased, and flax and hemp were now cultivated. Stock-raising so multiplied the number of cattle (45,000 head) that some were exported to the West Indies.

The colony's budget comprised few items: troops and fortifications, magistrates and civil servants, public works, transport, allocations to religious institutions, and miscellaneous grants. The total expense ranged from 300,000 *livres* in 1713 to 600,000 in 1749. The receipts comprised duty on wines, brandy, and tobacco; export duty on moose hides; property and seigneurial fees; profit on sales in the King's stores and in the royal fur-trading establishment at Tadoussac; and the sale of trading permits. That was all, for there were no direct taxes. These receipts averaged between 120,000 and 150,000 *livres* a year, which left an annual deficit of between 200,000 and 400,000 *livres.*

Certain particulars of the financial system may be noted. Canada was the first country in the Western Hemisphere to possess paper money, called "card money" because at the outset, in 1685, playing-cards were used. The value was written on each card, which was signed by the governor and the intendant. Payment for the surplus of imports drained the metallic specie; since the paper money did not leave the country, it was of advantage in avoiding the resort to barter during the winter months. In addition to the money the intendant could issue *ordonnances*—orders for payment, receipts, and acquittances issued for work or supplies. All this paper was convertible by the intendant into bills of exchange on the royal treasury. The whole system lent itself to abuses and peculation.

Resident at Quebec was a bishop, whose diocese included New France, Acadia, and Louisiana. Under his direction were 82 parishes in 1721 and 124 in 1756. The tithe was only a twenty-sixth of the product of the soil, and new land paid nothing for five years. Since this revenue was insufficient, twice out of three times, the King made up the balance. In the three towns of Quebec, Montreal, and Three Rivers, religious institutions looked after education and hospital care, while in the country districts a number of schools were scattered.

Colonization soon took advantage of peace: the parishes were peopled rapidly and the cultivated area stretched along the banks of the St. Lawrence from Rimouski to Coteau-du-Lac. A through highway between Quebec and Montreal was opened; another road went from Laprairie to St. John, whence the Richelieu led to Fort Saint-Frédéric, on Lake Champlain. Agriculture prospered: the land under cultivation rose from 77,000 *arpents* in 1720 to 180,000 in 1734; wheat jumped from 134,000 bushels to 737,000; and the cattle reached 80,000 head.

On the other hand, only a few industries managed to subsist: the porpoise-fishing and seal-hunting, the export of masts and ships' planking, and the manufacture of tar and resin. Only one mine, at St. Maurice, near Three Rivers, gave some results. Its forges produced pots, pans, and cannon-balls. Revived in 1732, ship-building succeeded well: the dockyards at Quebec furnished ships for Île Royale and Martinique, while the King's dockyard built shore-ships, frigates, and even sixty-cannon warships.

The important trade was still that in pelts, mostly beaver. Trading in other furs was free, but beaver skins remained under the monopoly of the Company of the West. The annual value of fur, only 520,000 *livres* in 1725, soon attained an average of 1,300,000. The trading was done by means of permits allocated by the governor and the intendant. The royal administration exploited certain territories, while conceding or leasing various western posts, sometimes even to the commandants of forts. A certain amount of contraband trade always went on with the English colonies, which paid higher prices and supplied merchandise of better quality.

The other branches of commerce did not amount to much: the sale of small ships and construction timber to the West Indies; the export of lumber, beef, and flour to Île Royale; and that of tar, resin, and iron to France. From the mother country came all manufactured products: cloth, furniture, instruments, clothes, and wines. The imports totalled an average of two million *livres* and always exceeded the exports.

The country continued to expand by exploration: after 1731 Pierre Gaultier de la Vérendrye and his sons explored the western plains from Winnipeg at least as far as South Dakota. But this growing colony still lacked adequate population. New settlers and demobilized soldiers amounted to only about a hundred colonists a year. Louis XV finally allowed the sending out of young men of good connexions who had gone wrong, as well as poachers and salt-smugglers, but this system was soon abandoned. In all, the immigrants of the eighteenth century did not exceed 5,000 men in sixty years. Only the high birth-rate reinforced the population, which grew to 24,000 in 1720, 42,000 in 1739, and 70,000 in 1758.

After a prosperous peace of thirty years, the War of the Austrian Succession came in 1741 to Canada like a fatal blow. To guard her territory, ranging from Labrador to the Rockies, there were only twenty-eight companies of marine troops, a total of 1,200 soldiers, while the militia could muster about 10,000 men. Quebec was the only fortified town; Montreal had a weak stone wall and Three Rivers a stake fence. Small forts, mostly log stockades, existed at Chambly, Frontenac (Kingston), Niagara, Detroit, and Michilimackinac. To protect her sea gateway, France had long fortified Louisbourg, the capital of Cape Breton Island. Thirty million francs had made a Gibraltar, so it was believed, of this little town of 3,000 inhabitants and 1,500 soldiers in a colony that existed on fishing, the total population of which did not exceed 6,000 souls.

It was here that hostilities broke out: the French privateers, with Louisbourg as their base, captured twenty-four Boston ships.

The post at Canceau was seized and a vain attack was made on Port Royal. Massachusetts reacted immediately. A flotilla carrying 4,000 men besieged and captured Louisbourg in June, 1745. France dispatched a squadron of thirteen ships, but a storm dispersed it, and an epidemic carried off 2,400 soldiers. The English garrison was captured at Minas. In Canada the war was limited to skirmishes along the borders of the English colonies and Iroquois raids against French settlements. Soon the Treaty of Aix-la-Chapelle (1748) restored the *status quo* and returned Louisbourg and Île Royale to France.

The war having doubled the colonial budget to 2,000,000 *livres* a year, France, in order to make Canada bear a portion of it, raised the duty on wines and liquors in January, 1747. The following year, import and export duties were placed on goods which had hitherto been exempt. All this doubled the revenue, bringing it up to 200,000 *livres* a year. The country continued to progress: the fur trade reached 3,000,000 *livres* a year; the rural districts, with 200,000 *arpents* of land under cultivation, produced an average of 800,000 bushels of wheat and contained 100,000 head of cattle. The exports—furs, flour, meat, lumber, and oils—amounted to 2,000,000 *livres* a year, and almost balanced the imports. The colony contributed to the royal treasury 500,000 *livres,* which about covered its normal budget.

But Canada had ceased to be a colony to be developed and had become a bastion to be fortified. France's main objective was to block the inland expansion of the English colonies: she set out to build forts in the remote forest, to supply the country with guns and troops, and to spend millions of *livres* for war when there was not a man or a sou for colonization. The expenditure leaped from year to year, and this financial prodigality allowed Intendant Bigot and the commissary Cadet to form the *Grande Société,* which, cornering the contracts for supplies, bought at official prices and resold at excessive rates. An ox was bought on requisition for 80 *livres,* but was sold to the King at 1,200. It was a reign of unrestrained malversation. Military expenditure and administrative misappropriation forced the budget up to a fantastic height. From 2,000,000 *livres* in 1748, it rocketed to 12,000,000 in 1754, to 24,000,000 in 1758, and to 30,000,000 in 1759.

A costly possession, New France constituted also a permanent *casus belli,* as she tried by a chain of forts to hem in the English colonies, whose population, overflowing their frontiers, was on the march to invade the Great Lakes region, capture the western fur trade, and cut New France asunder from Louisiana. Against the impending danger the governors erected Fort Beauséjour to the east and tried through the Abbé Le Loutre to entice the Acadians into French territory; while to the west, in addition to Forts Frontenac, Niagara, and Detroit, they raised Forts Presqu'île and Rivière-aux-Boeufs. As counter-preparation the British started building a post at what is now Pittsburg, but the French seized the place and made it Fort Duquesne. The young officer George Washington, with a party of Virginians and Indians, attacked a detachment led by Jumonville, and killed the leader with nine men. The crisis had arrived. Both France and Britain dispatched troops to America. In July, 1755, Braddock and Washington, marching against Fort Duquesne, were beaten by Dumas and the Canadians at the Monongahéla. In September, Colonel Johnson in turn defeated Dieskau and his troops at Lake Saint-Sacrement, and without a declaration of war British war-ships seized French vessels transporting troops to Canada.

In 1756 the war became official. Montcalm took command of the Canadian army: 3,700 regulars, 1,900 marine troops, and about 4,000 militiamen. Without delay he besieged and took Fort Oswego, the English bridge-head on Lake Ontario. In the following year he captured and razed Fort William Henry, on Lake George, the door to invasion from Lake Champlain. In the face of these French victories, Pitt, determined to conquer at any cost, closed the Atlantic to shipping from France and sent Amherst and Wolfe to attack Louisbourg with 12,000 soldiers and a naval squadron. At the end of seven weeks Governor Drucourt and his 5,000 men had to capitulate, and the way was now open for invasion by the St. Lawrence. In the interior, from New York, Abercromby marched with 15,000 regulars against the French forts on Lake Champlain, but Montcalm, ranging his 4,000 men behind a log abatis, defeated a force nearly four times as large moving northward from New York. This victory saved the colony for a time.

In 1759 Pitt organized mass attacks on Quebec, Carillon on Lake Champlain, and Niagara. Against these three armies numbering 40,000 men, supported by the English colonies with a population of 2,000,000, New France could match only 6,000 soldiers and 10,000–15,000 militiamen in a country of 70,000 souls. The fight seemed hopeless. Niagara had to capitulate, but the French commander at Carillon blew up his fort and that at Saint-Frédéric, and fortified himself at Île-aux-Noix. After building some small vessels, the English decided in October not to attack until spring.

The decisive struggle took place before Quebec, where Wolfe landed in June with 9,000 regulars from a fleet of over 140 ships. Behind the town walls and Montmorency retrenchment, Montcalm awaited the enemy. Wolfe attacked on July 31, but the assault was completely repulsed. The question of lifting the siege was now considered, but Wolfe decided to run the risk of scaling in the night, at Anse-au-Foulon (Wolfe's Cove), the cliff that leads to the Plains of Abraham. On the morning of September 13, 5,000 redcoats were lined up for battle. Immediately Montcalm gathered together his forces and marched against the enemy. But his incongruous army—soldiers, marine troops, and militiamen—lacking cohesion, withered under the brisk fire from the British lines. Shaken by the force of the fusillade, it broke before the bayonet attack and soon fled in full retreat. Wolfe was killed on the spot, and Montcalm, who was wounded, died in the next night, defeated for the first time in four years of fighting.

On September 18 Quebec capitulated, and the French army took up winter quarters at Montreal. In the spring of 1760 Lévis marched against Quebec, but the siege had scarcely begun when a British squadron carrying reinforcements entered the harbour. The French army retired to Montreal, where three British armies converged: ascending the St. Lawrence from Quebec, coming along the Richelieu, and descending the St. Lawrence. With 19,000 men at the gates, Governor Vaudreuil had to sign, on September 8, 1760, a capitulation which surrendered all New France, from the Gulf of St. Lawrence to the Rocky Mountains. In February, 1763, by the Treaty of Paris, Louis XV ceded definitively the whole of Canada to Great Britain.

But the work of France did not perish with the Conquest. In 1763 Canada was much more than a mere colonial settlement, and already contained the essentials of a new nation. In the course of 230 years of possession, from Cartier to Vaudreuil, the French, in spite of their small numbers, had succeeded in the adventurous and remarkable achievement of exploring the continent from Labrador to the Gulf of Mexico and from Acadia to the Rocky Mountains. In this immense territory they had opened up main routes of communication, developed the fur trade, and introduced Christian civilization to the indigenous tribes.

In the interior of the colony, which extended from Cape Breton Island to Detroit, they had established an administration nominally autocratic but tempered with a benevolent paternalism: no direct taxation was imposed, and only light consumption taxes were collected. Justice was administered with dispatch, with fairness, and at little expense. Economically, the seigneurial régime favoured the colonist and agriculturist in every way. In the towns there were artisans of all trades, and in certain branches—construction, goldsmithing, and sculpture—many remarkable craftsmen. The colony possessed good institutions of learning and hospitals in each town. The Canadians spoke a French of high quality, and Montcalm said that the social life in the towns compared favourably with that of the provinces of France.

Comparatively early—since the beginning of the eighteenth century—from the free life in a new country and the struggle against Nature's difficulties, the people of New France had acquired new habits of initiative, independence, and self-reliance. At the same time, new conceptions of social relations developed, due to the levelling of the classes that resulted from the similar working and living conditions imposed by the necessities of colonization.

Displaying a natural pride in the achievements of the pioneers, this moral and social French-Canadianism continued to grow and to assert itself with the years to such a point that travellers disembarking at Quebec were astounded and resentful at the spirit of assertiveness and independence of all classes of the colony's inhabitants. It reached the point where rivalry arose between the old-country French and the native Canadians in every sphere: military, administrative, economic, and even religious.

At the time of the Conquest, despite her small population of some 70,000, French Canada possessed all the essential elements, economic and cultural, of a political community different from that of the mother country, and even tending to throw off useless colonial restrictions. This people stood almost ready to assert its right to a separate nationality in America, distinctively French and Roman Catholic, evolving towards a particular destiny, worthy of the achievements of their forefathers: explorers, settlers, craftsmen, soldiers, and missionaries—men and women whose endeavours had erected the remarkable structure of their country.

CHAPTER IV

The British North American Colonies

BY A. L. BURT

THE BRITISH acquisition of New France, by military capitulation in 1760 and by treaty cession in 1763, posed a new and difficult problem for the British Government: how to fit into the Empire an old colony that had a European population of some 70,000 and was utterly alien in language, religion, laws, political institutions, and culture. The problem was so foreign to British experience that officials in London could not grasp it when they approached the task of providing for the administration of the newly-conquered Canada. They assumed that the colony was bound to lose its French character and its Roman Catholic religion. Such a transformation had taken place in Nova Scotia, with the founding of Halifax in 1749, the deportation of the Acadians in 1755, the arrival of settlers from New England, the convocation of the first Nova Scotia assembly in 1758, and the subsequent swelling of the New England influx.

No expulsion of Canadians was contemplated, but there was an expectation that large numbers of the surplus population in the old colonies would pour into Canada, changing her national character; and there was a lively hope, supported by circumstantial reports from the St. Lawrence, that the Canadians might easily be persuaded to see the true light of religion and turn Protestant. Therefore London proceeded to establish in Canada the same form of government that the other British colonies possessed. A governor and council were appointed, and the governor was directed to call an assembly as soon as circumstances would permit.

Law courts of the traditional English type were introduced, and they were to apply English laws.

London also greatly reduced the geographical size of Canada. All the hinterland south-west of the Ottawa River, except a little strip of what is now Ontario, was cut off in order to create an immense Indian reserve in the heart of the continent; and the southern boundary from the St. Lawrence eastward was drawn much as it is today, to preserve unoccupied Canadian territory south of this line for English settlement by annexing it to New England and Nova Scotia. Then, too, Nova Scotia was enlarged by the addition of the remaining parts of Acadia that France had just surrendered—Cape Breton, Prince Edward Island, and the region soon to become New Brunswick; the western boundary of this bigger Nova Scotia was defined as running up the River St. Croix to its source and thence straight north to the height of land. These boundary prescriptions from the St. Lawrence to the Bay of Fundy are important because they were to be copied twenty years later as a dividing line between the United States and British North America, but the boundary west of the St. Lawrence had to be changed before the American Revolution.

The attempt to govern Canada as if she were an ordinary English colony soon proved to be impossible because it rested on a false assumption. The French of Canada, fearful of their fate under the rule of a foreign and heretic power, instinctively rallied behind the Church, their only possible shield; and the lands of Canada, though officially advertised in the old colonies, drew no settlers from the south or anywhere else. The only British immigrants were those who went to engage in trade, a small and pushing urban minority who aspired to control the country because, according to English law, no Roman Catholic could hold public office or even exercise the vote.

As the governor, who had been military ruler of Quebec from its capture, was a warm friend of the French Canadians, he refused to call an assembly, which would have to be elected from and by this mercantile minority. The latter then raised such an uproar that they forced his recall, only to find that his successor, Guy Carleton, was equally opposed to an assembly and more capable of bridling them. But if an assembly was impossible, so also was the situation created by the failure to call one, for an assembly was legally essential for taxing and legislative purposes.

The English laws against Roman Catholics also struck at the jurisdiction, the revenue, and the property of their Church in Canada, the institution most precious to the vast mass of the population; and the application of English law to a society cast in the very different mould of Roman law caused no end of trouble. There was little difficulty with the English criminal law, since it affected only a few persons; but the effort to substitute English for French civil law produced hopeless confusion and threatened all the property in the colony.

It became more and more evident that a new constitution would have to be given to this old French colony to suit its character. Otherwise the Canadians would never become loyal British subjects and would seize the first opportunity to deliver the colony back to France, then Britain's chronic foe. The south-western boundary also had to be changed because the plans for the great native reserve broke down completely. Their failure left the interior without any government, and some kind of government was necessary to regulate the dealings of fur-traders with one another and with the red men. As this derelict region had belonged to Canada and most of its trade was still conducted from Montreal, the obvious solution was to reannex it.

Therefore the home government passed the Quebec Act of 1774. It restored to Canada all the territory down to the Ohio and out to the Mississippi. It dropped the idea of an assembly and met the need for a local legislature by giving the governor and the council a limited authority to enact laws. It opened the council and other public offices to Roman Catholics, who thus gained political emancipation in Canada more than half a century before they got it in Britain. It continued English criminal law and restored the old civil law as it was on the eve of the Conquest, leaving to the governor and the council the task of modifying these basic laws as might seem advisable. Because the old civil law required the payment of the tithe, in addition to protecting the other property rights of the Church, the Act declared, out of regard for the Protestant minority, that the Roman Catholic clergy could collect the tithe only from their own people. Because the new legislature had no elected chamber, it was forbidden to levy taxes. But the colony had to be provided with revenue; and this was done by a companion measure, the Quebec Revenue Act, which imposed customs duties and tavern-keepers' licence fees.

Very naturally, though quite mistakenly, Americans at once saw in the Quebec Act the design of a dastardly blow aimed through Canada at the back of the old colonies. Therefore, at the outset, the American Revolution thrust a fiery arm up into Canada. But the American forces that besieged Quebec during the winter of 1775–1776 were not strong enough to take it, and if by some accident or blunder they had got it they could not have held it against the powerful expedition that arrived from Britain in the spring of 1776 and swept them out of the country. If the newly-conquered Canadians had risen in revolt when the invasion gave them a chance, the outcome might have been different; but they preferred to remain neutral because they had even less love for the Americans than they had for the British.

As the scope of the war widened, something else kept Canada in the Empire. The entry of France into the war shook the foundations of British rule in this French colony, and simultaneously raised the prospect of a combined French naval and American land attack upon it. But whenever such a plan was proposed, one or the other ally vetoed it. It was first put off by American suspicion that it would restore French control of the St. Lawrence, which would work with Spanish control of the Mississippi to throttle the United States. When American desire overcame this suspicion and revived the project, France vetoed it, lest it establish the United States on the St. Lawrence and thereby undermine American dependence upon France. Thus the alliance that rendered Canada almost fatally vulnerable was politically, though not physically, incapable of striking the combined blow that might have robbed Britain of this colony.

Nova Scotia remained British for a different reason. The newly-arrived Yankees, who formed three-quarters of its population, would have thrown this colony into the American Revolution if they could. But living in little isolated communities that were scattered along the coast of what was virtually an island, they were beyond the reach of American aid, without which they were helpless against the power that the mother country could bring to bear upon them at any time. They were trapped, as the Acadians had been; and they reacted in the same way, begging to be allowed to remain neutral. Even more beyond the grasp of the American Revolution, thanks to British sea power, were Prince Edward Island, which had been granted to a few proprietors in 1767 and by their influence had been made a separate colony with its own governor, council, and assembly in 1769; and Newfoundland, which was more of a fishing station than a colony and had no resident governor until 1818 and no assembly until 1832.

At the close of the American Revolution, Nova Scotia experienced a second transformation. It became overwhelmingly British. The "Neutral Yankees," as they have aptly been called,[1] were not expelled, nor did they seek to depart when peace was restored. They were swamped in 1783 by the arrival of some 30,000 Loyalists, who increased the population threefold. About 9,000 settled on the St. John River, forming the nucleus of the province of New Brunswick, between 2,000 and 3,000 in Cape Breton Island, and almost all the rest in what was to remain Nova Scotia. Most of them were city-bred folk from the New England seaboard, and a high proportion had belonged to the upper class of the society they left behind. They had lost all their property, but they retained their education and their spirit. It was this select stock that really made the two provinces of Nova Scotia and New Brunswick, which have supplied an extraordinarily large percentage of the professional, political, and business leaders of the Dominion of Canada. In 1784 New Brunswick was severed from Nova Scotia and given its own governor, council, and assembly. Cape Breton was cut off at the same time, but it had a much smaller population and did not get an assembly until it was reannexed to Nova Scotia in 1820.

To the old Canada, the American Revolution also gave a new population, though it was less numerous. About 1,000 Loyalists settled in what is now the Province of Quebec, and nearly 6,000 laid the foundations of what grew to be Ontario. In contrast to those of the Maritime Provinces, most of these Loyalists were backwoods farmers from the interior of the old colonies, just the

[1] For notes to chapter iv see page 573.

people to open new country, and they were only the vanguard of a swelling migration of pioneers from the American frontier, which they drew after them into the upper region. At last, a quarter of a century after the Conquest, a rapidly growing English-speaking population appeared beside the French but separated geographically from them. The colony was assuming a dual character that called for a radical revision of the Quebec Act, but the loud cries that arose in Canada were so conflicting that again London was puzzled.

The British mercantile minority on the lower St. Lawrence once more clamoured for an assembly. These men knew that the great majority of the electorate would be French Canadian; yet they thought they could manage the chamber, for they counted on the backing of the rapidly growing settlement in the upper region and on winning enough support from the French, many of whom they persuaded to join in the chorus. On the other hand, the seigneurial class shouted against an assembly, and they too rallied a large following. Meanwhile the Loyalists on the upper St. Lawrence demanded a separate government for their part of the country, and the opposing camps below united in denouncing this demand.

The consideration that finally brought the home government to a decision was finance. The proceeds of the Quebec Revenue Act had fallen far short of what the colony needed, and the governor had to draw bills on the British treasury. This could not continue indefinitely, for the taxpayers in Britain would object; nor could Parliament impose additional levies, having enacted in 1778 that it would never again tax a colony. The only way left was to have the people tax themselves through elected representatives. This obvious conclusion led to another. The colony would have to be divided because one assembly for the whole would be unworkable. The country was too large and the difference between the older French society on the lower St. Lawrence and the new English-speaking society above was too great. Therefore, in 1791, an imperial order-in-council divided the country into Lower and Upper Canada, and Parliament endowed each with a legislative council and a legislative assembly.

By this time an important change was coming over the enormous territory that the royal charter of 1670 had given to the Hudson's Bay Company. The traders of that company had long been content to sit in their posts on "the Bay" and there collect the furs that the red men brought down to them; for it was not until towards the end of the French régime in Canada that French rivals, working overland from the St. Lawrence, appeared upon the scene, and the British conquest of Canada checked their invasion when it was beginning to worry the English company. The Hudson's Bay Company soon had to push inland again, however. Following the Conquest in 1760, British traders, attracted by visions of fortunes in furs, took over the trade from Montreal and carried their enterprise with tremendous energy into the West. For a few years these Montreal traders were beset by rivalries among themselves, causing much liquor and not a little blood to flow on the frontiers. They ended this fratricidal strife in 1784 by combining their interests in the North West Company, which possessed a driving power and a ruthless efficiency seldom if ever surpassed in the later history of business corporations in America.

The new Canadian company roused the old English company to fight for its life; and within a decade an intense conflict developed which took the form of planting rival fur-trading posts along the water-ways of this vast, lone land—throughout the watershed of Hudson Bay, which was the limit of the older company's charter, and wherever else Indians might be attracted and furs obtained. This competition spread British influence and control, and laid the foundations for Canada's acquisition of the West nearly a century afterwards. Since the only way into the West was through Hudson Bay, or by the long canoe-trail from Montreal, no settlement was yet possible, or any real government. The white men were ruled by their respective companies, to which the half-breed population, which now began to arise, was also attached; and neither organization attempted to exercise jurisdiction over the red men.

Though peace was signed between Britain and the United States in 1783, it was another thirty-five years before peace between them was really established; meanwhile the history of the British North American colonies was more or less that of a thinly-settled borderland where two jealous powers met and eyed each other suspiciously. The international boundary as defined in 1783 was open to dispute in many places; and, what was more serious, each power contemplated a new boundary settlement that would drastically curtail the territory of the other. Also, Americans were pushing into British North America, and British influence, operating from this base, was exercising an effective control over much of the unsettled interior of the United States.

Americans haunted the shores of the Maritime Provinces, where, as the result of American insistence on the retention of old rights, the Treaty of 1783 qualified British sovereignty by allowing Americans to fish in territorial waters and to land and dry their catch.[2] Other Americans, in search of land, pressed across the northern border of the United States. The government of Lower Canada, fearing an uncontrollable influx of squatters and seeing no other possibility of settling the empty region now known as the Eastern Townships, opened it to these pioneers. They came in the last decade of the eighteenth century and continued to come until they were stopped by the outbreak of war in 1812. Much greater was the American migration into Upper Canada, giving it a rate of growth many times that of any other British North American colony—and a predominantly American character. This American trek to British soil naturally encouraged the American hope of a drastic boundary revision.

The British influence in the interior of the United States was linked with the larger boundary question. By agreeing to run the international boundary through the Great Lakes, Britain formally ceded to the United States an immense territory that was still effectively British; then, in violation of the treaty, she retained control of it by keeping her garrisons there. At first glance it looks as if the British Government had negligently signed away the better half of Montreal's fur-trading empire (for in 1783 the merchants of that city were still drawing more pelts from south of the line than from the North-West), and, discovering this blunder in time, had tried to correct it by refusing to make delivery. But the treaty was negotiated and signed on a mutual understanding that the trade of this region would continue to be British. A general reciprocity agreement that would preserve it was deleted from the peace treaty for inclusion in a supplementary commercial treaty, which for various reasons was never concluded. One might therefore suppose that the failure to implement this understanding induced the British violation of the treaty; but it did not, for the latter occurred before the former was realized.

What caused the British violation was the discovery of another blunder. The Government in London had forgotten its red allies in this region. It had made peace without them and, worse still, had promised to the United States, with which they were still at war, the territory that they inhabited and that was guaranteed to them by a solemn British treaty of only fifteen years before. News of this betrayal soon penetrated the western forests, forcing a crisis for the governor in Quebec to face. He assured the Indians that Britain would not desert them, and to prove it he initiated the policy, later upheld in London, of retaining the military posts in the interior of the United States.

As the Indians beat back successive American attacks, British policy grew bolder—by mediation to extract from the United States a recognition of this territory as an Indian reserve under a British guaranty. The American Government would have none of it, and war between the two powers was narrowly averted in 1794, when American forces, at last victorious over the Indians, chased them past a British military post on American soil. Already, over in London, an agreement was being reached, in Jay's Treaty, whereby Britain withdrew her garrisons in return for an American promise not to interfere with the Canadian fur trade in this American territory, over which, as a consequence, American sovereignty was still qualified in favour of British interests. Not until after the War of 1812 did the United States win from the British the full control of this territory; meanwhile the war itself inspired in each power an ambition to push back the boundary of the other.

The War of 1812 seemed to imperil the very existence of the British North American colonies, but it did not. Until 1814 Britain was locked in a life-and-death struggle with Napoleon, and therefore could not be expected to send any appreciable reinforcements to the little garrisons that were widely scattered through these colonies and numbered less than 5,000 regulars. British North America was a long, thin line of settlement that was not even continuous, and it stretched for more than a thousand miles along an indefensible border. The United States had a population of 7,750,000, as against scarcely 500,000 in all these colonies. Of this half-million, the large majority were French, who had been sullenly neutral during the American Revolution and were now openly resenting the rule of their British masters; the minority included a large proportion of Americans, who formed the greater part of the population in Upper Canada.

British sea power, however, was an ultimate guaranty, not called upon because it was not needed, to make the United States disgorge even a considerable land conquest; and, long before the fall of Napoleon released a powerful army of British veterans for use in North America, the tight British blockade of the American coast was exerting such stifling economic pressure on the United States that it was paralysing the ability of the American Government to push the war on land. Nor was this the only cause of paralysis: internal division in the United States offset the external distraction of Great Britain. American opposition to the war was intense, and was concentrated in the North. It split New York and it dominated New England. Another cause was the incompetence of the administration in Washington, which hopelessly mismanaged what fighting resources it commanded.

The Maritime Provinces were immune from attack by sea or land, thanks to British sea power and the practical neutrality of New England; and to the people of these provinces, fighting in this war meant privateering, which brought more profit than loss. The only military activity in this quarter was the British conquest of a considerable portion of Maine in the autumn of 1814. At the other extreme, in the West, where the fur trade had preserved a strong British influence in American territory, and where American ineptitude had provoked a renewal of native hostilities on the eve of the declaration of war against Britain, an enormous section of the United States, from the Great Lakes to the Mississippi, was lopped off by the British and their Indian allies in 1812. There the British sway continued unchallenged throughout the rest of the war.

The two Canadas were the only vulnerable part of British North America, and for years their easy conquest had been confidently predicted by war-mongers in the United States. If the Americans had concentrated all their military efforts in a drive down the Richelieu on Montreal, only a few miles from the border, they could have snuffed out the native war in their own country and sliced off the whole of Upper Canada and the richest portion of Lower Canada. Success there would have given a strong impetus towards the capture of Quebec, which could not be relieved from overseas until the summer of 1814, and the fall of Canada's citadel would have locked Britain out of the whole land. This was what the British feared, and it caused them grave concern.

The American direction of the war was, however, so utterly incompetent that it struck at the western extremities of British power in the North rather than at the controlling heart on the lower St. Lawrence. The second American siege of Quebec, of which there had been loud talk in the United States, quickly became a forgotten dream, and the plans for an invasion of Lower Canada collapsed at a touch. It was on Upper Canada that the brunt of the war fell. The Americans conquered the south-west corner of that province, but were driven back when they invaded the Niagara peninsula, where the fighting was heaviest and most continuous.

The collapse of the big European war, with the fall of Napoleon in 1814, turned this little American war upside down. It blasted American hopes of extending the United States at the expense of British North America, and it raised British hopes of tearing away extensive portions of the United States. These included not only the conquered Maine district and the whole region from the Great Lakes to the Mississippi, but also territory south of the Great Lakes to give security against another American surprise attack when Britain's hands were tied. It was the Duke of Wellington who, late in 1814, decided that there was to be no such redivision of this continent. Fearing a renewal of the war in Europe, which came in 1815, he persuaded the British Government to make an immediate peace with the United States on the basis of the old boundary.

The Treaty of Ghent, signed on Christmas Eve, did little more than end the war. The real peace settlement came afterwards, in the Rush-Bagot Agreement of 1817 for disarmament on the Lakes and in the London Convention of 1818. The latter provided for the settlement of outstanding disputes over the fisheries and the boundary as far as the Rocky Mountains, and it implicitly laid the old ghost of special British trading-rights that had limited American sovereignty in the West. The war had taught a wholesome lesson in mutual vulnerability. The exposure of the United States on the seaboard balanced the exposure of British North America in the interior. But if war revealed the necessity for permanent peace between the two powers, it also reinforced in Canada the anti-American prejudice that dates from the American Revolution. Canadians could not forget that they had had to fight to save their country from being conquered by the United States, and this memory has contributed much to the growth of Canadian national feeling.

The British North American colonies were increased by one in the second decade of the nineteenth century, when the Scottish philanthropist, Lord Selkirk, established, on a large tract of land granted him by the Hudson's Bay Company, a settlement which proved to be the nucleus of the future province of Manitoba. This infant colony was twice replanted, after being uprooted by the Nor'-Westers, who saw in it a strategic move of the English company to cut the North West Company's communications and destroy its food supply, the pemmican which was made there by the *métis*. But the Canadian company, which employed the half-civilized *métis* in its violence against the settlers, was coming to an end; for the heavier transportation costs of the longer overland route from the St. Lawrence were telling in favour of the English company. The end came in 1821, when the older organization absorbed the younger. Montreal lost its fur trade, and the Selkirk settlement its enemy. But the colony grew slowly, and there were only about five hundred whites and nearly ten times as many half-breeds living along the banks of the Red and Assiniboine rivers in 1850.

The first assembly in what is now western Canada was granted in 1849, but not to the Red River settlement. During the American War of Independence and the subsequent settlement of large numbers of English-speaking Loyalists in eastern Canada, Captain James Cook and Captain George Vancouver had explored the Pacific Coast and paved the way for British settlement of what was to become the Dominion's most westerly province. The Russians had already inaugurated the trade in pelts of sea otter, which occupied a place in the history of western Canada comparable to that of beaver in eastern Canada. Angered by the incursions of British fur-traders upon a region of which for three centuries they had claimed the monopoly, the Spaniards in 1789 seized the property of Captain John Meares, including the *North-West America,* the first vessel launched on the coast of British Columbia. In the following year they were compelled to restore this property and admit British subjects' right to trade and settle north of the thirty-eighth parallel of latitude.

The territory, known as New Caledonia, was administered by the Hudson's Bay Company, and little was known or cared in England about its potentialities. By 1840 American settlement made it seem advisable, in the interests of the fur trade, to move the Company headquarters north from Fort Vancouver, on the Columbia six miles above its junction with the Willamette; and in 1843 Victoria was founded on Vancouver Island. The Oregon Treaty of 1846 defined the limits of the Hudson's Bay Company Territory, and in 1849 a colony was organized under the Crown, with headquarters at Victoria and with its own assembly. The Hudson's Bay Company, however, retained supremacy throughout most of the future province of British Columbia until the gold-rush of 1858 led to the organization of another colony on the mainland, with New Westminster as its capital.

Meanwhile there was striking development in the older colonies of British North America. The war against Napoleon gave a vigorous stimulus to their prosperity. Realizing the danger of continuing to depend on the Baltic for vital supplies of timber, Britain sought security by drawing them from these colonies. To do this as quickly as possible, by forcing labour and capital into the business, the British Parliament clapped prohibitive duties on foreign timber, thus giving colonial timber a monopoly in the rich British market. Thereupon the woodsman's axe bit furiously into the virgin forests of British North America, particularly in New Brunswick and Upper Canada, and a great colonial trade in timber sprang up where virtually none had existed before. The return of peace did not stop its expansion, for the British preference was continued and the British demand increased.

This substitution of one forest product for another as the staple of British North American trade was highly important. Furs had made Montreal the wealthiest urban centre in all these colonies, but had brought little benefit to any other part of them, whereas timber production enriched them as a whole and helped to spread settlement. It opened the country, it assisted pioneer farmers to find their feet, and it encouraged immigration from the British Isles by slashing west-bound passenger rates.

Immigration from the mother country was little more than a fitful trickle until 1815, when population problems began to worry the authorities at home, forcing a reversal of the traditional British policy of discouraging emigration. Then the trickle grew into a stream; and around 1825 the stream swelled into a full-flowing river, which soon transformed the British North American colonies. By 1850 their total population was multiplied to approximately 2,500,000—five times what it had been at the time of the War of 1812. Prince Edward Island now had about 63,000, Newfoundland nearly 150,000, New Brunswick a little over 180,000, Nova Scotia 275,000, Lower Canada 890,000, and Upper Canada 950,000.

Newfoundland, originally settled by fishermen from the southwest of England, was predominantly Irish, as it had long been. Its people dwelt along the coast, chiefly in and near St. John's, for the sea provided their only means of livelihood. Of late years they had added seal-fishing to their mainstay, the cod, for which the principal market was in southern Europe and the West Indies. Prince Edward Island, on the other hand, was almost wholly agricultural; but this "garden of the Gulf" was not so attractive to immigrants as it might have been if they could have obtained titles from the absentee proprietors. New Brunswick was less dependent on its timber than it had been. The southern third of the province was fairly well occupied by farms, and there was continuous settlement up the main river valleys and around the coast. On the last there was considerable fishing and not a little shipbuilding, while the port of St. John had a far-flung commerce.

Nova Scotia was much more mature than the other colonies by the sea; and its population was more distinctly Scottish, particularly in Cape Breton, where most of the people were Gaelic-speaking Highlanders. All along the much-indented coast of Nova Scotia were thriving fishing villages; and the land of the province, though not so good as that of Prince Edward Island, was well cultivated. The rich coal-deposits of Cape Breton and Pictou County supported a prosperous mining industry, the only one in British North America. But the golden age of Nova Scotia, which was then well begun, was based chiefly upon shipping, for the province had become the seat of a great ship-building industry. The vessels that came off its stocks included many of the finest that ploughed the ocean in the era of wood and sail, and they carried a goodly share of the world's commerce. When steam began to supplant sail, it was quite natural that, in 1840, an enterprising Halifax merchant, Samuel Cunard, should start the first line of transatlantic steamships.

The two Canadas, which became Canada East and Canada West on their reunion in the same year that the Cunard Line was founded, could also boast of a large commerce and an extensive ship-building industry, centred in Montreal and Quebec, respectively—by far the oldest cities of all British North America. Montreal, which had outgrown Quebec by the American Revolution, leaped ahead in the first half of the new century, attaining a population of nearly 60,000, much larger than that of any other city in these colonies. It lay in the midst of the oldest and most highly-developed agricultural region, and the improvement of the St. Lawrence ship-channel shifted trade up river from Quebec, making Montreal the commercial capital not only of the better part of Canada East but of Canada West as well. In further contrast with Quebec, which remained almost exclusively French, Montreal was nearly one-third English-speaking, and almost all its big business was in the hands of this minority, as it still is.

But winter, though it never locked up the ports of the Maritime Provinces, closed the St. Lawrence for five months in every twelve, and maritime activity played a relatively smaller part in the life of the Canadas as a whole, which was overwhelmingly agricultural. Instead of having to import wheat and flour, as did all the Maritime Provinces except the smallest, United Canada had a surplus for export. But this surplus was small, amounting to less than two bushels a head, which, as there was yet practically no export of meat or dairy produce, indicates how little more than self-sufficient agriculture was in those days before the introduction of farm machinery. The trees of the forest still provided the only article exported in large quantity from the St. Lawrence.

Lower Canada, whose population in 1815 outnumbered that of all the other British North American colonies combined, had much less need for immigration than any of them. Yet that province still had land that attracted new comers. British people from across the water completed the settlement begun by Americans in the Eastern Townships, much to the dismay of the French-Canadian leaders, whose people were beginning to need this space for their own expansion. The establishment of an English-speaking and Protestant bloc within this French-speaking and Roman Catholic province contributed to the racial strife that tore Lower Canada, as we shall see, until the middle of the nineteenth century.

Upper Canada gained more by immigration than all the other provinces put together, for it had far more undeveloped good land. By 1850, when most of this was taken up, the population of the province had grown tenfold since the War of 1812, and it was again completely changed in character. That war had severed the growing connexion between Upper Canada and the United States as with a knife, and subsequent immigration had flooded the province with people from the British Isles. But if they came as English, Scots, and Irish, and long retained the distinctive marks of their several national origins, particularly the Scots and the Irish, they came also to build a new life in the New World and it quickly made them over into good North Americans. Though the huge majority of them became subsistence farmers who owned their own land, they formed a society whose business and professional needs gave rise, before the middle of the century, to most of the towns and cities of the present Ontario.

Meanwhile there was a growing political ferment in all the colonies, culminating just before 1850 in what may best be termed the British North American Revolution. Though the American

Revolution, by giving birth to the United States, contributed greatly in the long run to the political emancipation of the remaining colonies in North America, its immediate effect had been to make British colonial policy more reactionary rather than more liberal. The fiery destruction of the best part of the old Empire burnt in upon British minds the fear of another American Revolution, and this fear dominated British colonial policy for more than two generations. Turning back to find the basic mistakes that had produced and might reproduce the tragedy, thinking Britons almost at once concluded that these mistakes were: letting the colonies at first develop virtually free of control, and attempting later to tax them. Therefore the British Government resolved never to tax a colony again, and never to let the remaining colonies get out of hand. The first resolve was not reactionary; the second was wholly so.

To keep a tight rein on the government of each colony, no important change in the traditional form of British colonial government seemed necessary or even desirable, for this form was derived from the model that centuries of experience had evolved in England. What did seem necessary was to make it work properly. Assemblies were more essential than ever, because of the decision that colonies must levy their own taxes; but now they were to be kept strictly in their place and never allowed to grow independent, as they had been in the lost colonies. No assembly was to have more than a limited power over colonial legislation. The legislative will of the popular chamber was to be restrained by the triple check of the upper chamber's coördinate authority, the governor's veto, and the home government's right of disallowance. Nor was any assembly to have even a voice in the way the government of a colony was administered. That was the business of the governor or lieutenant-governor, assisted by the advice of the council, which he selected; by the other public officials of the colony, any of whom he could replace; and by the instructions that the home government sent him from time to time. The members of the local administration were thus all answerable to him, and he in turn was responsible to London.

On the whole, this system operated well for many years after the American Revolution. It suited the character of the Empire as it had been altered by the loss of all the mature colonies. But the time came when things began to go wrong. The system was not static, and neither were the colonies. It degenerated and they developed, producing so serious a strain that some kind of revolution was inevitable.

What got out of control, upsetting the balance of the system, was the council. Its members, like all other appointed officials, were removable at will, but were allowed by hardening custom to hold their places for life. The one exception was the highest official of all. The governor could be only a temporary sojourner, because he was almost invariably a senior military or naval officer. If his administration was a failure, he was recalled; if it was a success, he was rewarded by promotion to a more important command elsewhere. As each new governor was a stranger to the land and its people, he had to lean on the permanent officials for advice on how he should carry out his orders from London. Moreover, these orders had to be based on some information about the colony; and this information was obtained from him and his predecessors, who in turn had got it largely from this very group of permanent officials.

So it came to pass that the government of each colony, though theoretically controlled by the mother country through the governor, fell into the hands of a close little oligarchy in the provincial capital—the members of the council,—who, with their friends and relatives, filled every important office except that of the chief executive. Legally they were all responsible to him and through him to the home government, but practically they were not, because he was a stranger and London was far off; and neither legally nor practically were they responsible to the assembly.

This perversion made the system doubly intolerable as the colonies approached what might be called the adolescent stage in their development. The result was a rising demand for self-government. At first it was not clearly formulated. Occasionally a popular leader suggested copying the American pattern with its election of the executive as well as the legislature, but gradually the movement became focused upon securing the British device of an executive comprising the leaders of the majority in the legislature, or "responsible government," as it was called.

In each province the demand encountered stiff resistance. The members of the ruling clique were clinging to office and power, and they held two honest convictions that, being shared by many others in the community and by the home government, made them the leaders of a real Tory party and gave them support from London. One was that self-government would be bad government, to prove which the antics of contemporary American democracy were cited. The other was that colonial self-government was incompatible with imperial unity. Here was the most formidable obstacle that the Opposition, or Reform party, had to fight—the invulnerable ghost of the American Revolution.

The struggle for self-government began much earlier in Lower Canada than in any of the other British North American colonies, and there the racial division invested it with a bitter intensity unknown elsewhere. The form of government pitted the French majority, who controlled the assembly, against the English-speaking minority, who out of self-defence rallied to the support of the ruling oligarchy; and each side feared that the other was determined to crush it. The conflict prevented the establishment of a system of public schools when the other provinces were creating their systems; it blocked legal reform in the one colony that was most encumbered by antiquated laws; it stopped public works, even the improvement of Montreal harbour; and generally it retarded the economic development of the country.

It came to a head in the Lower Canadian Rebellion of 1837, which touched off the Upper Canadian Rebellion of the same year. In no other province of British North America did the pressure for popular government precipitate an armed outbreak; and these two outbreaks, each the work of only a few hotheads, were quickly suppressed.[3] However, they were serious enough to startle the home government into sending out, with wide powers to take charge of the whole situation in British North America, one of the greatest British statesmen of the century.

Lord Durham's mission was short, but its results were lasting. Early in 1839, after his return to England, he submitted what is perhaps the most famous government report in the English language. It is the corner-stone of the modern British Commonwealth of Nations. Durham insisted upon a revolution in British colonial policy. The fear of letting the colonies have too much freedom lest this freedom destroy the Empire, he argued, was both false and dangerous. It would drive them out of the Empire. The only way to keep them attached to the mother country was to give their people the same liberty to govern themselves as the people at home enjoyed. Instead of a policy of force inspired by fear, he demanded a policy of freedom inspired by faith. This, he proclaimed, was the sovereign cure for the ills that had been troubling British North America and was the magic that would bind the Empire together. He was the first British statesman to see this fundamental principle, and seeing it he gave the idea to the British world.

Less far-seeing was another recommendation of this report. Unable to perceive how the French Canadians could be fitted into his scheme of self-government so long as they retained their separate nationality, and believing that this was destined to be submerged in the English-speaking sea of North America, Durham urged the reunion of the two Canadas, which would reduce the French to a minority position in the elected chamber and hasten the process of their assimilation. Accepting this part of the report, the home government passed the Union Act of 1840, and in the following year a United Canada was created by joining the two provinces. But the main recommendation of the report was too bold for official adoption.

Durham had not removed, but had simply leaped over, the intellectual obstacle at which the British Cabinet balked. Letting the colonies govern themselves as they wished meant letting them leave the Empire when they wished. To stave off the evil day, by giving the people in the colonies every possible satisfaction short of this liberty, the home government struck a belated blow at the colonial oligarchies. The custom that had allowed them to remain in office indefinitely was denounced, and the governors were instructed to make such judicious changes of advisers as would ease the tension between the executive and the popular chamber. But this was attempting the impossible. No governor, removable only by London, could be his own prime minister.

At last the home government had to face squarely the colonial demand, and it decided to let the colonies have what they wanted. The way was prepared by the free-trade movement in Britain, which triumphed in 1846. This revolution in fiscal policy, brought about by the needs of the mother country, consciously destroyed the closed economic system of the Empire, which had come to favour the colonies at the expense of the people in Britain. The adoption of free trade was Britain's declaration of independence of her colonies, and the logical sequel was to allow them to have political independence.

The Colonial Secretary, Lord Grey, was inspired by Durham's faith, but the other members of the Cabinet were not. Still obsessed by the logical conflict between imperial unity and colonial self-government, they had not conquered their fear of another American Revolution. It had conquered them and turned them face about. Realizing that continued resistance would sooner or later drive the colonies into a revolt that was bound to be successful because of their proximity to the United States, these men of little faith chose an earlier friendly parting as the only alternative to a later violent one. No legislation was necessary to effect this momentous transformation in the government of the colonies. A simple instruction from the Colonial Office to the governors, that the will of the assemblies should no longer be resisted, sufficed to establish the Cabinet system of government in the colonies. This was done in the middle of the century, and then Durham's magic began to work.

This British North American Revolution was effected quietly except in Montreal, the capital of United Canada. There a government responsible to the assembly meant much more than it did in the provinces by the sea. It meant the end of the effort to keep the French Canadians down. As the assembly was nearly equally divided between French and English members, and the latter were deeply split between a Tory minority and a Reformer majority, responsible government was impossible unless it was shared equally by the two races. The transfer of power from the Tories, who stubbornly believed in English supremacy, to a ministry that was half French Canadian so enraged the more extreme Tories of Montreal that they stirred up destructive riots against the government. These riots of 1849, which forced the removal of the capital from that city, were a blessing in disguise. 'Forty-nine now balanced 'thirty-seven, and a United Canada could begin a new page.[4]

CHAPTER V

The Dominion: Genesis and Integration

BY D. G. CREIGHTON

NATIONALISM is the theme that dominates the history of British North America during the second half of the nineteenth century. Ever since the American Revolution, men had dreamed of a union of the surviving British possessions in the new continent; but it was not until after the middle of the nineteenth century that this purpose—latent, only occasionally articulate, but powerful—found at last a set of circumstances which goaded it imperatively towards realization. Both internal and external factors, forces at once spiritual and material—the clash of cultures and the new spirit of nationality, democratic parliamentarianism and the success of the federal movement, the Industrial Revolution and the growth of the new national economics—combined at length to set the creative process in motion.

Against this gigantic back-drop of half a continent, a small, straggling population of less than four million people, captained by a few purposeful and resolute men, played out the most decisive episode in its collective history. First, under circumstances both urgent and favourable, came the achievement of formal political union; then, with ominously increasing difficulty, followed the rapid expansion and consolidation of the new nationality; and finally, in an atmosphere of disappointment and frustration, under the twin calamities of inward division and outward failure, the newly-created union was put into a position of desperate defence.

The first of these periods, beginning with the middle of the nineteenth century, despite the jarring shocks with which it opened, found British North Americans in, perhaps, a more favourable situation than they had ever before occupied. They were more solidly established, more reasonably adjusted to each other and to their environment, more conscious of themselves, their fundamental purposes, and their desired future than at any other period in their history. The prime division between English-speaking and French-speaking British North Americans continued; but there were few further complicating racial and cultural divisions; and, right down until the last census of the nineteenth century, British and French totalled about 90 per cent of the population. An inheritance of half a continent lay in prospect before them, but already they had made a few fertile fringes of it effectively their own. The frontier conditions of settlement had ended in New Brunswick and Canada West. The economic uncertainties and cultural disturbances of the threescore years of basic colonization were now over; and compact provincial societies, not unprosperous, fairly cohesive, each with its dominant set of values and its appropriate group of cultural institutions, could look forward more confidently to the future.

Politically also the future looked more settled, more certain, than it had been. It was more than sixty years now since the American Revolution had ended in the disruption of the first British Empire. A long, slow, difficult period of adolescence had followed for British North America. Those sixty years had been agitated by a war between Great Britain and the United States, and by rebellions in the Canadas; both had involved invasions, either official or unofficial, from the American Republic. Yet British North America had painfully survived all this; and in the 1840's the Ashburton and Oregon treaties retraced with more emphatic clarity the line which implied that America north of the Rio Grande was going to be not one but two. Continentalism by force had apparently been defeated. Continentalism by the adaptation or imitation of basic ideas had been rejected with equal decision. The period of groping, unhappy experimentation, during which William Lyon Mackenzie, almost despite himself, had been led to adopt eighteenth-century revolutionary formulas and to copy American revolutionary procedures, had ended in the defeats of

1837. Robert Baldwin and Joseph Howe, who were conservatives as well as liberals, imperialists as well as provincial autonomists, had been the instruments which confirmed British North America's fundamental preference for British institutions.

This choice was simply one more indication of the real character of British North America. The provinces were physically established in North America; but, however insignificant their size, and however problematical their future, they had never considered themselves as members merely of an isolated and localized American community. They were a part of the western European American world; they were bound by ties of deepest and most affectionate necessity to Europe. The original homes of the great majority of their people, the chief markets for their goods, the sources of their political ideas and institutions, the determining centres of their religious values and cultural standards, lay in Europe, and chiefly in the United Kingdom. Europe had always influenced them profoundly; and at no time was the fact better illustrated than in the last half of the nineteenth century, when the crucial decisions on the future of British North America were made. The appeal of the example of the United States was extinguished by the American Civil War. For French Canadians, the most potent influences of the period were probably the triumph of conservative forces, political and religious, in France, and the repeated pronouncements of the Vatican under Pius IX. And, for French and British Canadians alike, the prestige of British accomplishments and British institutions was accepted and unquestioned during all the middle decades of the century. The British North American provinces, in their own estimation at least, were not so much "possessions" as provinces in a transoceanic political and cultural community; and, though they had achieved a measure of political independence and were determined upon its increase, they conceived of their autonomy always within the limits of a still-integrated and vital imperial union.

It was with this character and this history that British North America entered the first stage of its own nationalist movement. Industrialism, liberal democracy, and nationalism were visibly remaking the world. Already the events which had occurred in Great Britain and the Empire in the 1840's had brought home to the British Americans the realization that a new, decisive, and dangerous epoch in their affairs had arrived. Despite the dramatic clamour of the events of the Continent, England breathed the spirit of the new age and anticipated its characteristic accomplishments more surely than any other country in Europe. In the 1830's the United Kingdom had reformed its domestic institutions. In the 1840's it turned to the institutions of Empire. Industrialism, free trade, laissez-faire, as expounded and defended with cool, doctrinaire clarity by Manchester Liberals, had apparently convinced almost an entire generation of English public men that the value of the Empire was highly problematical and that its costs were a certain loss. The corn-laws were repealed, the old mercantile system was abolished, and "responsible government" was conceded to the colonies.

In the years that followed, a strenuous effort was made to reduce the charges of colonial defence and to escape from the entanglements of colonial diplomacy; gradually it became apparent that Great Britain was prepared to transfer the Hudson's Bay Company's Territories to the colony, or group of colonies, which was willing and able to accept the responsibility. The full impact of Britain's age of reform had fallen upon British North America. It almost seemed as if the motherland were anxious to abandon her commitments on the new continent, as if she were eager to withdraw from her own Empire.

These shattering blows had, for almost the first time, forced British North Americans to shake off their satisfied complacency and to think and plan for their own future. At first, particularly in Montreal and among large sections of the commercial community, the desolate sense of abandonment was overwhelming. At first, the colonial instinct, rooted in British North Americans, for some secure and preferential relationship with a greater power was natural and insistent. Inevitably the recoil was from Great Britain to the United States. Its first political expression was the Annexation Manifesto of 1849, in which a number of prominent Canadians, chiefly merchants, advocated the political union of their provinces with the United States. The Manifesto, however, aroused little enthusiastic support: what the colonists really wanted was not political union but some substitute for the old colonial system, some form of relationship with the Republic which would confer commercial benefits without embarrassing political complications. The Reciprocity Treaty of 1854, which opened the United States and British North America to the free import of each other's natural products, amply satisfied this demand. It helped also to bring back prosperity, or, at least, it coincided with better times and booming markets.

But the Reciprocity Treaty had been the product of astute diplomacy and happy Anglo-American relations, and this concord among the English-speaking nations was doomed by the American Civil War. From 1861 on, the relations between Great Britain and her North American provinces on the one hand, and the United States on the other, rapidly deteriorated. The dispute on the *Alabama* claims, the explosion which followed the descent of a group of Southerners[1] from Canada East on the village of St. Alban's in Vermont, the machinations of the Fenian Brotherhood, who apparently hoped to liberate Ireland by the circuitous method of conquering British North America,[2] were all evidences of the exasperation of American opinion against Great Britain and her North American provinces. The Reciprocity Treaty was abrogated; a stiff passport system was introduced; and notice was given by the Republic of the intended termination of the Rush-Bagot Agreement limiting naval armaments on the Great Lakes. A war, deliberately begun or inadvertently started by some dangerous Fenian absurdity, might imperil the survival of British North America. A diplomatic submission of Great Britain to the United States would conceivably involve the surrender of a part, or even the whole, of British North American territory. The United States, which, for a while after 1850 had seemed to offer a welcome substitute for the old imperial preferences, now reappeared, more frightening because more formidable than before, in the old guise of a bellicose and acquisitive neighbour.

These two circumstances—the apparent withdrawal of Great Britain from her North American responsibilities, and the ominous unfriendliness of the United States—were the two principal political factors in the situation in which British North America now found itself. It was a perilous position. But it was also an age of

1 For notes to chapter v see page 574.

national movements, of new states and federations. And might not this revived federal technique be used to preserve the British inheritance in North America? It was half a continent—an imperial domain—which lay at stake. The continental ambitions of British Americans, which had been present, though quiescent, for a long time, were now quickened into activity by the apparent evidences of British neglect and American cupidity.

The expansionist urge was felt even in the Maritime Provinces, where the merchants and politicians of Halifax and St. John hoped that their ports would become the Atlantic outlets of a vast new hinterland; but its strongest expression came from Canada East and Canada West. For some time now the frontier of settlement had reached the limit of good land in the peninsula of Canada West; and, despite the vast sums that had been put into the St. Lawrence canals and the Grand Trunk Railway, in an effort to capture the commerce of the American West, it had to be regretfully admitted that the St. Lawrence Valley had failed to become the dominant international trade-route of northern North America. Inevitably there was discouragement, but discouragement never became a positive conviction of failure. Always there had been alternatives, and now the second alternative became at once preferred and inescapable. In Rupert's Land and the North-West Territories there were whole provinces where new immigrants and the sons of Canadians could make their homes. Out West there were plentiful materials for a new national economy which might be as rich as the old international commercial empire of the St. Lawrence had ever been.

The political pressure of the new age had made union more desirable. The economic techniques and resources of the new industrialism made it more possible than it had ever been before. The times were not only urgent but also propitious. The Industrial Revolution had come to British North America, bringing with it the first railways and the first tiny shops and factories. The beginnings of manufacturing created the hope and the prospect of a national economy more varied and complete, and therefore stronger and more enduring, than anything in the past; and the railway, the most characteristic creation of the age of steam and steel, would supply the appropriate chain of iron to bind the new economy and the new nation. From the first the British North American railways had been ambitious; and the design of a transcontinental which would run from ocean to ocean through British territory had stirred men's imaginations. But the building of the Intercolonial, which was to connect Canada and the Maritime Provinces and to provide the first great section of a national highway, had been repeatedly postponed because of disagreement among the provinces on the division of costs; and in the end both Canada and the Maritime Provinces had built railways which were aimed largely at North American rather than exclusively British North American markets. Now, in the new circumstances, it was time to revive the national plan. Union would, at one and the same time, remove these political misunderstandings and establish a financial base strong enough to support these costly national enterprises.

There was one last clinching argument. During the middle 1860's the cloud of uncertainties which hung over the whole future of British North America weighed oppressively on men's spirits; and union, plans for which had been inspired partly by these uncertainties, was surely the best way of ending them. In Prince Edward Island and Nova Scotia the peril was felt least, for their people were inclined to believe that Great Britain, if only in her own interest, would be obliged to defend them, as necessary to the maintenance of her maritime supremacy in the Atlantic. But in New Brunswick, with its long land frontier and its memories of recent border troubles, there was far more reason for uneasiness; and in Canada, which had sustained the brunt of the fighting during the War of 1812, and which British military experts now pronounced extremely difficult to defend, apprehension threatened at moments to become hysteria.

It was true that political union by itself could perform no miracles of self-defence. Without British assistance, less than four million British Americans could not hope to confront over forty million citizens of the United States. But now, as Great Britain had clearly indicated, unlimited British military assistance could not be counted on at all times as a right. It could be merited and justified only by strenuous colonial efforts at self-protection. And, once again, political union was the best assurance that the northern colonies would offer Great Britain the most effective coöperation in a joint defence of the British inheritance on the North American continent.

All these impulses towards union grew mainly out of the changed situation in the English-speaking world in which British North America now found itself. These impulses, born of fear and ambition, were powerful; but their potency was strengthened by the support of another incentive which had its roots in a totally different set of circumstances—in the cultural divisions of British North America. These divisions and the rivalries which they helped to provoke were among the most characteristic and important features of provincial life in the nineteenth century. Even in the Maritime Provinces, where the population as a whole was homogeneous in its British origin, religious controversies were sometimes a serious factor in politics; and in Canada, where two ways of life, often antithetical, confronted each other in immediate juxtaposition, there was always the danger that the most innocuous of issues might drive the two societies into a state of primitive fury. The problem of church and state—of education, religious organizations and endowments, and clerical influence—was twisted inextricably in the affairs of a province which was partly secular, partly Protestant, and partly Roman Catholic in its convictions.

The union of Upper and Lower Canada had sought to combine the two peoples and their philosophies in a single unitary state. But the union had survived—and even then with increasing difficulty—as an unacknowledged federal system. The two sections, Canada East and Canada West, had equal representation in the provincial legislature, and virtually equal representation in the provincial Cabinet. The inevitable results were balanced parties, close divisions, changing governments, and eventually a virtual paralysis of constitutional rule. The Canadians, by the very circumstances of their society and government, were the most determined federalists in British North America. On the one hand, their cultural differences kept them apart; and, on the other, the commercial system of the St. Lawrence united them in common enterprises and ambitions.

From the moment, in 1864, when they formed a coalition government with the express purpose of ending their constitutional difficulties, it was the Canadians who forced the pace. But for them, British North America might have passed through a stage of regional unions preliminary to the final achievement of national federation. The perambulating conference, which began in Charlottetown and ended in St. John in September of 1864, had been called ostensibly to consider the project of a legislative union of the Maritime Provinces, but the Canadians, who had invited themselves and were never officially members of the conference, dominated and mesmerized it with their persuasive, almost desperate, appeals for a general federation. Then, almost without a pause—for a pause might have permitted enthusiasm to decline or resolution to weaken—a new conference was called at Quebec; and there, in the last three weeks of October, the delegates hammered out the seventy-two Resolutions which were to form the basis of the Canadian federal union.

There was a hard check in this headlong progress when L. S. Tilley, Prime Minister of New Brunswick and an enthusiastic supporter of Confederation, was defeated by the forces of anti-Confederation in a general election in his province. But within scarcely more than a year, Tilley, helped by some material assistance from the Province of Canada and by British moral support, was back in office. Many of the Quebec Resolutions were none too popular in the Maritime Provinces; and all that Tilley, and Charles Tupper of Nova Scotia, were able to obtain from their respective legislatures was a general resolution authorizing the continuation of the negotiations for union. Armed with this, delegates from the Maritime Provinces met the Canadians again in London in the autumn of 1866. At this Westminster Palace hotel conference the Quebec Resolutions were substantially revised; and in the spring of 1867 the British North America Act, uniting the four provinces of Ontario, Quebec, New Brunswick, and Nova Scotia, was enacted by the imperial Parliament. Throughout the entire process Canada had stood out as the guiding and directing province; and from among the Canadians John Alexander Macdonald, who for ten years had been one of the principal leaders of the Liberal-Conservative party, emerged preëminent, alike because of his constructive statesmanship and because of his political dexterity.

Moderate conservatism was the spirit which informed the whole of the Canadian Confederation settlement. The defeat of the European revolutions of 1848, the campaign against "liberalism" in the Roman Catholic Church, and the sanguinary progress of the American Civil War were among the most potent external influences guiding the delegates. Democratic ideals and republican institutions had fallen to a new depth of disrepute in both Europe and North America. The old radical tradition of British North America had grown cautious by the middle 1860's; and George Brown, of the Toronto *Globe,* had weaned the so-called "Clear Grits" from their republican tendencies and had converted them into a body of moderate Reformers. Men like George Cartier, an old follower of Papineau, and Thomas D'Arcy McGee, an Irish rebel of 1848, could unite in affirming the importance of governmental authority and the value of monarchical institutions. American influences on Canadian federal union were almost exclusively negative. The Fathers of Confederation found their chief source of inspiration in the old constitutions of the British North American provinces, in the laws and conventions of the old colonial system, and in the organization of the Mother of Parliaments.

Perhaps the most significant feature of the new federal structure, the feature which Macdonald, the chief architect of the new constitution, never tired of emphasizing, was the commanding position of the central government and Parliament. All the principal parts of the new system—the federal institutions, the division of powers, the controls exercised by the federal government over the provinces—supplied evidence of the consistency with which the Fathers of Confederation had pursued the objective of a strongly-unified state. The Senate, the members of which were to be appointed by the central government, on the basis of equal representation for regions rather than equal representation for provinces, differed in all essential respects from its counterpart in the American system. Residuary powers of legislation were deliberately conferred, after a good deal of debate, upon the central authority rather than the provincial legislatures; and the power of appointing the lieutenant-governors of the provinces and of disallowing provincial legislation, which had been possessed by the imperial government, was transferred to the federal government. Certain limited guaranties respecting the use of the English and French languages were written into the new constitution; and education, the most contentious of the cultural subjects, was conceded, with guaranties for both Protestant and Roman Catholic minorities, to the provinces. It was hoped that these provisions, in their turn, would strengthen the central government by freeing it from old and contentious responsibilities which might endanger the great work of national development and integration.

Finally—and this was among the most serious of their convictions—the Fathers of Confederation believed that the importance of the new Dominion should be indicated not only by its position with respect to the provinces but also by its status in the Empire as a whole. The effort openly to realize this ambition in the title "Kingdom of Canada" was defeated as a result of the evident disapproval of the United States; but the thought was implicit in much of the British North America Act and explicit in many of the speeches in which the Fathers of Confederation explained and defended their federal scheme. With a glad, conscious sense of their release from the petty immaturities of provincialism, they proclaimed British North America's coming-of-age. It was a new nation they were creating—a new type of nation also—a nation which would be autonomous without being isolated. Inevitably the imperial relationship of the future, though its character was still hazy and uncertain, would differ profoundly from that of the past. But the belief that it must continue as a vital reality was, for British Americans, just as profound an article of faith as the conviction that its character would change.

On July 1, 1867, when the new constitution went into operation, Confederation was little more than a sheaf of blue-prints and a little basic stone-work and scaffolding. Almost everything remained to do. Only three of the British North American provinces had entered the union. Newfoundland, Prince Edward Island, and British Columbia remained aloof; Rupert's Land and the North-West Territories continued under the control of the Hudson's Bay Company. Though the general objectives of the new nation were sufficiently well understood, the national policies by which they could best be attained were still unsettled; the usages, practices, and conventions of the new state had not yet been formed; and, most important of all, a national spirit had somehow to be built up out of the discordant materials of sectional loyalties and provincial ways of life. Worst of all, the security, the separate identity itself, of the new union was not yet established, for the long shadow cast by the American Civil War still lay darkly over the English-speaking world.

Here was difficult, dangerous work—work of decades if not, indeed, of generations. It was perhaps fortunate—though fortune was powerfully assisted by astute political calculations—that Sir John Macdonald, who had taken so prominent a part in the framing of the union, should have been destined, as Prime Minister, to preside over the greater part of the first decades of its political existence. In the Province of Canada, Confederation had been carried by a coalition government; but after 1867 the old party divisions in general reëstablished themselves—the Reformers or Liberals on the one hand, the Liberal-Conservatives on the other. Macdonald was able to attract a good many of the veteran provincial leaders of pre-Confederation days into his following, and to gain solid support in the new provinces as they came into union. Far more clearly than his principal political opponents, George Brown, Alexander Mackenzie, and Edward Blake, he seemed to realize the necessities of his own place and age—the opportunities which were there for the taking, the risks which must be accepted. In the end, for better or for worse, he came almost to personify the new Dominion; and, with the exception of the five years from 1873 to 1878, his party, the Liberal-Conservatives, held office from 1867 to 1896.

One of the first tasks—the task upon the successful completion of which almost everything depended—was to end the incubus of dangerous uncertainty which seemed to press against the very life of the young Dominion. The bellicose expansionism which seemed so prevalent in the United States after the Civil War, and the emphatic determination of the British to centralize their military strength in the United Kingdom, combined to leave Canada in a state of ominous vulnerability. For a few years, and particularly during a few tense episodes, the position was grave enough; but, as things turned out in the end, appearances were a good deal more serious than realities. The United States never deliberately tried to push things to extremes; and Great Britain, despite the voluble protestations of her free-trade, laissez-faire extremists, never entertained a serious thought of abandoning all her commitments in North America nor of surrendering the Dominion which she had helped to call into being. The British regulars were indeed withdrawn from central Canada, though not before they had taken part in the military demonstration which ended the Riel Rebellion and clinched Canadian possession of the North-West; but Great Britain firmly, though gently, rejected all tentative American proposals for the annexation of all or part of Canada; and the Canadians and British exchanged formal pledges to come with all their forces to the defence of the British North American heritage. In reality the English-speaking world had no desire for, and no real expectation of, a fratricidal conflict. Finally the United States proposed that the *Alabama* claims and the other issues pending between the Empire and the Republic should be referred to a joint board of arbitration.

The Washington Conference of 1871, which Macdonald attended as one of the five British delegates, settled all the outstanding disputes among the English-speaking peoples, though not, to be sure, to the complete satisfaction of Canada. Macdonald had hoped that establishment of political concord between the Republic and the Dominion would be accompanied by a return to the favourable regulations which had governed their trade from 1854 to 1866; but the United States could not be induced to accept a reciprocity agreement of the old pattern. Macdonald signed the Washington Treaty with great apparent reluctance, but at bottom there can have been no serious doubt in his mind. For him the solidarity of the British people would have been a conclusive argument, even if he had not had a fairly reasonable economic case to present. The diplomatic and military unity of the Empire continued with no wish on the part of any number of Canadians to prevent it.

In the mean time the territorial expansion of the Dominion had proceeded apace. To attain its destined continental boundaries, to include within its limits the entire territorial inheritance of the British in North America—this was obviously the primary task of the new federation. It was a task undertaken with such vigour that the six short years which were required for its completion serve to conceal the difficulties which were encountered. Sometimes these difficulties were largely, if not entirely, fiscal. The secessionist movement in Nova Scotia and its famous leader, Joseph Howe, were appeased by a new financial arrangement between the Dominion and Nova Scotia. Still better terms had to be granted Prince Edward Island when, in 1873, it finally entered union; and the supposedly fantastic promise, to commence a Pacific railway within two years and complete it within ten, was made in 1871 when the entrance of British Columbia extended the Dominion to the Pacific.

These repeated rearrangements of the original financial settlement of Confederation, these vast obligations, far too lightheartedly assumed, the opposition claimed, were serious enough. But a really ugly incident in the territorial expansion of Canada came before the end of 1869, when rebellion broke out on the banks of the Red River, just at the moment when the transfer of the Hudson's Bay Territories to the Dominion was about to be completed. In a military sense the rebellion was unimportant, for it occasioned virtually no fighting; but its political consequences were significant and unhappy. The British and French half-breeds in the little community by the Red River had participated almost equally in the revolt; but its leader, Louis Riel, and one of his principal lieutenants were partly French, and a so-called "provisional government," of which Riel was the head, committed an act of tragic folly in the execution of one of its political opponents, Thomas Scott. Back in Quebec, French Canadians pleaded vehemently that Riel, in whom they saw another Papineau gallantly defending the rights of the minority, should be pardoned, while in Ontario English Canadians clamoured for the punishment of rebels and murderers. Thus, within three years of the first Dominion Day, the "nationalist" and cultural struggles, which Confederation had supposedly localized in safety among the provinces, had broken out again on a national scale and in the very heart of the programme of territorial expansion itself.

Yet the worst consequences of the revolt were somehow smothered in delay and inaction. Manitoba, a new province, prematurely created as a result of the rebellion, was added to the Confederation; and by 1873 all British North America, with the exception of Newfoundland, had entered the new federal union. The year 1873 saw also the defeat of the Macdonald Government, the formation of the first Reform administration, and the beginnings of a great depression. The slump, which was an economic tragedy for the new Dominion, was a correspondingly serious political misfortune for the Reform Government; and for four years the great work of national integration, which was obviously the next task of Canadian nation-building, made only the slowest and most stumbling progress. It was not until 1878, when Macdonald's return to office coincided with a brief, fortunate appearance of better times, that the programme was vigorously resumed. In Macdonald a genuine patriotism, a statesmanlike capacity for large ideas, and a certain robust, almost light-hearted adventurousness were combined. He took up the business of national integration with enthusiasm and pertinacity, and drove it rapidly forward in the next few years.

On the economic plane, the national objective was a strong, varied, and integrated economy. The settlement of the West on a large scale was the first step towards this goal; the second was a transcontinental railway which would link the new and the old regions; and the third was a protective tariff, which would defend the young economy, at least during its immaturity, against the competition of the more important industrial countries of the English-speaking world. These three policies, all of which deserve to be called "national policies," though at the time the tariff alone received that imposing title, were, with at least some measure of logic, parts of a related whole; but they were not, at the beginning, presented as a coherent programme and were adopted independently, with varying amounts of enthusiasm and protest. There was little dispute about either the desirability of western settlement or the methods by which it should be carried out; and British North America, having experimented with both free grants and land sales, swung back to the free-homestead system as the best means of competing with the United States for the swarm of immigrants from Europe. There was not even a great deal of disagreement, in principle, about the Pacific railway, though, of course, the terms on which it was to be built and the amount of government support it was to receive were contentious subjects susceptible of endless argumentation. The tariff was the really controversial measure. Yet, by a curious set of circumstances, the protective tariff was adopted before the construction of the railway had even begun.

For a long time the British North American provinces had made no serious departures from the principles of free trade. The Maritime Provinces, with their large merchant marine and rapidly expanding Atlantic trade, and the Province of Canada, with its St. Lawrence navigation system and its dream of a great commercial empire in the international American West, had the best of reasons for preferring a tolerant economic world with low tariffs and reciprocal give and take. True, there had always been duties on imports, but they had been low duties, for revenue only, applied because, in the rudimentary state of colonial government, there seemed no other practicable way by which a state could collect its funds. This happy condition of fiscal simplicity was first disturbed by the coming of the Industrial Revolution. The Industrial Revolution brought the first tiny manufacturing establishments to British North America, and it inspired the building of large public works, chiefly railways, to which, in the absence of rapidly available capital, the state had to give very substantial support. Within a short time the state's needs to finance its debts and the manufacturers' concern to defend their properties had united to produce a definite trend towards higher tariffs. And the serious depression which began in 1873 simply accelerated this tendency, for, on the one hand, it brought declining revenues to the state, and, on the other, it exposed Canadian business to dumped surpluses of consumer goods from the United States and Great Britain.

It is possible that, even under this double pressure, Canada might not have committed herself to a régime of high protection if other commercial policies had been available. In the past, British North America had placed its reliance either upon the reciprocal preferences of the old colonial system or upon the reciprocal free trade in natural products which had been secured by the Reciprocity Treaty with the United States; but these commercial privileges, to which a large part of Canada still looked back with longing regret, belonged to an age which had passed, or was passing, away. The new economic systems were either more extreme or more exclusive than they had been. England had adopted free trade, and the United States had sharply raised its tariff; in neither policy did there seem to be any opportunity for an exchange of fiscal privileges such as Canada coveted. It was true that before, and even since, the abrogation of the Reciprocity Treaty the Canadians had gone on hoping, and vainly striving, for its renewal. In 1871, at the Washington Conference, Macdonald had tried and failed; in 1874, on behalf of Alexander Mackenzie's Reform Government, George Brown tried again and failed once more. These repeated rebuffs and the desperate circumstances of the depression helped to make the slogan "Reciprocity of trade or reciprocity of tariffs" a popular rallying-cry. In opposition, the Liberal-Conservative party took up the cause of protection and won the general election of 1878. Next year, with the enactment of Tilley's new duties, the Dominion committed itself even more firmly to a career of economic nationalism.

Within two years—for Macdonald was now full of urgency to complete his programme—the Canadian Pacific Railway was chartered. Here, in sharp contrast with the matter of the tariff, which continued to provoke endless disputes, there was general agreement about basic policy; but the route of the national transcontinental had not yet been finally determined, and Macdonald and his Conservative colleagues insisted upon a provision which effectively emphasized its national character. Hitherto, Canadian railways, like Canadian canals, had been planned to compete for the traffic of the international American West; and if, as at first seemed likely, the Grand Trunk Railway had been awarded the Pacific contract, the line would probably have been prolonged to Chicago and so northward to the Canadian prairies. Upon this and all other such schemes the Government resolutely turned its back. The line, it was decided, must run through Canadian territory from start to finish; this condition, which of course necessitated building north of Lake Superior, was accepted by the group of capitalists, headed by George Stephen, Donald Smith, Duncan McIntyre, and R. B. Angus, who in October, 1880, signed the contract to build the Pacific Railway. The

Government agreed to concede a cash subsidy of $25,000,000, a grant of 25,000,000 acres of land, and a monopoly of traffic in the Canadian West. These were substantial concessions; but in return, at any rate, the nation obtained the services of a company which was to have a very distinguished record among North American transcontinentals. George Stephen and his associates were not speculators who were anxious to make a quick profit out of company flotation, land sales, or contracting. They were men of experience, ability, and resolution, who were determined to build and strengthen the railway as a permanent property. The line, which by contract they had been given ten years to build, was completed within five.

With the driving of the last spike on the railway, at Craigellachie in British Columbia, in November, 1885, the second of the two epochs in this crucial half-century in the history of Canadian nationalism was over. The first period had seen the establishment of a constitutional framework of political unity; the second had witnessed the working out and application of the fundamental policies of economic integration. There was sufficient wisdom and strength in these economic and political foundations to ensure the survival and the future development of the Dominion. But the men who had created the new nation and had watched over the early decades of its existence had hoped for something more than this: they had hoped not only for ultimate security but for immediate and striking success. And in this, during the ten years which followed the completion of the Canadian Pacific Railway, they were more and more grievously disappointed. A new period, a period of trials more terrible than any they had yet experienced, was now upon them; and the old century, which, for Canada, might then have ended in achievement and pride, seemed to be closing instead in failure and frustration.

Among the many causes—political, cultural, and economic—of these repeated reverses and this deepening disappointment, the long depression obviously occupies an important place. With only brief interludes of better times, it lasted from 1873 until practically the end of the century. The long decline of prices, the shrinkage of markets, the curtailment of credit, lay like a ponderous incubus upon the whole country. In the Maritime Provinces, where the depression coincided with the absolute decline of their old ship-building industry and carrying-trade, the effects were particularly severe; and in the West, when the brief rush of immigrants which had accompanied the building of the Canadian Pacific died away, the apparent failure of the whole policy of western settlement was made manifest. The West, the hope of Confederation, was empty still. The effort to compete with the United States for immigrants had evidently failed; the tragedy lay not only in the decline of immigration from Great Britain and Europe, but even more terribly in the movement of native-born Canadians to the United States. The country grew with distressing slowness. In 1871 the population had been 3,689,257. Twenty years later it had reached only 4,833,239.

In these circumstances Macdonald's national policies invited criticism and were vulnerable before it. In Manitoba and the North-West Territories the C.P.R. monopoly of railway traffic was bitterly attacked. W. S. Fielding, who acquired political power in Nova Scotia as the champion of the well-being of his province against the iniquities of protection, was merely a particularly striking embodiment of a protest against the tariff which was strong throughout many parts of the country. The whole concept of economic nationalization in Canada was under the severest trial; and, as the depression continued and deepened, Canadians, in their desperation, began to agitate for a return to the various forms of economic colonialism of the past. Imperial federation, which began to gain adherents in Canada during the 1880's, had its obvious economic corollaries; but, so long as England's devotion to free trade remained unshaken, there seemed little chance of a revival of the reciprocal benefits of the old colonial system.

For a long time there had appeared to be equally little hope of a renewal of the Reciprocity Treaty; but now it was argued that the United States, while it would certainly reject a partial measure, might be ready to consent to unlimited free trade. In 1887 a movement for the commercial union of the two countries began rapidly to gain support in Ontario and the Maritime Provinces. At first it was a non-political movement, led by such dubious apostles as Goldwin Smith, who for some time had been impatiently predicting the political union of the United States and Canada; but in the autumn of 1887 prominent Liberals began to discuss the proposal sympathetically. Up to that moment the Liberal party had never opposed protection in principle. But in 1887 Edward Blake retired from his post; and under Wilfrid Laurier, the new party leader, the fashionable commercial doctrine quickly prevailed. In the following year the Liberals committed themselves to unrestricted reciprocity with the United States, and the crucial battle for the national policies of Canada was now at hand.

While this attack against economic nationalism was openly declaring itself, a similar movement of protest against political centralization had been slowly gathering strength. The Fathers of Confederation, Macdonald among them, had expected that under Confederation the provincial governments would sink virtually to the level of municipal corporations; and after 1867 there was a strong and instinctive disposition on the part of the federal government to impose direction, if not exactly tutelage, upon the provinces. Lieutenant-governors, regarded as "Dominion officials," were appointed without concern for provincial susceptibilities. Provincial bills were frequently reserved by lieutenant-governors, and provincial acts were frequently disallowed by the federal government. During the 1880's a pet measure of the province of Ontario was three times disallowed by Ottawa; and the repeated efforts of Manitoba to break the monopoly of the Canadian Pacific Railway by chartering rival railways to the American border were annulled by the federal government in the national interest.

This strict supervision of provincial legislation was not the only example of the Dominion's evident assumption of paramountcy. There were other illustrations, equally clear, in the Parliament's extended use of its own legislative authority, under the residuary clause as well as under the enumerated powers—a use which seemed to find judicial approval in the decision of the Judicial Committee of the Privy Council (see p. 235) in the case of *Russell* v. *the Queen*. Yet centralization, however vigorously it was enforced, depended ultimately upon a spirit of national unity, which still had far to develop and which the national policies had not yet done much to promote. Several of the provincial premiers, with Oliver Mowat of Ontario at their head, were in frank revolt against the federal government; and they were able to appeal successfully to the still-surviving provincial loyalties of the Canadian people.

That these fervid appeals could be made to cultural values as well as to economic and political grievances was the final and possibly the greatest misfortune of these troubled years. Since the days of the Red River Rebellion, the latent animosities between English-speaking and French-speaking Canadians had been permitted to slumber; but now, as settlement advanced into the North-West Territories with the building of the Canadian Pacific Railway, an event occurred which awakened them into sudden and violent activity. The French half-breeds, who had trekked westward from the Red River to the banks of the Saskatchewan, became once more the centre of a formidable agitation against the federal government, and Louis Riel returned to lead them. The North-West Rebellion of 1885 was an open appeal to force; force, in the shape of several regiments of the Canadian militia, was required to subdue it. There could be no doubt, this time, of the complicity of Riel and his principal lieutenant. The only real question—and it was a question which divided Canada into two camps, mainly on racial lines—was whether the half-breed leader's evident delusions of grandeur could justify his pardon on the ground of insanity. The Cabinet, in its uncertainty, decided to let the verdict of the courts stand. Riel was hanged; and with his execution at Regina, in the autumn of 1885, the furious controversy in central Canada reached a point of hysteria which probably has no parallel in Canadian history. In a moment a "nationalist" agitation sprang up in the Province of Quebec. Honoré Mercier rode into power in the provincial House as the "nationalist" champion of his outraged compatriots; and Wilfrid Laurier, soon to be appointed successor to Blake, began to effect the transference of French Canada from the Conservative to the Liberal banner. The concord of 1867 between the two races had been broken, and during the nineteenth century it was never reëstablished.

These three matters—the depression, the Dominion-provincial

conflict, and the controversy over the "Regina scaffold"—formed the three sombre themes in the history of the decade of troubles which followed 1885. They were inextricably mingled in their development; they were stated over and over again, with variations, throughout the period; but one of them, the dispute of the provinces with the Dominion, reached and passed its most dangerous crescendo within a few years. In 1887 the first interprovincial conference in the history of Canada assembled at Quebec at Mercier's invitation. It had been planned, of course, as a Dominion-provincial conference; but Macdonald steadfastly refused to permit the federal government to be represented, and his disapproval was sufficient to ensure the absence of two provinces, Prince Edward Island and British Columbia. These defections gave the conference the somewhat equivocal appearance of a Liberal caucus; but even so it was a formidable gathering. Quebec's nationalist crusade, Ontario's constitutional grievances, Manitoba's campaign against the Canadian Pacific monopoly clause, and the agitation in the Maritime Provinces over the tariff—all these were represented at Quebec. The very fact of the conference—the assumption which underlay all its meetings—was in itself a denial of federal autonomy under the British North America Act. For the delegates assumed, without any legal or historical justification, that the Dominion was the product of a contract among the provinces, which could be altered at their pleasure. They proceeded, in a series of resolutions, to change it radically. Among other things, they recommended a sharp increase in provincial subsidies, the abolition of the Dominion's power of disallowance, and a change in the composition of the Senate which would give the nomination of half of its members to the provinces.

The provinces had been very aggressive. In fact, they had overshot the mark. Without the concurrence of the Dominion and the other two provinces, of which there was now no likelihood whatever, the imperial Parliament would never legislate on the basis of the Quebec Resolutions of 1887. The provinces were in the awkward position of not knowing exactly what to do with their own resolutions. But, at the same time, they did not stand alone in their embarrassment. The federal government, which was prepared to take a high line with respect to the constitution-mongering at Quebec, could no longer afford to ignore the provincial protest movement of which the Quebec Resolutions were simply the expression. The monopoly clause in the Canadian Pacific charter was revoked. On two important occasions the Dominion warily refused to be drawn into a further exercise of its power of disallowance. But these, on the whole, were small strategic retreats. Macdonald would never have surrendered any important part of his position. The real change which took place in Dominion-provincial relations in the last decade of the century came, not from any concession of the federal government, but from a series of decisions in the Judicial Committee of the Privy Council which, in effect, reversed the judgement in *Russell* v. *the Queen* and substantially reduced the value of the Dominion's residuary power.

If, in the matter of political centralization, the Conservatives suffered a partial defeat, they gained an almost complete victory in their defence of economic nationalism. Macdonald was prepared, and indeed anxious, to revive the old Reciprocity Treaty, with some necessary modifications; but he objected to unrestricted reciprocity with the United States for exactly the same reasons for which he disliked imperial federation of the colonies and Great Britain. Both policies, to him, were fundamentally wrong, for both would jeopardize the political autonomy which he had consistently sought for Canada. The belief that unrestricted reciprocity and commercial union were essentially the same and that each was inevitably a precursor of political annexation was by no means peculiar to the Conservatives. It divided prominent Liberals, with Edward Blake, the old leader of the party, opposed to the policy which his successors had adopted; and it must have created doubt and suspicion in the minds of a substantial body of the electors. Despite the depression, despite the quarrels and hatreds which had accompanied it, Canadians were not yet ready to give up the hopes of Confederation; and when, in the last election of his life, Macdonald appealed to their nationalist patriotism, he was returned once more.

It was not politics and economics but race and religion which had the most serious consequences, certainly for the Conservative party, and probably for the Dominion as a whole. The huge fires of the Riel controversy were not easily smothered; and in episode after contentious episode the long sequence of cultural disputes continued until the end of the century. Mercier, himself a political product of the Riel affair, determined to compensate the Jesuit Order for the confiscation of its property in the eighteenth century, and thus raised again the old issue of state endowments for religious purposes. The Equal Rights Association, organized to contest this particular piece of legislation, helped to rekindle the educational controversy in central Canada, and to transfer it to Manitoba, where particularly inflammable materials existed. There had been a large French-speaking half-breed minority in Manitoba at its inception, and, as a result, the province had been provided with supposedly appropriate educational institutions. In 1870 they had been satisfactory; but, in the mean time, immigration, though it had disappointed expectations, had decisively confirmed the British, English-speaking character of the province. The Manitoba legislature abolished the official cognizance of the French language and set up a system of provincial, non-sectarian public schools to which all were required to contribute, irrespective of religion. The Roman Catholic minority petitioned for the disallowance of the provincial legislation and attempted to have it upset in the courts. Having failed in both efforts, it appealed to the federal government to intervene, as it had the right to do by the British North America Act, to protect the educational rights of Roman Catholics by remedial legislation.

The long train of troubles which had begun with the North-West Rebellion found its appropriate climax in the ensuing controversy. In the end, the Manitoba school question broke the hold of the Conservative Government. Ever since the death of Macdonald in 1891, the party had been steadily deteriorating under the shifting leadership of four successive prime ministers. Now, at the penultimate stage of the decline, the Conservatives decided to sponsor remedial legislation in the hope of retaining the support of the Roman Catholic bishops and, through them, of French Canada. But the decade of troubles had not only roused the citizens of Quebec as Roman Catholics; it had also antagonized them as French Canadians. And to that sense of injured national pride, which was in large part a consequence of the Riel affair, Wilfrid Laurier, the native son, appealed with supreme success.

The general election of 1896, which ended the long period of Conservative rule and brought the Liberals into office, closed an epoch in Canadian history. A new government was in power; a new century and a new period of prosperity were about to begin. In fifty years Canada had passed through the genesis, the first growth, and the first tribulations of her national existence, and she was the stronger for having survived the long ordeal of inward division and outward failure.

CHAPTER VI

The Twentieth Century

BY C. P. STACEY

IT WAS the singular good fortune of Wilfrid Laurier and the Liberal party to come to power in 1896, at the moment when the long depression was ending and the country was on the eve of a period of unprecedented prosperity. New gold discoveries, particularly in South Africa, had inaugurated an era of rising world prices favourable to commercial and manufacturing enterprise. Particularly important for Canada, the price of wheat, which had long been depressed, now began to rise, and the early years of the twentieth century witnessed a wheat-boom.

At the same time, immigration began on a scale hitherto unknown. For generations Canada had taken second place to the United States as an attraction to settlers from the British Isles and the continent of Europe; but about 1890 the frontier phase of American history ended with the virtual exhaustion of free land south of the forty-ninth parallel. The tide of migration now set towards Canada, and the settlement of the western prairies began in earnest. With the dawn of the new century the stream of immigrants swelled to a flood. At this time, then, the United States, the United Kingdom, and Europe were all contributing in large proportion to that stream.

Isolated minority groups had already made their appearance —the Icelandic colony at Gimli, Manitoba, in the early 1870's; the Mennonites who came to Manitoba during the same decade; and subsequently, in the future Saskatchewan, the Doukhobors, with their odd customs and antinational bias. Some of the new comers showed a strong and perhaps natural tendency to settle in solid, homogeneous communities; and apprehensions were aroused over the difficulties of assimilation, as indicated by statistics of naturalization, school attendance, and literacy. The result was that restrictions were imposed on certain of the less assimilable groups and particularly, after the Vancouver riots of 1907, on immigrants from the Orient. However, the general stream of immigration continued to grow until almost the eve of the First World War, with Americans coming in large numbers after 1910. From all countries, the number of arrivals in 1912–1913 totalled over 400,000—the largest in Canada's history.

In these circumstances, the population of the Dominion for the first time increased very rapidly. By 1901 it was up to 5,371,315; and the Census of 1911 showed a total of 7,206,643. Alberta and Saskatchewan were organized as provinces in 1905. A new era had come to the Canadian West and the development of early-ripening wheats permitted the northward extension of settlement. The year 1905 was the first in which the Canadian wheat crop passed 100,000,000 bushels; in 1913 it exceeded 231,000,000. As recently as 1890 it had been only 42,000,000.

The mining frontier too was on the move. In the year in which Laurier came to power, placer gold was found in the Yukon, and the famous rush that followed raised that territory's gold production above 1,000,000 ounces in 1900. The Yukon development proved to be merely a flash in the pan, and it was long before Canadian gold again equalled the figure of 1900, but other metals soon more than compensated. In the early years of the twentieth century the almost incredible mineral wealth of the Canadian Shield began to be appreciated and exploited; the province of Ontario, and in due course Quebec and Manitoba also, profited enormously. The copper and nickel resources of the Sudbury area, discovered in 1883, were opened up; Canada soon attained a virtual world monopoly in the latter metal. The silver deposits around Cobalt were found in 1903. Following the discoveries at Porcupine a few years before the First World War, Ontario's gold production also developed rapidly.

This same period saw the effective beginning of the exploitation of Canadian water-power resources. The Hydro-Electric Power Commission of Ontario was established in 1906 to buy or produce electric power and sell it at cost to the municipalities. The Commission, a pioneer experiment in public ownership, proved a great success. The availability of cheap electric power in central Canada was an important element in the expansion of industry during the First World War.

Canada had had a frankly protective tariff since the Conservatives introduced the "National Policy" in 1878–1879. The Liberals, although they continued to pay some lip-service to free trade, maintained the tariff after their victory in 1896. Thanks doubtless in some degree to protection, but still more to the generally favourable conditions of the time, Canadian industrial production for the decade ending in 1910 showed what was considered in those days "an extraordinary growth."[1] Nevertheless, it remained for the First World War to produce the greatest development up to that point in Canadian history and to alter materially the balance between agriculture and industry.

The national expansion of the Laurier era, and particularly the opening and settlement of the West and the North, produced a new wave of railway construction. The 'eighties had given Canada her first and entirely necessary transcontinental line, the Canadian Pacific; the new wealth and enterprise and confidence of the first decade of the twentieth century gave her two more, the value of which was far more dubious—the Canadian Northern and the Grand Trunk Pacific, the latter joining at Winnipeg with the National Transcontinental from Moncton, New Brunswick. There was also additional building by the Canadian Pacific and by provincial authorities, with the net result that Canadian railway mileage doubled between 1900 and 1915. Experience was very soon to show that Canada had expanded her lines beyond her immediate economic needs or her strength. In 1919 the Canadian National Railways were organized and the Dominion Government took over the two younger transcontinentals. Socialist theory had nothing to do with the decision; the lines were simply incapable of functioning on a private basis.[2]

Few people anticipated such a result, however, in the years preceding the First World War. There was unlimited confidence in the continuance of the boom and in the future of the country

---

[1] For notes to chapter vi see pages 574–575.

generally. Surveying the progress made since 1900, indeed, Canadians seemed to have ample grounds for confidence. The country's population had risen from little more than 5,000,000 in 1901 to an estimated total of almost 8,000,000 in 1914. The Dominion's revenues of all sorts had risen from $36,000,000 in 1895–1896 to $168,000,000 in 1912–1913; and its export trade, which had been worth only $117,000,000 annually when Sir Wilfrid Laurier came to power, had increased substantially to $300,000,000 by the time of his fall.

Enough has been said to demonstrate how remarkable was the prosperity experienced in Canada in the first decade of the twentieth century. It was thanks to these favourable conditions, no less than to his own remarkable personality and qualities, that Sir Wilfrid Laurier maintained himself in power so long.[3] His Government was sustained in three general elections, in 1900, 1904, and 1908; and when it finally met disaster, in the famous campaign of 1911, it was not upon a domestic issue.

The Laurier administration was forced to concern itself with external problems to a larger extent than any previous Canadian government. Relations both with the rest of the Empire and with the United States called for careful handling during this disturbed and difficult period of world history.

Laurier came to power the year after the formation in the United Kingdom of Lord Salisbury's Conservative Government, in which Joseph Chamberlain was Colonial Secretary. It fell to Laurier, accordingly, to direct Canadian policy in relation to Chamberlain's active programme of imperial development. This programme included three main points. Chamberlain desired to create some form of permanent centralized imperial authority, a Council or Cabinet sitting in London which could speak for the Empire as a whole and exercise authority over all its component parts. He desired also an economic reorganization, conceived in terms of "imperial free trade," that is, abolition of all tariffs within the Empire, combined with imposition of tariffs against countries outside. Finally, Chamberlain wanted a unified system of imperial defence which would enable his Council in London to control the forces of the entire Empire, including the self-governing colonies.

The weakness of this programme, which admittedly had many supporters in Canada and elsewhere, was that it was founded upon a fundamental misunderstanding of the nature of the imperial association. Chamberlain and a good many other people seem to have thought of the British Empire as a nation. It was and is no such thing, but an association of nations—not one nationality but a partnership of nationalities; and, in attempting to recentralize the Empire, Chamberlain was looking backward rather than forward.

As Prime Minister of the largest and most developed of the colonies, Laurier felt himself charged with the important but somewhat ungrateful task of opposing the Chamberlain programme. In a succession of Colonial Conferences in London (1897, 1902, 1907) he was the spokesman of autonomy. It would be unfair to describe Laurier as anti-imperial; it would be truer to say that he had a sounder conception of the Empire than Chamberlain, and he defended that conception, which was founded upon long Canadian experience, with skill and success. It was in great part due to Laurier that the centralizing schemes were watered down until, instead of permanent imperial machinery which would certainly in due course have aroused colonial hostility, there emerged simply improved coöperation and closer understanding.

No new central authority was set up. The only machinery evolved was the informal procedure of the periodical Colonial Conference (later rechristened Imperial Conference), a consultative gathering, having no executive power, which gave the heads of the governments of the Empire the opportunity of discussing common problems around the table. Chamberlain's schemes for economic reorganization likewise produced little result. They met strong opposition both in England, where the public showed itself loath to abandon the free-trade policies adopted in the 1840's, and in the Dominions, which were unwilling to cast down the protective tariffs behind which their infant industries had developed. In 1898, however, the Laurier Government enacted the British Preferential Tariff, by which British goods entered Canada at a rate substantially lower than those of foreign countries.

Chamberlain's military projects had similarly limited results.

Laurier was decidedly unwilling to compromise on the principle that forces raised by the self-governing Dominions should be controlled by their respective governments, and he had no intention of handing over revenues raised in Canada to be spent in a manner over which the Canadian Government would have no control. Accordingly, no centralized military system was set up. Nevertheless, an important precedent was established in 1899 when the Laurier Government sent Canadian troops to fight in the South African War.

In this matter the position of Laurier was difficult. Before war broke out he had been subjected to strong pressure from Chamberlain to offer troops for service in the event of war; this he had resisted. There was strong feeling in his own Province of Quebec against any contribution to a war with the Boers; elsewhere in the country, however, it was felt, at least equally strongly, that Canada must contribute. When war actually came, the Government at once decided to send a contingent. The force sent was small, and the British Government was permitted to pay the major part of the cost,[4] but the venture had an importance far outweighing the size of the operation.

The question of naval defence requires special attention, if only because it provided an important issue of Canadian political controversy. Since the first Colonial Conference in 1887, certain of the colonies had been making cash contributions for the maintenance and enlargement of the naval forces of Britain. At the Conference of 1902 every important Dominion except Canada accepted this practice. Laurier, however, took the ground that "the proposals would entail an important departure from the principle of Colonial self-government," and told the Admiralty that his Government was considering establishing "a local Naval force in the waters of Canada." However, no immediate action was taken.

Popular agitation on the question grew with the German naval menace. In 1909 the Canadian House of Commons passed unanimously a resolution approving in principle "the speedy organization of a Canadian naval service" in close relations with the Royal Navy; and in 1910 Laurier introduced into Parliament a bill designed to create a Canadian navy. The Conservative leader,

Mr. (later Sir) Robert Borden, however, declared that, while still believing in a Dominion navy as a long-term policy, he considered that the existing situation required "immediate and effective aid" to the British Government in the form of money for the construction of battle-ships.

Borden's action placed Laurier in an exceptionally awkward position. Conservative "imperialists" accused him of lukewarmness towards the Empire, and French-Canadian nationalists in Quebec opposed any kind of naval expenditure as toadying to London. Laurier's bill was duly passed, but was not fully implemented, since the election of the following year, 1911, brought about his defeat. Though the naval issue, as we shall see, was not the primary one in the election, it was a serious embarrassment to him and certainly did him considerable harm in Quebec.

In place of Laurier's bill, the newly-formed Borden Government introduced a bill appropriating up to $35,000,000 for three dreadnoughts to be offered to the King for the common defence of the Empire. This passed the Commons, but was thrown out by the Liberal majority still surviving in the appointed Senate. Borden did not choose to carry the issue to the public in an election, and nothing further was done before the outbreak of war in 1914.

The great naval debate of 1909–1913 thus proved to be a singularly futile exercise. The Laurier policy, which could have provided Canada by 1914 with an effective little fleet, was not proceeded with; the Borden policy of "immediate and effective aid" produced no aid whatever. When war broke out, Canada had no naval force except two elderly and undermanned cruisers which had been acquired by Laurier as training-ships; and in 1914 the coast of British Columbia depended for defence upon war-ships provided by Britain, Australia, and Japan.[5] The whole affair demonstrated the immaturity of Canada at this period. It is hard to avoid the conclusion that political interests took precedence over the interests of national defence, but it seems clear also that the naval projects were not the result of a genuine demand from Canadian public opinion. Had they been so, the matter would scarcely have been allowed to rest where it did.

Relations with the United States also passed through an important transition during the Laurier régime. When Laurier formed his administration, Canada had been at peace with her great neighbour for eighty-two years. Nevertheless, the peace had not been wholly undisturbed, and as recently as 1895 there had been some apprehension of conflict. The foreign relations of Canada were still controlled by and conducted through the British Foreign Office, though the principle had been fully established that in negotiations affecting Canadian interests the Dominion should be both consulted and represented.

This situation came into the lime-light in 1903 because of the controversy with the United States over the Alaska boundary, which had assumed a new importance as a result of the Yukon gold-rush of 1898. Canada's contentions on the main point were not particularly well founded, although there was room for controversy on the exact position of the boundary; and had her case been rejected by a fair international tribunal, she could scarcely have complained. Unfortunately, the method by which the question was disposed of left her with a deep sense of grievance. The United States, under the administration of President Theodore Roosevelt, refused to consider arbitration, the procedure which President Cleveland had forced upon Britain a few years before in the case of the boundary between Venezuela and British Guiana. The best arrangement that could be made was an agreement to settle the matter by a majority vote of a tribunal of three "impartial jurists" from either side; and Roosevelt proceeded to appoint as the American members three political personalities who had already committed themselves on the issue. The British representatives were two Canadians and the Chief Justice of Great Britain; thanks to the vote of the latter, the award of the tribunal went against Canada.

The affair gave Canadians the impression that they had been made the victims of an unusually cynical piece of international bullying. It was not the first time that the settlement of an Anglo-American dispute had left the Canadian public angry with both the mother country and the United States. Laurier went so far as to say in the House of Commons that the affair had demonstrated the need for Canada to assume much wider control of her own foreign relations. He took no strong action to implement these views; nevertheless, there can be little doubt that the Alaska boundary award was a milestone in the growth of Canadian national feeling and eventually exercised considerable influence on the development of Canadian external policy. Fortunately, the point at issue was not so important as the Canadian public appeared to believe, and the award at least disposed peacefully of the last serious territorial question between the two countries, leaving the way clear for a further evolution of friendly relations.

A noteworthy development took place in 1909, when the Boundary Waters Treaty created the International Joint Commission, charged with settling questions connected with the boundary waters of Canada and the United States, or other matters which might be referred to it by the governments concerned. While the treaty was technically an Anglo-American agreement, the Commission which it constituted was purely Canadian American, so that Canada's direct influence upon the settlement of disputes with the United States was materially widened. The Commission has settled, peacefully, quietly, and unanimously, many matters which if neglected might have grown to be troublesome and even dangerous.

It was a Canadian-American question that caused the defeat of the Laurier administration. Both Laurier and President Taft had been subjected to pressure for reductions in tariffs, and in 1911 a reciprocity agreement, to be carried out by mutual legislation, was made between the two governments. It provided for free trade in natural products and for reciprocal reduction of duties on many food products and some manufactures. Such an agreement would have been very welcome to the Canadian public not many decades before, and in fact several unsuccessful attempts had been made to reëstablish reciprocity after the abrogation of the Treaty of 1854–1866. Now, however, the proposal resulted in a wave of opposition which surprised the Government and finally brought it down. The Conservative Opposition made free and reckless use of the argument that reciprocity in trade would lead inevitably to the political absorption of Canada by the United States. The manufacturers who had prospered behind the tariff wall threw themselves into the fight; and the foolish utterances of some American politicians, not excluding President Taft, afforded grist for the Conservative mill.

Undoubtedly, selfish interests and political ambitions played a great part in the campaign. At the same time, it must be recognized that these influences could not in themselves have carried the day. There was certainly much genuine concern over the ultimate effect of the agreement upon the British connexion and upon the development of Canada as a nation. Furthermore, the remarkable progress and prosperity of recent years had given Canadians a new faith in their country's ability to stand on her own feet and go her own way. The Alaska boundary affair had also kept alive Canadian distrust of the United States, evoking memories of many an earlier crisis and dispute. It was the last occasion, however, on which these ancient enmities exercised a very significant influence upon Canadian-American relations. The war which broke out in Europe three years later was to do much to set those relations upon a new and better footing.

The First World War was in many respects the most important event in Canadian history. It may almost be said to have turned Canada from a colony into a nation. It revolutionized her status in the British Commonwealth and in the world at large; it produced fundamental changes in her economic life; and it deeply affected the general outlook of her people.

Given the constitutional status of the Dominions as it existed in 1914, Canada's involvement in the struggle was inevitable. "When Britain was at war, Canada was at war." It by no means followed, however, that Canada was obliged to play an active part; this was a matter for decision by her Government and her Parliament.

Canadians of the generation of 1914 had done little thinking about international affairs. The Canada of that age is charmingly and nostalgically depicted in Stephen Leacock's *Sunshine Sketches of a Little Town,* and the country's mentality was in the main a small-town mentality. Discussion and understanding of European issues were limited, and the general ignorance of what these issues might mean for Canada was reflected in her extreme unreadiness for war. The country's traditions, though not entirely unwarlike, were quite unmilitary, and her government and people had never liked spending money on defensive preparations in time of peace. As we have seen, her naval policy produced much controversy but no ships; although increasing sums of money were spent upon her militia during the years preceding 1914, the force was deficient in both training and equipment. The country possessed only about 3,000 regular soldiers, and was in no position to bear any part of the first shock of war.

In spite of all this, it was with a relatively light heart that Canada followed the mother country into the conflict. Had her people known what lay ahead, there would have been less enthusiasm, though the result would have been the same. The country in 1914 was fundamentally united. Sir Wilfrid Laurier, the French-Canadian leader of the Opposition, associated himself with the Government in support of the cause, and it was only as time passed and the strain of the struggle grew that serious threats to national unity began to appear.

The Dominion's greatest contribution was the Canadian Expeditionary Force. The First Canadian Division crossed the Atlantic in 1914 and went to France early the next year. Later in 1915 the Canadian Corps was formed, and in August, 1916, it reached its full strength of four divisions. The Canadians served throughout on the Western Front, sharing the grim experiences and the heavy losses of that theatre from April, 1915, when the First Division stood up to the first German gas attack, until the armistice in 1918. As the campaign proceeded, the Corps played an increasingly prominent and costly part. It especially distinguished itself in the desperate fighting on the Somme in 1916, in the great "set-piece" attack which captured Vimy Ridge in 1917, in the deadly offensive at Passchendaele later the same year, and in 1918 in the resounding success at Amiens and the subsequent advance to victory.

The First Division in 1914 was placed under the command of an English officer, who was subsequently promoted to command the Canadian Corps when that was formed. Only in June, 1917, did a Canadian—Lieutenant General Sir Arthur Currie—become Corps Commander. This change, strongly recommended to the British authorities by the Canadian Government, reflected the growing national spirit within the Corps itself, a spirit which moved more strongly and became more evident as the war went on. The Canadian Corps and its victories and sacrifices became, in fact, the vehicle in war-time of a new Canadian national consciousness and national pride, and the memory of these things continued to be influential in peace.

In all, about 628,000 Canadians served in the armed forces in this war, and about 60,000—a very heavy proportion of Canada's small population—gave their lives. Like the United Kingdom, Canada long recruited her army by voluntary methods. By 1917, however, recruits were no longer coming forward in the required numbers, and conscription was then instituted. The measure was unpopular in many rural areas and throughout the French-Canadian community. The people of Quebec, having no racial ties with Britain and little sympathy with modern France, were decidedly isolationist; and, although many of them had fought as volunteers, compulsion aroused their fierce opposition. Sir Wilfrid Laurier took the field against the conscription policy. In the autumn of 1917 Sir Robert Borden formed a union Government of Conservatives and conscriptionist Liberals which appealed to the country in December. It won an overwhelming victory in the Dominion as a whole, but in Quebec it obtained only 3 seats out of 65. It was apparent that the conscription issue had placed a serious strain upon the unity of Canada.[6]

Meanwhile the Dominion was making an industrial contribution to victory which could not have been foreseen in 1914. The Imperial Munitions Board, an agency of the British Government, was set up to control war production, and under its direction there was an enormous output of artillery-shells and a considerable output of aircraft, while the Canadian ship-building industry, long moribund, came to life again. The extraordinary development was reflected in the growth of exports of manufactured goods from Canada to the United Kingdom: from $8,000,000 in 1913–1914 to $339,000,000 in 1917–1918. During these years Canadian industry made unparalleled advances. "The influence of the War upon the manufactures of Canada was profound and far-reaching, tending to promote the diversification of products and the production at home of many commodities which had been imported previously." [7] The ground gained during the First World War was never lost.

In certain respects the war was a great misfortune. Canada could ill afford the men she lost; the large immigration of the pre-war years was checked by the conflict and not resumed on the same scale after 1918; her national debt was quintupled in four years; the crisis of 1917–1918 strained the relations between her two great peoples almost to the breaking-point—a situation which continued to have serious repercussions in Canadian politics. On the other side of the ledger stood the strengthening of the country's economic structure, a great increase in national wealth, and a stimulus to the national spirit. Canada, in the words of an English historian, "earned what she reaped, but she reaped much. She gave greatly to the war and in turn the war gave much to her."[8]

Countries capable of placing formidable armies in the field cannot be treated as colonies. The war gave the Dominions both a stronger sense of their own power and importance and a greater appreciation of their own stake in the results of foreign policy; at the same time, it left Britain convinced that they must henceforth be considered partners and allies rather than dependencies. It thus greatly accelerated a process of imperial evolution which had already been under way.

Even while hostilities were still in progress, the new situation began to appear in the novel association of the Dominion prime ministers with members of the British Government as an Imperial War Cabinet; and the new status won on the battle-field was reflected in the Dominions' share in the peace settlement—a share which owed much to the determined initiative of Sir Robert Borden. The Dominions were represented at the Peace Conference of Paris, not only as members of a British Empire delegation but also as separate entities; and they signed the Treaty of Versailles in their own right. They were, moreover, separately admitted to the League of Nations, in spite of the fears of certain countries (notably the United States) that this was merely a device for increasing the voting-power of Great Britain.

The control of the Dominions over their own foreign policies was rapidly extended in the immediate post-war years. In 1920 Borden obtained the consent of the British Government in principle to Canada's sending a minister of her own to Washington, although action was not finally taken until 1926; and in 1923 Canada not only negotiated a treaty with the United States (the Halibut Treaty, establishing a closed season in the Pacific), but signed it without participation by a representative of the British Government.

The new status of the Dominions was formalized in 1926–1931. The Imperial Conference of 1926 essayed the difficult task of defining it, and produced the famous statement that Great Britain and the Dominions were "autonomous Communities within the British Empire, equal in status, in no way subordinate one to another in any aspect of their domestic or external affairs, though united by a common allegiance to the Crown, and freely associated as members of the British Commonwealth of Nations." After further discussion between the countries of the Commonwealth, the substance of these conclusions was enacted into law in the Statute of Westminster of 1931. This epoch-making enactment removed what may be termed the last legal disabilities of the Dominions and placed the cap-stone upon the edifice of their autonomy by establishing the legislative equality of their parliaments with that of the United Kingdom.[9]

The ending of the war brought new men on the scene and new developments, both political and economic. In 1920 Sir Robert Borden was succeeded as leader of the Conservative party and as Prime Minister by Arthur Meighen. The latter was defeated in a general election late in 1921. Sir Wilfrid Laurier had died two years before; and the new Liberal leader, Mr. William Lyon Mackenzie King, a grandson of the rebel of 1837, now became Prime Minister. Mr. King proved to be the dominant figure in Canadian politics until the end of 1948. Except for a short interim in 1926, he remained head of the Government until after the onset of the great depression in 1929; he was head of it during the Second World War and until he retired in favour of Mr. Louis St. Laurent, who was chosen as leader of the Liberal party in 1948.

Broadly speaking, the decade following the peace of 1919 was one of prosperity. It is true that the initial post-war boom collapsed somewhat heavily in 1921, but recovery was rapid. In the years that followed, much energy went into adapting to Canadian uses the recent advances of science and engineering, and organizing their results in national terms. For example, the development of motor transport led to heavy expenditures for road-building by the provinces and produced a new national industry—the tourist industry—founded largely upon the nearness of the great centres of population in the United States. Only during the Second World War, however, was a motor-road completed across the intransigent terrain of the Canadian Shield.

The invention of radio broadcasting presented special problems for Canada—the result of her vast physical extent, two languages, small population, and the proximity of the United States. By 1928 the question was pressing. Canadian programmes were in general available only to listeners near the large cities. "There was a tendency for the larger stations to become little more than agents for the big radio networks in the United States. . . . Canadian talent and Canadian interests were being largely neglected, and it appeared that on a basis of purely commercial operation, radio would be lost as an effective means of Canadian development."[10]

In 1929 a Royal Commission recommended a form of nationalization; in 1932 the Canadian Radio Broadcasting Commission was set up, and in 1936 it was replaced by the Canadian Broadcasting Corporation. The system thus instituted was characteristically Canadian, in that it was a half-way house between American and British practice, between private enterprise and public ownership. Local private stations were permitted, under C.B.C. regulation; advertising was allowed as a necessary means of revenue; but network broadcasting was limited to the Commission's stations. A chain of stations was built from coast to coast; much was done to encourage and develop Canadian talent and Canadian programmes; and a licence fee for receiving sets was authorized as a sustaining revenue for the Commission. This fee, although it was not popular, could be defended as a small part of the price of Canada's cultural independence.[11]

There was some broadening of Canadian cultural life in these years. A group of painters who before the war had been developing a characteristically Canadian technique now won some international recognition, and established the school known as the Group of Seven. Competitions such as the Dominion Drama Festival and organizations such as the Toronto Symphony Orchestra stimulated public interest, but in general the country was primarily absorbed in making money.

One source of prosperity was a further great development of mineral production in the Canadian Shield during the 1920's. There was a particularly striking increase in gold production, which continued through the depression years that followed. In 1930 pitch-blende was found at Great Bear Lake in the North-West Territories—a discovery very important in the light of subsequent developments of atomic energy. The exploitation of this and other resources of the North was assisted by a large expansion of air-transport facilities, and the "bush-pilot" became a notable Canadian character. Trans-Canada Air Lines (a government-owned corporation) was to launch its cross-country service in 1939. There was some further advance of the farm frontier, particularly in the Peace River country of Alberta; and the mechanization of agriculture went forward rapidly. At the same time the industrial and financial progress of the war period continued to bear fruit. By the late 'twenties the gross value of manufactured products actually exceeded that of the war-years. During 1926–1929 expansion in almost every field of commerce and industry was swift and feverish.

An interesting feature of Canadian political and economic life during the 1920's was the growth of farmer and labour movements in Canada, the former spearheaded by the political victory of the U.F.O. (United Farmers of Ontario) at the provincial elections of 1919, the latter stemming from the Winnipeg general strike of 1919 and the organization of the short-lived Canadian Labour party in 1921. The political aspects of these movements will be treated in chapter xiv, "Political Parties and Ideas" (pp. 331–352); in the economic field they expressed themselves in such organizations as the United Grain Growers Limited (an amalgamation in 1917 of coöperative marketing societies in Manitoba and Alberta) and the Saskatchewan Coöperative Elevator Company, culminating in 1923 in the Wheat Pool; the Ontario Milk Producers, and other producer societies; together with small local ventures in coöperative processing among fishermen, fruit-growers, and others, extended during the succeeding depression decade, and accompanied by the beginnings of consumer coöperatives.

In the world depression, inaugurated by the panic of 1929, Canada was a heavy sufferer. The national revenue fell from $460,000,000 in 1928–1929 to as low as $311,000,000 in 1932–1933; the gross value of manufactured products was cut in half, and the decline in the country's total exports was even greater. At the low point of the depression in 1933 it was estimated that 265 of each 1,000 Canadian wage-earners were unemployed.[12] One of the early effects of the depression was to drive the Liberal administration from power. The Conservative Government of Mr. R. B. (later Viscount) Bennett, which took its place, waged an uphill battle against the situation for nearly five years, until its defeat in the election of 1935.

In the early years of his administration, Bennett concentrated upon the tariff as a means of mastering the country's economic difficulties. He retaliated against the American Smoot-Hawley Tariff; and although his first proposals for a revision of imperial commercial policy were rebuffed by the free-traders of Ramsay MacDonald's administration, after the formation of the "National Government" in the United Kingdom in 1931 he was able to suggest an Imperial Economic Conference, which took place at Ottawa in 1932. The result, after considerable bickering, was a dozen inter-imperial trade treaties. Trade figures for succeeding years indicate that Canada benefited more than the United Kingdom by the Anglo-Canadian agreement, for British exports to Canada increased much less than those from Canada to the United Kingdom. During three years, Canadian imports from the United States decreased by 13 per cent, but remained nearly three times as great as those from the United Kingdom. In general, the Ottawa treaties increased the volume of inter-imperial trade appreciably but by no means tremendously; the Anglo-Canadian agreement did not fundamentally alter the Dominion's balance of external trade; and the results, so far as Canadian trade revival was concerned, were disappointing.

In Canada there had been abundant praise for the manner in which President Franklin D. Roosevelt had attacked the problems posed by the depression in the United States. Canadians admired the American "New Deal," often somewhat uncritically; and unfavourable comparisons with the attitude of the Canadian administration were wide-spread. In January, 1935, to the astonishment of the country, Mr. Bennett proclaimed a New Deal of his own, and thereafter pushed through Parliament a series of enactments including provision for minimum wages, unemployment insurance, and a forty-eight-hour week. The majority of these measures were, however, *ultra vires* the Dominion Parliament under the interpretation of the British North America Act, which had been developed by judicial decisions in recent years; the greater part of the legislation was ruled unconstitutional in 1937.

In the mean time the Bennett New Deal had failed to save the Conservatives from defeat in the election of 1935. The depression had produced in Canada a new socialist party, the Coöperative Commonwealth Federation (C.C.F.), organized in 1932; but, while this party obtained a fair proportion of votes and remained a permanent factor in political life, it was to Mr. King and the Liberals that the country as a whole turned. Socialism was not a major force in Canadian politics; and a particular difficulty in its way was its failure to gain ground in the conservative Roman Catholic Province of Quebec.

Mr. King's third administration, formed in 1935, was less aggressively protectionist than Bennett's. Following up an approach which Bennett himself had made towards the end of his administration, it immediately concluded a reciprocal trade agreement with the United States. In 1937 a revised Anglo-Canadian trade agreement liberalized that of 1932; and in 1938 new agreements were made with both the United Kingdom and the United States. The United States in turn was now able to make an agreement with Great Britain. "The greatest triangular exchange of commodities in the world had thus been 'frozen' in patterns of reciprocal advantage by three carefully drawn treaties at the end of 1938."[13]

The invalidation of Bennett's social legislation by the courts served to direct attention to one of Canada's thorniest internal problems, the distribution of powers between the Dominion and the provinces. The framers of the British North America Act of 1867 naturally did not envisage the problems of a modern industrial state—problems unknown in their time—and they believed that they had set up a strong central government which would have all the powers required for its tasks. Following Confederation, however, their intentions were defeated by two circumstances: the resurgence of demands for provincial rights and decisions in important constitutional cases which interpreted the British North America Act in a manner highly favourable to these demands, whittling down the power of the central government to make general laws for the "peace, order, and good government of Canada" to the point where it is effective only in a time of emergency, and exalting the importance of the power granted to the provinces to make laws concerning "property and civil rights." (See pp. 291 ff.)

In 1937 the Dominion Government attempted to clear the way for modernizing the constitution by appointing a Royal Commission on Dominion-Provincial Relations. After exhaustive investigation, the Commission reported in 1940.[14] Broadly speaking, it recommended that the Dominion should assume full responsibility for unemployment relief and should also assume all provincial debts. The provinces, in return, it suggested, should abandon to the Dominion the fields of personal-income and corporation taxes and succession duties, as well as the cash subsidies which they were receiving from the Dominion. In order to permit the provinces to "provide normal Canadian services on a Canadian standard with no more than normal Canadian taxation," the Commission proposed that each province requiring it should receive from the Dominion an annual "national adjustment grant."

This carefully prepared plan came to nothing. Early in 1941 a Dominion-provincial conference met to explore the possibility of reaching agreement upon it. It immediately became apparent that the representatives of the wealthier provinces, in particular Ontario and Quebec, would have nothing to do with the scheme, and after a fierce attack by Mr. Mitchell Hepburn, the Premier of Ontario, the conference ended. Later attempts to obtain general agreement had little better fortune. In 1940 an amendment to the British North America Act established the right of the Dominion to control unemployment insurance, and by 1947 individual financial agreements were completed by the Dominion Government with seven of the nine provinces. Beyond that point, nothing was done to provide a permanent solution for what one historian described as "the financial anarchy produced by the existence of ten taxing and borrowing authorities in a country whose economy cries aloud for central direction."[15]

Among all the developments in the period spanned by the two world wars, none was more significant than the change in Canada's attitude towards international affairs.[16] Canada, as we have seen, joined the League of Nations when the League was formed. This, combined with the ancient connexion in the British Commonwealth, gave the Dominion two links with the world at large which the United States did not have. Nevertheless, the existence of these links did not prevent the development of an isolationism akin to that which flourished south of the border. It may be said, indeed, that Canada pursued inside the League of Nations much the same isolationist policy which the United States pursued outside it. In the period between the two world wars the Dominion showed itself decidedly unwilling to accept any political or military commitments, either through the British Commonwealth or the League. Even had the country accepted such commitments, it had not the means of fulfilling them; for after 1918 it reduced its armed forces to their pre-war level of insignificance.

The isolationist tendencies of the period between the two world wars are clearly shown in the election campaign of 1935, which took place in the midst of the international crisis caused by the Italian attack on Ethiopia. The parties vied with each other in declaring their determination (as Mr. Bennett put it) not to be "embroiled in any foreign quarrel where the rights of Canadians are not involved"; the politics of fear were fully in control. Soon after the election, the Canadian delegate at Geneva, acting without any specific authority, proposed that the economic sanctions already in effect against Italy should be extended to include cutting off her supply of oil—the measure best calculated to interfere effectively with the Italian operations.[17] His initiative was disavowed by the Canadian Government. In these years, government policy was based upon the postponement of decisions in the interest of maintaining national unity. The formula employed was that, when the final crisis came, the representatives of the people in Parliament would decide.

As the situation in Europe went from bad to worse, political leaders found it possible and necessary to take a somewhat more positive line. Beginning in 1936, the Government undertook an extremely modest programme of rearmament, although it was careful to explain that its primary object was the defence of Canadian territory. The Munich crisis of September, 1938, was a severe shock to the Canadian people, and when Hitler, in defiance of all his engagements, occupied Czechoslovakia in the following March it seemed clear that war was unavoidable. It also became clear that Canadian public opinion had hardened to the point where it would both sanction and demand participation. At the same time, every political leader was aware that the Province of Quebec was much less disposed to intervene than the rest of the country, and every political leader remembered the election of 1917. On March 27 Dr. R. J. Manion, the leader of the Conservative Opposition, enunciated his policy in a newspaper interview. It was "full coöperation with Britain in war-time" combined with "no conscription of Canadians to fight outside our borders in any war." Three days later, in the House of Commons, Prime Minister King committed his Government to a policy of no conscription for overseas service in the event of war.[18]

This approach to the crisis was doubtless unheroic, and was open to the serious objection that it is dangerous to fight a war with a totalitarian state on a basis of limited liability. It was, however, singularly successful in preserving the unity of Canada. When fighting began in Poland on September 1, 1939, the Canadian Parliament was called, in accordance with the undertaking so often given. On September 10 the House of Commons approved without a division Mr. King's recommendation that the Dominion should take its stand with Britain and France. After one week of formal neutrality, Canada declared war on Germany.

Canada thus had made her choice, and it is worth while to try to analyse the reasons. It is a striking fact that while the United States and the other American republics were organizing a delusive "hemispheric neutrality" at the Panama Conference and declaring it to be the united policy of the Americas to keep the

"European" war out of the New World, the country occupying the northern half of North America was mobilizing for that war. For more than two years Canada was the only American country actively engaged in the struggle. In the light of later events, one may well conclude that she was the only one to take a realistic view of the issues in 1939. Certainly her decision is not one which Canadians need remember with any feeling but satisfaction.

The decision, however, was not taken on merely realistic grounds. In the crisis, the traditional British connexion—allegiance to the Crown and all that it implies—was certainly the most powerful single factor in the situation. Yet, in contrast with 1914, Canadians went grimly and reluctantly, knowing what they were in for, and gloomily resolved to see it through. Behind this determination there was more than mere emotion. There was considerable understanding, slowly and painfully arrived at, of the nature of the crisis confronting mankind. Canada's approach to this trial had rather closely paralleled that of the United Kingdom. The people of both countries shrank from the idea of another bloody war, and in both the policy of "appeasement," which seemed to offer the hope of escape, long had a powerful appeal. Both countries neglected their defences too long. In both, nevertheless, the steady progress of Hitler's brutal and cynical course of aggression roused a frightened and reluctant people at last to the realization that armed resistance to the menace could not be avoided. The process was gradual. Had war come at the time of Munich, it is certain that Canada would have joined Britain and France; it is also certain, however, that her people would have been less united in 1938 than they proved to be in 1939.

It was these large general considerations—traditional ties and the threat to freedom—that determined the Dominion's course. There were other factors that might have influenced it. Notably, there was an economic as well as a sentimental and political bond uniting Canada to Britain. The United Kingdom in 1939 was the Dominion's second-best customer—second only by a very small margin to the United States. Canada, a great producing country with a small home market, lives by exports, and her trade, essentially, was with Britain and the United States; by comparison, all her other external trades put together were almost negligible. The loss of the British market for her staples would be a staggering blow for the Canadian economy. Nevertheless, it was not on a calculation of economic profit and loss that the Dominion made its decision in 1939.

The war effort of Canada developed gradually. As in the United Kingdom, during the first few months less was done than might have been; and after Dunkirk there was a rapid expansion. Canada's unpreparedness in 1939 slowed the process of mobilization in both military and economic fields; it was, indeed, three years before the country was realizing anything like its full war potential. In the end, however, as expressed in terms of either mobilized man-power or production of war material, the national effort was greater than it had been in 1914–1918. During the war, slightly more than 1,000,000 Canadians entered the armed forces.[19]

Although before 1939 it had been widely suggested that Canada's share in the event of another war was unlikely to take the form of a large expeditionary force, the army again represented the greatest national contribution to victory. Its primacy now was less marked than in 1914–1918, for in the Second World War Canada maintained large naval and air forces of her own. The army, however, was not merely larger than these; it was more distinctively national. It fought under Canadian commanders up to the army level, whereas the individuality of the other services was, to a considerable extent, submerged in the Royal Navy and Royal Air Force with which they served.

Although Canadian troops went overseas as early as December, 1939, it was long before they saw action. As a result of the withdrawal of the British armies from the Continent at the time of Dunkirk, the main Canadian field force found itself committed for a long time to a garrison role in the United Kingdom. The first Canadian soldiers to go into action were in fact two battalions, sent from Canada, which helped to defend Hong Kong against the Japanese in 1941, and the 5,000 men who fought in the raid on Dieppe the following year. By this time a Canadian army headquarters had been formed in England. The Canadian force overseas eventually included two corps headquarters with corps troops, five divisions (two armoured), two independent armoured brigades, and numerous ancillary and special units.

During 1943 this army was divided. In July one division took part in the Sicilian campaign, and later in the year a Canadian corps was built up in the Mediterranean theatre. Until early in 1945 this corps fought in Italy under the Eighth Army, playing an important part in the operations that broke the Adolf Hitler and Gothic lines. It was transferred to north-western Europe before the final collapse of Germany. One Canadian division formed part of the assault force that landed in Normandy on June 6, 1944. In July the First Canadian Army "became operational" under the Twenty-first Army Group and was particularly heavily engaged during the Falaise battles which followed. That autumn it saw further heavy fighting in the struggle to open Antwerp, and in February and March, 1945, it played a large and costly part in the battle of the Rhineland. It continued to be heavily engaged until the German surrender.

The Royal Canadian Air Force made one of its greatest contributions to victory through the British Commonwealth Air Training Plan, which trained 131,500 air-crewmen for Canada, the United Kingdom, Australia, and New Zealand. Many of these Canadian airmen were, however, made over to the R.A.F. for service in British units. Although 48 R.C.A.F. squadrons served overseas, and thousands of R.C.A.F. personnel were attached to the R.A.F., the opportunities for Canadian airmen to rise to high command were rather limited.[20] A tremendous contribution was likewise made by the Royal Canadian Navy, which underwent an almost incredible expansion. At the outbreak of war it had only 15 vessels; by April 1, 1945, it had 404 in commission. Its main battle-ground was the Atlantic, where it played a large and increasing part in the fight against the German submarines.

Fortunately, Canada's casualty list was somewhat shorter in the Second World War than in the First. Between the three services, some 41,000 Canadians lost their lives. The R.C.A.F., with 17,000 fatal casualties, suffered particularly heavily in proportion to its strength.

Before the war ended it had produced, as in 1914–1918, serious strains upon national unity. The policy of avoiding conscription for overseas service, adopted with a view to maintaining that unity, long remained in effect. The wide powers over persons and property conferred upon the Government by the National Resources Mobilization Act, passed after Dunkirk, did not extend to compelling individuals to serve overseas; it authorized conscription for home defence only. In 1942 a national plebiscite released the Government from its commitments on this question; Quebec, however, unlike the other eight provinces, voted against release. The Government held the power to introduce full conscription in abeyance until the autumn of 1944, when shortage of infantry reinforcements became acute. After a last attempt to obtain the needed men by voluntary means, which produced a serious political crisis, compulsorily enlisted men were sent overseas. Nevertheless, of the 368,000 Canadian soldiers who served in Europe, all but about 13,000 were volunteers.

Canada's industrial effort in this war, although it got off to a somewhat slow start, owing in part to the complacency of the British Government in the early months, was in the end both much larger and far more diversified than in 1914–1918. Among the items produced were 794,000 motor vehicles; 900,000 rifles; 244,000 light machine-guns; 16,000 aircraft; 6,500 tanks and self-propelled guns; and 391 cargo vessels, 486 escort vessels, and 3,500 miscellaneous vessels and special-purpose craft. Manufacturing production reached "a much higher level than ever before."[21]

The deep mark left by the war upon the economic life of Canada is described in later chapters, but we may note here its contribution to the opening of the North-West Territories. The Alaska Highway, built by the United States Army Corps of Engineers in 1942–1944 under a Canadian-American agreement, was an important factor in this development. With it must be mentioned the two war-time chains of air-fields known as the North-West and North-East Staging Routes. The Norman Wells oil-field on the Mackenzie River was greatly developed as the result of the United States Canol project (1942–1945). Canada's greatest source of petroleum, however, is the province of Alberta, where production was considerable after 1930 and was enormously expanded during and immediately after the war.

The Second World War, like the First, significantly affected Canada's external relations. In particular, it brought her closer to the United States than ever before. Franklin D. Roosevelt was perhaps the first American president to be genuinely popular in Canada. He was so, we have seen, even before 1938, when he remarked that the United States would "not stand idly by" if Canada were threatened by aggression. The divergence between Canadian belligerency and American neutrality in 1939 proved to be a temporary phase, for the collapse of France threw the United States into panic and was indeed the end of American isolation. The Roosevelt plan of "all aid to Britain short of war" necessarily brought Canadian and American policy into close alignment. At the same time the two countries took joint measures for the security of North America. The meeting between Mr. Roosevelt and Mr. King at Ogdensburg on August 17, 1940, resulted in the establishment of a Permanent Joint Board on Defence which provided an effective organ for continuous consultation on mutual military problems. After the United States became an open belligerent, coöperation naturally became still closer. Some mention has already been made of joint-defence projects in the North-West. Had the war against Japan continued, a Canadian division would have served with the United States forces in the Pacific. At the time of the Japanese surrender, this division, which was to be organized and equipped on American lines, was preparing to move to the United States for training.

This Canadian-American coöperation did not end with the war. Serious controversies with Russia, which immediately began, left the Americans more conscious than ever before of the military importance of Canada. In February, 1947, it was announced in Ottawa and Washington that informal and limited military collaboration would continue. The Permanent Joint Board on Defence was continued, and arrangements were made for the exchange of officers and facilities between Canadian and American forces. Canada, however, did not give the United States possession of bases on Canadian soil. The arrangement between the two countries provided that each should continue to control establishments in its own territory. The American bases in the new province of Newfoundland, established before it became part of Canada, are a special problem. Discussion concerning possible alterations in their status is understood to be in progress at the time of writing.

Indeed, while a striking development of the post-war period in Canada has been the decline of the isolationism that was active before 1939, Canada's new sense of international responsibility has been but one form of a new and more mature affirmation of her national status within the British Commonwealth and the wider framework of the United Nations Organization. There is no more interesting illustration of the way in which past anomalies have been resolved than the passage of the Canadian Citizenship Act in January, 1947. This statute has established explicitly by law a dual loyalty which has always been tacitly recognized in the Dominion—that of the Canadian *citizen* who is also a British *subject*. The latter term, whatever its earlier meanings, no longer implies colonial inferiority; like much of the British constitutional phraseology, its meaning has expanded with a "freedom slowly broadening down from precedent to precedent."

Such acts among the nations of the Commonwealth may be milestones in the history of international law. The possibility of dual citizenship has been suggested in other quarters, as, for instance, between the United Kingdom and France. Such a development, if widely extended, might become an influence in breaking down the rigid concept of national sovereignty now outmoded by the hard facts of our twentieth-century world. In the light of these considerations, it is not surprising that Canadians should find the achievement of their national maturity merging naturally into the wider associations of the Commonwealth and the international order.

By no means unrelated to these far-reaching developments of the war and post-war years was the decision in 1948 of Newfoundland to join Canada as the tenth province of the Dominion. This oldest British colony, geographically and strategically a vital salient on British North America's Atlantic wall, had hitherto preferred to maintain its separate identity. In spite of a historic development parallel in many respects to that of the provinces which formed the nucleus of Confederation, Newfoundland had refused to join the union of 1867. Throughout its history it had been closely associated in peace and war with the British Isles; and its dominant maritime interests, no less than its spirit of sturdy independence, led it to doubt seriously the advantage of closer union with the Canadian provinces. For many years it enjoyed full rights of self-government and Dominion status.

The economic depression of the 1930's, however, brought this island, with its raw-material economy and colonial financial system, to the verge of bankruptcy. In 1934, by mutual consent of the Newfoundland and British governments, responsible government was suspended in favour of government by a commission of three members from the United Kingdom and three from the island. This was clearly a temporary arrangement, but not until after the end of the Second World War was permanent decision possible. Finally, in the summer of 1948, after two years of intense debate, Newfoundland went to the polls to choose among continuation of commission government, return to responsible government, and union with Canada on terms which had been made the subject of careful consideration with the Canadian Government. Commission government was eliminated in the first plebiscite, but it took a second referendum on July 22 to decide for confederation. The vote was close, but the majority was considered adequate; and on April 1, 1949, the union became effective. When Parliament opened in the autumn, the members for Newfoundland were in their places. The transition to the new régime in Newfoundland had been smooth, and there seemed no reason to doubt that the advantages of union would far outweigh the disadvantages on both sides.

Newfoundland's decision was of more than local importance. The Second World War, with its emphasis on air travel and transport and its shifting diplomatic balances, had tremendously increased both the strategic importance and the vulnerability of the island. In a world of sharply-increased international tensions, the decision to join in a larger political and defensive unit could probably not have been long avoided. To Canada the decision meant the completion of a process which had begun with the acceptance of the principle of responsible government just one hundred years earlier. That principle, worked out in all its implications, had made possible the integration of British North America by the will of its own peoples, and the creation of a Canadian nation stretching from sea to sea.

Part Three

THE ECONOMY

CHAPTER VII

Fundamental and Historic Elements

BY H. A. INNIS AND W. T. EASTERBROOK

Canada is a nation of great geographic, racial, and cultural complexity, as other parts of this volume have pointed out. In sharp contrast, its economy is relatively simple, and because of this simplicity is highly vulnerable. Through most of Canadian history, the demands of metropolitan centres in the Old World, and later in the New, have encouraged an intense preoccupation with one or very few exportable commodities and the transportation systems necessary to their exploitation. The physical environment provided enormous and highly-accessible supplies of staple goods and the river systems and countless lakes for their transportation. Ease of application of simple techniques to abundant natural resources strengthened the belief that the country was destined to fit, in a complementary way, into the mature systems of other areas. National policies underlined a singular lack of diversity in economic life by restricting economic and political expansionism mainly to the narrow limits imposed by geography and primitive techniques of production and transportation.

So long as Canada remained simply a source of supplies of fish and fur and lumber for the more economically advanced regions of the world, the enterprise of individuals and company organizations provided sufficient drive for an expansion which, in terms of markets and resources, was both natural and inevitable. When industrialism came to Canada in the 1840's with a shift to iron and coal, and wheat and railways and steamships, painful adjustment replaced continuous, almost uninterrupted expansion. There were staple commodities in abundance, and techniques could be borrowed, but the application of industrial technology to the exploitation of Canada's resources demanded capital expenditures that were enormous for an area so thinly peopled. To the south, the increasingly powerful and competitive United States, a country much more happily endowed by nature, forced the pace far beyond the ability of private enterprise to carry on without substantial state support. As a result, for a century an alliance of business and government has provided a pattern of expansion that goes back to the first penetration of the continent —a pattern unchanged in the emphasis on staples for external markets, but marked by new technical and institutional methods.

The economic beginnings which first brought Europeans to North America regularly in the sixteenth century and helped to determine eventual control of the northern half of the continent are found in the cod fisheries of the North Atlantic. The heavily salted cure for the Paris market, and later the sun-dried product for Spanish and Mediterranean ports and West Indies plantations, was the first staple exploited to meet European demands. With the end of effective Portuguese and Spanish competition late in the sixteenth century, the struggle for control of the North Atlantic region narrowed down to that between the aggressive commercialism of the English and the more inflexible centralism of the continental-minded French. The divisive character of the fisheries, an industry based on small units of enterprise, weakened all attempts at monopoly control by either power. The French were unable to construct a well-integrated commercial system on the basis of the cod fisheries, and the rise of New England as a competitive centre hastened the exit of France from North America in 1763. The fisheries also forced wide breaches in the mercantilist system of the English and, by increasing the elements of competition within the first British Empire, hastened its break-up in 1783. The fishing industry not only helped to determine the outcome of international conflict in this area; it led to the discovery of the rich fur resources of the continent and to the rise of the fur trade—a trade which was eventually to mark out the boundary line between the undiversified economy of the northern half of the continent and the more complex area of development to the south.

Just as Russian traders pushed across Siberia into the North Pacific area in search of sable and sea-otter furs, traders and trading organizations in North America drove westward from the Atlantic across the continent in search of beaver pelts. Before 1763 the French had developed a remarkably efficient trading organization based in the St. Lawrence region and reaching westward to the Saskatchewan River system. The English chose, on the other hand, a maritime type of expansion, striking at the excessively elongated system of the French from bases in the Hudson River area to the south and the Hudson Bay to the north. The vulnerable continental system of the French, with its heavy costs of transportation and undue reliance on the uncertain income derived from a luxury staple, was forced to give way. And when, in 1783, the American colonies chose a separate destiny, the fur trade to the north remained within the imperial system, an area too weak to strike out for itself and barely strong enough to withstand the pressure for absorption into the new nation rising to the south.

Canada as the weaker unit managed for a time, on the basis of her fur trade and water-transportation system, to achieve a continental unity of her own, dominated by Canadian fur-trading interests centred at Montreal and reaching from the Atlantic to the Pacific. As with the French, this transcontinental system based on the St. Lawrence failed to meet effectively the competition of the geographically favoured Hudson's Bay Company, and the North-West Company was submerged in that organization in 1821. Canada's first economic unity based on a staple had collapsed.

Different regions then turned to the exploitation of different resources. Western Canada and the Pacific coastal strip carried on with the fur trade. Nova Scotia concentrated on its fisheries. The financial interests of Quebec and Montreal, with their London connexions, shifted to the white and red pine of the St. Lawrence area, the adjacent sections of the Canadian Shield, and New Brunswick.

The change was made with little difficulty. The resources of the forest were easily accessible, and great rivers carried the roughly-squared timber to Quebec and St. John without the necessity of huge capital outlays on transportation systems. Expansion of the new industry coincided with the technological unemployment of early industrialism in England; and, beginning in the 1820's, large numbers of emigrants filled the holds on the return trips of the "coffin-ships" of the timber trade.

With immigration and the expansion of settlement in Upper Canada as far west as the Great Lakes, other products became available for export: at first, potash;[1] later, and more important, wheat. Following the end of the British preferential system in the 1840's and the decline of timber exports to Europe, wheat became the dominant staple of the St. Lawrence Lowlands. This continued until the last decades of the nineteenth century, when the opening of prairie lands and the beginning of large-scale prairie wheat exports necessitated agricultural reorganization in eastern Canada and closer orientation there to the expanding domestic market.

Unlike the earlier staples, it was clear from the beginning that wheat as a trading commodity would require extensive improvements in the transportation system of the St. Lawrence—improvements which could be made only with very heavy capital expenditures. Expansion became much less easy and automatic: further development could result only from deliberate planning. The drive or backing for change to such a policy was provided mainly by the commercial and financial interests centred in Montreal. Opposition to these interests came from the colonial aristocracy (military, ecclesiastical, and professional) and from the habitants of Quebec and the rural class of Upper Canada, all of them antagonistic to and suspicious of the aspirations of the commercial capitalist. The entrepreneurial interests won out, when the Act of Union (1840) united the provinces of Upper and Lower Canada and cleared away the obstacles to strong governmental support of transportation developments. The canal era of the 1840's reflected the faith of its promoters in the ability of the St. Lawrence system to carry to the seaboard not only the products

[1] For note to chapter vii see page 575.

of Canada but those of the expanding United States Middle West as well.

It was not an easy situation for the Canada of the 1840's. Threatened with the loss of British preferences, and faced with the vastly greater competitive power of the United States, the only alternative to stagnation, as the expansionists saw it, was a strong attempt to make the St. Lawrence system the chief continental artery of trade. Had this succeeded, Montreal would have become the great *entrepôt* of trade between North America and Europe. It was a bold attempt but, viewed retrospectively, a hopeless one. Montreal at no time seriously challenged Manhattan. The Erie Canal, completed in 1825, along with United States developmental policies, gave New York unquestioned preëminence. When it became obvious that the canals had failed, Canada hastened to build supplementary and, later, trunk railways linking the whole St. Lawrence area with Atlantic Coast ports.

Reciprocal trade relations with the United States, beginning in 1854, seemed to provide grounds for optimism; but the outcome of the Civil War left control of American national destinies in the hands of the protectionist North, and this, together with the beginnings of Canadian protectionism in the late 1850's, brought reciprocity to an end in 1866.

Canada in 1866 was very much on her own: she was burdened with a huge national debt incurred for a transportation system with an unused capacity which reflected its failure to capture United States traffic; she was committed to a policy of economic expansion which allowed of no turning back; and she feared a movement of population from the United States northward to the thinly-settled wheat-lands of western Canada or the Pacific coastal strip with its little-known resources. On the Pacific Coast, the spread northward of United States settlement had been stopped at the forty-ninth parallel, but, with the Fraser River and Cariboo gold-strikes and hope of other discoveries farther north, the pressure from the south continued. The Canadian prairies, a natural extension of the Great Plains, imposed no geographic barrier to the penetration of settlement from the United States.

It was apparent that the fur trade and mining activities of the Pacific Coast and the Shield, and the limited agricultural development of the Red River Valley and what is now southern Alberta offered no means by which western Canada could, unaided, preserve its great area for Canadian developmental purposes. Yet it must be retained, if only to achieve the full utilization of existing transportation facilities and to increase revenues for the servicing of the already unwieldy public debt.

The solution worked out in the years immediately following Confederation was an inevitable corollary or outcome of earlier decisions. In the 1840's Canada had elected to continue as an expanding area of commercialism based on export staples rather than to develop a more stable and diversified economy. The colony had embarked upon construction of transportation facilities which committed it to expansion as the only means of meeting their enormous costs. The Galt and Cayley tariffs of 1858 and 1859 had laid the base for protectionist policies, and the speed of United States expansion westward had increased the need of Canadian enterprise for such support.

To include and integrate the scattered western communities within a larger transcontinental system while there was yet time required the construction of a transcontinental railway network. It was to be based, like the transcontinental water-ways system of the Nor'-Westers and their French predecessors, on the St. Lawrence region, but it was faced with even greater difficulties. It must cross the non-revenue-bearing southern extension of the Canadian Shield and pierce the Rocky Mountain barriers to the Pacific Coast. Public support must aid private enterprise in its construction; the new staple, prairie wheat, would move eastward; and this must be counterbalanced by a westward movement of Canadian manufactures, protected from the entrance of American competition except at tariffs so high that they would themselves aid public financing. Public finance, transportation, and tariffs were thus closely-related and fundamental elements in an ambitious programme of nation-building in the northern half of the continent.

While the scope of Canada's endeavours was thus magnified, the essential pattern remained the same. The whole Canadian economy was to be geared, as with the southern United States, to the expanding industrialism of Europe. Whereas central Canada was to develop behind tariff walls a sector of its own to correspond with the industrial north-eastern region of the United States, the Canadian railways and their rates were designed primarily to encourage large-scale transportation of a major staple to the world market. And Dominion land policy, with its control of the resources of the Prairie Provinces, was directed to attracting the population and initiative necessary to develop that staple.

These policies and that development rested on a unique geographic environment, early subservience to the industrialism of Great Britain, and the presence of the almost overwhelming competitive power of the United States. It was the old, well-tried formula on a somewhat larger scale—a national programme expressed in terms of staples and transportation, tariffs and railway rates, land and immigration policies, and the buttressing of enterprise by governmental ownership and support. And its outcome could not be otherwise than an undiversified, rather lop sided economic development, exposed because of dependence on external markets to the vicissitudes of world market conditions and the vagaries of changing commercial policies and practices.

In the late nineteenth century and the early twentieth, gold and base-metal mining, production of pulp and paper, and hydroelectric power developments enormously strengthened the more favoured regions of the country, mainly central Canada and British Columbia. Striking advances were made in processing and manufacturing based on natural resources. And accompanying these changes was a sharp reorientation in markets. Canada's gold and non-ferrous metals, pulp and paper, have gone largely to the United States. There has been, at the same time, a marked reduction in the relative importance of wheat, a staple marketed principally in Europe. These changes in industry and in markets have meant for Canada a somewhat more diversified economy. On the other hand, reliance on the income from a few export staples destined for external consumption is fundamentally unchanged, and it is doubtful whether the pattern of Canadian economic development has been significantly altered.

It is true that there is greater complexity, but its significance is political rather than economic. The products of twentieth-century industrialism are derived from provincially controlled resources, and the richest and strongest provinces have the greatest stakes. Instead of being carried on the latitudinal transportation system which binds together the whole economy, the mineral and pulp-wood and paper products of central Canada are shipped to adjacent metropolitan markets in the United States. British Columbia also looks southward and outward for its markets for staple products. Even the wheat regions, with the choice of the Hudson Bay Railway and the Panama Canal via Vancouver, have alternatives to the use of the transportation system which made a national transcontinental economy possible.

The direct result has been an increase in regional tensions as the Dominion Government has sought to preserve a political unity based on iron and coal, wheat and railways and tariffs, against the divisive forces of the new industrialism. The economy has changed mainly in adding a few staples and the subsidiary developments based on or resulting from them, but the political significance of this change is very great and it suggests increasing difficulties as economic tendencies weaken, rather than support, political unity.

The presence of the United States as neighbour has been of the greatest significance to the problems and policies of federalism in Canada. It was fear of the economic and political penetration of the United States which forced the federal government to become heavily involved in the expansion of nineteenth-century Canadian industrialism. And it is the influence of United States markets, with their strong north-south pull, which, by increasing the strength of regionalism, complicates the task of the Dominion Government in protecting the unity so painfully achieved.

Dominion-provincial relations in Canada reflect the tensions produced by the conflicting interests of areas based on the old and the new industrialism. The Dominion Government has supported the former as the effective means of achieving and maintaining economic and political unity, and its importance as the economic basis of Canadian unity has not changed. But markets and resources and transportation factors have changed, and the changes increase the difficulty of preserving Canada's national entity.

A century ago Canada faced the necessity of making difficult decisions of long-run policy. The same problem has been posed again in the twentieth century, with the difference, however, that the time-worn device of state-supported expansion as an economic panacea has become less effective. Further transportation developments, in spite of the increased importance of air traffic and the use of the gasolene engine and the Diesel barge and tractor, seem to offer no opportunities for expansion comparable to those of the past. Tariffs appear to have reached the limit of their usefulness as weapons of fiscal policy; and railway rates, where they move at all, move upward and hence further strengthen regionalism. The chaos of the European market weakens any prospect of an early restoration of large-scale traffic across the Atlantic—traffic on which the Canadian economy once in large part depended. And quite apart from these difficulties, the heavy overburden of national debt precludes any easy adjustment to changing conditions.

It is obvious that Canada, in common with other industrial areas, has prospered by expansion, but that policies based on the assumption of an expanding world in terms of trade and output will no longer suffice if a more static or even retrogressive world economy is in prospect. It is, however, precisely at the point where adjustment appears as the prerequisite to further expansion that the significance of Canada's vulnerability to external actions and policies becomes apparent. So long as her economy remains sensitive to changes in economic and political conditions in the United States and, to a lesser extent, in the United Kingdom, and so long as she is unable to insulate herself against their influence to a significant degree, it is difficult to see how she can devise strong and independent national policies.

Over a long period, Canada has by her own actions steadily increased the influence of factors external to her economy, with the state as an active agent in promoting developments by which she could fit more effectively into a pattern of world trade. Her resources may be further developed, a new current of immigrants be encouraged to enter, and a new industrialism be fostered, but fundamental and perplexing difficulties remain. These difficulties are a product of the geographic and economic forces which encourage regionalism and have retarded the development of any great national autonomy or independence. Canada from the beginning seems to have been destined, economically, for a part in a larger system and, unless the United Kingdom recovers sufficiently to regain its nineteenth-century position as a counterpoise to the enormous weight of the United States in Canadian affairs, it is difficult to see how this system can be other than that of Canada's "great neighbour."

The economic aspects of regional conflict and lack of national autonomy have important implications for Canada's political life, even though they do not by themselves constitute a threat to her status as a separate and independent political entity. Quite apart from the intangibles of national feeling, tradition, and inertia, powerful interests on both sides of the border are strongly opposed to any merging of the two countries in one political unit. Each nation is a product of its own distinct historical evolution, and politically the patterns in the two countries have been profoundly different.

The significance of twentieth-century economic changes lies rather in terms of effective government of the country. Unless the Dominion Government and the provinces recognize the political significance of recent developments in production, transportation, and markets, and attempt, in the interest of unity, to distribute equitably the resulting profits and losses over the nation, effective national policies are out of the question. Weakness here must inevitably be reflected in the increasing strength of external influences in the economy. A strong political unity, on the other hand, promises a more influential "middle-nation" role in world affairs.

CHAPTER VIII

Eastern Canada

BY A. W. CURRIE

THE ATLANTIC SEABOARD includes the three Maritime Provinces of Nova Scotia, New Brunswick, and Prince Edward Island; the newly-associated island province of Newfoundland; and also the Gaspé peninsula of Quebec. In area the region, without Newfoundland, is roughly 60,000 square miles, or about the size of New England, which it resembles geologically and to some extent economically. The area of the island of Newfoundland is 42,734 square miles; that of its Labrador mainland, about 110,000 square miles. Substantially, all these provinces consist of either islands or peninsulas. Such communities tend to become insular in a sociological as well as a geographic sense. Moreover, this area has experienced almost chronic business depression over the last twenty-five years. As a result of geographic and economic factors the Maritime Provinces have developed strong and distinctive political, social, and economic characteristics.

Geologically the region is chiefly one of hard crystalline rock, heavily glaciated, with a general trend, or "grain," running from south-west to north-east. The Gaspé peninsula, eastern New Brunswick, Newfoundland, Cape Breton Island, and the backbone of Nova Scotia consist of dissected plateaux, rounded hills, and ancient mountain ranges rising to altitudes of from 1,000 to 4,200 feet. Central New Brunswick is a gentle downfold eaten into by the St. John River and its tributaries. Prince Edward Island and the littoral opposite it are fairly level sandstone plains. In the Annapolis–Cornwallis Valley, along the Petitcodiac between St. John and Moncton, and in numerous scattered patches, beds of reddish conglomerates, sandstones, and shales overlie the igneous rocks. The deposits of gypsum, salt, and high-quality bituminous coal are of great economic value. Newfoundland, which is geologically related closely to the mainland of Quebec and Labrador, has a considerable development of metalliferous rocks. The sunken coast-lines with their numerous harbours and the submarine topography off shore partly account for the success of the Seaboard fishing industry. Yet even with this wide variety in detail, the general build of the area is of more or less parallel bands of hard rock.

In view of the geology of the region, fertile soils are comparatively limited in area and dispersed in location. The sandstones have weathered down into fairly continuous stretches of arable land. The world's highest tides have gathered up silt from near the mouths of rivers and deposited it at the head of the Bay of Fundy and in the Minas Basin, forming fertile sea-marshes which have been reclaimed by dikes. And the forces of erosion have created a few fertile acres along a number of the river courses, notably the lower St. John. On the uplands, unfortunately, soil is either absent or is merely a thin mantle of glacial drift. In many poorly-drained lowlands and marshes the soil is "sour" or even waterlogged. All these conditions signify recent glaciation. In brief, despite "islands" of fertility, the Maritime Provinces suffer from poor soil resources.

The climate of these provinces is continental cyclonic, modified by the sea, which nearly surrounds them, and by their location on the eastern edge of the land mass. Typically (in Britain, for example) the presence of an adjacent body of water has a decidedly moderating influence on climate. But the prevailing westerly winds reach the Maritime Provinces from a huge area of land which becomes very cold in winter and hot in summer, and thus they bring a fairly wide range of temperature. Nevertheless, the ocean does have some influence, for it slightly reduces the extremes of temperature, delays the arrival of spring and autumn, and helps to create frequent fogs along the coast. At Halifax the average annual precipitation is 55 inches, cloudy days are common, the average temperature in January is 23° F. and in July 64°, and the frost-free period is 185 days. Temperatures usually become more extreme as one goes inland, while both the amount of precipitation and the length of the growing season decline.

The 1,600,000 inhabitants of the Atlantic Seaboard are of a number of stocks. Halifax is about equally divided between English and Scottish Protestants, and Irish and Scottish Catholics. Near Lunenburg, in south-western Nova Scotia, a large proportion of the people are of German origin; from Yarmouth to Digby, of French; and in the Annapolis Valley, chiefly of English ancestry. In Cape Breton Island and along the Northumberland Strait the majority of the people are of Highland Scots descent, and Gaelic is still spoken. Newfoundlanders have a strong Celtic strain, inherited from the old fishing colonies of Cornwall, Devon, and Brittany, with an infusion of Irish. The three chief religious groups—Roman Catholics, Anglicans, and United Churchmen—are so evenly balanced as to offer a basis for the apportionment of government posts. Prince Edward Island is also largely Scottish, though with a good many English and French. The original settlers in New Brunswick were United Empire Loyalists, the "displaced persons" of the American Revolution. In the northern part of that province, French-Canadian communities predominate, as they do in the Gaspé peninsula.

In brief, the Atlantic Seaboard is a veritable mosaic of cultural groups. Yet friction, it is important to note, is negligible in comparison with that existing from time to time between the English and French in the St. Lawrence Lowlands. Also, there are no groups like those on the prairies, which are still in the process of being assimilated into the Canadian way of life. In the Maritime Provinces, acculturation is reasonably complete. The various cultural groups have intermarried; they have moved about within the provinces for economic reasons; they and their ancestors have lived in the region for a hundred and fifty years or more; and the number of recent immigrants with divided loyalties is relatively small. The apparently strong attachment of the various groups to their home-lands is almost entirely sentimental, and of little practical importance in comparison with their mutual associations as Maritimers and Canadians.

The earliest economic development in the Seaboard region was connected with fishing. The wealth of the seas could be taken quickly, without elaborate equipment or advanced techniques, and by methods identical with those already in use in Europe. Unfortunately, neither this industry nor the fur trade which followed it was conducive to permanent settlement. Eventually a few French colonies were established near forts like Louisbourg and in the salt-marshes around the Minas Basin, the land of Evangeline. After the expulsion of the Acadians (1755) pre-revolutionary New Englanders came into the Annapolis Valley, but wide-spread settlement took place only with the influx of Loyalists and Scots in the 1780's and 1790's.

By 1800 the Atlantic Seaboard had emerged as an agricultural community, and in the next fifty years it became a great shipbuilding centre as well. The advent of iron and steel vessels and of the steam-engine doomed this era, the most prosperous in the history of the Maritime Provinces. By 1900 specialized agriculture had become well established in a few favoured areas, the steel plant at Sydney had been erected, and the fishing and lumbering industries had attained at least their present size. Then after 1920 the region began slowly to slip behind the rest of the country economically.

Maritime agriculture has been handicapped by climate, which restricts the number of products which can be grown, and by soil, which limits the area of production. The chief cash crop in the Annapolis-Cornwallis Valley is apples, which are normally exported to Britain. During the recent war the shortage of shipping-space raised serious problems for the producers of such a bulky commodity. Then, too, in the last few years Britain has been raising more of her own fruit. Further, Nova Scotia apples, partly as a result of the cloudy weather, are not brightly coloured. Though they appeal to Europeans, to most Canadians they are less attractive than rosy apples. In sum, this industry, a mainstay of agriculture in the Maritime Provinces for more than sixty years, is in danger of losing its old market and has difficulty in entering another, the St. Lawrence Lowlands, in competition with nearer sources of supply.

In Victoria and Carleton counties, up the St. John River about 125 miles as the crow flies, and in Prince Edward Island, potatoes are the largest single source of farm income. The soils and climate are particularly favourable to the growth of high-quality tubers. Provincial departments of agriculture and coöperative marketing associations have gone to great pains to reduce the prevalence of disease and to ensure the growth and export of only high-grade stock, whether for table purposes or for seed. The superior quality of this product commands a premium in many markets. On the other hand, prices vary a great deal from one year to another. Importing countries such as the United States and Cuba have levied duties against the Canadian article. Potatoes are bulky, expensive to haul to market, and usually face strong competition from locally grown supplies, since this vegetable can be raised in virtually every part of the continent.

In Prince Edward Island, fox-farming is a valuable addition to agriculture. Foxes are fed low-grade fish, farm animals that have outlived their usefulness, and specially prepared biscuits. Raising this type of live-stock is a risky business, however; being penned up, the animals quickly develop diseases unknown in their native habitat. Moreover, since they are still in process of domestication, they must not be molested any more than necessary. At first, some fox-farmers made large profits by selling breeding-stock to ranches being established elsewhere. After this demand had been satisfied, the Island industry began producing for the regular fur trade. Prices tend to fluctuate according to the dictates of fashion, but the steadily growing popularity of furs, the superior quality of pelts from semi-domesticated over those from wild animals, and the apparently dwindling supplies of skins taken by trappers have served to support the price.

Maritime Province farmers also carry on mixed farming both in the districts of specialized agriculture just mentioned and on the intervale soils scattered throughout the area. The output of dairy products is favoured by ample rainfall and good growing conditions for pasture, hay, and oats. In many districts, however, farm-steads are separated from each other by ridges of hard rock, making it expensive to haul cream and milk to butter and cheese factories. Production techniques both on farms and in processing plants are often out of date. On the whole, the Maritime Provinces fail to make the most of their natural advantages in dairying.

Near fishing villages and saw-mill towns a few farms are operated by the men when they are not working at their main occupation, or by the wives and children when the men are on the sea or in the woods, but the quality of output is low and the yields per acre are small. Owing to cloudy weather and low summer temperatures, wheat is nowhere an important crop, though a little is grown. French Canadians in northern New Brunswick and the Gaspé are largely self-sufficient.

Although the Atlantic Seaboard is not without prosperous farming districts, other parts of Canada are so favoured by nature that they can send their goods into this region and undersell locally grown supplies. The Maritime Provinces as a whole do not provide for their own requirements of grain, eggs, poultry, beef, or dairy products. In 1941 agriculture employed 32 per cent of the gainfully occupied males,[1] a higher proportion than in Ontario and Quebec (25 per cent) and British Columbia (16 per cent), but much less than on the prairies (56 per cent). Income per farmer is low, even with supplemental earnings from lumbering or fishing. Except in Gaspé and northern New Brunswick, the rural population has steadily diminished in numbers over the last fifty years, even in the districts of specialized agriculture. Abandoned and run-down farms are common, particularly on the poor soils of the uplands. As a whole, Maritime Province agriculture is not thriving, although there are important exceptions: fox-farming, potato-raising, apple-growing, and some dairying.

Fishing is not in itself a large employer of labour, but many coastal settlements depend upon it completely. The waters above the Grand Banks of Newfoundland and adjacent to the coast are among the world's richest pastures for commercial fish. A basic geographic difficulty is that a comparatively isolated area produces a perishable article for sale in distant markets. To reach these markets the fish may be preserved by canning, freezing, smoking, or salting, the last method being much the cheapest. Formerly, salt cod found a ready market in Canada, Spain and the Mediterranean countries, Brazil, and the West Indies, but nowadays, when fresh meat and fish are more readily obtained and incomes have risen, consumers are less willing to buy a relatively unpalatable food like salt fish. In the face of disappearing outlets, Canadian

[1] For note to chapter viii see page 575.

producers are experiencing strong competition from Iceland and Norway. The Maritime industry has tried to shift from cod to herring, haddock, and halibut, and from salt fish to the fresh or quick-frozen trade. In this new business the fisheries are handicapped by the long distance to the main market in the St. Lawrence Lowlands and by the scattered nature of their operations. It is difficult to ship by express direct from the many small ports along the Atlantic and Gaspé coasts or to bring freshly-caught fish to larger centres for freezing. Other riches of the sea are important, too—young herring (the so-called sardine), smelts, some salmon, tuna, and by-products like cod-liver oil and fish-meal as well as lobsters and oysters.

Forests provide work for almost as many men as do the fisheries. Nearly three-quarters of both Nova Scotia and New Brunswick and much of Newfoundland are still forested, chiefly with yellow birch, maple, spruce, white pine, balsam, and tamarack. The hardwoods are used for flooring, furniture, implement-handles, and the like; the softwoods are used mainly for news-print. Logging is a seasonal occupation, but many of the saw-mills and other woodworking plants operate throughout most of the year.

Mining gave employment to about 5 per cent of the gainfully occupied in 1941. Although some gypsum, salt, natural gas, and gold are mined, and copper and iron (particularly the latter) are important in Newfoundland, coal has the premier position, with 40 per cent of the total Canadian output of this product. The most valuable coal-fields are on Cape Breton Island not far from Sydney. In this field the seams dip gently below the sea without faulting or appreciable change in quality. At present some coal is obtained three or four miles from shore and can probably be mined at twice this distance. The reserves should meet the requirements at maximum annual output for about two hundred years. Unfortunately, submarine mines are expensive to work because of the cost of providing ventilation and light at the face of the coal, and the expense of tramways and power to haul the coal inward and upward to the foot of the shaft. Machinery is not used so extensively as in the United States, labour relations are far from satisfactory, and output per man-day is low. Consequently the cost per ton is high. Without a protective tariff against American coal,

Cape Breton mines would find it impossible to sell in the Montreal area, which is their chief outlet.

The coal-measures in the Pictou-Cumberland field between the head of the Bay of Fundy and the Northumberland Strait are excessively faulted. Though relations between management and men are reasonably good, and the mines are subterranean, costs are still high. Besides these local problems, the Maritime Province industry, like coal-mining everywhere, must meet the competition of fuel-oil, gasolene, and hydro-electricity; economies in the use of coal for raising steam; and increasing wage costs.

The coal-deposits at Sydney led to the establishment of the Seaboard's largest single manufacturing industry, an iron and steel works. Among the plant's advantages are easy access to high-grade iron ore from Newfoundland and eventually from Labrador, tariff protection for most of its goods, fairly acceptable labour relations, and water transportation to the St. Lawrence Lowlands and export markets. Among its disabilities, this plant has expensive coal and is comparatively remote from the large market in the industrialized Lowlands. It is not fully modern, having been erected primarily to make rails for Canada's expanding railway network, whereas the chief demand today is for plate, cold-drawn sheet, beams, and pipe. The Sydney works have not expanded as rapidly as the industrialization of the Canadian economy as a whole.

The region also has a number of creameries, fish-canning and -packing plants, wood-working establishments, foundries, textile mills, ship-yards, a sugar-refinery, and a large candy factory. Further, it has the usual bakeries, printing-plants, and other concerns to supply local needs. Most of the factories sell only in the Maritime Provinces and Newfoundland, and in the British West Indies; a few, despite the long rail or water haul, sell sardines, sugar, candy, and steel in the central Canadian market. A total of 11 per cent of the gainfully occupied of the Maritime Provinces were engaged in manufacturing in 1941.

The tourist business has grown rapidly in the last two decades. This region is relatively cool in summer and is close to thickly-populated New England and New York. Yachting, salt-water bathing, fishing, hunting, apple-blossom week in the Annapolis

Valley, and places of historical interest are some of the attractions. The Atlantic Seaboard has Canada's only Atlantic ports which are open throughout the year. They carry on an extensive trade with the United Kingdom, the British West Indies, and other parts of the world, though the bulk of Canadian transatlantic traffic is handled through Montreal, with a substantial amount through New York. Newfoundland and Labrador have landing-fields on the direct route to north-western Europe.

Notwithstanding its many lines of endeavour, the Atlantic Seaboard has failed to share fully in the prosperity of Canada as a whole. The population of Nova Scotia, New Brunswick, and Prince Edward Island has declined from 21 per cent of the Dominion total in 1871 to slightly less than 10 per cent in 1941. In the latter year they got not quite 7 per cent of the Dominion's salaries, wages, and the net income of individual enterprisers such as farmers and merchants. Economic and political problems in Newfoundland have been discouraging. Emigration to western Canada, Montreal, Boston, and New York has been heavy, but few new settlers have come from Europe to these provinces.

Some of the reasons for this comparative retrogression have already been hinted at: poor agricultural resources, the shift in dietary habits away from salt fish, the high cost of coal, the smallness of the local market, the long distance to the big consuming centres along the St. Lawrence, and, to go farther back into history, the change from wood and sail to steel and steam. The United States tariff has cut off the most accessible market for some Maritime Province goods and the Canadian tariff has benefited the central part of the country more than the Seaboard Provinces. The Second World War, like the First, created a tremendous but artificial prosperity. At its conclusion, unemployment soon sprang up in the Seaboard Provinces, although throughout the rest of Canada business was booming.

For more than sixty years the economic situation in the Maritime Provinces has caused persistent discontent, with periodic outbursts of special grievance and a tendency to blame Confederation for the region's difficulties. It is perhaps surprising that the political repercussions have not been greater. Party loyalties are very strong, however, and the protest movements that are prominent in the West have made little headway. The situation might change rapidly, however, if the older parties prove unable to deal with the basic problems of the area.

All three provinces have found themselves without the financial resources to meet the growing demands for public services of all kinds; and the same condition in Newfoundland was doubtless a factor in that country's decision in 1948 to join the Dominion of Canada. It is expensive to provide medical, dental, and nursing care, hospitalization, schools, and roads for the population scattered along the coast and in lumbering camps, a disproportionate number of which have low incomes or are elderly. At the same time, the sources of government revenue such as taxes on gasolene and corporate income are less lucrative than in other provinces. Even though provincial debts have been kept down to manageable size and the governments are run economically, a financial gap exists between what the exchequers have and what seems absolutely necessary to satisfy the vague but ever-broadening concept of decent standards of living. This gap can be met only through more assistance from the Dominion Government in the forms of outright subsidy, more generous federal old-age pensions, grants for public works, a guaranteed minimum price for fish, or lower freight-rates.

This aid is not, in the Maritimer's view, a favour or a gift. It is regarded, rather, as a proper compensation for the burden which the national tariff imposes on the consumer in the Maritime Provinces. The fact also must be taken into account that the present Canadian National Railways (formerly the Intercolonial) between Quebec City and Halifax follows a circuitous route which was chosen after Confederation for strategic rather than economic considerations.

The problems which the Maritime Provinces face are, in fact, unusually intractable because they are mainly of geographic origin. Moreover, their small population has given the Maritime Provinces an apparently weak voice in the councils of the nation, although they have contributed an unusually large proportion of able men to the public life of the country. The result of these economic and political circumstances has been a sense of frustration which has often expressed itself in criticism of Confederation, and for which it is difficult to see a permanent solution. There can be no doubt, however, that the strategic importance of the provinces on Canada's Atlantic flank make their welfare a matter of national, and even of continental, concern.

The St. Lawrence Lowlands are the economic heart of Canada. Their agriculture is more diversified and typically more prosperous than that of any other part of the Dominion. Their manufacturing is highly developed, and their financial institutions serve the entire country. They contain over half of the Dominion's total population and the region, though divided linguistically and culturally into two groups, forms an economic unit.

The eastern boundary of the Lowlands lies in the vicinity of Quebec City, and the western boundary, 600 miles distant, along the Detroit and St. Clair rivers. Their southern boundary is the United States and their general northern limit, the Laurentian Shield. A tongue of the latter stretches southward from the main mass into New York State, thus cutting the Lowlands in two. More specifically, the boundary between Lowlands and Shield runs from near Quebec City a few miles back from the St. Lawrence and Ottawa rivers to a point roughly 150 miles up the Ottawa from Montreal. There it turns south to cross the St. Lawrence River about 100 miles above Montreal. The boundary then re-enters Canada near the mouth of Lake Ontario and runs due west to the lower end of Georgian Bay. The section between Lake Huron and Lakes Erie and Ontario is bifurcated by the eastward-facing Niagara escarpment, which is a prominent feature of the landscape from Niagara Falls north-westerly to the peninsula which separates Georgian Bay from Lake Huron.

In effect, the Lowlands are three physiographic sections differing from each other chiefly in altitude. The section of which Montreal is the centre is from 100 to 300 feet above sea level; the rough parallelogram between Lake Ontario and Georgian Bay, from 250 to 1,000 feet; and the peninsula of western Ontario, between Erie and Huron, roughly 600 feet. In all three sections the topography is broadly similar, namely, a plain sloping gently towards the Great Lakes and the St. Lawrence River with some local variation in elevation. This topography is the result of the fact that detritus was spread out, but not always to uniform depths, in the lakes which formed along the front of the continental ice-sheets during the Pleistocene period.

The entire Lowlands have fertile soils, chiefly clay with some sand and loam. Varied types of soil exist within the same county and even on the same farm. The Lowlands have few minerals of importance beyond gravel, limestone in the Niagara escarpment, some petroleum and natural gas in western Ontario, and huge reserves of salt.

In consequence of this region's location within the belt of cyclonic storms, the climate is characterized by frequent changes of temperature, precipitation, humidity, and wind direction. This variability applies not only from day to day and season to season but also from year to year. Even so, the rainfall is always sufficient and the growing season is invariably long enough for vigorous plant growth. Over a period of years the mean annual temperature at Toronto has been 44.4° F., monthly averages being a minimum of 22° and a maximum of 68°. The mean annual precipitation is 32.33 inches, which is spread comparatively evenly throughout the year. The average length of the frost-free season is 200 days. Temperatures along the north shore of Lake Erie are slightly warmer than at Toronto. In the interior of western Ontario they are a little lower, and in the eastern sections of the Lowlands the winter average may be as much as 10° colder.

The total population of the Lowlands in 1949 was approximately 6,500,000, or double that in 1905. The rate of growth is higher among French-speaking than among English-speaking groups, but even among the former the rate of net natural increase seems to be falling off. In the Province of Quebec, persons of French racial origin constitute about 80 per cent of the population, and some counties where farming and lumbering predominate are almost solidly French. Citizens of Anglo-Saxon parentage live chiefly in Montreal; the numbers in Quebec City and in the smaller cities and rural areas directly east of Montreal are declining.

In Ontario the majority of the population is of English, Scottish, or North-of-Ireland descent. In both provinces, especially in the larger cities, there are growing numbers of smaller ethnic groups—Jews, Italians, Ukrainians, and Greeks. In the vicinity of Kitchener, 70 miles west of Toronto, there is a long-established and prosperous community of Canadians of German origin.

Important as cultural differences are, all parts of the Lowlands have had substantially the same economic history. Their early development was associated with staples such as furs, lumber, grain, and cheese. But since approximately 1900 in Ontario and 1920 in Quebec, manufacturing has made very rapid strides. Although agriculture remains important, the Lowlands today are a mature economy in the same sense, though not to the same degree, as New York or New England. This is shown by the variety of economic activities, the increasing urbanization of the population, and the occupations of the people.

Agriculture in the Lowlands is distinguished by its diversity. Most farmers raise a variety of products such as wheat, oats, barley, milk, butter, beef, hogs, poultry, wool, vegetables, and fruit, both for sale and for their own use. Certain crops may predominate in certain parts, but there is a variety in every area and on almost every farm. This diversity is due to the several types of soils existing within a comparatively small area, to the necessity of maintaining the fertility of the soil by rotation of crops, to the need which the farmer feels for making the fullest possible use of his time and his horses and machinery in order to maximize his income, and to the habits of self-sufficiency which the pioneers had perforce to acquire. In recent years, especially in Ontario, farmers have shifted away from production for use and towards production for sale, but mixed farming is still characteristic. Farmers use a considerable amount of machinery, but the type of agriculture precludes mechanization to the same extent as on the prairies.

In Lowland agriculture the dairy cow occupies an important position. The output of milk expanded threefold between 1900 and 1940 because of increasing urbanization and the change in consumers' dietary habits. The raising of dairy products is favoured by a climate suited to the growth of hay and oats, by ample supplies of drinking-water for cattle, by the ability and diligence of farmers and their wives, and, finally, by a large market in the cities near by.

The raising of other types of live-stock and poultry is important on many farms and for the region as a whole. Truck gardens are located near every large city. In the Niagara peninsula, and to some extent in other sections, farmers derive a large part of their income from peaches, pears, cherries, apples, and grapes, but even in these districts agriculture is diversified. Sugar-beets, tobacco, and corn are important in small areas particularly favoured by climate and soil, lying chiefly just north of Lake Erie.

On the whole, agriculture in the Lowlands is pretty consistently prosperous. Of course the Second World War and the large post-war demand for food from abroad have had a buoyant effect on the industry, but even in the 1930's it managed to hold its own. To be sure, farmers failed to get any return on their capital or, in some years, a decent wage, but they did not have to go on relief or live off their capital as was, unfortunately, often true on the prairies. The prosperity and relative stability of farm income is due to the generally level topography, the comparatively high percentage of tillable land, the favourable climate, the absence of serious droughts or wide-spread devastating frosts, the proximity of a large market, the skill and thriftiness of the farmers, and most of all to the diversity of products raised. It is not difficult to shift from one product, the selling price of which may be temporarily depressed, into another for which the prospects are better. The fact that much of the output is sold in the adjacent cities insulates the farmer in large degree from adversities occasioned by tariffs, quotas, and foreign-exchange restrictions in other countries. Because farmers are interested in selling several products, and are never in utter financial distress, coöperative marketing has not made the same progress here as on the prairies, where farmers soon get together whenever their main, and frequently their only, product suffers a price collapse or a crop failure.

Notwithstanding a satisfactory, even generous, income in comparison with farmers in other parts of Canada, the agricultural population of the Lowlands has declined steadily since 1891. Thousands have moved from farms to the near-by cities of Canada and the United States, drawn by the higher standard of living in urban communities, the attractiveness of city life, and the reduced need for farm labour on account of increasing mechanization. With the decline of the number of persons on farms, medical, educational, and religious services of a standard at all comparable to those in the urban areas are relatively more expensive to provide. Moreover, many of the farmers belong to the older age-groups in the population. This makes for declining productivity per man-day (unless it is offset by further mechanization) and also for a conservative attitude of mind, a reluctance to adopt bold and far-sighted methods for dealing with the sociological problems which have arisen from rural depopulation.

Although, generally speaking, the same products are produced and the same basic problems faced throughout the region, there are a few important differences between farming in Ontario and in Quebec. In the latter province, mechanization is not so general as in Ontario and farms are typically smaller. The farm buildings are likely to be less pretentious and the village churches much more imposing. The farm holdings are long and narrow (less than 50 by from 320 to 480 rods) and front along a river with additional tiers of farms abutting on road-ways a mile or more farther back. In Ontario the standard size is 80 by 200 rods, and farms are arranged between "side-roads" and "concession lines" in blocks 1.25 miles square, although there is much local variation due to topographic and other conditions. The difference in the appearance of the farm-steads in the two provinces immediately strikes the eye of the traveller.

In manufacturing, as in agriculture, the Lowlands produce a wide range of articles, including almost all Canada's automobiles, bicycles, railway locomotives and cars, farm implements, copper and brass and rubber goods, tobacco, books and magazines, and leather wares; and a high proportion of steel, textiles, furniture, and paints. Other regions in Canada process raw materials which are bulky and perishable (milk, fish, fruit, vegetables, and logs) before sending them long distances to market. They manufacture their own perishable and bulky finished goods (bakery products, newspapers, aerated waters, and so on). But the St. Lawrence Lowlands supply them with most of their other manufactures except what are imported from the United States or Britain.

As a manufacturing centre the Lowlands have the advantage of a large and prosperous market of their own and a location towards the geographic centre of Canada. They have cheap water transportation for about eight months each year down the St. Lawrence to the Maritime Provinces and the export market as well as up the Great Lakes to the prairies. They benefit from being able to borrow manufacturing and selling techniques from one of the world's most advanced industrial economies located just across the border in the United States. They can also draw upon the reserves of skilled labour trained in universities, technical schools, and industry. Finally, they can readily assemble the numerous parts which go into automobiles and industrial machinery.

The area's chief drawback is lack of fuel. It has no coal of its own, and its reserves of petroleum and natural gas are inadequate. It can, however, import coal very cheaply from adjacent parts of the United States or from the Maritime Provinces. It has the inestimable advantage of ample supplies of cheap hydro-electricity. Moreover, it possesses, either within its boundaries or in the Shield near by, such important industrial raw materials as grains, dairy products, live-stock, hardwood and softwood forests (for furniture, news-print, and rayon), salt, copper, nickel, and iron. Also, it has better access than outlying regions to investors and financial institutions.

To emphasize the manufacturing advantages of the St. Lawrence Lowlands is not to suggest that this part of the economy is without problems. Many Canadian plants are smaller than their American counterparts. While they may escape some of the unwieldiness of size, they cannot derive all the gains of large-scale production. Consequently, so the manufacturers insist, they need a tariff to protect them from outside competition. However that may be, Canadian producers in selling abroad frequently profit from the British preferential tariff, the arrangement whereby Great Britain, the Dominions, and the numerous colonies grant each other more favourable customs duties than they apply to imports of non-Empire origin. In order to take advantage of this system, many American firms have set up branch plants in Canada.

The degree of dependence of Canadian manufacturing on tariffs at home and within the Empire cannot be determined with any accuracy. Undoubtedly, in numerous cases, notably in news-print, artificial rubber, and aluminium, Canadian producers need have no fear of foreign competition. In other instances manufacturing thrives chiefly because of artificial barriers to trade. At all events, Canadian manufacturers view with apprehension any radical change in present tariffs which might come about as a result of the unwillingness of consuming groups within Canada to continue to pay the higher prices occasioned by the tariff or the resurgence of economic nationalism abroad. This perturbation will doubtless be intensified as soon as the immediate post-war demand for goods has been satisfied and a bitter struggle for markets develops. The problem of freeing international trade without ruining tariff-protected industries within various countries is not peculiar to Canada.

In the development of manufacturing in the Lowlands the use of hydro-electric power has played a vital part. The largest generating plants are below Niagara Falls, and along the Ottawa, Gatineau, St. Maurice, Saguenay, and other rivers which flow from the Shield onto the plain. The greatest potential source yet to be exploited is along the St. Lawrence between the foot of Lake Ontario and Montreal. Negotiations have been carried on for several years between the governments of Canada and the United States looking forward to the utilization of this power and the construction of a water-way which will, it is hoped, allow ocean-going steamships to penetrate to the upper Great Lakes. The waterway might obviate the necessity which commonly exists at present for trans-shipping western grain and other goods from lake to smaller river steamers at Lower Lake ports and again from the latter to ocean carriers at Montreal. The power aspects are, however, more important, on the whole, than navigation. Although almost every factory in the Lowlands gains from having a cheap supply of clean, readily available energy, the electro-chemical (carborundum), electro-metallurgical (aluminium), and news-print industries are the largest individual consumers. The use of electricity is wide-spread in stores, in homes, and on farms.

In Ontario most of the electricity is generated and distributed under a public-ownership system popularly known as the "Hydro" (see pp. 358 ff.), which is controlled jointly by the provincial government, a semi-autonomous commission, and the various municipalities served. Its success has attracted world-wide attention. Until recently, hydro-electric development in Quebec was almost entirely under the control of private capitalists, but in 1946 their property in Montreal was expropriated and a public enterprise was formed to take over their activities.

The size of the Lowlands' population, the diversity of its agriculture, and the development of its manufacturing have inevitably stimulated activity in transportation, trade, and finance. The head offices of the Canadian National and Canadian Pacific railways, which own 90 per cent of the nation's milage, are both in Montreal. The largest wholesale houses, the most important mail-order concerns, and the biggest department and chain stores are centred in either Montreal or Toronto. Similarly, all the chartered banks and the dominant financial institutions, such as the trust, insurance, and mortgage companies and the investment banking-firms, have their chief offices in one of these two cities. These enterprises have branches across Canada, in Newfoundland, the British West Indies, and many other countries. The concentration of financial power along St. James Street (Montreal) and Bay Street (Toronto) has often given rise to resentment in other parts of the country—a feeling not unlike the animosity towards Wall Street in the United States.

The Lowlands, in a word, are approaching a state of economic maturity. The region does not rely on one or a few staples; it has developed advanced techniques of production and is relatively independent of outside capital. As a result, its problems of public finance are less acute than in other parts of Canada. The centres of wealth and big business, Ontario and Quebec, can tax corporate and personal profits even when this income is derived in part or entirely from other provinces. The comparative congestion of population, while it increases some expenses of government, makes on the whole for many economies. Ontario and Quebec consider that they have no real need to approach the Dominion treasury for assistance. At the same time, these two provinces (including the parts of the Shield which are legally incorporated in them) have 60 per cent of the seats in the Canadian House of Commons. It is practically impossible for any political party to form a government in Ottawa without a substantial block of supporters from one, and probably from both, of these provinces. From a political as well as an economic point of view, the Lowlands are therefore in a very strong position in relation to the rest of the country. The resulting disequilibrium is the most difficult problem in Canadian federalism.

The traveller from the St. Lawrence Lowlands into the Canadian Shield moves into a quite different geographic and economic environment. Fertile plains, prosperous agriculture, advanced manufacturing, and a thickly-settled population are replaced by a plateau 1,000 to 2,000 feet above sea level, broken by innumerable rounded hills rising 200 to 300 feet above the ruling level of the land. There are thousands of lakes, usually with picturesquely irregular outlines, hundreds of swamps, and dozens of rivers following haphazard courses and breaking into many rapids. A few struggling pioneer farming areas with a polyglot population cluster around several thriving but dispersed mills and mining camps. Throughout the rest of the region are only scattered log cabins, the crude homes of prospectors and trappers.

The area of the Shield is no less than half that of Canada. It takes in all the Province of Quebec north of a narrow strip along the St. Lawrence and Ottawa rivers. It incorporates all Ontario north of Lakes Superior and Huron except the Hudson Bay Lowland, but includes the tongue, previously described, which outreaches southward to touch the St. Lawrence River for 60 miles below the outlet of Lake Ontario. And it comprises those parts of the Prairie Provinces and North-West Territories which lie, roughly speaking, north and east of a line drawn from the south-east corner of Manitoba to near the mouth of the Mackenzie.

The Arctic Archipelago and the Lowlands lying to the south of Hudson and James bays are not geologically parts of the Shield. The former seems to consist chiefly of stratified rocks with some outcrops of ancient gneisses and schists. For the most part it has no great altitude, though there are some high mountains (10,000 feet) in Ellesmere Island. The Hudson Bay Lowland extending inland for as much as 350 miles is flat and poorly drained. The economic potentialities of both these geologic provinces remain as yet unexplored in detail. Bituminous and lignite coal and gold, copper, and mica have been found, but the only resource of any present value is furs. It is convenient, though not wholly satisfactory, to treat these regions as part of the Shield.

The Shield itself is composed of very old crystalline rocks planated by centuries of erosion and then heavily glaciated in the Pleistocene period. As the continental ice-sheets slowly advanced, they scoured off the residual soil, smoothed down the topography, striated and polished the rock surface, and, by scattering debris irregularly over the surface, completely disorganized the drainage. The result was the formation of the numerous lakes which are everywhere a characteristic feature of the region. Clay and other fine, stratified deposits, accumulated in the large temporary lakes left by the retreating glaciers, now form what are known as clay belts.

In its more southerly parts, that is, below a line drawn from near the mouth of the Mackenzie to Churchill, Manitoba, and from the upper part of James Bay roughly to the Straits of Belle Isle, the Shield is covered with balsam, spruce, and jack pine. In its northern part, including sections of the Archipelago adjacent to the mainland, the native growth is of the *tundra* type. In winter, of course, the northern lands are thinly blanketed with snow, but during the summer acres of ground are covered with flowering plants of about 250 species, principally lupine, heather, saxifrage, and flowering moss. In sheltered spots along river banks, poplar and Richardson willow grow, though more slowly than specimens farther south, but in the lower Archipelago the few trees are gnarled, twisted, and often prostrate. The northern islands and a few hundred square miles west of Hudson Bay are comparatively barren.

The climatic conditions which prevail over such a huge region are difficult to describe except in very general terms. Everywhere the summers are short and warm, and the winters are long and frosty. At Cochrane, on the forty-ninth parallel, 60 miles west of the Ontario-Quebec boundary, the average temperature in July and August (66° F.) is nearly as high as at Montreal, but the average length of the frost-free period is not much more than half as long. Winter temperatures are a few degrees lower than at Winnipeg and Montreal and the cold is much more persistent. The cyclonic storms which bring spells of warmer weather to the Lowlands and even to the prairies are less common on the Shield. Spring is delayed, but comes with a rush when it does arrive.

Precipitation rarely exceeds 30 inches annually, but evaporation is slight.

In the *tundra* the climate is even more severe than in the forested parts of the Shield. At Lake Harbour on Baffin Island the average during July is only 10° above freezing (i.e., 42° F.) and the January average is 10° below zero. In fact, temperatures averaging below zero may be expected from November to April. Though the summer is short, it is bright. At 70° North Latitude, roughly along Canada's Arctic shore, the sun is above the horizon at all times between May 17 and July 28. Conversely, in winter the sun is never visible from November 25 to January 18, though the moon and stars and at times the spectacular aurora borealis give light enough for intermittent hunting. Also, because the sun is not far below the horizon, during part of this time there is a kind of twilight for a few hours each day. Throughout the *tundra* precipitation is light, about 10 inches.

For obvious reasons the economic history of the Shield has been dictated by climate and geology. For nearly two and a half centuries before 1900, the only economic activity was concerned with the fur trade, the course of which is traced in the historical chapters. It is interesting to note that, although the Hudson's Bay Company now functions as an ordinary commercial firm, it still, despite competition, dominates the fur trade of the Far North. Although fears are sometimes expressed over future supplies, there is no clear evidence yet of a serious decline in animal population. Fur-bearing animals still thrive in the Shield because the forests provide cover for large numbers of mice, lemmings, rabbits, birds, and other creatures on which some of the fur-bearers feed. The bark of trees and the roots of plants in the numerous lakes supply a good diet for beaver and musk-rat. However, it is reasonable to expect that continuous trapping will reduce the number of animals and, of course, cutting away the pulp-wood pushes them farther back.

Although the fur trade was the Shield's original source of wealth, it is now far exceeded in importance by mining. Even in the 1880's, silver was being produced in large amounts from Silver Islet in Lake Superior, and copper-nickel ores had been revealed at Sudbury north of Lake Huron. In 1902 more silver lying in veins near the surface (grass-roots) was found at Cobalt, 250 miles north of Toronto. By 1925 this district had become the world's fifth largest producer, rivalling mines which had been in production for two hundred years. In the last twenty years Cobalt's silver output has declined rapidly because of exhaustion of the more valuable argentiferous ores and the depressed world price of silver.

Meanwhile, the gold discoveries in the crystalline rocks at Timmins and Kirkland Lake, roughly 120 miles north of Cobalt, and at numerous other points throughout the Shield have brought hundreds of companies into existence. Of the dozens of mines listed on the Toronto and Montreal stock exchanges, most are mere "holes in the ground." The few which do come into production last no longer than fifteen years on the average. Yet "good mines die hard." One which was estimated to have a life of three years in 1924 and of four more years in 1929 is still operating profitably.

The nickel at Sudbury has become increasingly valuable; at present Canada supplies over 80 per cent of the world's total requirements. The same ore-body produces copper, a little gold and silver, and about 40 per cent of the world's platinum and palladium. This is apparently Canada's, if not North America's, most nearly permanent metal-mining project, with its output assured for at least another century.

Gold, copper, zinc, and silver are found together at Flin Flon on the Saskatchewan-Manitoba boundary and at Rouyn 25 miles east of the Ontario-Quebec border. In both areas the reserves are large. The ores are geologically so complicated that the problem of separating the different minerals from the gangue and from each other defied solution until in 1923 a Canadian company perfected the flotation process.

From 1900 to 1923 about 5,000,000 tons of iron ore were mined 120 miles north of Sault Ste. Marie and just east of Lake Superior. About twenty times this amount had to be left behind because its ferrous content was too low for practical use. None of the several methods which have been devised for beneficiating the ore is sufficiently economical to be a commercial success, but with the assistance of a small subsidy offered by the Ontario government the abandoned mines began to come back into production. During the Second World War a large mine was opened at Steep Rock, 135 miles west of Port Arthur. An enormous deposit of rich ore has been discovered on the Labrador-Quebec boundary, and a railway 330 miles long will be built from the Gulf of St. Lawrence to make it accessible. In short, it appears that within a very few years, when the high-quality ores of Minnesota are exhausted, Canada may supply a large part of the iron-ore needs of the huge United States steel industry.

In 1930 radium was discovered near the east end of Great Bear Lake, 28 miles south of the Arctic Circle. Canada's output of this vital and beneficent element added to the world's supply and forced a reduction of 60 per cent in its price. The same ore-body contains uranium, which before 1945 was of very minor importance, used as an alloy in steel and as the yellow colour in pottery and glass-ware. The development of the atomic bomb immediately brought Canada's uranium resources to the world's attention. Possession of the ore and the coöperation of Canadian scientists with those in the United States and Britain to release atomic energy thrust upon Canada part of the responsibility for controlling the use of the epoch-making discovery. As a first step in control, the government set up a publicly-owned company to mine and sell uranium either to friendly foreign governments or to the Dominion's own atomic-energy plant at Chalk River, 100 air-miles north-west of Ottawa.

In addition to the minerals mentioned, the Shield produces graphite, talc, mica, and feldspar. Only a small part of its enormous area has been carefully surveyed, and undoubtedly much wealth yet remains to be disclosed. However, geologists are of the opinion that the Shield becomes less richly mineralized towards the geographical centre of the mass. Workable deposits are most likely to be discovered in a broad band around its periphery (south and west sides), which has already received the most attention from prospectors.

Be that as it may, mineral deposits sooner or later become depleted and the people depending on them for livelihood must move elsewhere. Long before the reserves are physically exhausted, a mine may become worthless because of the discovery in some other part of the world of higher quality or more favourably located ores, or the development of new techniques in treating them. Hard-rock mining is not a satisfactory basis on which to build an economy. Although there is no immediate danger that the prosperity of mining in the Shield will disappear, there is no definite assurance that it will be permanent.

All the southern sections of the Shield are covered with softwood forests. These provide the chief raw material for a large news-print industry which normally has produced 40 per cent of the world's output. The growth of this industry was stimulated by the presence of large markets in the near-by cities of the United States and Canada, and by the depletion of the pulp-wood reserves in the north-eastern part of the United States.

Mining and the manufacture of news-print in the Shield are greatly assisted by low-cost hydro-electric power. Rivers tumble over rocky ledges. Precipitation is fairly regular at all seasons and from year to year. The forest cover reduces evaporation and retains water about its roots, thus further equallizing the flow. The many lakes act as storage basins. There are no other sources of energy within the Shield, and coal and oil are expensive to bring in from outside. Although dams, generating plants, and transmission systems are expensive to construct, interest rates have been declining in recent years. For these reasons hydro-electricity, already important in the Shield, will probably become of increasing value, since only a small percentage of the potentialities of the region have been developed. Because hydro-electricity can be transmitted for distances up to 300 miles at less expense than any other type of energy, it will encourage manufacturing in the Lowlands, which are already making use of this resource.

The future of agriculture in this region is a matter on which wide differences of opinion exist. On the one hand are those who emphasize that most of the Shield has no soil of any depth. Even where deep soils do exist—that is, in the former beds of the Pleistocene lakes—they are usually of heavy clay, cold, and generally inhospitable to plant growth. Furthermore, agriculture is limited by the short growing season. Though the long periods of sunshine during the summer at these northerly latitudes partially offset the shortness of the frost-free period, the temperature may drop sharply on even the warmest days. Rainy weather in the late summer frequently prevents harvesting, seriously reducing quality and yields per acre.

On the contrary, some geographers consider that these areas will sooner or later be thickly settled and prove capable of supporting as many people per square mile as those parts of Europe which correspond with them climatically. The soils may be improved by open or tile drains or by working organic material such as straw or animal manure into the clay. Frosts killed field crops in southern Ontario in the pioneer days, but with the spread of settlement and the cutting back of the forests the menace of frost disappeared. The same result may come about in the Shield. In any case, farmers there can sell pulp-wood off their land and so get cash for a living until they have cleared enough land to maintain their families. Obviously the region will never be a cereal-producer like the prairies. Nevertheless, it can easily grow hay, barley, and roots and so has possibilities for raising dairy products.

Whatever the long-run prospects may be, farming in the Shield up to the present has been only moderately successful. French Canadians have gone into the flat-lying lands west and south of Lac St. Jean. In the Clay Belt near Cochrane and in smaller districts elsewhere, English- and French-speaking Canadians have also settled. In the last ten years their farms have begun to take on a new air of prosperity, of stability. Yet progress is slow, owing to climatic conditions, the lack of capital for drainage and buildings, and sometimes the inexperience of the farmers. Only a very small fraction, certainly not over 5 per cent, of the potential agricultural land is being farmed. The largest Clay Belt contains about 70,000,000 acres lying along the northern transcontinental line of the Canadian National Railway for a width of about 50 miles and a distance of 75 miles in Quebec and 130 miles in Ontario. In large measure the extent of future settlement will hinge on how willing native-born Canadians are to accept central Europeans as immigrants. It will depend, too, on whether the latter will remain on soil which will give them a standard of living generous in comparison with what they have been accustomed to, but below that prevailing in cities and on farms in the rest of Canada.

Settlement in the Shield has been too recent for its people to have developed any unique political, social, or cultural characteristics. A high proportion of the people are rootless: they move from one mining camp or news-print town to another. They are of numerous races also. English-speaking Canadians still constitute the leaders in politics, trade, and the professions and the executives in mine and mill. French-speaking Canadians have some of the political and professional positions, and are ideal bush-workers. Scandinavians are beginning to enter the managerial and professional groups. Poles, Hungarians, and others are chiefly unskilled. Wages per day are high, but so is the cost of living even in normal times because substantially all food, clothing, and other supplies must be hauled in. Money is liberally spent, and thriftiness of the sort practised by the Quebec habitant or Ontario farmer is unknown. Moral standards are sometimes less rigid than in the older districts.

The Shield has no economic unity in the same sense as the Maritime Provinces or even the St. Lawrence Lowlands. Its mining magnates may try to bring pressure on the government for legislation favourable to that industry, but the people as a whole have no particular demands on the Dominion exchequer nor any marked attitude towards international and Commonwealth relations. Neither have they any pronounced views on the tariff, another political question on which in the past Canadians have divided politically. Among the reasons for this lack of regional consciousness are the newness of the settlements, the heterogenous character of the population scattered in a number of pockets over an immense territory, the absence of a disastrous depression which in other regions served to pull people together, and the subdivision of the Shield among four or five provinces, each with its own administration, and the North-West Territories, which are administered from Ottawa.

The future of the Shield remains uncertain. Hydro-electricity, a perpetual asset of undoubted value, gives little employment once the structures are completed. This power will be used in manufacturing, but only on the edge of the Shield or in the Lowlands, not in the heart of the Shield itself. The fur trade will continue to give work, but to only a small dispersed population as it has done for over two hundred years. Agriculture has done fairly well on a small scale, but it has not yet proved that it can support a large population at standards acceptable to Canadians generally. Mining and news-print manufacturing—the two industries on which the Shield chiefly depends—are based on wasting assets, though forestry is not necessarily an exhaustible resource. They have been expanding rapidly for the last quarter of a century, and their prosperity shows no signs of immediate abatement, but they are not wholly sound foundations for a permanently prosperous economic life.

The tremendous expansion which has taken place in the northern area of the Shield has brought serious sociological and other problems in its wake. These are complicated by the requirements of national defence, since this region has assumed a new and unforeseen importance in world strategy. The future of the Arctic, and of the Arctic peoples, may be radically affected by these developments.

CHAPTER IX

Western Canada

BY VERNON C. FOWKE

THROUGH the heart of the North American continent the central plain stretches from the Gulf of Mexico to the Arctic Ocean: 3,000 miles long and 400–800 miles wide, its western boundaries are marked by the towering peaks of the Rocky Mountains, its eastern limits—from south to north—by the valleys of the Mississippi and Red rivers and by the westward-bulging Canadian Shield.

Centrally located in this gigantic plateau is the north-central plain, an irregular oval in shape and 400,000 square miles in area. This region straddles the international boundary on a north-west south-east axis from Hastings, Nebraska, to Edmonton, Alberta. Topographically it is a vast, level or gently-rolling territory sloping downward, the northern portions to the north and east, the southern parts to the south and east. Its temperatures display mid-continental extremes of seasonal variation. It is distinguishable from the remainder of the continental plateau by vegetation and rainfall. In natural vegetation it constitutes, with minor notable exceptions, a treeless grass-land. Its rainfall varies widely from place to place and from year to year, but, with an annual average which nowhere exceeds 20 inches, its condition ranges from semi-arid to arid. Early travellers called this region the "Great American Desert."

Aridity, however, cannot be an unvarying attribute of a region which may produce a billion bushels of wheat in a single year. Nor is the annual variation of rainfall exceptionally great on the plains. Rather, the peculiar climatic feature of the area is that the annual rainfall varies around an average figure which is critical for ordinary agricultural practices.[1] Were this average appreciably lower, the region would be a genuine desert without cultivation except on irrigated lands. Were the average appreciably higher, the annual rainfall would seldom shrink to the level of drought. As it is, crop production on the plains moves in unpredictable cycles with years of ample rainfall scattered among moisture-deficient years or series of years.

That part of the north-central plain which thrusts north-westerly across the international boundary forms the heart of the central Canadian plain. Ninety years ago Captain Palliser described it as a "more or less arid desert" jutting as a triangle into British territory north of the forty-ninth parallel of latitude. To this day it is frequently called "Palliser's Triangle," or "the prairies." Its soil is fertile and varies from light to dark brown in colour. Its average annual rainfall varies in different places from 11 to 15 inches. Around it on the east and north lies a crescent-shaped park belt roughly 100 miles in depth. Still a grass-land, with deep, black, fertile soil, the park belt is dotted throughout with patches or "bluffs" of trees and shrubs. Its rainfall is higher than that of the Triangle, with an annual average varying from 15 to 20 inches in different localities.

Beyond the park belt lie the forest regions with soils unsuitable for agriculture except in certain limited areas. Most significant of these exceptions is the upper valley of the Peace River, where tracts of fertile, black park soil comprising several million acres lie separated from the outer margins of the park belt by hundreds of miles of rugged forest lands. These portions of the upper Peace may be regarded as the northern outposts of the continental grassland plains—the last significant frontier, perhaps, of North American agricultural settlement.

Apart from the Peace River Valley, those portions of the Canadian plain described above are drained into Hudson Bay by the Saskatchewan-Assiniboine-Nelson river system. North of the park belt the continental plain narrows to a 400-mile-wide corridor between the mountains and the Canadian Shield. This 1,000-mile corridor corresponds roughly with the Mackenzie River Valley:

---

1 For notes to chapter ix see pages 575–576.

it is wooded, its soils are sandy and gravelly in contrast to the fertile clays of the short-grass plains, and its terrain is more rugged. Thus the physical features of the northern plain differ so markedly from those of the central plain that its economic life requires separate treatment. (See pp. 207 ff.)

The Canadian portions of the central plain lie entirely within the three provinces of Manitoba, Saskatchewan, and Alberta—the Prairie Provinces.[2] This term sharply underlines the significant elements of the region in the modern Canadian economy. Of the total area of these provinces (750,000 square miles, or 450,000,000 acres of land area) well over half is covered by forest and Precambrian Shield and not more than one-fifth is grass-land plains, or prairie area proper. The Precambrian Shield in western Canada is without agricultural possibilities. Under the forests lie grey, leached soils largely unfit for agriculture. It is doubtful if more than one-third of the total acreage in the three provinces can be utilized agriculturally. In 1941 the total area of farms in the Prairie Provinces was 120,000,000 acres (27 per cent of the total area) and 65,000,000 acres were improved. Yet the agricultural development of the plains region has had such an impact upon the Canadian economy in the present century that the three provinces are the "Prairie Provinces," a synonym for the Canadian wheat economy, and Prairie Provinces they would remain though their northern boundary were moved to the Arctic Ocean.

Before the Europeans came, the plains were inhabited by nomadic, non-agricultural Indians—the Plains Indians of North American history. Buffalo from mighty trampling herds, hunted with arrow and spear, provided these Indians with food, clothing, and tepee shelter. Horses, introduced to Central America by the Spaniards in the sixteenth century, escaped, multiplied, and spread northward over the continental plains far in advance of their former masters. The Plains Indian took as readily to the horse as the horse took to the plains. By the later eighteenth century the horse had become an integral part of the culture of the Plains Indian from south to north. Warlike and of studied cruelty, relying upon stealth and speed, the Plains Indian found in the horse an ally which enabled him long to harry and retard the line of European advance.

The Indian way of life, adapted to the plains environment, was self-contained. Europeans sought commercial advantage rather than self-sufficiency in the New World. The competitive search for furs drew them to the forested margins of the central plains and to the plains themselves. Prairie rivers carried the traders from forest belt to forest belt and the river valleys yielded furs. Plains Indians acted as middlemen and carriers. Buffalo meat, concentrated and preserved as pemmican according to Indian lore, provided merchant and carrier with staple food. The mid-continental location of the plains imposed a tremendous transportation burden upon the fur trade from its earliest days. The burden of transportation has dominated the economic life of the area ever since.

The fur trade brought Europeans to the wooded margins of the Canadian plains in the seventeenth and eighteenth centuries; and, throughout most of the nineteenth century, fur-traders still dominated the region. Since 1900, hundreds of thousands of European immigrants have settled there, however, to develop one of the great wheat-exporting regions of the world. Yearly spring plantings of some 25,000,000 acres and a long-run average production of 15.6 bushels per acre provide the Prairie Provinces with an annual crop of wheat averaging upwards of 400,000,000 bushels. In quality the product is hard red spring wheat, high in protein content and favourably known in world markets for strength and blending qualities. Three times since 1940 (and once before, in 1928) the Canadian plains have produced a wheat crop in excess of half a billion bushels. Plains farmers produce less than one-tenth of world wheat supplies, but export as much as two-thirds of their annual production. In the late inter-war years Canadian exports represented 35–40 per cent of the total world trade in wheat.

Canadian historians will characterize the first three decades of the twentieth century as the period of the creation of the prairie wheat economy. The agricultural conquest of the Canadian plains during this period was so spectacular in its proportions that it stimulated and integrated the economic life of the whole Dominion. Within that generation the Canadian population all but doubled, to total 10,377,000 in 1931. Meanwhile the population of the Prairie Provinces increased more than fivefold, to a total of 2,354,000. In 1901 only 8 per cent of all Canadians lived on the plains. By 1931 nearly a quarter were there. Table 1 indicates the extent and rapidity of population growth in the Prairie Provinces after 1900.

TABLE 1

POPULATION OF PRAIRIE PROVINCES AND PERCENTAGE OF RURAL TO TOTAL POPULATION, 1901–1946

Year	Manitoba	Saskatchewan	Alberta	Total	Rural population as percentage of total
1901	255,211	91,279	73,022	419,512	75
1906	365,688	257,763	185,195	808,646	70
1911	461,394	492,432	374,295	1,328,121	65
1916	553,860	647,835	496,442	1,698,137	64
1921	610,118	757,510	588,454	1,956,082	64
1926	639,056	820,738	607,599	2,067,393	64
1931	700,139	921,785	731,605	2,353,529	62
1936	711,216	931,547	772,782	2,415,545	63
1941	729,744	895,992	796,169	2,421,905	62
1946	726,923	832,688	795,007	2,362,941	61

SOURCE: Dominion Bureau of Statistics. *Census Reports.*

The expansion in prairie population was associated with immigration from the British Isles, from northern and western Europe, and from the United States in numbers so large as to rank among the greatest population movements in human history. From 1900 to 1930, immigrants to Canada totalled 4,500,000—three times as many as in the previous half-century. In one year, 1913, there were 400,000. Of the thirty-year total, an estimated 1,250,000 came from the United States.[3]

The wheat economy did not spring spontaneously upon the central plain. The Selkirk settlement in the Red River Valley made but fitful progress for decades after its start in 1812, handicapped by a disheartening array of natural hazards such as drought, frost, flood, hail, and grasshoppers. Lack of transportation facilities and markets added to the difficulties. Plans put forward by eastern Canadians after 1850 for western economic development included the construction of a railway from the St. Lawrence across the plains to the Pacific Coast, the adoption of a land policy which would permit land to pay for railway construction and at the same time encourage immigration and settlement, and the institution of an experimental farm system which would attack the natural hazards confronting western agricultural production. Confederation in 1867 provided the constitutional framework within which these plans were effected. Results remained disappointing, however, until the end of the century.

The occupation of the Canadian plains after 1900 relied heavily upon techniques which had been gradually perfected by the Americans for the mastery of their plains region. Significant instruments in this category were the chilled-steel plough to break the tough prairie sod, the bare summer fallow for the conservation of moisture, the self-binding reaper, the endless-belt elevator and the box-car for the bulk handling of grain, and the steel-roller mill for reducing the flinty spring wheat to flour. As free land

TABLE 2

NUMBER AND AREA OF FARMS AND ACREAGE UNDER FIELD CROPS, PRAIRIE PROVINCES, 1901–1946

Year	Number of farms	Area of occupied farms (Millions of acres)	Average size of farms (Acres)			Area of improved land (Millions of acres)	Area under field crops (Millions of acres)
			Manitoba	Saskatchewan	Alberta		
1901	55,200	15.4	274.2	285.1	288.6	5.6	3.6
1906 *	......	....	....	....	....	...	...
1911	199,200	57.7	279.3	295.7	286.5	23.0	17.7
1916	218,600	73.3	288.5	353.8	339.3	34.3	24.6
1921	255,600	87.9	274.5	368.5	353.1	44.9	32.2
1926	248,200	88.9	270.6	390.1	370.5	49.3	35.0
1931	288,100	109.8	279.2	407.9	400.1	59.7	39.9
1936	300,500	113.1	271.4	399.6	405.2	60.9	40.2
1941	296,200	120.2	291.1	432.3	433.9	65.5	38.4
1946 †	269,700	117.9	....	472.7	....	...	...

SOURCE: Dominion Bureau of Statistics. *Census Reports*.
* Not available. † Preliminary.

of better quality became scarcer in the United States, attention turned increasingly to the Canadian plains, where the American system of rectangular survey had long since been adopted. Marquis wheat, cross-bred and selected by Dr. Charles Saunders of the Dominion Experimental Farms, was generally available by 1910. This variety was at least the equal of Red Fife for yield and for milling and baking qualities, and had the added advantage—decisive for certain areas—of ripening earlier.

Table 2 sketches the main outlines of the agricultural occupation of the Canadian plains after 1900. As indicated in the table, the rate of settlement and land improvement was particularly rapid from 1901 to 1911, but remained high until 1931. The area in farms in the Prairie Provinces increased sevenfold and improved lands elevenfold from 1901 to 1931. In 1936 there were 300,000 farms in the Prairie Provinces, though the number declined over the next ten years, owing partly to the abandonment of submarginal land but more particularly to the amalgamation of occupied lands into larger farm units. The table shows the persistent increase in the size of prairie farms, particularly in Saskatchewan and Alberta. The most active areas of agricultural expansion after the middle 1920's were the Peace River Valley and the northern frontiers between park and forest belts.

Increased wheat acreage formed the basis of prairie expansion. Wheat plantings (virtually all in the Prairie Provinces, and spring-sown) increased from 4,300,000 acres in 1901 to 8,900,000 in 1911, to 17,800,000 in 1921, and to 26,400,000 in 1931. Wheat shipments abroad increased from negligible quantities in the 1890's till by 1920 they were the largest single contributor to Canadian export values. In value, wheat exports yielded $9,700,000 in 1901, $129,-200,000 in 1921, and $250,000,000 in 1926. During 1926 Canada exported on the average 1,000,000 bushels of wheat per day.

The occupation of the central plain called for capital as well as for settlers. Much foreign and eastern Canadian capital was invested directly in western enterprise. Even more was invested in the industries of the eastern provinces and British Columbia, which expanded tremendously in response to prairie farm demands. British and foreign investments in Canada increased from $1,250,000,000 in 1901 to more than $7,000,000,000 in 1931. Capital and labour found profitable occupation in the construction of many thousands of miles of railway, including two additional transcontinental lines and a network of branches within the Prairie Provinces; in transporting, housing, and equipping millions of immigrants; in providing equipment for scores of thousands of new prairie farms; and, finally, in the creation of the many hundreds of market centres which sprang up on the townsites selected by railway companies at eight- to ten-mile intervals along the railway lines.

The occupation of a new region is but the first step towards the mastery of its natural and economic hazards. Much that the Americans had learned in the settlement of their plains region was helpful in the settlement of the Canadian West, but much remained to be learned. Despite the adoption of summer fallow for moisture conservation, recurring seasons and cycles of drought remain the greatest natural hazard over a substantial part of the Canadian plains. Series of years with rainfall well above average prompted the settlement and cultivation of areas where failure of cereal production was in the long run inevitable. Homesteading reached a peak in Alberta and Montana between 1909 and 1919, when rainfall conditions were unusually good and when cost-price relationships were exceptionally favourable to wheat production. Early in the 1920's much of the land at the heart of the Canadian prairies was abandoned or allowed to return to grass. More was given up in the 'thirties.

During the 1930's a prolonged combination of natural and economic difficulties bearing upon the wheat economy resulted in regional disaster. Throughout this decade the natural hazards which individually constitute the lesser handicaps to wheat production—weeds, rust, smut, grasshoppers, saw-flies, cutworms, hail and frost—continued to exact their unmeasurable but certain toll. Drought, however, reduced crop after crop to total failure. All the Prairie Provinces suffered severely, but Saskatchewan the most, with its wheat production for the years 1930 to 1938 inclusive reduced below an annual average of ten bushels per acre. In 1937 the wheat crop averaged less than three bushels per acre in Saskatchewan and but six and one-half bushels per acre for the three provinces. Carefully tended summer fallow, long regarded as the final bulwark in the battle against drought, turned against its creators and, drifting before light breeze or driving wind, converted the country-side into a region of desolation overhung by a choking, blinding pall of dust.

Short crops coincided with world-wide depression and the collapse of indispensable European markets. For the ten years after 1929 prairie farmers received an average of $240,000,000 a year from the sale of their produce, compared with an average of $540,000,000 for the years 1926 through 1929. For the "bumper" crop of 1928 they received $612,000,000. For each of the years 1931,

1932, and 1933 their income was $170,000,000. In December, 1932, No. 1 Northern wheat, the best grown in Canada if not in the world, sold at Fort William for less than 40 cents a bushel, which, after deducting transportation and handling charges, represented a price to the farmer of 25 cents or less.

A brief summary of the incidents of the 1930's emphasizes the precarious nature of the prairie wheat economy with its reliance on uncertain rainfall and almost equally uncertain foreign markets. Portrayal of these incidents also provides a background against which to record the advance that has been made since that period towards mitigating the worst threats to prairie farm security. Much is still to be learned and much already known remains to be made effective. Nevertheless, the progress to date inspires reasonable confidence. Jointly contributing to this progress have been the cumulative experience of a highly-intelligent farming community, the enterprising nature of producers of farm implements, the persistent and enlightened research of agricultural scientists, and the guidance and financial support of provincial and Dominion governments.

The crucial and stubborn problem of rainfall deficiency is under multiple attack. In the most arid areas cereal production has been abandoned and the lands have been restored to grazing purposes. Apart from the park belt, in the areas not so converted, the average farm has increased greatly in size over the original homestead unit of 160 acres (the "quarter-section"), which was ever an inadequate unit on the short-grass plains. In Saskatchewan the average farm increased in size from 285 acres in 1901 to 473 acres in 1946. (See table 2, p. 197.) The arithmetical average tells little about the size of actual units. Preliminary estimates suggest that of 125,700 farm units in Saskatchewan in 1946 there were 30,000 farms of 160 acres, 40,000 of 320 acres, and 50,000 of 480 acres or more.[4] The smaller farms are concentrated in the park belt and the larger units are typical of the prairie areas. Consolidation of farm units has taken place partly by purchase and partly by rental. In 1901, 90 per cent of all occupied land in the Prairie Provinces was operated by owners; in 1941, 62 per cent was so operated.

Plains farmers rely more than ever on summer fallow for moisture conservation and weed control, but the bare, ploughed summer fallow which made soil-drifting inevitable has been replaced by "trash-covered" fields prepared by means of the tractor-drawn one-way disk.[5] Advances in machine design and simplification of cultural practices as exemplified by the changes in summer-fallow methods have greatly increased the acreage manageable by one man and have reduced the costs of growing wheat. A complete set of machinery for a prairie farm may now consist of a tractor, a

TABLE 3

NUMBER OF TRACTORS, HARVESTER COMBINES, AND MOTOR-TRUCKS, PRAIRIE PROVINCES, 1921–1946

Year	Tractors	Harvester combines	Motor-trucks
1921	38,485	.....	.....
1926	50,136	.....	5,640
1931	81,659	8,897	21,517
1936	81,657	9,827	21,293
1941	112,624	18,081	43,363
1946	142,833	44,289	54,718

SOURCE: Dominion Bureau of Statistics. *Census Reports,* as cited in *Brief of Argument of the Province of Saskatchewan in Opposing the Application before the Board of Transport Commissioners for Canada* (Regina, 1947), p. 55.

tiller combine (a one-way disk fitted for simultaneous planting and cultivation), a harvester combine and swather, and a motor-truck for hauling to market—all mounted on pneumatic tires for easy draught and effective operation. Park-belt farms, smaller and with cultivation impeded by tree growth, are less adaptable to full mechanization than are prairie farms. The newest types of equipment, however, are found throughout the wheat-growing area. Table 3 shows the rapid advance in the mechanization of prairie agriculture over the past twenty years.

The Dominion Government now leads the attack upon the problem of drought throughout the plains. Against the background of the desperate plight of prairie farmers in the 1930's the Dominion established the Prairie Farm Rehabilitation Administration[6] with a programme for the improvement of prairie agriculture by means of alterations in cultural practices, land utilization, and water conservation. The Land Utilization Branch of the P.F.R.A. has created seventy-seven community pastures, which cover 1,500,000 acres of lands deemed unfit for cultivation because of aridity or because of erosion resulting from earlier cultivation. Settlers have been moved and those left in the neighbourhood of each pasture have grazing grounds for live-stock. Community pastures carried 80,000 head of stock in 1946, yielding grazing revenues of $200,000.

The water-conservation activities of the P.F.R.A. embrace "small-water developments" and "large-water developments." Under the former, the Government has assisted in the creation of 35,000 small dams and dugouts for the preservation of spring run-off waters on individual farms. Large-water proposals envisage the damming of rivers which cross the plains to control their flow for irrigation and power production. Four main projects concern the St. Mary's, the Bow, the Red Deer, and the South Saskatchewan rivers with the ultimate possibility of placing 2,000,000 acres of land "under the ditch."[7] The St. Mary's development is under construction; the others form parts of a long-run plan. Obviously there is no intention of converting the wheat economy to an irrigated region. The hope is that through water conservation the plains area may be made self-sufficient in live-stock feeds even through a succession of drought years.

Drought will persist, and the Dominion Government has underwritten a scheme of crop insurance designed to establish a floor below which the income of the individual prairie farmer cannot be driven by crop failure. Space permits few details, but under the Prairie Farm Assistance Act of 1939[8] the individual farmer may receive a cash grant up to a maximum of $500 in any year. The actual amount of the grant, if any, depends, first, upon whether the circumstances constitute a "national emergency" or a "crop-failure year" within the meaning of the Act, and second, upon the average yield on a *township* basis and the seeded acreage of the individual farmer. Growers pay a levy of 1 per cent of the sale price of all wheat, oats, barley, and rye which they market. Deficiencies are paid from general taxation. Table 4 summarizes the main financial results of the Prairie Farm Assistance scheme over its first eight years of operation.

Agricultural scientists wage an endless and far-from-futile battle against plant diseases, insect pests, and weeds. The most spectacular success in research for the wheat economy in recent years was the development in the mid-thirties of rust-resistant varieties.

Wheats resistant to the saw-fly may be in prospect. Controls of natural hazards have advanced far, but remain inadequate.

The basic handicaps of the plains economy are transportation distances and uncertainty of markets. Little progress has been made in dealing with the problem of distance since the almost entire cessation of railway construction twenty years ago. Coöperative activity in marketing has been a constant feature of western Canadian agriculture. Wheat-growers early in the century organized a farmer-owned company to sell grain on commission.

TABLE 4

RECEIPTS AND PAYMENTS UNDER PRAIRIE FARM ASSISTANCE ACT FOR FISCAL YEARS 1939–1940 TO 1946–1947

Province	Receipts from 1 per cent levy	Awards	Total awards as percentage of total receipts
Manitoba	$ 4,233,000	$ 1,772,000	42
Saskatchewan	14,653,000	54,503,000	372
Alberta	7,315,000	16,422,000	225
Total	$26,201,000	$72,697,000	277

SOURCE: Ottawa dispatch, December 13, 1947, citing Report of Auditor General of Canada.

Later they formed elevator companies and built or purchased hundreds of local and terminal elevators. In the 1920's they established "pools" which handled members' grain in pool elevators, pooled these grains according to grade, and sold through their central selling agency direct to foreign buyers. Early in the 1930's pooling was necessarily abandoned, but the farmers' companies own upwards of 2,000 local elevators along with great terminal houses at Fort William, Port Arthur, and Vancouver through which they handle half of the western wheat crop. Coöperatives are prominent in the marketing of live-stock, dairy products, wool, forage-crop seeds, and honey, as well as in the purchase of farm equipment and supplies including live-stock feeds, repair parts, and motor-fuel. A coöperative oil-refinery is well established at Regina. The Saskatchewan Coöperative Producers, Limited (formerly the Saskatchewan Wheat Pool), has embarked upon the processing of farm products such as flax-seed for oil and wheat for glycol, and the milling of wheat into flour and mill-feeds.

Agricultural coöperation, with no "cure-all" ambitions, is a permanent, integral part of the plains economy. Its comparative conservatism fails from time to time to satisfy the more radical of the farmers, whose revolt may express itself in a variety of ways. An example of such revolt—extreme perhaps—was the month-long delivery strike sponsored by the Alberta Farmers' Union in the fall of 1946 in support of demands for parity prices for farm produce.

The Winnipeg Grain Exchange, which recently celebrated its sixtieth anniversary, is the long-run storm-centre of the plains farmer's fight for economic security in marketing. One of the world-famed institutions which provide for grain transactions on both cash and futures bases, it symbolizes for prairie farmers the impersonal workings of the price system and the grain trade. As such, it receives much of the blame for the price fluctuations which bedevil prairie agriculture.

Farmers have long agitated for the prohibition of futures trading and for the marketing of their wheat by a monopolistic national board on the model of the Canadian Wheat Board of 1919–1920. A federal Wheat Board was established in 1935, but without monopoly control until September, 1943, when, simultaneously, futures trading in wheat and some coarse grains ceased in Winnipeg. Legislation in 1947 extended the Wheat Board's monopoly control over wheat until July 31, 1950.

Meanwhile the bulk of Canadian wheat exports go to Britain under the Anglo-Canadian wheat contract of 1946, which provided for minimum exports of 600,000,000 bushels over the four crop years 1946–1947 to 1949–1950. A price of $1.55 per bushel basis No. 1 Northern Fort William for the first two crops was eventually raised to $2.00, same basis, for the 1948–1949 crops. Wheat grown in the years 1945–1949 inclusive is, in effect, being marketed in a five-year governmental pool upon which farmers to date have received advance payments of $1.75 per bushel, basis No. 1 Northern Fort William. There is also a scale of lower prices for grades of lower quality. Furthermore, out of his selling price the farmer must pay transportation and handling charges from his local elevator to Fort William, so that the prices mentioned are by no means to be regarded as net. The position of the Grain Exchange in the prairie economy after July, 1950, cannot be predicted, but neither farmers nor grain-traders consider the issue sufficiently settled to permit relaxation of their publicity and political efforts.

The Second World War had important effects on prairie agriculture. With the temporary loss of western European markets and with the British shifting their demands to live-stock and its products instead of wheat, Dominion Government controls were established which cut prairie wheat acreage by 40 per cent and greatly stimulated live-stock production. Whereas, in the late 'thirties, prairie farmers obtained two-thirds of their cash income from wheat, by 1942 that proportion had been cut to 30 per cent with the newer emphasis on sales of hogs and cattle. Much of this shift, however, was only temporary, and in the post-war years the region promises to remain predominantly a wheat economy with live-stock and dairy products continuing to be of considerable secondary importance, particularly in park-belt areas.

A substantial cash income, up to a billion dollars a year (1944 and 1946), secured within the framework of price control, has lasting significance for prairie farmers and has permitted them to liquidate indebtedness, to acquire acreage and machinery for farm units of more economic size on a debt-free basis, and generally to consolidate their economic position. The expansion of industrial employment in eastern cities and in Vancouver facilitated the transfer of surplus population out of the prairie region. British contracts for the purchase of wheat, meats, cheese, and eggs give assurance that the problem of markets will not become acute during the immediate post-war years.

Agriculture, with particular emphasis on wheat-growing, is the predominant economic activity of the central plain and accounts for upwards of three-quarters of the net value of production in the Prairie Provinces. By the early war years (1942) manufacturing contributed one-seventh of the total, though this was less than 8 per cent of the net value of manufacturing in Canada. Other economic activities exist in considerable variety, but are of minor importance. Among these are mining, lumbering, fishing, and trapping.

More than one-third of the population of the Prairie Provinces is classed for census purposes as urban rather than rural. Yet the distinction is the purely formal one that persons who live in cities, towns, or incorporated villages are classed as urban and all others as rural. Many of the "urban" dwellers of the plains, therefore, will be found living in groups ranging in numbers from a few score to a few hundred. In the Prairie Provinces only three cities have populations approaching or in excess of 100,000, and but one other has a population in excess of 50,000.[9] Cities, towns, villages, and hamlets—the last not classed as urban—are the prairie market centres where manufactured and processed goods, fresh fruits, and vegetables are exchanged for agricultural products, chiefly wheat. Direct descendants of early fur-trade posts, these market centres number hundreds rather than half-dozens; the bead-work pattern which they form on prairie maps is threaded on railway steel instead of on ribbons of flowing water. Though not defended by fort or palisade, they yet post gaunt and tireless elevator sentinels to overlook the plain.

Mineral production is of significance in the Prairie Provinces, and unproven prospects inspire confidence that future mining development may be great. The base- and precious-metal production of the Shield portion of the Prairie Provinces has been dealt with in chapter viii, "Eastern Canada" (see pp. 185 ff.). Widely scattered over the prairies proper and in the foot-hills are tremendous reserves of bituminous, sub-bituminous, and lignite coal, but production is hampered by lack of markets, since Canadian industry is concentrated in the eastern provinces and depends on American sources of coal near by. Turner Valley in southern Alberta has long produced oil, though in trifling amounts in comparison with annual Canadian imports. Active prospecting in recent years has opened promising new pools, including one at Leduc, Alberta, near Edmonton, which is already rated as a field worth $500,000,000.

Beyond the prairies are forest resources, fisheries, and furs. Hundreds of small mills produce lumber and railway ties. There are some industries, chiefly engaged in processing agricultural products and in refining fuel for agricultural use. Fisheries in northern lakes are capable of great expansion. Furs contribute to the livelihood of widely-scattered northern peoples. Relatively, however, the contribution of all these activities to the economic life of the Prairie Provinces remains small.

Beyond the circling park belt the continental plain stretches north-westerly a thousand miles to the Arctic Ocean. Corridor-like between the Mackenzie Mountains and the Canadian Shield, this section of the plain constitutes the Mackenzie River Valley.[10] Europeans travelled its water-routes first in search of furs. St. Lawrence traders reached the Arctic via the Mackenzie in the late eighteenth century and found productive fur territory in its head-water valleys safely beyond the limits of the Hudson's Bay Company's charter rights. Amalgamation of the Hudson's Bay and North West companies in 1821 established monopoly control over the trade which for another hundred years provided almost the only contact between this region and the outside world. The creation of the wheat economy in the Prairie Provinces after 1900 left the Mackenzie Valley practically untouched. Trapping and fishing provide to this day the basic native livelihood. Trading and administrative work remain the central purposes for all but a few of the population clusters which have formed upon the river transportation system. In 1941 the population of the North-West Territories was 12,000, of whom 2,300 were whites and the others Eskimoes or Indians. Of the total, perhaps 7,000 were in the Mackenzie Valley.

After 1920 pontoon-equipped aeroplanes revolutionized the movement of persons in the northland and permitted prospectors to reach countless regions formerly remote and inaccessible. The demand for fuel prompted test drillings along the Mackenzie River beyond Fort Norman, where oil seepage had first been noted many years before. Drilling in 1920 produced commercial quantities of oil, and later tests indicated an area of great promise. As mentioned in chapter viii, pitch-blende—source of radium and uranium—was discovered at the eastern end of Great Bear Lake in 1930, and in 1933 the Eldorado Gold Mines, Limited, established a reduction mill on the property at Port Radium and a refinery at Port Hope, Ontario. Gold was discovered on the shores of Great Slave Lake in 1935. Fact and fiction concerning the richness of the ore-bodies in the region prompted a pre-war gold-rush to Yellowknife, the lake-shore centre of the strike. Gold discoveries on Lake Athabaska established Goldfields in the 1930's, but its marginal ores supported operations only under the unusually depressed cost conditions of the 'thirties. Four summer-producing oil-wells at Fort Norman supplied fuel in the pre-war years to Port Radium and Yellowknife and to an increasing proportion of river vessels which were converted to its use.

The Second World War struck sharply at the economic life of the Mackenzie Valley. Gold, radium, and furs yielded war-time precedence to many other commodities. Mining at Port Radium was suspended in 1939. Yellowknife lost personnel and in time its mines were placed upon a maintenance basis only. Goldfields became, and has remained, a ghost town. Other war requirements, however, provided stimulation which far outweighed the tendencies towards retrenchment.

The significance of Alaska and north-western Canada for hemispheric defence was readily apparent after the Japanese attack upon Pearl Harbor late in 1941. The amazing development of north-western communications in the subsequent months, and in particular the construction of the Alaska Highway in 1942, should not lead one to overlook the pioneering work done in pre-war years. By 1939 the Canadian Government, utilizing a knowledge of the routes long familiar to Canadian bush-pilots, had prepared a detailed plan for an air-route linking Edmonton with the Yukon and Alaska. Upon the outbreak of war the implementation of these plans was rushed rather than dropped by the Government, with the result that at the time of the attack on Pearl Harbor it was possible to offer to the Americans an air-route from Edmonton to Alaska. In consultation between the Canadian and American governments early in 1942 it was agreed that the Americans would extend and improve the air-route, and also would take a major share in building a highway capable of carrying heavy military traffic. By a remarkable effort the highway was opened from the end of steel at Dawson Creek, British Columbia, to Fairbanks, Alaska, a distance of 1,533 miles, before the end of the year.

The agreement between the Canadian and American governments in connexion with all such joint works on Canadian soil was that at the end of the war the American interest in them should be liquidated and that they should be turned over completely to Canada at a valuation to be agreed upon. This arrangement was fully and honourably carried out, the American Government accepting very reasonable terms in view of the fact that the value of these works and the need for them were radically reduced by the return of peace.

The Alaska Highway lies outside the Mackenzie River Valley. In effect the Valley and the Highway run parallel, separated by mountain ranges. Yet the construction of the Highway had great significance for the Mackenzie area. The vulnerability of the Pacific supply-routes which had prompted construction of the inland highway to Alaska also encouraged the search for adjacent sources of fuel for aeroplanes and for motor transport. Norman Wells on the Mackenzie River, beyond the mountains from the Highway, was the only prospect within thousands of miles. Simultaneously with the construction of the Alaska Highway, then, the Americans laid plans for the Canol project. This project envisaged the expansion of oil production at Norman Wells to its maximum, the establishment of a refinery at Whitehorse on the Highway, and the construction of a pipe-line and highway some 600 miles through the Mackenzie Mountains to supply the refinery with crude oil from Norman Wells. The project was completed at tremendous cost. Sixty producing wells were added to the former four in the Norman Wells area. Pipe-line, highway, and refinery were constructed. In addition, distributive pipe-lines were laid from Whitehorse to Fairbanks, to Skagway, and to Watson Lake. A winter road for tractor trains was constructed along the Mackenzie Valley from Fort Smith to Norman Wells, with a branch to the Alaska Highway at Fort Nelson and one to Grimshaw on the Peace River. In 1944 there were 600 persons at Norman Wells. In 1945 the entire Canol project came to an end. The Whitehorse refinery and its pipe-line were closed. Most of the wells on the Mackenzie were capped.

War-time developments in atomic research centred attention on uranium and its Canadian source in the pitch-blende properties of Port Radium. The mine and mill, closed at the start of the war, were taken over by the Dominion Government in 1942 and a working force of 200 men was established.

Some observers, viewing the idle pipe-line and mountain roadway of the Canol project, the capped wells and the vast rows of abandoned construction equipment at Canol and Fort Norman, argue that the war had no lasting effect upon the Mackenzie Valley. The effect was transitory for the most part. But not entirely. The oil resources of Norman Wells have been clearly established. A chain of landing-fields constructed during the war makes wheel-mounted aeroplane transportation possible from Fort McMurray to Fort Norman. Tractor trains have come into common use as a means of winter transport in the Mackenzie Valley, and roads which were opened for such equipment in the Canol development may more readily be maintained than constructed. A refinery remains at Norman Wells, and on the basis of more readily available fuel a great proportion of the river fleet of tugs and packet-boats has come to rely on oil rather than on wood for fuel. Port Radium has achieved world importance as a source of materials essential to atomic developments. Yellowknife boasts of the world's largest body of gold ore and has renewed its war-interrupted mining-boom. With a population of 3,000 it is moving to a new town-site and installing a million-dollar water and sewage system.

The Mackenzie Valley will become increasingly important to the Canadian economy. To gold, oil, and pitch-blende must be added known resources of coal along the lower Mackenzie; and salt and one of the world's largest deposits of high-bituminous tar-sands near Fort McMurray.

Agricultural prospects are restricted by soil and climate, but vegetables and coarse grains are grown as far north as Aklavik. Summers are short and rainfall is under 14 inches a year in most of the Valley. Yet growing conditions are surprisingly favourable. Norman Wells, north of 63° North Latitude, has spring as early as Gaspé in 49° North Latitude. A provisioning agriculture may be expected to develop in the Valley in association with any substantial development of the mineral or other resources of the region.

The Pacific slope, which includes British Columbia and the Yukon, comprises a distinct geographic and economic Canadian section between the central plain and the Pacific Ocean. Briefly described, this region is a rugged plateau lying between parallel mountain ranges—the Coastal Range falling precipitously to the Pacific and the Rocky Mountain Range separating the plateau from the central plain. The interior plateau has an elevation of

3,000–4,000 feet above sea level, but is deeply gashed by rivers and is surmounted by secondary mountains. In the southern part of the province the interior mountain ranges separate valleys which are narrow but of considerable importance because of agricultural or mineral resources. Alaska separates the Yukon from the Pacific Ocean, and the Alaska Panhandle, stretching south along the coast, occupies the northern half of the coast-line of British Columbia. A chain of partially submerged mountains off the coast forms an archipelago of well-forested islands. Of these, Vancouver Island, 285 miles long, and the Queen Charlotte Islands are the largest.

The economic life of the coastal region has rested for the past century upon a few basic industries made possible by specific natural resources. Reliance upon a narrow range of extractive enterprises creates all the opportunities and difficulties associated with staple production. Quick and multiple monetary returns have often rewarded the enterprising investor. Dependence upon distant and foreign markets has rendered the returns uncertain and has subjected the region to wide fluctuations in economic welfare. The opening up of resources in rugged and isolated areas calls for heavy private and public developmental expenditure. Market fluctuations have frequently made the accompanying burden of debt oppressive. Primary industries typically rely upon wasting assets. The leading staple industries of the Pacific slope today are lumbering, mining, agriculture, and fisheries. Though at present in second place, mineral production has, by new and promising discoveries, frequently provided the incentive to development. Settlement, the cultivation of land, lumbering, and the construction of roads and railways have commonly awaited the imperative demands based upon the extraction of mineral wealth.

The first European economic interests in the Northern Pacific region were in furs and the fur trade. By the mid-nineteenth century the Columbia and Fraser rivers were firmly established as fur-trade routes under the control, by that time, of the Hudson's Bay Company. The discovery of minerals, however, gave the first impetus to settlement and more diversified economic expansion. Prospectors working northward from California after the gold-rush of 'forty-nine found the yellow metal at the mouth of the

Fraser River and in the Queen Charlotte Islands. Farther inland, gold was found on the Thompson and upper Fraser rivers in 1858, with an ensuing rush of gold-seekers which included an estimated 30,000 persons from California. The continued search for the mother lode opened the Cariboo deposits in 1860, and for several years this northern interior region was the scene of extensive and highly-profitable mining activities. Deposits on the Fraser and Thompson rivers and in the Cariboo were worked by the placer method, the gold particles being separated from sand and gravel by water and gravity in a variety of ingenious contrivances.

In the 1880's and 1890's mining developments reached boom proportions in the Boundary district, situated in the Kootenay Valley adjacent to the state of Washington. Silver, gold, copper, lead, and zinc were found in this region in various hard-rock combinations presenting new and intricate problems of extraction. Instead of placer mining these ores required hard-rock reduction processes which involved blasting, crushing, and smelting. Transportation costs encouraged the construction of smelters near by to be used in place of the more distant American facilities.

News of gold discoveries on the Klondike and other tributaries of the Yukon River in 1896 precipitated a rush of gold-seekers to that region. This rush, the most spectacular in Canadian history, drew 30,000 miners to placer diggings just below the Arctic Circle and created Dawson City with a population of 10,000. Rich surface deposits yielded fabulous rewards to crude and wasteful hand-powered efforts, but with the early exhaustion of these deposits Yukon gold-mining became a big-business activity possible only by means of capital resources sufficient for the purchase and operation of gigantic dredges and steam plants for thawing the soil.

Despite superficial differences, the successive mineral discoveries influenced the economic life of the Pacific region in much the same way.[11] Prospectors and miners swarmed into the areas of promise. There they required to be provisioned, clothed, and sheltered. Mining activities—whether placer or rock—required timber and sawn lumber. The extraction of base metals imposed the additional requirement of smelter installations. Obviously the machinery and many of the supplies necessary for mining and smelting operations could not be produced locally and had to be transported into the area, frequently over very difficult terrain. As for food-stuffs and lumber, from the very beginning of mining activity in a region there was often the alternative between local production and importation. Mining developments were commonly accompanied by agricultural and lumbering activities. Herds of cattle were driven up the valleys from the United States for slaughter and to stock the valley grass-lands. Cereals were grown and local flour and grist-mills were established. Timber was cut and processed in newly-constructed local saw-mills.

With all possible expansion of subsidiary industries in the mining areas, demands for the establishment or improvement of transportation persisted and forced heavy expenditures of public funds and the provision of public guaranties for the encouragement of private expenditure. The gold-rush to the Cariboo in the 1860's entailed the construction of a costly wagon-road which left the colony heavily burdened with debt. A generation later, the threat that the mining area of the Kootenay Valley might become economically tributary to the neighbouring portions of the United States centring on Spokane inspired the construction of the Crowsnest Pass railway from Lethbridge, Alberta, to Nelson, British Columbia. The Canadian Pacific Railway constructed this branch with the aid of federal subsidies. After its completion in 1897 the Kootenay mining centres secured the bulk of their provisions from Alberta, and coal and coke for their smelters from Fernie in the mountain pass.

The establishment of the wheat economy in the Prairie Provinces after 1900 instituted a new era in the economic life of British Columbia, and the population more than doubled in the ensuing decade, with a record increase of 213,823, unchallenged until the 'forties. The wide-spread publicity given to mineral strikes in the Kootenay, and more particularly the fabulous accounts of the gold discoveries in the Yukon, called attention to economic opportunities in the Canadian North-West and thus contributed to prairie agricultural settlement. The expanding provisions market of the Kootenay Valley provided more tangible encouragement to prairie producers. In turn the annual establishment of prairie farm-steads by the tens of thousands offered profitable markets for many products of the Pacific slope. Lumber and shingles were required in great quantities for the almost exclusively wooden housing structures of prairie farms and market centres. Before 1914 these uses absorbed 70 per cent of the total production of wood products in the coastal province. Posts of British Columbia cedar were used with barbed wire from eastern Canada to build thousands of miles of prairie fences. Tree fruits such as apples, pears, and cherries, and small fruits such as raspberries, strawberries, blackberries, and loganberries have been, and remain, indispensable to Canadians on the plains. Prairie markets rely heavily on sugar and syrup refined in Vancouver, and on coffee, tea, and spices imported into and packaged in that city.

The integration of the coastal and prairie economies which characterized the first twenty years of the present century has not been maintained. The British Columbia economy advanced tremendously in the 1920's. The prairie markets remained important, but relatively much less, as a result of the tremendous expansion of export sales.

Economic expansion of the coastal region after 1920 was chiefly related to increases in the output of base metals and forest products. War-time demands after 1914 had directed intensive research efforts towards the improvement of metallurgical processes. The skills thus acquired relating to the extraction and utilization of base metals made possible the profitable multiplication of output totals for British Columbia mineral areas in the 1920's. Between 1920 and 1929 the British Columbia output of copper more than doubled, silver tripled, zinc quadrupled, and lead increased ten times. By the end of the decade the province was producing approximately one-tenth of the world's requirements of lead and zinc.[12] The demand which prompted this expansion in mineral production was almost entirely an export demand.

The Panama Canal became fully effective after 1920 and revolutionized the lumber industry of British Columbia. Before the opening of the Canal, high ocean freight-charges had largely excluded Pacific timber from the industrial centres of the North Atlantic, and railway rates had restricted its inland movement to the Prairie Provinces. Less than one-fifth of the timber produced in British Columbia reached export markets. The reduction in ocean charges which followed the full utilization of the Panama Canal made the North Atlantic markets accessible to British Columbia lumber-producers.[13] British Columbia lumber production nearly doubled during the 1920's, and the export proportion increased to nearly one-half of the total.

Export markets encouraged the expansion of other industries in British Columbia after 1920. Pulp and paper went to the United States and the Orient. Nearly all the province's catch and pack of fish and a substantial proportion of the total production of apples went abroad. Mining and news-print production stimulated the installation of hydro-electric power equipment till, in 1929, per capita production of such power in British Columbia was the highest in the Dominion. The population has increased steadily, having almost quintupled in the first four decades of this century and, by 1946 estimates, topping the million mark. Table 5 indicates the growth in the population of British Columbia.

TABLE 5

POPULATION OF BRITISH COLUMBIA, 1871–1946

Year	Population	Year	Population
1871	36,247	1921	524,582
1881	49,459	1931	694,263
1891	98,173	1941	817,861
1901	178,657	1946	1,003,000 *
1911	392,480		

SOURCE: Dominion Bureau of Statistics. *Census Reports.*
* Intercensal estimate.

Four primary industries constitute the foundation of the coastal economy. These are forestry, mining, agriculture, and fisheries. Hydro-electric power is developed particularly for the production of minerals and pulp and paper. Manufacturing has become increasingly important with emphasis upon the processing of local raw materials. Other activities such as ocean shipping and catering to the tourist trade are of great importance in particular parts of the coastal region. In the late pre-war years the four primary industries mentioned above accounted for two-thirds of the net value of production in British Columbia and the Yukon. Manufacturing provided one-fifth of the total. During the war-years coastal manufacturing expanded till it provided upwards of one-half of total net production. Meanwhile primary production expanded absolutely, but declined in relative importance.

Timber resources covering 75,000,000 acres are of prime importance to the province of British Columbia. These resources vary greatly in accessibility and quality. Douglas fir trees, 3 to 6 feet in diameter and from 150 to 225 feet high, are monarchs of the coastal forests. They have long been regarded as the best lumber species in the region. Stands of timber currently considered as poorer in quality, such as western hemlock, spruce, and cedar, cover greater areas. In the pre-war years Douglas fir was cut at the rate of one and a half billion board feet annually from total accessible reserves of an estimated eighteen billion feet. The trees cut were from two to three hundred years old. The total annual cut of all varieties averaged above two and a half billion feet. Of the total acreage of timber only a small fraction carries mature accessible timber of good quality. Depletion of Douglas fir reserves leaves extensive stands of hemlock, spruce, and cedar available for cutting.

Despite the Panama Canal, British Columbia is thousands of miles from the export markets upon which its timber-producers must rely. Any reduction in the quality of timber exports must, therefore, increase the difficulty of the maintenance of these markets. Depletion caused by fires, over-cutting, and the lack of an effective policy of reforestation has aroused deep concern in British Columbia. It can be recognized, however, that both the accessibility and the usefulness of timber resources may be altered favourably by improvements in the industrial arts. Mechanization of logging operations has in recent decades steadily extended the range of economic operations. New knowledge concerning the utilization of wood frequently increases the economic importance of "inferior" timber. In addition to vast quantities of lumber and timber, British Columbia forests provide upwards of one-half of the Canadian output of shingles, large quantities of sash, doors, and plywood, and the raw materials for three large pulp-mills.

The dynamic influence of mineral developments on the coastal economy over the past century has already been indicated. Placer mining has given way to lode mining. Base metals have superseded gold in importance. Gold and silver are nevertheless produced in widely-scattered localities in substantial quantities. The output of gold was expanded in the 1930's following the increase in its American price. The world-famous Sullivan mine in the Kootenay region provides the ore from which the Trail smelter extracts over 90 per cent of Canada's lead production. This ore is also rich in zinc, silver, cadmium, bismuth, and additional minerals. High-grade bituminous coal-bodies have long been worked on Vancouver Island and in the Crowsnest area of the Rockies. Mineral production in the province has problems associated with a heavy reliance upon foreign markets, the complexity and limitation of known ore-bodies, and the difficulties of prospecting and promotion in mountain areas.

The last of the coastal export industries to be mentioned is the fisheries. The island chain down the coast of British Columbia forms a natural breakwater and protects the feeding-grounds for many species of fish. Salmon, taken as they leave the ocean to ascend the rivers to their freshwater spawning-grounds, are by far the most important of the Pacific catch. Halibut, herring, and pilchard constitute a substantial proportion of the total value of fisheries. Fresh salmon and halibut go from Prince Rupert to eastern markets in express refrigerator-cars. The great proportion of the salmon, however, is canned, totalling 1,500,000 to 2,000,000 cases a year, or 60 per cent of the Dominion's salmon-pack. Britain and European countries provide the chief outlet for canned salmon. Conservation of fishery resources presents peculiar difficulties because it requires international action. Mining and transportation development in the interior have caused river contamination and obstruction which have seriously threatened the salmon industry through interference with spawning. A concrete fish-way recently constructed at Hell's Gate on the Fraser holds much promise for the conservation of Pacific salmon. For the study and solution of such problems Canada and the United States have set up permanent joint international commissions for the salmon and halibut fisheries. These commissions have done excellent work.

Mining, forestry, and fisheries perpetuate the export-staple tradition of the early coastal fur trade. Agriculture in British Columbia, in contrast, has traditionally been a subsidiary industry relying far more heavily on domestic than on export markets. As might be expected, agriculture in the province is varied in character and regionally scattered. Market gardening, mixed farming, and dairy farming are carried on in the lower Fraser Valley and on Vancouver Island, catering to the urban markets of Vancouver, New Westminster, and Victoria. Cattle-ranching is found in the Cariboo. Fruits are grown extensively in the Okanagan and Creston valleys and on Vancouver Island. The province has small, highly-specialized wheat-growing areas. Mixed farming is wide-spread. The subsidiary nature of agriculture in British Columbia is emphasized by the degree to which farmers supplement their cash income in occupations such as logging, mining, and construction.

The mountainous nature of the Pacific region reduces agricultural acreage to extremely small proportions. Of the total provincial land area of 235,000,000 acres, 4,250,000 acres are considered to be suited to cultivation. An additional 10,000,000 to 15,000,000 acres may be suited to grazing. In 1941, about 4,000,000 acres were in farms in British Columbia, with 900,000 acres improved. Difficulties which confront agricultural expansion are evident in the diffusion of fertile land throughout the various river valleys, many of them cut up badly by serpentine watercourses. Rainfall is inadequate in the interior valleys, with an annual average as low as seven inches in certain places. Irrigation is necessary for agriculture in such regions, and possibly 70,000 acres are irrigated in the province. For a variety of reasons, however, mountain conditions render irrigation difficult and costly.

Though British Columbia ranks third among Canadian provinces in manufacturing output, the comparison should not be allowed to mislead, since the total gross output of the province's manufactures approximates only 7 per cent of the Canadian total. The figure for British Columbia does, however, approach the total for the Prairie Provinces as a group. The opening of the Panama Canal stimulated manufacturing and processing in the coastal cities, Vancouver and New Westminster. Of outstanding importance in the industrial life of the province are saw-milling, fish-curing and -packing, the manufacture of pulp and paper, slaughtering and meat-packing, and the refining of petroleum products. The preparation of locally produced fruits, vegetables, and dairy products, and of imported tea, coffee, and spices, along with a substantial bakery output, make British Columbia a significant contributor to the food industry of the Dominion. Shipbuilding and ship-repair, which occupied fifteenth place in the scale of industrial output before the war, jumped to first place during the war-years, employing 25,000 workers—one-quarter of the total industrial labour force—and producing one-fifth of the total industrial output of the province in 1944.

The economic effects of the Second World War on the Pacific region can best be analysed sectionally. In the Yukon the main impact was centred on Whitehorse at the head of navigation on the Lewes-Yukon river system. The construction there of a large airport, and a refinery and pipe-line system in connexion with the Canol project, along with the establishment of supply depots for the Alaska Highway, turned this peaceful northern settlement of 500 persons into an American military construction camp of 8,000. But the Canol refinery and supply-lines have been closed, the construction armies are gone, and the future of the Alaska Highway is uncertain. Comparatively little remains of the wartime boom. Whitehorse is still linked with the outside world by the narrow-gauge mountain railway built from Skagway at the turn of this century. It is also connected with the end of steel in the Peace River area by the Alaska Highway. Moreover, it occupies a strategic position on the North-West Staging Route for air transportation from Edmonton to Fairbanks, Alaska. Upwards of 300 air-miles down the Yukon River is Dawson, capital of the Yukon. Near this city, up to a dozen huge dredges work ponderously through the tailings and earth-deposits to wash out the gold left by wasteful earlier miners. During the war only three dredges were operated, each manned by a crew of about seventy. The population of Dawson in 1941 was 1,000. In 1901, soon after the peak of the Klondike gold-rush, its population exceeded 9,000. These figures typify the Yukon as a whole. In 1901 the Yukon held more than 27,000 persons. Two-thirds of these were gone by 1911. In 1941 the total population was less than 5,000.

Prince Rupert, the western terminus of the northern branch of the Canadian National Railways, situated on the British Columbia coast immediately below the Alaska Panhandle, was another centre of war-time economic revolution. Here, as with most of the northern war-time development, Alaskan defence was the urgent goal. Shortage of ocean tonnage and the exposed nature of Pacific shipping-routes strongly suggested the possibilities of a deep-sea port less than eighty miles from Ketchikan, Alaska, and fully linked with Canadian and American transcontinental railway systems. To enable this port to meet the colossal shipping requirements of Alaskan defence the Americans spent more than $20,000,000 on its facilities in the early war-years. Through these facilities were moved millions of tons of materials, heavy equipment for the Alaska Highway, coastal guns for the Alaska Defence Command, bombs for the Japanese campaign, equipment for the Whitehorse refinery, and hundreds of miles of pipe for the Canol project. Prince Rupert embarked 75,000 military personnel for Alaska. The city's pre-war population of 6,500 all but doubled. Confidence among the city's business men that the war-time impetus would last relied heavily on the prospect of diverting from Seattle a substantial proportion of the Alaska trade. Prospects are favourable for a marked development of the region centring on Prince Rupert with proposals for the construction of a huge cellulose plant near by, and for two pulp-mills on the coast of Alaska north of Prince Rupert.

Seven out of every ten British Columbians live in the lower Fraser Valley and on the southern end of Vancouver Island. Half of the total provincial population is concentrated in the metropolitan area comprising Greater Vancouver, New Westminster, and Victoria. Ship-building and aeroplane production along with a great variety of closely-related productive activity drew scores of thousands of workers from the Prairie Provinces to this area during the war. The population of Vancouver proper increased from 275,000 to 340,000 between 1941 and 1947, an increase of almost one-quarter. This increase was by no means at the expense of other urban and rural sections of the province. Over the same years the total population of the province increased by more than 200,000, or 27 per cent. Regions dependent upon gold-mining were forced to retrench during the war, but areas producing and refining base metals, such as that centring on Trail, were of vital importance to the Allied war effort.

Although much of the war-time stimulus to the Yukon economy was transitory, and the degree of permanence of the influence on the Prince Rupert area may be uncertain, the stimulus to the lower Fraser River and Vancouver Island will for the most part be lasting. The population movement from the Prairie Provinces to the coastal region was well established before the war. Employment opportunities in war industries consolidated the movement. The closing of aeroplane factories and ship-yards in Vancouver caused no large-scale exodus of people. A compensatory expansion in a wide range of peace-time industries provides continuing employment. Many of the new comers to the province have established themselves on small subsistence agricultural holdings. If one can assume the maintenance of any reasonable level of world trade in the years to come, the ports of Vancouver, New Westminster, and Prince Rupert and the province of British Columbia as a whole will occupy positions of major and increasing importance within the Canadian economy.

CHAPTER X

Trends and Structure of the Economy

BY BENJAMIN H. HIGGINS AND ARTHUR LERMER

THE ORIGINS of the Canadian economy are to be found in the integration of sharply-separated areas that have been brought together under heavy pressures, internal and external, which still operate powerfully. Their workings have at times been clearly seen, and can best be understood, therefore, if we consider them in their historical perspective.

Prior to the Confederation of 1867, the discontinuous areas of settlement which made up British North America were almost completely separated economically. They were, however, faced with enormous problems which seemed insoluble by provincial means alone. In the Canadas the intensive development of the St. Lawrence Canal system had virtually necessitated the union of the provinces in 1841, but the commercial possibilities of the water-way were seriously threatened by the American Drawback laws of 1845 and 1846, which enabled Canadian imports and exports to pass freely through American territory, thereby taking advantage of the lower ocean freight-rates at New York. Before the canals were completed, however, the era of railways had begun, and the intensive building programme of the 1850's was designed to restore, not to supplant, the St. Lawrence as the vital artery of communication which could compete with its American rivals. It is not surprising that the 1850's brought also proposals for rail connexion between the Canadas and the Maritime Provinces and even chimerical suggestions for an all-British rail-route and telegraph line from the Atlantic to the Pacific.

Meanwhile, the abandonment by Britain in the 1840's of the old system of colonial preferences hastened intercolonial tendencies, as we can see clearly in the negotiation of the Reciprocity Treaty of 1854, which included both "Canadian" and Maritime Province interests. During the 1850's the principle of colonial tariff protection began to gain adherents, and the idea of intercolonial reciprocity took root. The impossibility of solving the problems of railway finance by provincial or local effort, the active interest of certain British investors in the idea of union, and the danger of losing the West to the United States were among the influences which drove British North America powerfully towards Confederation, and which make 1867 a milestone in the economic as well as the political and cultural history of the country.

The population of Canada, as recorded by the Census of 1871, the first after Confederation, stood at upwards of 3,600,000 people. Four-fifths of these lived on the land, where they engaged in agriculture and extractive occupations. In the entire country there were only nine cities with more than 10,000 inhabitants, and none with more than 50,000. Superimposed on this rural foundation was a structure of secondary industries consisting of such manufacturing, handicraft, and service enterprises as were naturally sheltered from outside competition.

In the Maritime Provinces the chief occupations were fishing, lumbering, ship-building, and the carrying-trade. The latter, in 1866, provided full-time employment for approximately 13 per cent of the gainfully employed in Nova Scotia and about 7 per cent in New Brunswick. Fish was a staple export to the West Indies and was supplemented by lumber, potatoes, and miscellaneous products. Cod dominated the fishing industry, and Nova Scotia was the leading province, with more than 24,000 men employed in fishing in 1881. As the heavy trade in square timbers diminished with depletion of the supply of accessible forest, a demand for sawn lumber arose to take its place. Agriculture, though important, remained subsidiary to fishing and lumbering.

New Brunswick confined itself almost wholly to lumbering. Forest products comprised nearly 70 per cent of its total exports in 1866. Much of its ship-building, too, was for export, and it was a common practice to design rough ships for the timber-trade with the intention of disposing of both ship and cargo. In this way about half of all ships constructed were exported. Saw-mills sprang up at the mouths of the great rivers, and many farmers derived a large part of their income by providing the lumbering industry with hay, oats, and potatoes.

Within the Maritime Province economy, Prince Edward Island had adapted itself by withdrawing entirely from the sea and devoting itself to supplying its neighbours with a part of their requirements of agricultural products. At the time of Confederation the Island's population, number of farms, occupied acreage, and volume of grain production were substantially the same as at present, although some emphasis has since been placed on the production of specialized commodities (e.g., foxes and dairy cattle).

In Ontario and Quebec, lumbering and agriculture occupied the majority of the population. For a time lumbering had taken a leading role and, combined with ship-building, had made Quebec one of the world's foremost timber ports, but after the middle of the century agriculture gained predominance and by 1860–1865 provided four-fifths of all exports. Dairying began to emerge as a manufacturing interest. By 1867 cheese factories were being established, and their exports continued to increase to the end of the century. Ontario's woollen mills also flourished, but the use of homespuns was wide-spread, and in 1870 farms produced a total of 7,500,000 yards of woollen cloth.

On the Pacific Coast the feverish days of pioneer gold-mining in the Fraser and Cariboo fields were gone; gold production, though still important, had for the time being reached its climax. Small amounts of timber were being exported to the United States, and Nanaimo, on Vancouver Island, boasted a thriving coal-field. Of fishing little existed besides a solitary canning factory and a few whaling enterprises. Manufacturing consisted of a small number of saw-mills and grist-mills, breweries, and distilleries.

The mineral wealth of Canada in 1867 was little developed and largely unknown. Gold was mined in British Columbia and, at the opposite shore, in Nova Scotia. Silver was being profitably worked on the north shore of Lake Superior, and copper ores in the Eastern Townships of Quebec. Iron was extracted from the bog-ores north of the St. Lawrence, and from the magnetites of Marmora and other points in Ontario. Nanaimo, on Vancouver Island, annually produced some 30,000 tons of coal; Nova Scotia, 600,000 tons. In Ontario, petroleum fields yielded small quantities of oil. The search for additional wells led to the discovery of salt deposits, and in 1867 western Ontario produced ninety barrels of salt each day.

TABLE 1

OCCUPATIONS BY PERCENTAGE DISTRIBUTION, 1871

Occupation	Ontario	Quebec	New Brunswick	Nova Scotia	Av. of Canada
Farming, lumbering, fishing	51	52	51	52	51
Manufacturing, handicrafts	14	11	12	10	13
Construction and unskilled labour	18	17	18	15	18
Mining			..	2	..
Service	17	20	19	21	18

The extent and character of manufactures were determined primarily by the distribution and abundance of raw materials, but lack of transportation made the development of large-scale enterprise negligible. Lack of transportation was, on the other hand, a protection to the small, isolated industries which were scattered throughout the towns and villages, and which were also aided by the prevailing low revenue tariff. Industrial establishments ranged, in order of value, through flour-mills, saw-mills, boot and shoe factories, tanneries, foundries, bakeries, woollen-mills, blacksmith-shops, and many others. Simple agricultural implements and tools were widely manufactured. Establishments, however, were small; the average value of invested capital, in 1870, was only $1,900.

The dominant characteristic of economic life was the high degree of self-sufficiency of the local community. Local industries engaged in barter, and thus remained relatively untouched by business fluctuations. When prices fell and production for export became unprofitable, it was always possible to fall back on the family farm in order to obtain the minimum requirements of food, clothing, and shelter.

The framers of the Confederation agreement evidently anticipated that the new country would grow in economic strength through the increase of its self-sufficiency resulting from internal trade. They expected that manufacturing would assume much greater importance in an economy which heretofore had relied mainly on staple production, that immigration would increase, and that the credit position of the Dominion would improve. They were convinced that the economic activities of the various provinces rendered them capable of becoming markets for each other's special products. The Dominion Government was, by the British North America Act, given authority to regulate trade and commerce, although, in apparent contradiction, the control of property rights and civil rights was vested in the provinces.

Although there was no doubt of the intention to extend westward, the means of communication which were to make this possible were not, apart from a reference to Canadian canals, defined with any degree of clarity or certainty prior to Confederation. The Quebec Resolutions of 1864 referred to the immediate completion of the long-delayed Intercolonial Railway, of which only 374 miles were then in operation in the Maritime Provinces. Although many considered the Intercolonial simply a necessary inducement to federation, others held that it would provide the West with an invaluable winter route to the seaboard in the not-unlikely event of bonding privileges being withdrawn by the American Government. The failure to deal with railway development in the West arose partly from the unfamiliarity of the Quebec delegates with the nature of such undertakings, and partly from the unresolved status of the North-West Territories, at that date still a part of the domain of the Hudson's Bay Company. With the completion of Confederation, however, events moved rapidly. The West was acquired; Manitoba, British Columbia, and Prince Edward Island entered the union as provinces, a Pacific railway was projected, and by 1885 the Dominion was not only rounded out in continental extent, but was spanned from Atlantic to Pacific by a band of steel.

In the course of the pre-Confederation debates, much had been made of Canada's manufacturing prospects. "In fact," said Tupper in the debates of 1867, "the possession of coal-mines, together with other natural advantages, must, in the course of time, make

Nova Scotia the greatest emporium for manufactures in British America."[1] The Western Provinces were equally confident. On the strength of this optimism, considerations of protection were largely ignored in the early years. Reliance, instead, was placed on natural advantages that the country was deemed to possess by virtue of its natural resources and geographical position. The

TABLE 2

Imports and Exports, 1868–1875

Fiscal year	Imports	Exports
1868	$ 73,000,000	$58,000,000
1869	70,000,000	60,000,000
1870	75,000,000	74,000,000
1871	96,000,000	74,000,000
1872	111,000,000	83,000,000
1873	128,000,000	90,000,000
1874	128,000,000	89,000,000
1875	123,000,000	78,000,000

manufacturers shared in the nation's prosperity until 1873, and the scale of their operations grew modestly but steadily. Little foreign capital was utilized, and the processing of farm products continued to hold first place. The most notable development in this field was the rapid growth of cheese factories. Cotton manufacturing prospered and products were diversified. In 1870 there were 41,000 establishments, with more than 187,000 employees and a total production of over $221,000,000.

As table 2 indicates, there was a substantial and more or less constant excess of imports over exports from 1868 to 1875. Since the amount of invisible exports and imports was negligible, the period saw a steady flow of outside capital into the country. Sir George Paish commented, in 1911, "Practically the whole of the capital which has been spent on railway construction in Canada has been provided by the investors of Great Britain."[2]

The greatest excess of imports over exports occurred between 1871 and 1875, which were years of heavy investment and industrial growth. The Intercolonial Railway was being built and work had begun on the Canadian Pacific Railway. During these five years, imports reached a total excess of $172,000,000.

[1] For notes to chapter x see pages 576–577.

Up to 1876 flour was the most important export, and tobacco and raw textiles led the list of imports. Imports increased steadily from 1869 to 1873, whereas exports revealed a tendency to move in bursts and then to hold steady. One such period was from 1869 to 1872. The so-called unfavourable balance of trade during this period showed a high inverse correlation with the degree of prosperity, a condition typical of an immature but expanding debtor country. The composition of imports and exports, in terms of percentages based on 1900 prices, is given in table 3.

TABLE 3

IMPORTS AND EXPORTS, 1869–1875
(Percentage)

Principal classes	Imports	Exports
Agricultural	27.0	12.3
Animal	7.5	24.1
Fibres and textiles	26.5	0.9
Wood and paper	...	38.7
Iron and steel	12.8	1.2
Non-ferrous metals	1.1	1.8
Non-metallic minerals	5.0	2.9
Chemicals	2.3	...
Miscellaneous	17.8	18.1

The Canadian banking system may be said to date from 1867, although in its more rudimentary form it began much earlier. Just before Confederation the Bank of Montreal had undertaken to act as the financial agent of the Canadian Government, substituting the government issue of notes for its own. The division of powers under the British North America Act gave to the federal government control over banking and currency, and committees of both Houses were appointed to determine policy. Their reports showed a diversity of opinion. Eastern bankers favoured the American system with its independent local banks; Westerners preferred the existing system, which provided a very elastic basis of paper currency. Sir Francis Hincks, appointed Minister of Finance in 1869, proposed a currency system based on government issues, designed to provide maximum security without sacrificing the elastic quality. The arrangement with the Bank of Montreal was terminated in order to appease the Ontario bankers. In 1871 two bills were introduced creating and establishing a permanent government paper currency. When the acts became law in 1870, Canadian banks were committed to the British type of banking structure.

An outstanding feature of the Bank Act was the stipulation of double liability. It also regulated the capital requirements, establishing a minimum of $500,000, and regulated the conditions of its procurement. One-third of the bank's reserves were to be in Dominion notes, but the size of the reserve was not specified. Conditions were laid down for the making of returns, accompanied by a warning to the public that this in itself was not a guaranty against mismanagement. An essential feature of the system was the freedom to establish branches. Hincks considered this of the greatest importance for the development of commerce in so large and thinly-populated a country, and to this end kept the initial capital requirements as high as possible.

With a sounder banking and currency system, the prosperity of the country was marked in 1870 and 1871. Confidence grew to optimism, and optimism led to speculation. The paid-up capital increased from $30,000,000 in 1869 to over $58,000,000 in 1874. Increasing supplies of currency assisted speculation in insurance and utilities corporations, and this magnified the reaction of the economy to the crisis of 1873.

In fiscal policy, efforts to restore reciprocity with the United States, which had come to an end in 1866, continued to engage government attention. The pre-Confederation policy of protection instituted by Alexander Galt in central Canada had been justified on the grounds that heavy government expenditures to improve water and rail transportation had raised the price of exports and reduced the cost of imports. The resulting benefits, he argued, should be used to reimburse the government by way of the higher 20 per cent tariff. The hope that the tariff would also assist domestic manufacturers gave to Galt's policy the name of "incidental protection." Such industrialization as had been achieved by 1871, however, depended little on tariff protection. About 12 per cent of manufacturing employees were in naturally sheltered industries; another 43 per cent were employed in initial processing of domestic raw materials and were unaffected by tariffs. Special protection had enabled certain industries to achieve a degree of self-sufficiency: among them, agricultural machinery, boots and shoes, brewery and distillery products, and tobacco.

In negotiation for reciprocity with the United States, Canada relied on two strong bargaining levers: the inshore Atlantic fisheries and the free use of the St. Lawrence water-way, in return for which she sought mutual markets. The conversations in Washington in 1866 lapsed without achieving an agreement, but Canada continued to permit the passage of American commerce through the Canadian canals, and the fisheries were left open to American exploitation on payment of a fee which frequently proved uncollectible. Negotiations again broke down in 1869. A brief retaliation was attempted by the imposition of duties on coal, salt, and bread-stuffs in 1870, but it was quickly abandoned. The Washington Treaty of 1871 settled the fisheries question on the unsatisfactory basis of a payment of money compensation to Canada, the amount to be determined by arbitration, but the idea of reciprocity was cursorily rejected, and Canada's trade relations with her neighbour continued with relatively little change for the next eight years.

The years 1873–1896 were a time of world stress and strain. For twenty-three years the secular downward trend in prices brought one crisis after another. The depressions were long and severe, the recoveries short and sickly. It has been estimated that throughout this period England had only five months of prosperity for every twelve months of depression. The first warning of the end of the so-called "Prussian boom" in coal, iron, and steel was the Vienna crash of May, 1873. Wall Street followed suit in September with its "Black Friday," and the number of bankruptcies was staggering. Thousands of factories closed, throwing vast numbers of workmen into unemployment. Strikes of extreme bitterness and violence occurred in many countries. Railroads suffered heavily, and the loss to stock-holders in 1877 was estimated at a round billion dollars.

The slump which began in 1873 lasted six years and was succeeded by a further collapse from 1882 to 1888 and another in 1896. Throughout the "great depression," prices continued to fall, and a severe stringency in the international money-market checked economic expansion and curtailed foreign trade.

Financial difficulties were closely interwoven with the supply and usage of gold. England had long since adopted the gold standard, and after the Franco-Prussian War Germany and most other European countries followed suit. The demand for gold did much to create a scarcity, and the volume of world production became a significant factor in economic life. The increase from 1851 to 1875 coincided with buoyant prices, and derived chiefly from the discovery of the American and Australian fields. Although gold production almost held its own during the subsequent period, it did not keep pace with the great industrial expansion and could not support prices.

TABLE 4

WORLD PRODUCTION OF GOLD, 1801–1910

Period	Annual average
1801–1850	£stg 5,100,000
1851–1875	25,000,000
1876–1895	24,500,000
1896–1905	58,100,000
1906–1910	84,800,000

Apart from gold, much European overseas investment proved unsound for reasons varying from fraud to over-optimism. Turkey and Egypt repudiated bonds held chiefly in England. The great financial house of Barings was saved from ruin only by assistance from the banks when South American republics defaulted.

As the two depression decades wore on, trade continued to fluctuate, but joint action by banks and financial institutions averted fresh panics. By 1896 the secular trend reversed itself and falling prices ceased to threaten seriously commerce and industry.

In Canada favourable terms of trade contrived to hold off the worst effects of the depression for almost three years after the Vienna crash. The most serious immediate repercussion was a cessation of international investment which compelled the Mackenzie Government itself to commence construction on the Canadian Pacific Railways, private capital being refused. Lumber exports also suffered, falling as much as 50 per cent, and bringing hardship to dependent agricultural districts. Otherwise the country really benefited, as falling costs of manufacturing and transportation brought down import prices more rapidly than prices of the predominantly agricultural exports.

After 1875, however, Canada could no longer escape the maelstrom. Crop failures added to the difficulty. Imports declined both in value and in volume. After a recovery from 1880 to 1883, they maintained a steady level, with slight evidence of decline. Exports varied according to price changes. The unfavourable trade balance decreased, and in 1880, when business was at its worst, the balance was actually favourable.

TABLE 5

IMPORTS AND EXPORTS, 1874–1895
(Millions of dollars)

Fiscal year	Imports	Exports	Fiscal year	Imports	Exports
1874	128	89	1885	109	89
1875	123	78	1886	104	85
1876	93	81	1887	113	90
1877	99	76	1888	111	90
1878	93	79	1889	115	89
1879	82	71	1890	122	97
1880	86	88	1891	120	98
1881	105	98	1892	127	114
1882	119	102	1893	129	119
1883	132	98	1894	123	118
1884	116	91	1895	111	114

SOURCE: *Canada Year Book, 1913*, pp. 227–228.

During the latter part of this period, canned fish displaced flour as the most important export, and for a time iron and steel manufacture increased in importance. Tobacco and raw textiles remained as the leading imports up to 1890, but after 1880 coal and iron and steel increased steadily. McDiarmid[3] points out that after 1873 the barter terms of trade began to turn in Canada's favour, though American producers gained on the Canadian market at the expense of both domestic and British competition between 1874 and 1878. Exports to Britain increased while imports dropped; with the United States the situation was reversed.

Between 1873 and 1885 the purchasing power of Canadian exports in terms of imports was steadily rising, since animal and wood products, which constituted important categories in Canadian exports, held a slight upward tendency, while imports were chiefly of manufactured goods, and of iron and steel products, which followed the general falling trend of world prices.

It was, on the whole, a traders' depression. The business failures, of which there were many, were mainly in commercial rather than industrial circles, and there was a general absence of the panics that prevailed elsewhere. Viner[4] comments on the "less spectacular but steady growth of business enterprise in Canada, and . . . the inward flow of capital." Canada's acute financial and industrial depression in 1892–1895 he attributes mainly to "the collapse of a real-estate boom, a succession of crop failures, and a decline in business activity in sympathy with the disturbed economic conditions then prevalent in the United States." In 1895, for almost the first time since Confederation, exports exceeded imports, an indication that the inward flow of capital had been checked.

TABLE 6

NET BARTER TERMS OF TRADE, 1874–1895

Fiscal year	Import price as percentage of export price	Fiscal year	Import price as percentage of export price
1874	131.3	1885	108.1
1875	127.8	1886	105.6
1876	121.7	1887	101.4
1877	121.5	1888	94.4
1878	112.5	1889	100.8
1879	113.8	1890	98.9
1880	116.7	1891	100.2
1881	116.1	1892	95.0
1882	109.5	1893	95.6
1883	107.4	1894	92.8
1884	109.0	1895	88.5

Of outstanding importance in the depressed period of the 'seventies and 'eighties was the adoption of Macdonald's "National Policy," the significance of which was brought out clearly in chapter v, "The Dominion" (pp. 107 ff.). Like the opening of the West and the construction of a transcontinental system, the new policy had a profound effect in charting the future course of the Dominion. In a real sense it was the product of unfortunate world conditions and of the uneven and unhappy relationship with the United States impinging on a young country already beset with geographical difficulties; but added to these were such pressing immediate circumstances as problems of public finance, the failure to obtain a renewal of reciprocity with the United States, and the conviction that the Canadian home market and manufacturing industry were being imperilled by American competition and that Canada was being used as a dumping-ground for American goods. Politically, Macdonald's new policy allied conservatism with the manufacturing element, instituting a trend which has continued to run through Canadian politics.

The election pledges which Macdonald made in 1878 were redeemed by raising tariffs on a large number of finished products. Duties were increased to 30 per cent on cottons and were doubled on woollens. Rates on furniture went up to 35 per cent, pig-iron was made to pay $2 a ton, and manufactured iron and steel products were protected to the extent of 25 per cent. On goods not otherwise provided for, the 17.5 per cent rate rose to 20 per cent, but many special rates were imposed, and the whole tariff structure became much more complex. The implementation of the National Policy coincided with the end of the depression period, and to it went credit for the revival of 1879–1883. More important contributory causes, however, were improvement in world demand and the coincidence of good crops in Canada with exceedingly bad ones in Britain.

Dominion revenues also improved, the tariff yielding 50 per cent more in 1881 than in 1878. The programme of industrialization was closely related to settlement and transportation policies calculated to foster the growth of the home market. A new syndicate, formed by private interests, was granted a railway charter in 1880, and by 1885 the Canadian Pacific transcontinental was completed. There were now more than 10,000 miles of steam railway in Canada.

Adequate revenues were not long maintained. An inevitable result of investment in developmental projects was an increase in revenue for the treasury, which in turn encouraged further public works. Sooner or later, however, the flow of investment was checked, and revenues fell with falling imports. Such a development followed the completion of the Canadian Pacific. The substantial surpluses of 1881, 1882, and 1883 were replaced in 1886 by a deficit. The recurrence of depression in 1884 fostered misgivings; the National Policy had not proved a cure-all, and agitation began for a commercial union with the United States.

In the wake of the renewed depression came strife and bitter discord between sectional and religious groups, and in the sphere of constitutional relationships the Dominion suffered a series of defeats at the hands of provincial antagonists, led by Oliver Mowat, Premier of Ontario. By 1884 the decisions of the Judicial Committee of the Privy Council, which apparently was steeped in the doctrine of states' rights, had denuded the Dominion Government of most of its residuary powers and had awarded them to the provinces. The National Policy was revised upwards until by 1887

TABLE 7

GAINFULLY EMPLOYED, TEN YEARS OF AGE AND OLDER, 1891

Occupation	Number employed	Occupation	Number employed
Agriculture	735,000 (45%)	Service	203,000 (12%)
Fishing, trapping, logging	42,000	Professional	59,000
Mining, quarrying	15,000	Personal	125,000
Manufacturing	237,000 (14%)	Clerical	24,000
Construction	86,000	Labourers	116,000
Transportation	61,000		
Trade and finance	88,000	All occupations	1,615,000

SOURCE: *Canada Year Book, 1937,* p. 132.

it reached its apogee and a measure of stability. Renewed depression again created acute political and economic unrest, however, and fundamental changes in tariff policy were hotly advocated, with the extremes of imperial federation on one side and commercial union with the United States on the other—a proposal to which the Liberals had for the moment committed themselves in the modified form of unrestricted reciprocity. In the election year of 1891 Macdonald was, in fact, forced to translate the tariff-reciprocity dispute into terms of loyalty and treason to win a verdict for his national Canadian-British system. Fortunately, this was the nadir, and slowly, especially during the last half of the decade, conditions improved. The change proved to be the beginning of a new period.

Before leaving the discussion of the long period of depression which began in 1873, we should note some changes which, though gradual, were significant. Under the dragging weight of depression the occupational structure altered. (See table 7.) Lumber declined and agriculture expanded, with increasing emphasis on live-stock and dairy products, and with less on grains. Those engaged in agriculture, which in 1881 comprised 46 per cent of the gainfully employed, decreased in percentage through every subsequent census. On the other hand, both manufacturing and service occupations displayed an opposite trend. Historically, as Colin Clark has demonstrated, this phenomenon is associated with increasing material wealth, and, to a large degree, growth in secondary and tertiary occupations is a rough guide to the growth of real income. Associated with this trend was the movement from rural to urban communities.

TABLE 8

RURAL AND URBAN POPULATION, 1871–1891

Year	Rural	Urban
1871	2,966,914 (80%)	722,343
1881	3,215,303 (74%)	1,109,507
1891	3,296,141 (68%)	1,537,098

As agriculture expanded in scope, it underwent important changes. Grain production lost ground to mixed farming, and the early beginnings in live-stock, dairying, and fruit-farming reached important proportions by the end of the century. Better transportation facilities encouraged shipment to Great Britain, and cheese vied with live-stock in the export trade. In 1880 more than 30,000 cattle, 10,000 sheep, and 40,000,000 pounds of cheese reached the United Kingdom. In the Maritime Provinces, fruit-farming developed and Annapolis Valley apples found British markets. Occupied lands increased from 36,000,000 to 45,000,000 acres, and again by a third by the end of 1891. In the West, ranching was begun both in British Columbia and in present-day Alberta; by 1892 there were a quarter of a million cattle on the western prairies. The first prairie wheat was shipped in 1876, but rapid advance in wheat-farming was checked for another twenty years by transportation difficulties, low prices, and the inability of farmers using eastern methods to master the problems posed by western conditions.

In manufacturing the transition was as pronounced as in agriculture. Manufacturers marked time in the 'seventies, but enjoyed a revival in 1879 under the National Policy and the improved conditions in the United States. Despite the subsequent collapse in 1882, the Census of 1891 showed substantial expansion. Large-scale production was emerging. Establishments with an output of less than $2,000 increased production, but nothing like the 69.6 per cent achieved by establishments with outputs that exceeded

TABLE 9

MANUFACTURING INDUSTRIES, 1881–1891

	1881	1891	Percentage increase
Number of establishments . .	49,722	75,968	51.8
Capital	$165,303,000	$354,620,000	114.0
Number of employees	254,935	370,256	44.4
Wages paid	$59,429,000	$100,663,000	67.8
Cost of raw materials	$179,919,000	$256,119,000	42.3
Gross value of product	$309,676,000	$476,259,000	53.5

SOURCE: O. J. McDiarmid, *Commercial Policy in the Canadian Economy* (Harvard Univ. Press, 1946), p. 185.

$50,000 in the intercensal decade. Most favoured by the National Policy, the cotton industry by the 'eighties was capable of supplying twice the domestic demand for certain varieties. Saw-mills and furniture factories grew in number, and pig-iron production was established under a bounty granted in 1883. A syndicate was formed to control the cotton market. The oatmeal millers formed an association which introduced the "pool," and binder-twine and cordage producers adopted a similar device. Where tariffs did not allow for such control, agreements were sometimes reached with American firms, for example by undertakers, coal-dealers, watch-jobbers, and rubber-manufacturers.

In growth of population the period from 1873 to 1896 lay between the third (1831) and fourth (1911) peak periods. Though increases were vital to Canadian prosperity, they had to await a new era of economic expansion. Table 10 demonstrates the outcome of thirty years of adverse economic conditions. The disparity between actual increase and estimated natural increase resulted from net emigration to the United States, which for eight decades attracted very large numbers not only of native-born, both French-

and English-speaking, but of recently arrived immigrants. Immigration propaganda and an open-handed land policy in the 1880's provoked a rush of settlers into the prairies. Macdonald believed that the expenses of railway construction could be borne by the disposal of 100,000,000 acres of land, 25,000,000 of which had already been granted to the Canadian Pacific syndicate. Construction of this railway encouraged a boom which brought tens of thousands of new comers: 60,000 arrived in 1882; approximately 3,000,000 acres were claimed. Then falling prices, increased world

TABLE 10

POPULATION MOVEMENTS, 1871–1901

Decade	Population at beginning of decade	Actual increase	Natural increase (est.)	Immigration	Emigration
1871–1881	3,689,000	636,000	799,000	342,000	505,000
1881–1891	4,325,000	508,000	686,000	886,000	1,064,000
1891–1901	4,833,000	538,000	612,000	321,000	395,000

wheat production, and frost and drought took their toll. In the Maritime Provinces the decline of the West Indies trade and the rise of steam vessels at the expense of the wooden ship were discouraging factors which go far to account for the decreased rate of population growth from 13.5 per cent in 1871–1881 to 1.1 per cent in 1881–1891; thereafter it barely held its own. Farms returned to forest, and villages shrank. In Quebec the residents succumbed to the lure of New England industries.

By 1901, Canada, which began at Confederation with a population of some 3,500,000, had grown to only 5,371,315. For thirty years she had added almost as much to the population of the United States as to her own.

With the opening of the twentieth century, Canada stood on the threshold of a new era. The period dominated by the interests of subsistence farming, of lumbering, fishing, and a very limited though growing external trade was passing; a period of rapid growth affecting every aspect of the national economy was about to begin. As always, in Canadian affairs, world conditions had a profound influence. After 1896, the trend in world prices began a great rise which continued, with few set-backs, to 1920. For this there was a variety of reasons. Industrialism, fattening on a host of technological improvements, experienced what amounted to a second Industrial Revolution. The population of Europe grew at a phenomenal rate, nearly tripling between 1800 and 1930, owing to growth of productivity, reduction of the death-rate, and progressive banishment of pestilences; these developments hastened urbanization. The discovery of gold in the Transvaal in 1896, and later in other countries, including Canada, poured a flood of the precious metal into the world's currency systems. The commercial and industrial growth of America, Germany, and Japan was part of this ebullient era, and in the search for markets and raw materials the Great Powers struggled and jockeyed for political as well as commercial advantage.

TABLE 11

NET LONG-TERM CAPITAL MOVEMENT, 1900–1913
(Millions of dollars)

Year		Year		Year	
1900	+29.8	1905	+109.5	1910	+308.2
1901	35.1	1906	102.3	1911	343.4
1902	40.3	1907	91.1	1912	316.1
1903	51.7	1908	218.1	1913	541.7
1904	58.9	1909	249.4		

From 1900 to 1914 Canada shared in all the stimulating effects of this world-wide expansion, and in particular it fell to Canada to provide an increasing part of the world's food. With the end of the American frontier period, pioneers had to seek the Canadian West. Prices of agricultural products rose, and rose faster than those of manufactured products. Ocean freight-rates fell, and interest rates had never been lower. Canada was the principal target for British capital, and large quantities flowed in, chiefly into federal, provincial, and municipal securities or railroad bonds, although much was also applied to industry, mining, and lumbering. Of settlers' capital, the greater part came from the United States. With cheap capital eager to enter the country and a world awaiting her products, Canada stood on the brink of unprecedented progress and prosperity.

An over-all view of Canada's foreign trade during these years shows the United States replacing the United Kingdom as the chief supplier of imports, while Great Britain, on the other hand, purchased an ever-increasing quantity of Canadian goods, chiefly wheat. Canadian exports to Great Britain doubled between 1896 and 1906. From 1896 to 1914 to all countries exports rose from $105,000,000 to over $400,000,000, but during most of the period the value of imports was even greater.

TABLE 12

EXPORTS AND IMPORTS, 1896–1913
(Millions of dollars)

Fiscal year	Imports	Exports	Fiscal year	Imports	Exports
1896	118	121	1905	267	203
1897	119	138	1906	294	257
1898	140	164	1907	260	205
1899	163	159	1908	371	280
1900	190	192	1909	310	262
1901	190	196	1910	392	301
1902	212	212	1911	472	297
1903	241	226	1912	559	315
1904	259	214	1913	692	393

SOURCE: *Canada Year Book, 1913,* p. 228.

The consistent excess of imports over exports after 1902 was made possible largely by the growing volume of long-term investment. The reverse situation had obtained from 1896 to 1901, while Canada was recovering from the preceding depression years, liquidating part of her foreign indebtedness and paying interest. Throughout the period, however, terms of trade remained favourable, as indicated in table 13.

The Canadian balance of international indebtedness was in extraordinarily large measure adjusted to the borrowings in Great Britain through triangular transactions with the United States. British funds made available to Canadians through the floating of loans were used to buy New York exchange, which was in turn used to pay for increased imports from the United States. The adjustment of the British balance of international indebtedness to the capital investments in Canada was similarly effected through increased British exports to Latin America and the Orient, which were in turn paid for by increased exports from these regions to the United States and from the United States to Canada.[5]

A potent factor in the development of the Canadian West was urbanization of the United States and exhaustion of its supply of fertile lands. To the stream of European immigrants was thus added an increasing flow of Americans, attracted by seemingly limitless lands, for which Red Fife wheat and summer fallowing

TABLE 13

IMPORT PRICE AS PERCENTAGE OF EXPORT PRICE, 1896–1913

Fiscal year	Percentage	Fiscal year	Percentage	Fiscal year	Percentage
1896	94.4	1902	94.0	1908	94.1
1897	92.2	1903	93.6	1909	87.9
1898	91.6	1904	95.0	1910	87.5
1899	93.9	1905	97.6	1911	89.4
1900	100.0	1906	95.0	1912	88.8
1901	98.6	1907	96.1	1913	89.7

provided means of exploitation. Wheat-growing was the great achievement of the West. In 1900, 25,000,000 bushels were grown; in 1911, 190,000,000.

In 1906 the entries for homesteads, some of course destined to be cancelled for non-fulfilment of conditions, covered an area equal to that of Massachusetts and Delaware combined; in 1908 a Wales was given away; in 1909 five Prince Edward Islands; while in 1910 and 1911, in homesteads, pre-emptions and veteran grants, Belgium, the Netherlands and two Montenegros were carved out of the wilderness. . . . By 1912 there was comparatively little land open for homesteading except in the northern half of the prairie provinces.[6]

TABLE 14

GAINFULLY EMPLOYED, TEN YEARS OF AGE AND OLDER, 1901 AND 1911

Occupation	1901	1911	Occupation	1901	1911
Agriculture	715,000	933,000	Service	236,000	321,000
Fishing, trapping, logging	43,000	77,000	Professional	74,000	99,000
Mining, quarrying . .	28,000	62,000	Personal ...	148,000	200,000
Manufacturing	299,000	372,000	Clerical	58,000	106,000
Construction	89,000	150,000	Labourers ...	126,000	317,000
Transportation	82,000	158,000	All occupations	1,782,000	2,723,000
Trade and finance . .	99,000	221,000			

SOURCE: *Canada Year Book, 1937*, p. 132.

In concert with the general advance, markets expanded; though the number of manufacturing concerns fell off, the larger scale of operations more than compensated. Specialization was becoming possible, and subsidiary industries were growing up. Production for domestic consumption was greatest, in order of importance, in iron and steel, textiles, tobacco, and boots and shoes. Nothing resembling a self-contained iron and steel industry had appeared, largely owing to absence of developed ore-bodies, but many of the processing stages were well developed in Nova Scotia, at Hamilton in Ontario, Trail in British Columbia, and elsewhere.

TABLE 15

MANUFACTURING INDUSTRIES, 1900–1915
(5 or more hands)

	1900	1910	1915
Number of establishments	14,650	19,218	15,593
Capital	$446,916,487	$1,247,583,609	$1,958,705,230
Number of employees	339,173	515,203	(Not recorded)
Wages paid	$113,249,350	$241,008,416	$283,311,505
Cost of raw materials	$266,527,858	$601,509,018	$791,943,433
Gross value of products	$481,053,375	$1,165,975,639	$1,381,547,225

A resurgence of gold-mining began with the Klondike discoveries of 1894 and the rush three years later to Quartz and Bonanza creeks. When the more accessible deposits were worked out, hydraulic methods were employed. Even the old Cariboo workings of British Columbia were reopened. Lode-mining was introduced in the Rossland and Boundary districts, and British Columbia achieved an average gold production of $5,000,000 a year. In 1903 a chance discovery of silver during railway construction at Cobalt, Ontario, marked the real opening of the Precambrian Shield to the miner. Within a few years gold discoveries, such as those at Porcupine and Kirkland Lake, launched the hard-rock mining of the Shield fully on its way in what was to be one of the greatest mining developments of the twentieth century. Coal production, though less important, rose to nearly 13,000,000 tons in 1910, mostly from Nova Scotia. Forty years after Confederation, mineral production was ten times its original size and exports had increased thirty-fold.

Matching in importance the growth of mining was the rapid rise of the pulp and paper industry made possible not only by the extent of Canadian forests but by water-power resources which were to make Canada one of the most important producers of cheap hydro-electric power in the world. The pulp and paper industry was first developed at Three Rivers, in Quebec, with its good spruce supply, transport facilities, and market location. The sulphite process had been introduced in 1887, and the 1890's saw the pulp industry enter the Niagara peninsula. Railways aided by opening hitherto inaccessible territories, and the United States provided a market which later was to prove almost insatiable. By 1913 Canada supplied the United States with almost 10 per cent of its news-print requirements, principally from northern Ontario and Quebec, New Brunswick, and British Columbia.

The railways, as we have seen in chapter vi, "The Twentieth Century" (p. 126), did not remain untouched by the pervasive and irrepressible optimism of the times. A new programme of building was undertaken, and within a few years the country had acquired three transcontinental railways instead of one, and the ingredients of its perennial railway problem. As part of their expansive activities the railways shared with the Government and private individuals responsibility for the intensive colonization propaganda which, in the decade 1901–1911, increased Canada's population at an annual average of 183,500, a rate never equalled before or since. Colonization had long been an essential element in broad government plans, but heretofore results had been disappointing. Now advertisements in thousands of American periodicals extolled the country, and free excursions allured farmers. In Europe, railway companies established their own colonization departments. Many immigrants came from Lithuania, Poland, Italy, Romania, Hungary, and Russia, but both the United States and England contributed. From the former, in 1897, came 9,000; in 1912, 133,000. The majority of British emigrants, by 1912, selected Canada as their destination. From 1897 to 1912 the total immigration was over 2,250,000, with 961,000 from the United Kingdom, 784,000 from the United States, and 594,000 from other countries.

This great influx of new comers left permanent effects on the distribution of population in the country. Between 1901 and 1911 the Maritime Provinces accounted for only 2 per cent of the total population increase, Ontario and Quebec 38 per cent. Western Canada, on the other hand, accounted for 60 per cent as against 9 per cent in the preceding decade. The areas brought under settlement were sometimes unwisely chosen, for instance some of the prairie-dog belts, but on the whole the Dominion's land policy of preëmption grants proved satisfactory in laying the foundations of the prairie West, and in particular of Alberta and Saskatchewan, which were created as provinces in 1905. Almost as marked as the westward trend was the trend towards urbanization. Especially affected were the larger centres, notably Toronto and Montreal, the importance of which was emphasized through their commercial, financial, and industrial services to the growing hinterlands of which they were the focal points. Throughout the country, in these years of general prosperity and industrial activity, the growth in population acted as a damper on the trend towards higher labour costs, and producers acquired a cheap and plentiful labour market that enabled them to reap the full benefit of rising prices.

The boom years before the First World War made clear the singular relationship between government revenues and the nature of Canada's international trade. Some 71 per cent of Dominion revenue was raised by customs duties and another 14 per cent by excise duties. Thus the financial position of the federal government fluctuated with the volume of imports. The boom years, with heavy imports, mostly from the United States and thus subject to maximum tariff rates, brought frequent surpluses in the budget. This affluence encouraged public works, principally railways, but also public buildings, roads, harbours, and public utilities, many of such a character that private investment was likely to be unwilling or unable to attempt them alone. It was evident, however, that sooner or later the Dominion must seek a wider tax-base, and that these lavish investments would be put to the test of productiveness as the field for further investments narrowed, and obligations for interest and repayment increased. That day was forestalled by the advent of war.

The period under review was marked by interesting developments in tariff policy. The manufacturing preëminence of the United States made competition difficult for Canadian manufacturers, especially in view of Canada's inability to create a self-sufficient iron and steel industry, and reliance on supplies from the Pittsburg area. In 1902 the manufacturers began a campaign for further protection. A commission was appointed to study the problem, and the manufacturers' proposals met with powerful and effective opposition from western farmers, who, as staple producers, selling in a world market beyond government control, could expect nothing more from protection than higher prices for manufactured products. As a result, the new tariff did not go far towards meeting the manufacturers' wishes. The Taft administration at Washington reopened reciprocity discussions with the Laurier Government, which had campaigned for freer world trade, and in 1911 a proposed agreement was presented to Parliament for ratification.

Few at the moment of its presentation would have predicted its defeat, but the proposal soon aroused such sharp opposition that in the ensuing election of the same year Laurier was decisively beaten. Reciprocity was, it is true, not the only issue, and during the campaign loyalty slogans were revived and bandied about with all the zeal of 1891. In spite of these complex and emotional elements, however, the decision did undoubtedly represent a determination on the part of the majority of the Canadian people to protect the national economy which they had been creating on east-west lines with so persistent an effort and in the face of heavy odds.

Tariff relations with Great Britain were of a different order, though not unconnected with the same problem of the national economy. As early as 1897, preferential tariff treatment was established for Great Britain and other countries offering reciprocal terms. The unconditional offer to Great Britain elicited her cooperation, and in 1898 the tariff was replaced by a specifically British preferential tariff. Again in 1907 the tariff was revised, fixing preferential rates approximately one-third lower than general rates, and in 1912 preferential treatment was extended by agreement with other parts of the British Empire. A final weapon in the arsenal of fiscal devices was the anti-dumping duty, introduced in 1904 and amended in 1907. It countered the disposal of surplus goods at less than domestic prices by imposing a special duty sufficient to reëstablish price equality.

Despite increases in population and urban trends, however, and despite efforts towards diversification of industry and development of internal and external trade, Canada was still, in 1914, both politically and economically immature. The next four years were to accelerate enormously the rate of economic change. War brought heavy burdens and tragic losses, but it was to have a more marked effect on the national life than two or three decades of peace.

By present standards, Canada's economic effort in the First World War was on a small scale. The number of enlistments per capita was nearly as great as in the Second World War; but, whereas in the Second World War nearly half of the national income was devoted to war purposes, Canadian war expenditures, at home and abroad, exceeded 10 per cent of the national income only in the last year of the First World War. Even including British outlays through the Imperial Munitions Board, war expenditures in Canada never reached 20 per cent of the national income.

Similarly, there was no approach in the First World War to the doubling of total production which took place in the Second World War. The value rose from $1,600,000,000 in 1914 to $3,700,000,000 in 1918, with all the main categories sharing in the rise, but with wheat and munitions leading, and national income rose from $2,200,000,000 in 1914 to $3,714,000,000 in 1918. But these increases resulted mainly from a rise in prices, and actual physical production does not seem to have increased by more than 20 per cent during the war period.[7]

It is hard to explain why inflation failed to call forth a larger expansion of production, especially in view of the persistent lag in wages behind prices, and the prevailing excess capacity and unemployment. Apparently, by 1913 Canada had reached the end of an investment boom based on foreign lending, and would have had a serious depression had war not come.[8] As it was, national income fell from $2,359,000,000 in 1913 to $2,253,000,000 in 1914, and even in 1915 national income was slightly below the 1913 level.[9] However, the shift from capital expansion to exporting which war entailed was in complete accord with long-run requirements for the Canadian economy. Large-scale government operation of war-production plants and allocation of resources may be a partial explanation of the more striking performance in the Second World War; certainly the greatest expansion in the earlier war was in munitions manufacturing, in which government ownership and control bulked largest. On the other hand, excess capacity in 1914, despite imminent depression, may simply have been much less than in 1939.

Canada's chief economic contribution during the First World War was a substantial increase in exports to Britain. The value of total exports trebled, and in the last two years over 40 per cent of the net value of manufactured goods was exported, as compared with 6 or 7 per cent in pre-war years. Munitions exports alone amounted to nearly one-third of net manufactures. In 1917 between one-quarter and one-third of the shells fired on the Western Front were of Canadian manufacture. The value of other manufactures exported rose fivefold; the value of agricultural exports, threefold. Even allowing for doubled export prices, these figures suggest a significant increase, reflected in changing trade balances.

TABLE 16

CANADIAN TRADE BALANCES, 1914 AND 1918

	1914	1918
Total		
Imports	$ 619,000,000	$ 963,000,000
Exports	455,000,000	1,586,000,000
Balance	—164,000,000	623,000,000
United States		
Imports	396,000,000	792,000,000
Exports	177,000,000	441,000,000
Balance	—219,000,000	—351,000,000
United Kingdom		
Imports	132,000,000	81,000,000
Exports	232,000,000	861,000,000
Balance	100,000,000	780,000,000

During the First World War, as during the Second, Canada reversed her international credit position, changing from net borrower to net lender. Early in the First War Canada borrowed in England to cover costs of maintaining and equipping Canadian troops there. Heavy British purchases of munitions and supplies resulted in an exchange of roles, and in the fiscal years 1918 and 1919 advances to England were $112,000,000 and $221,000,000, respectively. Most famous, perhaps were the wheat loans of 1917 and 1918, under which Canadian banks advanced $100,000,000 against purchases of wheat, the second loan being essentially a renewal of the first. Such loans to Britain more than offset Canadian borrowing in New York. The first American loan, floated through J. P. Morgan in July, 1915, consisted of $45,000,000 in one- and two-year notes at 5 per cent, sold at par and at 99.5, respectively. Such high rates on short-term obligations did not fail to bring criticism on the Finance Minister, but he answered that Americans were not yet used to buying Canadian Government securities, and were not even convinced that the Allies would win.

Direct controls played a small role in the economic policy of the First World War. An Order-in-Council of 1916 forbade accumulation of "unreasonable" stocks of goods and required hoarders to sell excess holdings at "just" prices. In 1917, threats of a short wheat crop and famine prices led to the establishment of a Board of Grain Supervisors to coöperate with the Allied purchasing agency in rationing the available supply between domestic and foreign markets. A Food Control Office, set up in the same year, though mainly investigatory, rationed certain commodities among processors and dealers. A fuel controller was appointed to worry about the new pressure upon the supply of coal when the United States entered the war. Strikes and lock-outs were prohibited. In 1918, rentals were brought under supervision. Price-fixing seems to have been more extensive immediately after the war, under the Combines and Fair Prices Act, than during the war itself.

In the financial sphere the main item of direct control was the Order-in-Council of 1917 forbidding the issue of new securities by provincial governments, municipalities, or corporations without the consent of the Ministry of Finance. The object was apparently more to assure an adequate market for government bonds than to exercise discriminatory control over new investment. In the final year of war, public works were discouraged, though without striking success on provincial and municipal levels.

There was no formal exchange control, though transactions in foreign exchange were strictly curtailed to prevent panic and confusion. In the first few months, when heavy British capital withdrawals drove the pound sterling to a premium, Canadian borrowing in London operated as a mitigating factor. Later, when the pound was subject to downward pressure, Canadian loans combined with American to sustain it. To maintain the Canadian dollar in New York, American branches of Canadian banks were required to contribute $100,000,000 in gold to the Department of Finance, loans were floated in New York, and a large cash balance was held there with which to buy Canadian dollars from time to time when the need arose. A precursor of the triangular arrangements of the Second World War was the agreement under which Great Britain was permitted to use part of the proceeds of American loans to pay for Canadian munitions. Some attention seems to have been paid to the French franc as well; customs duties of French goods were avoided because France needed dollar exchange, and subscriptions were made to French loans. The net effect of these measures was to keep the Canadian dollar at a slight discount in New York most of the time, while in the fall of 1915, 1916, and 1917 it even went to a premium.

TABLE 17

EXPENDITURES AND TAX REVENUES, 1915–1919

Fiscal year	War expenditures	Total expenditures	Tax revenues	National income
1915	$ 61,000,000	$284,000,000	$ 98,000,000	$2,324,000,000
1916	166,000,000	331,000,000	125,000,000	2,677,000,000
1917	307,000,000	529,000,000	175,000,000	3,302,000,000
1918	344,000,000	650,000,000	197,000,000	3,714,000,000
1919	447,000,000	727,000,000	236,000,000	4,211,000,000

The tax system with which Canada entered the First World War now seems highly primitive. Customs duties plus excises on liquor and tobacco accounted for 90 per cent of total revenue. The anti-inflationary powers of taxation were not understood and were little used as an instrument for economic control. Per capita tax collections rose only from $16.50 to $27.41 during the war, and at no time did receipts amount to 10 per cent of national income. While tax collections approached 60 per cent of war expenditures in the fiscal year 1918, at no time during the war did they exceed 30 per cent of total government expenditures. Measured against income-creating expenditures in Canada of the Dominion and British governments combined, the percentage recaptured in taxes would of course be still smaller.

In the fiscal year 1915, efforts to raise additional tax revenue were restricted to increases in tariffs and excises. Actually, revenues fell off by nearly $30,000,000, owing to the fall in national income. In 1916 a Business Profits War-Tax was introduced, but it yielded only $150,000,000 during the entire period of the war. In the fiscal year 1918 a tax on personal incomes was levied for the first time in Canadian history. It was regarded as a considerable burden at the time, but the rates now seem ridiculously light. Single persons were permitted an exemption of $2,000 and married couples $3,000; the normal tax of 4 per cent was paid on the excess up to $100,000; the surtax on higher incomes ran up only to 25 per cent. In 1919 the exemption for married couples was reduced to $2,000 and the rates were slightly increased. Even in this last fiscal year of the war, special war-taxes raised only 18 per cent of total current revenue.[10]

For the most part, Canada financed the First World War by a mixture of borrowing and monetary expansion. Under the Finance Act of 1914, the banks were relieved of the obligation to pay out gold or Dominion notes on demand, and were permitted to issue their own notes in any amounts, with a tax of 5 per cent on circulation in excess of paid-up capital; they could also get Dominion notes against approved securities. Since the banks could get more than 5 per cent on their loans, the tax was not an effective curb on note expansion. The only limit to deposits was the customary reserve ratio, which was not hard to maintain under the circumstances; and the small number of Canadian banks kept the drain on reserves through the clearing-house within bounds. The printing and circulation of $96,000,000 additional Dominion notes contributed to bank expansion by swelling reserves.

Despite the liquidity of the money-market, the Finance Ministry embarked upon its programme of large-scale domestic borrowing with much trepidation. Before the war the Government had never raised so much as $5,000,000 by public subscription. Until November, 1915, the only domestic borrowing was a direct loan of $5,000,000 from the Bank of Montreal. Net $50,000,000 was called for, and the banks were allotted half of the issue on the assumption that the public could not be counted upon for more than $25,000,000. To everyone's surprise, the loan was heavily over-subscribed. The Government accepted $100,000,000, and returned $4,000,000 of the banks' allotment. Encouraged by this success, the Government borrowed on an ever-increasing scale throughout the rest of the war.

Between the First and Second World Wars the Canadian economy followed the usual pattern: minor recession, inflationary primary post-war boom, deflationary primary post-war depression, recovery, secondary post-war prosperity, and deep and prolonged secondary post-war depression.

Payment for war materials already produced, completion of war contracts, high costs of demobilization, decontrol of food and fuel, and general optimism contributed to a primary post-war boom characterized by continued monetary expansion and rising prices. The down-turn came in the autumn of 1920, and 1921 was a year of deep depression. Recovery set in at the end of 1922, however, and 1923 was moderately prosperous, but with business failures still at a high level and with continued depression in agriculture and fishing. In 1924, recession, bordering on depression, set in again, but losses of income and employment were recovered in the following year.

The period from 1926 to 1939 had three major phases and one minor cyclical phase: prosperity from 1926 to 1929; a down-swing from 1929 to 1933; recovery from 1933 to 1937; and the minor recession and recovery of 1938 and 1939. In the course of the three major cyclical phases, the Canadian economy suffered fluctuations of income and employment as severe as any in the world, with the possible exception of the American, and no major group of the population was spared. It does not necessarily follow, however, that the whole period of the 'twenties and 'thirties must be regarded as a delayed and painful readjustment to the distortion brought about by the war and post-war boom of 1915–1920. Indeed, the only serious maladjustment left by the war was excess acreage under field crops, and it was an excess largely because self-sufficiency programmes abroad narrowed the export market. These self-sufficiency programmes were, of course, partly the result of the war; but an unexpected change in demand for a major product is not what is usually implied by "war-time distortion" of an economy.

In the realm of prices, while a process of gradual, irregular, and frequently interrupted narrowing of price margins can be discerned in the 1920–1937 period, price movements were too diverse to make readjustment of the war-time price structure a dominant causal factor.

As for the occupational distribution, there was very little distortion due to war, and very little readjustment afterwards. The decennial census figures for 1911, 1921, and 1931 show the following striking facts: (1) there was more change in the second decade than in the first; (2) the change was in the same direction, except in trade and transportation, where the fluctuations could be due as much to cyclical as to war influences, and in any event are too small to be significant. The figures show certain trends operating throughout: the decline in the "three f's" (farming, fishing, and forestry); the gradual decline of the relative importance of manufacturing and the increasing importance of services; a decrease in the number of male employees and an increase in the number of female employees relative to total population. The relative loss of construction employment from 1921 to 1931 might be attributable in part to postponement of construction during the war, the consequent building boom in the 'twenties, and the depression in the construction industry in the 'thirties; but there is nothing that can definitely be labelled as "readjustment" to war-time disturbances.[11]

In agriculture, especially in field crops, the war unquestionably left an inheritance of maladjustment, which might be called "distortion." Field crops, dairy products, and farm animals were the most profitable agricultural products during the war and suffered the most intense depression afterwards. In 1920, field crops provided some three-quarters of agricultural revenues, dairy products about 13 per cent, and farm animals about 7 per cent. The area under field crops rose from 33,000,000 acres in 1914 to 60,000,000 acres in 1921, with wheat responsible for about two-thirds of the total acreage. Wheat acreage increased from 10,300,000 acres in 1914 to 17,400,000 in 1918, but continued to rise after the war as farmers tried unsuccessfully to combat price collapse with higher output.

The increase of wheat acreage during the First World War proved a serious problem in the face of a contraction of exports from an average of $261,200,000 in 1915–1917 to $141,400,000 in

1937–1938. It might be said that it proved a problem whenever the price of wheat dropped below $1. Yet Canada's chronic agricultural difficulties can hardly be called "readjustment to war-time distortion." There has been little readjustment, and acreage has tended to go up when prices are high and even for a short while after they drop.

If Canadian economic development from 1919 to 1939 cannot be regarded as a process of war-time distortion and post-war readjustment of the internal economic structure, was it instead, as was then and is still widely supposed, largely a matter of reaction to "outside influences"?

It is unquestionably true that Canadian national income tends to vary directly both with exports and with export surplus. However, the primary post-war boom and depression cannot be explained solely in these terms. In 1918 and 1919, both exports and export surplus fell below the 1917 level, but national income continued to rise. In 1920 the export surplus was negative, while income was at its peak. The movements of long-term capital varied still less closely with income in these years. In the following years, income and foreign trade did move closely together, but the export surplus, which is perhaps more significant for the level of employment than volume of exports, was much more unstable, and it is clear that the instability accounts for a considerable share of the fluctuations in income and employment during the inter-war period.

Moreover, as has been clearly shown by Mr. R. B. Bryce of the Department of Finance, the balance of trade is not the only kind of "outside influence" affecting Canadian economic fluctuations.[12] Prior to 1914 and again in 1921–1923, the most important outside influence was foreign investment in Canada. Investment, whether financed domestically or abroad, has its own effects on income. Also, the ease of shifting from Canadian to American or British securities in normal times makes the Canadian stock- and bond-markets highly susceptible to fluctuations in London and New York, especially in view of the very close relationship of Canadian business and financial thought and public opinion generally with the state of mind in Great Britain and more particularly in the United States.[13]

There can be no doubt that Canadian economic conditions are profoundly affected by outside forces and that this fact greatly complicates the problem of maintaining full employment without inflation in Canada. Yet there can be no doubt, either, that the determinant of Canadian national income is the volume of total expenditures at home, from whatever source, and the close relationship between Canadian and foreign economic fluctuations in the past is no basis for a defeatist attitude towards Canadian economic developments in the future.

Fluctuations in domestic private investment were also of great significance, at least after 1926. Between 1926 and 1929, private investment in plant and equipment expanded by more than 50 per cent, from $605,000,000 to $978,000,000. It then dropped to a level scarcely more than 20 per cent of its 1929 peak, not recovering even its 1926 position until the Second World War. Inventories, while not so big in absolute amount, showed still greater fluctuations in percentage terms, and the instability of private investment was apparently even more important than variations in the foreign-trade position as a causal factor in inter-war economic fluctuations.

In the primary post-war boom and depression the fiscal policy of the Dominion Government was unquestionably a significant factor. Both expenditures and deficit continued high in 1919; after 1920 expenditures were cut, while tax-rates were raised, and a surplus was produced. In the secondary post-war boom and depression (1926–1933) governmental policy played a mildly aggravating role, while recovery after 1933 was probably aided slightly by the measures adopted by government.

In the secondary post-war prosperity and depression, Dominion revenues followed the cycle. The over-all figures, however, disguise somewhat the true nature of federal tax policy in the period; for regressive taxes, such as customs, excises, and sales-taxes, were the ones that fluctuated cyclically, while the progressive taxes on income and profits moved in a partially counter-cyclical manner. The business-profits taxes, left over from the First World War, were cut more than in half between 1926 and 1929, and gradually disappeared in the ensuing down-swing. Income taxes were fairly stable in the up-swing, but rose substantially from 1929 to 1931, and even in 1933 were still above the 1926 level. From 1933 to 1939, income taxes more than doubled.

The change in structure of revenues in prosperity, so far as it was effective at all, was such as to retard the expansion of consumption while stimulating savings and investment. Since investment cannot increase indefinitely without a growth of the market for its final products, federal tax policy in prosperity would seem to have made some small contribution to the factors leading to collapse. During the down-swing, federal tax policy, in and of itself, was an aggravating factor. Revenue from taxes on consumption fell mainly because income and consumption were falling, while the increase in yield of income taxes reflected an ill-timed increase in tax-rates. During recovery, the rise in taxes on both consumption and investment acted to some degree as a brake on progress towards full employment.

Federal government expenditures as a whole followed no clear-cut cyclical pattern during the inter-war period, but declined in such a way as to emphasize the down-swing of 1921–1922 and to retard recovery in 1923–1925; their increase accentuated expansion in the prosperous years 1926–1929 and offset somewhat the deflationary forces in operation between 1929 and 1933; their cuts delayed recovery in 1934; while fresh increases added to the expansionary forces from 1935 to 1939.

In the inter-war period, debt policy followed much the same erratic pattern as expenditures. Since deficits tend to have an expansionary effect and surpluses a deflationary effect, whereas *decreases* in the deficit tend to have a contractionary effect and *decreases* in the surplus an expansionary effect, the federal debt policy accentuated the down-swing of 1921–1922, retarded recovery in 1923–1924, imposed a break on expansion from 1926 to 1929, offset somewhat the contraction of 1930–1933, and imposed a slight limitation on the recovery of 1934 to 1937. In 1938, a year of mild recession, the reduction in the Government's deficit would act as an aggravating factor.

Dominion public-investment policy in the inter-war period was highly erratic. Expenditures on gross investments and maintenance increased steadily during the prosperous years 1926–1929 and continued to rise to a peak in 1930. During the down-swing of

1930–1933 they contracted sharply to little more than one-third of the 1930 volume, and in 1937 were still less than one-half. In the minor recession of 1938, Dominion public-investment policy was slightly compensatory, since outlay for public investment increased in that year.

On balance, the fiscal policy of the provincial governments between the wars was such as to aggravate rather than alleviate economic fluctuations. Revenues show a strong cyclical pattern, with expenditures fluctuating still more violently.[14] Provincial debt increased slightly more in the down-swing than in prosperity, and rose more in the 1933–1937 recovery than in either of the earlier phases.

Municipal expenditures as a whole, and municipal capital outlays as well, were considerably more stable during the inter-war period than those of the Dominion and provincial governments, partly because of the relative stability of municipal revenues. Taxes levied by the twenty-seven larger cities continued to increase through 1932. Even on a per capita basis, tax-levies rose until that year. The main effect of the increase in levies was an increase in tax delinquency, leaving revenues more or less unchanged.

The relative stability of municipal fiscal policy did not arise from any deeper conviction at the municipal level that government should play an active role in offsetting fluctuations in private spending. On the contrary, the municipalities considered the employment problem only as it presented itself in the form of increased costs of unemployment relief and social services, on the one hand, and increased difficulty in maintaining revenues, on the other. Municipal governments quite properly considered unemployment to be a national problem, and were inclined to resent the relief burden it imposed on them. However, the relative stability of their expenditures helped somewhat to impose limits on the violence of the fluctuations in the economy as a whole.

No story of the great depression in Canada would be complete without reference to one of its chief institutional products, the Bank of Canada. As in other countries, the general public, governmental officials, and even professional economists in Canada sought an explanation of the great depression in defects of the monetary system and inadequate or misguided control of the credit mechanism. In 1933 a Royal Commission on Banking and Currency in Canada was set up to study the desirability of monetary reform and particularly the desirability of establishing a central bank. The Report of the Commission (Macmillan Report) expressed the view that the financial system should be able to handle the seasonal fluctuations in volume of business, to withstand the vicissitudes of a highly-regionalized economy, to provide for the financing of external trade, to help provide the necessary mechanism for borrowing at home or abroad, to control domestic speculative tendencies and foreign-exchange rates, and to participate in international coöperation regarding financial policies which might affect world prices of Canadian exports and other matters.

From 1853 to 1914, the Commission felt, these requirements had been reasonably well fulfilled under the gold standard. The lack of rediscount facilities, however, meant that external cash reserves could not be increased quickly and that consequently Canadian banks were dependent on liquid assets outside Canada. Thus the country's ability to maintain the gold standard was partially dependent upon external factors. The Commission also deplored the absence of any single institution charged with responsibility for regulation of credit and currency in the interests of the country as a whole, and for maintaining the external stability of the country's currency. The chief recommendation of the Commission was that a central bank should be established, and this was done in 1934.

The purpose of the new bank, as stated in the preamble to the Act of incorporation, was "to regulate credit and currency in the best interests of the economic life of the nation, to control and protect the external value of the national monetary unit and to mitigate by its influence fluctuations in the general level of production, trade, prices and employment, so far as may be possible within the scope of monetary action, and generally to promote the economic and financial welfare of the Dominion." The Bank was accorded the usual powers of a central bank: to rediscount commercial paper and make loans to commercial banks on approved short-term paper; to engage in open-market operations; to

TABLE 18

GROSS NATIONAL EXPENDITURE AT MARKET PRICES, 1938–1946

(Millions of dollars)

Item no.	1938	1939	1940	1941	1942	1943	1944	1945	Revised prelim. 1946	Prelim. 1947
1. Personal expenditure on consumer goods and services	3,714	3,817	4,334	4,979	5,508	5,822	6,235	6,782	7,682	8,711
2. Government expenditure										
a) War—goods and services, excluding Mutual Aid, etc.	36	70	549	1,129	2,222	3,096	3,410	1,876	1,736	1,462
—Mutual Aid, U.N.R.R.A., and Military Relief	....	....	....	....	1,002	518	960	1,041	107	38
b) Non-war	685	690	633	647	661	685	735	841	....	....
3. Gross home investment										
a) Plant, equipment, and housing	576	554	713	995	931	828	756	865	1,321	2,042
b) Inventories	7	329	368	218	333	—42	—83	—294	475	780
4. Exports of goods and services	1,358	1,449	1,792	2,458	2,347	3,443	3,566	3,576	3,170	3,538
5. Imports of goods and services	—1,257	—1,328	—1,626	—1,967	—2,275	—2,858	—3,539	—2,895	—2,850	—3,576
6. Residual error of estimate for reconciliation with table 1, item 9	+21	....	—23	—56	—242	—248	—220	—178	+15	+57
7. Gross national expenditure at market prices	5,141	5,581	6,740	8,403	10,487	11,244	11,820	11,614	11,656	13,052

SOURCE: Dominion Bureau of Statistics. *National Accounts, Income and Expenditure, 1938–1946* (Ottawa, 1947), and *Preliminary, 1947* (Ottawa, 1948).

Item 3*a*. See footnote, item 7, table 1.

Item 3*b*. Includes grain held by the Canadian Wheat Board.

Item 4. Excludes Mutual Aid, U.N.R.R.A., and Military Relief.

Items 4 and 5. Minor adjustments have been made to the figures of current receipts and payments shown on page 23, *The Canadian Balance of International Payments, 1926–1944* (Ottawa, 1945), Dominion Bureau of Statistics, to achieve consistency with the other component series.

deal in foreign exchange, coin, and bullion; to deal in short-term securities without limitation; and to act as fiscal agent for the Dominion Government and, by agreement, for any provincial government. The Bank was accorded a monopoly of the note issue, and the notes of the chartered banks were to be gradually retired until they amounted to no more than 25 per cent of their paid-up capital. The Bank was nationalized in 1938.

In terms of the share of total resources devoted to war, Canada must be accounted one of the major belligerents of the Second World War. The enormous growth of government responsibilities in war-time resulted in an expansion of total government expenditures from less than 15 per cent of gross national income in 1938 to over 40 per cent in 1944. At their peak in 1944, war expenditures reached $4,400,000,000 (over $350 per capita), including nearly $1,000,000,000 for aid to other Allied nations. The armed forces were swelled from a mere handful of 10,000 to over 750,000 men and women in 1944; and the number of workers in war industry grew from 121,000 in 1939 to 994,000 in 1944.

Before the war, Canada had no war industries worthy of the name, was producing less than one plane a week, and had built no sea-going vessels for twenty years. By the end of 1943 she was producing 80 fighting aircraft and 6 ships per week, as well as 10,000 tons of chemicals and explosives, 4,000 military vehicles and 450 armoured cars and tanks, and large quantities of other war material. Canada had become the fourth industrial country among the United Nations, with the two largest blast-furnaces in the British Empire, a rate of industrial production double the pre-war rate, a steel production double that of pre-war, an aluminium production six times pre-war, and—despite a decline both in acreage cultivated and in agricultural employment—an expansion of agricultural production by some 60 per cent.

This rapid expansion of industrial production did not begin immediately after the declaration of war. When war broke out, Canada was emerging only gradually from a decade of economic depression with a high proportion of idle and under-employed resources. Furthermore, as Professor K. W. Taylor of the War-Time Prices and Trade Board explained, "Our principal allies showed little interest in large additional supplies of foodstuffs, and indicated only moderate interest in the development of Canadian sources of supply for war material."[15] Thus Canada had little encouragement until the summer of 1940.

The overrunning of Norway, the fall of France, and the drastic British losses at Dunkirk, however, completely changed the situation. Great Britain was suddenly desperately in need of whatever material assistance she could get; during the last half of 1940 the Canadian war-production programme got under way with direction and vigour; during early 1941 the economy moved into full employment; by the end of that year, unemployment and excess capacity had virtually disappeared.

Because of the enormous expansion of total production permitted by the prevalent excess capacity and unemployment when war began, the standard of living of Canadians as a whole did not decline seriously during the war. There were many shortages, especially of housing, other durable consumers' goods, and luxury items. There was a noticeable decline in the quantity and quality of services, and in the quality of some commodities. Yet the physical volume of civilian consumption as a whole rose during the war by about 15 per cent; the lower-income groups, at least, were better off in material terms during the war than they had been in the immediately preceding depression years.

In the first budget-message of the war, the principle of financing the war as much as possible on a pay-as-you-go basis was laid down. During the first two years of war, however, while unemployment and excess capacity still existed and a full-scale war-production programme was not yet established, it was considered both permissible and desirable to produce some increase in the supply of money as a deliberate part of war finance. It was felt that monetary expansion would help to lubricate the war machine as it gathered momentum, and that no threat of serious inflation could develop so long as unemployment and excess capacity were wide-spread. In accordance with these principles, tax increases were moderate in the first two years of war, as table 19 indicates. After 1940, however, and especially after 1941, when full employment prevailed, the Canadian Government relied largely on increases in income-tax rates to sterilize increases in income and check inflation. In 1942 the system of income-tax collection was shifted to a pay-as-you-go basis.

From 1942 until 1944, when the "refundable portion" of the tax was cut in half, the structure of the Canadian income tax (including compulsory savings) was about the same as in Australia; slightly higher than in the United Kingdom for incomes between $4,000 and $20,000 per year and slightly lower in other brackets; and considerably higher than in the United States (including the New York State income tax).

TABLE 19

FEDERAL INCOME TAX, MARRIED PERSONS WITH NO CHILDREN, 1939–1944

Income	Pre-war[1]	1939[1]	1940[1]	1941	1942		1943		1944	
					Fixed	Savings	Fixed	Savings	Fixed	Savings[2]
$ 1,500	...	...	$ 30	$ 75	$ 54	$ 54	$ 108	$ 108	$ 108	$ 54
3,000	$ 45	$ 50	208	400	292	150	584	300	584	150
5,000	177	200	604	1,000	689	250	1,378	500	1,378	250
10,000	784	882	2,336	3,080	1,881	500	3,762	1,000	3,762	500

1 Includes Ontario. (In 1941 provincial taxes were removed under federal-provincial agreement.)
2 In 1944, compulsory savings were cut in half.

In 1941 a Dominion inheritance tax was introduced for the first time. The corporation income tax was raised from 15 per cent to 18 per cent, and in addition a tax on excess profits was imposed, amounting to 12 per cent of total profits plus 100 per cent of profits in excess of the average for the fiscal years 1936–1939, or another 10 per cent of total profits, whichever was greater. This combination of provisions meant that no corporation could earn and keep more than 70 per cent of pre-war profits. However, 20 per cent of profits in excess of 116.66 per cent of the pre-war "standard" profits was refundable after the war emergency had ended.

Before the war, Dominion finance leaned heavily on commodity taxes; the federal government derived about two-thirds of its total revenues from tariffs, general sales-taxes, and specific taxes on liquor and tobacco. The war afforded an opportunity for reducing the regressiveness of the federal tax structure. Pursuing its stated policy of imposing the burden of war finance in accordance with ability to pay, the Government avoided general increases in commodity taxes. Taxes were increased on certain "luxury" goods and services; to help conserve American dollars, a 10 per cent "war exchange tax" was imposed on non-Empire imports, and automobile taxes were sharply increased. In the main, however, the increase in commodity tax receipts reflects expanded outlays rather than higher tax-rates.

As a consequence of increased rates and higher incomes, total revenues rose nearly sixfold from the fiscal year 1940 to the fiscal year 1945. Over the six fiscal years of war, Canada covered some 56 per cent of her federal expenditures from current revenue, more than either the United States or the United Kingdom.

The great increase in personal income-tax burden in 1941 meant that discrepancies among the income-tax structures of different provinces caused serious inequities in the sacrifice made by persons of similar incomes. Accordingly, the Dominion negotiated an agreement with the provinces, valid for the duration of the war emergency, under which the provinces vacated the fields of personal and corporate income taxes, and received instead annual subsidies, equal either to the amounts actually collected from these taxes during the fiscal year ending nearest December 31, 1940, or to the amounts paid by the province for net debt service (less succession duty collections) during the same period. The Dominion also undertook to recompense the provinces for losses on gasolene taxes (and later on liquor taxes as well) resulting from Dominion rationing and similar restrictions.

The Dominion Government spent nearly $19,000,000,000 during the six fiscal years of the war, and, having covered only $10,600,000,000 with current revenues, had total deficits of some $8,400,000,000. Some $300,000,000 of old debt matured during the war, which was met by new borrowing. Moreover, cash requirements exceeded expenditures;[16] in all, the direct and guaranteed funded debt rose from $4,700,000,000 on March 31, 1940 (or, a year earlier, $4,400,000,000), to $14,600,000,000 at the end of the fiscal year 1945.

Over the same period, however, the average rate of interest on outstanding debt fell from 3.5 per cent to 2.6 per cent, and consequently the interest burden rose only from $115,000,000 (fiscal 1940) to $273,000,000 (fiscal 1945). As a percentage of national income the debt service rose only from 2.4 to 3.0 per cent; as a percentage of revenues it fell from 20.4 to 10.1 per cent.

In Canada the war-time reduction in interest rates depended much less on a change in debt structure than in the United States or the United Kingdom. Only some 25 per cent of the borrowing was in the form of short-term obligations (one year or less), as compared to 38 per cent in the United States and 53 per cent in the United Kingdom. Moreover, only 14 per cent of the increase in debt went to the central bank and only 17 per cent to the commercial banks, as compared to 9 per cent and 32 per cent in the United States. The United Kingdom was more successful in placing obligations outside the banking system, however: the central bank took only 7 per cent and the commercial banks only 15 per cent of thc war-time increase in debt.

Throughout the war the Bank of Canada followed a policy of providing the chartered banks with the cash necessary to maintain reserve ratios within the customary range of 9–12 per cent, while meeting all legitimate credit needs of private enterprise and at the same time lending to government whatever was required. The result was a growth of central-bank holdings of government securities from $163,000,000 in August, 1939, to $1,625,-000,000 in August, 1945. Over the same period, chartered bank portfolios of governments grew from $1,187,000,000 to $3,415,000,-000. At the latter date, government securities of Canadian banks constituted 52 per cent of total assets, compared to 58 per cent for American banks and 61 per cent for British banks.

The growth of bank holdings of government securities was accompanied by a small (11 per cent) increase in domestic loans, and consequently the volume of money increased substantially. The active circulation of notes increased from $207,000,000 to $966,000,000, deposits from $2,532,000,000 to $5,172,000,000. The total supply of money thus swelled by 116 per cent, which compares to 115 per cent in the United Kingdom and 165 per cent in the United States.

High taxes and war-loan campaigns were supplemented by a battery of direct controls. To stimulate, organize, and control war production, the Department of Munitions and Supply had powers to allocate strategic materials, to impose limitations on the use of other scarce materials, and to determine priority ratings. The allocation of man-power was controlled by the national selective service, in coöperation with the Inter-Departmental Committee on Labour Coördination. A War Emergency Training Programme was set up to provide additional skilled workers for war industries.

Regulation of both prices and supplies of civilian goods and services was administered by the War-Time Prices and Trade Board. Prior to November, 1941, price controls were selective, certain scarce commodities of particular importance in low-income budgets were subjected to price ceilings and rationing, but no over-all price ceiling seemed necessary so long as unemployment and excess capacity existed. The cost of living had risen only 8 per cent up to April, 1941, and the wholesale price level only 20 per cent. In the summer and autumn of 1941, however, prices began rising more sharply, and more comprehensive action was required to prevent general inflation. Accordingly, in December, 1941, a "Maximum Prices Regulation" fixed prices on a wide range of goods and services at the highest lawful price at which they had been sold in the four-week "basic period" (September 15 to October 11, 1941). Rentals were also fixed at their October 11, 1941, level.

Restrictions on consumer credit had been introduced shortly before the general price ceiling. A down payment of one-third of the purchase price was required for most durable goods, and payments had to be completed within six to fifteen months, including a minimum charge of 3/4 of 1 per cent per month on the total amount financed.

A general wage ceiling was introduced at the same time as the price ceiling. Employers were forbidden to reduce wages below the November 15, 1941, level, or to raise them without the permission of the National War Labour Board. The regulation made provision, however, for a cost-of-living bonus, amounting to the lesser of 25 cents a week, or 1 per cent of the weekly wage, for each 1-point rise in the official cost-of-living index. One such bonus was declared in July, 1942, and another in November, 1943. After that the bonus system was replaced by a "basic wage" incorporating bonuses granted up to that time, which was to remain fixed for the duration except in cases of "injustice."

The general price ceiling was supported by rationing, purchase limitations, and subsidies. Ration cards were issued for gasolene, sugar, tea, coffee, meat, butter, conserves, and certain canned goods. Liquor was rationed by provincial authorities. Purchases of automobiles, tires, radios, refrigerators, and other scarce consumer durables were subject to permit, and the production of such items was limited. Subsidies were paid through the Commodity Prices Stabilization Corporation, Limited, a Crown company under the direction of the War-Time Prices and Trade Board and responsible to the Minister of Finance. One of the first functions of the subsidy system was to offset the "squeeze" on wholesalers and manufacturers involved in imposing a simultaneous price ceiling at all stages of production and distribution, while retail prices lagged behind wholesale prices and wholesale prices lagged behind manufacturers' costs. In November, 1942, subsidies were used to reduce prices of milk, oranges, tea, and coffee, in order to lower the cost-of-living index and avoid a cost-of-living bonus to wage-earners at that time. Subsidies were also used to offset rising costs of imports.

The Canadian battle against war-time inflation must be accounted a success. The cost of living rose only 20 per cent during the war, less than in Australia, the United Kingdom, or the United States, and very much less than in Canada during the First World War. Wholesale prices rose 47 per cent, about the same as in the United States, but considerably less than in the United Kingdom or in Canada during the First World War. The post-war story is less happy: the cost of living rose over 30 per cent and wholesale prices over 60 per cent in the three years following the war; and some argue that tax reductions and the scrapping of direct controls in 1946 and 1947 have proved premature in the light of subsequent developments.

Control of foreign exchange was planned very early, as officials of the Canadian Government anticipated that war would bring a serious shortage of American dollars. The Foreign Exchange Control Board was established on September 15, 1939, with the

Governor of the Bank of Canada as its chairman, and the Bank as its technical adviser. By that time the Canadian dollar had depreciated about 10 per cent in New York, and the official rate of exchange for the duration of the war was established with a premium on the United States dollar of 10 per cent buying and 11 per cent selling.

The most difficult period for the Board was between mid-1940, when the United Kingdom ceased gold shipments as partial payment for the growing surplus of Canadian exports to Britain, and April, 1941, when the Hyde Park Declaration came into effect. As a result of the Declaration, war materials sent to Canada for manufacture into war supplies for Great Britain could be financed through Lend-Lease; and the American Government agreed to buy direct from Canada munitions, strategic materials, aluminium, and ships. Thus the Declaration diminished Canada's need for American dollars and at the same time increased their supply.

Canada gave to the United Kingdom and other United Nations a total of over $4,000,000,000 worth of Canadian goods and services to assist her Allies in the joint war effort. This figure includes an interest-free loan of $700,000,000 and a billion-dollar gift to Britain in March, 1942, and some $2,500,000,000 in Mutual Aid, U.N.R.R.A., and Military Relief from 1943 to 1945 inclusive. This assistance, which normally would have yielded foreign exchange convertible into American dollars, added considerably to Canada's own war-time dollar problem. However, deliveries to the United States under the Hyde Park Declaration, together with an unprecedentedly high net inflow of American dollars in capital account, yielded such a substantial flow of American dollars that Canada ended the war with a reserve of American dollars.

The Second World War accelerated the trend, already discernible in the inter-war period, for Canada to become an essentially manufacturing, rather than an essentially agricultural, country. According to the Department of Reconstruction, "in Canada, the most striking result of the war is the rapid expansion of productive capacity in the manufacturing industry."[17] In 1918, agriculture contributed 44 per cent of the total net value of

Canadian production; manufacturing, 33 per cent. When the Second World War began, agricultural production had already shrunk to 22 per cent of the total, while manufacturing had grown to 39 per cent. In 1943, well over half of the net value of Canadian production consisted of manufactured goods; agriculture, despite a 60 per cent increase in the value of agricultural production, accounted for only 20 per cent of the total.

The Canadian exports problem has been well stated by Homer S. Fox, the Commercial Attaché of the United States Embassy in Ottawa.

> Wartime industrialization has basically altered the Canadian economy. One of the world's great producers of foodstuffs and raw materials, Canada has now become a leading industrial nation as well. Many of the country's major postwar problems arise from and center on this fundamental change. . . . Prior to World War I . . . exports of raw materials were nearly double the total exports of fully or semi-manufactured goods. . . . By 1944, . . . exports of manufactures were nearly three times those of raw materials, although the latter were in turn three times the corresponding exports in 1930. . . . In addition to the great expansion of physical plant, there has been a large increase in the variety of articles manufactured and in the skill and industrial "know-how" of both management and labor.[18]

The redistribution of employment demonstrates the same phenomenon. Agriculture and construction were the only major fields of employment to suffer a war-time decline. From the beginning of the war to July, 1944, when industrial employment as a whole increased nearly 60 per cent, male agricultural employment fell about 20 per cent and construction employment about 12 per cent. The decline in construction can reasonably be interpreted as a temporary war-time phenomenon, but the decline in agricultural employment took place in the face of an enormous increase in agricultural production, based largely on an export demand that cannot be expected to continue indefinitely at its war-time level. The decline represented a long-delayed rationalization of agricultural production and a redistribution of population to meet the new structure of Canadian national income. Over 120,000 people left the Prairie Provinces for other parts of the country during the war.[19] It is also worthy of note that employment in primary industries exclusive of agriculture rose only 10 per cent during the war and fell from 10 per cent to 7.5 per cent of total employment.

The shift in employment from agriculture to manufacturing, while highly desirable in the light of the factors stressed above, means that Canada has become to an increasing degree a *competitor* of the United States and the United Kingdom in the manufacturing field. Britain has declared her intention of expanding exports at least 75 per cent above the pre-war level. The United States also seems to be counting on a continued high volume of industrial exports. It will therefore be necessary for Canada to discover specialized fields of manufacture where she has a relative advantage over *both* Britain and the United States, if high levels of exports are to be maintained.

A glance at a chart showing the course of any of the major economic quantities (income, employment, production, prices) during the first three post-war years reveals a striking fact: despite the greater degree of control exercised on the economy in the transition period, the usual post-war pattern of minor recession and inflationary primary post-war boom has been followed again; but because of more adequate controls, the amplitude of fluctuations has been very much less than is typical of post-war periods.

The disjointed cessation of hostilities, first in Europe and then in Asia three months later, and the recognition that V-E Day was in sight some months before it actually came, made the preliminary "recession" phase longer than usual. Employment in manufacturing began to decline later in 1944, before the war was actually over, and declined sharply throughout 1945. It expanded again during 1946 and early 1947, but remained well below the war-time peak. The fluctuation in manufacturing employment was partially offset by expansion in other fields, notably agriculture and services, including trade, finance, and transport. Total employment reached its peak at the end of 1944. Excluding the armed services, employment was at its recession low in October, 1945, at which time it was a bit over 10 per cent below the war-time peak. Demobilization was rapid, but was accompanied by withdrawals from the labour force.

As a consequence of this constellation of developments, recorded unemployment reached a peak of some 6 per cent of the labour force in the autumn of 1945. Total unemployment was presumably significantly higher, especially if "disguised" employment is included. During the summer months of 1946, unemployment fell rapidly, and by the end of the year essentially full employment had been restored. Unemployment increased again during the ensuing three months, but this increase was partly seasonal and partly the result of shortages arising out of wide-spread strikes. By June of 1947, "full" employment ruled once more, and prevailed to the date of writing.

Other indices show a similar pattern of post-war behaviour. Gross national income fell from $11,800,000,000 in 1944 to $11,400,000,000 in 1945, and $11,200,000,000 in 1946; but in 1947 gross national income was up to $13,375,000,000, and indications are that the 1948 figure will be considerably higher. The drop in total production during 1945 and 1946 was greater than these figures indicate, since prices, after a very slight decline following the cessation of hostilities, resumed their upward course in October, 1945, and rose faster during 1946 than at any time since 1941. Total production dropped about 17.5 per cent between 1944 and 1946. Similarly, the expansion of income in 1947 and 1948 is largely the result of accelerated post-war inflation; wholesale prices rose over 16 per cent in 1947, and 3.75 per cent in the first half of 1948.

There were marked disparities in the post-war developments of different regions. In the Maritime Provinces, employment followed a downward trend from the middle of 1943 to the middle of 1945, recovered considerably less during late 1945 and 1946 than in the country as a whole, and declined sharply in the first half of 1947. From V-J Day to March, 1946, unemployment increased much more in the Maritime Provinces than in any other region, and the improvement in the next few months was less than in any other region. In late 1946 and early 1947, unemployment in the Maritime Provinces rose close to the 1946 peak, while in all other regions the seasonal peak in 1947 was well below that of 1946. In the spring of 1947 the ratio of unemployment to employment in the major Maritime industrial centres was one and a half to fifteen times the national average. The inevitable post-war decline in ship-building, reduced harbour activity caused by the dwindling volume of foreign trade and the seasonal shift of shipping to Montreal, coal shortages owing to strikes, the relatively greater dependence of Maritime industry on war contracts, the reappearance of secular and structural problems temporarily alleviated by war-time demands, and a relatively low rate of current capital formation (which was partly a result of all the other factors) were among the reasons for the peculiarly acute employment problems of the Maritime Provinces.

In Quebec the course of employment and unemployment was very close to the national pattern. Industries where employment had been abnormally expanded by war-time orders, such as munitions, ship-building, and aluminium, suffered sharp post-war setbacks; but reduced employment in these industries was partially offset by expansion in consumer durables, construction and services of all kinds, together with sustained high levels of activity in textiles, iron and steel, chemicals with peace-time uses, and pulp and paper.

Ontario suffered less dislocation of employment during reconversion than the other three industrialized regions. Some of the smaller war-inflated centres, such as Fort William, Port Arthur, and Oshawa, experienced ratios of unemployment to employment two to five and a half times the national average, but the province as a whole suffered no greater (percentage) decline in employment or increase in unemployment than occurred in the national economy; and the province enjoyed a more rapid and more complete recovery from the mid-1945 trough than the country as a whole. High demand for consumer durable and capital goods, of which Ontario produces a greater share than any other region, accounts in large degree for the relatively favourable post-war economic history of the region.

The post-war employment pattern in the Prairie Provinces has been unique. Employment fell very slightly from the fall of 1944 to mid-1945, and expanded slowly but fairly steadily thereafter. Nevertheless, between V-J Day and March, 1946, unemployment increased about as much in percentage terms as in the national economy. In the major cities, where the few Prairie Province industries are mainly concentrated, the ratio of unemployment to employment was considerably lower than the national average;

unemployment apparently occurred mainly in agriculture. The combination of rising employment and simultaneously swelling unemployment suggests a substantial "back-to-the-farm" movement on the part of men and women demobilized from the armed forces and released from war industry.

British Columbia has undergone the most violent war and post-war fluctuations in employment of all regions. War-time industrialization was more rapid in British Columbia than in other regions, and since it consisted mainly of industries like ship-building and aircraft that were directly dependent on war-time demands, the post-war recession was particularly sharp. Unemployment however, did not increase very much more in percentage terms than in the country as a whole, indicating substantial withdrawals from the British Columbia labour force. The recovery in employment did not begin until the summer of 1946 in British Columbia, partly because of the reluctance or inability of former war-industry workers to move into mining, logging, fishing, and agriculture, where jobs were available. The recovery was rapid once it started, but was less complete than in the national economy.

The story of Canada's economic growth from Confederation to the First World War is primarily an account of geographic expansion, settlement of new territories, and discovery and exploitation of new natural resources. The story of Canadian economic development since 1913 is the story of a nation's approach to industrial maturity.

In the course of a single generation Canada has changed from a country producing and exporting mainly primary products to a country producing and exporting mainly manufactured goods. This development is the natural one for a country that starts its life with the great advantages of abundant resources and a small, vigorous population. Economic growth in such countries requires foreign capital to begin with, but, as high levels of income are reached, the nation is able to save enough to finance its own economic expansion and even, as with Canada, to become a net foreign lender as well.

The general course of Canadian economic development would probably have been much the same had there been no major wars in the twentieth century, but the changes would probably have been less rapid. The two world wars, far from distorting the Canadian economic structure, accelerated trends that were clearly discernible before each war began. They provided opportunities for profitable expansion of industrial plant and equipment by enlarging the world demand for industrial products while reducing some of the traditional sources of supply. Perhaps even more important, the opportunities for large-scale industrial production afforded to Canada by war revealed to Canadian workers and managers a highly-significant fact: given a market big enough to permit the use of the best large-scale production techniques, Canadian industry could compete successfully in many lines of manufacturing with any country in the world. Plant and equipment installed for war purposes tends to be used in peace-time; the two world wars helped to get Canada "over the hump" that any nation must climb if it is to overcome the handicaps of small size in industrial production and develop a highly-industrialized economy.

There is every reason to suppose that Canada's future will be one of continued industrialization. However, the pace of industrialization has been and will continue to be very uneven from one region to another. The income and employment of several vast regions will still depend mainly on the production and export of primary products in the foreseeable future. To be prosperous, Canada must produce and export increasing quantities of *both* primary and manufactured goods for many years to come.

Nor is the present dual nature of the Canadian economy the only problem arising out of Canada's approach to economic maturity. There are several factors that may make the maintenance of a high level of income and employment after the boom is over more difficult than it was before the First World War. In 1913 Canada had come to the end of a period of enormous expansion, based on opening up the West, and financed in large degree by foreign capital. The construction of railways and highways, new cities and towns, the provision of agricultural implements, and the other needs attendant on the development of a new frontier called for investment in huge quantities. During the 'twenties the last stages of this expansion of the West were completed; indeed, signs of retraction already appeared. During the 'thirties it became clear that Canada's western frontier had been over-extended in some respects. Wheat prices fell to 40 cents a bushel, farmers burned wheat for fuel, one-third of Saskatchewan's families were on relief. Instead of opening up new areas for cultivation, the governments of the Western Provinces made strenuous efforts to remove families from sub-marginal lands, in order that those lands might be reconverted to grass. During the first years of the Second World War the Government actually found it necessary to *support* the price of wheat.

In sharp contrast to developments in the First World War, wheat acreage, during the Second, was considerably reduced. On the other hand, acreage under coarse grain and flax was increased somewhat, and exports of bacon and beef were increased drastically. Perhaps some of these gains can be sustained; but as European live-stock is replenished and the food emergency in Europe disappears, it is doubtful whether present exports of Canadian meats can be maintained. There is little reason to hope that opportunities for agricultural expansion in the Canadian West will afford any sizable outlet for investment. But the possibilities of the Canadian North and Arctic must not be left out of consideration in any forecast of future development. Little more has been done than to scratch the surface of the region, but it has already had a far-reaching effect on the economy of the country.

The decline in the rate of population growth has contributed to the difficulty of finding profitable outlets for private investment in Canada. The population is no longer growing as fast as it did before the First World War. The natural rate of increase has been cut nearly in half since 1921. Canadian cities, which grew over sixfold between 1871 and 1921—more than doubling every twenty years—grew only 12.2 per cent during the 'thirties. There were 601 urban communities in which the population actually declined during that decade. Consequently, private investment in housing, transportation, and public utilities, formerly based in large measure on the prospect of a growing population, will be less attractive after war deficiencies have been met than it was during the period of rapid population growth. The declining rate of population growth is reflected in the fact that only in the last two years of the boom of the 'twenties, and at no time during the 'thirties, did the value of building permits and construction contracts reach the level of 1912.

Besides these problems arising out of a changing economic structure, Canada, like most other countries in the world, faces a chronic shortage of American dollars. Her balance of payments is dominated by the large import surplus from the United States and the large export surplus to the United Kingdom. Before the Second World War Canada used her sterling surplus to offset her dollar shortage. Now that sterling is not convertible into dollars, Canada has great difficulty in obtaining enough American dollars to pay for all the things that Canadian households and firms would like to buy from the United States. As a result, it has been necessary to retain control of foreign exchange, to restrict capital movements and travel in the United States, and to limit imports of certain classes of American goods.

For maintaining high and stable employment in the long run, Canada has four main requirements: encouragement of exports, stabilization of consumption at a high and rising level, stabilization of private investment, and public investment to accelerate national development and to offset fluctuations in private investment.

A minimum volume of exports of one-half the war-time peak, or 15 per cent higher (60 per cent by value) than pre-war, has been suggested as an aim arising from "an expansion of total world trade, within which other countries as well as Canada can increase their exports,"[20] and dependent to some extent on the reduction and removal of barriers to world trade. Imports as well as exports should rise as the Canadian economy expands. Nevertheless, for some years at least, Canada might occupy the position of a creditor nation. The Export Credits Insurance Corporation was established in August, 1944, to provide the export trade with protection against contingencies that cannot be considered ordinary business risks, including war or revolution in the country of the foreign importer, blocking of funds or transfer difficulties, protracted default in payment by the foreign importer, or total insolvency of the foreign importer. The Corporation is not designed to protect

Canadian exporters or financial institutions against the usual risks of competition.

Social-security measures designed to maintain consumer incomes should help to stabilize consumption. Among these are unemployment insurance, family allowances, pensions and other assistance to war veterans, and farm floor prices. Old-age pensions have been paid since 1927 to British subjects aged seventy or over. At the Dominion-Provincial Conference in 1945, the Dominion Government proposed a federally financed national old-age pension plan, to provide $30 a month for persons aged seventy and over, plus a Dominion-provincial old-age assistance plan for persons aged sixty-five to sixty-nine. A national public health insurance scheme, financed mainly by the Dominion and administered mainly by the provinces, was also proposed. Unemployment insurance was introduced in 1941, and in 1945 the Dominion proposed a broadening of the coverage and a prolongation of benefits. The Family Allowance Act of 1945 provides monthly payments to lower-income families in respect of children up to sixteen years of age.

Special assistance is provided for private investment in housing under the National Housing Act of 1944. The Government contributes 25 per cent of mortgage loans to owner-occupiers or builders of rental projects. The Government's share is provided at 3 per cent, the share of the private lending institution is provided at 5 per cent, making the effective rate to borrowers 4.5 per cent. The Government will also lend at 3 per cent interest to private limited-dividend corporations (with dividends limited to 5 per cent) to cover up to 90 per cent of the lending-value of low-rental projects. These loans are amortized over fifty years. Insurance companies have been authorized to make direct investment in housing projects, and to borrow from the Government on the same terms as limited-dividend corporations, but are guaranteed a minimum return of 2.5 per cent and are not limited to 5 per cent dividends. The Government also undertakes to cover half of the loss borne by a municipality in buying slum areas and reselling them to limited-dividend corporations for low-rental projects. Under a 1946 amendment, the Central Mortgage and

Housing Corporation, which administers the Housing Act, was authorized to make direct loans to purchasers of houses, but little use has been made of this power.

To stimulate private investment, taxes on business profits were reduced after the war, and special depreciation allowances granted for tax purposes to firms converting war plants to peace-time uses. To assist the financing of private investment, the Government established the Industrial Development Bank in August, 1944. The Bank was designed to meet needs for medium and long-term credit of a kind not ordinarily provided by the chartered banks or other lending institutions. Its purpose was not to salvage shaky firms, but to assist sound industrial enterprises unable to obtain their requirements from other sources on reasonable terms and conditions.

The Dominion Government's proposals to the Dominion-Provincial Conference on Reconstruction emphasized the need for community planning to help provide a "shelf" of soundly-planned projects for a time when prospective employment conditions suggest a need for increased public investment expenditures. Undertakings to develop national resources, to add to capital equipment, and to raise conditions of living should increase employment during slack periods in private industry. Grants were offered to the provinces for planning public investment, and further grants to assist in their execution if it was timed in accordance with national policy to combat inflation and unemployment. The full instrumentation of these and of social-security proposals is still awaited in a new Dominion-provincial financial agreement.

The disappearance of Canada's reserves of American dollars during 1947 and the growing passive balance of payments with the United States necessitated new measures to conserve dollar exchange early in 1948. Exchange control had, of course, been retained throughout the transition period; but after January, 1948, restrictions on travel in the United States and on capital transfers, which had been relaxed somewhat, were tightened again. In addition, imports of certain commodities from the United States were restricted by outright prohibition, quotas, or taxes. The commodities selected for restriction were of a sort that could ultimately be produced in greater quantities in Canada, or for which sources outside the United States could be developed. It would appear, therefore, that Canada has embarked on a long-range programme of industrial and trade development that would make the Canadian economy less directly dependent upon imports from the United States. As this chapter has indicated, such a development is quite consistent with the whole trend of Canadian economic development since 1913, which has been one of increasing industrial maturity.

Part Four

POLITICAL AND CONSTITUTIONAL SCENE

CHAPTER XI

The Federal Constitution

BY R. MACGREGOR DAWSON

THE CONSTITUTION and government of Canada, which had a corporate beginning in 1867, combined for the first time in history the Cabinet system with a form of federalism. Responsible, or Cabinet, government was a continuation of an earlier inheritance from England; federalism was an adaptation of what had been practised in the United States for approximately eighty years. This double influence has never ceased to operate upon Canadian government, and it has been clearly displayed in the general forms which the constitution, using the term in its broadest sense, has assumed. Thus, while a substantial part of the constitution is contained in the pages of a written document, the British North America Act, there is another part, no less extensive and, if anything, more important, which appears in various guises and is often no less intangible and elusive than its English parent. Any understanding of the constitution of Canada must therefore begin with some appreciation of its nature, its diversity, and its inherent complexity.

The British North America Act had as its primary purpose the creation of a federation and the allotment of powers to a central or Dominion Government on the one hand and to component provincial governments on the other. It also set forth in incomplete detail some of the branches of the Dominion Government and provided in general terms for their operation. Finally, the Act broke up the former Province of Canada into the two new provinces of Ontario and Quebec, and equipped them with a temporary constitution which they were free to alter after their governments had become established. It does not, however, pretend to be a comprehensive document such as, for example, the constitution of the United States, and a literal-minded student attempting to learn about Canadian government by nothing more than a conscientious examination of the Act would be shocked to find that the Dominion is ruled as follows:

The executive government and authority of Canada is vested in the Sovereign, who is apparently represented by a Governor General (secs. 9, 10). The latter is assisted by a Council, which he chooses, and summons, and removes (11), and which advises him in his work (12, 13). The Sovereign is Commander-in-Chief of all naval and military forces in Canada (15). The Governor General appoints the Speaker of the Senate (34) and virtually all the judges (96). He appoints all the members of one house of the federal legislature (24), and these members hold office for life (29). The other legislative body, the House of Commons, is called together by the Governor (38); this house can be dissolved by him at any time and a new election ordered (50). All money bills must first be recommended by the Governor before they can be passed by Parliament (54). The Governor may assent to legislation; he may refuse his assent; or he may reserve a bill for the consideration of the King-in-Council in Great Britain (55–57); he may also disallow any provincial act or refuse his assent to any provincial bill reserved for the signification of his pleasure (55–57, 90). The same general powers are exercisable by the provincial lieutenant-governors, who are appointed by the Governor General and are accountable to him (58, 59, 90).

Canada would thus appear to suffer from a dictatorship, the autocratic rule of one central figure, the Governor General, acting in place of the Sovereign, who governs the Dominion with little reference to or control by the people. The only popular element is apparently supplied by a House of Commons, which meets when the Governor desires, considers financial legislation which he recommends, and can be forced into an election whenever he deems it desirable. While it is true that by the Act the Governor is advised by his Council, the exercise of the foregoing powers is vested in him alone. Such was substantially the nature of the executive government before 1848; today not one of these statements is literally and completely true. The garments are those of a hundred years ago, but the constitution is a living thing and can be understood only by a study of the changes which have accompanied the growth of responsible government. Most of these changes are found in the unwritten provisions of the constitution.

Today there is virtually no question on which the Governor General acts according to his own judgement or on his own responsibility. He acts on the advice, not of the entire Council mentioned in the British North America Act, but of a part of it, and a part chosen in such a way as to tie it into the very fabric of the House of Commons. This part of the Council is the Cabinet, a body never mentioned in the Act. It is chosen not by the Governor but by the Prime Minister, the leader of the party or (rarely) of the coalition commanding a majority in the House of Commons. The Prime Minister is the most important political figure in Canada, yet he does not appear in any part of the written constitution. The Prime Minister and his Cabinet must always have the support of the House of Commons; and all members of the Cabinet, including the Prime Minister, must have seats in that body or in the Senate. Most of the Cabinet members are also heads of executive departments, for the work of which they are severally (and jointly also) responsible to the House of Commons.

Since senators are appointed by the Governor on the recommendation of the Cabinet, a party coming into power after a prolonged term in opposition will probably not be able immediately to command a majority in the Senate. The powers of the latter body, however, are delaying rather than final, and the final legislative authority resides in the elected House.

Custom or constitutional usage is thus an indispensable part of the Canadian constitution; it is dominant in some fields, and its operation may substantially modify the meaning of some of the explicit written provisions. This is in the best English tradition, and similar practices may be found in other parts of the British Commonwealth. While such reliance on custom may give a potential elasticity to the constitution, this does not necessarily follow, for a fundamental principle such as the parliamentary responsibility of the Cabinet is as rigid and unchangeable in fact as any clause in the written constitution.

There was a time in Canadian history when any British statutes, if they so stated, would apply to Canada and would override any Canadian enactments. Such statutes have been rare, however, since the passage of the British North America Act by the British Parliament in 1867, and their passage or continuance, except at the desire of the Canadian Parliament, legally ceased with the enactment of the Statute of Westminster by the British Parliament in 1931. The British North America Act is an exception to this rule, and it is still amendable only by the British Parliament, pending the adoption of some satisfactory method for amendment in Canada. An occasional statute applicable to the Dominion may still be passed at Canada's own request, sometimes in association with other parliaments in the Commonwealth, as, for example, the Declaration of Abdication Act, 1936. Closely related to these British statutes are a few British orders-in-council which also remain a part of the Canadian constitution, most notably those passed many years ago to admit certain provinces to the federation.

Another and much more extensive section of the constitution is composed of statutes enacted by the Canadian Parliament. These naturally cover a wide field, from the creation of courts to the conditions of admission to the Civil Service; from the franchise to the establishment of government departments; from the salaries of public officials to grants made to provincial governments. Nor can the provincial statutes be ignored, for they comprise the greater part of the provincial constitutions and are limited only by the controlling terms of the British North America Act. Dominion and provincial orders-in-council, authorized by the statutes of their respective legislatures, present further material of a constitutional nature.

The decisions of the courts, which interpret both the British North America Act and all ordinary statutes, form no inconsiderable part of the unwritten constitution. For in Canada, as in the United States, this function of the judiciary involves not only the right to give greater precision to the terms of a statute but also the power to set aside all legislative and executive acts which go beyond the legal grant of power, and particularly the grants contained in the British North America Act. The importance of this function is naturally greatly enhanced by the federal nature of the constitution, for the courts hold the balance on all questions of disputed jurisdiction between the Dominion and the provinces.

There thus emerges a hierarchy of legislative powers and corresponding strata of laws, each of those at the lower levels being subordinate to and deriving its authority from the one above. While the Dominion and provincial legislatures thus exercise coördinate authority under the terms of the British North America Act, the courts will see that they keep within the scope of the authority so delegated, and will set aside any laws which they consider to be *ultra vires* or beyond the powers of the enacting legislature. Similarly, orders-in-council of the Dominion and provincial governments must be legally authorized by Dominion and provincial statutes, respectively, and a minor legislative body, such as one exercising jurisdiction over a municipal area, must be able to demonstrate that its powers have been legally delegated by a proper authority under the British North America Act. In this sense the Act, like the constitution of the United States, is quite literally "the supreme law of the land" and the duty of the courts is to interpret its terms and maintain that supremacy.

Even so, the written constitution in Canada and the judiciary who interpret it have not acquired the same dominating position as in the United States, for the British North America Act contains no comprehensive "bill of rights" clauses on the American model. Special constitutional protection, it is true, is accorded to the use of the English and French languages in the Dominion and in Quebec, and special safeguards have been accorded to sectarian education; but the rights of freedom of speech, freedom of assembly, trial by jury, and similar liberties of the citizen depend not upon the written constitution but on statute and on the common law. This protection has, on the whole, been adequate; although in recent years there has been a growing feeling—aroused in the main by occasional provincial excesses—that some special constitutional guaranties would add materially to the security of a number of these rights.

The enumeration of the diverse elements which comprise the Canadian constitution is still not complete. To the statutory law and its judicial interpretation must be added substantial sections of the common law, which was transplanted from England over two hundred years ago and has been thriving ever since in its new environment.[1] To the constitutional usages or conventions must also be added a supplementary section of general ideas and principles of democratic government which are commonly held and which merge with those conventions and are frequently found to be inseparable from them. The privileges of Parliament and its precedents, rules, and procedure form another section which is confined within a fairly narrow but far from unimportant field.

The extent and nature of constitutional change and adaptability are in large measure determined by the nature of each of these manifestations, and the manner of their growth is, on the whole, fairly obvious. One of these, however, the amendment of the written constitution, needs a few words of explanation.

Formal amendment of the British North America Act is carried out by the British Parliament, although such action will be taken (according to long-established custom and the terms of the Statute of Westminster) only at the request of the Parliament of Canada. Strangely enough, the conditions under which Canada will make this request are not entirely clear. At times the theory has been advanced that all the provinces must indicate their acceptance of a proposed amendment before the Canadian Parliament can properly approach Great Britain in such a matter. While this theory has no legal foundation and can produce only the most slender justification in past practice, assuredly no Dominion Parliament would feel morally free to initiate amendments to certain parts of the written constitution without first securing at least a measure of provincial agreement. In this class would be placed such amendments as those dealing with a transfer of provincial powers or, most important of all, any which affected the special position of the French and English languages. One positive statement on this matter can be made, however, without reservation of any kind. The only barrier to the acquisition by Canada of complete control over the amendment of its own written constitution is the inability thus far of the Canadian people to draft a method of amendment on which they will be in general agree-

[1] For notes to chapter xi see pages 577–578.

ment. Once that is done, the British Parliament will speedily insert the amending clause in the Act and relinquish with relief the purely nominal functions which it is now compelled to discharge. Even the present situation, anomalous as it is, does not in fact, therefore, impair the actual sovereignty of the Canadian people.[2]

The Canadian constitution is based unmistakably on the British idea of a union or identification of the executive and the legislative powers, or, more specifically, of the Cabinet and the House of Commons.[3] All members of the Cabinet, according to a convention of the constitution, must have seats in Parliament, and all but one of them (by a further convention) must have seats in the House of Commons. The Cabinet, under the leadership of the Prime Minister, directs the business of the Commons; it introduces the greater part of the legislation; it has complete responsibility for the initiation of taxes and the recommending of expenditures. It is, however, always responsible to the Commons, which may at any time call it to account. The moment it loses the confidence of the Commons, it must resign or advise the Governor General to dissolve Parliament and hold a general election: that is, the House must get a new Cabinet in which it has confidence, or the Cabinet must find a new House which will give it support. The fundamental sympathy between the Cabinet and the House of Commons is therefore an indispensable condition of the entire system.[4]

The same sympathy does not, however, exist between the judiciary and the executive or the legislature; indeed, especial care is taken to ensure that the judiciary will be protected against any untoward influence from either of the other branches of government. This assurance against interference is provided in some degree by the terms of the British North America Act, but it receives powerful reinforcement by statute and constitutional custom and procedure. Although this is superficially in accord with the idea of division or separation of powers which characterizes the constitution of the United States, it is actually the British tradition which is dominant. Despite the British doctrine of parliamentary sovereignty, the courts in that country have been rendered virtually independent through a long-established abdication of controls by the executive and legislative branches, and the Canadian practice stems historically from this source. Thus, while the weight of Canadian government unmistakably favours the idea of union of powers, this must be read as subject to one very important exception in the statutory and conventional independence accorded to the judiciary.

Although the essential principles of Cabinet, or responsible, government are found in the customary practices of the constitution, the federal structure of Canadian government rests on the express legal terms of the British North America Act as interpreted by the courts. This structure, however, presents certain novel features which depart in some measure from federalism in its most orthodox manifestation. The provinces, while broadly equal in status and powers, are not identical in all these respects. Thus at one time they did not all own the natural resources within their borders; their representation in the Senate has never been the same;[5] the Dominion has often made separate and unequal financial arrangements with different provinces; and the French language enjoys a preferred position in Quebec which it possesses nowhere else except, in certain respects, in the Dominion Government itself.

Nor do the provinces have complete control over their own governments. The Lieutenant-Governor in each province is appointed, instructed, and, if necessary, removed by the Dominion Cabinet. The Dominion Cabinet also has the power to disallow or nullify any provincial statute within a year, although it has used such power sparingly. Aside from these and one or two other minor peculiarities, the provinces are equal and autonomous, and in general exercise their powers independently of the Dominion Cabinet and Parliament.

The distribution of powers between the Dominion and the provinces is, of course, the dominant feature of the federation. It is on the surface fairly simple, but in actual application and interpretation it has proved to be extremely complicated. As in most federations, the primary purpose was to grant to the central government jurisdiction over all subjects of general or common interest, while giving to the provincial governments jurisdiction over all matters of local or particular interest. There was, however, a decided tendency in 1867 to strengthen the hands of the Dominion authorities at provincial expense—a lesson which the founders of the federation drew from experience in the United States. The American difficulties which by 1861 had culminated in the Civil War were, in the opinion of Canadian observers, directly traceable to the excessive emphasis which had been placed in that country upon the powers and importance of the states. Canada, it was thought, could avoid a similar catastrophe by departing somewhat from orthodox federalism and by weighting the distribution of powers heavily in favour of the central government.

The Dominion Parliament was therefore given a general power to enact laws "for the peace, order, and good government of Canada" in relation to all matters not assigned exclusively to the legislatures of the provinces under the British North America Act. As examples of this comprehensive grant, twenty-nine specific powers were listed. These specific powers (together with one or two others which occur elsewhere in the Act) included public debt, the raising of money "by any mode or system of taxation," borrowing money, regulation of trade and commerce, navigation and shipping, banks and banking, patents, copyrights, defence, criminal law, railways, canals, telegraphs, and postal services.

The provincial legislatures for their part were given jurisdiction over a modest list of specific subjects which included the amendment of the provincial constitution[6] (except for the office of Lieutenant-Governor); borrowing money on provincial credit; direct taxes; hospitals and asylums; administration of justice in the province, including the constitution, maintenance, and organization of provincial courts; municipal government; property and civil rights; and certain other subjects, including "generally all matters of a merely local or private nature in the province."

Concurrent power was to be exercised in relation to two topics—immigration and agriculture. Either the Dominion or the province or both could legislate in these fields; in the event of a conflict, the law of the Dominion would override that of the province to the extent of the conflict.

Education received special consideration. It was given explicitly to the provinces, but subject to the limitation that each province was bound to respect any legal rights in denominational schools possessed by any class of persons at the time of union. If a province did not observe this guaranty, the sectarian minority could appeal to the Dominion; and the Dominion Parliament was empowered to enact legislation to enforce the provisions of this section of the Act.

These were the chief provisions whereby the Act endeavoured to distribute power between the central and the provincial authorities. A few of their complexities will be outlined to give a more accurate idea of the situation and to indicate the vital function discharged by the courts as interpreters of the text of the British North America Act.

In the first place, some apparent contradictions occur in the distribution of powers. Property and civil rights are entrusted to the provinces, but banking, patents, copyrights, and other matters which would normally come under property and civil rights are given to the Dominion. This difficulty has not proved to be serious, for particular enumerations are taken as exceptions to the general; the provinces thus have jurisdiction over property and civil rights, except banking, patents, and so on. The provincial power to impose direct taxes has not been considered, however, to limit the Dominion power to raise money by "any mode or system of taxation," and both authorities, therefore, may impose direct taxes. A direct tax has been interpreted according to nineteenth-century terminology as that which is "demanded from the very persons who it is intended or desired should pay it"—a definition which is impossible to apply with accuracy.

Secondly, the courts have held that on many topics only the particular circumstances—the object and scope of the legislation—will determine where jurisdiction lies. This is known as the "aspect" doctrine: subjects which "in one aspect and for one purpose" may come under Dominion control may in another aspect and for another purpose come under the province. A province may thus be allowed to legislate on one aspect of a certain subject because it relates to property and civil rights, and the Dominion may legislate on a different aspect of the same subject under its power to enact the criminal law. Jurisdiction over certain labour questions, the control and sale of liquor, the regulation of insurance companies, the marketing of natural products, has in this way been split between Dominion and province. Effective legislation and administration in such fields are thus extremely difficult.

The most troublesome question by far, however, has been the interpretation placed by the courts on the residual power. The Dominion Parliament was given the power to legislate "for the peace, order, and good government of Canada" (that is, a general legislative power) on all matters not given by the Act exclusively to the provincial legislatures; the topics which were enumerated as belonging to the Dominion were stated as examples of this general grant—"for greater certainty, but not so as to restrict the generality of the foregoing terms of this section." The residual power was thus clearly vested in the Dominion, with a list of specific illustrative powers added for the sake of clarity. But the courts in interpreting the Act split the grant to the Dominion into two parts: the twenty-nine enumerated powers and the general power to enact laws for the general welfare of Canada. The specific powers of the Dominion were held to override any of the provincial powers, and the provincial powers were held to override the general power of the Dominion.

The latter interpretation would not, perhaps, have been very serious had one of the provincial powers not been "property and civil rights," a comprehensive heading which would be affected incidentally by almost any legislation which the Dominion might try to enact under the "peace, order, and good government" clause. The result has been that "property and civil rights" has covered virtually all the unallotted territory, and the provinces have thereby come to exercise in effect the residual power.

One use, however, was found for the "peace, order, and good government" clause: the courts decided that in it lurked an emergency power which the Dominion could assert in times of grave national peril. On such rare occasions, peace, order, and good government would override any of the explicit provincial powers. It was under this authority, for example, that the Dominion was able to exercise almost complete power during and after the two world wars.

The results which have flowed from this restricted interpretation of the residual power have been far-reaching. Most of the more "modern" powers of government were not mentioned in explicit terms in the British North America Act, and they might easily have been given to the Dominion under the "peace, order, and good government" clause. Following the interpretation given above, they have for the most part, irrespective of their national significance, been given to the provinces under "property and civil rights." The regulation of trade and marketing within the province, workmen's compensation, industrial disputes, trade-union legislation, hours of labour, wages, unemployment insurance, health regulations, and other topics have been declared to be under provincial control. The Dominion has thus been severely crippled in any endeavour to deal with many of the problems presented by modern industrial and economic conditions, and it has been the provincial powers which have proved to be elastic and adaptable. It must, however, be confessed that the majority of the Canadian people are apparently in sympathy with this strengthening of the provincial government, and in only one instance—unemployment insurance—has the constitution been amended so as to permit the Dominion to take jurisdiction over what has been a provincial topic.

A further consequence of this accretion of provincial powers has been a correspondingly tremendous drain on provincial finances. At the time of Confederation the provinces yielded to the Dominion by far the greater part of their revenue; for approximately 83 per cent of the income of all provinces had been derived from customs and excise taxes, both of which were passed over to the Dominion under the new constitutional arrangements. The Dominion assumed, of course, a substantial number of the functions which had hitherto been paid for by the federating provinces, including those which were considered likely to prove the most costly in the future. The provincial loss in revenue was nevertheless far greater than the relief derived from the shifting of expenditures, and it was not expected that the provincial budgets would balance without substantial Dominion assistance.

The Confederation agreement therefore gave to the provinces three major sources of revenue: (1) Fees, royalties, permits, Crown lands, and small services performed by the province. (2) Direct taxes. These were not considered to be very productive, and were looked upon as a reserve which the province might use when necessary. (3) Annual grants or subsidies paid by the Dominion. Some of these payments depended on the size of the provincial debts which the Dominion had absorbed at Confederation; others varied with the estimated cost of the provincial governments; some were adjusted to anticipated provincial revenues and other local factors; and one—the most important—took the form of a per capita grant to each province. These payments have since been adjusted and readjusted many times in response to provincial agitation, and in recent years have been augmented by conditional subsidies or grants-in-aid made by the Dominion for specific purposes, usually on the condition that a province must meet the grant with another and, as a rule, equal contribution devoted to the same purpose.

The outstanding characteristic of all these financial arrangements is that they have never been static, and there has always been severe pressure from one province or another to induce the Dominion to increase the payments. These agitations have been caused mainly by an inability of some of the provinces to balance their budgets; and while in earlier years this inability may have been brought about by extravagance, it has occurred more recently through the operation of forces over which the provinces have had little control. This shortage of funds has long since turned the nominal power to levy direct taxes into a very real one, and these taxes have been of such dimensions that they have yielded substantial revenues. They have, indeed, been so productive that the Dominion (which, it will be recalled, may exercise unlimited powers of taxation) has also entered the field, and by the levying of sales-taxes, income taxes, and, most recently, succession duties has severely lessened the provincial capacity to raise revenue from these sources.

The underlying cause of recent financial difficulties in the provinces has been the inability of provincial revenues to defray the cost of provincial functions, a fundamental lack of equilibrium between different aspects of the constitutional distribution of powers. The original functions of the provinces under the British North America Act have become enormously enlarged, and to these have been added many new functions which have been made necessary by a changing economy and a changing conception of the function of the state. A provincial load, which had been steadily growing more onerous, was made virtually insupportable by court decisions which extended provincial jurisdiction under the broad interpretation of "property and civil rights." Thus, while all the provinces in 1874 spent $4,000,000 a year on education and public welfare, provincial expenditure on these subjects by 1937 had multiplied over sixty times and was approximately $250,000,000 a year.[7]

A situation already difficult has been complicated by the fact that, owing to economic differences, the provinces have not been equally embarrassed by this financial stringency. The gap between the economically fortunate and those which are less fortunate is indeed wide. The wealthier provinces (Ontario, Quebec, and British Columbia) have been able both to take on new duties and to enlarge the old without serious inconvenience; but the remainder (and even here, some far more than others) have proved unable to make ends meet, and the activity of their governments had to be carried on under lower standards and at a lower level of efficiency. The world depression of the 1930's thus found most of the provinces in an extremely vulnerable financial position, rendered more precarious in the Prairie Provinces by a succession of crop failures. To cope with unemployment problems, the Dominion was forced to give some assistance to all provinces, with more substantial contributions to those most heavily afflicted. The depression emphasized what had already become evident: if the Confederation was to function effectively under modern conditions, constitutional revision on a fairly radical scale would have to be undertaken in the immediate future.

This process of revision, which had its beginnings in 1937, was still in progress ten years later. In 1937 the Rowell-Sirois Commission was appointed by the Dominion Government to investigate the economic and financial basis of Confederation, the distribution of federal and provincial powers, and the financial relations of these governments. The report of the Commission was focused mainly on the two chief problems mentioned above—the position of the provinces in relation to the Dominion and the difficulties raised by the economic inequalities of the provinces.

It suggested, for the first, a transfer of certain functions accompanied by a transfer of taxing powers; and for the second, special payments by the Dominion to the more needy provinces which would enable them to maintain certain basic services at what was considered to be a minimum level for the entire Dominion.

The report was presented after war had broken out. When it was rejected by some of the provinces at a special Dominion-provincial conference, further consideration was temporarily shelved. Forced by the necessities of war to take decisive action in order to utilize the nation's resources to the best advantage, the Dominion made temporary financial arrangements with the provinces and launched a number of its own measures which gave effect to several of the Rowell-Sirois recommendations. These were primarily for the duration of the emergency; but there is no doubt that the more extensive powers exercised by the Dominion during the war convinced the Government of the desirability of a much greater measure of centralized control than had been contemplated before the war. With this end in view, the Dominion brought forward new proposals soon after the cessation of hostilities; but prolonged consideration at another Dominion-provincial conference failed to bring about general agreement.

In 1946–1947 the Dominion made fresh overtures to the provinces along substantially the same lines; but these proposals were to run for a trial five-year period (instead of three, as previously suggested) and could be accepted by the provinces individually. The offer involved a large annual Dominion grant on a per capita basis in exchange for the relinquishment by a province of its corporation taxes, income taxes, and succession duties; to this was added the promise of increased Dominion activity in assisting certain social services and promoting economic development in the province. While the basis of the annual payments was not the same for all provinces, the difference did not rest on "provincial need," but represented rather the best bargain which both contracting parties were able to obtain at the time of negotiation. The many problems associated with provincial economic inequality are therefore not adequately met by these proposals. By the end of 1949, seven provinces had accepted the terms of the Dominion Government; but the two largest and wealthiest provinces, Ontario and Quebec, still remained aloof. Newfoundland, because of its recent accession to the federation, has not yet made its agreement with the Dominion, although such action was expected within a short time.

The solution of the vexed Dominion-provincial problem is thus still unknown; it will doubtless be determined by the experience of the trial five-year period as tempered by the unpredictable attitude of the provinces of Ontario and Quebec. In short, Dominion-provincial relations, which have never been settled or tranquil, are at present passing through a transitional stage with the lines of final settlement still indistinct and uncertain.

CHAPTER XII

The Machinery of Government

BY HUGH MCD. CLOKIE

THE CANADIAN POLITY presents several distinctive facets according to the point of view from which it is regarded. Considered as an American country, Canada is unique in being a monarchy among republics, in possessing Cabinet government on a continent where separated powers or presidential domination prevail, and in retaining a close association with a non-American imperial power. On the other hand, as representative of the British tradition, Canada is noteworthy for her special application of the American principle of federalism, for leadership in developing autonomous status within the British Commonwealth, and for her long-continued, peaceful coöperation with the United States. Then, too, considered as a member of the world's community of states, Canada displays an interesting dualism of nature—internally by virtue of her bi-national culture, and externally through concurrent membership in the United Nations and in the British Commonwealth of Nations.

These various aspects of the Canadian political scene indicate some of the great constitutional problems that spring from the country's background. From the earliest days the rulers of Canada have been forced to wrestle with the complex consequences of British heritage, mixed population, and American environment. Indeed, a superficial glance at Canadian institutions might tempt one to conclude that the result is more of a disordered medley of inherited and borrowed devices than a coherent and intelligible system. But, despite appearances, the existing institutions—whether inherited, borrowed, or improvised—are actually woven into an orderly pattern, intelligible enough to those familiar with the elementary assumptions and understandings of British constitutionalism. Basically, the Canadian constitution is founded on British principles, which make possible the combination of monarchical forms with democratic practices, provide for the dominance of the popular chamber in a bicameral legislature, ensure the control of administration by leaders of the parliamentary majority, protect the independence of the judiciary, and permit some degree of permanence or professionalism in the Civil Service. On closer examination it will be found that, although incongruities exist in form and appearance, they are primarily of an illusory nature.

When one penetrates the surface of the constitutional system, the most striking characteristic will be found to be its adaptability. For eighty years or more the major institutions and organic processes have remained relatively unchanged, save for numerical enlargements. Yet during this period Canada has been extended westward to the Pacific and northward to the Arctic. Canadian status has been revolutionized by emergence from colonial dependence on Britain to independent statehood with little more than a shift in emphasis and in the functioning of the formal organs. Likewise, the transformation of the economy from a fairly primitive reliance on one or two staple raw materials to large-scale agricultural and industrial production has proceeded with slight disturbance of the normal political processes.

It is true, of course, that through these years the spread of democratic concepts has given new meaning and significance to some aspects of the constitutional system; but the nature of the party system, the operating mechanism, has remained essentially what it was shortly after Confederation. Despite fluctuations of fortune, the same two political parties have dominated the political scene since 1867 and have together retained the allegiance of the greater proportion of the electors. The two parties have had fewer than a score of leaders between them, and their hold on the public is indicated by the fact that there have been but twelve prime ministers (eight Conservative and four Liberal), and that the terms of office of four of these ministers totalled about three-fourths of the whole period.

The stability of the country's institutions and politics indicates the exceptional conservatism of the Canadian people. This conservatism has sometimes been attributed to the long years of submissive colonialism or to the emigration of the more aggressive pioneers, but other influences are probably more decisive. Indeed, in constitutional durability Canada displays no greater conservatism than Britain or the United States; if in policy and politics she is less inclined to innovation than Britain, she is certainly more radical than her neighbour to the south. There are, however, two factors that impose serious restraint on change: the racial complexity of the populace and the regional structure of the economy. Any serious or sudden change in policy or organization is likely to be viewed with alarm by some important cultural or regional group, so that Canadians are conservative by necessity rather than by innate disposition. There is little constitutional idolatry, for a consciousness of historical continuity prevents the obvious enthusiasm that Americans profess for their constitution as an ancient revelation. The work of the Fathers of Confederation is not revered by Canadians as the culmination of political wisdom; it is admired as a statesmanlike approach to the problems of the day; it is clung to, in default of any better, for its continuing utility; and it is appreciated most for its capacity for extensive growth and adjustment under almost revolutionary circumstances. At the same time, its deficiencies and inadequacies are only too well understood.

Canada, it is often said somewhat apologetically, is a difficult country to govern. The statement is probably true of every country. In Canada, however, it means that the attempt to govern democratically, that is, by popular consent, necessarily carries with it the recognition that the central government should not unduly disturb the accepted conditions of life in the various parts of the country, and, when changes have to be made, that they should be distributed over the whole community so as not to fall with undue severity upon, or with discrimination against, any particular section, group, or set of interests. This is but the essential conservatism of democratic practice among a people whose divergencies are both notable and tolerantly acknowledged.

Needless to say, while Canadians share some of the constitutional incongruities of British conservatism, their institutions have also been influenced by the pervasive force of federalism and by the existence of a written foundation of fundamental law. The evident consequence has been to qualify certain English dogmas, such as parliamentary sovereignty, the unity of the Crown, and the ultimate responsibility of one Cabinet for coördination of all administrative activities. Furthermore, the statutory formulation of the institutional framework, particularly in the British North America Act of 1867 and its amendments, has contributed not so much a rigidity to the system as a legalism that pervades its discussion. Reliance on judicial interpretation for determining the respective spheres of central and provincial governments has tended to carry over into other phases of constitutional construction even when such a process is neither appropriate nor necessary.

It has been noted that the Canadian system is essentially of the Cabinet type, though operating within the limitation of a federal distribution of powers laid down in a fundamental document.[1] As elsewhere, the Cabinet is the small group of politicians, sixteen to twenty in number, who have the confidence of Parliament and are entrusted with the national administration. On behalf of the public, therefore, the Cabinet exercises such powers of the Crown as relate to Canada as a whole or pertain to the Dominion Government within the federal system. In this capacity the Cabinet is referred to as the Committee of His Majesty's Privy Council for Canada. The Privy Council consists of some seventy or eighty gentlemen, chiefly members of former ministries, who never meet as a body but whose constitutional functions as advisers of the Crown are performed exclusively by the score or so of ministers of the day who make up the Cabinet.

The concept of the Crown occupies a position of unusual significance in Canadian constitutional theory. The Crown is much more than a symbol of association with other members of the British Commonwealth, important as this may be; it is the legal point of reference for state authority in a polity where the several aspects of power—legislative, executive, and judicial—are dispersed among numerous Dominion and provincial organs. While a certain amount of harmony is produced by the principles of

[1] For notes to chapter xii see pages 578–579.

federal law and parliamentary usage, the major theoretically unifying element is the Crown by virtue of its being a participant in all legislatures, the nominal repository of executive functions, and the fountain of justice. In all these phases of regal power pertaining to Canada generally or to the Dominion Government in particular, the authority of the Crown is invoked solely by the Canadian Cabinet.[2]

The King's personal participation in the functioning of the Crown for Canada is necessarily rare and is reserved for exceptionally significant occasions: a royal visit, the outbreak of war, the periodic appointment of a royal representative for Canada. When the personal attention of the King is required, it is requested by the Canadian Prime Minister directly or through the Canadian High Commissioner at London. But, since an absentee monarch can know little or nothing of Canadian affairs and is not in close contact with his ministers in Canada as he is with his British advisers, he cannot play the same role that he does in Britain. The complete elimination of British ministerial advice on Canadian matters, formally recognized in the Balfour Report of 1926, has thus left the King in a position of relatively isolated splendour so far as Canadian government is concerned. In the slight connexion which the King may occasionally have with the conduct of Canadian affairs, he is guided exclusively by his Canadian ministers.

In matters relating to the British Commonwealth as a whole, the Canadian Cabinet necessarily shares with other governments the privilege of advising the Crown. When there is agreement among the several governments—as in the abdication crisis of 1936 or the proposed royal marriage of 1947—the advice is given by concurrent action rather than in joint form on behalf of all Commonwealth members. Where unity does not prevail or where national pride requires a demonstration of separate action—as at the outbreak of war in 1939—the powers of the Crown are, at the option of the Canadian Cabinet, exercised for Canada alone. In this connexion it may be remarked that Canada makes no contribution to the financial establishment of the monarchy.

Except for the occasional resort to the King for special reasons, the Cabinet's control of the prerogative is attained by way of advice to the royal representative in Canada. The Governor General, whose appointment is entirely a matter of arrangement between the King and his Canadian ministers, is now endowed with all royal powers relating to Canada. This status is fully recognized in the new letters patent of 1947 under which the Governor is not merely entrusted with the duties originally stipulated in the British North America Act, but is also empowered to perform any function that the King might perform. Despite this status, however, the Governor General is not technically a viceroy, for his formal authority is not exercised in his own name but in that of the King. In practice, then, and regardless of what the Act of 1867 may appear to say in distinguishing between the duties of the Governor General and the powers of the King, the Governor acts for the King in the regular conduct of Canadian public business. He does so, too, in accordance with the same constitutional rules that the King would follow. He receives no instructions from Westminster and makes no report thereto.[3] Just what discretion is left to the Governor General in the face of Cabinet advice is as much disputed in Canada as is royal discretion in Britain. It need not be asserted that the Governor General is completely a rubber stamp for the Cabinet's decisions, though the shortness of tenure (usually five years) and the fact that he is appointed on the responsibility of the Cabinet evidently tends to weaken his position.

The one essential privilege retained by the Governor General is that of selecting a Prime Minister who can form a Cabinet agreeable to Parliament. But the opportunity for making a real choice arises only once or twice in a generation, for the leadership of the majority party is a matter of common knowledge. It can occur, nevertheless, on the death of the Prime Minister, on the disintegration of the majority party, or when there are three or more parties none of which possesses a majority. What discretion this gives a Governor to dismiss a ministry, refuse a dissolution, or reject nominations to office (to name some disputed points) is necessarily vague. The controversial events of 1926, when Lord Byng refused a dissolution to Mr. King, are still debated. The most that can be said is that the relationship of Cabinet and Governor is a delicate one, calling for wisdom, judgement, and fair dealing on both sides. The primary responsibility of the Governor is to obtain and keep a ministry capable of conducting His Majesty's Government with the support of Parliament. It is obvious, on the other hand, that a ministry should not involve the Crown in illegal, unconstitutional, or improper conduct; but it is equally obvious that the Governor's resistance to his ministers' demands is a last resort for emergencies only.

Despite the episode of 1926, which was interpreted by some as creating a constitutional crisis indicative of undue intervention by an outsider in domestic affairs, there has been little demand for the appointment of a Canadian as Governor General. For the time being, at least, Canadians are content with a transitory governorship that is attractive only to members of the royal family, retired British generals, or the socially ambitious. The impotence of the post renders it unattractive to active British politicians, and its ceremonial obligations make it too strenuous for those past their prime. Eminent Canadians who have withdrawn from public life have hitherto been excluded from appointment, partly because their known partisanship might cause difficulties for the Cabinet or its successors and bring the Crown into disrepute, and partly because such an action might be interpreted as severing one of the symbolic ties connecting Canada with Britain and the Commonwealth.

If the legal status of the Cabinet springs from its role in controlling the exercise of the powers of the Crown, its political importance flows directly from its parliamentary background. In this respect, though Parliament comprises King, Senate, and House of Commons, it really means nothing more nor less than the Commons, for it is in the Commons that the basic features of ministerial responsibility operate.

Though the Senate appears at first sight to resemble the American upper chamber, especially in its restricted membership (ninety-six senators)[4] and semi-federal distribution (though with equality for four regional divisions rather than for the constituent provincial units), the similarity is quite illusory so far as power is concerned. The Senate is as impotent as the British House of Lords, of which it is the Canadian equivalent and which it emulates as a revising and delaying body. Whether the Cabinet has a partisan majority in the Senate is sometimes fortuitous, depending usually on how long the ministers have been in office, for the life-tenure of senators (at the nomination of the Prime Minister) makes it a slowly-changing record of past party fortunes. The Cabinet, however, fears no vote of want of confidence in the Chamber, nor do the senators profess to utilize their nominally equal legislative voice.

Two indications of the Senate's inferior status may be cited. In recent years it has been usual for but one minister to be a senator. He has no departmental duties, but serves as government leader, spokesman, and manager in that House. Further, the slight regard for the Senate's legislative powers is indicated by the lateness in the session with which bills from the Commons reach the Senate. Yet it must be admitted that the possibility of Senate amendments to government measures—or even their complete rejection—is a consideration that every Cabinet must bear in mind.

The real centre of gravity to which the Cabinet is drawn is the House of Commons; this, it is hardly necessary to say, is because the latter is the reflection of public opinion as registered at the previous election and as it will be again at the next. The constitutional relationship of ministers to Parliament is essentially what one would expect in a Cabinet system of the British variety. In general, parliamentary business is transacted in accordance with the rules that prevail at Westminster. Members of the House are seated at desks arranged so that the Government and its supporters, sitting on the speaker's right hand, face the Opposition across the chamber.

The bi-racial basis of the population is recognized by the use of both French and English in parliamentary proceedings, though French is employed less to influence the House than for personal and partisan controversies among the French-speaking members. It is, however, always used on formal occasions such as the moving or seconding of the Speech from the Throne, which presents the Government's policy at the beginning of each session.

The speakership (on ministerial nomination) is usually alternated between the two races from Parliament to Parliament, and, since the speaker's partisanship is only temporarily suspended, his rulings are often debated acrimoniously and are even challenged on occasion by appeal to a vote of the House. A greater parade of standing committees (of which there are twelve) is made than at Westminster, but the government takes care to maintain a party majority in all of them. The Cabinet maintains decisive control over parliamentary proceedings and has the assurance of a majority that it can—within the limits of time and of due provision for opposition criticism and questioning—secure the passage of such legislative proposals, financial measures, or administrative provisions as it may decide on. Cabinet dominance, however, should not be interpreted literally as dictatorship, for not only does the whole parliamentary process tend to foster discussion and reasoned argument if not to promote compromise and conciliation, but the Cabinet must satisfy its own supporters and conduct itself with an eye to the public that will have to be consulted at the next election. The consideration that the ministers may themselves be in opposition at a not-too-distant date is necessarily a sobering thought for any government.

The Cabinet is of course a party body. But this is not considered a matter of reproach, as the House is itself composed of partisans; indeed, the ministers have the confidence of the House only because they have a majority there. Furthermore, the Cabinet's hold on the Crown and the Senate, as well as its influence with the Commons, depends on its party complexion and leadership. While the Cabinet retains the support of a partisan majority, it is fairly secure in office; when it loses the support of this majority, either by party disintegration or, as is more usual, after an election, it becomes powerless and retires. It is, therefore, in the particular connexions of the Cabinet to its party in the House that the distinctive characteristics of Canadian politics are most clearly seen.

The House of Commons consists of members elected in single-member constituencies (with two historical exceptions—Halifax, N.S., and Queen's, P.E.I.) by the registered adult citizens, of whom approximately 70 per cent cast their votes. Up to the present the number of seats has fluctuated roughly according to the decennial census of provincial populations, with a standard of representation set by Quebec's fixed quota of 65 members. In 1946, however, a constitutional amendment removed some of the existing anomalies, eliminated the use of Quebec as the standard, and substituted a fixed number of 255 seats,[5] which are to be distributed among the provinces according to population, though still with protection for the smallest provinces, and more particularly Prince Edward Island. The House of the future will thus be slightly larger than in the past—it has been 245 for some twenty years—and this enlargement, while increasing Quebec's quota, makes it unnecessary to reduce the representation of more than one province. The distribution of seats within each province is accomplished by Dominion legislation, but the details are arranged by bi-partisan committees with a minimum of gerrymandering.

Members of Parliament are chiefly local men; women are a rarity. They need not be residents of their constituencies, but are almost always residents of the province in which their constituencies are located.[6] They are hardly to be described as professional politicians, for they enter Parliament late in life, at least so far as the major parties are concerned in most provinces. One out of three has had experience in local politics (though now rarely in the provincial legislature), but this has not provided a full-time or remunerative career in the American fashion. Candidates, of course, have the backing of local party organizations, but there is not usually a "machine" well nourished by patronage. Indeed, the sitting member is more likely to be the master of his local organization than its servant. Members are, moreover, from the better-educated section of the community, half of them being university products, and are often from the learned professions, most frequently the law. Farmers are the second largest group; but representatives of organized labour are still not numerous, even in the new socialistic party, the Coöperative Commonwealth Federation.

Members of Parliament, then, are most often successful middle-aged men who have made a place for themselves locally and are closely connected with the prevalent interests of their regions. Each has been fairly free, within the very broad limits of party tendencies, to conduct his campaign for election in the manner best suited to his particular locality—a practice that frequently produces divergence of opinion within the party and requires careful handling by the leader.

Under these circumstances it might be expected that parliamentarians would display considerable independence in their political conduct in Parliament, but they seldom do so. Independent candidates, that is, those without a national party affiliation, are rarely successful except in Quebec, and party candidates, once elected, display in Parliament a notable subservience to the bonds of party discipline. Regularity of conduct in the direction decided within the party is not merely commended by the leaders; it is expected by the public, for it is understood to be the very condition of party government of the Cabinet variety. When voting for a candidate the elector knows that he is also voting for the candidate's party leader as prospective Prime Minister. The successful candidate knows that it is his duty to support his party, especially when in power, and believes, as do his constituents, that it is only by consistency in this respect that he can gain influence in party counsels and keep the interests of his constituency before the party chieftains. Accordingly, though Canadian parties resemble American in being a medley of special pressures and regional interests, fortified no doubt by traditional prejudices and assumptions, in their parliamentary working they approximate far more closely to the unity of British parties.

The older Canadian political parties have made little continuous effort to enlist the personal participation of the masses except at election time. Even representative conferences are held only for such exceptional occasions as the choice of new leaders. Political headquarters hardly exist. Party organization centres chiefly about the leader, who is the major bond of unity between the numerous elements and factions that bear the same party name. Allegiance to the party, and more particularly to the party leader, is elevated to such a degree as to be a distinctive feature in the Canadian political scene. Indeed, a party without a leader is quite impotent, as the Conservatives found in the interregnum between the withdrawal of Mr. Bennett and the selection of Mr. Bracken. Loyalty to the leader is continuous and is not dependent on success at each election; a party that changes leaders at every set-back suffers accordingly.

It would be an overstatement to say that the leader makes the party, though it is evident that he shapes and colours it to an exceptional degree. The leader is recognized as the authority to enunciate party policy, determine election strategy, and direct parliamentary tactics. The solidarity of the party depends on his skill in gathering together the several disparate elements in some kind of harmony. The parliamentary caucus of the party provides the opportunity for leader and followers to resolve their differences; the whips have the task of keeping the individual members in line day by day.

The maintenance of party discipline is obviously most imperative in the party in power, for the responsibilities of office outweigh the pressure of local influences and personal whims of parliamentarians. Conformity is therefore most definitive in the majority party, save when some great issue arouses deep-seated passions—as conscription in war-time has done among Quebec members. In the last resort, too, the Prime Minister has the privilege of invoking a dissolution of Parliament before its maximum five-year term expires. A few desertions from the party may not be fatal to a ministry unless its majority is very small, but no government can feel secure unless its support is continuous and willing. An election must come some time and the Prime Minister will no doubt weigh the state of party unity among other political considerations in choosing an opportune time for his appeal to the people. For the private members, especially the older ones to whom entrance to Parliament is the climax of a career rather than its commencement, dissolution brings not only expense and labour but hazard, for the high casualty rate (some 30 per cent) may mean the end of parliamentary life.

As the local attachments of the ordinary member of Parliament enhance the functions of the party leader in formulating national party policy, so the general composition of the parliamentary majority confers a notable freedom on the leader of the majority in the selection of ministers. It often happens that in forming a Cabinet the Prime Minister will find it necessary to go outside Parliament to secure a minister or ministers of appropriate calibre, experience, or popularity to fill a particular post or to represent a certain province. Such appointees, of course, must procure election to Parliament—not always an easy task, as General A. G. L. McNaughton found in 1945 after becoming Minister of National Defence. But the very fact that such non-parliamentary appointments occur indicates that the Cabinet is not necessarily a group of outstanding party men who have made their reputations in Parliament itself. Even the party leader may have been taken from another field, as was Mr. Bracken, who in 1942 was chosen leader of the Progressive Conservative party at a party convention while he was still Premier and leader of the Progressive party in the province of Manitoba.

The Cabinet is to be regarded, then, as a body of party men, selected by the Prime Minister because they represent the several sections of the country, its races, religions, and interests (in fairly well-established proportions), and are prepared to carry on the public business in unison. The Prime Minister is something more than *primus inter pares;* he is almost in the position of a president surrounded by subordinates because he, and he alone, draws his prestige from a national following.

Yet despite this, the standard British rules of unity, secrecy, and collective responsibility are recognized as applying to the Canadian Cabinet. The ministers present a united front in public at least, and the entire Cabinet goes out of office when a Government is defeated. Furthermore, a minister who carries personal disagreements outside the Cabinet may be dismissed if he does not resign. He is not, it should be remembered, primarily an administrator but preëminently a politician. Indeed, once in office his success depends almost as much on his parliamentary showing as on the capacity to direct the work of an administrative department.

Part of a minister's parliamentary task is to defend general Cabinet policy and not simply measures that concern his own department. The over-all control exercised by the Cabinet requires that no minister should commit the Government to policies of importance on which other ministers have not been consulted. Much of the work of a department is, of course, routine and noncontroversial, but when it does involve matters of policy the minister is to be considered as a representative of the Cabinet with the duty of coördinating his department's activities with the plans of the Government as a whole.

Special Cabinet committees for special topics are often employed to work out agreed policies on subjects affecting government policy in several departments. During the Second World War such committees and sub-committees became a prime mode of administrative integration—a purpose that was also served by the establishment of a Cabinet Secretariat to coördinate the planning and enforcement of Cabinet decisions.

Although all ministers are nominally equal in the Cabinet, they actually carry responsibility and exert influence in proportion to their personal capacities and the importance of their respective departments. The Department of External Affairs, for example, was up to 1946 held by the Prime Minister, and has been not only more secretive than most government agencies but less open to parliamentary scrutiny. Finance undoubtedly ranks second, especially in view of the profound consequences of government fiscal policies on the country's economic life; it was the minister in charge of this department who assumed major control of consumer rationing and price control during the Second World War. Justice and Agriculture are always of first-class importance. During the Second World War, Labour, the Defence ministries (National Defence was then divided among ministers for the Army, Navy, and Air), and the specially created Department of Munitions and Supply were also numbered among the key ministries. After the war the Defence ministries were reunited, Munitions was succeeded by Reconstruction, and new social-service departments —National Health and Veterans' Affairs—came into prominence.

Peace-time reorganization reduced the number of departments to seventeen,[7] but the membership of the Cabinet continued at twenty: the Prime Minister gave up External Affairs to another minister, the leader of the Senate continues without portfolio, and the former office of Solicitor General (administratively subordinate to the Ministry of Justice) has been revived. The parliamentary assistants, established during the war to aid the six most overburdened ministers, do not have seats in the Cabinet; whether these appointments will be continued is not yet clear.[8]

The role of the ministry in connecting Crown and Parliament has been explained. Ministers also serve as the channel for relating Crown and Parliament to administration. As members of the Cabinet, the ministers make the large decisions of executive policy and guide the Crown in the exercise of its prerogative and statutory powers. At the same time, as political heads of departments, they represent the interests of the particular administrative establishments. Likewise, as leading members of the Parliament that provides funds, enacts laws, and inquires into numerous phases of executive performance, they stand between parliamentary critics and anonymous and silent administrators, defending departmental conduct, explaining needs, and assuming responsibility for every aspect of government action.

A minister is not assigned to a department because of his expertness in the subject administered—even the Minister of Justice need not be a lawyer—but as a parliamentarian of a particular party stripe. How much influence the minister will exert depends, therefore, on his interest, initiative, and capacity to master the intricacies of his department. The day-to-day control of a department is handled by a permanent official, usually known as deputy minister, though in the departments of External Affairs and of the Secretary of State he is called under-secretary. Beneath these permanent heads are thousands of civil servants of various categories and qualifications. The Civil Service, swollen by war activities and new social services to unprecedented heights—well over 100,000, two and a half times the figure preceding the Second World War—has a high degree of security of tenure and protection from most partisan influences. In character it may be said to lean more to the American static type of specialized recruitment than to the English type of progressive careerism. Periodically there are outbursts of criticism at the growth of bureaucracy and public objection to the possible entrance of political influence in government services, especially as the state engages in new administrative activities. Frequently the result is an effort to establish independent administrative boards and commissions outside the general departmental structure. But the nature of ministerial responsibility in Parliament tends to offset any devices directed to separating administration from policy-making. In recent years, too, the combination of wide administrative powers of regulation, enforcement, and adjudication has provoked serious controversy and discussion, but without producing satisfactory solutions for what are undoubtedly among the most vital problems of modern government.

The Canadian judiciary, while showing some traces of federalism, is organized differently from that of the United States. The American vertical cleavage into federal and state courts is virtually unknown [9] in Canada, where the line of division is primarily horizontal, and appeals may therefore be taken from the provincial courts to the Dominion appellate court. Minor courts are purely provincial; the county courts and the higher provincial courts of original and appellate jurisdiction are constituted and organized by the province, but their judges are appointed and paid by the Dominion; and the highest court of appeal in the Dominion, the Supreme Court of Canada, is completely under the control of the federal government.

At the top of the system is the Judicial Committee of the Privy Council, a survival from colonial days, which still functions in London as a court for a large section of the British Commonwealth and Empire. Its continuance as a part of the Canadian judicial system now rests entirely with the Canadian Parliament, and is not in any way imposed by Canada's Commonwealth connexion. The future of the Judicial Committee in the Canadian system is very uncertain. Appeals in criminal cases were stopped in 1933; and the Cabinet has announced its intention of cutting off appeals in all other cases by securing the passage of the necessary statute. This will apparently be effected in 1950.

The high standing and independence of the judiciary have always been conspicuous merits in Canadian government. The first characteristic is derived in large degree from the fact that all judges are appointed by the executive. This usually means appointment by the Governor General in Council, that is, the Dominion Cabinet; but minor judicial offices and magistracies are filled by the corresponding authority in each province. While party affiliation is almost always considered in making the choice, this has rarely been allowed to prejudice the quality of the appointments. Judicial independence has been encouraged in various ways, the chief of which are tenure during good behaviour, and an elaborate and difficult method of removal by joint address of both houses of

Parliament for the superior court judges, and a somewhat easier method for the removal of county and district court judges. Canada has thus been strongly influenced by the traditions and practices of the British judicial system, and has remained singularly untouched by the more radical judicial experiments in many of the state governments of the United States.

CHAPTER XIII

Local Government

BY K. GRANT CRAWFORD

There are as many systems of local government as provinces in Canada and, although the general basis of organization is similar, there are numerous variations in detail. The variations result from influences and conditions peculiar to the individual provinces; the similarity is due to the common background of experience of the inhabitants. Local government in Canada lacks a long tradition, for parts of the country have been settled for less than half a century, and even in the older regions local self-government is little more than a hundred years old.

Under the French régime and in the early years of the English era, in what are now the provinces of Quebec and Ontario, there were no significant institutions of local self-government on the modern pattern. Such institutions were not to be expected under French rule, for they would have been a contradiction of the prevailing policy of centralized control; under British rule they were not provided because there was no local demand for them and it was British policy to retain as much as was feasible of the methods of government which had been in effect previous to British acquisition of the country.

Following the influx of the Loyalists and others from the Thirteen Colonies during and after the American War of Independence, the new settlers began to demand some measure of local self-government resembling that to which they had been accustomed. The municipal institutions in the American colonies had been based upon the English experience of the early settlers, modified to meet conditions in the colonies. The justices of the peace, who were appointees of the governing authority, combined judicial and administrative functions, on the English pattern, and played an important part in all the early American systems of local government. In the New England colonies, however, the town meeting of all the inhabitants and their elected select-men became an effective local power, even though their decisions often had to be approved by the justices. The majority of the Loyalists who came to what is now Ontario had been accustomed to local government of the New England type, and argued that they had not sacrificed their status and possessions in loyalty to the Crown only to be deprived of the means of self-government. Their very presence in Canada refuted the assertions of those who held that such democratic innovations as local self-government were dangerous and must be relentlessly opposed.

Although provision was made in Upper Canada in 1793 for town meetings of the inhabitants to appoint a number of local officers and to deal with a few minor matters, no substantial advance occurred until after the Rebellion of 1837. Lord Durham in his famous Report emphasized the urgent need for local government institutions in both Lower and Upper Canada, and provision was subsequently made for a system of elected district councils for Lower Canada (Quebec) in 1840 and Upper Canada (Ontario) in 1841. This system marks the beginning of Canadian local self-government.

Not for another forty years was any effective move made to establish local government institutions in the Maritime Provinces, where, except for the cities, local administration continued to rest in the hands of justices of the peace. Development on the prairies came even later as settlement spread and the provinces were created; it was influenced largely by the system in Ontario, whence came most of the early settlers in the West. In British Columbia, settlements were scattered because of the topography, and the area organized into municipalities has been relatively small. The municipal system which evolved, however, is a modification of that established in the central provinces. In Prince Edward Island the limited area has made it possible to govern the whole province from the provincial capital, with the result that no provision has been made for local government institutions except in a few urban centres and except for local school authorities throughout the province.

Since large tracts of land have not yet been populated, a relatively small proportion of the area in some provinces has been organized into municipalities. In Nova Scotia and New Brunswick the entire land area has been so organized, but in Ontario, the most populous province, the proportion is 10 per cent, and in British Columbia only 0.5 per cent. Even in the latter two, however, 96 and 75 per cent, respectively, of the population lives in organized municipalities.

The Canadian unit of local government is the municipality; the inhabitants of this area are, by law, constituted a municipal corporation. These corporations are endowed with the characteristics common to all corporate bodies and have, in addition, such special powers and duties as the respective provinces see fit to give them. The powers of the municipal corporation are exercised by an elected council. Other corporate as well as unincorporated bodies provided by statute form a part of the machinery of local government, and to these bodies the provinces have assigned special, limited fields of activity.

All these municipal bodies, of which the municipal council is the most important, derive their existence and authority from the provincial legislatures, for, in the allocation of powers under the British North America Act, the sphere of legislation relating to municipal institutions was placed under the exclusive jurisdiction of the provinces. The provinces, however, are, in turn, subject to the limitations which the same Act has imposed upon them. Thus, while a province may grant to a municipal corporation almost any of the powers which the province itself possesses, it cannot grant to its municipalities powers which come within the exclusive jurisdiction of the Dominion. The municipal corporations have no assured status in that the provincial legislature which creates them may extend or reduce their powers and can even dissolve them. There are no constitutional restrictions on the legislature's jurisdiction over municipalities, provided the provincial legislature keeps within its own sphere of legislation. One consequence of this situation is that the relationship between the

ASPECTS OF THE CANADIAN SCENE

National Film Board

PARLIAMENT BUILDING, OTTAWA

Malak

SKIING WITHIN SIGHT OF OTTAWA

National Film Board

CONFEDERATION SQUARE, OTTAWA

Canada Wide

HOUSE OF COMMONS IN SESSION

National Film Board

HALIFAX HARBOUR

Canadian Pacific Airlines

MONTREAL HARBOUR

Canadian Pacific Airlines

UNIVERSITY OF MONTREAL

Aluminum Company of Canada

SAGUENAY WATER-POWERS

Provincial Publicity Bureau, Quebec

ON THE ISLE OF ORLEANS

National Film Board

CHATEAU FRONTENAC, QUEBEC

National Film Board

AT THE UNIVERSITY OF NEW BRUNSWICK

Canadian Pacific Railway

PARLIAMENT BUILDING, WINNIPEG

National Film Board

UNIVERSITY OF SASKATCHEWAN

British Columbia Government Travel Bureau

LOOKING NORTH FROM VANCOUVER

National Film Board

APPLE ORCHARDS NEAR KAMLOOPS

National Film Board

NEAR BANFF, ALBERTA

Canadian Pacific Railway

BOW RIVER VALLEY, ALBERTA

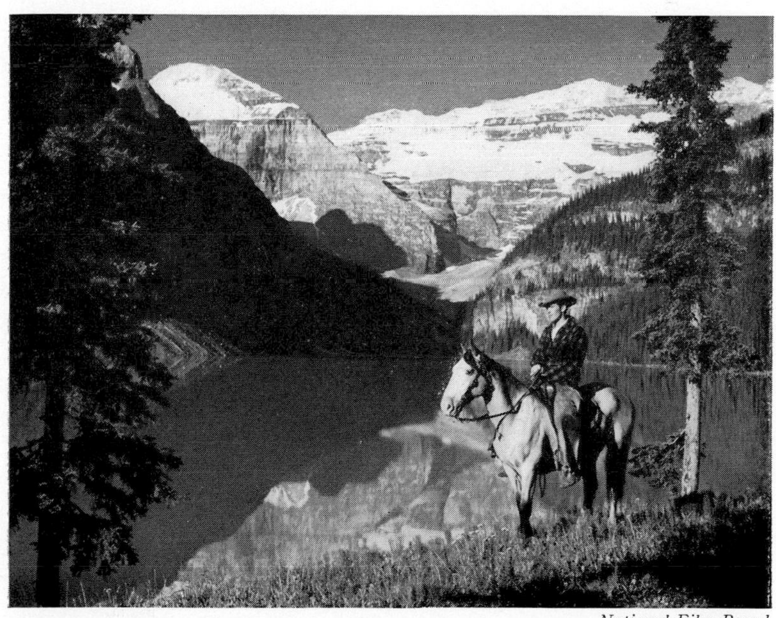

National Film Board

LAKE LOUISE

National Film Board

AIR FREIGHT, NORTH-WEST TERRITORIES

National Film Board

FLYING AMBULANCE

National Film Board

WESTERN HARVEST

Editorial Associates Ltd.

GRAIN ELEVATORS, PORT ARTHUR

Photographic Survey Corp'n Ltd.

ST. CLAIR RIVER AT SARNIA

National Film Board

WELLAND CANAL

National Film Board

PAPER-MILLS, NEWFOUNDLAND

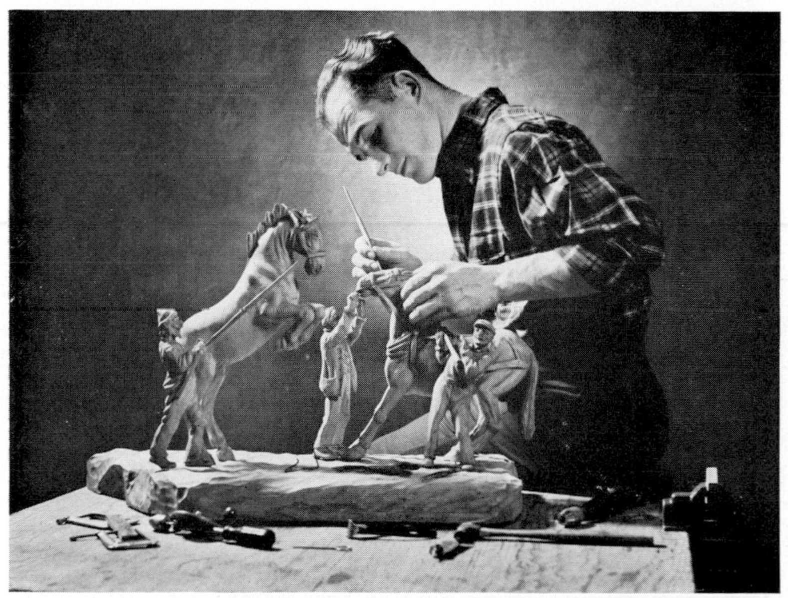

Canadian Pacific Railway

WOOD-CARVER, QUEBEC PROVINCE

Canadian Pacific Railway

SMELTING WORKS, BRITISH COLUMBIA

National Film Board

ASBESTOS MINE, QUEBEC PROVINCE

national and the municipal government is normally through the medium of the provincial government.

Except for a degree of uncertainty in some of the newer fields of legislation, there is a fairly definite division of responsibility for governmental functions between the Dominion and the provinces, but the scope of jurisdiction and responsibility of the municipalities is subject to constant change according to provincial policy as expressed through legislation. Provincial legislatures have placed certain obligations upon the municipalities which they have created, and have also provided them with a wide range of powers the exercise of which is optional with the local councils. But the functions which do not clearly rest upon any of the three levels of government create problems for the municipal authorities. Governments exist primarily to meet the needs of the people whom they serve, and most of such needs arise or their results take effect where those people reside. Consequently, when needs develop for which no level of government has provided or accepted responsibility, the citizen naturally turns to the government to which he has ready access—the municipal government. As a result, municipalities are constantly having to assume responsibility for functions which are not clearly theirs, but for which neither of the other levels has provided. The residual responsibility, though not the residual power, frequently, in fact, rests upon the local level of government. Among the problems thus created, the financial one is very serious (this point is dealt with more fully in chap. xvii, "The Social Services," pp. 390–407), and municipalities are constantly appealing to their provinces for relief from the growing tax burden on real property, which is the major source of municipal tax revenue.

Where the provinces have given assistance, they have naturally required that they be given some supervision over the municipal operations. Two factors, in particular, have encouraged this trend. One was the extensive assistance required by the municipalities to finance unemployment relief costs in the depression years and the necessity for supervision over municipalities which fell into default in meeting their obligations—a supervision extended eventually over all municipalities as a protection against similar defaults in the future. The second has been the growing awareness of the interdependence of all communities and the realization that many problems, such as those of health, social services, and community planning, cannot be effectively isolated by municipal boundaries. It is essential that provincial action be taken to maintain at least minimum standards in the areas of education, public health, and social welfare.

This constant extension of provincial supervision and regulation has been met by the growing resistance of local authorities, mitigated in some provinces by the increase in provincial grants for municipal activities. It is still the opinion of a substantial number of citizens that the higher standards resulting from provincial control and the accompanying grants may prove too expensive if the growing centralization undermines the self-reliance of the local government and weakens what is generally regarded as the foundation-stone of the democratic system.

Because there is a constant if gradual expansion of settlement and a progressive concentration of population in urban communities, all except the three Maritime Provinces provide for the creation of new municipalities in previously unorganized territory, and all provinces make provision for changing the status of urban centres as their population increases. Municipalities fall into two classes, rural and urban. Rural municipalities in the several provinces are designated as counties, parishes, townships, rural or municipal districts, or district municipalities. The area of rural municipalities varies greatly between provinces, but most of them are much smaller in the two central provinces of Quebec and Ontario than elsewhere. These two provinces have a two-tier form of local government in which the county—not to be confused with the county in Nova Scotia and New Brunswick, where it is the basic rural unit of government—functions as the local government authority for certain purposes, and the townships, villages, and towns lying within the county area are quite independent of the county municipality with respect to the functions which the province has assigned to them.

Urban municipalities, in ascending order of population, are villages, towns, and cities. In general, the larger the population the greater the extent of the powers with which the municipality is endowed. Population requirements vary, but in most provinces it is necessary to have a population of 5,000 to 15,000 to be elevated to the status of a city. Cities in provinces which have a two-tier organization of municipal government are entirely independent of the county. Of the total of 4,018 incorporated municipalities, 1,650 are urban and 2,368 are rural, but 54.34 per cent of the population lives in urban centres. While there are only 55 urban municipalities of 10,000 population or over, they contain 38.52 per cent of the entire population.

The qualifications for electors and members of councils and other municipal bodies, as well as the electoral process, are controlled in detail by provincial legislation. The usual requirement is that municipal electors be either owners or tenants, but property qualifications are low enough so that almost any owner or occupier of property is qualified as an elector; in three provinces no property qualification whatever is required. In general, voters must be British subjects and twenty-one years of age, although in Saskatchewan the age requirement is only eighteen years.

A person who is qualified to be an elector may be a candidate for municipal office unless he falls within one of the three classes of those who are specifically disqualified: those whose position might subject them to a conflict of interest in carrying out their public duties, as with persons employed by the municipality or having a contract with the municipality; those holding certain public offices, such as officers of the courts of justice; and those whose personal character makes them unsuited to be representatives, namely, bankrupts, habitual drunkards, and those convicted of criminal offences punishable by imprisonment. A common basis of disqualification is failure to pay taxes owing to the municipality. In two provinces the property and other qualifications required of the head of a municipality are higher than those applying to candidates for other offices.

The municipal councils are composed of the head (mayor, reeve, warden, chairman, overseer) and the other members (controllers, aldermen, councillors). Although the head of the council has certain specific responsibilities placed upon him as an individual by statute, he has no powers, with a few minor exceptions, except as he acts as a member of the whole council. It is the council as a whole, acting as a unit in accordance with the decision of the majority, that exercises the powers of the municipal corporation, and it is upon the council as a whole that the duties of the corporation are imposed. While in three provinces (Quebec, Manitoba, and British Columbia) the mayor has a veto on the actions of his council, all such vetoes can be overridden by a majority vote of the council.

It is general practice, except for a part of the Montreal city council and in the filling of vacancies occurring between elections, for all members of the council to be elected to office by the electors. Usually they are elected to the position which they finally occupy, though in county councils the head of the council is not elected as such, but is chosen by members of the council from among their own number. County councils in Quebec and Ontario are elected by indirect election. They are composed of representatives of the local municipalities (those other than cities) which make up the counties. In Quebec the county council is composed of those elected as mayor in each of the local municipalities, and in Ontario of those elected as reeve and deputy reeve of the local municipalities. Thus, in these two-tier systems of county government, a mayor or reeve or deputy reeve acts on two governing bodies, for he is a member of the local council to which he was originally elected, and by virtue of his local office he also sits as a member of the county council. The head of the county council, known as the warden, is elected by the members of the county council from among their own number.

All the municipal electors have an opportunity to vote for the head of the municipality, but the other members of council may be elected either by general vote or by the electors in one of the geographical sub-divisions of the municipality known as wards, or, in rural areas, parishes or divisions. In the Maritime and Prairie Provinces, where the basic rural unit is large in area, elections are by divisions and there is considerable variation in the total personnel of councils. In Quebec and Ontario, where the basic rural unit is relatively small, election is by general vote and the councils have a uniform fixed personnel, being seven and five, respectively. In urban municipalities there is great variation in practice, but among the larger urban centres slightly more elect on the general-vote basis than on the ward basis. Canadian urban councils are not large, the normal personnel being from seven to fifteen, although there are exceptions: Montreal with one hundred members, Toronto with twenty-three, and Hamilton with twenty-one. County councils have a larger number, though even the largest, York County in Ontario, has only fifty-one members.

The term of office varies from one to four years. The more common terms, however, are one or two years with a preference for the one-year term. In some rural municipalities in both the eastern and the western provinces, the term may run to three or even four years; in the western provinces such terms are usually staggered, with one-third of the total number being elected each year. Even where the longer term applies to aldermen in urban centres, the head of the municipality is usually restricted to a one-year term, although it is the practice to concede a mayor a second term if his service has been reasonably satisfactory.

In some municipalities there is open participation by political parties in municipal elections, but it is not usual for municipal elections to be conducted admittedly on a party basis. A candidate's status with the local branch of the provincial or national parties may have a material effect on his prospects of success, but the public resents the suggestion that municipal elections are being run on party lines. With the exception of labour candidates and adherents of the Coöperative Commonwealth Federation, it is exceptional for any municipal candidate to hold himself out publicly as a supporter of, or to be supported by, a particular political party, whatever the arrangements behind the scenes.

Municipal councils, except those with a very small membership, operate on a committee basis. Under this plan the council is divided into standing committees of three to five members, the number of committees varying from one municipality to another. It is not the practice to appoint those who are not council members to such committees. There is no typical number of committees, but Finance, Works, Administration, Welfare, and Fire and Light committees are common to most municipalities. The duties of the committees are to supervise those activities of the corporations which the council puts under their jurisdiction, to confer with and advise the responsible executive officials, and to report their recommendations to the council. The council may adopt or reject such recommendations, but it is the final authority and is not in any way bound by committee recommendations.

In the larger cities of Ontario and in British Columbia municipalities of over 15,000 population, provision is made for the election of controllers. These controllers, who are four or two in number, are elected by general vote of the electors. While they form a part of the council, they also, with the head of the municipality, constitute a board of control to which are allocated many of the executive duties of the council as distinct from its legislative duties, but the actions of the board are subject to approval by the whole council.

The municipal council is the senior unit in the machinery of municipal government, and its scope of operation is wider than that of any other, but it is not the sole unit. The various provinces have made legal provision for other special-purpose bodies, most of which are corporate. Some are elected by the municipal electors or certain portions of the electorate, and others are composed of appointees of the council or other public bodies. The number of such special-purpose bodies varies from province to province; within any one province they are more numerous in the larger urban centres than in rural municipalities.

The educational function is usually under the jurisdiction of a specially elected body, and the health function is often handled by a body appointed for the purpose. A wide range of other functions, such as parks, libraries, police, and utilities or municipal enterprises, are usually so administered. These special-purpose bodies, whether elected or appointed, have varying degrees of independence ranging from educational bodies, which are completely independent of council both in policy and finance, to other bodies which are dependent on council's wishes in the matter of finances and correspondingly responsive to its wishes in matters of policy. The greatest degree of independence normally rests with the educational bodies, owing to the prevailing provincial attitude that educational standards are a matter for provincial determination even though the necessary finances are provided locally, and also owing to the complications which result from the existence of separate school systems based on religious differences. The degree of independence of the other bodies depends on a variety of circumstances and influences which may have been effective when provision was made for the establishment of the independent boards. Some of these bodies were created for the purpose of removing the activities under their jurisdiction from the financially restrictive control of the municipal councils; in others the councils requested the transfer of functions to special-purpose bodies to effect better results or to relieve themselves of politically embarrassing problems.

In addition to special-purpose municipal bodies functioning within one municipality, there is a growing use of specially created bodies having jurisdiction in two or more municipalities. These are of two general types, the first being those created to handle some activity common to a number of adjacent municipalities in an area including an urban centre and the surrounding urbanized area: such are planning boards, the Montreal Metropolitan Commission, or the Greater Winnipeg Sanitary District. The second type is designed to enable a number of smaller municipalities to combine to increase the efficiency and share in the burden of services which they could not afford to carry individually. The health units in Ontario which perform the public-health functions for an area including a number of municipalities are examples of this type. In the central provinces the same purpose is attained in some degree by operations of the county level of local government.

The conduct of municipal enterprises is assigned largely to special-purpose bodies. Such enterprises include the supply and distribution of water, the generation and (or) distribution of electricity, the production and distribution of gas, the operation of harbours, *abattoirs,* markets, hospitals, transportation systems, and telephone systems. Those most commonly occurring are the supply and distribution of water and electricity. An unusual example of the latter is the Ontario hydro-electric system, which is a municipal mutual enterprise under which electrical energy is produced for and distributed to the municipalities by their agent, the Hydro-Electric Power Commission, the local distribution being the responsibility of local commissions, which are usually elected. This system serves some 922 municipalities with 2,608,000 horsepower. Canadian municipalities have not entered the field of housing to any appreciable degree.

The execution of the policies adopted by the municipal councils rests with permanent paid officials, the greater number of whom are part-time officers, as the majority of the municipalities are relatively small. Even in the small municipalities, however, it is an increasing practice to combine a number of offices in one individual and thus make it possible to pay sufficient to retain him on a full-time basis. Certain officers—clerks, treasurers, assessors, and auditors—must be appointed by the municipal councils. The appointment of additional types of officers is left to the discretion of the local council according to local needs. The officers whom the councils are obliged to appoint are statutory officers and are required to carry out their statutory duties in accordance with provincial law; within the ambit of their statutory duties they are not subject to the direction of their council.

The appointment and dismissal of municipal employees rest with the council, except for a limited number of officers whose tenure depends on some provincial authority. There is no election to the paid municipal staff, nor appointment and dismissal by the head of the municipality. Certain offices may be filled only by persons possessing professional qualifications or by those who can comply with standards established by the province. An office for which almost all provinces have established requirements is that of auditor. In practice, municipal employees in Canada have a high degree of security in office, although legally their appointments are usually at the pleasure of the council. There is virtually no dismissal from office resulting from changes in the political complexion of councils, which is in part due to the generally accepted rule that those in paid municipal office do not—at least openly—participate in political activity.

As the problems of local government have increased in complexity, both the provinces and municipal officers have become conscious of the necessity of raising the standards of performance of such officers if local government is to meet the problems with which it is faced. Consequently, there have evolved a number of employee organizations designed to raise professional standards. These organizations are in addition to the provincial municipal associations, the main purpose of which is to act as a liaison between the municipalities and the province in matters of legislation and policy. Several provinces have taken steps to assist in the effort to raise the standards of qualification and performance of permanent municipal employees by sponsoring short training courses, by establishing standards of qualification for those to be appointed to certain offices, and by encouraging the professional organizations with financial support.

Effective local government of the Canadian type requires an active partnership of three factors: the electors, their elected representatives, and the permanent staff. The interest and the participation of the citizens are indispensable for good and efficient government, yet here, perhaps, is the weakest of the three factors. Although, under special circumstances, the participation of the electors may rise to a higher figure, normally not more than 30–40 per cent, and frequently less, of the electors exercise the franchise. This is not necessarily a true measure of citizen interest, but it is one indication. A wide-spread effort is being made through radio programmes, newspaper publicity, and study groups to arouse and sustain interest in local government, its administration, and its problems.

The main functions of municipal councils are legislative and administrative. Important as is the legislative function, it is of secondary importance in the life of the people whom the council exists to serve. The primary function is to provide services for the protection or convenience of the inhabitants, for, as the concentration of population increases, the citizens become increasingly dependent on municipal services. The municipal corporation is required by provincial legislation to maintain roads and streets according to a certain standard; failure renders the corporation liable for damages to persons injured thereby. In addition, however, there is a wide range of optional activities and services which tend to increase in number and extent as the needs of the inhabitants increase and as experience proves the effectiveness of the municipal corporation as a community service agency.

Expansion of settlement in the rural areas and growth of urban centres have been comparatively rapid, and many large cities have developed where but a few decades ago there were only farm lands. This rapid expansion has been accompanied by an insatiable demand for roads, schools, drains, waterworks, sewers, lighting systems, and all the other physical structures which form the framework essential to community development. During the same period the protective services such as police, fire-protection, sanitation, and public health have been organized to meet the needs of a rapidly expanding population.

Canadian municipalities have not advanced as rapidly as some others in providing for cultural and recreational needs. There is a limit to the accomplishments possible in a given period and with limited funds, and the insistent demand has been for an ever-expanding physical plant and protective services. There is evidence that municipal councils, having provided for this structural basis, are now prepared for expansion in social services, but the extent of their response will depend mainly on the resolving of the problems of municipal finance.

The greater part of the municipal revenue is derived from locally imposed taxes, although some provinces make substantial grants towards the cost of education, health and welfare services, and highway construction and maintenance, and in some urban municipalities considerable net revenues are derived from enterprises such as water and electrical works. The objects which may be taxed by municipalities are determined by the respective provinces; the extent of the tax-levy, subject to a maximum limitation, rests with the local authorities. The major source of municipal taxation is real property, which provides the entire tax revenue in most rural municipalities and approximately 90 per cent in urban communities.

The concentration of municipal taxation on this restricted field leaves little flexibility for adjustment to meet changing conditions and establishes a real if undetermined limit on the total burden of taxation which it is possible to impose. It is not reasonable to expect that the situation will be relieved by provincial action extending the scope of municipal taxation, for the provincial need of additional revenues is increasing even more rapidly than that of the municipalities, and if new sources of taxation are tapped it is to be expected that the provinces will absorb them for their own purposes. Despite the arguments against the justice of charging the costs of municipal services almost exclusively against real property, the fact remains that real-property taxation has to date provided the necessary revenues, and no satisfactory alternative or supplementary source has been proposed.

Municipal taxes are levied upon the assessed value of real property, which is determined by assessors appointed by the local councils, subject to appeal to local revising bodies composed of members of the council or persons appointed by the council and usually subject to a further appeal to the judiciary or provincial administrative boards. Provision is made for equalizing the assessment to establish a just relationship between the basis of assessment used in one municipality as compared with that in another to permit an equitable distribution of the cost of functions which are borne jointly by a number of municipalities, as in the local municipalities comprising a county.

In practice there are wide variations between municipalities within a province in the standard of valuation of property for assessment purposes, but there are also variations in the legal basis of assessment as between provinces. Thus while in all provinces the legal basis for assessment of land is the full actual value, yet in the four most westerly provinces buildings and improvements on land are legally assessed on a basis varying from 60 to 75 per cent of the actual value. The value for assessment purposes is always the capital value rather than the rental or income value, and real-property taxation is levied against the owner rather than against the occupant.

The common types of municipal taxation in Canada are real-property taxation, which is found in all provinces; business taxation, which occurs in seven of the provinces; and personal-property taxation, which occurs in five provinces. The basis of business taxation varies widely, but in general this tax, which is usually at the same rate as that on real property, is levied upon a business assessment related either to the assessment or to the area of the real property occupied by the business rather than to the volume of business done. Its significance is indicated by the fact that it represents only 8 per cent of municipal taxation in Ontario, where it is of greater importance than in any other province. Personal-property assessment in the provinces where it occurs represents as much as 20 per cent of the total municipal assessment, the average being 10 per cent.

Numerous classes of real property are exempt from municipal taxation: Crown properties, municipal and educational property, and property owned by religious bodies. Exempt properties represent between 10 and 30 per cent of all real property, but in areas where there are extensive holdings by the Crown the burden of providing services for holdings which yield no tax revenues becomes onerous. This problem has been intensified by the increase in the holdings of Crown companies during the recent war and the continuous expansion of government enterprises. Constant demands are being made by the municipalities that the Crown, as represented by both the province and the Dominion, should make payments in lieu of taxes even though the constitution specifically exempts the Crown from taxation; these demands are met with equally constant refusals.

The municipal council is the tax-levying and tax-collecting authority both for its own needs and for those of the special-purpose bodies, some of which have the right to require the council to raise whatever sums of money they demand. Where there is a two-tier form of local government, it is the lower tier, or the local unit, which is the collecting authority. The methods of collection include an individual demand for payment; the imposition of percentage penalties for non-payment; the levying of taxes by distress and the sale of goods and chattels; by suit in the courts; by order upon a tenant to pay over any rents to the taxing authority; and by the sale of the real property to realize the taxes owing, subject to redemption by the original owner within a specified time upon payment of the equivalent of the tax-sale purchase price plus interest and costs.

The greater part of municipal taxation is levied upon the assessed value of real property on the principle of taxing according to the capacity to pay, on the assumption that ownership of real property is a measure of that capacity. This source of tax revenue is supplemented by another system of taxation based on benefit received. The latter taxes, generally described as local improvement or special assessment taxes, are widely used in urban communities to provide for pavements, sewers, and similar works, and services such as street-cleaning. Such taxes are levied against the owners of property, not on the basis of the assessed value, but according to the number of feet of frontage of the real property abutting on the street where the work or service is performed.

On the average, taxation provides approximately 83 per cent of municipal revenues, but some municipalities derive a large portion of their revenues from enterprise operations. This source of income is not so great as it might be because of the widely-held opinion that public enterprises should supply service as nearly as possible at cost. In some provinces, provincial grants and subsidies towards the cost of particular services are important. It is expected that, following financial adjustments between the Dominion and the provinces, there will be a readjustment of the financial relationship between the provinces and their municipalities.

One of the major problems of municipal financing has been that of long-term debt. Municipalities have the right to issue bonds repayable over a period of years as a means of financing capital construction. As a result of the financial difficulties experienced by many municipalities during the depression years in the 'thirties, there has been a tightening of provincial controls, and all provinces now exercise control over the local debt-incurring power. The total debt of municipal and school corporations, which in 1944 was $1,627,380,931, has been gradually decreasing in the last decade. One unique feature of municipal financing in contrast to that at the other two levels of government is that a municipality which incurs a long-term debt is required to provide annually for the repayment of part of the principal either by means of a sinking-fund or by the redemption of some of the securities outstanding.

Public demands for improved standards of service, the continuous expansion of the scope of municipal service, and the changing attitude of the public with respect to the proper sphere of governmental activity have combined to increase the number and complexity of the problems of the municipalities. There is a gradually increasing demand for expanded cultural, recreational, welfare, and educational services and for better housing and health measures, as well as for programmes of conservation and community planning, but there are sharp differences of opinion among the electorate in regard to the extent of municipal responsibility in such activities and on the method of financing them.

Municipal government might be said to be at a point between

two eras. Circumstances have forced municipal bodies to concentrate on physical construction and the protective services. Opinions have not divided on the reasonableness of providing a municipal fire-fighting service or paving streets, but rather on the degree of service for which it is feasible to pay. With respect to newer types of municipal activity, there are sharp differences also on the principle of municipal responsibility, and municipal representatives are not likely to move effectively until public opinion has more definitely resolved these differences.

There is also the problem of providing finances for new undertakings. So long as the greater part of the municipal revenues is obtained by direct taxation of the group which owns real property, that hesitation is likely to continue. The municipalities maintain that a greater portion of the cost of social services should be borne by the senior levels of government, since the problems involved result from their policies, and their varied sources of taxation make it possible for them to distribute the burden more equitably. The answer is assumed to be greater financial assistance by the provinces to the municipalities. An alternative solution, less damaging to self-government, may be found in a redistribution of functions between the provinces and their municipalities. Under such a redistribution the provinces would assume the entire responsibility and cost of functions which are so controlled and regulated by the province as actually to be provincial functions, but which are now carried on or financed through the agency of the municipalities with varying degrees of provincial assistance.

Whatever the eventual solution of the basic financial problem, it is increasingly evident that circumstances will compel a readjustment of provincial-municipal relations in the not-distant future. Any general programme of municipal improvement on the part of local authorities must await such a readjustment, which, in turn, is dependent upon action by the respective provinces.

CHAPTER XIV

Political Parties and Ideas

BY FRANK H. UNDERHILL

POLITICAL PARTIES emerged in the British North American colonies during the struggle for self-government in the first half of the nineteenth century. Reformers in each colony strove for colonial control over domestic colonial affairs and sought to wrest power from the local land-holding, commercial, banking, and ecclesiastical oligarchy. Conservatives identified their own aristocratic monopoly of power with the maintenance of the British connexion, and denounced the Reformers as disloyal American republicans and democrats. The "responsible government" which was won in the 1840's was the British Cabinet form of parliamentary government; and Canadian politicians continued to conduct their political parties, as their other political institutions, upon the British model. Canadian Liberal leaders in the nineteenth century were likely to be well versed in the teachings of Fox, Macaulay, Mill, Cobden, and Gladstone. Conservative leaders were likely to quote Burke and Disraeli and Salisbury. And the Cabinet system, which makes the tenure of office dependent upon the day-to-day maintenance of a majority in an elected legislature, tended to impress a British structure, with British standards and ideals, upon Canadian parties. To this day the two historic parties have retained their British names, Liberal and Conservative.

At the same time, as the eastern colonies expanded and consolidated themselves into a nation stretching across the northern half of the North American continent, the North American environment gave an American quality to the actual practices of the Canadian parties. The tasks to be performed by statesmanship in

Canada and the United States were essentially the same, and differed greatly from the tasks confronting statesmanship in the older countries of Europe. Immigration and settlement, westward expansion, the building of roads and railways across empty territories, the separation of church and state, the establishment of municipal government and state-supported education in new communities, the exploitation of virgin natural resources through the dynamic energy of business men backed by state assistance, industrialization, and the struggle of interests between eastern industry and western agriculture—it has been on these questions that politics have turned in both North American countries. Without conscious imitation, Canadian Conservatives have spontaneously given expression to the ideas of Hamilton and Clay and Mark Hanna. Canadian Liberals and Radicals have rather more consciously found inspiration in the ideas and methods of Jefferson and Jackson, Wilson and Roosevelt.

Besides these North American sectional, economic, and class issues, Canadian statesmanship has had to deal with a special minority community in French Quebec—a minority which is almost a nation in itself, defending its religion, language, and culture against the pressure of an unsympathetic environment, and evolving in defence of its peculiar institutions a philosophy of minority rights very like that of the South of Calhoun and his successors in the United States.

This continental complexity of interests has made the task of building and maintaining a nation-wide political party very much the same in Canada and in the United States. "The most common and durable source of factions," declared James Madison in the *Federalist* (No. X), "has been the various and unequal distribution of property. Those who hold and those who are without property have ever formed distinct interests in society. Those who are creditors and those who are debtors fall under a like discrimination. A landed interest, a manufacturing interest, a mercantile interest, a moneyed interest, with many lesser interests, grow up of necessity in civilized nations, and divide them into different classes, actuated by different sentiments and views. The regulation of these various and interfering interests forms the chief task of modern legislation, and involves the spirit of party and faction in the necessary and ordinary operations of the government."

It is the similarity of the various and interfering interests in the two countries that produces the similarity in their political parties. The function of the party leader has been to discover the terms on which as many as possible of these interest-groups can be induced to work together in a common policy, to emphasize what the groups have in common rather than what divides them, to conciliate discontented groups within his own party, and to woo discontented groups in the rival party or parties.

Whether the results of this process in Canada should be described as British institutions adapting themselves to a North American environment or as American institutions disguised in British clothes is perhaps only a matter of taste. The Cabinet system of government makes for parties with more effective central leadership and discipline, and discourages the group aberrations and revolts which characterize the internal history of American national parties. But the continental scale of politics tends to turn Canadian parties into composite aggregations of groups kept together by an opportunistic group-diplomacy which is more familiar in Washington than in London. Canadian students will continue to argue endlessly on the relative importance of British and American influences upon their political practices, and on the degree to which a distinctive Canadian way of doing things, differing from both models, can be said to have established itself in the Canadian corner of the North Atlantic Triangle.

The party system of the new Dominion of Canada after 1867 was an expansion of that which had developed in the smaller Province of Canada under the Act of Union of 1840. Union brought French Canadians and English Canadians together in the same representative legislature, and confronted leaders with what has been the fundamental task of Canadian politics ever since: the building up of political parties that can collect votes from both French and English, Roman Catholics and Protestants. The first effective political party of this character was the Reform coalition led by LaFontaine from Lower Canada and Baldwin from Upper Canada. This first experiment in coöperation, which won responsible government for the colony, never quite grew from an uneasy coalition into an organized party. Early in the 1850's, with the retirement of its original leaders, it went to pieces.

Out of the ensuing confusion of competing sectional groups a new bi-racial coalition which called itself the Liberal-Conservative party was constructed by 1854. Its two chief architects were John A. Macdonald from Upper Canada and George Étienne Cartier from Lower Canada. Cartier brought into the new party the majority of the French Canadians, strongly organized into a communal group under the leadership of their Church. Macdonald brought the Upper Canadian Tories with their Loyalist anti-American traditions, along with a small group of Baldwin Reformers who belonged mostly to the business community. They were joined also by most of the English in Lower Canada, led by the Montreal business group. Cartier himself, as solicitor of the Grand Trunk Railway, supplied a link in Montreal between Church and business. Both Montreal business and the Upper Canada Tories had been strongly anti-French before this; but the skilful Macdonald-Cartier leadership managed to keep racial and religious differences subordinated in a policy of vigorous economic expansion for the colony.

Over against this governing coalition, which kept its hold on office with only a few breaks until 1896, an opposition gradually consolidated itself. In Lower Canada a group of young French-Canadian intellectuals and professional men launched an ultra-democratic Rouge movement with ideas partly derived from the Paris of 1848, and entered into a losing fight against the domination of politics by the Roman Catholic Church. In Upper Canada the frontier agrarian discontent which had supplied William Lyon Mackenzie[1] with rebel supporters in 1837 found a new expression in the Clear Grit movement.[2] Grittism began with a demand for simple, economical government and an extension of elective institutions on the American model. After George Brown, the publisher of the Toronto *Globe,* joined the movement, it took on a pronounced anti-Catholic tone. The fact that Upper Canada was growing more rapidly than Lower Canada but that the two sections had equal representation in the legislature gave the Grits

---

[1] For notes to chapter xiv see page 579.

a grievance which they exploited to the full in the cry for "Representation by Population." Against Macdonald-Cartier conservatism, which it declared to be a corrupt alliance of the Roman Catholic Church with the Bank of Montreal and the Grand Trunk Railway, the *Globe* championed the interests of "the intelligent yeomanry of Upper Canada," and at the same time supported the claims of Toronto as a commercial and transportation centre against Montreal.

By the 1860's a deadlock had been produced in the legislature, and out of this came the coalition which achieved Confederation. Brown and the Grits joined with Cartier and Macdonald to negotiate a union with the Maritime colonies. But the Rouges refused to have anything to do with the coalition or its grandiose project, and the Grits remained in it for only a few months. It was Macdonald who established the closest personal relations with the political leaders of New Brunswick and Nova Scotia; and it was Macdonald who formed the first government of the new Dominion at the head of a Conservative party which now included elements from the Maritime Provinces and was soon to include supporters from Manitoba and British Columbia. The Grit-Rouge opposition also acquired allies from the outlying sections and grew into the Reform or Liberal party. It took about a generation after 1867 for this Liberal-Conservative two-party system to establish itself completely over the whole extent of the new nation, but by the 1890's every little Canadian boy and girl was being born either a little Liberal or else a little Conservative.

Since Confederation, the history of Canadian political parties falls into three periods: a Macdonald era, a Laurier era, and a King era. The retirement of the Right Honourable W. L. Mackenzie King in the summer of 1948 from the leadership of the Liberal party leaves room for the beginning of a fourth era. Mr. King retired after a prime-ministership which had lasted longer than that of any political leader in any British country since the institutions of parliamentary Cabinet government were first established in Britain in the early eighteenth century. He came into office as the result of the first general election after the First World War, in 1921. He and his party colleagues formed the Government of the country from that date to 1948, save for a few weeks in 1926 and a longer interval of five years, 1930–1935, when the Conservatives were in office.

This long hold on office by one of the two major parties under a single leader has been characteristic of Canadian politics since 1867. It seems to demonstrate the immense importance of the political leader in the functioning of Canadian parties. The Conservatives governed the country continuously from 1867 to 1896, with one unhappy Liberal interval of office during the depression years of 1873–1878. During all this period, until his death in 1891, they were led by Sir John Macdonald, who won six general elections for them—in 1867, 1872, 1878, 1882, 1887, 1891. From 1896 to 1911 the Liberals were in office under Sir Wilfrid Laurier, who led them in four successive election victories—1896, 1900, 1904, and 1908. After his defeat in 1911, there followed a unique ten years in which the Conservatives under Sir Robert Borden carried on the Government without the support of Quebec; they were reinforced in 1917 by a coalition with most of the English-speaking members of the Liberal party. In 1921 Mr. King led a revived Liberal party to victory. The new feature of the King era was the emergence of a variety of new minor parties which disrupted the simplicity of this historic two-party system and which the old parties have not yet been able to absorb or eliminate.

Macdonald's Conservative party earned its right to direct the fortunes of the new nationality by its courageous and imaginative nation-building policies. Under its leadership the bounds of the Dominion were extended from ocean to ocean. To consolidate this continental domain and to preëmpt it against American expansion from the south, the Canadian Pacific Railway was built in the 1880's from Montreal to Vancouver—an adventure which still staggers the imagination, a railway across an empty and unsurveyed continent connecting a little colonial community of four million at the eastern end with a still smaller community of a few thousand on the Pacific. In the depression of the 1870's the policy of tariff protection was adopted to rescue the Canadian economy from its vulnerability to American pressure and to build up a well-balanced economic structure, with urban manufacturing supplementing agriculture and the extractive processes. By a stroke of genius this protective policy was termed the "National Policy."

There was little that could be called conservative about all this. Macdonald's conservatism was a Hamiltonian policy of nation-building through an alliance of state power with the energies and ambitions of the great business interests.

The Liberal Opposition criticized particular aspects of these measures and opposed some of them outright. They exhausted the armoury of Cobdenite arguments against the tariff, pointing correctly enough to the danger of creating a new privileged class of protected manufacturers. Correctly enough, also, they predicted the evils that would result from a railway monopoly in the West and from the over-intimate ties between a powerful railway corporation and a political party. They denounced the régime of corruption and scandal which accompanied the Macdonald policies, for the price of Macdonald's nation-building was a demoralization of Canadian politics similar to that in the contemporaneous period in the United States after the Civil War.

Inevitably, perhaps, these criticisms created the impression that Liberals were not so keen on building up a great Canadian nation as were Conservatives. When they got into office themselves in 1873, the world depression ruined their opportunity to show what they could do in the economic expansion of the country. But undoubtedly the Liberals of Alexander Mackenzie's generation were never quite at home with the bustling crowd of contractors and speculators who wanted to build up the country by appropriating a slice of its natural resources to exploit for their own profit. The Liberal Opposition's support of reciprocity with the United States, and of provincial rights as against Macdonald's centralizing tendencies, also put them, or seemed to put them, on the anti-national side.

By 1896, five years after Macdonald's death, the Conservative party as a constructive force had gone to pieces. Laurier was able to win office for the Liberals by attracting the support of the majority of his fellow French Canadians. He and his predecessor in the leadership of the party, Edward Blake, had been gradually reorienting it away from its Grit anti-Catholic bias; and in 1896 he carried Quebec in spite of the fact that he was opposing his Church on the difficult issue of Manitoba schools. The Liberal party became henceforth the national party of French-English coöperation.

Laurier also abandoned for the time the Liberal pro-American outlook on commercial policy. He took over the National Policy of protection with slight modifications. In fact, his chief modification was a brilliant political device. He established a tariff preference for British goods in the Canadian market over American and other foreign imports; and by this British preference he stole from the Conservatives their chief campaign weapon, the Union Jack, to the waving of which they had long claimed an exclusive right. But the British preference was never allowed to operate so as to subject Canadian manufacturers to too much British competition, which in their eyes was just as undesirable as American competition.

Laurier also committed his Government to a grandiose transcontinental railway-building policy, and lined up railway and banking magnates behind his party just as Macdonald had done behind his. In the great wheat-boom of the early 1900's the Liberal party was able to assume the role of the nation-building party, the dispenser of prosperity, the benevolent creator of economic opportunity for everyone. Until Laurier suddenly took up reciprocity again in 1911, to be immediately repudiated by the business interests whom he had courted, there was little in these early years of the twentieth century to distinguish the two historic Canadian parties except that one was in and the other was out. Both had become composite parties of the standard American type, attempting to appeal to every interest-group in the country.

How deeply the Laurier generation of Liberals had become imbued with the gospel of prosperity under business leadership was shown by two significant facts. There were hardly any repercussions in Canadian politics from the raging campaign which American muck-rakers and reformers were conducting at this time against the evils of business in politics. And there were even fewer signs of Canadian liberalism taking up the humanitarian social-security programme which formed the main policy of contemporary British liberalism.

In one field there did seem to be a deep difference of principle between the two parties. Laurier fought against the programme of the new imperialism which had become popular in Britain. He prevented the Imperial Conference from developing into any form of centralized imperial government. While he rather reluctantly sent Canadian troops to the South African War in 1899, he refused to enter into imperial commitments for future military action; and in 1910 he took steps to begin the construction of a Canadian naval force. The alternative policy of contributing to the British navy was adopted by the Conservatives. Yet, after 1914, when Canada was led into the European war by a Conservative Government, it was Borden, the Conservative Prime Minister, who carried Laurier's policies to their logical conclusion. The British Commonwealth of Nations emerged in 1919, a loose association of self-governing states with no fixed treaty obligations to one another and no central organs of government. The Dominions achieved a right to a voice of their own in international conferences and a separate membership in the new international organization, the League of Nations. Mr. King was able to carry this process further without raising any violent party conflict. By the 1940's Canada had gone beyond Dominion status: she was equipped with a diplomatic service of her own, and her international contacts were no longer those of a junior partner in a Britannic firm, but of a nation participating actively in world affairs. And all this had been accomplished to the accompaniment of parliamentary debates remarkably academic in character and without parties seeking mandates from the electorate for opposing policies.

The First World War, however, put a strain upon Canadian national unity from which the historical two-party system found it difficult to recover. The two established parties, with their North American habit of collecting votes from all possible interest-groups without too fine a regard for principle, had worked fairly well down to 1914 as unifying agencies in a loosely-knit national community; and each had come to pursue policies which never deviated very far to the right or left of centre. But after 1917 the French Canadians felt so strongly about British overseas wars that the party responsible in that year for conscription was unable to regain an effective foothold in the French community for more than thirty years. Industrial workers and consumers in the urban areas suffered from the high cost of living and became furious at the failure of governments to do anything about it. Farmers felt that they were being victimized by an inequitable distribution of income from war production and that their grievances were ignored in Ottawa. Among all classes the emotional and intellectual upheaval of war created an atmosphere of restlessness, of willingness to make political experiments. The immediate result was an insurgent movement, primarily agrarian, that put farmers' governments into office in Alberta, Manitoba, and Ontario, and sent sixty-five "Progressives" to the first post-war federal Parliament in 1921.

This was the problem which Mr. King, the successor of Laurier in the leadership of the Liberal party, had to meet. The Conservatives were routed in the election; but his party had not enough seats for a majority, and depended upon the Progressives, who formed the second-largest group in the House. The skill with which he manoeuvred in this situation saved the Liberals as at least one national party which could still successfully appeal to all sections and classes. He enjoyed the support of the French Canadians in even greater degree than had Macdonald or Laurier. The western Progressives he treated sympathetically as impatient Liberals with whose main aspirations—for freer trade, against imperialism, against monopolistic big business—his own party had always been in accord. He invited them into the government fold, where they could be more influential than in opposition. In the end the two men whom the Progressive party elected in succession as leaders found their way into the Liberal Cabinet. Progressivism, which had swept like a prairie fire from the Rockies eastward until it was stopped by the fire-break of the Ottawa River, was divided, once it reached Parliament, in its conception of its own function. Moderate leaders wanted to build up a genuine low-tariff party—liberal with a small l—and were willing to negotiate with Mr. King. A more radical element, coming mainly from Alberta, with some support in Ontario, expounded a new political theory of government by coöperating economic groups. It looked upon the Progressive movement not as a party in the old sense, but as the first expression of a new order—the representatives of the interests of the agricultural group, who were prepared to negotiate with other organized interests, presumably inside some kind of economic cabinet. This, said the expounders of the new faith, would produce a more genuine democracy than the sham democracy of two old-type parties both controlled by eastern big business.

These internal divisions, combined with the post-war return to normalcy, led to a rapid disintegration of the Progressive movement. By 1930, except in Alberta, the old parties were in the ascendant again in the provinces; and at Ottawa the Progressive contingent had shrunk to a mere handful. The first challenge to the old party system had been triumphantly defeated.

Depression, however, in the 1930's threw up further political expressions of discontent. Progressivism was reborn in the Coöperative Commonwealth Federation (the C.C.F.). And the Second World War, following close upon the depression, apparently shook the Canadian voter still more violently from his hereditary allegiance to the old parties. The failure of insurgency after the First World War to blast the old system from its place induces scepticism as to the likelihood of any far-reaching changes in political habits coming out of this second period of unrest and expectancy. But during those years of confusion two great developments in the structure of Canadian democracy were taking place outside the realm of politics. Farmers, especially the wheat-farmers of the prairies, were building up a powerful coöperative organization for the marketing of their products. And in the cities trade-unionism was going ahead with gigantic strides. Sooner or later, it seems certain that organized farmers and organized workers will turn their attention to political action to protect their own interests, and whenever such action is undertaken, the balance of power in the group-diplomacy which constitutes Canadian politics will be profoundly altered.

The results of the general election of 1945 are given in table 1. The Independents from Quebec Province mostly supported the Liberal Government, thus giving the Liberals about sixty seats from Quebec, which is what they steadily won there after the conscription issue of 1917, except for one election in 1930. Even without the support of the scattered Independent membership, the Liberals had a majority throughout the duration of the Parliament elected in 1945. And their security in office was increased by the fact that the Conservatives and the C.C.F., the two main opposition groups, were normally more opposed to each other than either was to the Government. In this, as in all recent elections, the percentage of the popular vote cast for each party differed widely from the percentage of seats won by it. In 1945 the Liberals got 41 per cent; Conservatives, 29 per cent; C.C.F., 15 per cent; Social-Crediters, 4 per cent; others, 11 per cent, of the total vote.

TABLE 1

NUMBER OF SEATS WON IN GENERAL ELECTION OF 1945

Party	Nova Scotia	New Brunswick	Prince Edward Island	Quebec	Ontario	Manitoba	Saskatchewan	Alberta	British Columbia	Yukon	Total
Liberal	8	7	3	54	34	10	2	2	5		125
Independent Liberal				2							2
Progressive Conservative *	3	3	1	1	48	2	1	2	5	1	67
Independent Progressive Conservative				1							1
Coöperative Commonwealth Federation	1					5	18		4		28
Independent C.C.F.									1		1
Social Credit								13			13
Bloc Populaire				2							2
Labour Progressive †				1							1
Independent				4					1		5
Total	12	10	4	65	82	17	21	17	16	1	245

SOURCE: Based on *Canadian Parliamentary Guide*, 1948.

* The party which is officially known as Progressive Conservative since its last national convention has gone through a bewildering number of changes of name in recent years. It was founded in 1854 as Liberal-Conservative, and is ordinarily referred to as the Conservative party.

† The Labour Progressive party emerged under this title after the Communist party was declared illegal by the courts in the 1930's. The one member elected by the party in 1945, from a Montreal constituency, lost his seat later when convicted in the courts during the highly-publicized Soviet spy trials.

The new phenomenon has been the presence of two new parties in addition to the Liberals and the Conservatives. The Coöperative Commonwealth Federation, the Canadian socialist party whose name is always popularly shortened to C.C.F., and the Social Credit party both emerged in western Canada in the depression years of the 1930's. There are other small party groups whose voting support is not large enough to show as a significant percentage of the whole electorate. Notable among them are the

Labour Progressive party (Communist), active since the early 1920's in the bigger industrial and mining centres; and the *Bloc Populaire Canadien,* an expression of extreme French nationalist feeling in Quebec with a radical social policy, which also came into being in the depression years. By 1948 the *Bloc* was pretty well replaced in the Quebec provincial field by another nationalist party, the *Union Nationale,* headed by M. Maurice Duplessis, with a vaguer economic policy but a greater practical capacity for political organization and a more powerful demagogic appeal in exploiting the sentiment of provincial autonomy.

The Conservative party provided the official leader of the Opposition in the Parliament of 1945. But one marked feature of the last quarter of a century has been the fact that only the Liberal party has continuously succeeded in maintaining itself as a fully national party in the sense that it draws substantial support from all regions. In 1945 the Liberals won 18 of the 26 seats in the three Atlantic provinces, 54 of Quebec's 65 seats (plus most of the Quebec Independents), 34 out of 82 in Ontario, 14 of the 55 seats in the three Prairie Provinces, and 5 out of 16 in British Columbia. The Conservatives, on the other hand, won three-quarters of their representation, 48 seats, in Ontario, the only one of the nine provinces with a Conservative Government. In Quebec's 65 constituencies they ran only 29 candidates and elected only 1. In the Maritime Provinces they won 7 out of 26 seats, in the Prairie Provinces 5 out of 55, and in British Columbia 5 out of 16. The distribution of Conservative votes has not been as one-sided as these figures might suggest, and the size of their vote in most elections since 1917 has entitled them proportionately to a larger representation than they have obtained. This has been their justification through the lean years for claiming to be still a nation-wide major party.

The two new parties have so far been even more sectional in their parliamentary representation than have the Conservatives. Of the 28 C.C.F. members elected in 1945, Saskatchewan provided 18; British Columbia, 4; Manitoba, 5; and the whole of Canada east of Manitoba, only 1. All 13 of the Social Credit members were from Alberta. Obviously, on the basis of these figures, neither the C.C.F. nor Social Credit can claim to be a nation-wide party. The

C.C.F. has polled large numbers of votes in Ontario, but in 1945 it failed to win any seats there. And neither group has succeeded in making any effective impact upon French Quebec.

The Social Credit movement swept into power in Alberta in 1935. The Government which it ousted from office there was neither Liberal nor Conservative but the U.F.A. (United Farmers of Alberta), which had itself ousted the Liberals in 1921. Thus Alberta has been outside the realm of the two old parties for almost thirty years. The Social Credit leader was a Calgary school-principal, William Aberhart, who had made himself famous by leadership of a Sunday Bible-class whose meetings were broadcast on the air, and who in the early years of the depression had imbibed the social-credit doctrines expounded by an Englishman, Major C. H. Douglas. At the depth of the worst depression which western agriculture had ever experienced, his party promised to deliver Alberta farmers from their sufferings by a credit of $25 a month to every citizen. The metaphysical intricacies of the orthodox teaching as to the nature and function of credit and currency, and the various heresies which have seduced some mistaken individuals from the true faith since 1935, cannot be explained here. The Social Credit Government, once in office, failed to carry out its promised benefactions in credit, but it has remained firmly in office. From being a rather fantastic millennial movement of the left, Social Credit has moved far to the right in recent years. After entering the lists as champion of the farmer against big business and the parties dominated by big business, it now campaigns as the defender of individualism against the threat of socialist totalitarianism as represented by the C.C.F. Its efforts between 1944 and 1948 to spread the gospel into neighbouring provinces and into the East were an almost complete failure.

The Coöperative Commonwealth Federation was founded in 1932. Small local socialist labour groups had come and gone in the big Canadian cities for years before this, in unsuccessful efforts to imitate the British and European labour movements. Trade-unionism in Canada was weak in the industrial field, and politically it followed the tradition established by Gompers in the United States. Canadian farmers had indeed entered politics after 1918, but the Progressive movement had disintegrated from lack of a clear purpose. The C.C.F. was launched in Calgary at a meeting of some of these labour and farmer groups of western Canada who had survived the political discouragements of the late 1920's and who were now convinced that no programme short of a full socialist one would emancipate farmers and workers from the disastrous effects of capitalist booms and depressions.

Because socialist terminology was unpopular in North America, and because it was starting in life as a federation of groups aiming at the coöperative commonwealth, the new movement took the clumsy name of Coöperative Commonwealth Federation, which, fortunately for itself, has been shortened by general consent to C.C.F. It chose as its first leader J. S. Woodsworth, a former Methodist minister and since 1921 Labour M.P. from Winnipeg. Woodsworth had made himself known in the days of the Progressives as the best-informed and ablest of the western radical leaders. In 1933, at a national convention in Regina attended by delegates from Ontario and the East, it adopted a comprehensive socialist programme set forth in what has become known as the Regina Manifesto. By this time a good many middle-class intellectuals had joined the movement, and some of them drafted the Regina programme. It was an attempt to formulate in language applicable to Canadian conditions a Fabian socialist policy such as the British Labour party had worked out for Great Britain. The programme did not include nationalization of land, since all were agreed on the family farm as the most efficient and socially desirable unit of agriculture. It emphasized the conception of planning, with government regulation of the economy as a whole, government ownership or control of monopolistic or semi-monopolistic industries, government boards in charge of external trade, a full social-security system, and a national labour code. Constitutional parliamentary methods were to be used to bring about the transition to the new social order.

There were Marxian elements in the C.C.F. for whom this programme was not full-blooded enough. In its early days it had a great deal of trouble with "fellow-travellers," and it has not yet entirely eliminated them.

The first main appeal of the C.C.F. was to the prairie farmers, and it was in Saskatchewan that it won its first political victory.

In 1944 it captured the provincial government from the Liberals who had held office almost continuously since the province was founded in 1905. In June, 1948, the C.C.F. Government in Saskatchewan was reëlected to office, though with a considerably reduced number of seats. The movement has been strong also in the industrial areas of Vancouver and in Winnipeg, where the Winnipeg strike of 1919 started Labour into politics. But it failed for some time to make progress in eastern Canada among either farmers or trade-unionists. Only a handful of members were elected in any general election down to 1945. Then the party, under the leadership of Mr. M. J. Coldwell of Saskatchewan, won 28 seats, and was particularly successful in winning votes among the men of the armed forces.

Since the outbreak of the Second World War the threat of the C.C.F. has forced the two old parties to form a Liberal-Conservative coalition in both British Columbia and Manitoba in order to hold these provinces against it. In the Ontario provincial election of June, 1948, it won a remarkable series of victories in Toronto and some of the main urban areas—victories due principally to the active intervention for the first time of the C.C.L. (Canadian Congress of Labor, connected with the American C.I.O.) trade unions.

The adoption by the C.C.L. unions of the C.C.F. as their political party, following the mode of procedure of the British trade unions in the early 1900's in joining the new Labour party, may be a turning-point in the history of the C.C.F. But the A. F. of L. unions remain true to the Gompers tradition. As trade-unionism becomes stronger in the C.C.F., the party will undoubtedly be troubled by tension between its labour and its farmer wings, not to mention the difficulties which both may find in working harmoniously with the growing middle-class elements which have joined the movement. By 1948, however, it formed the provincial government in Saskatchewan, functioned as His Majesty's Opposition in all the other provinces west of the Ottawa River, and hoped, by forcing Liberals and Conservatives into coalition in the federal field, as it had done in two of the provinces, to become one of the two major parties itself.

In the mean time, there is one obstacle that has proved to be insurmountable to all the political parties except the Liberals. This is the Province of Quebec. Canada has been governed almost continuously since 1867 by a national party, the nucleus of whose strength has come from a majority of French votes in Quebec, with majority support also from the Atlantic and Western Provinces and with the Ontario majority usually in opposition. During the King era the Liberal party was stronger than in earlier days in Quebec and weaker in the West, the home of the new protest movements.

The threat to Liberalism in Quebec for the last forty years has come mainly from local French Catholic nationalism. It started with the movement organized by M. Henri Bourassa against Laurier's sending of troops to the Boer War in 1899. Laurier was eventually defeated in 1911 by an alliance between anti-British Bourassa nationalists of Quebec and the strongly imperialist Conservatives of English Canada, an alliance of which many present-day observers have been reminding themselves. When Laurier opposed conscription in 1917 he recaptured French nationalist support for the Liberal party. But a more virulent anti-English separatist nationalism sprang up in the depression of the 1930's, fed on the economic grievances of a province in which most of the natural resources were in the hands of English-Canadian business men.

Mr. King's greatest achievement as a national statesman was his success in carrying the two Canadian communal groups through the Second World War without any such tragic English-French split as occurred in 1917. But in provincial politics Quebec fell into the hands of a new *Union Nationale* party under the leadership of M. Maurice Duplessis. Many of the leaders of this extreme nationalist movement came from circles that were once Conservative. In the controversial issues of Dominion-provincial relations, which were never quite pushed off the stage by the war and which revived as soon as the war was finished, M. Duplessis formed an anti-Liberal and anti-Ottawa axis with Mr. George Drew, the Conservative Premier of Ontario.

At the national Conservative convention in September, 1948, Mr. Drew was elected leader of the federal Conservative party. He succeeded Mr. John Bracken of Manitoba, who had been chosen leader in 1942 in an effort to strengthen the Conservative appeal to the West. Mr. Drew's strategy was plainly to extend into the federal field the Drew-Duplessis alliance which had worked so well when the two men were provincial premiers. Quebec and Ontario in their total population and wealth far overtop all the other provinces put together. It was generally supposed, too, that the Social Credit leaders in Alberta were not unfriendly to the Drew-Duplessis forces. A radically new political alignment in Canadian politics seemed to be in the making.

But the Canadian electorate would have none of it. The election of June 27, 1949, resulted in a sweep for the Liberals such as had never been equalled in Canadian history. Out of 262 seats in the new House of Commons they won 193. Newfoundland, the new province, gave them 5 of its 7 seats; the other three Maritime Provinces gave them 21 out of 27 seats; Quebec, 68 out of 73, Ontario, 56 out of 83; the three Prairie Provinces, 32 out of 53; British Columbia, 10 out of 18. The Conservatives won only 41 seats, of which 25 were in Ontario. The C.C.F., suffering badly in Saskatchewan and failing to make progress in Ontario, was reduced to 13 seats. Social Credit won 10 seats in Alberta.

This was a sweep in seats won. As usual, the division of the electoral vote showed a rather different picture. Incomplete figures (at the time of writing) gave the Liberals 49.5 per cent of the votes, the Conservatives 30 per cent, and the C.C.F. 13.6 per cent. If to the Conservative votes be added the "Independents" in Quebec who were mostly Duplessisites, the Conservative percentage of the vote was rather better than it had been in 1945. The C.C.F. percentage went down, while the Liberal percentage rose markedly. On any calculation the result was a remarkable victory for Mr. St. Laurent, the Liberal successor of Mr. King. His fellow Quebeckers repudiated the Duplessis forces overwhelmingly, apparently delighted to have a French Canadian once again as Prime Minister. And Ontario repudiated Mr. Drew. Evidently the Liberal party is still, as it was in the King era, the party that divides Canadians least.

The advent of the C.C.F. has been important for other reasons than its threat to become a new major party. It has tried to develop organizational practices which will give a real voice and influence to the rank-and-file members of the party. Unlike the old parties, which have collected funds from wealthy individuals and corporations, it finances itself by regular membership dues and by many small contributions from individual members for special purposes. The controlling body of the party is a national convention of delegates which meets biennially. The convention elects or reëlects the national leader, as well as a small executive council, at each biennial session. It formulates party policy and draws up a campaign platform for each election. In each province an annual provincial convention performs parallel functions for the provincial sphere. All human organizations tend in time to become oligarchical in control; but the C.C.F. has so far combined a skilful leadership at the top with a genuine democratic base, and its rank-and-file members express themselves vigorously at conventions.

The new party publishes a weekly or fortnightly paper in each of the provinces west of the Ottawa River. Equally important, it has a small secretariat who engage in economic and social research, with the assistance of many voluntary specialists from the universities, and who produce memoranda and reports for the use of parliamentary members, councils, and conferences. The party publishes more books and pamphlets than Canadian politics has ever seen before. Its local clubs carry on study-groups in winter, and its provincial organizations conduct summer schools. The amount of organization and propaganda in the intervals between elections is something new in Canada. The British Labour party, of course, forms the model in all this democratic activity. Like their British fellows, the C.C.F. leaders and followers still consider themselves a movement as well as a political party.

Organization in the old parties has become highly oligarchic; until recently, except for the distribution of patronage, party machines have remained quiescent between election campaigns. Canadian parties are more closely controlled by parliamentary leaders, provincial or federal, than are American parties; and local bosses do not play so prominent a part. But as national organizations the Liberal and Conservative parties have remained loose federations of not very active provincial machines. The group of leaders in Ottawa determine national policy for them, and the provincial machines get out the votes at elections. What proportion of party funds is raised nationally and what provincially, what may be the sources and the size of such funds—all this is part of the *arcana imperii* which has not been revealed to the Canadian public.

Neither of the old parties has anything that really parallels the regular convention system of the C.C.F. Since Confederation the Liberals have held three national party conventions. The first was in 1893, for the purpose of pulling the party together after its disastrous espousal of Unrestricted Reciprocity; it led to the victory of 1896. The second was in 1919; its purpose was again to unite the party after the split of 1917 over conscription. It was at this convention that Mr. Mackenzie King was chosen party leader; and the result was the victory of 1921. The third convention came in August, 1948. It chose Mr. Louis St. Laurent to succeed Mr. King as leader, thus reviving memories of the Laurier régime when, for the first time, a national party sat in the seats of government with a French Canadian as leader. Mr. St. Laurent had been Minister of External Affairs. After the convention his chief departmental official, Mr. Lester Pearson, resigned from the Civil Service to enter politics as Minister of External Affairs. This notable accession of strength to the Liberals and the reorganization of the party under an outstanding French Canadian were evidently steps to equip the party for the struggle which was seen to be coming.

The Conservatives chose their leaders and drafted their platforms in parliamentary caucuses at Ottawa until 1927. In recent years they have held four national conventions—in 1927, 1938, 1942, and 1948. Each successive convention chose a new leader. This sudden addiction to the convention habit was probably to be explained not by a Conservative conversion to American party practices, but by the continuing difficulty which thwarted the party from the end of the First World War in finding either leader or platform which could collect enough votes from the electorate. The 1948 convention, however, with its plan of aligning Ontario and Quebec under Conservative leadership, seemed to mark a new era. But the Drew-Duplessis alliance was decisively rejected by both provinces in the 1949 election.

Canadian party conventions draw up platforms, but these are the most American phenomena in Canadian politics. Nobody in the party or outside pays much attention to them; and party policy is really enunciated before each election in the addresses of the party leader.

Canadian party conventions, both in new and in old parties, are, of course, devices for working up party enthusiasm. The smoke-filled hotel room can also, no doubt, be discovered at all of them by the inquiring newspaper-man. But they have not as a rule been occasions for either the cynical trading of bloc votes or the hysterical mass demonstrations which make the American quadrennial conventions the wonder of the world. Voting is done by ballot, oratory is less confined to the sacred incantations of party, and the proceedings generally are those of business-like, if sometimes excited, adults.

Such is the complex picture of Canadian party politics in 1949. Conservative hopes of a revived party with substantial support in all sections—the Maritime Provinces, Quebec, Ontario, and the West—met with bitter disappointment in the election of June 27. The Liberals remain the only effective nation-wide party. And a two-party system requires two fairly well balanced national parties. The C.C.F. hopes of becoming the second party, and thereby becoming also the Opposition, on the disintegration of the Conservatives, turned out to be equally unrealistic. Had the C.C.F. been successful, this would have tended to make the pattern of Canadian politics more like the British and less like the American. The main division would then run between left and right, between radicals and conservatives (conservatives with a small c, a group that would include a great many Liberals with a capital L), between socialists and anti-socialists.

But all the Canadian parties now profess to be progressive, all present advanced social-security programmes, all propose some degree of state regulation of the economy for the benefit of the masses. All the other parties are angling for the same votes and the same interest-groups which socialists may consider to belong to them. Whatever their moral indignation at the potential iniquities of totalitarian socialism, the parties on the right will continue to move in the socialistic direction; their ritualistic incantations of individualist faith have less and less connexion with their actual practices. And whatever its moral indignation at the actual iniquities of monopoly capitalism, a socialist party which, in the process of becoming a national party capable of government, has made adjustments to the points of view of French Catholics, individualist eastern farmers, and a perplexing variety of middle-class groups may not be so clear-cut in its doctrines as the C.C.F. seems, to both friends and enemies, to be at present. Under whatever new forms, the old group-diplomacy will continue. The two-party system of the 1950's or 1960's, if a two-party system crystallizes out of the multi-party confusion of today, may look to historians remarkably like the two-party system of the days of Macdonald and Laurier.

CHAPTER XV

The State and Economic Life

BY ALEXANDER BRADY

IN MODERN CANADA the activity of the state has hitherto been shaped by the pioneer nature of the country, the physical structure of the half-continent, the imperial sweep of settlement after 1867, the influence of the interacting ideas and institutions of Britain and the United States, and the quick response of the whole society to the advance of western industrialism. State action is similar to that in the other Dominions or indeed to that of other northern countries with moving frontiers of settlement. The special distinctions that exist are rooted in differences of geographic position, physical environment, and cultural quality. Here there is space for only a brief sketch of the general theme. The role of the state in the economic life of Canada is really the modern history of Canada, and all the chapters in this book throw light upon it.

Notable is the presence in numerous forms of protective or neo-mercantilist policies with both political and economic ends. From the establishment of the federal state in the 'sixties of the last century, the commercial, financial, manufacturing, labour, and even agrarian groups have exerted persistent pressure to transform a simple colonial economy into one integrated and national. This national aspiration has involved not merely protective tariffs, adopted in the 1870's and ever since maintained, but also bounties for struggling industries, prohibitions on the export of raw materials in order to stimulate domestic processing, the building and administration of canals, state aid to or direct participation in the construction of railways in order to exploit soils and forests and mines, the public generation and distribution of hydro-electric power, and the fostering of agriculture. Most of these state policies were concerned with creating and maintaining a continental economy wherein trade would flow east and west across the continent within the political boundaries of a growing nation.

Here we witness the familiar process whereby national economic policies are shaped in any modern democratic state, whether of Europe or of the New World. Special interests, conscious of their disadvantages and anxious for succour, argue their case before the public or directly exert upon governments such pressure as they can command. The organized groups of Canada are anxious to protect their economic identity against the formidable competition of rival groups in the United States. They are always conscious of a hard and unremitting struggle for survival in a continental environment wherein American industrialism, fed by rich natural resources, is an imperial and ever-expanding power. The concept of Canadian nationality has lent coherence to the numerous claims of these interests for protection, and in public debate has given such claims a more attractive complexion.

Protection, however, has extended beyond the sphere of material interests. The establishment of the Canadian Broadcasting Corporation (1936), patterned in the main upon the British, was designed to afford protection and encouragement to many elements of cultural life. It has ambitiously but quietly sought to foster in the populace some sense of a national community and a national culture, both of which have seemed menaced by the power and success of the private broadcasting companies in the neighbouring country. While the proximity of the United States is only one of many influences, it is a major one, written clearly not merely in the fiscal but in all phases of state activity.

Varied circumstances have tempered the policy of fiscal protection. The agrarian interest, although weakened by regional fissures, has always had considerable weight in politics, and has been prompt to withdraw support from parties that seek what it regards as an extravagant protection of secondary industry. It has not been reticent in demanding protective duties for its own products, but large sectors of the rural community concerned with production for export have always supported freer trade, if not free trade.

The growing political power of the wheat areas in the West during the early decades of the twentieth century strengthened such views in Ottawa, and in particular helped to revive interest in the idea of trade reciprocity with the United States.

The division of Canada into geographic and economic regions has also helped to modify the protectionist impulse, for rarely do all the regions obtain a similar benefit from a specific form of protection, and some regions disclaim ever receiving a major benefit from protective tariffs. A cautious policy that will appease as many sections as possible becomes politically imperative in order to ease the strains of the federation and save it from disruption. Such a policy has been dictated no less by the kindred need of maintaining a balance between Canada's commercial relations with the United States and those with Great Britain. Imperial preference, introduced in the 'nineties, was motivated not merely by sentiment for the motherland, or special economic interests shared with Great Britain, but by the necessity of exerting a bargaining influence upon the United States. From the 'seventies of the last century to the present, tariffs as an instrument in nation-building have been used with opportunism in performing a difficult task.

In Canada public ownership is closely related to protection in that most of it was undertaken in connexion with public utilities, such as railways and electric power, in order to quicken development in primary and secondary industry and to create an economy more integrated and diversified, able to stand on its own feet alongside the young, powerful economy of the neighbouring Republic. The factor of competition between American and Canadian transport routes has always been present, and helps to explain the fostering solicitude of government. Nation-building through the tying together of scattered settlements and the opening up of fresh territories has been the primary motive for railway subsidies or direct state construction. The unity of Canada has required railway lines no less than the Roman Empire required roads; they have been the main agency of colonization and industrial diversification. To the men who established federation in 1867, they were imperative to bind the Maritime Provinces to the St. Lawrence Valley and the western lands to the urban areas of the East, creating a continental market within which a national economy could be built.

But, in a new country, lines had to be pushed ahead of available traffic, involving hazards of heavy capital investment from which private enterprise shrank without state support. The Intercolonial Railway, completed in 1876 and built directly by the Government to connect Halifax with Quebec and Montreal, illustrates that combination of political and economic design which is implicit in all state-sponsored railways. Judged by the yard-stick of private business, it was never a commercial success. But it is almost irrelevant to assess it by the criterion of deficits or surpluses, since it was primarily a political achievement that served well the ends of a national government seeking to create an integrated community. Its administration was never brilliant and was always handicapped by competition with water-transport and shorter rail-routes through the United States, and by political interference, especially political patronage and the insistence of the Government on low rates in order to lessen the hostility of the Maritime Provinces towards other federal policies.

The transcontinental Canadian Pacific line was begun by the Government, but it was soon transformed into a private enterprise, much aided by public land-grants and capital. The land-grants were intended to make the railway no less responsible for colonization than the Government itself. The later transcontinental lines, the Canadian Northern and the Grand Trunk Pacific, were similarly assisted by the federal and provincial governments. The eastern branch of the Grand Trunk Pacific was built directly by the Government, and its route and terminus were in part determined by political considerations and regional claims. Generous public aid through land-grants, cash subsidies, and bond guaranties helped to double railway milage between 1900 and 1915, an increase which resulted in excessive capacity and created heavy overhead costs that could not be met from current revenues. The financial plight of these railways during the First World War brought them under the Government as the guarantor of their bonds, and between 1918 and 1923 the present Canadian National Railways took form, incorporating the Intercolonial with other lines. In this instance public ownership was virtually predetermined by the former lavish aid to private corporations, which in turn was derived from the perennial pressure exerted on the Government by commercial, industrial, and agrarian interests determined upon an expanding and continental economy. Historical cause and effect have here a singular lucidity.

What has been the record of the Canadian National Railways? It is obvious that the system suffers from serious disadvantages when compared over the last quarter of a century with the great private road, the Canadian Pacific: it had a larger milage of light traffic lines; its equipment and property were at the outset in wretched physical condition; it faced throughout vast territories the task of creating goodwill among shippers and the public; as a government-owned railway it was subject to embarrassing pressures from various organized groups, which hampered effective management; and, finally, in 1922 it was simply a collection of different lines, built for competition, which had to be welded into a genuine unity. Inevitably, the Dominion was compelled annually to pay millions of dollars in deficits. But the Canadian National Railways are not to be judged merely by the test of profitable returns on investment, since, like other lines, they have been an instrument of nation-building, drawing together widely-scattered communities and making possible the exploitation of natural resources remote from the industrial heart of Canada. Credit, moreover, must be given for a notable improvement in their character. They became a distinguished railway system.

What happened within the national sphere happened also within the regions, especially in Ontario and Quebec. In Ontario the province constructed and operated the Temiskaming and Northern Railway, which was planned to quicken and integrate the development of a provincial economy and to bind the growth of the northern region, with its forests and mines, to the financial and industrial metropolis of Toronto. By 1913 the railway was extended to tide-water at Moosonee on an estuary of James Bay, and since then it has helped to open up the resources of the northland and to consolidate Ontario's industrialism.

Despite periodic flurries of opinion on the issue, the state-owned railway operates across the continent virtually side by side with the Canadian Pacific, accepting the same system of rates but in some degree competing in the quality of service. Thereby a giant railway monopoly is avoided. In times of economic adversity an amalgamation of the railways is advocated under either public or private management, but the powerful railway unions have hitherto resisted such a solution, fearing a reduction in staff. Other regional and group interests would also be sharply affected by amalgamation, and hence private enterprise and public policy continue to be mixed in the railway operations of Canada.

In the administrative organization of state railways Canadian experience may not afford so rich a variety as that found in Australia, but it has interest. Canada, on the whole, has discarded the direct operation of the lines by a department of the Government, a system which had exhibited the ills of political patronage in the days of the Intercolonial Railway. When the Canadian National Railways were established, provision was made for a public and independent board, appointed by the Government, resembling the organized directors in a private corporation, and fully answerable for administration. But while the Government did not attempt to control the day-to-day operations, it could not avoid a perennial interest in the performance of the management because of the profound importance of the railways to the public and because it paid the deficits. In 1932 the Duff Commission condemned the large board on the ground that it provided too much opportunity for regional pressures to assert themselves, and recommended instead a small body of three trustees. This institution in turn worked ill, and was replaced by a larger body, whose performance is under the annual scrutiny of a standing committee of Parliament.

State provision of electricity has a developmental role somewhat similar to that of railways, and the hydro-electric power system of Ontario easily holds pride of place. It represents the most impressive experiment in public ownership and is influential in other like ventures not merely within Canada but in the United States. Collectivism in the hydro-power of Ontario, in contrast to private enterprise in the hydro-power of the neighbouring state of New York, is a provincial complement to that national policy pursued by governments at Ottawa since the 'seventies: the public construction of canals, the building or subsidizing of railways, and the provision of protective tariffs and bonuses for secondary industry. It received its initial impulse from the small manufacturers, merchants, and municipal councillors of southern Ontario, who, in a province without coal, were zealous to exploit the sole major source of power in order to further a sturdy industrialism and a robust urban life. The insecurity of relying solely on American coal, periodically accentuated by stoppages and strikes in the mines of Pennsylvania, alarmed the public and influenced its action. In the early years of the century there was a prevalent fear that private companies financed in the United States might exploit the spectacular waters of Niagara and create a local aggregation of industry beneficial principally to American interests.

During the first decade of the century the urgent need of cheap power for industrial expansion was decisive in creating a drive for public ownership. The expanding market for goods on the new agrarian frontiers of Saskatchewan and Alberta impelled manufacturers in Ontario to support any measures that enabled them to lessen their costs and enlarge their output in the face of American competition. Heavy investment of capital in transmission lines was necessary in order to utilize in Toronto and other urban centres the water resource of Niagara; under government guaranty such capital was obtainable at relatively low rates. The chief creator of the public hydro-system, Adam Beck, always emphasized that cheap power was not to be had if private companies were permitted to command the situation and extract profit on watered stock. To be cheap, power must be sold at cost, and from the outset sale at cost has been the cardinal trait of the Ontario system. Public ownership was designed to eliminate profit-taking from the distribution of electricity. Such has been the interpretation placed upon the popular slogan that did such doughty service on many a political platform— "The water-powers of the province for the people of the province." In their more ebullient moods, politicians even spoke of making electric power as free as air, but this language was merely the customary hyperbole of a popular appeal.

The administrative instrument for this collective ownership of power is the Hydro-Electric Power Commission of Ontario, which since 1906 has existed as a body corporate of three members, appointed by the Lieutenant-Governor in Council and holding office during pleasure.[1] From the outset the tie with the provincial government has been intimate. At least one of the commissioners must be a Cabinet Minister, and up to 1935 the capital used was advanced by the Government. After 1935 the Commission began to raise its own financial requirements. Adam Beck, the remarkable chairman of the Commission from its inception in 1906 till his death nineteen years later, was for part of the period a Minister of the Crown as well as chairman of the Commission. But Beck was always determined to make "the Hydro" as autonomous as possible in order to protect it from a political interference fatal to efficiency. Hence he emphasized that it was strictly a coöperative enterprise of the numerous municipalities[2] in the province, existing only because these municipalities freely contracted to buy power from the Commission at prices fixed to cover the costs of generation and transmission. Through their payments for power the municipalities liquidated the borrowings made by the province for generating plants and transmission lines.

Yet in only a limited way is the actual administration of the system operated as a coöperative enterprise. The provincial Commission, under the authority of a provincial statute, exercises a decisive jurisdiction over the councils and commissions engaged in distributing electricity within their local areas. It controls wherever necessary the rates of municipalities which purchase power from the Commission, directs the use of profits in reducing rates, and insists on a uniform system of book-keeping. At every turn it makes them cling to its interpretation of the principle of power at cost, and more than once in the exercise of its authority it has clashed with the city of Toronto.

As a result of its essential nature the hydro-system was never remote from miscellaneous pressures, on the one hand from the provincial government and on the other from the municipalities. Adam Beck, through the weight of his personality and the skill of his leadership, created in all parties a strong following which shielded the administration and policies of the

[1] For notes to chapter xv see pages 579–580.

hydro-system from becoming a political football. Indeed, he was one of those men, rarely met with in political life, who, fortunately for Canada, was able to make his cause transcend the bounds of party. But soon after his death the management of the system came under intense political fire. The expanding consumption of electricity in the 'twenties, quickened by the growing industrialization in southern Ontario, began to strain the existing generating capacity, and a continued growth in the demand threatened to create an acute shortage of power. This threat drove the Commission to make contracts with private corporations in Quebec for the purchase of current generated in the Ottawa and St. Lawrence valleys.

In the early 'thirties the sharp onset of depression quickly changed the immediate outlook, reduced the demand for power, and left the Commission saddled with heavy contractual arrangements. Here was a situation politically exploitable, and a Liberal party, out of office in the province for a quarter of a century, was not unwilling to exploit it, encouraged doubtless by the prevalent ignorance of the public on the subtleties of the production and distribution of power. It was charged on the hustings that the Conservative leaders had accepted gifts for the party treasury from the Quebec "power barons" with whom the contracts were made, that the actual prices paid were excessive, and that the integrity of public ownership was menaced by dealings with private companies. The electoral triumph of the Liberals brought not merely a revision in the contracts but the dismissal of some high officials in the hydro-system for being implicated in bad policies. Thus in a brusque and almost brutal manner the authority of the Government over the hydro-enterprise was demonstrated. Such incidents in the early 'thirties exposed the weaknesses in the former administration of the system, among them the failure of the Commission to publicize adequately what it was attempting, and the no less serious error of pushing the permanent officials into a position in which they became embroiled in political controversy.

But on the whole no serious political interferences with the administration of the hydro-system have been revealed. Certainly, although mistakes have been made, no political corruption has reduced the quality of its performance. The engineer has generally been left with adequate freedom to perform his technical task. The Commission has been fortunate in securing distinguished engineers, whose utilization of the provincial water resources has made possible a steady industrial advance. The municipal distribution of the system increased from 2,500 horse-power in 1910 to 2,608,000 in 1945, and the number of coöperating municipalities from ten to more than nine hundred. Isolated generating stations have been linked by a vast network of transmission lines, and from hydro-power in country and town the economy of Ontario has received a remarkable stimulus.

Although the experiment of Ontario in public ownership profoundly influenced other provinces, the character and the pace of public policy in each province have varied greatly in accordance with physical, industrial, and cultural circumstances. Quebec for some decades shrank from entrusting the state with the electrical industry. In this province, industry was less diversified and there were fewer small manufacturers, merchants, and workers scattered in many towns and eager for cheap power. In Quebec, moreover, hydro-electric power at widely-distributed sites was developed incidentally by large companies concerned with other industries such as pulp and paper, asbestos, cement, and mining. Once firmly established in the production of electricity, these giant corporations were not easy to dislodge, and in any event the French electorate was not greatly stirred by the evangel of public ownership that was prevalent in the English-speaking community. In the early years of the century, public ownership was considered to be closely akin to socialism, and socialism was frowned upon by most of the Roman Catholic hierarchy as something sinister.

Yet in the 'thirties, under the sharp spur of new social discontents and a fresh upsurge of French-Canadian nationalism, a movement was launched for greater provincial control and ownership of water-power. In 1935 a commission of three members was appointed to coördinate the activity of power companies in the province and to supply electricity to the largest possible number of citizens. This was the first of a series of measures which culminated, in 1944, in the creation of the Quebec Hydro-Electric Commission and the expropriation of the wealthy Montreal Light, Heat and Power Company, a supplier of electricity and gas in metropolitan Montreal. Behind such action was the mounting influence of a national and popular creed which declared that the humble French-speaking people of the province were being exploited by the wily English-speaking capitalists dominating the board-rooms of the power companies. Provincial autonomy and self-assertion, as well as the prospect of cheaper power, thus seemed to dictate the need of public ownership. Drifting away from old loyalties, Quebec tardily began to emulate the example of Ontario. Yet, apart from the Montreal, Light, Heat and Power Company, great private electric companies continued to exist in the province, and their demise is still not near.

In some of the other provinces, notably in Manitoba and Nova Scotia, public and private ownership of power exist side by side, but in the last twenty-five years the trend has been towards a wider jurisdiction by public bodies.

The heavy taxation by the federal government of private power companies during the Second World War sometimes strengthened the case of the advocates for public ownership, since it was assumed that under provincial management the revenue which flowed to Ottawa could instead be used to extend the local consumption of electricity. The specious simplicity of this argument made it popular, and it harmonized well with the sentiments of those who were anxious to build up provincial institutions. But more important in the long run was the growing necessity in all provinces to integrate and simplify the generation and distribution of electricity and to extend its use to as many citizens as possible. In Manitoba and Nova Scotia, for example, the pressure for wide-spread rural electrification has tended to enlarge the activity of the public commissions, because they are best able to build lines into areas of low population density, where the development of an adequate load is inevitably slow. In this situation a public authority with public capital can meet the costs of service better than a private company.

Early in the present century public ownership in utilities other than electric power had already begun. The properties of the Bell Telephone Company in the three Prairie Provinces were purchased and administered by the governments. Here the special pressure came from farmers. Their amenities of life could be greatly enlarged by the telephone, but they were prompt to realize that a private company would shrink from providing service to a thinly-scattered rural population. Hence the risks of telephone service were made a collective responsibility. Within the same region other forms of assistance were offered: public elevators, credit facilities, debt-adjustment boards, the encouragement of coöperatives, and experimental farms.

Despite the individual organization of production on the typical prairie farm, successful growing of wheat on the great plains has always been peculiarly dependent on numerous aids from provincial and federal governments, including the provision of railways, the regulation of railway rates, the grading of grains, the supervision of marketing, and in the last generation the stabilizing and bolstering of prices for the product. It is little wonder that the western farmer is much more of a conscious and zealous collectivist than his fellow-agrarians of Ontario and Quebec. He opened up a hard frontier, which has remained hard. Through the state he has endeavoured to lessen or even to pool the risks of his highly-commercialized and precarious agriculture. In this endeavour he has often been encouraged by industrialists in eastern Canada, for to them a prosperous agrarian frontier in the West has been crucial. Significant, in addition to other forms of government aid, is the prairie farm rehabilitation programme, inaugurated under federal legislation in 1935 to rehabilitate farm lands in the dry and soil-drifting districts of the West; it constitutes one of the first attempts on a major scale to conserve agrarian resources by direct public action.

Labour legislation has been moulded by the peculiar influences of the social environment and the federal system. Until the last decade the growth of the Canadian labour movement, unlike that in its sister Dominions of Australia and New Zealand, has been delayed by regional fissures, racial divisions, the mobility of labour in the hopeful era of the open and accessible frontier, and perhaps most of all the agrarian nature of the economy for many decades after 1867, wherein the rural labour force has felt no urge to seek organization. Farm labour has been provided mainly by the farmer and his family. The hired man who may supplement the toil of the proprietary family has never been a suitable recruit for the ranks of organized labour. Where he is anything more than a temporary labourer on the land, his homely ambition is to possess a farm of his own, and hence his concern is less with his fellow-labourers than with the class of producers which he is anxious to join. In the Canadian country-side there has been nothing equivalent to that dynamic agent of pressure, the Australian Workers' Union; indeed, there has been no organization worthy of mention because no large units exist like the sheep-stations of the Australian outback, employing a rural proletariat.

Consequently, strong labour organizations have come only with the progress of urban industrialization, a progress much stimulated by the two world wars of the twentieth century, especially the second. Thus in 1937 the number of organized workers in Canada was 383,000, which was the largest figure of any year up to that date. By 1944 the number had almost doubled.

Yet the ranks of urban labour are always weakened by the dispersal of the population in towns and cities across a continent, rendering organization difficult and exposing the movement to regional cleavages. The division into English-speaking and French-speaking groups impairs coöperation in central Canada, where the great metropolitan centres exist and where most of the industrial population is concentrated. The Roman Catholic unions of Quebec often have a different view of the goals sought through the state by the unions of the neighbouring Ontario. They are much less state-conscious, much less inspired by the secular philosophies of labour in North America, and, because of their Catholic leadership, much less militant. They are disposed to emphasize social collaboration rather than class struggle. But here again a fast-growing industrialism is introducing significant changes. The position of the Catholic unions is being challenged by the aggressive invasion of unions from English-speaking Canada and the United States, and the French workman in the industrial town is responding to social stimuli that differ from those traditional in rural Quebec.

The boundary between Canada and the United States is rarely a barrier to the migration of ideas, least of all in matters of labour organization and social pressures. The international unions of

North America have created funnels whereby influences from the United States easily flow into the Canadian labour camp, sometimes with the effect of checking its national cohesion. British influence has always been present and often potent, owing to the fact that hitherto British immigrants provided much of the union leadership; but varied and pervasive influences from the United States are evident in the present active lobbying by labour and in its past tendency to avoid direct political action, a tendency now clearly on the wane.

Such circumstances, combined with the divisions of jurisdiction explicit in the federal system, determine the character of labour law. Most of the legislative power dwells with the provinces in virtue of their control over property and civil rights. Laws have been passed on the employment of women and children, minimum hours of work, wages, factory inspection, workmen's compensation in accidents, and conditions under which a stoppage in industrial work is legal. In brief, the Canadian labour code is mainly a complicated structure of provincial codes, but in substance it is similar to that found in other countries of the English-speaking world. The security of trade unions under the law came more slowly than in Great Britain; but the enactments, when made, tended to follow British models, with the most significant variations in Quebec, which through its Civil Code has a distinct legal tradition.[3] The broad trend, most evident in the 'thirties and 'forties of the present century, is clearly towards protecting the unions as free associations, enabling them to exert their maximum power in industry and the state. Provincial legislation, much influenced by the National Industrial Recovery Act of the United States (1933) and by the Wagner National Labor Relations Act (1935), has been reasonably effective in protecting the right of workers to join unions and in compelling employers to negotiate with them.

Besides the provincial enactments, there were the Dominion amendments to the Criminal Code in 1939, making it illegal for an employer to dismiss or threaten to dismiss a workman simply because of his membership in a lawful trade union. With its increased powers during the emergency of the Second World War and under pressure of labour, the Dominion Government sought to strengthen trade-unionism and protect its personnel, notably in the War-Time Labour Relations Regulations of 1944, which proclaimed the rights of employees and employers, formulated rules for collective bargaining, and provided machinery for conciliation in industrial disputes. These Regulations set the pattern for post-war legislation in the Dominion and the provinces.

The most significant early federal legislation, which influenced all subsequent enactments, even when these go beyond it in scope, was the Industrial Disputes Investigation Act of 1907. This provided for compulsory investigation of disputes in industries in which stoppages of work diminish the welfare of citizens in general. But no attempt was made to compel parties to a dispute to accept the recommendations of the conciliation boards. Canada did not follow the precedents of Australia and New Zealand in providing for compulsory arbitration under the state. Underlying Canadian legislation was the assumption that conciliation would adequately serve the public interest by advancing a settlement. The statute was circumscribed by the limited jurisdiction of the Dominion Parliament in labour matters, but over the years it has had an important ameliorative effect on industrial struggles. and its essential elements are still retained in Dominion and provincial legislation.

Social services in their evolution have been affected by the same basic forces that shape the character of labour law. Since social services are treated at length in chapter xvii (pp. 390–407), only a few general observations are needed here. In Canada, as in the other democracies of the English-speaking world, notable spurts occurred in the rise of public social services as a consequence of three related events in the twentieth century: the First World War, the depression in the 'thirties, and the struggle against Nazi Germany. Of these, the depression was notable because it greatly enlarged the range of state action and made imperative heavy levies upon the Dominion treasury in Ottawa to aid the provinces and municipalities in providing relief payments.[4]

Attempts in the national sphere to follow the example of the United States in its generous social-security measures and industrial regulation were, however, frustrated by the rigidity of the federal constitution. The draftsmen of the British North America

Act had not envisaged national social services, which consequently remain limited by the letter of the law. In 1937 the enactments sponsored by the Bennett Government, the nearest equivalent in Canada to Roosevelt's New Deal, were in the main declared to be *ultra vires* of the federal Parliament. Nothing, therefore, was achieved comparable to the contemporary revolution in the social services of the United States or to the sweeping innovations embodied in the social-security legislation of New Zealand. Apart from any restraining influences within the community itself, the federal system of Canada was a barrier to drastic national change.

Yet expenditures on social services inclusive of education were steadily on the increase, costing the nation by 1939 more than a quarter of all public spending. The annual expenditures of Dominion, provincial, and municipal governments on public welfare and relief, excluding education, were in 1913 some $15,000,000; in 1930 they were $83,000,000; by 1937, $236,000,000. This increased public spending inevitably came to be reflected in taxation. In 1925 federal, provincial, and municipal governments were raising in taxes some 14.7 per cent of the national income. By 1938 that percentage had increased to 19.7.[5]

The Second World War, through its economic and social consequences, created much public debate on the necessity for social reform, aroused public sentiment, and deepened the pressure for national action. Extensive publicity was given to the Beveridge Report and its implications. Democratic strategy, it was argued, required more effective social services. But more important than such general debate was the rapid emergence of a war economy which speeded the process of industrialization, still further enlarged the chief cities, and created a more powerful labour movement clamorous for social-security measures. The Rowell-Sirois Commission, whose monumental report was completed in 1940, prescribed a realignment of constitutional powers and financial responsibilities in order to place social services on a sounder basis; but attempts both during and after the war to implement its recommendations encountered stubborn opposition in the central provinces and some of the outlying provinces. Two important steps, were, however, taken during the war in the establishment of unemployment insurance (1940), patterned in the main upon the British system, and in the provision (1944) for the payment of monthly family allowances out of the Dominion treasury.

The problem of state action in the sphere of social services inevitably becomes a constitutional issue, and that, in turn, a problem of achieving sufficiently wide agreement in a federal community. The major jurisdiction still dwells with the provinces, but most provinces are experiencing a decrease in their financial power to implement the far-reaching schemes of social amelioration demanded by advancing industrialism. While no province, least of all a province on the lean federal periphery, seeks to get sharply out of step with its fellows, there is an obvious lack of uniformity in the range and quality of services from province to province. The wealthy can afford to be generous, but the poor must be parsimonious. Ontario and Quebec, enriched by their industrial diversity, are strong enough to enact such social legislation as they deem suitable for their needs.

In social services, as in public utilities, Quebec in particular has its own distinctive views and peculiar procedures, determined by Roman Catholicism, its Civil Code, and its nationalist traditions. Here a well-established practice of activity by the religious orders in providing many services has hitherto weakened the political impulse to look to the state and especially to Ottawa for assistance. Charity, inspired and organized by the religious communities, is regarded as a more desirable dynamic than the philosophy of state collectivism, and it provides hospitals, orphanages, and asylums. In the smallest social cell, the parish, the *curé* directs the application of local charity, and in the larger social units the bishops provide appropriate organization for social amelioration. The Church, an indefatigable upholder of private property as an agency for developing personality, looks suspiciously on the enlargement of state functions, especially those which threaten to draw away influence and responsibility from itself. It readily sponsors coöperative enterprise among all portions of the population, but it fears the growth of the secular Leviathan. Nevertheless, even in Quebec the role of the state grows ever larger, for with the march of industrialism private charity is inadequate to cope with the modern problems of social service, particularly during periods of depression.

The conclusions are self-evident. Since 1867 Canada as a state has become more collectivist in character, owing mainly to those economic and social forces which explain collectivism throughout the Western world. There is nothing singular in this phase of her evolution, nothing in the role of her government that cannot be paralleled elsewhere, especially in countries, like the Dominions, with moving frontiers of settlement and development. She accepts as a matter of course that the state must become "the universal intervener," the chief instrument of economic coördination and direction, particularly in adverse times. She also responds to the urges of an industrial society, the incitements of nationalism, and the claims of democracy, but she responds with those subtle variations that derive from the quality of her community and the influence of geography. Much of her state intervention has been concerned directly with the building of a national economy over half a continent, alongside the United States, and with the aspiration to maintain independence and balance within that economy.

In recent decades the most distinctive and important trend pertains to welfare legislation and social services. Here as elsewhere in the Western world there has been a widening concept of welfare, an ever-growing sense of public responsibility for the ill-favoured individual or for the ordinary individual as a citizen. The change is profound from the simple colonial economy of 1867, with its reliance upon the capacity of the rural family to provide a livelihood and shelter for its members, to the complex economy of the present, with its accelerated tendencies to devolve upon the state the responsibility for personal security. Regions as well as individuals expect and demand security, and are subsidized by the national government through transfers of income from more affluent regions.

This collectivism is throughout empirical, shaped by the thinking of those who are concerned with the practical problem of the moment and the exigency of given situations. Hence all political parties in turn have furthered it, and in this matter the labels of Liberal and Conservative are almost irrelevant. Political leaders have responded to concrete necessities, mass pressures, and the inevitable reorientation in public sentiment with the expansion of an industrial civilization.

The rise since the 'thirties of the Coöperative Commonwealth Federation (commonly known as the C.C.F.), inspired by a socialist sentiment and determined to reduce private profit-making, has introduced more ideological discussion on the role of the state, but it is only a symptom of the new social forces that are beginning to change the programmes and actions of the older parties. The C.C.F. has been nourished by intellectual food of mixed origin —the ideas of British liberal socialism, the aspirations of American reformers associated with some of the Protestant churches, and the traditions of agrarian democrats anxious to curb big business. Whatever its own future as a third party, its ideas and feelings will have an influence in this generation in helping to reshape the functions of the state into a more collectivist mould.

Finally, it is to be emphasized that, owing to the federal structure of the state and the bi-national character of the community, Canadian state collectivism is not highly centralized. The federal government at all times exercises powerful controls over the economy through the currency, tariff, and taxation, but, so long as the federal system survives, it is forbidden to operate directly in some spheres except in periods of national emergency and war. Significant differences exist among the policies of the provinces. Each provincial government is held accountable to its electorate for the development of local natural resources and the provision of most social services, a circumstance which prevents a highly-centralized and top-heavy state.

But any growing trend towards collectivism in the next generation will increasingly be related to the strains of the federation. As the provinces, especially those on the periphery, enlarge the functions of their governments, they will inevitably look to the national treasury for financial assistance. Conversely, as the central Parliament endeavours to hold the national economy in balance, it will seek more controls over local policies and provincial incomes. What government does and how the federation works will continue to be two inseparable issues in the Canadian state.

Part Five

SOCIAL AND CULTURAL INSTITUTIONS

CHAPTER XVI

The Canadian Community

BY SAMUEL DELBERT CLARK

RECENT STUDIES of Canadian-American relations, particularly in the social field, have served to give emphasis to the importance of the continental environment in the development of a common way of life on the North American continent. Indeed, one is almost tempted to begin a chapter such as this with the bald assertion that the Canadian community is but a pale reflection of the American community, and that if the reader wishes to learn something about it he need only refer to the extensive body of literature relating to social institutions and social behaviour in the United States. Nothing, it would seem at first glance, could be said about the Canadian community which has not already been said about the American.

Certainly, in many ways the Canadian community has been a northern extension of the American; population movements and the sharing of a common environment have led to a close similarity in social development. Exploitation of their North American resources has been a joint enterprise of the two peoples. There has emerged not two separate cultural systems—an American and a Canadian—but rather a number of distinctive forms of community organization, related more to underlying conditions of economic life than to political developments.

On the Atlantic Coast, exploitation of the fisheries early led to the development of a form of community organization—the fishing village—which differed little in New England and Nova Scotia. In the continental interior the trade in furs made much the same social demands whether the traders were operating out of Albany or Montreal. The timber-lumbering industry of New Brunswick and the Ottawa Valley grew up in close relationship to that of Maine, Vermont, and, later, Michigan and Wisconsin. The agricultural settlement of New Brunswick, the Eastern Townships, and Upper Canada, while later, drawing much from direct immigration from Europe, was, in the beginning, part of the great western movement of agricultural peoples which led after 1790 to the occupation of upper New York State, western Pennsylvania, and the new states of Ohio, Tennessee, and Kentucky. The discovery of gold in the Fraser River Valley in the 1850's followed the discovery of gold in California, and the mining camps in British territory differed little from those which had grown up in the American West. Wheat-farming on the plains of Canada gave rise to a society much like that which developed out of wheat-farming on the plains of the United States. Out of the Industrial Revolution there grew up in English-speaking Canada cities which had little to distinguish them from those which had grown up across the border.

The forms of community organization which developed in Canada represented the adjustments of the population to their North American environment. Like similar forms across the border, they were the products of social experiments forced upon a people faced with new conditions of living. The effort to build societies on a common front brought the populations of the two parts of the continent close together. Though their cultural heritages were different, particularly before 1760, cultural differences tended to disappear upon settlement in America. The move from the Old World to the New, and from one area of the New World to another, often involved an almost complete break with the past. The very character of the settlement of America made for little continuity in the development of forms of social organization.

The settlement of America did not take place gradually. Rather, there were long periods when movements of population came almost to a halt. Wars and political uprisings, lack of transportation, ignorance of resources or failure to develop technological means of exploiting them, speculation in land, and the resistance of large economic organizations such as fur-trading companies to developments which threatened their monopolistic positions were some of the factors which held back the spread of population across the continent. When the barriers to migration did break down, the movement of population tended to be a flood. New means of transportation, technological developments in methods of production, realization of resources hitherto unknown, the up-swing of the business cycle, or sudden climatic changes were sufficient to attract attention to new areas of the continent and to set under way a mass movement of people.

Thus the settlement of America might be thought of as having taken place in a series of great "rushes." The sudden occupation of the Fraser River Valley after 1857 and of the Klondike after 1897 by gold-seekers are two of the best examples of such rushes in the settlement of Canada, but other areas—the St. Lawrence Valley after 1660, the Annapolis Valley and the south shore of Nova Scotia after 1760, the St. John and Miramichi valleys and the Great Lakes region after 1800, the Red River and Assiniboine valleys after 1880, the western prairies and the industrial city after 1900, the Canadian Shield after 1920—were occupied in much the same fashion by mass movements of population. It is true that settlement began long before the mass movement set in, but the simple forms of social organization established by the pioneers were swept aside by later comers. With thousands of bewildered people suddenly thrown together, strangers to one another and to the environment, pressing problems had to be solved hurriedly. New conditions forced an abandonment of traditional ways of thinking and behaving. In many respects the population began anew the task of building up a social system.

It is true that the loss of the Old World social heritage was offset in some degree by borrowings from the culture of the native. In North America, however, the native culture played no such role as in South America, where social continuity was secured through the absorption of the old society by the new. In North America, for the most part, the white man looked upon the Indian as a nuisance to be got out of the way; the Calvinist doctrine of predestination, in particular, offered an easy justification for the ruthless extermination of a race who were not of the elect. Only here and there, chiefly where the Roman Catholic attitude towards the native tended to prevail over the Protestant, were efforts made to draw upon the experience of the aboriginal inhabitants. In Canada there was no such military slaughter of the Indians as in the United States, but deprivation of their means of livelihood and the spread of disease served as effectively to decimate the Indians and to place them in a position of subjection. In much of Canada today Indian place-names are all that is left to remind one that the land was once occupied by the red man.

This sharp break with the past has accounted for much that is distinctive in American life. Out of the new societies growing up in America have come the challenges to Old World ways of doing things and Old World ways of thinking. Such societies have been the chief breeding-grounds of the great American economic, political, social, and religious movements. The break with the cultural past has been evident in the development of the Canadian as of the American community. Movements of social reform have spread from one side of the border to the other. Canada has shared with the United States in the frontier revolt against established society.

Geography has drawn the two countries together socially, yet there are many striking differences between them. Powerful forces have operated to bring about a distinctive development of many important aspects of Canadian society. The influence of these forces was most evident in the frontier—the very area where a common way of life showed most signs of developing. In the United States—or in that part of America which later became the United States—few restraints were imposed upon the opening up of new areas of settlement. Population moved in freely, and there was little interference from the outside in the building of the new society. People were left largely to rely on their own resources. In Canada, however, the risk of absorption by the southern neighbour was too great to permit the unrestricted development of new areas of settlement.

The frontier was a great leveller in a political as well as in a social sense; it tended to destroy Old World political loyalties and thus to weaken Old World political attachments. The movement for the political independence of the British colonies in America before 1774 was a reflection to some extent of the separatist political tendencies of the frontier, but the political independence of the colonies, especially after the collapse of the French Empire in America, involved no great danger of the intrusion of a foreign power. For Canada, however, such intrusion was always a real danger. Before 1760 the lines of the French Empire reaching into the interior of the continent lay exposed on the south to attack from the English-speaking colonies. After 1760 British control of the interior through the St. Lawrence was similarly challenged by the independent-minded Atlantic Seaboard colonies and, after 1784, by the new Republic of the United States. The Quebec Act of 1774, the American War of Independence, the long struggle after 1784 for control of the western posts, and the War of 1812–1814 revealed the intensity of the conflict for lines of communication reaching into the interior. Outlying settlements in British North America, in New Brunswick, Upper Canada, the Eastern Townships, and the Red River Valley, on the Pacific Coast, and even on the western prairies, faced the threat, as had the earlier French settlements, of absorption by their neighbour to the south.

Because of this threat the grip of political authority could not be relaxed within new areas of settlement in Canada as it tended to be south of the border. The Canadian frontier grew up within the protective custody, first, of the French colonial Empire, then of the colonial Empire of Britain, and finally, after 1867, of the Dominion itself. Thus the fur-trading posts of New France, the fishing villages of Nova Scotia, the lumbering camps and agricultural settlements of New Brunswick and Upper Canada, the mining towns of the Pacific Coast and of the Klondike, and the prairie farm communities of the West did not develop merely as economic areas of production and exchange; they were also important outposts of Empire or nation. Defence constituted, along with trade, a determinant of lines of community development and forms of social organization. An army, or at least a special constabulary force, usually followed close upon the heels of the frontiersman; indeed, many of the earliest settlements, for instance that of the Richelieu Valley in New France and of Perth in Upper Canada, were affected by military organization. Other agencies, particularly the Church, played an equally important role in maintaining political control in frontier areas.

The result was to make for the more orderly development of the Canadian than of the American frontier. The radical departures from accepted practice which were characteristic of the behaviour and thinking of American frontier populations in political organization, justice, family life, cultural relationships, and religious organization were less evident in the Canadian frontier population. The conservatism of the country as a whole operated as a powerful force in checking innovations.

In political organization, however, the spirit of revolt and experimentation has not been lacking. Support of the revolutionary cause by large numbers of Nova Scotians and French Canadians in 1776, the movement of political disaffection among many Upper Canadians during the War of 1812–1814, the Gourlay agitation and the rebellions in Lower and Upper Canada in 1837, the rise of the Clear Grit movement after 1850, the Red River Rebellion of 1870 and the North-West Rebellion of 1885, the defiance of Canadian political authority by miners' associations in the Klondike in 1900, the rise of farm political movements in western Canada after the First World War, the Winnipeg general strike in 1920, and the growth of the Social Credit movement in Alberta and of the C.C.F. movement in western Canada and industrial Ontario after 1932 are indications of the strength of the challenges to constituted authority. But such movements of revolt, in contrast with similar movements in the United States, were arrested before they could make their influence significantly felt in the political life of the country.

In the United States, support of political reform offered a means of strengthening the political structure of the nation; the Republic was in effect a product of revolution, and movements of political reform after 1784 served to sharpen politically the divorce from the Old World and to make American institutions more distinctive. In Canada, however, reform movements threatened to draw the population more closely to their southern neighbours and to weaken if not destroy the political ties of Empire or, after 1867, of nation. This was true even when such movements drew their inspiration from the Old World, as, for instance, in New France before 1760, in Upper Canada during the 1830's, and in western Canada after 1920. The attack upon political institutions implied a challenge to constituted authority, and the danger was great that a state of confusion would lead to the intervention of the southern neighbour. William Lyon Mackenzie and Louis Riel are obvious examples of reform leaders who, though advocating ideas only partly American in origin, found themselves leading movements which derived much of their support from across the border.

Thus the effort to build up a political system in Canada which would remain independent of the United States involved the imposition of strong checks upon revolutionary tendencies. New France was isolated from revolutionary France through the building up in the colony of a powerfully centralized political and ecclesiastical system. The British colonies and, after 1867, the Canadian nation were similarly isolated from outside revolutionary influences by the maintenance of a strong system of political control, supported by the Church, a privileged upper class, and, before 1870, the British army and navy. Whereas the American nation was a product of the revolutionary spirit, the Canadian nation grew mainly out of forces of a counter-revolutionary character.

In the development of institutions of law and order, similar forces of conservatism operated to restrain the influence of the frontier. Areas developing beyond the reach of the law have not been unknown in Canada. In the fur-trading interior of New France, the transient fishing settlements of Cape Breton and the east shore of New Brunswick, the lumbering camps of the St. John, Miramichi, and Ottawa valleys, the shanty towns of Irish canal-workers, the mining camps of the Fraser River Valley and the Klondike, and the congested areas of the growing cities, widespread lawlessness and disorder developed. Crime was an expression of the emancipation of the population from the traditional controls of an Old World society. Efforts to enforce the law assumed the character of interference from outside; the authority of the police and the courts was challenged by that of the gang, the vigilante committee, and the mob. Yet, in contrast with the United States, such challenges to constituted authority were never strong enough to lead to a general break-down of law and order. The fire-arm was much less important in Canada than it was in the United States in defending the frontiersman from the North

American Indian and from his fellow frontiersman. Seldom in the Canadian frontier did force pass out of the hands of the state. The Vigilante Committee organized in San Francisco in 1857 or the gang rule of Soapy Smith in Skagway in 1897 has no true parallel in Canadian experience.

The reason was that frontier settlement in Canada rarely extended far beyond the reach of the military forces of Empire or nation. The United States had no pressing reason for providing military protection to outlying settlements; border warfare, whether with the Indians, the Spanish, the Mexicans, or, before, 1760, the French, was left mainly to the settlers. The vulnerability of the Canadian frontier, however, forced early attention to problems of defence, with the result that law-enforcement agencies could usually rely upon the support of military forces. Thus about the fur-trading posts of New France, in the agricultural settlements of New Brunswick and Upper Canada, and in the shanty towns of Irish canal-workers the army played an important role in maintaining order. In the isolated fishing settlements of Nova Scotia, policing was a function of the navy. A force of Royal Engineers put an end to lawlessness in the mining camps of British Columbia. Settlement of the western prairies and the gold-rush to the Klondike took place under the close control of the North-West Mounted Police. Even in Canadian cities, serious threats to law and order have been met by the decisive use of force.

The result was to establish a tradition of respect for the institutions of law and order. The population generally did not feel the need of taking the law into its own hands through mob action or the organization of vigilantes. There was lacking that intense jealousy of local rights which in the United States made it difficult for federal forces to intervene. The way in which the Royal North-West Mounted Police came into being was in striking contrast with the Texas Rangers. In the United States the frontier bred a spirit of liberty which often opposed efforts to maintain order. In Canada, order was maintained at the price of weakening that spirit.

The institution of the family has found support in much the same set of conservative forces which have upheld the institutions of law and order. With the family, as with other forms of social organization, the disturbing influence of the frontier made itself felt. The rapid increase in the Canadian divorce rate in recent years is a reflection of family disorganization which is closely related to urban growth and the weakening of puritan values. Before the turn of the century few divorces were known, but family disorganization as a social phenomenon reaches back to the beginnings of the Canadian community. By its very character the frontier tended to be a society of males: the fur-trading post, the lumbering camp, the agricultural settlement, the mining town, the ranching community, and even the manufacturing city (as distinguished from the more mature urban community with a diversity of economic interests) were made up predominantly of men in the age group from eighteen to forty. In such areas, large sections of the population lived entirely outside the family system, and there developed such substitute forms of social organization as prostitution and the partnership of two men to meet needs ordinarily satisfied within the family. The disorganizing effects of such developments upon the mores of the community were evident, for instance, in the rural society of New France brought into close contact with the fur-trading frontier, the agricultural settlements of New Brunswick which grew up alongside timber and lumbering camps, the old fur-trading and governmental centre of Victoria which served during the gold-rushes as the disembarking point and supply centre of the mining population, and the urban community developing in relationship to manufacturing and the new northern frontier of mining and pulp and paper. The two great wars have only accentuated the effect upon family life of the disorganizing influences growing out of conditions within the Canadian community.

The much lower divorce rate in Canada than in the United States, however, indicates a greater stability in family organization, which has been as true of the past as of the present. The restraining influence exerted upon Canadian frontier development had the effect of limiting the degree of emancipation from moral values. Controls of social class and the church lent strong support to the controls of a traditional morality. There was less readiness to accept unconventional forms of behaviour in matters relating to the family. Whereas in the United States the frontier spirit of experimentation led to a modification of forms of family life and to a tolerant attitude towards deviations from traditional moral standards, in Canada such a spirit was severely checked through the pressure of strong forces of social conservatism. Frontier patterns of revolt against the controls of a formal family system, as for instance among the *coureurs de bois* of New France or within the bohemias of the urban community, tended to be confined to the peripheral areas of society and to have little effect upon behaviour generally.

The strength of the puritan tradition in Canadian society has not been unrelated to the strength of the aristocratic tradition; the spirit of equalitarianism generated within the frontier situation, like that of libertarianism, was greatly moderated by the opposing spirit of conservatism. Canada shared with the United States in the great democratic movement, with its almost fanatical emphasis upon the principle that all men are equal. The frontier provided unfavourable ground on which to build an elaborate structure of social classes, which broke down under the influence of the common experience of frontier life. The social worth of the individual was measured in terms of accomplishment rather than in terms of family background. Thus, in New France, seigneurs had difficulty in maintaining a social status which set them apart from the lowly habitants or, indeed, from the bush-rangers. In the new agricultural settlements of the Maritime colonies, the Eastern Townships, Upper Canada, and, much later, the western prairies, upper-class families were forced into close social association with families of lower standing, and differences in social worth quickly disappeared along with differences in economic worth. Even more, in such highly-mobile areas as mining towns and industrial cities, an inherited class structure tended to disintegrate in the face of powerful forces of equalitarianism. Yet, in spite of the strength of such forces, the aristocratic principle has persisted as an important organizing influence in Canadian society.

The strength of the military interest in itself served to emphasize the importance of class distinctions. Because the frontier was usually garrisoned by military forces, there was present from the beginning a strong influence operating against democratic tendencies. The military emphasized and lent support to distinctions in status. In the town of Quebec under the French régime, and in the British colonial centres of Halifax, Fredericton, Kingston, York (Toronto), and Victoria, the army or navy, with its officers in smart uniform, gave the local society a colour and dash which were lacking in American frontier communities. Even in the new Canadian frontiers, the Klondike, the western prairies, the industrial city, and the northern mining communities, the military tradition, as represented, for instance, by the Royal Canadian Mounted Police, had some influence upon social class relationships.

Efforts to strengthen the political ties of Empire or of nation led to deliberate attempts, through land-grants and political preferments, to create and strengthen an aristocracy in the colonies of New France, Nova Scotia, Prince Edward Island, New Brunswick, Upper Canada, and British Columbia, and, later, in a less obvious fashion, in the Canadian nation. The democratic movement, it was felt, was liable to draw Canadian people closer to their neighbours to the south; and a privileged upper class was a bulwark of loyalty and conservatism. Though the economic forces of the frontier tended to the destruction of class differences, as, for instance, in the Upper Canadian backwoods community of the 1830's, the effect was neutralized in some degree within a political and military system of class privilege; many upper-class persons who proved unsuccessful as farmers obtained appointments in the government or the army. The frontier had two things of value to offer—land and offices—and both were often reserved for a privileged few.

The strength of the aristocratic tradition in Canada, though not easily measured, is revealed in the political attitudes of the population, the educational institutions, the patriarchal organization of the family, and the respect for old and established leaders. Though few Canadians would consciously subscribe to a society based upon class distinctions, the belief in the social superiority of certain groups underlies much of their thinking. There has been lacking in Canadian experience that explicit rationalization of an equalitarian philosophy which in the United States was a product of revolution. The aristocratic tradition was too deeply rooted in the political philosophy of Empire to be destroyed by the equalitarian forces of the frontier.

In Canada, as in the United States, the frontier acted as a great melting-pot of different cultures whereby the population was forced to conform to a common pattern of thought and behaviour. Though New France after 1660, Upper Canada after 1800, and the western prairies and industrial cities after 1900 were settled by people of diverse cultural backgrounds, a common cultural type soon emerged in these different areas. Assimilation proceeded even more rapidly in such highly-mobile areas as the mining frontier. The break-down of cultural differences on the frontier hastened the development of a single Canadian type.

Yet the persistence of ethnic differences suggests that assimilation did not proceed unchecked. The separation of the two chief cultural groups, the French-speaking and the English-speaking, offers the best example of the preservation of inherited ethnic loyalties within the Canadian cultural system, but ethnic separatism has not been a characteristic of the French Canadians only. Throughout English-speaking Canada there has been a similar tendency towards the preservation of inherited cultural attachments among English, Irish, Scots, Americans, central Europeans, and Asiatics.

Such a tendency has been a reflection of the colonial character of Canadian society. Assimilation in Canada meant an increasing conformity to American values of life and standards of behaviour. Efforts to check American influences in Canadian cultural life thus involved the strengthening of the supports of ethnic group loyalties. British colonial policy offered no real encouragement to the assimilation of the French-Canadian population, particularly after 1774, when assimilation would have meant the more rapid spread of American revolutionary ideas in the colony. Similarly, in Nova Scotia, New Brunswick, and Upper Canada the chief bulwarks against the growth of the American revolutionary movement were the Old World loyalties of the population; state support of an upper-class social system offered one means of keeping such loyalties alive. Since 1867, paradoxically, the security of the Canadian nation has depended upon discouraging a too-strong Canadian nationalism. Preservation of English and Scots and Irish group loyalties served to perpetuate the colonial attitude of the Canadian people and thus to check the spread of American influence. In the United States the Briton hastened to become a good American; in Canada he has been encouraged to remain a good Briton. Nor has any vigorous effort been made to assimilate continental European peoples in Canada, except through the public schools; as with the French Canadians, the break of continental Europeans from their cultural past has tended to expose them to American influences. The maintenance of the political attachments of Empire or nation depended upon the cultural isolation of the population within the American continental system, and such isolation has been secured most effectively through the preservation of Old World loyalties.

Finally, the religious development of Canada, in contrast with that of the United States, has reflected the influence of strong conservative or traditionalist forces operating to check the influence of the frontier. In Canada, as in the United States, the frontier was a breeding-ground of new churches and sects. The failure of Old World churches to gain leadership in frontier areas, and the weakening of traditional social values and forms of social organization encouraged the population to join whatever religious groups made their appearance. Sects developed naturally out of the frontier situation in response to the need for new and satisfying group loyalties. No Canadian frontier escaped the phenomenon of religious upheaval.

In New France, it is true, restrictions upon the settlement of Huguenots made impossible the development of any religious movement outside the Roman Catholic Church, but much the same sort of spirit as sectarianism found expression within the Jesuit Order. Later religious movements, both within and outside the Church, have similarly tended to weaken the Roman Catholic ecclesiastical structure in Canada; schisms among central European Catholics in western Canada are recent examples of sectarian development. Among Protestants, of course, religious division has been much more pronounced. The history of Protestantism in Canada has been characterized by a series of religious upheavals which have precluded the development of unity within the church as a whole. Even to list the names of the sects which have appeared at different times would be impossible. Schisms within churches have been succeeded by new schisms to add to the confusion. The recent growth of movements such as the Pentecostal, Pentecostal-Holiness, Nazarene, Apostolic, Church of God, Four Square Gospel, Christian and Missionary Alliance, and Jehovah's Witnesses demonstrates the continuing state of disunity of the Protestant body.

Nevertheless, a considerable degree of stability has been characteristic of the religious organization of the Canadian community. The large denominations have succeeded in maintaining a strongly influential position in spite of the weakening effects of religious division. Soon after Confederation the various branches of Presbyterians and Methodists came together in two great national churches. The Baptists, the Disciples of Christ, and even the Salvation Army and the Pentecostals gradually lost much of their extreme separatist character in accommodating themselves to the secular social structure. The union of the Methodist, Presbyterian, and Congregational churches to form the United Church of Canada in 1925, and the more recent formation of the Canadian Council of Churches mark a culmination of developments reaching back to the beginnings of Protestant religious organization in the country.

Powerful political and cultural forces served to support the denominational organization of religion and to check extreme manifestations of religious division. The church, as distinguished from the sect, closely identified itself with the interests of Empire or nation. By its very nature it depended upon the maintenance of the traditional loyalties. In offering support to established political attachments, it was able to command, in turn, a measure of political support. Thus the Roman Catholic Church in French Canada, the Church of England in the British colonies, and more recently the United Church of Canada enjoyed many of the privileges of a state church, whether or not legally established. Maintenance of the political ties of Empire or nation has depended upon the maintenance of a system of ecclesiastical control in the Canadian community.

Movements of religious division, on the other hand, have been viewed as threats to traditional political attachments. By its otherworldly appeal, the sect tended to deprecate the importance of such secular interests as the state; it sought the full and undivided loyalty of its followers. When the sect was American in origin, the political implications of its teachings were particularly disturbing. Lack of interest in the welfare of the state was assumed to be a disguise for attitudes of political disloyalty. Thus the full weight of the traditional political and social order was brought to bear, directly and indirectly, against the development of sectarian movements. The result was to make for the rapid accommodation of such movements to secular interests. The New-light-Baptists, the Methodists, the Disciples of Christ, and the Salvation Army early broke with the parent churches in the United States and shifted from a separatist position to seek closer ties within the Canadian community. Where such ties were not secured, as in the Jesuit Order in New France and the Riel group in the North-West Territories, the sect was virtually outlawed by the state.

The effect has been to give a conservative character to religious organization in Canada. The hold of tradition has been strong, and new forms of religious organization and new types of appeal have received little encouragement. Fanaticism has been confined mainly to the fringes of society. On the other hand, Canada has been unfriendly to a too-liberal approach to religious teachings; such movements as Unitarianism have made little headway. Religious organization has been built closely into the political and social structure of the community, and change has come slowly in the face of resistance from powerful interests identified with the established order.

The strength of the ties with the Old World is exemplified in the maintenance of the imperial connexion. Canada has no revolutionary tradition. At no time in their history have the people turned their back on the past and placed their whole faith in the future. The lack of such an emotional experience has affected the development of all aspects of Canadian society. It is this which accounts for what is most distinctive in the national character.

CHAPTER XVII

The Social Services

BY ELIZABETH S. L. GOVAN

SOCIAL SERVICES on a national scale have received comparatively little attention in Canada until recent years, partly because the North American environment gave them little encouragement, and partly because constitutional interpretations have assigned most of the powers in connexion with them to the provinces.[1] The origins and early development of social services in Canada are therefore as diverse as the provincial communities themselves. In particular, the differences between Quebec and the English-speaking provinces are based on sharp contrasts in social philosophy, community organization, and systems of law.

In the early days of French colonization the Roman Catholic Church followed close on the heels of the explorers, and with it came the personnel and the spirit which built the social-service organization of the Quebec of today. The French people transplanted their tradition of law and charity to the New World, developing their social legislation on the foundation of the French Civil Code, and their organization for welfare services upon the parish and the religious orders. The governor took the initiative in paying for the maintenance of foundlings, the control of begging, and the organization of temporary relief committees to give assistance in emergencies, but other matters were left in the hands of the Church. Under British rule no attempt was made to introduce the English poor-law in Lower Canada, and the Church continued to expand its activities, assisted after 1801 by govern-

[1] For note to chapter xvii see page 580.

ment subsidies, in the care of the sick, infirm, insane, and foundlings. Local gaols and Houses of Correction were established by the provincial authority, and the apprenticeship of children was legalized.

In Nova Scotia and New Brunswick the English poor-law, with its deterrent philosophy, residence and settlement laws, and use of the workhouse, was transplanted to the young colonies, and still has strong influence. In Upper Canada the districts provide Houses of Correction for vagrants, idlers, and disorderly persons, but less responsibility was placed upon the local community than in the Maritime Provinces. Public funds supported the insane in the gaols, to some extent the destitute immigrant, and in an emergency the unemployed. Grants were given to public hospitals and private institutions, which developed on the English pattern. The penitentiary was the first provincial institution, followed by an asylum for the insane. Houses of Industry and orphanages were organized under private auspices, and apprenticeship took care of the majority of dependent children.

By the time of Confederation there were institutions for the care of immigrants, the sick, the insane, the blind, the deaf and dumb, orphans, and the aged, but they had developed largely through the efforts of churches or private charitable agencies. Provincial activity was limited to the penitentiary, the insane asylum, and the making of grants to private organizations. Local authorities controlled gaols, Houses of Correction, and, in Montreal, a House of Industry. In emergencies, temporary local committees were appointed to deal with outdoor relief or epidemic.

It is not surprising, then, that when the British North America Act was drawn up, the Fathers of Confederation gave little thought to the social services as they are known today. "Hospitals, asylums, charities, and eleemosynary institutions" were specifically assigned to the provinces; the "property and civil rights" clause, included in the specification of provincial powers, covers most of the rest. The federal government can legislate for the common good in matters of national concern, while the provinces are responsible for problems of local importance: social services traditionally have been considered to belong to the latter group. The federal government can also make financial grants, and it was on this basis that the system of family allowances was introduced in 1945. The only actual change in the original Act, as far as the division of powers is concerned, was the amendment of 1940, which enabled the Dominion to legislate for unemployment insurance.

At the same time, the financial arrangements provided in the British North America Act have given the federal government much greater financial resources than those of the provincial and local authorities. In modern times the social-service programme of any nation has been the field in which demands upon public finances have increased most markedly; and to the extent that the programme is not based upon pre-payment, and in the area of economic security particularly, it becomes most expensive when the national income is curtailed. Thus the constitutional division of responsibility places the financial burden upon the governmental units least capable of meeting its demands. The variety in the wealth of the provinces and differences in sources of wealth have made the problem of agreement upon changes in constitutional and financial powers the focus of political struggle. Federal financing means a redistribution of income among provinces and, apart from conflicting philosophies in regard to the desirability of a social-security programme, tends to arouse provincial competition rather than coöperation.

The responsibility for social services which the constitution gave to the provinces has been delegated by them to the municipalities, compulsorily in Nova Scotia and New Brunswick, permissively elsewhere, but generally with the provincial governments relieving themselves of the major task. Tradition in both England and France demanded that the needy should be cared for locally, either by governmental authority or by private charity, and this pattern was transplanted to the New World. While the local community remained an isolated and a necessarily self-sufficient group in the wilderness, while the lack of transportation prevented movement of population, and while a pioneer rural economy provided work for all who could work and rendered indigent only the sick, the infirm, and the very young orphan, local responsibility was a feasible system of organization, and private charity could carry that part of the burden which the family itself could not assume.

In Canada, however, as elsewhere, these conditions changed. Rapidly growing industrialization, particularly in Ontario and Quebec, brought increased economic insecurity. As communications improved, seasonal occupations, due largely to climatic conditions, set labour moving and made local residence laws inapplicable. Droughts and industrial failures with devastating local effects weakened the local community financially at the very time when there were abnormally large calls for aid. Urban areas grew beyond the stage in which it could be argued that the local administration had personal knowledge of local indigents. Western agriculture and Canadian geographic conditions in general produced many areas of scattered population to which "community" could have no meaning and where the provision of such facilities as hospitals became a very expensive burden.

Nevertheless, as long as the rural economy predominated, business cycles might reduce standards of living, but they did not bring complete destitution to the point of starvation. As industrialization proceeded, Canada was still developing untouched natural resources, and prosperity and increasing standards were accepted as normal. The depression of 1921–1924 was considered to be an abnormal aftermath of the war and was dealt with as such rather than as a warning of the economic insecurity which comes with industrialization. The pioneer spirit still prevalent in Canada tended to idealize individual self-sufficiency and to trust in a policy of laissez-faire.

The bitter experience of the 1930's brought the realization that Canada was now part of a world economy and must share in the ill effects as well as the advantages of that situation. Gradually it became obvious that the local community was unable and unfit to carry the burden imposed on it, and that provincial revenues were inadequate to support the necessary programme of social services. The Dominion Government had financial resources but lacked constitutional authority, and the issue of Dominion-provincial relations thus arose in an acute form.

The constitution does give the Dominion Government responsibility in social services for Indians, mariners and passengers on foreign ships, criminals, and members of the armed services (active and retired) and their dependents. These groups were placed under federal authority because of their relationship with external affairs, treaties, defence, and federal criminal law. Work with Indians follows well-established lines, and the personnel of foreign ships does not present a large problem. Federal criminals are few in comparison with the offenders controlled by the provinces. After the First and Second World Wars, however, service personnel were of considerable numerical importance and have received liberal treatment.

Besides these responsibilities, the federal government has participated in social-service programmes by using its power to make grants and to legislate for the common good. This is demonstrated particularly in pensions for the aged and the blind, government annuities which can be purchased by individuals, and family allowances. These are parts of a permanent policy, as are also unemployment insurance and employment bureaux. In grants for unemployment relief, drought or flood relief, and aid to transients, careful statements are made to avoid creating precedents which might imply federal responsibility.

Apart from this limited federal planning, the provinces have been forced to work out their own patterns. The tendency has been to tackle problems in segments, dealing with comparatively small categories of people whose need could not be denied, rather than by over-all planning. Sometimes one province experiments, and the others follow by conservative steps. Canada has seemed reluctant to adopt forms of social security which require national planning, national spread of risk, and large-scale financing.

From the time of Confederation until 1930, there was some tendency in all the provinces except Quebec to transfer responsibility from local to provincial authorities, mainly through the further development of provincial organizations. The institutions caring for handicapped groups, such as the insane, the blind, the deaf and dumb, and for offenders against the law were extended to meet, often inadequately, the needs of the growing population throughout the country, with some coöperation between provinces whose populations did not warrant separate facilities for special groups. Although many of the original institutions were organized under *ad hoc* boards, they have in the main now been brought under the direct control of a government department. Expenses are met by the province only or by joint provincial and municipal contributions. Private institutions exist side by side with the provincial ones, and are the pattern in Quebec, where the break-down of private responsibility resulted in 1921 in a system of heavy subsidies to religious and lay organizations, paid by the province but collected in part from the municipalities. Where the municipality contributes, the question of local residence is an important issue.

Increasing industrialization brought provision for workmen's compensation, a particularly acceptable form of social insurance, since it aided the more concentrated and less self-sufficient industrial population. Financed by a levy on employers, it relieves the state of the responsibility for those injured or diseased as a result of their employment. The Ontario Act of 1914 has been copied by all the provinces except Newfoundland, which is almost entirely agricultural in its economy. Administration, of which the costs are also borne by the pay-roll assessment, is generally under a commission. Coverage is compulsory for the enumerated industries, some of which have numerical limitations. Benefits are related to earnings, being two-thirds (three-quarters in Saskatchewan) of the average wages for total disability, with minimum rates fixed but no maximum in amount or duration. All the provinces include a provision for dependents' allowances and tend to be generous in their definitions of dependents. Medical benefits are financed from the same fund, except in British Columbia, where the employee makes a contribution, and are available without limitation and regardless of eligibility for cash benefits. The doctor is usually chosen jointly by the employer and the employee, with medical referees available at the Commission. Compensation is based on the view that industrial accidents are a legitimate part of costs of production, and hence all accidents are covered except those due solely to the wilful misconduct of the employee and not resulting in serious disability or death. Civil damages are not available for accidents covered by insurance, and appeal is to the Commission and not to the courts. The acceptance of this type of social insurance and the generosity of its benefits as compared with other forms of social assistance give recognition to the growing industrialization in the country, and are probably less a subject of controversy because the cost to the public is hidden in the employer's contribution.

Mothers' allowances followed workmen's compensation, being adopted first in Manitoba in 1916. All the provinces except Newfoundland now provide such allowances. The legislation is based upon the principle that the mother is the best person to bring up her own children, and hence most provinces have a "character" clause. Unfortunately, since there is little organized coördination with the child-welfare programme (see pp. 404 ff.), the mother declared unfit by the mothers' allowance administration may still maintain control of the child. Eligibility is limited to mothers who pass a means test and who have dependent children, and has gradually been extended from widows, the original group, to various families in which the father is no longer the support because of physical incapacity, insanity, desertion, or imprisonment. Only half of the provinces include any allowance for the father if he is in the home, the other half ignoring his presence entirely. Five years' residence in the province is generally required, and reciprocal arrangements exist between only two provinces.

Maximum amounts are set either by statute or by the administrative authority, and in Manitoba alone is any attempt made to calculate the need on a budgetary basis. The administration is centralized, with some provision for municipal coöperation in receiving applications. Finance is entirely provincial, except in Alberta, where the municipality is required to contribute 20 per cent of the pension, and in Quebec, where it may be, but to date has not been, required to contribute 5 per cent. The three Maritime Provinces have made suggestions that federal financial assistance should be given in this field.

Pensions for the aged and the blind have been adopted by all the provinces following the offer of the federal government, in 1927, to help with finances to the extent at first of 50 per cent, later of 75 per cent, of the pensions. This system demonstrates one of the ways in which, when experience has shown the difficulties of divided jurisdiction, the federal government has tried to sponsor uniform social services through its financial power. The federal Act lays down the conditions of eligibility upon which the subsidy will be granted. Administrative organization must have federal approval, but the costs remain with the provinces, and the federal control depends entirely upon the audit: the federal authority was the treasury, until 1946, showing that the control is purely financial. The Act specifies the means test, age limitations, residence, and maximum pension. Provincial legislation is free to go beyond this at its own expense, but has usually done so only to the extent of adding a cost-of-living bonus and providing for medical care. In Quebec the decision on the award of a pension can be appealed to the court—a recognition of the right of the citizen to the assistance which has not yet been given in other forms of aid or in other provinces.

Under this system of financing, the tendency has been for the provinces to limit their expenditure to those for whom the federal government will give reimbursement, and to economize on administration costs, offering little in the way of the individualized services which the recipients often need in addition to financial assistance. Reciprocity between the provinces is a condition of the federal subsidy, but the great differences in the percentage of the aged receiving pensions suggests wide variation in the application of the means test.

There has been considerable agitation for an improved system of caring for the financial needs of the aged, an increasing problem in Canada as elsewhere. The federal government has tried since 1908 to compensate in part for its inability to establish old-age insurance by organizing state insurance on a voluntary basis in the form of annuities. This has won such wide-spread support that much private insurance is based upon the plan that the individual first holds the maximum government annuity of $1,200 a year. Suggestions have also been made officially for a federal scheme of non-contributory pensions with no means test, but this would depend upon provincial agreements on financial changes, and has not proved acceptable.

Workmen's compensation, mothers' allowances, and pensions for the aged and the blind are the three forms through which the provinces have given financial assistance. They demonstrate the tendency for one province to model its legislation upon that of another, although the copying may not take place until twenty years later. Those provinces which have acted later have usually placed the responsibility for their delay upon their financial position, which again reflects the disproportion between provincial responsibilities and powers of taxation and stresses the wide divergence among the provinces in financial capacity.

Until the depression of the 1930's the measures outlined above were the limits of provincial social services for the destitute, except for the indirect help given by grants to private organizations. Local authorities were responsible for all other care. In varying degrees they relied upon Houses of Refuge, or, in the Maritime Provinces, workhouses, and upon public outdoor relief and private agencies, church and lay. The problem was considered to be the care of the unemployable, as destitution resulting from unemployment was not recognized. Provincial institutional care and public assistance relieved the local authority to some extent, and the burden of caring for the remaining cases was supposed to be insignificant. In some areas no provision at all was made; others varied greatly in adequacy of assistance, conditions of eligibility, residence, and so on. Little serious attention was given to the problem as a whole. During the early 1920's the post-war depression overtaxed these facilities, and provincial and federal governments were forced to help financially in order to prevent municipal bankruptcy, but this was usually accepted as a temporary emergency which would not be repeated.

The first years of the depression of the 'thirties were regarded in the same way. The greater industrialization of the East made it suffer more severely at first, but drought and restricted markets brought the West into the same situation. Municipalities which had relied upon subsidized private organizations were gradually forced to take greater responsibility, particularly in Quebec, and to alter their conceptions of unemployed and unemployable. Many of the municipalities found themselves approaching bankruptcy; in order to save their credit they demanded and received provincial help.

As the depression continued, some of the provinces were forced into the same financial position from which they had attempted to rescue the municipalities. They appealed to the federal government, which alone seemed to have financial resources to deal with the emergency. From 1931 to 1941 the federal government made annual "emergency" grants, which the provinces distributed among the municipalities for direct relief, relief work, and various smaller schemes such as land settlement and vocational training. For a short period it also took direct responsibility for transients, who, in spite of the desirability of free movement of labour, were faced with residence laws which made them ineligible for assistance. The terms and conditions of federal grants varied from year to year, being for the most part a percentage of expenditure on direct relief or on wages for relief work. The federal government did not contribute to administrative costs and it left the provinces to set standards.

The provinces used their power in a variety of ways, but made no contribution towards administration except in bankrupt or unorganized areas. Generally they treated the situation as an emergency, at least until the second half of the decade. The Maritime Provinces clung to their old poor-law organization. Quebec, without an actual poor-law, pursued many poor-law principles, demanding that wherever possible work must be performed in return for relief, and that relief must be below the wages for local unskilled labour. Ontario belatedly tried to set a standard of adequacy, even if a low standard, to demand certain administrative reforms, and to develop a small supervisory field-staff. Only the wealthier and more compact municipalities developed any permanent organization. Provincial administration in unorganized areas provided the basis for departments of public welfare, some of which emerged from the depression to organize integrated programmes.

The most constructive result of these years of turmoil was the determination of the federal authority, backed by public opinion, that a national system of unemployment insurance must be established. When the first Act was declared unconstitutional, an amendment to the British North America Act was obtained and the Unemployment Insurance Act came into force in 1941. At the same time, as a necessary corollary to an insurance plan, a national employment service was established, based upon the diverse provincial systems which had previously been operating with some financial help from the federal government.

Unemployment insurance is financed by approximately equal

contributions from employers and employees. The federal government adds an amount equal to one-fifth of the other total contributions, and pays the costs of administration. Roughly 75 per cent of the wage-earners are covered; private domestic servants and agricultural labourers are excluded because of administrative problems. Benefits are available, after a nine-day period, for insured persons capable of, available for, and unable to obtain, suitable work. The amount of benefit is about two-thirds of the average wage, slightly increased for workers with dependents; the period of benefit is roughly one week for every five for which contributions have been paid in the preceding five years. Administration is in the hands of a commission, which also, by an amendment in 1946, is responsible for the National Employment Service. The country is divided into regions for administrative purposes, with numerous offices to make staff readily available to the local insured. The employment offices attempt to link worker and job regardless of geographic divisions, so that, for example, the needs of the rural employer may be met by a person seeking work in the city.

Unemployment insurance represents the acceptance by the federal authority of its responsibility for the employable unemployed. With its adoption, Dominion grants to the provinces for public assistance ceased. Some provinces have continued to contribute financially to local relief; Quebec and the Maritime Provinces have assumed that all persons not eligible for insurance benefits are unemployable. Hence these provinces have practically withdrawn their contribution, placing the entire burden upon the local unit. Some municipalities in their turn, where this responsibility is not a legal mandate, have discontinued public relief, holding that the obligation properly belongs to private organizations, church and lay. In point of fact, one-quarter of the wage-earners are not in insured occupations. Another group receives insurance benefits which do not recognize the difference between the needs of a family of two and that of three or more, and which totals only about two-thirds of what was itself a minimum subsistence wage. Others have drawn the benefits for the full time for which they were eligible, and are still unemployed and in need of assistance.

It is often suggested that the federal government should accept responsibility for all unemployed, either indirectly through the continuation of subsidy methods, or directly, which would have the advantage of close coördination with the employment offices, the use of existing administrative organization, and the avoidance of the invidious distinction between employable and unemployable. However, even under the local authority, changing public opinion has in some degree removed the stigma previously attached to public assistance, resulting in the trend towards cash allowances and more adequate assistance. In many larger cities, public-welfare departments are now well established and capably administered.

The control of wages and industrial conditions is a matter of provincial jurisdiction, and there is no national minimum wage. The federal government, however, has taken a definite step to improve the standard of living by instituting a system of family allowances, using its constitutional power to legislate for the general good. These allowances are made for all children under sixteen years of age, with certain residence qualifications. Unlike other legislation, the Family Allowance Act includes Indians, Eskimoes, and non-citizens. The child must be living in a family group (that is, not in an institution) and must be attending school if of school age. The amount varies from $5 to $8 a month according to the age of the child. The money must be spent on the welfare of the child; it is not intended to finance basic maintenance, which remains the responsibility of the parent, but to provide "extras" contributing to his welfare but beyond the resources of most bread-winners.

Allowances are paid regardless of family income. To upper- and middle-class families they mean no greater assistance than the old system of income-tax deductions for dependents, which they largely offset, but to families below income-tax level they are a great boon. Reports show that, since the first payments in 1945, regularity of school attendance and the purchase of milk and children's clothing have increased. The policing of the Act, necessary because of the stipulation that the money be spent on the child's welfare, has presented problems, as applications and payments are made by mail: following a precedent established during the Second World War in investigating allowances to dependents of members of the armed services, use is made of private welfare organizations, with payment to them for services rendered.

Public health and medical care are social services which have both economic and health implications. Public health is the concern of all levels of government. The Dominion provides technical assistance in research, and deals with interprovincial and international health problems. The provinces administer hospitals for mental diseases and tuberculosis (with private hospitals also functioning in these fields); they supervise other hospitals, giving leadership, technical advice, and laboratory services; and they administer health grants. The municipalities provide public-health services and some hospitals. Private organizations also sponsor hospitals and visiting-nurse services.

Health problems were first dealt with publicly only in emergencies, with emphasis upon the danger of the communication of diseases through immigrants; temporary local boards of health were created to deal with such situations. Gradually, in each province, such boards became permanent and took over the health control of the community. In scattered rural areas where local organization is financially weak or lacking, several provinces have assisted in establishing local health units, administered by the province and financed jointly by the province and the local community. This means a type of coöperative planning which has been lacking in the welfare field, but which is now possible in Ontario under an Act passed in 1948. Public-health services have been very well developed in the larger urban centres, and their success and the great need of the rural areas have encouraged the newer development.

The same difficulties of power, finance, tradition, and philosophy operate in the provision of medical care. Nowhere in Canada does any form of social insurance compensate the worker for loss of earnings during illness, except under the limited terms of the workmen's compensation laws. Interest in health insurance has been aroused in varying degrees throughout the provinces since 1919, when the first provincial commission was appointed to study the subject in British Columbia, but the original opposition of the Canadian Medical Association, now considerably modified, and the combination of the old question of Dominion-provincial relationships, the shortage of facilities and personnel, and the problems of a scattered population have postponed developments. In recent years, however, some constructive experiments have been made. Among higher-income groups there is avid acceptance of privately organized, non-profit medical services and hospitalization insurance. For indigent groups, provision is gradually being made for medical care as part of the public-assistance programme, through local health officers, payment to hospitals, or contracts with the local medical association. Free care is increasingly provided at provincial or provincial and municipal expense for such services as pre-natal examinations and treatment of tuberculosis, venereal diseases, and mental diseases—conditions in which the community, and not only the individual, is vitally interested. The lower-income groups have to date been the most neglected.

It is in the health field that the scattered population of the rural community suffers most. Because of the greatness of the need and the willingness to experiment, Saskatchewan and Alberta have developed the "municipal doctor" system. Under this system a local area may levy a special tax to subsidize or pay the salary of a resident doctor who would not otherwise be tempted to risk private practice in the locality. If he is a salaried doctor his services are free to all who pay the tax; he often acts as health officer also. In some areas the province pays the salary or makes grants towards it. Developing from this in Saskatchewan came local hospitals with facilities free to taxpayers, and, in 1947, a provincial hospitalization scheme whereby all citizens receive free hospital care in return for payment of a special tax, which for indigents is paid into the fund by the province. A similar plan was launched in British Columbia in 1949.

Various official and unofficial proposals have urged a comprehensive health-insurance programme on either a national or a provincial basis with federal subsidies for minimum standards. One province passed an act which never became operative; another legislated to make possible provincial participation in a projected federal scheme. There is wide public interest, but provincial jealousy of federal power, interprovincial feeling, financial considerations, and the difficulties of instituting a comprehensive programme throughout the country have hindered progress. The recent National Health Grants programme is planned to increase facilities and personnel as a preparation for further measures.

Problems of finance, responsibility, and scattered population also affect child-welfare services. Private children's aid societies have been authorized by provincial acts and have been given police authority to apprehend neglected children and to accept their legal guardianship; the municipalities (in Nova Scotia and Ontario the province also) are liable for maintenance. Such societies started in 1893 with the Ontario Act. This has served as a model in the other provinces (except Newfoundland), though the Quebec Act, passed in 1942, has never been proclaimed, and Saskatchewan has recently changed its policy. Provinces have supervised, imposed standards, and contributed financially in varying degrees. At the same time they have delegated to the societies certain functions in regard to adoption of children and assistance to unmarried mothers. These societies are organized in city, county, or regional units. In the rural areas particularly, as the only local social agency, they may be called upon for other services such as family welfare and temporary placement of children. They have, from the time of their organization, concentrated upon foster homes, using shelters only for temporary accommodation. They represent a peculiar development of an officially recognized private agency which obtains the largest part of its funds from public sources but over which the public authorities have little control.

As such societies have not been formed in all areas, even in the provinces which authorize them, and as the less populated or unorganized areas have been least likely to have such services, each of the provinces, with the exception of Quebec, has assumed responsibility for the child-welfare programme in a greater or lesser part of its territory, so that the provincial department performs the functions of a society in areas where no society exists. In some provinces this is a separate service; in others it is coördinated with other provincial social services.

Overlapping services, competition for foster homes, the desirability for closer coördination with other services such as mothers' allowances, and the growing feeling of municipalities that they wish more control over the care of the children whom they must support are leading towards a comprehensive public programme for child welfare. Only in Ontario has the area covered by the societies even approximated the organized territory within a province. Most of the work elsewhere has been limited to the larger centres and adjacent districts, so that provincial authority has had to function rather extensively. In Alberta, although societies have nominally existed in some areas, the province has had full, co-extensive power and has made use of it. In Saskatchewan, guardianship of children was transferred in 1946 from the societies to the province; Ontario municipalities are becoming increasingly restless in their demand for larger control; and increased provincial grants have brought closer supervision and greater power to the New Brunswick government. Thus one province after another is moving towards a public programme.

Quebec alone has followed a different pattern of development. Most of the needy Roman Catholic children are looked after in institutions under the Church, with government subsidies paid on a *per diem* basis through the Bureau of Public Charities. The Bureau has nominal power to set up standards, but is carefully prevented from interfering in anything which might be considered a matter for Church control. Minority religious groups work through private agencies, many of them under lay control, which receive public subsidies in the same manner. Adoption is more restricted than in the other provinces, as strong feelings of family responsibility and obligation have defined closely the type of child who may be adopted.

Handicapped children are generally dealt with as problems of health or education rather than under child-welfare organizations. Schools for the deaf and blind come under the provincial education department, hospitals for mental defectives under the health department. Local school-boards are encouraged by provincial grants to establish special classes for the handicapped who do not require institutional care. Private agencies supplement an inadequate programme.

The system of justice presents a mixed picture. The federal government is responsible for criminal law and conducts institutions for prisoners serving sentences of more than two years. Provincial governments administer civil law and shorter-term penal institutions, and municipalities provide gaols and "lock-ups" for temporary detention. A Royal Commission on Penal Reform reported in 1939 that in many of these institutions the emphasis was on punishment rather than on rehabilitation. There was no classification except on the basis of the duration of detention; educational and vocational training facilities were lacking, and parole and probation organization were inadequate. The Second World War postponed action upon the recommendations, but some progress is now being made on both provincial and federal levels.

Federal legislation, passed in 1908, allows municipal authorities, with provincial consent, to establish juvenile courts with jurisdiction over those under the age of eighteen years, except those charged with crimes punishable by death. Most of the provinces have made use of this legislation only for those under sixteen years, and only in the larger centres. Where such special courts are not provided, juveniles are tried in private, separate sessions of the adult court. In the larger cities in Quebec, juvenile courts have been expanded into social-welfare courts which assume additional jurisdiction over certification of the insane, appeals concerning old-age pensions, and family conciliation. Family, or domestic-relations, courts are linked with juvenile courts in a few centres in other provinces. These courts are socialized in varying degrees. The best have the services of child-guidance clinics and probation officers; others differ little from adult courts in their methods and outlook. Juveniles cannot be detained with adult offenders, and each province has some form of juvenile training-school or reformatory, sometimes its own, sometimes under church control. Costs are borne by provincial or provincial-municipal funds.

Recreation is probably the area most recently recognized by the public as a social responsibility, with interest stimulated during the Second World War. Municipalities have powers in regard to parks and playgrounds, and the most advanced have used these powers to provide not only facilities but supervision. The federal National Physical Fitness Act of 1943 provides federal funds up to a certain maximum to match provincial contributions towards approved programmes. This action has stimulated provincial participation in a field previously considered solely a municipal responsibility. The programme has usually been administered under the provincial department of education, first through the schools, sponsoring both group and mass activities, and then for adults. National fitness has been interpreted as physical, mental, moral, and spiritual; hence the programmes are wide and varied. Grants are made to local authorities or to private organizations with acceptable recreational facilities and projects.

This is a picture in outline of the problems and the progress of Canada and her provinces in the organization of social services. Because of differences in cultural background, emphasis on individualism, and political issues, public opinion is divided on the desirability of a comprehensive social-security programme. There is, however, far greater interest than has ever been in evidence before. There is a definite trend towards public responsibility for increased assistance to private organizations, towards provincial responsibility for relief of local authorities, and towards federal leadership. Needs have been recognized and an effort is being made to overcome the difficulties. Social services have become a vital issue in public and political discussions, and the progress made in the last few years has by no means satisfied the public demand.

CHAPTER XVIII

The Cultural Pattern

BY WALTER HERBERT

THE CULTURAL PATTERN of a nation is a mosaic of many intricately adjusted parts, touching almost every aspect of the national life. In commoner usage, however, the term culture is associated chiefly with the fine arts, and it is mainly in this sense that the word is used in this chapter.

Whether there is a Canadian culture in the full meaning of the term has been much debated by Canadians themselves. Certainly there is not yet a well-defined pattern based on a common tradition. Elements from various sources are mingling, and signs are not lacking, especially in recent years, that a truly Canadian culture is developing. But at what point and in what proportions the elements will unite is not yet clear. Several rivers, joining to form a greater stream, may continue to maintain their individual characteristics throughout many miles of the major stream's course. The modern traveller high above the earth can see the waters green, blue, or yellow with mud, and eventually trace their mingling, but for a time it is the spectacle of their diversity in unity which intrigues him. So it is with the tributaries in the stream of Canada's cultural development. The stream moves on, the elements mingle, but the diversity of the component parts is still of primary interest and importance.

The experience of Canada in this process of cultural development is by no means unique. In each of the American nations the elements, derived chiefly from European sources, have been moulded under the pressure of the environment into new and distinctive cultural patterns. In Canada the component elements, the details of time and circumstance, differ, often sharply, from those of her American neighbours; the process in essence is the same.

The Canadian cultural stream as it appears today, except in the Province of Quebec, is predominantly Anglo-Saxon, with strong influences from the United States and the United Kingdom evident in virtually every aspect of the life and thought of the Canadian people. Dominant in the Province of Quebec, and extending in many ways beyond its borders, is the culture of French Canada with its distinctive qualities resting firmly on more than three centuries of development in the New World. To this biculturalism, with its subtle and pervasive influences, is added the fact that in some parts of the country the traditions and attitudes of central and northern Europe are by no means negligible.

Among the influences which impinge on Canadian culture today, those from the United States are by all odds the most powerful. They appear to be building a substantial superstructure upon the cultural foundations created by British influences during the nineteenth century. Projected incessantly, even if unintentionally, across more than three thousand miles of international border, they sometimes seem objectionably aggressive to Canadian sensibilities. This reaction against American influence has been one of the chief incentives in the creation of something distinctively Canadian in the cultural, as in the political, sphere.

It would, however, be a distortion to picture the Canadian attitude towards American influence as merely one of reaction or resentment. Indeed, it might well be argued that the reverse is more nearly true. Much that comes from the United States is North American rather than American in the narrower sense, and Canadians instinctively recognize themselves as North Americans; much also is good, and Canadians, for the most part, know the United States too well to accept the unqualified condemnation of everything American which has too often been made by the superficial foreign observer. The Canadian, therefore, realizes that he must try to understand his giant neighbour in both his virtues and his defects, that he can neglect that understanding only at his peril, but that he cannot expect an equal understanding from that neighbour in return.

Hollywood movies, of course, are the shock-troops of American culture and, with their incredible mixture of the refined and the shoddy, they set many fashions for Canadians to follow. Even in the backwoods hamlets of Quebec, where other non-French influences have failed to make headway, the Hollywood film, with French subtitles, has insinuated itself into the warm hearts of the solid habitant people. American-made motion pictures are shown everywhere, and Canadians appear to welcome them heartily, although English and Continental films hold a very high place. American radio broadcasts enter the lives and thoughts of nearly every Canadian family daily, bringing grand opera, symphonic music, gangster plays, and all the other manifestations of the catholic American taste.

American magazines provide much of the current literary fare in Canada; the fine-arts section of one publication, for instance, makes a valuable contribution to Canadian popular knowledge and aesthetic appreciation; other United States magazines, with very large sales in Canada, throw almost exclusive emphasis upon the artistic importance of the female human form. Comic strips, or "funnies," provide much of the extra-mural education of junior Canadians. The daily papers in Canada include a considerable amount of news of United States origin, and supply their readers with syndicated columns of popular American journalists. The shelves of Canadian book-shops are crowded with American books; some are imported from the United States and others are Canadian editions printed in Canada for the Canadian branches or agents of American publishers. The constant influx of millions of American tourists to Canada, who bring with them an apparent sense of well-being and of contentment, suggests to many Canadians the probable excellence of the American cultural environment. Through numerous media and in countless ways, some subtle, some barbarous, Canada is receiving the full impact of the "American way of life," and in many respects these influences have enriched Canadian life.

The superficial impression created by all this is that the average English-speaking community in Canada differs little from its United States counterpart; but this is an illusion which is soon dissipated by closer observation. Since the American Revolution, and even before, American and British influences have always been mingled in the Canadian scene, but for a century British influences were predominant. Even up to 1914 the influence of London on Canadian developments was extremely important, even if not always direct. During this period of a century and a half, Canada was thoroughly impregnated with the British cultural tradition. Colonial officials brought the *mores* and preferences and prejudices of England and Scotland to the new land and established firm and lasting fashions in intellectual and aesthetic matters. Schools were established in the English tradition; schoolmasters from England and Scotland guided the tastes of young Canadians and exercised a notable influence in community development. Scottish clergymen for the Presbyterian Church in Canada and English clergymen for the Church of England in Canada aided materially as well as spiritually in establishing a bed-rock of British cultural tradition; and even today English and Scottish traditions and personnel are of great importance in the universities and churches of Canada.

For a century and a half, preferential trade arrangements gave English publishers almost monopolistic opportunities to dominate the Canadian literary market. British literature, painting, drama, and music became firmly established as Canadian preferences, not through the process of selection, but by virtue of the absence of comparison with the arts of other nations.

The strength of British cultural influences in Canada may be appreciated if it is remembered how persistent they were in the United States even in the nineteenth century. In Canada they were intensified and prolonged by the conviction that they were a bulwark against Americanism and that, adapted and modified in the North American environment, they would be a vital element in a true Canadianism. In cultural as in political developments, the lack of a revolutionary tradition produced a sharp difference between Canada and the United States. Admiration for British cultural tastes is thus still basic in English-speaking Canada. Many Canadians do not realize this; some realize and approve; others realize and deplore. However that may be, the cultural influences which enter the Canadian scene—even those from the United States—will continue to be imposed on an underlying foundation of British tradition which is still substantial.

In spite of the predominance of British and American cultures, however, Canada does not fit neatly into the Anglo-American pattern, nor has she ever done so. Approximately one-third of her people are of French background, reared in the French language, and thoroughly attached to French cultural traditions. Through three and a half centuries they have proudly and militantly maintained their cultural identity, and since 1763 have successfully resisted temptations to become assimilated with the English-speaking majority. Although the Province of Quebec is the home of most of the French-speaking Canadians and is the centre of their culture, French-language communities are found elsewhere in Canada, especially in New Brunswick, Ontario, Saskatchewan, and Alberta. The French language enjoys customary and official usage in Quebec, and has an equal status with English in the deliberations and proceedings of the Parliament of Canada. Litigants are entitled to plead in either English or French in Canadian courts of federal jurisdiction. All bank-notes and postage stamps in Canada are bilingual. Montreal, the second largest French-speaking city in the world, is bicultural as well as bilingual. French literature, music, painting, and drama are dominant; Anglo-American culture is secondary.

French Canadians do not maintain close cultural ties with France, and have not done so since the Canadian territories were ceded to the British by the Treaty of Paris in 1763. Modern France is admired and followed in some measure by the Quebec intellectuals, but for the generality of French Canadians the tie with Paris is vague and sentimental. The underlying Gallic culture of French Canada is essentially the tradition of seventeenth-century and mid-eighteenth-century France, and in rural Quebec it continues to thrive without substantial adulteration by the passage of time or by separation from the fountain-head. In the larger urban centres of the province, French culture must withstand the pressure of Anglo-American influence; and that it succeeds so admirably in holding its own is a matter of wonderment. French

Canadians maintain their own vigorous and highly-artistic culture along with, but not mingled with, the dominant Anglo-American culture of the rest of Canada. As a people they accord much greater importance to cultural matters than do their Anglo-Saxon compatriots, and are in many respects the leaven in the Canadian cultural dough.

Other national cultures have contributed more or less directly to the Canadian pattern. Among the groups which came to British North America in the eighteenth century are the Hanoverian Germans who settled around Lunenburg in Nova Scotia two centuries ago, and the Pennsylvania Germans who trekked to what is now western Ontario after the American Revolution. More extensive, however, were the settlements of the tens of thousands of Europeans who came in the great migration during the two or three decades preceding 1914. Bringing with them the ancient cultural traditions of their forefathers, these people and their descendants readily adapted themselves to their new homes. Settled mostly on the prairies, communities are nevertheless to be found in all parts of English-speaking Canada, many with evidence of German, Ukrainian, Swedish, Icelandic, and other cultural influences.

These immigrant peoples were warmly appreciative of their national customs, literature, music, dances, and handicrafts, and generously contributed their talents and artistry to the cultural life of the adopted land. Canadians who are two and three generations removed from the original immigrant stock have made, and are still making, notable contributions to Canadian literature and music, and they are the inspiration and mainstay in non-French handicraft arts in Canada. Their net contributions are not always directly traceable, but the lists of competent Canadian artists in music, painting, drama, and literature include many with family names which are neither Anglo-Saxon nor French in origin.

Canada's cultural development has thus been extraordinarily complex; its origins and main influences have come not from within but from without. As a result, cultural development has been imitative and unoriginal. This was true also of other American countries, but in Canada historical circumstances prolonged the immaturity of the earlier stages into the present century. Only in recent years have there been signs of the emergence of vigorous, original, creative powers among Canadian artists.

For a people who have been occupied mainly with the physical task of transforming a vast and rugged land into a modern community, Canadians have produced a surprisingly large amount of indigenous writing, although little of it is of broad literary importance, and much of it, both in English and in French, has been self-conscious and imitative. Characteristically, Canadian writing in the English language has been profoundly influenced by the traditional reverence for British and American literary fashions. French Canada's cultural isolation forced a measure of independence upon her writers, but the major part of their work was self-regarding and provincial and has had little recognition beyond the Province of Quebec. In recent years, however, Canadian writers of both languages have broken sharply from custom and tradition, and a new era in Canadian creative writing seems now to be emerging.

It is a fact of no small importance that the first Canadian works were written in French by explorers, missionaries, and settlers; for these early works, many of them reports and journals, are the frame upon which much subsequent Canadian writing has been hung. Frequently they are themselves notable literary productions, replete with impressive and skilful descriptions of the newly-discovered land, inspiring accounts of pioneer life, and uplifting expositions of faith and idealism. Champlain's accounts of his voyages and explorations are justly renowned, as are the remarkable records of the French Jesuit missionaries of the seventeenth century, the *Relations,* and Marc Lescarbot's *Histoire de la Nouvelle-France,* first published in Paris in 1609. In the eighteenth and nineteenth centuries there were notable additions in English: Samuel Hearne's *Journey from Prince of Wales Fort* and Sir Alexander Mackenzie's *Voyages from Montreal . . . through the Continent of North America, to the Frozen and Pacific Oceans.* Such works have not only been widely read for their own sakes but have proved to be a mine of information and a stimulus to the historical novelist. F. D. McDowell's *The Champlain Road* and Philip Child's *The Village of Souls,* both set in the seventeenth century, are successful novels based directly on source material.

Canadians have been writing histories of their country for more than a century now, and a number of their works are of high quality. While much remains to be done, especially for particular areas and periods, there is a relatively large and important body of historical writings which deal with Canada as a whole. Among them are F. X. Garneau, whose *Histoire du Canada,* first published in the 1840's, has had a profound influence on French-Canadian thought; G. M. Wrong and Thomas Chapais, who wrote in the earlier decades of this century; and A. G. Doughty, who wrote and edited much, but also made an important contribution to the cultural life of the country as Dominion Archivist. During the past two decades numerous works of modern scholarship have radically broadened and altered the interpretations of Canadian history, and in recent years works of high quality based on this specialized research have appeared for the general reader.

Closely related to formal history are the writings of public men. A number of nineteenth-century political leaders in Canada were prolific and able authors who created a literature of political discussion of no mean interest. Outstanding is the name of Joseph Howe, the great Nova Scotia leader, whose discussions of imperial and colonial relations lie in the tradition of Burke and rise at points to a level scarcely below that of the master himself. In the present century the name of J. W. Dafoe will be remembered, though unlike Howe, who also began as a journalist, Dafoe remained a political journalist throughout his life.

Biography and the literature of reminiscence have been somewhat neglected in Canada, mainly, it would appear, because of the very moderate financial reward they offer. Much has been written for magazines and newspapers about eminent persons and the passing scene, and has suffered the customary oblivion of periodical literature; but full-length books in permanent format, recording the lives of prominent Canadians, are rare. This is a matter of concern and regret to thoughtful Canadians, who realize that much of the intimate story of their country is passing away unrecorded with the demise of every "old-timer."

Canadian intellectuals have produced a not unworthy share of competent scholarly writing; their contributions to research and restatement, particularly in the social sciences and the humanities, are well regarded in academic circles. Until recent years, however, much of Canadian writing in this category was published in the United Kingdom and the United States.

Belles-lettres have been traditionally popular in Canada, and the essayist, English or French, has been a literary figure well liked and understood. While much of this kind of writing has appeared in periodicals and thus is not usually regarded as a part of the permanent body of Canadian literature, it is also true that many essays have been preserved in lasting format. The out of doors is a frequent topic, as in W. H. Blake's *Brown Waters.* Rural life and customs in Ontario are delightfully described by Peter McArthur in *Familiar Fields,* and Quebec is depicted with equal charm by Georges Bouchard in *Other Days, Other Ways,* by Claude Mélançon in *Charmants Voisins,* and by many others. Ships and the sea were the themes of Archibald MacMechan in *Sagas of the Sea* and other volumes. Canada's best-known literary critic, William Arthur Deacon, some years ago issued *Poteen,* an excellent volume of essays and sketches. Bruce Hutchison's *The Unknown Country,* originally published in the United States, became a best seller in Canada; her inhabitants showed great interest in Mr. Hutchison's description of their "unknown" country.

Much of Canada's critical and interpretative writing appears in journals of high literary quality sponsored by the universities of Toronto, McGill, Queen's, Laval, Ottawa, and Dalhousie. These publish a variety of excellent essay material which is always scholarly but seldom narrowly academic. First-rate comment on current politics, economics, and culture—much of Canada's best incidental writing—is found in *Saturday Night, Culture, International Journal, Canadian Geographical Journal, Canadian Forum, Here and Now, Canadian Art.*

Although Canadian novelists have rarely gained wide-spread recognition, or even a livelihood, from their literary efforts, they have been more numerous than is generally realized; and on the whole the Canadian novel has been elemental and vigorous. Most of the novelists have used the background and problems of their own communities and have not ventured into cosmopolitan or sophisticated fiction. This accounts, perhaps, for a certain dulness in their treatment of large themes. Canadians persisted in their devotion to an outmoded type of emotionless fiction during the first quarter of this century, when writers elsewhere were increasingly concerned with controversial themes of social significance. It is remarkable, for instance, that, although Canada made a notable sacrifice of her blood and substance in the First World War, no Canadian novelist succeeded in reflecting the great spiritual and emotional disturbance which was experienced by the country. Only in the last twenty years have Canadian novelists revealed greater vigour of style and broader originality of themes. They are just beginning to write books which deal skilfully with subtle human relationships, philosophical problems, and subjects of universal interest.

The temperamental variance between the citizens and institutions of the two cultures in Canada is now being treated with deftness and understanding by both French-Canadian and English-Canadian novelists; a basic problem which has hitherto been left to uninformed prejudices is thus brought directly to the hearts and minds of the Canadian people. Hugh MacLennan's *Two Solitudes,* which deals with this theme, has gained a very wide audience. Gwethalyn Graham's *Earth and High Heaven* posed the problem of anti-Semitism; her highly-successful novel was one of the first to depict a trend now current in the popular fiction of North America. In French Canada the picturesque tale describing the simple charm of habitant life is now being succeeded by such realistic novels as Gabrielle Roy's *The Tin Flute,* set in lower-class Montreal, and Roger Lemelin's *The Town Below,* based on life in the Lower Town, the old French-Canadian section of Quebec City. At his recent death, following a life of varied experience and prolonged hardship, Frederick Philip Grove left a number of serious and realistic autobiographical novels which are likely to take on added importance in the future.

The books mentioned above have currently gained an audience not only in Canada but beyond. Other Canadian novels have won a place as standard works of fiction in the English language. Stephen Leacock, with his *Sunshine Sketches of a Little Town,* and a score of delightful companion volumes, added notably to the gaiety of the nations and gained wide-spread honours as a humorist. The *Anne of Green Gables* stories, by L. M. Montgomery, and *Beautiful Joe,* by Marshall Saunders, continue to bring joy to children in many lands. Robert W. Service's *The Trail of '98* and Ralph Connor's *The Sky Pilot* have been published in many languages and seem likely to be perpetual good sellers. Mazo de la Roche's numerous novels dealing with the Whiteoaks family are always in demand in lending-libraries and book-shops throughout the world. William Kirby's *The Golden Dog* (1872) and T. C. Haliburton's *Sam Slick* (1836) have gone through many editions and reprintings to meet a never-failing popularity with readers in Canada, the United States, and Great Britain.

Canadian poetry, in English and French, is substantial both in volume and in quality, although it is not widely recognized in important anthologies. The early poets used the local scene almost exclusively as their theme, extolling the beauties or rigours of the country-side and praising the stoicism of the pioneers. Nostalgic references to England or Scotland or France recurred throughout these early Canadian lyrics. Nationalistic undercurrents appeared in French-Canadian poetry much earlier than in the work of the English-language poets, mainly, perhaps, because the French-speaking population in Canada was acutely conscious of having been abandoned by Paris long before the Anglo-Saxon Canadians even considered severing the political and cultural ties with London. Much of the French-Canadian poetry deals with love of country, duty to race, and devotion to language and religion, but Canadian poetry in the English language pays scant attention to such themes. Strangely enough, however, the single Canadian poem which is best known throughout the world was written by an English-speaking Canadian and deals with the theme of patriotism—*In Flanders Fields,* by John McCrae.

The earliest Canadian poetry was contained in unwritten Indian lore and French folk-songs. A great deal of this material must be presumed lost, but much of it has been revived, recorded, collected, and published in recent years by Canadian scholars. An important body of early indigenous song has been preserved in *Songs of the Haida,* collected and translated by Hermia Fraser, and *Songs of the Coast Dwellers,* by Constance Skinner. Dr. Marius Barbeau, the distinguished ethnologist of the Canadian Government, has been assiduous in the collecting of early songs and poems, and some of his research has recalled lyrics of Old France which were lost to the country of their origin for two centuries or more. William McLennan also is noteworthy for his preservation of early Canadiana. Recently the National Film Board of Canada, an agency of the federal government, made recordings of hundreds of early, unwritten Canadian songs, poems, and folk-tales.

Pioneer life in Canada and the beginnings of a local tradition were treated in the nineteenth century by a large number of poetically inclined Canadian writers, many of them poorly schooled and isolated, but moved by deep emotion. None of this poetry is considered important; but all of it must be accepted as earnest and purposeful, and probably not less competent than the average poetry written elsewhere. Remembered poets of the early Canadian school include Susannah Moodie, Oliver Goldsmith (grand-nephew of the English poet), Charles Heavysege, Charles Sangster, and Charles Mair. The last-named was perhaps the advance agent of a new school which was to be inspired by the rapid development of the country in the latter part of the nineteenth century and which was to express a new nationalistic element in Canadian writing.

The only Canadian woman poet of note before the turn of the century was Isabella Valancy Crawford. She achieved real power and depth in describing nature. Sir Charles G. D. Roberts, who wrote tales of animal life which sold widely in Canada, the United States, and England, was at his best when describing the Canadian scene. His cousin, Bliss Carman, also wrote most often of nature; his verse is extremely melodic. Another nature poet, Archibald Lampman, is now rated highly by modern critics; his best-known poem is probably *Heat*. E. Pauline Johnson, a descendant of the tribe which left the Mohawk Valley for Canada during the American Revolution, composed intensely patriotic verse. Duncan Campbell Scott, an official in the Department of Indian Affairs, based some of his most successful poems on Indian subjects.

Since the beginning of the twentieth century, the lyrics of Canadian poets, both romantic and sophisticated, have been in a more cosmopolitan vein. Marjorie Pickthall's poetry has delicacy and perfection of form. Audrey Alexandra Brown has chosen wide-ranging subjects; her verse is rich and melodic. The poetry of Tom McInnes is vigorous and varied. Among French Canadians, Alfred Deroches and Louis Dantin have produced poetry more cosmopolitan than that of their predecessors.

Robert Service portrayed the picturesque life of the mining camps during the Yukon gold-rush at the turn of the century. His poetry had a great vogue; interest in it was revived during the building of the Alaska Highway, when booksellers in Edmonton had difficulty in obtaining sufficient copies of his poems to satisfy their American customers.

At the present time the writing of poetry is thriving throughout Canada, and the number of anthologies, collections, and chapbooks being published indicates a surprisingly large reading public as well as a sizable fraternity of native poets. The best-known Canadian poet at work today is E. J. Pratt; his epics of the sea and shorter poems have recently been published in a collected volume available in Canada, the United States, and England. Earle Birney has published several notable volumes of verse.

Even the modern poetry, however, is divided into schools. While the lines are not closely drawn, such poets as Pratt and Birney, A. S. Bourinot, Leo Cox, Robert Finch, Guy Sylvestre, Charles Bruce, and Frederick Watt might be considered to belong to the more conventional school; and F. R. Scott, A. J. M. Smith, Dorothy Livesay, Anne Marriott, L. A. Mackay, A. M. Klein, James Wreford, Patrick Anderson, Patricia K. Page, and Ronald Hambleton, to the experimental, and in some instances political, school.

A widely-held belief among students of Canadian literature is that indigenous creative writing has been seriously hampered and retarded by the slow development of the book-publishing industry in Canada. It is less than a hundred years old, and only within the past thirty years has it achieved importance. Before 1914 most of the books sold in Canada were imported; Canadian publishing supplied less than 15 per cent of the total. Today, however, the situation is reversed; the preponderance of books sold in Canada are published in Canada—some as original ventures by Canadian publishers and others as Canadian editions of American, British, or French books. The English-language publishing houses in Canada are less devoted than they formerly were to jobbing the works of parent or patron companies in London or New York and more inclined to initiating the publication of books of Canadian origin.

An important modern development has been a new, mutually appreciative relationship between Canadian writers and Canadian publishers. The former are finding new confidence in the publishers' initiative and understanding, and the latter seem to show greater respect for the commercially exploitable calibre of Canadian writing. The efforts of the Canadian Authors' Association and the Canadian Library Association have undoubtedly played an important part in improving the writer's market in Canada. Recently, the Canadian Government has taken the first steps towards the establishment of a National Library—cheering news to all who have at heart the cultural advancement of Canada.

The Second World War caused a great increase in French-language publishing in Canada. When France and Belgium were occupied by the Nazi forces and the normal supply of French books to North and South America ceased, Montreal publishers were permitted, by special copyright arrangements, to produce books for world distribution on behalf of Continental French publishers. The consequent unprecedented boom in the production of French literature in Canada kept Montreal printing-presses running at top capacity throughout the war-years. Although the post-war resumption of business by publishers in France altered this situation materially, the fillip given to Montreal publishing seems, at this date, to have had permanent effects, and Canada's largest city appears to be established as a French-language publishing centre of world-wide importance.

The situation of the theatre in Canada is paradoxical, with a vigorous theatre movement thriving under circumstances which are usually considered inimical. Canada has no professional theatre in the broad sense, and the majority of her people, urban as well as rural, never see a professional performance. The expense of moving theatrical companies and stage equipment from one to another of Canada's widely-separated cities is prohibitive in view of the limited box-office receipts in most of the cities, which are relatively small; and only occasionally does a venturesome company journey from New York or London for a brief appearance in Toronto or Montreal.

Canadians, nevertheless, are a theatre-minded people and have developed an amateur movement of impressive proportions and competence. A surprising number of successful actors and actresses playing in professional ranks elsewhere have received their basic training in the little theatres of Canada. Little-theatre groups, composed entirely of unpaid actors, directors, and technicians, organized under non-profit auspices, flourish in all Canadian cities and many smaller communities. Drama groups in universities and colleges are notably successful, and educational authorities in most parts of Canada are favourably disposed towards dramatic training as an important element of the school curriculum. A number of provincial government bureaux and at least one office of the federal government are directly concerned with assisting community organizations in sponsoring the amateur theatre.

These various expressions of interest in the drama exist without being even loosely knit together in a nationally organized form; but they all draw inspiration from the annual Dominion Drama Festival, which stimulates keen rivalry among competing groups and arouses nation-wide interest and support. The national festival, the climax of a series of regional festivals, is held each year. Plays in French and plays in English, three-act plays and one-act plays, compete on equal terms for the festival's top honours. Regional and national festivals are judged by distinguished, bilingual drama critics—usually brought from London or New York. The Dominion Drama Festival is an event of far-reaching importance in the development of Canadian culture, as it is one of the few manifestations of truly national concern in the arts.

During the week of the Dominion Drama Festival, theatre-minded Canadians have the opportunity of exchanging views and experiences in committees and round-table discussions. The subject of a national theatre has been vigorously discussed at such meetings, and has aroused wide-spread interest. The Capital Planning Scheme, which is now in process of realization, and which will make Ottawa one of the world's beautiful cities, would provide suitable headquarters for the stimulation and promotion of all aspects of theatrical arts in Canada.

As playwrights for the theatre, Canadians have not been strikingly successful, although interest in this form of creative writing is rapidly growing. Annual competitions are numerous and popular, and one of the coveted prizes of the Dominion Drama Festival is a special award for the best play written by a Canadian. Well-taught courses in dramatic composition are offered at several universities—Queen's, Mount Allison, Alberta, and Saskatchewan—and at the Banff School of Fine Arts. In radio drama Canadian playwrights have met with conspicuous success. Their works are heard frequently over the major networks of both Canada and the United States, and a large number of Canadian-trained dramatists occupy important posts in the creative workshops of the large American broadcasting companies.

Musically, Canada is thoroughly mature in some ways, but comparatively undeveloped in others.

Among French Canadians there is an instinctive, light-hearted, and uninhibited turning to music to express both individual and group emotions, and in parts of western Canada the folk-music of continental Europe plays an important part in family and community life. The majority of Canadians, however, are influenced by Anglo-Saxon reticence, and do not naturally find an emotional outlet in musical expression, except perhaps in choral singing.

No account of the musical life of Canada is complete without reference to choral music. In English-Canadian communities the mainspring of choral organization has usually been a leader or chorister trained in the British Isles. Canadians have derived their enthusiasm for group singing from other European countries as well; there are several fine Ukrainian choirs, for example. The Mendelssohn Choir of Toronto, led by Sir Ernest MacMillan, does not have its counterpart on this continent. Emphasis is placed on choral music in the churches, and amateur, semi-professional, and professional groups—mixed choirs, men's and women's choruses, boys' choruses, and school choruses—abound. This enthusiasm and the extremely valuable training in choral work are having a profound effect upon musical appreciation and the status of music in Canada.

In musical appreciation as a listener's art, Canadians are generally well advanced and competent; and are eager to provide themselves with adequate musical pleasures. As elsewhere, radio broadcasting is the chief continuous source of musical entertainment, but the Canadian appetite for "live music" is noteworthy. Musical performances in the cities range from simple and dignified recitals of vocal and instrumental soloists to impressive concerts by great choirs and orchestras. In the smaller centres, performances are less frequent and less polished; but it would be difficult to discover anywhere in Canada an organized community which does not provide some form of live musical entertainment. Many individual musicians and concert groups are achieving high standards of performance, a fact which is evidenced by the willingness of critical audiences to accept these Canadians on the same terms as they do distinguished foreign artists.

Musical education occupies an important place in the curricula of all the provincial departments of education, and public funds are generously provided for musical studies. The socially desirable aspects of music in the community are widely recognized by Canadian educational authorities, and the trend is towards an expanding programme for the training of teachers and gifted students. Canadian universities and conservatories are now able to offer a thorough and diversified musical education, and rarely is it necessary for advanced students to go elsewhere to complete their studies.

The Royal Conservatory of Music of Toronto is generally recognized for the excellence of its teaching and its high professional standards. It offers undergraduate and graduate training in virtually every branch of music; and its Senior School for professional students includes classes in operatic performance and production. The Conservatory, which is associated with the University of Toronto, has been the key institution in musical education throughout English-speaking Canada. Its enterprising extension services have reached out to distant parts of Canada, as well as to the cities and towns, and have provided uniform teaching standards of inestimable value to the sprawling and sparsely-populated country. Its courses of study have been almost universally accepted in Canada as a basis for teaching, and they are supplemented by an admirable system of local examinations conducted by the Conservatory's itinerant examiners. Recently, several smaller regional conservatories and university faculties of music have achieved sufficient teaching strength to assume increasing responsibility for musical education in their own areas, thereby permitting the Toronto Conservatory to concentrate on advanced professional training and graduate studies.

In Montreal the Conservatoire Nationale de Musique et de l'Art Dramatique, sponsored and generously supported by the Quebec provincial government, provides free tuition, under internationally known teachers, to a number of advanced students.

However advanced Canada may be in music appreciation and musical education, she is under-developed in musical composition. The same factors which account for a certain lack of originality in literature have retarded creative musical writing: devotion to ancestral musical fashions and personalities, the weight of American and British influences, and the absence of music publishers in Canada. Another factor is the simple failure to recognize the importance of giving positive encouragement to anything so intangible as indigenous musical composition. On this point, Sir Ernest MacMillan, Canada's best-known musician, said recently: "We still need to become conscious as a people of the importance of creative work; for, in the long run, it is creation rather than performance that 'places' a nation musically. It is always true that the most important, though perhaps least spectacular, developments in any musical life are those in the field of musical composition. Canada has had composers in the past, some of whom have produced very interesting and even distinguished work, but on the whole our role has been that of an importer."[1]

Dr. Healey Willan was one of the first Canadian composers to win recognition abroad. While he has composed in many fields, including operatic works, he is best known for his church music. Dr. Graham George has composed operas. Claude Champagne has written symphonic works; J. J. Gagnier, orchestral and band music; the Rev. Placide Vermandère, church music. Barbara Pentland and Harry Somers have composed for strings and full orchestra; Arnold Walter and Harry Freedman for orchestra; Oskar Morawetz for orchestra and piano. Arrangements of French-Canadian folk-songs are a specialty of Sir Ernest MacMillan and Hector Grattan. Of the younger composers, John Weinzweig,

[1] For notes to chapter xviii see page 580.

Alexander Brott, and G. Coulthard Adams have won success in international competition. A group of youthful musicians have done excellent work for the films, particularly for the National Film Board: Robert Fleming, Maurice Blackburn, Louis Applebaum, and Eldon Rathburn.

Dancing, as a pastime, enjoys varying degrees of popular interest and support throughout Canada. The people of French or Ukrainian background are the most enthusiastic, the Anglo-Saxons less so. Festivals of folk-dancing are frequent and well patronized, and group dancing is taught in public schools in every part of Canada. All the dance forms are imported from other countries: some are the nostalgic, traditional steps brought by immigrants from Europe; others are ephemeral modern movements brought into Canada by the motion-picture industry. The only indigenous dance forms are those of the Indians, and these are performed only upon ceremonial occasions, by and for the Indians.

The dance as an art has, however, gained general support in recent years, and a dozen schools of ballet are now operating successfully in Canadian cities. The Winnipeg Ballet School and the Volkoff Ballet School in Toronto, both established in the middle 1930's, have attained teaching and performing competence that is recognized both at home and abroad; many of their graduates are star performers with noted ballet organizations throughout the world. Original choreography and musical composition by both schools have won commendation from competent foreign critics. The annual Ballet Festival, which brings together groups from distant points of Canada for a week of public performances, commands public interest and financial support. In many respects the art of the ballet would seem to be little suited to the Canadian scene and temperament, and yet it appears that the ballet may develop into one of Canada's most popular arts.

Painting is the most nationally expressive of all the arts in Canada, for within the general circumference of painting is a small, recognizable arc which is distinctly Canadian in manner. The catalogue of the National Gallery of Canada contains a section describing the works of the "Canadian School" of painters—a bold attitude for Canadian officialdom to take, but a justifiable and necessary one. In referring to Canadian painting, there is no suggestion that Canadian artists have devised new methods or have set universal fashions for others to follow. It means only that much of their painting has a specific content, a manner of portraying locale and atmosphere, which are unmistakably Canadian. Much of this specific content, especially in the painting of the past quarter of a century, has been inspired by the impressive qualities of the Canadian landscape. It is an error, however (made frequently and carelessly by both critics and laymen), to underestimate the quantity and excellence of Canadian painting which deals with subjects other than the local landscape.

The country's art history dates from recorded times when white explorers and settlers first came to the New World. Early French art in Canada, patronized by the Church, was mostly ecclesiastical, untutored, and unambitious, and cannot be considered in any sense the basis of the excellent painting of modern French Canada. The earliest works by English artists were mainly reportorial drawings and paintings by military men and surveyors. In many instances rendered by partially trained craftsmen, they were admirable examples of the fastidious verisimilitude which was an English vogue of the day. Representative works from these early days have been preserved in substantial numbers, and are exhibited in art galleries and museums.

The first Canadian painters to gain personal recognition and prestige were Paul Kane and Cornelius Krieghoff. Kane, who as a boy came from Ireland to make his home in what is now Toronto, became noted for his faithful recording of the personalities and customs of Indian tribes in all parts of the land which subsequently became Canada. He even made a hazardous trip across the Rocky Mountains in 1846 to do a series of paintings of the Pacific Coast Indians. Krieghoff, a youthful immigrant from Germany who made his home in Montreal about 1840, became a renowned painter of the atmosphere and customs of the devout, light-hearted people of rural French Canada. Both artists were highly competent, technically and intellectually, and their works are prized today and sought by collectors.

In the footsteps of Kane and Krieghoff followed other Canadian painters who, after attending art schools at home, went abroad for advanced training. They absorbed the attitudes of European masters, learned their methods, and returned to paint the Canadian scene viewed through European glasses. Much of their painting was, of course, technically good, but it breathed too little of the spirit of Canada and displayed too much of the influence of aged Europe. During this period, the second half of the nineteenth century, Canadian art was generally dull and purposeless.

By 1900 a few men in Toronto and Montreal sensed the beginnings of a positive "artistic national feeling" among Canadian painters; but this was not recognized by the general public or by art critics elsewhere. In the Toronto Art League a number of men, led by William Cruickshank, Robert Holmes, Charles Jefferys, and Fred Brigden, were speaking openly and painting boldly in defiance of conventional adherence to styles not suited to the Canadian scene; and in Montreal the followers of the distinguished Maurice Cullen were becoming rebellious and provocative advocates of a "Canadian manner" in painting. For the first two decades of the century an incipient Canadian art movement simmered below the surface.

A definite and open break from conventionality came in 1913, when a small band of Toronto painters, led by J. E. H. MacDonald, inspired by the remarkable personality of Tom Thomson, and subsidized by Dr. J. M. McCallum, began to work together with the object of portraying the glories of Canada's northland "in a manner befitting." In the first flush of its eagerness and inspiration, the group was dispersed by the First World War. Thomson, whose talent certainly approached genius, met accidental death after only four years of spectacular painting. Public interest was, for the time being, limited to propaganda posters and official war records. But immediately after the war the painters came together again, more mature and experienced but still fired with their pre-war ambition. After repeated visits to the Algoma country and the north shore of Lake Superior, the group produced a magnificent collection of fresh, bold, eloquent canvases which delighted their friends and shocked their critics.

Early in 1920 the name "Group of Seven" was adopted by Lawren Harris, A. Y. Jackson, Arthur Lismer, J. E. H. MacDonald, Franz Johnston, Frank Carmichael, and Fred Varley; and in May of that year the Group held its first exhibition in the Art Gallery of

Toronto. Reaction was immediate, violent, and disapproving. To Canada's conventional critics and unsophisticated public, the country's first band of art revolutionaries became known as the "Hot Mush School," and their early works were described as "a portrait of the inside of a drunkard's stomach." Scorn and abuse rained upon the names and works of the Seven. But they were convinced that they were right in wanting to paint Canada in a spiritual and emotional manner which could not possibly stem from the Paris *ateliers*.

The understanding directorate of the National Gallery of Canada befriended the Group in the face of bitter opposition. An exhibition in London brought forth unexpectedly favourable comments from Britain's canny critics. Paris looked and admired. Some artistically knowing Americans openly expressed warm admiration. Such praise could not be ignored, and Canada, slowly and reluctantly, came to acknowledge the Group of Seven as her own true sons. Today the Group, individually and collectively, occupies the topmost place of esteem in the Canadian art world and enjoys the almost-universal approval of critics in the many countries where its works have been exhibited.

The Group of Seven, as a physical entity, passed from the scene after ten vigorous and eventful years, but the Group as an influence on the cultural life of Canada is unlikely ever to be forgotten. During its brief span it inspired young painters to express their love of Canada on canvas, broke down the colonial rigidities of art criticism, and stimulated a remarkable new public interest in Canadian art. Possibly the work of the Group has become too nearly synonymous with "Canadian art," with the result that some people believe that all Canadian canvases depict solemn vistas, tortured pines, or endless snows. But this situation need cause no concern. The direct impact of the Group's example upon young Canadian painters will lessen with the years, and already there is talk of revolt against the stultifying influence of the Group of Seven! This is good, not bad. It can now be seen that a variety of influences, some indigenous and some foreign, are modifying the methods and spirit of today's Canadian School of painting, and the temptation to thoughtless imitation of the Group no longer presents a problem.[2]

Although the Group invariably and properly receives the lion's share of attention in any review of Canadian art, other painters, pursuing their separate ways without publicity, were doing distinguished work at the same time. One of these in particular cannot be ignored: Emily Carr, whose profound paintings of forest landscapes are among Canada's greatest works of art. Trained in art schools of the United States, England, and France, Emily Carr returned to Canada to lead a detached and lonely but intensely active artistic life in the remote parts of her native province of British Columbia. Her most admired canvases, painted in the later years of a comparatively long life, are highly personal in interpretation and original in technical performance. Her paintings are prized by art galleries and collectors in the United States and Canada, and to a lesser extent in England. She died in 1945.

The current art scene in Canada is one of unprecedented animation, with public interest and professional activity reaching high levels in all parts of the country. In the cities, art schools are hardly able to cope with the registration of students, and new schools are being established in rural centres. The fine-arts departments of the universities are working overtime to provide advanced professional training; special courses in painting at summer schools are swamped with applications; prizes and bursaries for painters are becoming more numerous; exhibitions are more frequent and better patronized; the press shows a new willingness to treat art as news; and sales of canvases by Canadian artists, at good prices, are higher than they have ever been. All this is gratifying to those who have waited anxiously for acceleration in Canada's artistic unfolding. But it is well to heed the cautioning of Robert Ayre, editor of *Canadian Art:* ". . . the arts, in all their branches, were never more alive in Canada than they are today . . . they have advanced in self-consciousness toward maturity, but, while we have some justification for satisfaction, we Canadians need not be in too great a hurry to pat ourselves on the back, because we still have a long way to go."[3]

Although Toronto and Montreal are still the two chief centres of artistic activity, a number of other communities now demand recognition as creating, teaching, and exhibiting centres.[4] Added significance is attached to this new factor of decentralization by the fact that groups of Canadian artists in various cities are working independently, with little intercommunication, and are revealing an unexpected variety of influences and trends. In Vancouver a surprising number of recent paintings depict sombre Mexican themes and tones. In Montreal a strong school favours the most advanced Parisian non-objectivists.

Highly-reputed art galleries are maintained in Toronto and Montreal, and lesser institutions are found in other Canadian cities. All are dependent upon popular public support. In most of the provincial capitals, museums and archives maintained by government funds include important collections of historical paintings. A large number of such works are collected, too, in the National Archives in Ottawa.

The National Gallery of Canada at Ottawa performs a notable, but generally unappreciated, service. Not content with providing merely a repository for canvases, the Gallery has followed the constructive policy of encouraging Canadian painters and stimulating public interest, both at home and abroad, in Canadian art. Its extension services, which include travelling exhibitions, inexpensive reproductions of paintings, documentary films, and radio broadcasts for school-children, have been a very important factor in developing Canada's art consciousness. The National Gallery was established by the Parliament of Canada in 1880, and is still housed in temporary quarters. Parliament has never appropriated adequate funds to the institution, and it is astonishing that so much has been achieved at so small a cost to the public treasury.

It is regrettable that Canada is not well provided with literature on native art and art exchanges. The quarterly magazine *Canadian Art* is excellently edited and offers valuable informational services to its limited number of subscribers, but its financial resources do not permit the publication of colour reproductions of contemporary painting.

Canada is not yet well served by national art organizations. The Royal Canadian Academy of Arts, chartered in 1880, has functioned mainly as a somewhat high-brow and conventional mentor to Canadian art and has had little positive influence. The conferring of its honorary recognition, R.C.A., upon a painter is not without practical value, however; and most Canadian painters consider it a compliment to be invited to exhibit in an Academy show. The Federation of Canadian Artists, a recent development, has as its aim the banding together of the whole Canadian art fraternity, regardless of schools, styles, and media, in a professional society. The Canadian Group of Painters, which emerged directly from the dissolution of the Group of Seven, in 1933, is an informal brotherhood of mature artists, in all parts of Canada, who assault the bastions of reaction and defend the fort against *avant-garde* violence. Regional organizations, such as the Ontario Society of Artists, the Maritime Art Association, the Art Association of Montreal and Les Amis de l'Art, in Montreal, have been vigorous and effective in their own localities.

Sculpture is probably the most neglected and ignored of the fine arts in Canada, despite the fact that a strong specialized interest in it has been evident from the earliest times. Wood-carving, mainly for church ornamentation, was a notable form of artistic expression in the early days of French Canada, and the influence of the pioneer wood-carvers has persisted through the years into modern Quebec's substantial commercial wood-carving industry. The designing and sculpturing of stone and metals have always attracted a select group of Canadian artists, but public recognition of their work has been negligible. Monumental figures are found in parks or contiguous to public buildings, but for the most part the architects and builders of Canada's edifices have been neglectful of the art of the sculptor.

Although Canadian sculptors have found favour to a considerable degree with critics and patrons in the United States, Europe, and Latin America, they have received scant recognition from art galleries and private collectors in Canada. In the work of a number of Canada's currently prominent sculptors there appears something of the Canadian content which characterized the paintings of the Group of Seven a quarter of a century ago; this is notably so in sculptured impressions of Canada's north country.

The Sculptors' Society of Canada, a small but well-established professional organization, fosters public appreciation of high artistic standards and takes a special interest in the teaching of sculpture in several Canadian art colleges.

The totem-pole carvings of the Indian tribes of Canada's Pacific Coast region, some of the most spectacular of all primitive artifacts, have recently received attention from official sources. Although scholarly research has been conducted for years by the distinguished Canadian ethnologist, Dr. Marius Barbeau, and his colleagues, the complete story of the totem-poles still remains to be told.

Architecturally, Canada is one of the "have-not" countries. The profession of architecture is well taught in a number of universities and is fostered by the substantial and distinguished Royal Architectural Institute of Canada, but it has been discouraged, by public apathy, from making any substantial creative contribution. As with the other arts, however, some change for the better in public attitude has been noted in recent years, particularly in relation to planned community development.

With the single exception of Quebec rural houses, with roofs designed to shed heavy snow-fall, there is little effort to adapt buildings, aesthetically or functionally, to geographical or climatic peculiarities. Most Canadian communities include examples of almost every style of dwelling built in the temperate zone, from California sun-houses to Siberian snow-lodges; and the total impression is a careless, undistinguished *mélange*. The purpose of house-building in Canada has been to provide shelter against the cold of winter and the rain of summer, and little time or expense has been devoted to "frills." In Canada, as in every country, a few show-places built by the wealthy have been designed and created with surpassing architectural skill and artistry.

Public buildings throughout Canada are generally uninspired and imitatively functional, and only rarely does a visitor note with pleasure the beautiful *décor* of an edifice erected by government or private enterprise. Noteworthy exceptions include the Parliament Buildings in Ottawa, several university campuses, a number of Manhattan-style office buildings in the chief cities, and a few of the older churches in the Province of Quebec.

Grain elevators are sometimes referred to as "genuinely Canadian" in design, particularly in books of travel and tourist literature. The tall, stark country elevators are conspicuous landmarks throughout the prairie region, and stately concrete granaries arrest the eye in such widely-separated places as Montreal, Fort William, Port Arthur, Churchill, and Vancouver. Canadian architects and builders have taken the leading part in developing and perfecting these important functional buildings, though the structures are neither original with, nor exclusive to, Canada.

There is no agreement among critics on the degree of prestige which should be accorded to handicrafts, but so far as these involve creative artistry of high order they earn recognition as elements in the cultural life of Canada. Rug-making, leather-working, embroidery, metal-working, book-binding, and wood-carving engage the talents of a large number of craftsmen who reproduce many traditional designs. Each racial group is making its distinctive contribution. The national government and the provincial governments are wisely interested in the promotion of these artistic and economically valuable crafts, and substantial sums from the public treasury are made available for teaching and exhibitions. Handicraft societies thrive as local, provincial, and national bodies.

The cultural situation cannot be viewed without a respectful glance at two appendages of the national government, the Canadian Broadcasting Corporation and the National Film Board. The C.B.C., a publicly owned utility operated by an independent commission which is responsible directly to the Parliament of Canada, is endowed by statute with potential monopoly control over all broadcasting activities in Canada. This control is exercised only in a limited, regulatory manner. While the Corporation owns and operates a string of powerful broadcasting stations across Canada from Newfoundland to Vancouver Island, most of the stations are privately owned and managed. The C.B.C. operates two national networks in the English language and a smaller network in French; and by special arrangement with the Canadian Government it provides a powerful, multi-language, international, short-wave broadcasting service.

The Corporation performs a vital function in presenting indigenous music, drama, and literature, and in stimulating public interest in cultural matters. Although its programming is notably catholic in content and is aimed at providing a wide variety of listening fare, its avowed policy is to include a substantial proportion of Canadian creative work—always subject to the qualification that such work must measure up to high standards of professional competence. The C.B.C. is the chief source of encouragement to Canadian composers. It commissions the writing of special musical works, and has given *première* performances of many native compositions, ranging from simple *divertissements* to complete operas and symphonic suites. Adaptations of stage classics and original radio plays by Canadians are among its most popular presentations. The works of Canadian short-story writers likewise receive encouragement from the C.B.C. Privately owned stations also endeavour to make good use of Canadian material and talent.

The National Film Board of Canada, one of the world's leading agencies in the production of documentary films, offers many opportunities to competent Canadian artistic talent. On the Board's large staff is found an able group of writers, musicians, dramatists, graphic artists, and film-art technicians, the majority of whom are Canadian-born. The Board has created a distinguished series of documentary films dealing with cultural activities in all parts of Canada, and wide distribution of these films has enhanced the Canadian's knowledge of his own cultural heritage.

One important fact relating to cultural development in present-day Canada needs to be added. Elsewhere in this book it is mentioned that under the terms of Canada's written constitution, the British North America Act, education falls within the exclusive jurisdiction of the provincial governments. The interpretation of this clause has at times caused seriously strained relations between the federal and provincial governments, and the national authorities are now inclined to avoid giving provincial governments reason to complain of "interference" in education. It is believed by many students of Canadian affairs that the reluctance of Canada's federal government to take suitable action to stimulate public interest in the arts is founded in cautious respect for provincial rights.

CHAPTER XIX

Education

BY WATSON KIRKCONNELL

EDUCATION in Canada represents in large degree an extension of the civilizations of the countries from which her peoples came. The *mores* of the major immigrant nationalities of the past three hundred years have contributed differing attitudes towards education. These have influenced one another and have been influenced in turn by the conditions inherent in Canadian life.

The French colonists brought with them the seventeenth- and eighteenth-century French conviction that education and the Catholic faith were closely bound together. The later French trend, under Napoleon, towards a state system of education organized under a strongly-centralized administration in all grades had little influence in French Canada, to which immigration from France virtually ceased after 1760. Great importance was attached to the work of teaching-orders of the clergy in training the youth of the community, especially at the secondary level. Parochial elementary schools were the norm, and there was little disposition to attempt universal popular education.

Among the United Empire Loyalists who after 1783 flocked into the Maritime and Great Lakes areas the most prominent single inclination was that of Puritan New England, where colonial legislation, as far back as 1642 and 1647, had set up state schools and made the education of all children compulsory. This disposition was reinforced by the strong educational convictions of colonists who came from Scotland, where a system of national schools dated from the sixteenth century. The simplicity of Scottish life had made all classes content to use the common schools, and even in secondary education the stress was on day-schools rather than on boarding-schools. The early colonists from England had no such interest in universal education, but were more concerned with higher schools and colleges for a social *élite*. Among the Irish immigrants to Canada there was reflected the controversy over religious instruction that convulsed Ireland during the nineteenth century, especially after the Roman Congregation's decree *De Propaganda Fide* of January 11, 1846, declaring that nonsectarian religious instruction was dangerous to youth.

The framework within which these various forces have developed was provided in 1867 by the British North America Act, which, in the distribution of authority between the provinces and the federal government, assigned education to the individual provinces. The one exception has been the federal provision of schools for the aboriginal Indian population, who are the wards of the Dominion Government and are under the care of the Indian Affairs Branch of the Department of Mines and Resources, Ottawa.

In one sense, there are as many systems of education in Canada as there are provinces. Generally speaking, however, there is a marked pattern which is common to the schools of the predominantly English-speaking provinces[1] and to those of the English-speaking minority in the Province of Quebec. The standard educational ladder consists of eight grades in a public elementary school and four or five grades in a public secondary school. The school, in Ontario and British Columbia, ends with the thirteenth grade; in the other provinces it has only twelve grades. Throughout all these years, education is free, and the pupil is obliged to attend until he is fourteen, fifteen, or sixteen years of age, depending on the province in which he lives. The financing is handled mainly by the municipalities in which the schools are located, but with an increasing measure of assistance from the provincial treasury. An increasing number of urban school-boards are providing an intermediate school or junior high school, comprising grades seven and eight (and sometimes nine), in which an earlier stress is laid on manual training, domestic science, and even foreign

---

1 For notes to chapter xix see pages 580–581.

languages. At the high-school level there is an increasing disposition to establish three parallel types of education—academic, technical, and commercial. The latter two, while maintaining some elements of general education, are more specifically slanted in the direction of occupational training for industry and commerce.

The foregoing system of free compulsory education is the natural fulfilment of Scottish and New England traditions. From Irish Catholicism, strengthened by the growth of French Roman Catholic minorities in some provinces, came a struggle for separate denominational schools. These are most clearly recognized in Ontario, where they are widely established in elementary education and have even (as at Hamilton, Ontario) broken into secondary education. The English predilection for private boarding-schools has never been extensively realized in Canada, and only 2 or 3 per cent of the school population attends such institutions. There are approximately forty such schools of English Protestant origin in Canada, including such well-known establishments as Lower Canada College, Bishop's College School, Trinity College School, Ridley College, and Upper Canada College, for boys; and Bishop Strachan School, Alma College, Havergal College, Moulton College, and the Ontario Ladies' College, for girls.

For the French-speaking majority in the Province of Quebec, who contribute one-fourth of all the children in Canada, the educational system differs sharply from the one outlined above. The elementary schools comprise only seven grades, after which the educational highway parts into three distinct branches. (1) Those looking forward to a life in the factory, on the farm, or in the home take a four-year course in technical, agricultural, and domestic-science schools. (2) Pupils who desire eventually to register at Laval University or the University of Montreal in the faculties of letters, law, medicine, dentistry, philosophy, theology, or canon law must enrol for an eight-year course in a classical college, or *collège classique,* where they undergo a rigid and rigorous course in four languages (French, English, Latin, and Greek), mathematics, science, history, fine arts, scholastic philosophy, and religion. The first four years are at the high-school level and terminate in matriculation examinations. The second four-year period constitutes the undergraduate course in arts for Laval or

Montreal, and is crowned with the degree of Bachelor of Arts. These classical colleges are conducted by religious communities of the Roman Catholic Church, and are self-financed except for an annual grant of $10,000 each from the provincial secretary. Students pay fees, and most of them are in residence. (3) A third choice open to those who complete the seventh grade is to pass on into the provincial high schools for a further four or five years, after which they may enrol in a normal school (for training elementary school-teachers) or in one of the higher schools of applied science, commerce, or agriculture. These higher schools have university affiliation and their courses issue in university degrees. Graduates of the classical colleges may likewise enrol in them, and often do; but graduates of provincial schools are not eligible for registration in the other university faculties.

In working out school problems, especially in the English-majority provinces, many effective methods have been devised. (1) In extensive rural areas where the population is too thinly scattered to maintain a large number of competent small schools, the consolidated school has been introduced. The children of the district are brought by bus to this central school. (2) Along remote railway lines a railway school car stops periodically on local sidings, and a specially qualified teacher instructs the children of trappers, section-gangs, lumber-men, and small farmers. (3) Provincial systems of correspondence courses are available to still more remote communities, to long-term patients in sanatoria, and to students of school age who are unable to attend school because of physical disabilities. The courses are free, and books and supplies are provided without charge by the provincial department of education.

The character of the school system has passed through two main phases. From the middle of the nineteenth century to about 1920, there was a continuous striving towards a rigid uniformity in methods and text-books, controlled at every level by government examinations and government grants, designed to surmount the manifest inefficiency of the pioneer period. In Ontario, for example, the system was based in part on that of Prussia and in part, at the secondary level, on that of England.

Since 1920 the predominant pedagogical influence has been

that of the United States. The "project" method has become increasingly prevalent in the elementary schools. At the secondary-school level, intelligence and aptitude tests are combined with vocational guidance to direct students into collegiate, technical, or commercial avenues of training. In approved schools, governmental control is so far relaxed that the average student writes no provincial examination until, and unless, he desires university matriculation at the very end of his school career. Some provinces have organized a series of educational radio broadcasts, and documentary films from the National Film Board and other sources are widely used. In the curriculum, the tendency is to replace the earlier disciplinary regimen, based on languages and mathematics and science, with an allegedly functional training for citizenship, which is much less exacting in standards and more immediately vocational in content.

Agencies, partly unofficial, have come to supplement the regular educational process at both ends of the age-spectrum. Kindergartens were introduced about 1882, and have since been incorporated by many towns and cities into their regular schools, sometimes as a distinct kindergarten year and sometimes in a combined form known as the kindergarten-primary. Even earlier work, at the nursery-school level, has sometimes been carried on with notable success, for example in connexion with the Psychology Department of the University of Toronto. At the other extreme is adult education, which enables the mature members of the community to pursue various courses of study and to develop hobby techniques. From England came the system of mechanics' institutes in the early 1840's. Few of these remain in Canada, but university extension lectures (as instituted by Cambridge University in 1873) and the more specific tutorial classes of the Workers' Educational Association (also English in provenance) have continued to flourish on Canadian soil. Frontier College was formed in 1900. Most recent of all is the formation in 1935 of the Canadian Association for Adult Education, affiliated with the World Association for Adult Education, London, England.

Community interest in both elementary and secondary schools has been much stimulated in recent years by the growth of home-and-school associations, through which parents manifest their interest in the work of the school and often give tangible support to its projects. There is no attempt to interfere with administration. The aim is rather to establish sympathetic and friendly relations between parents and teachers in the interest of the welfare of the school-child. This home-and-school movement in Canada began in 1916 in Toronto, and now has hundreds of branches throughout the country.

TABLE 1

ORGANIZATION OF PROVINCIAL EDUCATION

Province	Administrative authority	Permanent executive official
Nova Scotia	Council of Public Instruction (Executive Council)	Superintendent of Education
New Brunswick	Board of Education	Chief Superintendent of Education
Prince Edward Island	Board of Education	Chief Superintendent of Education
Quebec	Council of Education (with Catholic and Protestant committees)	Superintendent of Education (one for Catholics and one for Protestant schools)
Ontario	Minister of Education	Deputy Minister of Education
Manitoba	Minister of Education	Deputy Minister of Education
Saskatchewan	Minister of Education	Deputy Minister of Education
Alberta	Minister of Education	Deputy Minister of Education
British Columbia	Council of Public Instruction	Deputy Minister of Education

Other aspects of education, independent of the provincial systems, may be found in private trade-schools, including those under the Apprenticeship Act, and the numerous private business colleges that prepare young people for secretarial and stenographic work. In 1942 there were 27,226 students enrolled in private business colleges in Canada.

That there is at least a superficial uniformity in the organization of provincial education[2] across Canada is suggested by the summary in table 1. Underlying all such resemblances, however, are marked differences of economic level between province and province, and between city and country, which create great disparities in the educational opportunities of young Canadians in different parts of the Dominion. The equalizing of such opportunities is bound up with the whole unsolved problem of federal-provincial relationships. The provinces are jealous of federal interference with their constitutional control of education, yet it is only by a levelling up of educational budgets through federal subsidy that the poorer provinces can hope to match the salaries and facilities of the wealthier provinces. No easy or assured solution is in sight.

It is at the level of university education that the diversity of the Canadian tradition is most clearly discernible. The initial impulse of almost all higher education in Canada came from the Christian churches, and as these themselves varied in language, background, creed, and dogma, the academic institutions they set up were similarly varied. In the course of subsequent Canadian history, the world trend towards state-supported secular universities has affected church colleges in different ways. Some have dropped religious auspices entirely; others have affiliated or federated themselves with secular (usually provincial) universities; still others have energetically mobilized and integrated their resources under ecclesiastical control.

Thus the Church of England early took a lead in establishing colleges on an Oxford or Cambridge model that were to serve not only as centres of scholarship but as nurseries for an Anglican consciousness. In order of foundation,[3] the Anglican institutions were: King's College, Windsor, Nova Scotia (1788); King's College, Fredericton, New Brunswick (1800); King's College, Toronto, Ontario (1827); Bishop's College, Lennoxville, Province of Quebec (1843); Trinity College, Toronto (founded in 1852 after the secularization of King's, Toronto);[4] Huron College, London, Ontario (1863); and St. John's College, Winnipeg, Manitoba (1871). The Church of England found, however, that its adherents were a minority, even among Canadian Protestants; and the subsequent history of the colleges has varied greatly in accordance with denominational strength and policy in different parts of the Dominion. King's, Windsor, became the University of King's College, but was moved to Halifax, where it lives on a common campus in close association[5] with Dalhousie University. King's, Fredericton, is today the secular provincial University of New

Brunswick. King's, Toronto, secularized, became the nucleus of the University of Toronto, the largest university in the British Commonwealth. At Lennoxville, Bishop's University is the only Anglican university in Canada still carrying on independently on its own campus. The University of Trinity College is a federated college in the provincial University of Toronto. Huron College became the nucleus from which grew the secular University of Western Ontario, and of this it is now an affiliated college. St. John's College, Winnipeg, is an affiliated institution of the University of Manitoba.

The Church of Scotland in Canada was largely responsible for the early history of Dalhousie University, Halifax; of Queen's University, Kingston; and of Manitoba College, Winnipeg. All three came into being, at least in part, as an attempt of Presbyterianism to protect itself against institutions predominantly Anglican in policy. When the threat of Anglican domination passed, the Scottish tradition of state education gathered strength. Dalhousie and Queen's became non-denominational universities; Manitoba College surrendered its arts work to the University of Manitoba.

Methodism has clung more tenaciously to its institutions, but even here there has been compromise and accommodation. Mount Allison University (1858), at Sackville, New Brunswick, still maintains an independent existence as a denominational university, now under the United Church of Canada; but Victoria University (1836), after half a century of work at Cobourg, Ontario, moved to Toronto as a federal unit in the University of Toronto. Wesley (now United) College, Winnipeg, was from the outset an affiliated college of the University of Manitoba. In all three the United Church of Canada has succeeded the Methodist Church as the ecclesiastical sponsor.

Alone among the Protestant denominations, the Baptists have held strictly aloof from academic affiliation. In Nova Scotia, where the Baptist concentration is greatest, a Baptist institution, Queen's College, was incorporated in 1838, but the name was changed to Acadia in 1841, and the university still flourishes at Wolfville. In Ontario, McMaster University was founded in Toronto in 1887, but did not begin its main period of growth until its removal in 1930 to Hamilton, the chief centre of the country's heavy industry, where it is the only institution of higher learning and serves a municipal rather than a denominational constituency.

The greatest diversity of all and the greatest conservatism are found among universities and colleges under Roman Catholic auspices. This large religious community, representing half of the Canadians of school and college age, is divided by language (English and French) and by national background (French, Irish, Highland Scottish, Polish, and Ukrainian). Further diversity is added to the collegiate structure by the activities of several teaching-orders, especially the Jesuits, the Sulpicians, the Oblates of Mary Immaculate, the Basilians, the Eudist Fathers, the Holy Cross Fathers, and the Clerics of St. Viateur. To this must be added the canon-law requirement, operative in Quebec, that every diocese must have a classical college (leading to the B.A.), with the result that the secular clergy found and operate such colleges wherever the teaching-orders have failed to do so.

Academic history among the Canadian Catholics began in Quebec in 1635, with the founding of the Collège des Jésuites (closed in 1775). In the mean time, in 1663, Bishop Laval had set up the Séminaire de Québec, the root from which have grown both Laval University (charter of 1852) and the University of Montreal (1878, charter of 1920). Control of the two French-language universities rests with the bishops of the ecclesiastical provinces of Quebec and of Montreal, respectively. Arts and science instruction up to the level of a pass Bachelor of Arts degree is provided in an extensive system of classical colleges, mostly residential, forty-one for men and thirteen for women, located in many centres and taught either by religious orders or by the secular clergy.

Outside the Province of Quebec, the chief Roman Catholic universities are the bilingual University of Ottawa (1849), with ten affiliated arts colleges in Ontario, Saskatchewan, and Alberta; and St. Francis Xavier University (1866) at Antigonish, Nova Scotia, whose constituency is largely Highland Scottish. Irish Catholicism is represented chiefly by St. Michael's College, Toronto, federated in the University of Toronto; St. Patrick's College, Ottawa, affiliated with the University of Ottawa; Assumption College, Windsor, affiliated with the University of Western Ontario, and St. Mary's College and Mount St. Vincent College, Halifax.

St. Paul's College, Winnipeg, affiliated with the University of Manitoba, has a mixed Irish, Polish, and Ukrainian constituency. Other Catholic institutions are the Université St. Joseph (bilingual), Memramcook, N.B.; the Université du Sacré-Cœur (French), Bathurst West, N.B.; the Collège Ste. Anne (French), Church Point, N.S.; St. Dunstan's College (English), Charlottetown, P.E.I.; St. Thomas College (English), Chatham, N.B.; St. Boniface College (French), affiliated with the University of Manitoba; and St. Thomas More College and Campion College, affiliated with the University of Saskatchewan.

The earliest appearance of non-ecclesiastical higher education was the non-denominational private foundation of McGill College (1821), for whose soul the churches of England and Scotland wrestled for a time. As McGill University, it was to become the wealthiest of Canadian institutions, with an endowment comparable to that of some of the more affluent American colleges. The King's colleges at Fredericton and Toronto were presently translated into secular provincial universities; Dalhousie and Queen's dropped all religious auspices, except for a divinity school near by; and the church colleges of London and Winnipeg grouped themselves around secular universities.

In each of the three most westerly provinces, Saskatchewan, Alberta, and British Columbia, the development of which came later than that of the East, a single provincial university, secular and non-denominational, was set up, with the sole right to confer degrees in the province. The University of Saskatchewan (1907), the University of Alberta (1906), and the University of British Columbia (1915, with an earlier McGill affiliation) are thus closer approximations to American state universities than are any of the other institutions thus far discussed.

The imprint of Old World universities, as well as of churches, was set upon many of the Canadian universities in their early years. The three King's colleges and Bishop's College were modelled after the Oxford residential, tutorial, and ecclesiastical system; Trinity and St. John's looked to Cambridge; at Dalhousie and Queen's and McGill the influence of Scottish universities was very strong. Throughout a century of existence these forces were continually reinforced by the importation of professors from the transatlantic exemplar universities. Particularly after 1900, the influence of American universities grew increasingly strong, partly through the bringing in of American professors and partly through the training of Canadians in American graduate schools. As part of the general cultural *Anschluss* and *Gleichschaltung* of Canada to the United States that has been going on for half a century or more, the undergraduate life of Anglo-Canadian universities, especially in the provincial institutions, has

TABLE 2

INSTITUTIONS OF HIGHER EDUCATION

University	Full-time students	Faculty	Volumes in library
Acadia	896	60	87,000
Alberta	4,210	399	106,000
Bishop's	210	19	20,000
British Columbia	8,986	292	170,000
Dalhousie	668	140	67,923
King's College	166	12	32,000
Laval	4,975	810	824,706
McGill	7,110	853	447,199
McMaster	1,121	71	61,500
Manitoba	6,495	350	116,000
Montreal	5,460	580	250,000
Mount Allison	881	82	53,741
New Brunswick	1,350	95	17,000
Ottawa	2,300	198	130,000
Queen's	3,019	185	214,473
St. Francis Xavier	874	35	35,000
Saskatchewan	4,204	165	93,000
Toronto	17,111	1,329	448,786
Trinity College	675	36	42,500
Victoria	2,690	58	100,000
Western Ontario	2,935	285	167,500

SOURCE: *Britannica Year Book,* 1947.

been rapidly assimilated to American practice in such matters as initiations, athletics, class or year organizations, and social activities. In this, the press and the cinema have played a major part. In curriculum and academic discipline, however, which rest with faculty and senate rather than with the more impressionable undergraduate, the native Canadian tradition has proved more persistent.

The relative size of the major Canadian institutions of higher education may be gauged from table 2.

Undergraduate work in arts and science tends to be carried on at two levels, pass (or "general") and honours. In the pass courses the ideal is a general education, without undue concentration in any one field. Some universities have laid down a rather rigid prescription, especially in the first two years, that every student is to receive at least a modicum of English, foreign languages, mathematics, science, and philosophy or psychology. Others leave an elective system wide open, with the result, for example, at the University of Toronto, that a student can evade the humanities altogether. At the University of Manitoba, on the other hand, a pass student could take his entire course in the humanities. No other area of university curriculum is undergoing such energetic scrutiny today as the pass course in arts, and the next few years may see some interesting changes and experiments.

The honours degree, on the contrary, has assumed a high degree of specialized organization. In McGill, Bishop's, and the English-language universities of the Maritime Provinces, honours courses are identical in length with pass courses, but involve a much higher degree of concentration in a chosen field and are limited to a small group of high intellectual quality. In the remaining English-language universities of Canada the honours courses require an extra year of study and sometimes even separate instruction and examination in the area of concentration. The number of students who enrol for such courses has increased greatly. At Toronto, for example, the honours courses normally enrol over half of the student body. The Toronto honours degree resembles the Oxford "honour school" and the Cambridge "tripos." The aim is a liberal education by the path of specialization, and enrolment is encouraged by the provincial recognition of many such courses as the college prerequisite for senior posts in secondary education in Ontario. Some historians of Canadian education are inclined to regard the honours courses as the most typically Canadian development in higher education, influenced strongly in the first place by Oxford and Cambridge, but adapted resolutely to Canadian circumstances and needs.

In the French-language colleges there is a Canadian development of another tradition, stemming from the University of Paris and the French *lycées,* but altered greatly on Canadian soil. The *collèges classiques* of Quebec offer an approximation to the classics and philosophy course in the French *lycées,* but the educational process is much shorter in France, where students normally take their baccalaureate at the age of seventeen. In the Quebec colleges, on the other hand, the length of the course is increased so as to correspond exactly with that of all English-Canadian pass courses, except those in the universities of Ontario and British Columbia. The *collège classique* degree conferred by Laval or Montreal is essentially a pass or general degree. Unlike that of the Anglo-Canadian universities, it imposes a rigid curriculum initiating the student into all disciplines: French, English, Latin, Greek, history, mathematics (up to the calculus), nine sciences, art, philosophy, and religion. Unlike the classical colleges of France, which it otherwise resembles, it ends with a comprehensive two-year course in Thomistic philosophy. It should be borne in mind that all the foregoing courses must be taken by all students. There are no electives and no exceptions. Specialization comes later.

Graduate studies are the product of various forces. Until a generation ago, the Canadian graduate who wished to prepare himself further for university teaching turned for advanced studies to Oxford or to an American graduate school. A scattered few looked to German or other Continental universities. French-Canadian scholars went to Paris, Louvain, or Rome. Those who frequented American or Continental universities tended to bring home an ideal of advanced research. Those who went to Oxford, on the other hand, tended to stress fruitful undergraduate teaching in the honours courses and to regard research with suspicion. The last thirty years, however, have seen the rise of graduate schools in Canada—especially at Toronto, McGill, Montreal, and Laval—with stress both on the research thesis and on scholarly course work. Most of the universities carry work as far as the Master's degree; but few, apart from those just mentioned, carry men to the doctorate in arts and science. Toronto alone offers the doctorate in all fields—humanities, natural sciences, and social sciences. McGill tends to restrict itself to the natural sciences, the social sciences, and history. At Laval, Montreal (and Ottawa), the doctoral work is limited mainly to French, classics, and philosophy.

A striking feature of graduate work is the place given to mediaeval studies, especially in the Pontifical Institute of Mediaeval Studies on the campus of the University of Toronto and in the Institut d'Etudes Médiévales Albert le Grand, under the Faculty of Philosophy at the University of Montreal. Students from all over the world come to share in this study and research.

The problems involved in any extensive graduate work in Canada grow out of the vast distances within the country and the relative impecuniosity of the universities. Almost all institutions possess a handful of men who would be capable of giving instruction and guiding research at the doctoral level, but few could attempt this in more than one or two departments. Limitations of staff and the burden of undergraduate teaching, moreover, leave little time or strength for advanced work. Library resources are inadequate for the most part. Much thought is now being given to a possible pooling of staff personnel for graduate work, either by agreements on departmental specialization by different colleges, or by professorial exchange, or even by the direction of graduate students to more than one institution in order to have fruitful contact with additional instructors. Distance is the chief enemy, especially in western Canada.

Besides general and advanced education in the humanities, social sciences, and pure sciences, a wide range of professional faculties and schools is maintained by the universities of Canada These may be summarized as follows.[6]

Agriculture.—There are nine colleges or faculties of agriculture in Canada. With the exception of the Nova Scotia College of Agriculture at Truro, with two years only, they give a four-year course at university level leading to the degree of Bachelor of Science in Agriculture. Each institution undertakes special research in the agricultural problems of its area, and all have made contributions to agricultural science. The institutions are as follows: the Nova Scotia College of Agriculture, Truro; Macdonald College, Ste. Anne de Bellevue, affiliated with McGill University; the Ecole Supérieure d'Agriculture at Ste. Anne de la Pocatière, affiliated with Laval University; the Institut Agricole d'Oka at La Trappe, affiliated with the University of Montreal; the Ontario Agricultural College at Guelph, affiliated with the University of Toronto; the College of Agriculture at the University of Saskatchewan; and the faculties of Agriculture at the universities of Manitoba, Alberta, and British Columbia.

Architecture.—Three universities—Toronto, McGill, and Manitoba—confer the degree of Bachelor of Science in Architecture. In Montreal there is also a five-year French-language course in architecture at the provincial Ecole des Beaux-Arts, which is not affiliated with any university.

Commerce.—Most of the English-language universities offer courses in the Faculty of Arts (sometimes in a special "school") leading to a degree of Bachelor of Commerce. In the French-language system, Laval University has an Ecole Supérieure de Commerce and the University of Montreal its Ecole des Hautes Etudes Commerciales.

Dentistry.—There are faculties of dentistry at Dalhousie University, McGill University, the University of Montreal, the University of Toronto, and the University of Alberta.

Engineering and applied science.—Eight of the English-language universities and two of the French ones have faculties of engineering and applied science. In Nova Scotia the advanced work in engineering is handled by the Nova Scotia Technical College, at Halifax. The other institutions offering courses in engineering are McGill University, Ecole Polytechnique (the University of Montreal), Laval University, Queen's University, the University of Toronto, and the universities of New Brunswick, Manitoba, Saskatchewan, Alberta, and British Columbia. While each of them offers most branches of engineering, some have special branches suited to their region. The University of Saskatchewan, for example, instituted a course in ceramic engineering with a view to developing the ceramic clays of that province.

Fisheries.—Laval University maintains an Ecole Supérieure des Pêcheries at Ste. Anne de la Pocatière, giving a four-year course for the degree of Bachelor of Science in Fisheries. Dalhousie University, in coöperation with the Fisheries Research Board of Canada, offers a graduate course leading to the Master's degree.

Forestry.—The universities of New Brunswick, Laval, Toronto, and British Columbia give courses in forestry leading to the Bachelor's degree. Special attention is paid to the forestry problems of the region in which the school is located.

Fine art.—Courses in fine art, especially in art appreciation, are to be found in most of the universities. At Mount Allison and the University of Toronto it is possible to secure a Bachelor's degree with specialization in fine art. There are also a number of colleges of art, without fixed academic standards of entrance, which are devoted to the technical training of painters and sculptors. Among the best known are the Nova Scotia College of Art, Halifax; the Ecole des Beaux-Arts, Quebec; the Ecole des Beaux-Arts, Montreal; the Ontario College of Art, Toronto; the Winnipeg School of Art; the School of Decorative and Applied Art, Vancouver.

Home economics, household science.—All the English-language universities listed above as offering courses in agriculture also offer degree courses in household science or home economics. In Ontario there is a Faculty of Household Science at the University of Toronto, as well as instruction in connexion with the Ontario Agricultural College at Guelph. In the Maritime Provinces, degree courses in household science are given at Mount Allison, Acadia, St. Francis Xavier, and Mount St. Vincent. The University of Montreal has five regional schools in which a Bachelor's degree can be taken; Laval University offers a degree course at the Ecole Supérieure de Sciences Domestiques at St. Pascal, Province of Quebec.

Law.—There is no faculty or school of law in Prince Edward Island. In Ontario the provincial law school, Osgoode Hall, is operated without relation to any university. The other provinces have faculties of law in the administration of which the provincial law societies coöperate with the following universities: Dalhousie, New Brunswick, Laval, Montreal, McGill, Manitoba, Saskatchewan, Alberta, and British Columbia. The University of Toronto also has a School of Law in the Faculty of Arts.

Library science.—Full-time library schools are operated by McGill University and the University of Toronto. With one year of study, students who are already university graduates may obtain the degree of Bachelor of Library Science. The University of

Montreal has an Ecole de Bibliothécaires (1937), which issues a diploma.

Medicine.—Eleven of the universities provide a full course in medicine: Dalhousie, Laval, Montreal, McGill, Ottawa, Queen's, Toronto, Western Ontario, Manitoba, Alberta, and British Columbia. Of special eminence in graduate research are the Banting Institute and the Connaught Laboratories at the University of Toronto, and the Institute of Neurology and Neurosurgery at McGill University.

Music.—Degrees in music are awarded by Dalhousie, Acadia, Mount St. Vincent, Mount Allison, Laval, Bishop's, Montreal, McGill, Toronto, and Saskatchewan. Such degree courses stress the theory and history of music. Special training in musical execution is provided by a number of large conservatories of music, especially in Toronto and Montreal.

Nursing.—By a combined course of university attendance and hospital training, students are able to obtain the degree of Bachelor of Science in Nursing at certain universities: British Columbia, Alberta, Saskatchewan, McMaster, Ottawa, Queen's, St. Francis Xavier, and Mount Allison. McGill, Western Ontario, and Toronto have schools of nursing with special courses for graduate nurses. A similar course is given in French at the Institut Marguerite d'Youville, in affiliation with the University of Montreal. The University of Toronto also has special courses in occupational therapy and physiotherapy.

Optometry.—Three-year courses are given at the Ontario College of Optometry, Toronto, and Ecole d'Optométrie, Montreal.

Pedagogy or education.—Most of the universities operate faculties, colleges, or departments for the training of teachers for secondary schools. While the training of teachers for elementary schools is usually given in normal schools (which are not affiliated with universities and require only secondary-school standing), the university faculties of education require at least a pass arts degree for entrance. Some universities—McGill, Toronto (the Ontario College of Education), Manitoba, Saskatchewan, Alberta, and British Columbia—offer further pedagogical study leading to graduate degrees. At the University of Toronto such advanced training is facilitated by an Institute of Child Study. The training of bilingual teachers (English and French) is stressed in the Normal School of the University of Ottawa. Degrees in pedagogy are also available at two *instituts pédagogiques* affiliated with the University of Montreal.

Pharmacy.—Schools, colleges, or departments of pharmacy are operated in connexion with Dalhousie, Laval, Montreal, Toronto, Manitoba, Saskatchewan, Alberta, and British Columbia.

Physical education.—Courses for prospective teachers of physical education are offered at Toronto, McGill, and Saskatchewan.

Social work.—There are six schools of social work, operating either as part of, or in close collaboration with, a local university—Dalhousie, Montreal, McGill, Toronto, Manitoba, and British Columbia.

Theology.—Canada has some sixty-four theological faculties or colleges of university grade giving theological instruction. The Protestant institutions are as follows: Church of England, eleven; United Church of Canada, nine; Presbyterian, two; Baptist, two; Lutheran, two; total, twenty-six. These do not include the more elementary schools of "Bible-college" type. The Roman Catholic institutions number thirty-eight. Of these, seventeen are administered by the secular clergy and twenty-one by clerical communities. Advanced graduate work in theology has been organized at Toronto in the Toronto Graduate School of Theological Studies, a collaborative enterprise of the Anglican, United Church, and Presbyterian theological colleges in that city.

Veterinary science.—Undergraduate and graduate courses in veterinary science, leading to the Bachelor's, Master's, and Doctor's degrees, are provided at the Ontario Veterinary College, Guelph, in affiliation with the University of Toronto. French-language students take corresponding courses at the Ecole de Médecine Vétérinaire, La Trappe, affiliated with the University of Montreal.

Ancillary to all formal systems of education are the services of the libraries of the country. In spite of the early organization of mechanics' institutes and similar local associations, large-scale development of library services was for a long time hampered by the same geographic and economic factors which delayed political maturity. With the growth of urbanization, conditions improved, particularly in the larger and wealthier centres, but half of the population is still without library services, and the public libraries of most of the remainder are supported by their municipalities at a rate far below the minimum standard recommended by international authorities. The four largest municipal libraries are the Toronto Public Library (700,000 volumes in twenty branches), the Hamilton Public Library (200,000 volumes in five branches), the Ottawa Public Library (200,000 volumes in five branches), and the Bibliothèque Saint-Sulpice (150,000 volumes) in Montreal. Only four university libraries (Toronto, Laval, McGill, and Queen's) contain more than 200,000 volumes. Provincial libraries range in size up to that of British Columbia, with 200,000 volumes. The Library of Parliament at Ottawa contains about 500,000.

In spite of deficiencies, there have been some very encouraging developments in recent years. Most notable was the long-overdue decision of the federal government in 1948 to create a National Library, a step taken in response to a wide-spread demand from the Canadian Library Association and many other organizations, as well as from the press. The policy was to be initiated by the establishment of much-needed bibliographical and library services, particularly a union catalogue.

Efforts have also been made in many parts of the country to bring books to individuals or communities where library facilities are lacking. Provincial libraries in British Columbia, Saskatchewan, Manitoba, Ontario, and Nova Scotia have arrangements for sending single volumes or boxes of selected books to community centres or responsible persons who arrange for their circulation and return. Regional libraries have been especially useful in rural communities, where the purchase of enough books to give an adequate selection could hardly be justified by the number of possible readers in any one place, but where a wide choice can be offered by exchange of books among local libraries and by circulation through schools and post-offices, and even by bookmobile and book-van. Prince Edward Island afforded the model, perhaps, but there are successful units in British Columbia, including the well-known Fraser Valley system; in Alberta, where work was started in the Peace River region; and in Saskatchewan, where an Act of 1946 provides for government assistance wherever local groups are ready to take their share of responsibility.

In spite of difficulties, the professional morale of librarians has, on the whole, been high. It was mainly through the agitation of librarians themselves that professional schools were established. In the American Library Association, which has met in Canada several times, Canadians have held high offices, including the presidency, and unquestionably have contributed their share of information and ideas. The Canadian Library Council, organized in 1934, and the Canadian Library Association, in which it was merged in 1946, have been of great service to Canadian education by their work in the compilation of bibliographies, book lists, and book and periodical indexes, and have coöperated with publishers, service clubs, and other groups in arranging book fairs, children's book weeks, and Canadian book weeks, to arouse public interest in reading.

More attention has, on the whole, been given to art galleries and museums. The National Gallery of Canada, at Ottawa, was set up in 1880; its lending services place its extensive resources at the disposal of all parts of the country. The National Museum of Canada, at Ottawa, and the Royal Ontario Museum, at Toronto, both house fine collections. Provincial archives and museums in the cities of Halifax, St. John, Quebec, and Victoria are worthy of note; and important municipal and private galleries and museums are to be found in Toronto, Montreal, Vancouver, and other centres.

Closely associated with the higher ranges of science in Canada is the National Research Council, set up in 1916 to foster, stimulate, and coördinate scientific and industrial research. One of its major activities has been the provision of scholarships for research workers, in order to build up a large body of scientific experts; as a result many hundreds of researchers have proceeded to the doctorate and have had a stimulating effect on the graduate schools in science. Grants to individual professors and institutions have served to encourage permanent centres of research, not otherwise predictable, in some of the smaller universities. The National Research Council operates independently some eleven laboratories across Canada. One of its most important functions is to organize and coördinate national coöperative research programmes, in which many government departments and many organizations may have an interest. This function is carried out through associate research committees composed of the leading experts in each field of research. These committees seem to be a peculiarly Canadian invention, and have proved to be very effective.

There have more recently come into existence the Canadian Social Science Research Council (1940) and the Humanities Research Council of Canada (1944), seeking to provide stimulus and encouragement in their respective disciplines. Neither has sought or received financial assistance from government sources, but they have been aided by funds from foundations in the United States.

Another agency coördinating and stimulating Canada's intellectual life at its higher levels is the Royal Society of Canada, founded in 1882. It is composed primarily of senior scholars and scientists, elected to membership in some one of five sections: (1) humanities and social sciences in French; (2) humanities and social sciences in English; (3) chemical, mathematical, and physical sciences; (4) geological sciences; and (5) biological sciences. Its obvious models are in part the Royal Society of London for Improving Natural Knowledge and in part the British and French academies. To these influences from the two major traditions of its historical background it has added a peculiarly Canadian emphasis on geology, which, in keeping with the immense geological resources of the Dominion and the notable work of the Geological Survey of Canada, founded in 1842 by Sir William Logan, is given a section to itself.

More active, perhaps, are the Canadian Historical Association, the Canadian Political Science Association, the Canadian Geographical Society, the Canadian Institute of International Affairs, and comparable scientific and academic associations, the appearance and far-ranging activity of which have been striking features of Canadian intellectual life during the past few decades.

CHAPTER XX

Religion and Religious Institutions

BY ARTHUR R. M. LOWER

RELIGION is one of the most important factors in the shaping of a culture. In no country is this more evident than in Canada, whose historical experience is conditioned by the uneasy association of two religious opposites, French Roman Catholics and English Protestants. The English cultural group is itself divided into a Protestant majority and a Roman Catholic minority; and Catholics as a whole are divided by linguistic and historical differences among themselves. Add to this delicate balance of creed and culture a pioneer experience which has not yet been concluded, and which conserves the spirit of achievement commonly identified with puritanism, and the result goes far towards explaining the prominence, throughout Canadian history, of religion, formal and informal, organized and unorganized.

Canada is a state founded on one of the deepest of historical experiences, the conquest of one people by another. As a result of the British conquest of New France in 1763, the country came to be shared by two national-cultural groups with two languages, two prevailing religions, and two ways of life—one, the French, the older and the conquered; the other, the English, the Protestant, the conqueror. While the attitudes which the words imply have lost some of their rigour, Canada remains a country of two peoples, two languages, and two predominant religions.

This situation has deeply affected every aspect of Canadian history: in fact, it is Canadian history. Politically, it has thrust suspicions, jealousy, and mistrust into the forefront of public life, and only with extreme difficulty has the Canadian ship of state weathered some of the storms cradled in the ocean of race and religion. A notable example was the fight over separate Roman Catholic schools in Manitoba, upon which, in large degree, the general election of 1896 turned. Religion has resulted in the federalization of the Cabinet, whereby not only must each race have its quota of portfolios, but some of the secondary racio-religious groups must also have theirs. Thus at Confederation, in 1867, the necessity arose not only for due quotas of French Roman Catholic and English Protestant ministers, but also for an Irish Catholic minister and a special Protestant representative for the English of the Province of Quebec.[1]

Constitutionally, the racio-religious situation is reflected in three clauses of the country's fundamental instrument of government, the British North America Act of 1867: sections 51-1, 93, and 133. The first of these gave a fixed membership to Quebec in the House of Commons; the second guarded the school rights which religious minorities possessed at the time the Act was passed; and the third provided for the equality of the English and French languages in Parliament, in the courts, and in the legislature of the Province of Quebec. Confederation was achieved only through this understanding between the races on fundamentals, and while it is possible to argue that its terms are limited and that there is a distinction between religion and race, the plain truth is that it never would have been accomplished had not the French minority assumed that it was being given a coördinate place with the English and that its religion was being put on an equal footing with that of the English. In Canada, as elsewhere, "Catholic" is a larger term than "French," but so large and homogeneous is the French group that in practice it is difficult to separate the two. Not all Roman Catholics are Frenchmen, but all Frenchmen (or almost all) are Roman Catholics.

The outstanding fact is that, despite the deep divisions of the Canadian people, they have been able to live together with comparatively little armed strife. The only conflict of serious proportions was the Rebellion of 1837, which was disapproved by all but a minority of the French, and was not religious in its causation but rather economic, political, and cultural in the broadest

[1] For notes to chapter xx see pages 581–582.

sense. Ten years after the conflict came virtually complete internal self-government for the Province of Canada, with French ministers sharing the responsibilities along with English; and thirty years after, or in 1867, came Confederation, which gave a large measure of autonomy to the provinces and thus relegated the English minority within the Province of Quebec to a position of negligible political power.

At Ottawa, capital of the new Confederation, the two races met on equal terms, and it was not long before the national parties cut completely across racial and religious lines. Canada has had among her prime ministers Conservatives who have been Roman Catholics and Conservatives who have been extreme Protestants, just as she has had Liberals of both religions. The national parties have been successful in preventing the growth of political parties organized along religious lines (there has been nothing in Canada like the old German Centre party); if for no other reason, they deserve the deep gratitude of the country.

Roman Catholicism in Canada has everywhere been confronted with Protestantism. Even the remote country-side of Quebec, where a word of English is seldom heard and few Protestants exist, never loses consciousness of the aggressive Protestant world just over the horizon. The result has been, and still is, a zeal hardly to be found elsewhere in the Roman Catholic world today. Charges of slackness, of lapses from morals, of venality, which are frequently made against the priesthood of countries wholly Catholic, are seldom heard in Canada.

Canadian Catholicism, French or English, does not closely follow the European pattern. In a country like Italy, large numbers in all classes, especially among the intellectuals, have apparently fallen away from the Church. Others give it nominal allegiance: even if the women of the family, as a matter of feminine habit, remain more or less faithful, the men, apart from a few ceremonial occasions, seem to give the Church a wide berth. This pattern seems to extend into most European countries and, beyond Europe, is said to prevail in the urban areas of South America. It has as yet made relatively slight impression upon Canada. Among English-speaking Catholics there is no anti-clericalism, and church-going is assiduously practised by men and women alike. In this group there is little suggestion of the superstitious primitivism of the southern Latin countries, and for the obvious reason that English-speaking Catholics are either middle class or steadily passing into the middle class. In French Canada the country people remain as attached to the Church as were their forefathers, and in certain limited respects their attachment is on a rather primitive peasant level.

In the cities, especially in Montreal, the Latin pattern is beginning to appear. There is a proletariat to whose depths the Church may fail to reach, and there is an *élite* whose conforming observances are becoming somewhat mechanical and among whom may be found men who no longer conform. They, however, are the exception, and the Catholicism of French Canada, pressed on all sides as it is by English Protestantism, still stands strong and zealous. It is a religion by no means as superstitious or primitive as that of, say, Spain, and it is observably penetrated by the puritan spirit of the English continent.[2]

The Roman Catholic world of Canada, as the reader will have concluded, is no tight unit. The major factor of division within it is language. Of the total population of Canada in 1941, 43.2 per cent were Roman Catholics. Of the latter group, 67.7 per cent were French, with the remainder divided among people of a great variety of racial origins and languages. Among these, the Irish Catholics led, followed by English, Ukrainians, Scottish, Polish, and Italian Catholics, in the order named. Each of these groups, except the English, has something of racial distinctiveness, but all (with slight exceptions among the Italians) assimilate to the English-Canadian, not to the French, way of life. The increasing significance of Roman Catholics of the English pattern was recognized in 1946 by the Pope when he nominated a second Canadian Cardinal in the person of an "English" Archbishop (of Highland Scottish descent): at the centre of the faith, the English and the French Catholics of Canada, disproportionate though their numbers are, were thus equated.

In a single chapter it is impossible to comment upon the characteristics of the various sub-groups within Roman Catholicism, but it should be pointed out that the rural-urban division or that of native and non-native-born might be more significant than the division into language groups.[3] The average urban Catholic congregation in the non-French areas by this time probably contains some mixture of all the racial strains. In the country, especially in the West, the original settlements retain their religious and linguistic affiliations and hence their own peculiarities. In Canada the most outstanding of these is the rather large percentage of persons whom the census waveringly classifies now as Greek Catholics, now as Roman. This group, mostly Ukrainian in origin, is only loosely affiliated with Rome.

The characteristics of Canadian Roman Catholicism, however, are most plainly displayed in French Canada, which consists in a homogeneous group of nearly four million people, who have been in the country for three centuries and comes close to forming a nation within a nation. French-Canadian Catholicism, save for the exceptions noted above, retains many of its mediaeval aspects. The wayside shrines, the numerous churches and the constant sound of bells, the clergy in habits of brown or white or black, the places of pilgrimage with miraculous powers ascribed to them, all heighten the impression of mediaevalism. It is further reinforced by the prominence given to the scholastic philosophy in higher education, by the complete clerical control of education, and by the cheerful allegiance given to the Church. Quebec is perhaps unique in the modern world, a virtual theocracy.

Thus it is not surprising that the French Canadian Catholic Church has been ultramontane from the beginning. François de Laval, first Bishop of Quebec (1658–1688), allowed no spark of Gallicanism to enter his province while he reigned there supreme, and under his successors it received no encouragement. New France from the first has been a faithful ward of the papacy, and that allegiance, weakening the emotional attachment to the Crown of France, made the adjustment under the English flag much easier.

Even under such circumstances, however, Quebec has not escaped its anti-clericalism, nor, indeed, its free-thinkers. Papineau, the principal figure of the rebellion period of the 1830's, was not a practising Catholic, and the party that founded itself upon his movement, the *Parti Rouge* (prominent *ca.* 1850–1870), contained a group that was both anti-clerical and sceptical. The Church was too strong for it; its hour was brief and there were few who did not soon return to shelter in the fold. Today, under the impact of urbanism, scepticism on the part of the intellectuals again seems to be on the increase, but it is not yet conspicuous.

Protestantism in Canada shares the common characteristics of Protestantism everywhere, but it has been influenced by the circumstances of North American life and by the parent churches, European or American. In a new country, where men must fight their personal fight against nature, individualism is naturally strong. Since a new civilization had to be built up out of the forest, the sense of purpose was equally strong. It is this sense of objective, transferred to the religious sphere, which men call puritanism, and a puritan attitude is one which all pioneer countries apparently develop: the Roman Catholicism of seventeenth-century New France was puritan in its seriousness. It opposed the frivolities, such as dancing and the theatre, which military officers from France tried to introduce. The colony of New France had too great a task in hand—winning a continent for God and for France—to bother with frivolity. Similarly, in modern Soviet Russia, the sense of immediacy induced by concentration on an objective has brought a willing acceptance of austerity, and some aspects of the strait-laced morals which are commonly regarded as puritan.

Add to all this, in English Canada, the Calvinistic heritage of most of its people, and the character of English Canada as a country founded and rooted in puritanism is easily explained. English Canadians are generally industrious, thrifty, orderly, efficient, self-controlled, and unimaginative. Idle dalliance they tend to regard as mortal sin, and their characteristic products are not poets but engineers and business men.[4] In the middle of the twentieth century, this earnest country, emerging from the chrysalis of pioneering, is finding that there are more things in heaven and earth than are dreamed of in the puritan philosophy. Modern English-speaking Canada, vigorously smashing her inherited inhibitions, provides a spectacle which is sometimes frightening, sometimes ridiculous.

If Protestantism has kept Roman Catholicism on the *qui vive*, the reverse is also true. In Canada the spirit of the Reformation has never died. In small social groups, each person is uneasy until he finds out the religion of the others present, for a chance word might injure amicable relations. The day has gone by when Catholics and Protestants were constantly "at daggers drawn," but they still feel self-conscious in one another's presence, and on either side are organizations the major purpose of which is to keep the ancient fires alight. In Canada, religion can never be, as it is in England, a private affair. "Going over to Rome" cannot be viewed as merely a personal experience: it is also treason to the group.

Other characteristics of Protestantism derive from the North American frontier experience rather than from the Reformation heritage. Religion has not been highly intellectualized in Canada. It has always been possible, especially in larger cities or in educational centres, to hear sound intellectual sermons, but for the most part preaching has been old-fashioned in tone. Yet when the so-called higher criticism began, at the end of the nineteenth century, to penetrate the Canadian Protestant world, it aroused no great opposition among the mass of church-goers: there was nothing comparable to the American fundamentalist movement or the determined stand of whole communities (as in Tennessee) against "subversive" doctrines like evolution.

As Protestantism has worked away from its original fervours, it has introduced ritualism. To the Anglican Church this procession from zeal to formalism is an old story, but to the other denominations it is new. There can now be found in Canada non-Anglican churches in which the position of the baptismal font is considered important; this certainly would not have been true a generation ago. Many people, if they cannot have emotion, demand form, and with form sometimes goes beauty. Neither in architecture nor in service, however, has Canadian Protestantism achieved much on the aesthetic side: most of its buildings are as ugly as the sin they reprobate, and the sudden overlay of ritual in plain nonconformist environment sometimes achieves the same result.

Anglicanism (the Anglican Church is the state church of England on colonial soil), whether Canadian or American, has, in the aesthetics of religion, preserved much of the dignity and beauty of ritual and edifice which are its heritage from the mediaeval past. But Anglicanism has been affected also by the frontier ideals of homespun simplicity mixed with the warmth of neighbourly fellowship, so that, except in a few localities, it is Low Church in form and often manifests as much evangelical fervour as Methodism—and far more than Presbyterianism.

Protestantism everywhere tends to divide into innumerable sects, for the ultimate logical Protestant denomination consists of one person—the individual face to face with God. In few countries has this been more evident than in Canada. The Dominion Census of 1941 lists some seventeen different and recognized denominations, then lumps together dozens more under the heading "other." Most of those listed are small, however, and the dispersion of Protestantism is not really so great as the innumerable conventicles of its minor sects would indicate. Thus, in 1941, of the 55.20 per cent of the Canadian population which was Protestant, 90.34 per cent was comprised within five denominations: Anglican, Baptist, Lutheran, Presbyterian, and the United Church of Canada. The two largest Protestant churches—the Anglican and the United—together accounted for 63 per cent of the Protestant total. The innumerable minor sects made up, all told, only 9.66 per cent of the Protestant population.

The importance of this minority should not, however, be minimized. At present the minor sects consist in people who demand a highly-emotional, simple religion of sentiment and salvation, people whose educational and economic status is low. Sects take over large churches in down-town areas of the great cities, or turn old buildings into meeting-houses. These, in contrast with the failure of the older denominations, they fill. The old Methodist camp-meeting preachers of the early nineteenth century gave their hearers a spiritual diet of hell-fire and damnation, and strong pioneer appetites found it satisfactory sustenance: the modern sects give their urban audiences religious "soap-opera," and our more sentimental and self-pitying age finds it highly congenial. But just as Methodists, with the lapse of time, became prosperous and dignified (so that they now dispute over the position of the baptismal font), so the descendants of present members of the sects, a century from now, will probably have made their emotional services into ritualistic occasions, complete with surpliced choirs. Like nearly all Protestant denominations, the sects are in great part phenomena of race and class.

Protestant denominations in Canada which have their parent churches abroad have come to differ appreciably from them. Canadian Anglicanism has been less majestic and superior than English Anglicanism in its attitude towards nonconformists. Canadian Methodism has not been so prim as English Methodism. Canadian Presbyterianism was never so dour, intellectual, and stiff as Scottish Presbyterianism. This does not mean that Canadian churches are mere extensions of American churches: they have their own individuality. A semi-state church in early English Canada, the Anglican, set a standard of dignity for all the leading denominations which was absent in the United States. The presence of a large Roman Catholic and French population heightened evangelical consciousness, making against ritualism but for responsibility. In Canada, as contrasted with the United States, experimentalism was much less marked, fission did not go so far, energies were less widely scattered, sobriety and dignity were more conspicuous. So far as the writer knows, no Kentucky snake-cult has appeared in Canada, no Father Divine. But this has not prevented Canada from producing (for export to the United States) certain conspicuous figures in this nether world of Protestantism, notably Aimee Semple McPherson, the picturesque evangelist of the 1930's.

The balance is not all in favour of the more northerly of the two English-speaking countries, however, for the inventiveness, audacity, imagination, and courageous tenacity necessary to create a religion like Mormonism has found little counterpart in Canada. Canadians are preëminently safe and sane people: they are not the people for daring, half-crazy experimentation, and when Mormonism eventually reached Canada it came as a simple rural religion the worst vagary of which was not polygamy but soft money.

Pioneer individualism is closely related to pioneer ability to organize: each rests on the strong but adaptive qualities necessary to conquer the wilderness, and individualism, anything but anarchic, supplies the driving-power for the coöperative task. In both Canada and the United States these qualities have been carried up from the pioneer farm to the highest levels of society.

No peoples can organize themselves more quickly for war or for peace than can those of North America. In Canada the numbers to be organized have remained small, and the result has been obvious in the tendency for national bodies quickly to appear. The Dominion is itself an example of this. Canadian political parties spread with rapidity to the Pacific Coast in the wake of federalism. So did the Canadian Manufacturers' Association. Banks soon covered the country with their branches. Higher education becomes more and more closely organized—even French Canada finds it hard to resist being drawn in.

The churches have been no exception to this trend. Anglicanism, owing to its origins, has been one creed from the beginning. But both Methodism and Presbyterianism, each so divided in its homeland and in the United States, soon after Confederation came together in Canada into great nation-wide churches—the Methodist Church of Canada and the Presbyterian Church in Canada. In 1925 these churches, along with the Congregational Church, went farther and formed the United Church of Canada.[5] Even those stubborn individualists, the Baptists, have come close to a national organization. As the half-century mark is reached, the only major Protestant denomination that still remains divided—on the racial lines of its European origins—is the Lutheran, and there are now signs that it, too, is becoming Canadian. The nationalization of Protestant bodies has inevitably produced Erastian churches, whose tendency to identify the state with themselves and themselves with the state is not very healthy, but this is a stage that must be worked through. Sooner or later the Protestant conscience asserts itself, whatever the state, and then complete Erastianism ends.

All the foregoing is but another way of saying that Canadian Protestantism reflects a strongly middle-class and puritan society.

Religious development in Canada divides into several well-marked periods:

1. The wholly Roman Catholic and French period, before the English Conquest (1763).

2. French Catholicism, with some Protestant intrusions in the Province of Quebec, and the beginnings of Protestant colonization in other provinces, 1763–1820.

3. The growth of Protestant provinces: Nova Scotia, New Brunswick, Prince Edward Island, and Upper Canada.

4. The period of Protestant ascendancy, 1830 to the present. This long period, in which the major part of Canada's growth occurred, is marked by the following important phenomena: (*a*) the shift of Protestantism from a minority position to a majority—a shift accentuated by Confederation (1867) and by the great immigration of the early twentieth century; (*b*) Catholic recovery in former New France, with French occupation of former English country-sides; (*c*) the possible emergence of equilibrium after 1918.

At the beginning of the French régime, in the early seventeenth century, the French Government, under Henry IV, accorded various charters and trading-rights to individual Huguenots: these were swept away in the Roman Catholic revival under Louis XIII, and it became the policy of the French Government, rigorously adhered to, to allow no Huguenots to enter the colony. During the second half of the seventeenth century the foundations of the French-Canadian Catholic Church of today were firmly laid by Bishop Laval, whose intense anti-Gallicanism was reflected in the ecclesiastical province which he created in his own image. All his priests were "missionaries" who were never allowed to obtain any legal rights in their benefices and who were moved about at his discretion. To Laval more than to any other one man, Canadian Catholicism owes its missionary zeal, its ardour, and its puritan spirit.

Towards the middle of the eighteenth century a certain relaxation of zeal was observable: this did not go far, but it did admit of the residence of a few Huguenot merchants in the colony and a lessening of austerity in public and private manners.

After the Conquest it seemed, for a brief interval, that the Roman Catholic religion might be proscribed. The question was, Would the penal laws of England, which permitted virtually no toleration, be applied in their full rigour? English government in the 1760's was in confusion, however, and the rapidly changing administrations of the day developed no continuity of policy. Local governors used their common sense, and there was no interference with Roman Catholicism as a private creed. Within a few years after the Conquest, on the roundabout suggestion of certain officials in London, a French priest went to France and was quietly consecrated Bishop of Quebec. Returning to Canada, he received official recognition in the title "Superintendent of the Romish Church." This, however, with the passage of time imperceptibly yielded to "Bishop of Quebec." Eleven years after the Conquest the Quebec Act restored to the French church many of the rights (though not all the property) it had possessed under the king of France. The version of Canadian history generally upheld in the Province of Quebec—that the aftermath of Conquest was unspeakable oppression and tyranny, combined with religious persecution—is almost completely a myth, and French historians would do a service to their country and their scholarship if they tried to dissipate it.[6]

The English Protestant population of the Province of Quebec remained negligible until the arrival of refugees from the American War of Independence (the United Empire Loyalists). These German, Dutch, Irish, and English Protestants were settled upon the upper St. Lawrence; a few years later, in 1791, they were given a provincial organization of their own, Quebec being divided into Lower and Upper Canada. In the original province the English population remained inconsiderable until the Great Immigration which began soon after 1820 and continued for a generation. This new flood from the British Isles raised the English Protestant population in Lower Canada from a few thousands to a maximum of 30–35 per cent of the total, and Montreal by mid-century had almost become an English city.

Nova Scotia came to the English Crown under the Treaty of Utrecht, in 1713, but it did not receive any English population of importance until during the Seven Years' War, when New Englanders migrated there to take over the lands of the expatriated Acadians. These New Englanders were frontiersmen and Baptists: they stamped their character on the Annapolis Valley and other parts of Nova Scotia. In the 1770's English Methodists from Yorkshire settled in the Isthmus of Chignecto; about the same time, Scottish Highlanders, both Catholic and Presbyterian, occupied Cape Breton and the adjacent mainland coasts. The capital, Halifax, consisted in an upper crust of Tory Anglican officials and merchants, and a lower class of Catholic Irish. These migrations gave the religious pattern to Nova Scotia which it has ever since retained. New Brunswick, which was originally settled by United Empire Loyalists—who might have been Anglican or anything else, depending on the "preachers" who did, or did not, visit them, —was more affected by later immigrations than its sister province. In the Great Immigration (*ca.* 1820–1850), which added in large number to the population of all the provinces except Nova Scotia, many Irish, both Catholic and Protestant, came to New Brunswick. Prince Edward Island from the first was Scottish (Catholic and Presbyterian) and French.

The Loyalists who settled in Upper Canada were either Lutherans (Hessian mercenaries and Dutch), nominal Anglicans, or, more commonly, it would appear, nothing in particular. Methodist missionaries from New England began to preach among them in the 1790's, and by 1812 Methodism was probably the strongest denomination, numerically, in the province. It was, however, far surpassed in influence, wealth, and culture by the Anglican Church, to which nearly all officials belonged. Anglican officialdom soon formed a little provincial aristocracy, which managed to monopolize most of the good things and to provide a classical education for its sons. The group came to be called the "Family Compact," but it was not peculiar to Upper Canada, for there were Anglican "Family Compacts" in all the provinces, just as there had been in many of the American colonies before the Revolution.

In Upper Canada, the heat generated between the Anglicans and the humbler Protestants, chiefly the Methodists, provided the major political dynamic down to the 1840's. Strife centred mainly around the control of education and the disposition of the lands set aside for the use of "a Protestant Clergy," the so-called Clergy Reserves. Anglicans claimed a monopoly of these lands (with a gesture in the direction of the Established Church of Scotland); Methodists took the lead in disputing their claim.

The leaders of the two denominations, Archdeacon Strachan for the Anglicans and Egerton Ryerson for the Methodists, battled vigorously in press and pulpit for several years, and the controversy became an important factor in preparing the ground for the Rebellion of 1837. But Ryerson was of Loyalist parentage, and he soon dissociated himself and his Methodist followers from the extreme group. Even so, the Anglican slur of "republicanism" and "disloyalty" stood ever ready for use.

Under such circumstances, it is good to find men like Chief Justice Robinson carefully distinguishing between the political and the religious rivalries of the two denominations.[7] Robinson was an ardent Anglican, but he fully recognized the service which the Methodists rendered to provincial society in carrying the gospel to the remotest corners of the backwoods, and he was at all times ready to help them in the extension of their religious efforts. Dissension in Upper Canada was due not to religion but to denominationalism.

Just after the middle of the nineteenth century the "Clergy Reserves" issue was settled, and denominational tempers were allayed. Meanwhile, both Methodists and Presbyterians had established their own institutions of higher learning. Throughout the rest of the century the Protestant denominations lived together in reasonable amity. Nothing is more noticeable today than their *rapprochement:* there is even discussion, in a preliminary stage, about a possible union of Anglican and United churches.

The situation in Upper Canada, already rendered bitter by the issues of republicanism and loyalism, was made still more difficult by the immigration of tens of thousands of new settlers from the North of Ireland. These settlers brought with them all the belligerence accumulated in two centuries of warfare against Irish "papists." They transferred Ireland's historic misfortunes to Canadian soil, but, finding the comparatively few "papists" of Upper Canada foes hardly worthy of their steel, they turned their attention to the French Catholics of Lower Canada. There had been singularly little friction between French Catholic and English Protestant until the Irish came to Canada. Their Orange Order has seen to it that strife never entirely dies down. At the middle of the twentieth century, feelings are not so high as they were between 1837 and 1897, but they are still strong, and there are few months in which some rabid Protestant is not denouncing "priest-ridden" Quebec, with resultant counterblasts from extremists in French Canada. This, to put it mildly, does not make for national unity, and its relation to Christian brotherly love seems obscure. Another interesting effect of Irish immigration was the friction between French-Canadian and Irish Roman Catholics where they came into contact, which often has developed animosities as bitter as those between Protestants and Catholics.

In the Dominion of Canada (1867) the former Province of Canada was divided into the two provinces of Ontario and Quebec. With the addition of Nova Scotia and New Brunswick, in which the Protestants had a majority, the influence of Roman Catholics was reduced. In the Assembly of the Province of Canada, Roman Catholic members, whether English or French, had not found that race or party prevented them from uniting on important religious issues. They had been able, with fair regularity, to get their way: thus in 1863, a non-party, bi-racial majority, made up of members from both halves of the province, secured the passage of an act extending the system of separate (or Catholic) schools in Upper Canada. After Confederation, no Catholic combination, even had it occurred, could have forced its measures through the Parliament of Canada. The generation following Confederation was marked by several legal battles between the two faiths and by two armed outbreaks which, though not primarily religious, had important religious implications. (See also chap. v, "The Dominion," pp. 112, 119, 122.) In all these, Catholicism met defeat.

In 1869 the Dominion Government completed its negotiations for taking over the lands of the Hudson's Bay Company. Within the Territories was a small settlement of *métis,* or half-breeds, at the junction of the Red and Assiniboine rivers. Gross mismanagement by the government of the day gave these people the impression that in coming into the Dominion they would lose their lands. They refused to admit Canadian officials and set up a provisional government under Louis Riel, which executed Thomas Scott, one of its opponents. Scott was an Orangeman, and the act was regarded throughout Ontario as a planned piece of "papist" malevolence. Ottawa sent an armed expedition to Fort Garry, Riel left the country, the rising evaporated, and fortunately no more blood was spilled. But no one was hanged for Scott's death, and in consequence Ontario Orangemen redoubled the salvoes of hatred which they kept firing at "French papists." Quebec's response was to make a strenuous effort, through immigration and political influence, to gain control over the new province of Manitoba, which, in 1870, was organized as a result of the Riel episode. All to no avail, for within ten years Protestant immigration had swamped the *métis* and the French language, thus winning the English battle for the West.

When Riel led the Saskatchewan Rebellion in 1885, the religious fight was already lost, for by that time there was no possibility of making the prairies a French-speaking Roman Catholic area. The principle of separate schools was, however, incorporated in the arrangements made for Saskatchewan and Alberta when they were created provinces in 1905, with the result that in Catholic districts the public schools have practically become Catholic schools.

Meanwhile, in 1871, the province of New Brunswick had decided to abolish certain school privileges theretofore possessed by Roman Catholics. Its legislation was upheld by the highest courts and since then there have been no "separate" schools in New Brunswick, though the "public" schools in Catholic districts tend to be virtually Catholic schools.

On Riel's execution, after the second rebellion, a wave of nationalism swept over Quebec; the result was the return of a provincial government openly devoted to favouring French and Catholic interests. This government decided to award to the Catholic authorities of the province a considerable sum of money in compensation for the Jesuit lands sequestrated after the Conquest. Once again the passions of Ontario Orangeism were aroused and efforts were made to get the federal government to disallow the Act.[8] D'Alton McCarthy, the leader of the movement, failing at Ottawa, turned to the West and succeeded in blowing up again the fires of anti-Catholicism lighted by the rebellions: the school policy of the Manitoba government was the result.

Whatever its proponents might say in its defence, this policy was essentially a bid by a few extremist politicians for electoral popularity among the Ontario Orange elements at the expense of the long-enjoyed school privileges of the French (which, in the main, consisted in the privilege of doing without schools). It was transferred to the Dominion stage in 1895, when, after a series of legal struggles, it became necessary for the Dominion Government to pass legislation in negation of Manitoba's policy. The resulting battle convulsed Parliament and the country, and exhibited Canadian politics in their most confusing form. The Conservative Government, headed by a former Grand Master of the Orange Order, attempted to coerce Manitoba by legislation favouring the Roman Catholics: the leader of the Opposition, the French Catholic Wilfrid Laurier, who had been championing provincial rights, refused to be a party to the coercion of a province. In the election which followed, in 1896, he was damned by the French clergy and elected by the French people. With some difficulty he managed to pour enough oil on the waters to quiet the country.

Soon afterwards Ontario Orangeism found its emotions absorbed in the balmy atmosphere of Queen Victoria's Diamond Jubilee (1897) and in the hot currents of the Boer War (1899). This war brought a renewed wave of imperialism to English Canada and of nationalism to French Canada. Both emotions were in reality religious in that they were deeply felt, were unconnected with material interest, represented devotion to a way of life, and lived on the mysticism of racialism.

After the Boer War, English Protestantism found its energies going in new directions. Those were the years when the Canadian prairies were being settled, and thither went tens of thousands of people from Ontario. Material development acted as a lightning-conductor and the country enjoyed a few years' surcease from racial and religious strife. When, in 1903, the Alaska Boundary Award went harshly against Canada, both races, to their surprise, found themselves possessed of common sentiments, each discovering a measure of Canadianism in common antipathy to both English and Americans.

Such a union could not last, and subsequent events put the severest possible strain upon the relations between English Protestants and French Catholics (see chap. vi, "The Twentieth Century," pp. 135 ff.). It is true that they centred around Canada's relationships with the Empire, and that the differences were more racial than religious, but the strong tendency of English-Canadian Protestants to identify the terms "French" and "Catholic" modifies the importance of the qualification.

If the manner in which great issues have been settled leaves any doubt that Roman Catholicism lost weight in the country after Confederation, a statistical test removes it. In 1851 the proportion of Roman Catholics in the Province of Canada (Upper and Lower Canada taken together) was 49.6 per cent. In 1861 it was 48 per cent; in 1871, 46 per cent. In the provinces which came together to form the Confederation (Nova Scotia, New Brunswick, and Canada), the proportions of Roman Catholics in 1851 and in 1861 were 46.1 per cent and 44.2 per cent, respectively. At the first census after Confederation, in 1871, this proportion had fallen to 41.5 per cent. Since then, in the country as a whole, it has fluctuated little, as table 1 indicates.

TABLE 1

ROMAN CATHOLICS IN CANADA, 1851–1941
(Percentages)

	1851	1861	1871	1881	1891	1901	1911	1921	1931	1941
Ontario and Quebec . .	49.6	48.0	46.0	45.0	43.4	45.7	48.4	49.8	49.9	53.0
All Canada .	46.1	44.2	41.5	41.2	41.2	41.5	39.3	38.5	38.5	41.7

Further analysis shows that in the period from 1871 to 1901 the numbers of English Catholics in Canada were almost stationary: it was the French who maintained the numerical weight of the religion during this period. In the twentieth century the French have continued to show remarkable fertility: despite three decades of heavy Protestant immigration (1900–1930), the proportion of French-speaking Canadians to the total population has not greatly changed. Catholics whose origins go back to the British Isles have added very modestly to their numbers, as may be seen in table 2.

It is obvious from the table that non-French Catholicism in Canada has, for weight of numbers, depended during the twentieth century on European Catholics of the recent immigration. Among the millions who poured into Canada from 1901 to 1931, many were of Catholic background: table 2 indicates the remarkable addition they have made to Canadian Catholicism. Before 1901 it was divided rather simply into groups of French- and English-speaking communicants. Today it is polyglot. If the returns for 1931 and 1941 are accurate, the new comers are not quite so faithful to their Church as were the older Catholics. The proportion of Poles who returned themselves as Catholics in 1931 was 84.2 per cent, but in 1941 it was 80.8 per cent. Similarly, Ukrainian Roman Catholics decreased from 67 per cent to 62 per cent. It is apparent

TABLE 2

INCREASE IN CERTAIN RELIGIOUS GROUPS, 1901–1941

	1901	1941	Percentage increase
French Catholics	1,649,000 *	3,378,000	104.8
Other Catholics	580,000	1,614,000	178.2
"British" Catholics	473,000 *	770,000	62.8
Non-British, non-French Catholics	107,000 *	844,000	688.7
Protestants	2,929,000	6,155,000	110.1

* Figures marked with an asterisk are approximate. The Canadian census correlates religion and racial origin only for 1931 and 1941. Before that, other methods of computation must be used. These are, chiefly, the high degree of coincidence between the terms "French" and "Roman Catholic"—97 or 98 per cent—and the almost completely "British" origins of non-French Catholics before 1901. The approximations are believed to be close.

that European Catholics will not provide an important balance to French Catholicism in fertility, for they seem to be reducing their rate of increase with extreme rapidity: from 1931 to 1941, a decade of no immigration, it was scarcely more rapid than that of "British" Catholics. If the "British" Roman Catholic group

TABLE 3

SOME RATES OF INCREASE, 1931–1941

	French Catholics	"British" Catholics	Other Catholics	Protestants
1931	2,849,000	689,000	747,000	5,720,000
1941	3,378,000	770,000	844,000	6,155,000
Per cent increase	18.8	11.7	14.3	7.6

were further subdivided, the statistics would show that the Irish Catholics increased during the decade by only 4.9 per cent—well below the low level of Protestants.

A statistical examination thus seems to show that, as compared with the middle of the nineteenth century, Roman Catholicism has by the middle of the twentieth century fallen into a somewhat more emphatic minority position and that its English-speaking group has lost appreciably in proportionate weight. Whether this will be compensated by the energy of the new comers who entered in the twentieth century remains to be seen. Few acute observers would hold that the entire group of non-French Catholics in Canada is as important in the nation's life today as it was two generations ago.

French Catholics, in contrast, have been able by their reproductive powers to maintain their proportionate place, and today, as a century ago, they easily lead all other components of the population in fertility. Not only that, but during the last three-quarters of a century they have won back from English (and mainly Protestant) possession large areas of the country-side. Today the Eastern Townships of Quebec, bordering Vermont and New Hampshire, are once more French: the New Englanders who settled them a century and a half ago have proved easy victims to the French in this struggle for survival. Large sections of the Ontario side of the Ottawa Valley have likewise become French. In New Brunswick the French have increased from 15.72 per cent of the total in 1871 to 35.81 per cent in 1941. In northern Ontario the region from the Quebec border westward to Hearst has within the last generation been colonized by French Canadians. In the West, however, they have not held their own.

Along with this remarkable reversal of the verdict of the Conquest of 1763, both in Quebec and outside it, has gone a proportionate increase in influence. French-Canadian Catholicism is homogeneous and apparently self-confident. Less than 3 per cent of the members of the race have failed to remain within the fold. Zeal is strong both at home and abroad, and the foreign missionary effort of the group is said to be among the highest in the world. Curiously enough, zeal does not spill over into attempts to proselytize the neighbouring English: the French attitude seems to be that one's religion is one's own affair, and that, while it is the duty of a good Catholic to extend its bounds through reproduction, it is not his task to interfere with his neighbours' beliefs.

Intellectually, French-Canadian Catholicism, until recently, has not been remarkable, but, as the sense of inferiority that results from conquest is shaken off, it is finding itself both intellectually and culturally; the contributions of French Canada to literature, painting, and allied arts are far in excess of those of Catholic English Canada. The papacy presumably knows its own business best and probably was well aware of trends when it created an English cardinalate in 1946 in Canada: to the non-Catholic it would nevertheless appear that the Catholic centre of gravity is, and must for an indefinite time remain, in French Canada.

For Canadians, the interests of a historical summary of the positions of the two faiths will most likely be found in the conclusions drawn. How, it will be asked, do the two faiths compare today? Is there any likelihood of a major shift in their relative positions, leading to the dominance of one of them?

The answers may be found in statistical history. For nearly a century the two faiths have been in relative equilibrium and the two races have maintained approximately the same relative positions. Thus, while local shifts have occurred and will occur, it is unlikely that there will be a major change in the balance. Even in New Brunswick, where the rapid increase of French Catholics has often led to the conclusion that the province will soon be wholly French, it is almost mathematically certain that the French will not attain equality of numbers until the year 2000, if then. Every year that passes subjects the two races and faiths to the same environmental, political, and social influences. The utmost which can be accomplished by evangelical zeal in either camp is delay of the rate at which the gap between the two patterns of life is narrowed. In French Canada, language and tradition enable a strong rear-guard action to be fought. In English Canada, this is not possible, and in habits of life, including rate of reproduction, political attitudes, and moral outlook, the two groups steadily approximate.

It is probable that French Canada is undergoing the same process, though at a slower rate. Modern industrialism and urbanism are subtly affecting the former simplicity of the French way of life, driving it gradually into approximation to the English. Moreover, both races and creeds have found much in common. In the last century, Protestantism has moved far from its European origins and in most of the denominations it has taken on its own Canadian shape.

In finding that they are children of the same soil, with the same political roof over their heads, French and English, Roman Catholics and Protestants, are very slowly discovering their common interests. Nationalism is proving a bridge. A century ago or less, many, perhaps most, Protestants were contemptuous of their French fellow-citizens as poor, downtrodden, "priest-ridden" peasants, and did not try to conceal their contempt. Today such religious and social intolerance is passing. Many Protestants will concede that there may, after all, be something in a way of life which does not consist entirely in "dollar-chasing." Catholics will occasionally admit the inadequacy of a merely rural ideal, or a way of life which cannot do much to improve the earthly circumstances of the individual. These changes look towards approximation.

There is, moreover, a common fear, shared by all Catholics and by many Protestants, of communism. Protestants emphasize the tyranny that it implies, Catholics the atheism. To the hurt of Protestantism, which it divides, and more emphatically to the hurt of Protestant liberalism, this fear of the great unknown, the foreign unknown, is driving Canadians together, emphasizing that polarization of the world which is occurring elsewhere.

The present state of religion in Canada (in contradistinction to the present balance between Protestantism and Catholicism) reflects the great world currents of thought and action, but with a time-lag which arises from the immaturity of Canadian society. In neither Protestantism nor Catholicism have trends progressed as far in Canada as they have in the Old World. Canadians are not yet a people of ideas—they are too new, too insecurely combined. Consequently, the ideas of Europe, the creative continent, come to them after a rather long interval of time and are often mediated through Great Britain and the United States. As an example, German Biblical criticism made little impression in Canadian theological schools for two generations after it had reached its height in Germany, and then its chief exponents were from England.

European conditions cannot, therefore, prevail in Canadian religion, either Protestant or Catholic. To the Catholic from France, the French-Canadian church is apt to appear credulous and naïve. Intellectually, this charge cannot be made against Protestantism, the major denominations of which are now abreast of good European thinking in theology, the relation of religion and science, and similar matters. But paganism, indifference, and atheism (which can proceed as easily from a Catholic as from a Protestant background) are not yet as characteristic in Canadian life as they are in older and more sophisticated communities. Protestants in Canada seem to show greater interest in the church than do Protestants in older countries. Church attendance in Canada is much larger, proportionately, than it is in either Great Britain or the United States. The Protestant church apparently draws in more young people than in either of the other countries. Most people have some kind of connexion, real or nominal, with the church, and those who put themselves down in the census merely as "Protestant" are few; those who return "no religion" are fewer still. In Protestant Canada, anticlericalism is never encountered and, except in extreme circles (as among Communists), while often there is sharp criticism, there is virtually no hostility to the church.

It would be hard to prove Canadian Protestantism to be "the opiate of the people." That function may be left to the moving-picture theatres. Evangelical Protestantism, far from putting a man to sleep, keeps him only too wide awake. Not only does it impose the most tremendous of all burdens on him—his own absolute responsibility for his fate, finite and infinite—but it constantly throws at him the challenge that he is his brother's keeper, and makes him feel that the world's safety and salvation depend not on his rulers or his boss or his priest but on him. It is the inability of so many people to measure up to the challenge of Protestantism that constitutes the danger and accounts for the decline in the church, not any weakness in the Protestant principle.

Absence of hostility to the church (accompanied by mere indifference and the loss of the old, simple faith, common to a scientifically educated generation everywhere) has perhaps been purchased by a too-ready acquiescence of the churches in the demands of the state. To every Canadian Protestant church, except some of the minor sects like Doukhobors and Jehovah's Witnesses, the state's command has become almost a rule of conscience, tending to override individual judgement. In the last two wars only a few hardy souls dared to stand out against the decrees of the state and fight for the dictates of their own consciences. It is not hard to explain the attitude: the Protestant churches so far identify themselves with the state—it is *their* state—that divergence is hardly conceivable. Catholicism still stands on its international position, but it has made many retreats and is today far more under the influence of the state than it was centuries ago. Here again, church and state in Quebec are close to being one, and in emergencies the line of cleavage runs, not between church and state, but between the two Canadian divisions of the state—province and Dominion; or between the two peoples—English and French.[9]

Certain psychological attitudes are common to all religions. Of these, mysticism is one. In days gone by, French-Canadian Catholicism produced its share and more than its share of mystics; the annals of the seventeenth century, with its missionaries, martyrs, and devoted founders of nunneries and monasteries, are full of them. Today they are less abundant, and in English Catholicism their absence is conspicuous. Even in French Canada they tend to be outnumbered, if not obscured, by those who proclaim not the mysteries of the faith, but those of the race. Mysticism in Protestant circles has run a similar course. In Canada, Protestant mysticism has always been of the frontier variety, consisting in intense religious experiences which have often caused the recipients to indulge in grotesque emotional displays, such as shouting, "speaking with tongues," or rolling on the ground. Protestant mysticism, usually confined to simple pioneer people, emotionally starved except for the opportunities conveyed by a heady evangelicanism, has tended to exhibit grotesque parallels to the Dionysiac cults of antiquity. The withdrawn philosophic mystic, the Kierkegaard, the Keble, the Barth, is not a common phenomenon on Canadian soil. When the English Canadian gets an education, he leaves emotional religion and mysticism behind and goes in for something "practical"—social service, politics, stock-broking, or bridge-building. The Canadian air is hard on mystics: the winters are too cold and there is too much work to do.

As a result, most denominations, even the Catholic, have a utilitarian atmosphere. They stress good works and the social gospel. The most dynamic creed in Canada has undoubtedly been Methodism, and Methodism began by converting the frontier

Loyalists and inducing them to live orderly and more or less sober lives. A century ago it launched the temperance crusade and ever since it has been closely identified with opposition to alcohol. Until the twentieth century it brought up its young people in an atmosphere that did not permit smoking, card-playing, dancing, theatre-going, or attendance upon horse-races. In the early twentieth century it launched a foreign missionary movement the zeal of which was comparable to that of the Counter-Reformation or the Crusades. Its adherents were strong supporters of the League of Nations. Many of them were active in progressive movements in politics, so that today former Methodists constitute perhaps the most important single component in Canada's social-democratic party, the C.C.F. Methodism (since 1925 merged in the United Church of Canada) has always supported every form of good work. It has been essentially a social religion and as such is remarkably well adapted to the Canadian outlook on life. While it remained a separate denomination its character was so clear that it might be singled out for special mention, but what is said of Canadian Methodism applies in greater or less degree to virtually all the Protestant denominations, except that few Anglicans or Presbyterians have considered that conformity to the entire list of Methodist taboos was necessary for Christian conduct.

This chapter is concerned with Canadian religion, not with Canadian lack of religion. However, a word must be said on this most common of modern phenomena. Notwithstanding the relatively vigorous state of the Canadian church as compared with those of other lands, paganism has spread into Canada, as everywhere else. During the generation between the two wars, Canadians, like Americans, seemed to be determined to kick their institutions to pieces. They made fun of their politicians; they jeered at their preachers and the faithful who followed them, and mocked their parents' decorous youth. In a hundred ways they attempted to cast off the puritanism in which they and their forbears had been steeped. There was no sophistication about Canadian sin: it was just ugly. How far paganism has gone, no one can tell. The divorce rate mounts steadily. Sex crimes, the immoderate and often illegal consumption of alcohol, "wild" parties, and other excesses, all continue to increase. No doubt

Canadians, like others who repent a youth which has been too well spent, will not stop until they have run the gamut, sown their wild oats, and had opportunity to reflect on their course of action.

The present age is a constant whirlwind and it is impossible to predict which of its many aspects will eventually dominate. Paganism must have its day, presumably, but there is little danger of Canada's becoming a pagan country. Paganism is, as it were, skin-deep: it has been present in every age, but not in every age has it been possible to indulge publicly in pagan practices. When release has been obtained, the present fit will wear off and the more permanent characteristics of the people will again manifest themselves. No longer will it be possible for a great church to fulminate against, say, the theatre, and expect much of a hearing—that is just an aspect of growing up, and the days of innocence are passing. But the stern northern climate will continue to impose its own seriousness of purpose, making its people fight hard to establish decent conditions of life; and their inherited tradition of altruism, carried over by the school, the university, the church, and other agencies (not least, the state), will impel them to the type of liberal humanism which their best spirits have always had most at heart.

The future will not be to mysticism: there are few dark corners in our present age of electric light. It will not be to mere ritualism —the Canadian is too practical-minded to become much interested in rites and ceremonies. The future will be to a liberal humanism which keeps in view the old familiar goal, *Mens sana in corpore sano.* This attitude has had its sharp struggles with pure commercialism, and whenever a pitched battle has occurred, it is the free enterprising society of commercialism which has been defeated. Liberal humanitarianism has been moving steadily into politics for many years, and it is rapidly giving us the social-service state. Vigorous objection is always made to each new measure in the programme (such as family allowances), but these measures steadily increase. They are not the mere voting of the money of the rich majority by the poor minority: they reflect Canadian Protestant mentality, and the indications are that Canadian Catholic mentality, if not naturally preoccupied with social humanism, finds it relatively easy to accept it.

Can society live on such conceptions? Liberal humanism provides no patent, doctrinaire blue-print for life: it cannot rival communism in the assuredness of Utopia. But it is far from the "each-for-himself" philosophy that in certain countries has prostituted the good term "liberalism": it has long since left mere individualism far behind and is definitely an idealist philosophy. But it is far more concerned with heaven here below than with heaven hereafter. As such, is it enough? Must Roman Catholicism return to the mysticism of former centuries? Must Protestantism recover for itself, before it becomes respectably entitled to the name religion, the spiritual ecstasies of another age? In short, must supernaturalism reign again?

These are questions which cannot be answered here. Increasing disturbance in the world, increasing danger, may bring greater emphasis on the mystical in religion. But a practical people, still with numerous jobs of construction to complete, placing strong emphasis on the importance of material welfare, retaining a confidence in science and "progress" which has been lost by peoples who have suffered a harsher fate, will find it difficult to reconvert to mysticism and other-worldliness. Canadians feel that there will always be enough mystics to keep their outlook from becoming merely mechanical and purely crass. If the atmosphere which covers the practical Canadian landscape can nourish two generations of people to whom no sacrifice was too great in the cause they conceived to be right and just, then mysticism and its traditional belief may possibly be left to take care of themselves.

Protestant, liberal humanism fits exactly the technological civilization of our day. It is dynamic, adaptable, equalitarian, and optimistic. It does not embrace all Canada, but its spirit is not without influence in those parts of the country which do not know it directly. It has moved far enough away from the old days to meet Catholicism with tolerance and communism with discussion. It is more flexible than either of these world religions, and now that the Second World War and the pressures of the social situation have broken the smugness of its Calvinism and the rigours of its individualism, it may have a long future. No country could be more thoroughly committed to this liberal humanism than is Canada.

Part Six

EXTERNAL RELATIONS

CHAPTER XXI

Historic Factors

BY GEORGE P. DE T. GLAZEBROOK

THE PHRASE "external relations" is common Canadian usage, and is more applicable to Canadian circumstances than "foreign affairs." Throughout the various colonial stages, Canada was strongly influenced by a variety of relations with other areas, but, because of her status, she could not be described as having her own foreign policy. Even for the later years as a sovereign state, the phrase "external relations" is more suitable, since it covers relations with other parts of the British Commonwealth as well as with foreign countries. While the phrase is therefore convenient, it has tended to confuse not a few Canadians by concealing the fact that in modern times Canada—like other states—has a foreign policy, with all the problems of responsibility which that implies.

The starting-point of North American history is always to be found in Europe, and Europe provided Canada with what is the basic factor in any country—its people. For a century the white population in Canada was all French; and from then until the middle of the eighteenth century the French continued to occupy the greater part of the territory. Only near the end of the century did the picture show a material change, caused by the coming of the political exiles from the Thirteen Colonies, who became known as United Empire Loyalists. Immigration, which had been on a small scale during the French régime, now became important in volume and significantly diversified. By the middle of the nineteenth century the majority of the population was of British stock, born either in Canada, in the British Isles, or (in small numbers) in Newfoundland. As emigration from France had long since ceased, the effect of immigration was to swell the British element. Canada was thus composed of two linguistic and cultural groups. Small minorities came throughout the nineteenth century, and even before it, from other countries; but it was only with the ending of the long depression at the turn of the century that a vigorous immigration policy began to allow for far-reaching diversity. By 1911 the census showed that 5.6 per cent of the population had been born in Europe, with a much smaller, if more conspicuous, minority from Asia.

Canada, however, had only a small share in the mass movement from Europe to America. Not only did the United States receive the great majority of the new comers, but it also drew steadily on the population of Canada. The United States Census of 1860 showed a quarter of a million Canadian-born, and the drain continued so steadily that, from Confederation to the twentieth century, in only one year was immigration greater than emigration.[1] The immigration of Americans, which began with the Loyalists, also continued, although it was proportionately less than the exodus to the United States. The consequent mingling of peoples has been in itself an important aspect of external relations.[2]

Deductions from population statistics must be cautious. The Germans in Canada are, for the most part, old settlers with no continuing interest in their fatherland. The French retained a very limited interest in their motherland, while that of the British-born was much stronger. Some groups, such as the Doukhobors, have had less reason to retain sympathy for their country of origin; and the southern Irish were Irish rather than British. In the midst of these cross-currents there has been an absence of such influences on foreign policy as that of the Italian element in the United States. Suspicion of the United States which originated with the Loyalists has been balanced by migration both ways, as well as by other close connexions between the two peoples. On the whole, the only positive influence on external policy created by immigration has been that of the people from the United Kingdom, which has not been offset by any comparable force. For, although the French Canadians, making up the other large racial group in Canada,

[1] For notes to chapter xxi see page 582.

have checked the weight of the pro-British drive, they have not set against it a similar attachment to their country of origin.

One clear result of the European origin of the Canadian people has been the importation, throughout Canadian history, of European ideas. New France was never a replica of old France and never slavishly followed the ideas of the older society. In some respects, indeed, she resisted the tendency of French thought, particularly that of the rationalists of the eighteenth century and even more so that of the Revolution. Even the Third Republic, which was designed as a compromise, aroused suspicion in Canada because of its apparent radicalism. Yet, for all that, the stamp of the French mind can be seen on every page of the history of French Canada. If at times current ideas might be rejected, the French-Canadian outlook on the individual, the family, the state, law, and education was neither British nor North American. It was modified by both these points of view, it is true, but cannot be explained by either. Canadians of British origin, because of continued immigration and political affiliation, were even more deeply affected by their motherland. Early newspapers were full of English material (often whole columns copied from London papers), and the book-shops advertised the latest accessions of English books, which were the principal reading until their monopoly was challenged by American literature.

Canadian institutions strongly reflect their European origins. All the principal churches, for example, were transplanted in the colonial days. Roman Catholicism was the religion of virtually all Frenchmen in the New World as in the Old: indeed, more so, since Protestantism was but briefly permitted in Canada during the French régime. The English likewise brought the Established Church of their country, as they did the major and some of the minor nonconformist bodies. The forms of government were variations first on French and later on English models. Even the adoption of the federal principle in 1867 did not alter that fact, for both provincial and central governments followed the British parliamentary system in all other essentials and in countless details. Many of the techniques of the New World came from the Old. The tools that were brought by the early settlers from Europe revolutionized the life of the area, and the transformation can be followed through with the adaptation of the discoveries of the Industrial Revolution, with banking and commercial methods. Houses and public buildings reflect in a modified form the styles of France and England.

Canada has been in succession a part of two empires, the French and the British. Politically there have been few lasting effects of the first attachment, though it left a considerable cultural heritage. Some traces remain, particularly in the civil law of the Province of Quebec. The main imperial impact, however, has come from membership in the British Empire. The second British Empire, which followed the break-down of the first through the successful revolt of the Thirteen Colonies, left to be answered the question how progressive communities of the same stock as in the British Isles could find their destinies within the bounds of an imperial structure. At first there appeared the same strains and stresses which had been fatal before the American revolt, and a similar difference of interest between the metropolitan power and the colonies. A new conception of empire was needed if a second collapse was to be avoided. As one looks back on it, the answer to the conundrum seems obvious and easy, but it did not seem so then. Both in the United Kingdom and in Canada there were wide divergences of opinion as to the wisest course to follow, and honest doubts whether there could be designed an empire different from all those that experience had known. The gradual evolution of a Commonwealth of Nations was made possible by restraint, original thinking, and faith on both sides of the Atlantic.

The external relations of Canada have always been affected, in different ways and at different times, by the imperial connexion. For nearly a century after the fall of French power, Canada was part of a mercantile empire governed from London. There were both advantages and disadvantages in this position. The commercial and financial power of London, combined with varying trade privileges, facilitated the export of Canadian staple products. In the period of British free trade the loss of a protected market was balanced by the flow of British capital to finance the canals, railways, and other public works of Canada. It was then, and perhaps must remain, a moot point whether Canada gained or lost over the whole period from the fact that her relations with other countries were handled by the British diplomatic service. It is, however, a matter of record that military and naval defence were provided effectively and without raising the question of taxation that had loomed so large in the dispute between London and the Thirteen Colonies. With the acceptance, soon after the First World War, of the principle of equality of status, a new—or perhaps a modified—relationship between the self-governing units came into effect in foreign policy.

Because Canada was founded as a colony, she was from the first subject to the vicissitudes of the foreign relations of the metropolitan power. With the brief exception of the years 1760 to 1775, it happened that that power, whether it was France or England, was seeking to extend or maintain its position in North America. In the French period the series of European wars in the mid-eighteenth century spilled over into North America, where the competitive expansion of the colonies added a local rivalry. The British conquest of Canada did not put an end to this disturbed situation, since the politico-economic struggle for the West was carried on by the successor government in Quebec and by the independent governments on the Atlantic Coast. During the Revolutionary War and again during the Napoleonic Wars Canada was invaded from the south; while these attempts were successfully resisted, they left for generations an apprehension that American expansionism would again take the form of armed invasion.

The difficulty of establishing boundaries between Canada and the United States was inherent in the geography of the continent. Starting on the one hand from Atlantic bases and on the other from Northern Atlantic and St. Lawrence River bases, the Europeans had been disputing over an interior reached by converging lines of approach. It was not that physical geography bore no relation to political rivalries. The St. Lawrence–Great Lakes system, continued by the rivers of the prairies, was the spine of Canadian penetration and offered a rough sketch for a northern state. The problem was rather the details of boundaries in the areas where a combination of settlement, claims, lack of obvious natural lines, and incorrect maps left ample room for dispute. Throughout the century and a quarter of boundary negotiations the Canadian interest was in the hands of the British authorities.

In two of the main cases—that of the Pacific slope and the later Alaska question—the British Government was faced with a chauvinistic American attitude that raised the particular points at dispute to the level of high policy.

An important turning-point in the history of Canada's position in the continent was the Washington Conference of 1871. It was as part of the British attempt to lower the temperature raised by incidents during the Civil War that the Joint High Commission met. Contemporary Canadian opinion—official and unofficial—saw the Conference as a means of obtaining advantageous settlements on matters of particular interest: trade, fisheries, and indemnity for losses resulting from the Fenian raids. In the short view the results of the Conference, as seen from Canada, were highly unsatisfactory. On the other hand, the most difficult problem for Canada was one of defence against what appeared to be a further epidemic of American imperialism, and the fact that the Conference did much to smooth Anglo-American relations proved to be of the greatest significance in ensuring Canada's future security. Followed as it was in the next twenty years by the acceptance in London of peace with the United States as a basic principle of policy, the Washington Conference was the effective beginning of the period in which Canada no longer felt the pressure of American expansionism in the form of the threat of forced annexation. It did not, and could not, mean an end to the influence of the United States on Canada; for two countries so close, so similar, and with so many ties could not live in water-tight compartments. And, as the divergence in population and wealth widened, it was inevitably the greater that influenced the less.

Canadian external relations have in all periods been affected mainly by two Great Powers, the United Kingdom and the United States. Until the late nineteenth century, that too often meant seeking the support of the former against the latter. In the twentieth century the Canadian objective has been to avoid a clash between British and American policies, bearing in mind the disastrous results for Canada if she were forced to choose between the two. It is this triangular relationship that, more than any other one factor, dominates Canadian external policy. From this follows the importance of examining Canadian interests in relation to those of the United Kingdom and the United States. The area of common ground is wide. All have inherited, and all have adhered to, the same conception of the rights of man, the same belief in the sacredness of the individual, the maintenance of civil liberties, the protection of religious toleration. All have opposed the Great Leviathan, the state as power, the totalitarian state. Predominantly middle-class societies, they have been proponents of industry and trade. Canada, which, like the United Kingdom, has had an economy dependent on external trade, has found her markets and her sources of imports very largely in these two other countries. All three states have sought a world safe for the free individual, safe for the merchant. Canadian foreign policy has thus been tied, by interest as well as necessity, to the policies of the United Kingdom and the United States.

At all times the continuance of the strength of the British Empire has been an assumption in Canadian thinking. Even if the dependence of Canada on the power of the Empire was not always appreciated in periods of tranquillity, any threat to that strength was likely to bring a quick response; in fact, support was several times offered when the Empire could hardly have been said to be in danger. The Crimean War brought volunteers for service as well as demonstrations of loyalty, and in the Indian Mutiny a regiment was raised in Canada. By the time of the South African War the skies were more cloudy, since a difficult military operation was being conducted by the United Kingdom in the face of scarcely-veiled hostility from European powers. The Liberal Government of Sir Wilfrid Laurier, not without reluctance, dispatched two contingents to South Africa, besides relieving the British garrison at Halifax and permitting the recruiting of more Canadians for imperial units. The Government, though pressed by its Quebec supporters not to intervene in a British war, was forced to do so by the strength of the demand in other provinces for action. It is noteworthy that in the election of 1900 the Liberals lost seats not because of what the Government had done, but because it was held not to have done enough.

German hostility, which had been a factor during the Boer War, became the major consideration after the break-down of negotiations for an Anglo-German alliance. For the first time in the century, British naval supremacy, which had been a fixed condition in all Canadian thought on foreign relations, was threatened by German building and plans; and for the first time in Canadian history it became necessary to find a method of reinforcing the Royal Navy, which stood as much for the defence of Canada as for the strength of the Empire as a whole. From 1909 two successive Canadian governments wrestled with ways and means of supplementing the heavy naval expenditure of the United Kingdom; and while the failure to achieve any results may suggest a lack of applied realism, it leaves untouched the conviction that Canadian and imperial defence were identical.[3] The First World War even more obviously involved Canadian interests, and while there were differences of opinion as to the nature and extent of Canadian participation, there were no two opinions on the necessity for participation in some form.

The full participation of Canada in that long struggle was not the result of a new outlook on foreign affairs, nor did it effect any. The objectives shared by Canada with the United Kingdom and the United States were as valid as ever, and were all the more precious since they had been maintained in battle. There were, however, changes in degree if not in kind. The impact of a great war brought an even fuller appreciation of the importance of external relations. It brought, too, a more active consideration of the constitutional status of Canada. Was it logical that a country that had proved its ability to act as a principal in warfare should be deprived of a direct voice in foreign relations? And if it were not logical, how could the situation be remedied? There was a surfeit of loose talk on the proper status that Canada should have—loose because it was often divorced from a recognition of the fact that participation in international relations assumes adequate diplomatic machinery and a readiness to accept responsibility for its actions. Status was a necessary condition of function, but the one without the other was meaningless.

In the inter-war period the scene is obscured by the parallel developments of constitutional authority and external policy, the two at times becoming confused. In spite of that, however, certain trends in policy can be detected. On the whole, the compelling factors were still the position of Canada in the British Empire and on the North American continent. Canadian policy in that period was therefore largely derivative, the only peculiar element being the constant attempt either to compromise between, or to reconcile, the policies of Britain and the United States whenever those policies showed serious differences. Thus at the Paris Peace Conference the Canadian delegation assumed the duty of emphasizing in the British Empire panel the necessity of considering American opinion. In the League of Nations Canada, in the absence of American representation, stood for a North American view on Article X, arguing that the obligations under it were unduly severe for a country so remote from the sources of international friction. The question of the renewal of the Anglo-Japanese alliance brought the Canadian Government squarely up against the possibility of a divergence of policy between the United Kingdom and the United States. When the Imperial Conference of 1921 gave an opportunity for discussing it, the Canadian representative successfully argued that renewal was undesirable because of American objections to the alliance.

Canada followed, too, the drift towards isolation pursued fully by the United States and in lesser degree by the United Kingdom. Though believing in the League of Nations in general, Canadians continued to view with misgivings the commitments that membership entailed. When the draft Treaty of Mutual Assistance was presented for comment, the Canadian Government criticized its terms and added that "so far as it purports to impose a future obligation to take specific action in circumstances incapable of present definition, it would be hopeless to expect the people of Canada to accept it." When the Geneva Protocol succeeded the draft treaty, the Government promised its continued support of the League, but thought that the Protocol, with "its rigid provisions for application of Economic and Military sanctions in every future war," was undesirable. "Among the grounds for this conclusion," the reply went on, "is the consideration of the effect of non-participation of the United States upon attempts to enforce sanctions and particularly so in the case of contiguous countries like Canada." The change marked by the Locarno treaties from general to regional security agreements was more in harmony with Canadian thinking. The Government did not take advantage of the clause empowering it to adhere to the Treaty of Mutual Guaranty signed at Locarno, nor would it have been consistent with Canadian policy to have done so, for with every succeeding case it was becoming more apparent that Canada was not prepared to accept commitments to military and economic sanctions all over the world.

In his note of acceptance of the Pact of Paris of 1928, the Secretary of State for External Affairs drew a distinction between support of collective action in general and acceptance of sanctions in undefined cases. He pointed out that Canada, through membership in the British Commonwealth, friendship with the United States, and ample territory, was in a position that could be endangered only by a world war. Against such a contingency the League developed a habit of coöperation, an acceptance of publicity in international affairs, and machinery for conciliation, but the Covenant might not be interpreted as imposing other burdens on member states "automatically or by the decision of other states."[4] This position, stated in the period of optimism and prosperity midway between the wars, was unchanged in the years of depression and crisis that followed. Against the aggression of Japan, Italy, and Germany, Canada was no more—and perhaps hardly less—willing than the United Kingdom or the United States to be committed to war as a means of maintaining the settlement. The policy of appeasement—if it could be called a policy—was one that was not resisted by the Canadian Government of the day, and the Munich agreement brought in Canada, as in other countries not immediately affected, a sigh of relief that peace had not been broken.

So far as the Second World War was a result of the failure of the collective system, it was caused by the cautious policy shared by Canada with the Great Powers with which she had been most closely associated; for, unlike the period before 1914, the Canadian Government had had the means of participating actively in world affairs. Not only had it been demonstrated that United Kingdom policy could be influenced by Canadian views, but the League of Nations afforded a forum where small powers as well as large could and did raise their voices on matters of general interest. Furthermore, Canada in the inter-war period was achieving both the constitutional position and the machinery that would enable her to conduct relations with other powers directly rather than through United Kingdom channels. Separate representation at the Peace Conference was followed in 1923 by establishment of another precedent when a Canadian plenipotentiary alone negotiated and signed a fisheries agreement with the United States. This procedure was regularized by the Imperial Conference of 1923. In 1926 a further Imperial Conference put on record the equality of status of the self-governing countries of the Commonwealth in foreign as well as domestic affairs, and the Statute of Westminster in 1931 removed certain anomalies so that the legal position would accord with the political position. A small diplomatic service was begun with the establishment of a legation in Washington in 1927. Appropriately, it was by decision of her own Parliament that Canada entered the Second World War.

Even more than the First, the Second World War hastened Canada's participation in external affairs, since in the First War the emphasis was on constitutional status, and in the Second on function. Left for more than a year as the sole active belligerents against Germany and her allies, the countries of the Commonwealth were obliged to act with speed in the diplomatic sphere as well as in military and industrial matters. Canada was, in fact, during that time the second in importance of the states opposing Nazi conquest. One of the early needs was a more complete diplomatic service. Supplementing the long-established office in London, high commissioners were sent to the other Dominions and to Newfoundland. Missions were opened in South America, and temporary consulates in Greenland and in St. Pierre and Miquelon. By 1945, besides complete representation in other parts of the Commonwealth, there were thirteen embassies, two legations, a military mission in Berlin, and three consulates. In that year, too, Canada was represented at twenty-seven international conferences and meetings. During the same period the Department of External Affairs, which had been very small before the war, grew rapidly to meet the even greater increase of work.

In the war and post-war periods, when the uncertainties of her status in world affairs had been removed, it becomes easier to analyse Canada's foreign policy. In a public lecture in 1947 the

Secretary of State for External Affairs defined the principles of Canadian policy and their application.[5] For the first, he gave the rule that external policy should not destroy national unity; then followed belief in the conception of political liberty, respect for the rule of law, an appreciation of human values, and willingness to accept international responsibilities. Applying these principles, Mr. St. Laurent touched first on the position of Canada within the Commonwealth, which should be preserved "as an instrument through which we, with others who share our objectives, can co-operate for our common good in peace as in war." Secondly, he drew attention to the importance of maintaining good relations with the United States and accepting responsibility as a North American nation without believing that the continent could live unto itself. The support of French recovery is a Canadian interest, not only out of sympathy but because of its value to Canada. The application of a belief in international organization had been shown by active participation in many of those organizations.

It will be observed that these principles are traditional, that they can be found at work in earlier periods. The differences, as compared with earlier periods, are two: the very fact that by 1947 it was considered to be appropriate so to analyse the principles of policy; and the solid relationships of these principles to Canadian responsibilities and capacities. A good example of the latter is the attitude of Canada to the United Nations Organization. Whereas, in the past, the Canadian Government had tended to emphasize the danger of commitments in the League of Nations, it now evidenced willingness to accept a wide responsibility in the new international body. A firm definition of this attitude was made by the Secretary of State for External Affairs in a statement of October 1, 1947, when Canada was elected to the Security Council. Many questions might arise, he declared, "having their origins far away from our shores. At first glance these might not appear to affect directly the interests of the Canadian people." So far, however, as they were factors in world security, they were "of first importance to the future of this country."

The obligations and responsibilities involved in election to the Council had already been faced by a Canada more conscious than ever before of the relation between authority and responsibility. The first was emphasized by Prime Minister Mackenzie King in the summer of 1944, when the future United Nations Organization was being sketched. Representation on the proposed Council (as on other international bodies) should, he argued, be based not on the unreal distinction between great and small powers, but on the "functional idea." It was the power of contributing towards peace that mattered, not an arbitrary listing. The other side of the picture—responsibility—came up at the San Francisco Conference with reference to the proposal that the Security Council could call upon all members of the United Nations to participate in the imposition of sanctions. The Canadian delegation took the view that states should be able to participate in the formulation of decisions that would lead to the employment of their armed forces, and proposed an amendment to that effect. The result was Article 44 of the Charter.[6] Here is a marked contrast in tone with the Canadian policy of twenty-five years before with respect to Article 10 of the Covenant.

The same contrast may be seen in the drawing up of the treaties of peace. An expert delegation, well provided with preparatory studies, found that the procedure at the Paris Conference held in the summer of 1946 made little provision for general discussion of the treaties. This experience led the Government to propose that there should be a more satisfactory method for constructing the all-important treaty with Germany. The Government's object was not—as it had once largely been—to secure an admission of Canada's status, but rather to take an active part in the making of clauses that would in the future affect its own affairs. In a submission to the special deputies of the foreign ministers, the Government claimed that the Canadian people, even if they so desired, could not isolate themselves from the question of a German peace settlement. Their vital concern with wars originating in Europe had been demonstrated twice in a generation, and distance could give them no escape from the consequences of a bad peace. The body of the submission that followed was an expression of preliminary views on the principles that should be followed in the settlement.[7]

We see, therefore, that national maturity brought no fundamental change in the interests of Canada in world affairs or in the principles on which her policy had been based. The change consisted rather in a growing appreciation of the necessity of assuming responsibility for the pursuit and maintenance of interests and principles already deeply embedded in the country's historical development.

CHAPTER XXII

The North Atlantic Triangle

BY JOHN BARTLET BREBNER

JUST AFTER Christmas, 1897, John Hay, the American Ambassador in London, sent off to General John Watson Foster, international lawyer and occasional diplomat in Washington, a gossipy, confidential note about the recent collapse of negotiations for the control of pelagic sealing in the Pacific: "They frankly avow their slavery to Canada and chafe under it," he said, referring to the British diplomats, "and yet they rather resent our talking to Canada directly, and make this a pretext for declining adhesion to the Convention. . . . It is far more to Canada's advantage than ours to be on good terms with us. Lord Salisbury, in a private conversation the other day, compared her to a coquettish girl with two suitors, playing off one against the other. I should think a closer analogy would be to call her a married flirt, ready to betray John Bull on any occasion, but holding him responsible for all her follies."[1]

Most Canadians would have been startled had they known of the characterizations of their national policy which came so nonchalantly from Lord Salisbury and so waspishly from Mr. Hay, for, as they looked back into the past, it seemed to them that Great Britain had always found it easy and desirable to subordinate Canadian rights and aspirations to Anglo-American understanding, and that British North Americans had been conspicuously unable to prevent this. Their catalogue of real or imagined grievances against Great Britain was a long one: surrender of territory and of important lines of communication by the divisions of the con-

1 For notes to chapter xxii see pages 582–584.

tinent which took place in 1763, in 1783, after the War of 1812, in 1842, and in 1846; the loss of a preferential market and the outright anti-imperialism which accompanied free trade; willingness to open their inshore Atlantic fisheries to Americans; unwillingness to press Canadian claims for compensation from the United States arising out of the Fenian menace of 1864–1871; and even the obvious preference for the United States over Canada as a field for migration and investment.

No doubt it would have been equitable for Canadians to set indispensable aid in their resistance to American expansionism over against the catalogue of failings, but the weakest in a trio of nations seldom thinks in that way. Because it can be abused, and has on occasion been abused, such a nation may conclude that it is always abused, and may cast about for ways by which it can make use of the interests of one of its powerful partners against those of the other. British North America had been doing just that with modestly increasing success from 1760 to the end of the nineteenth century.

It was no accident that both Great Britain and the United States had reached the stage of recognizing the "nuisance value" of Canada in 1897, for a new balance of the forces embracing all three was in rapid process of acknowledgement and adjustment. Ever since the Republic had won its independence of the Kingdom, perceptive minds on both sides had recognized that the two countries needed each other in many reciprocal ways, as market or supplier, as lender or borrower, and in avowed or tacit alliance to keep open commercial opportunity in areas which other powers would have liked to close to them. It had not been easy for most Americans or Britons to acknowledge this; they had fought the War of 1812 before they combined in the vast prohibition of the Monroe Doctrine; but, no matter how provocative politicians like Palmerston and Polk had been in their public utterances, differences over Texas, California, and Oregon had been settled with unexpected ease and promptness. Even the ominous situation which grew out of British contributions to the destructive activities of Southern sea raiders during the Civil War was terminated within six years, although the settlement required a humiliating and costly admission of wrongdoing in the face of rather exultant truculence.

In fact, the Treaty of Washington of 1871, by which Great Britain seemed for the first time to recognize the United States as a Great Power, was the corner-stone of the Anglo-American understanding which had slumbered for a decade or so, only to reëmerge during the clash of rival imperialisms in the Pacific during the 'eighties and to challenge all beholders during the increasing international tensions at the end of the century. In the process the United States began to formulate active and fairly consistent foreign policies, and Great Britain abruptly altered her own to a pattern which was clearly adjusted to the role which the United States was assuming on the international stage.

On the one hand, Great Britain was emerging from her isolation (which the Canadian, G. E. Foster, had in January, 1896, echoingly pronounced "splendid") because she needed friends. On the other hand, the United States, having erased the internal frontiers which had absorbed its energies for so long, discovered that it had made new frontiers in the Pacific and the Far East and that, in order to exert its powers there, its navy must possess, not only a short cut through the Isthmus of Panama, but mastery of the Caribbean Sea. By a rapid sequence of events between 1895 and 1903 which included American support of Venezuela in extorting territory from British Guiana, the South African War, the Spanish-American War, repression of Filipino rebellion, and monopolistic seizure by the United States of a canal route across the Isthmus of Panama, the world was notified that Mahan's writings on sea power were working like ferments in American foreign policy, that Great Britain and the United States were assisting each other's aims and palliating each other's offences, and that Great Britain, in order to seal this understanding, was willing to surrender her treaty rights and to bow to treatment which came close to dictation.

Canada's misfortune was to misinterpret this situation. She did so for quite understandable reasons. In the first place, the revival of British imperialism which began with Disraeli's Crystal Palace speech of June 24, 1872, and which overwhelmed Mr.

Gladstone, its avowed opponent, within a decade, had raised great hopes in Canada—hopes which were multiplied by the calculated imperial pageantry of Queen Victoria's jubilees of 1887 and 1897, by Rudyard Kipling's chanting verses, and by the "Rideau Hall set," or the Governor General's *entourage* at Ottawa.[2] Moreover, world prices ceased falling in 1895 and started upwards in 1896, bearing Canada towards unimagined prosperity after an ordeal of almost twenty-five years which had been so grim that no matter how many hundreds of thousands of immigrants poured in, almost enough of them and of their predecessors poured out to the United States to hold the population stationary. The new prosperity was keyed to the omnivorous British market, not to north-south traffic with the United States. From Pacific to Atlantic the water-ways and the railways, into which much of the national wealth had been poured, began to earn dividends for themselves and to bring wealth to Canadians by moving products (chiefly wheat) to the seaboard. Sir Wilfrid Laurier, the Prime Minister, boasted that whereas the nineteenth century had favoured the United States, the twentieth would favour Canada.

Canada's new confidence first revealed itself conspicuously, a year or so after John Hay's complaint to Foster, during the meetings in Quebec and Washington of a Joint High Commission which tried unsuccessfully to settle a great variety of differences among Great Britain, the United States, Canada, and Newfoundland. When Hay and the Americans offered the Canadians what Laurier himself said was "a very fair treaty" of the commercial reciprocity which Canada had been avidly pursuing since 1865, the proposal was rejected, with some self-gratification on the Canadian side over escape from dependence, and some angry surprise on the American. In the same mood and on the same occasions, the Canadian delegation failed to press for a settlement with the United States upon some port on the Lynn Canal from which they might cross the Alaska Panhandle to the now roaring gold-camps of the Klondike. Apparently they expected Great Brittain to secure this for them as a makeweight during her impending retreat from the Isthmus of Panama and the Caribbean, but when they failed to obtain that help, they went ahead anyway with a strained claim of their own, only to encounter in the *manner* of the boundary award of 1903 an outrageous, unnecessary, and successful piece of bullying at the hands of Theodore Roosevelt with which Great Britain found it politic to connive.

This rude lesson in power politics coincided with the beginnings of what might be called the resistant phase in Canada's assertion of external as well as internal autonomy. During it, Canada, whether personified by the Liberal Prime Minister, Laurier, or the Conservative, Sir Robert Borden, stubbornly repelled increasingly urgent British assumptions that Canada's course in the world could be controlled by centralized British or British imperial direction. As chapter vi, "The Twentieth Century" (pp. 129 ff.), reveals, this was a difficult course to follow, particularly during the South African War, the crisis of 1912–1913 in Anglo-German naval rivalry, and the mounting stringency of the First World War; but until 1917 the determining factor in the Canadian balance of forces was the resistance of the defensive French-Canadian minority to action which might be construed as forwarding merely British interests, and both Laurier and Borden dextrously accommodated their procedures to this substantial portion of their electoral mandates.

Actually, it would seem, the civilization and culture of the United States then constituted a more serious threat to French-Canadian values than did the international position of Great Britain, but the scattered voices which were raised in warning against American ways were drowned out by the furore of the anti-British "nationalists" in Quebec. In addition, the United States had helped to lull apprehensions by an abrupt swing away from Roosevelt's bludgeoning into dignified acceptance of Canada as a distinct international entity in a permanent International Joint Commission of 1909 for the judicial regulation of the use of the lakes and rivers which they shared, and in the conclusive settlement by the Permanent Court of Arbitration at The Hague in 1910 of the conflicting claims to the North Atlantic fisheries. Even after Canada had exultantly rejected, by the spectacular process of a general election in 1911, a legislative agreement for Canadian-American commercial reciprocity which President Taft had driven through Congress at the cost of a special session, the United States allowed the statute to remain on the books for another decade.

If Canada declared her independence of the United States in 1911, and of Great Britain in 1912 when the Liberal majority in the Senate refused to approve a contribution to the British navy except after another general election which the Conservative Prime Minister, R. L. Borden, decided not to risk, the coming of war in August, 1914, ended her luxury of mere negation.[3] Of the Canadian people, 55 per cent were of British origin; 12 per cent were British-born; and the 28 per cent of French origin knew that Great Britain had stepped to the side of France. Even though many French Canadians condemned France for the worldliness and anticlericalism which had characterized her since the parting in 1763, a singularly unanimous Canada plunged into the war on a scale which was to bring strain within two years, strain which became focused on the increasing discrepancy between French-Canadian and British-Canadian support of the war effort, and which culminated in deep schism.

Canada surprised herself and outside observers by the magnitude of her contributions of men, money, and goods to the First World War. Long before the war ended, it had become obvious that Canada's growth and initiative had made her a national entity which must be internationally recognized. If Laurier had ushered Canada into the community of nations, it was Borden who had to make them recognize her—no easy task where Great Britain and the United States were concerned, for they were so obsessed by the exercise and the interplay of their preëminence in the world that they could seldom direct undivided attention to the adulthood of their junior partner. Nonetheless, Borden drove himself to the limit of his energies and achieved success.[4]

At a meeting of the Imperial War Cabinet on the afternoon of December 30, 1918, Borden, after listening to a "violent invective" against President Wilson by Prime Minister W. M. Hughes of Australia, "expressed the opinion that it would be most regrettable to enter the Peace Conference with any feeling of antagonism towards President Wilson or the United States . . . and I repeated that the best asset we could bring home from the war would be future good relations between the British Empire and the United States." Those good relations must be accompanied by precise and formalized recognitions of a sovereign Canada, and Borden had to fight hard to secure these.

In his relations with Great Britain, Borden had to contradict every British assumption that Canada would take orders, whether this involved the political education of his Governor General, the Duke of Connaught, or angry instruction of the New Brunswick–born Chancellor of the Exchequer, Mr. Andrew Bonar Law.[5] He had to assert and exercise Canada's extra-territorial sovereignty in military and naval affairs and lay the ground for its formal recognition within the Commonwealth in 1929 and 1931.[6] He had to check the attempts of the British Government to requisition Canadian shipping[7] and to reject a plan for coördinated imperial naval defence which the Admiralty had worked out by mid-1918 and continued to press unavailingly for another couple of years with singular indifference to, or unawareness of, Canadian policy. Among British statesmen, only Lloyd George and Lord Milner seemed capable of recognizing, and retaining as a factor in their habitual thought and action, the complete sovereignty which Canada was exacting as her right.

Washington was another matter; in fact, the masters of the New York money-market seemed to see more Canadians and to have a far more active interest in their problems than did the national administration. With the entry of the United States into the war in April, 1917, however, the pattern began rapidly to change. By October of that year Borden was bringing to a head his efforts to secure British approval for specifically Canadian diplomatic representation at Washington, efforts which produced the Canadian War Mission of February 2, 1918, and were to produce the joint announcement in the British and Canadian parliaments, on May 10, 1920, that Canada would in future have a Minister Plenipotentiary of her own at Washington who would also act for the British Ambassador in his absence. This diplomatic representation did not become actual until 1927 (with the substitution for the British Ambassador withdrawn), but Borden's point had been made.[8]

During the excitement of the war-years, and particularly while he was keyed up by membership in the small Imperial War Cabinet and the British Empire delegation at Versailles, Borden sometimes "talked big" with his British and American associates. Thus on August 13, 1918, Lloyd George "suggested that we should take over the West Indies and I acquiesced," and on February 3, 1919, he seriously discussed with George Louis Beer, the American expert on dependent territories, the exchange of the Alaska Panhandle for some West Indian islands.[9] The grim aspect of the relationship with the United States, however, was economic: the fact that Canada bought and borrowed more in the United States than she sold and lent there, and that only when Great Britain was capable of paying in negotiable exchange for her adverse trade balance with Canada could the latter pay her bills in New York. Fortunately or unfortunately, New York and Washington were eager to lend in 1917 and subsequent years, so that Canadians of the Borden era caught only a glimpse of what has been overwhelmingly their greatest economic problem since 1929.[10]

London and Washington had to be brought together to serve as Canada's sponsors in the international community, and this again was Borden's achievement, with Lloyd George and Milner helping to overawe (temporarily) the incredulous British Foreign Office and to find a place in President Wilson's busy mind for the novel idea of Canada acting as a national entity. The long, difficult process involved plenipotentiary membership in the Peace Conference, signing the peace, holding up the King's ratification until his Canadian Parliament had authorized it on behalf of Canada, and membership in the Assembly of the League of Nations and in the International Labour Organization. In several senses its symbolic peak was the signature, on May 6, 1919, by Clemenceau, Wilson, and Lloyd George of a declaration that "upon the true construction of the first and second paragraphs of that Article [IV of the League of Nations Covenant], representatives of the self-governing Dominions of the British Empire may be selected or named as members of the Council."[11] In A. G. Dewey's words, "Dominion nationalism emerged from the shelter of the Imperial Conferences, where it had enjoyed the privacy of a strictly family matter, and asserted itself before an international assembly."

The attainment of recognized international autonomy in 1919 opened a new phase in Canadian statehood, for henceforth the responsibility for, and consequences of, action or inaction must be accepted by Canada herself, no matter how habitual and tempting it might be to ascribe them to others. Yet, though the formalities of the triangular relationship with Great Britain and the United States had changed, and the actual balance of forces among the three had significantly altered, Canada was not powerful enough to bend either, let alone both, of her partners to her will, except occasionally by the old technique of playing one against the other. The "sound sense of the possible," which one Canadian historian[12] sees as the core of his country's survival, was to be variously tested during the next twenty years. The beginning of that period was exhilarating; the middle was humiliating; the end was heroic.

The most conspicuous discrepancy among the parties to the triangle was that Great Britain and Canada were members of the League of Nations, whereas the United States was not. Translated into superficial terms, this meant that the two former were supporters of "collective security" and the last was "isolationist." By 1922, however, only Great Britain acted as if "collective security" meant some commitment to positive action, and even she was more conspicuous for unburdening herself of old and new responsibilities. She was prepared to invest some of her energies in the League if it showed signs of working to stabilize the kind of world which it was in her interest to have. Canada acted as if the peaceful world she wanted had been created by the fact of the League and needed no help from her except advice. The United States tried to act as if there was very little world beyond its own boundaries. British isolationism came partly from the taxpayers' inability and refusal to countenance much expenditure abroad in any cause, and partly from sheer wishful suppression of the knowledge that isolation was impossible for Great Britain. American isolationism had deep roots in the escape from Europe of most of the people and in their very recent and insufficient realization of the inadequacy of the Atlantic and Pacific oceans as insulators against large political disturbances which began beyond them. Canada, as a North American state, tapped much the same roots, and the ties of sympathy and interest between part of her people and those of Great Britain were heavily offset by the apathy and even the hostility of other parts.

The exhilaration of Canada's course from 1918 to 1931 came largely from telling the mother country what the Dominion would not do. Although during that time Canadians were compensating for their material inferiority to the United States by a conviction of moral superiority, frequently it proved convenient to reinforce the Canadian case with Great Britain or in the League by stating that it harmonized with American wishes, and that Anglo-American understanding would be a blessing all round. This would have been even more exhilarating if Canada had been able to influence the United States either positively or negatively, but that was too much to expect in any large sense. Yet the Pacific Halibut Treaty of 1923 marked a necessary advance. This treaty was negotiated between the United States and Canada directly, and Canada succeeded in preventing the British Ambassador at Washington from signing it. Her view that her own negotiator was sufficient was accepted at an Imperial Conference of that year, but the Senate and the State Department of the United States took some time to adjust their procedures to this new, independent sovereignty of Canada. Once the step had been taken, however, it proved simple enough, subsequently, for Canada to act as a sovereign entity with the United States in treaties, conventions, and executive agreements on a variety of matters, ranging from the conservation of wild life to the development of the St. Lawrence water-way and even to quasi-military understandings.

It is in these mixed lights that Canadian international behaviour between the wars should be seen. Canada fought Article X of the League Covenant (the guaranty of territorial integrity and existing political independence) from March, 1919, until she was defeated at the League session of 1923. She refused to become involved in Anglo-Turkish relations without consideration of the whole matter by her Parliament. She successfully opposed the draft Treaty of Mutual Guaranty and the Geneva Protocol in 1924 and 1925, largely on the expressed grounds that they would make her relations with the United States difficult. In 1925, Article IX of the Locarno Treaty was drafted so as to excuse Canada from obligations unless she chose to assume them, and the leader of the Conservative Opposition, Arthur Meighen, carried the case for avoidance of commitments to its limit by urging that the dispatch of Canadian troops overseas be prohibited unless it were authorized by Parliament after a general election on the issue.[13]

It is probable that an event of 1921–1922 may have contributed substantially to Canada's confident withdrawal from precise responsibilities. In 1921 Great Britain proposed to renew the Anglo-Japanese alliance, and had won the support of the other Dominions and India at a summer conference in London, when Meighen of Canada, a minority of one, successfully opposed it. He did so by reviving a proposal which he had made in February, only to have it turned down by Winston Churchill, then Colonial Secretary. Meighen argued that, although the alliance had been drafted so as to preclude an Anglo-American war, and had been modified to meet the requirements of the League of Nations, it was objectionable to Canada and to the United States on much the same grounds, notably because it gave tacit approval to Japan's recent political and economic aggression against China. A multi-lateral Pacific agreement would be in closer harmony with the League of Nations idea. Why not shelve the alliance in favour of a multi-power Pacific conference which might well tempt the United States from its isolation, thereby reviving Anglo-American understanding for the sake of world order (and Canada's deliverance from anxiety)?

When Lloyd George decided that that gamble was justified, he persuaded the Conference to reverse itself, and opened negotiations with Washington which briefly preceded the efforts of Charles Evans Hughes, the American Secretary of State, to bring about a Pacific conference. By the summer of 1922 a series of multi-power treaties had effected substantial naval disarmament and ratios of naval armament among the Great Powers, as well as an agreement to respect existing rights in the Pacific, to settle future disputes by joint action, to respect the sovereign independence and territorial integrity of China, and to uphold the principle of the Open Door. In this whole matter, Canadians little more than glimpsed an intricate interplay of political power in which their North American position had endowed them with leverage on London and, indirectly, on Washington, which was far beyond normal expectations. Moreover, a general election in 1921 replaced Meighen by a distinctly more cautious Prime Minister in Mr. Mackenzie King. The significance of the incident to Canada, therefore, was that it contributed to an already rather uncritical reliance on collective security which involved little beyond correct sentiments from Canada.

The matter to which Canadians were devoting their unremitting attention between the wars was their position in an economic triangle the component corners of which kept changing in character and strength. The First World War had accelerated the decrease in the relative strength of Great Britain, which had begun about 1873, into an absolute decline which reached the point of inroads on capital by 1938. The same war had stimulated American extractive and industrial productivity for export to such astounding heights that the United States had been transformed from a substantial debtor nation to an immense creditor. Canada, although still with a debtor economy (now predominantly to the United States), had expanded productivity to a point which enabled her to finance the war mainly by internal borrowing and inflation and to look forward with some confidence to becoming a creditor economy.

Everything, however, depended upon the ability to export about one-third of Canadian production to a world in which most nations were trying to increase their economic self-sufficiency. Since Great Britain provided the striking exception, Canada tried to earn in that almost free market most of what she needed to meet her characteristic trade deficit with the United States. In Canada, manufacturing had outstripped agriculture in net value of production by 1920; it was soon pressing close to the net value of production in all primary production combined (agriculture, forestry, fisheries, trapping, mining, and electric power); and it surpassed that total in 1940. That meant that Canada was herself processing grains, meats, fish, milk, timber, and ores on the one hand, but also that she was building automobiles and other complex manufactures on the other. Yet, even when her production of gold and her large takings from American tourists were added to her American receipts from news-print, nickel, food-stuffs, and so on, the more productive Canada became, the greater was her deficit with the United States. The principal single cause for this anomaly lay in an intricate complex of geographical and other factors which made Canada deficient in coal and petroleum and kept her iron and steel industries much less efficient and versatile than those of her neighbour. A busy Canada meant enormous imports of coal and petroleum, and of crude, semi-processed, and manufactured American iron and steel.

The situation was made worse by the stubborn way in which the United States clung to an almost prohibitive protectionism and to other forms of economic nationalism which lagged behind its altered circumstances. Not until the War of 1939 was nearing its end did the American Government systematically endeavour to shape comprehensive economic policies appropriate to the international position which the United States had obviously attained by 1918. Between the wars, Republican administrations evoked world-wide tariff retaliation by the increasingly prohibitive American structures of 1921, 1922, 1930, and 1932. Canada reciprocated in self-defence and, after a failure in 1930 to persuade Great Britain to adopt high-tariff protection as the basis for a system of imperial preference, got her way at the Ottawa Conference after the American increases of 1932.

The United States elected the Democrats late in that year, however, and in 1934 began trying to buy its way back into the Canadian and British markets through tariff concessions. These, in the form of three bilateral trade treaties, had, by 1938, begun to restore a beneficial flow of goods in the North Atlantic Triangle. By that time Anglo-American trade, after a century and a half of unchallenged preëminence, was being surpassed in magnitude by Canadian-American trade. Yet if, as the Second World War was speedily to demonstrate, Great Britain could not indefinitely enable Canada to balance her payments in the United States, either Canada would have to learn how to buy less from the United States or the United States would have to learn how to buy more from Canada. After all, the hospitable British market, backed by Britain's solvent position before 1938, had been the mightiest single factor in the greatest economic triangle on earth.

The great shock and subsidence in the international economy which occurred in 1929, and which clouded the succeeding decade, opened a phase of brigandage in international politics during which the discrepancy between Canadian desires and Canadian powers was humiliating. In rapid succession, tyrannical oligarchies led Japan, Italy, and Germany into careers of cumulative aggression in defiance of existing political arrangements. When outraged Canadians turned confidently to the machinery of collective security for remedy, they discovered that it would not work, largely because their powerful American and British associates would not make it work.

Manchuria and Abyssinia provided two vivid demonstrations. In regard to the former, Canada started out in a righteous, assured way at the special Assembly of the League in 1932, only to find that Great Britain and the United States would neither act singly nor together to curb Japan, thereby crippling the League. The subsequent somersault in Canadian policy at Geneva bewildered the Canadian public and embarrassed the Conservative Government which had failed to prepare them for it. After the Italian attack on Abyssinia, the same Government began by vigorously supporting a strong effort to stop Italy through internationally maintained sanctions. Then, when the Baldwin Government in Great Britain went deliberately counter to the recently expressed wishes of its own people and bowed to Mussolini's threats by declining to risk its navy (and American understanding) in making the sanctions effective, the succeeding Liberal Canadian Government was left even higher and drier than before. As W. A. Mackintosh remarked of Canada, early in the summer of 1939, "Yet in large measure she is still on the world's circumference. She can support world policy better than she can initiate."[14]

From 1935 to 1939 Canadian humiliation deepened until it hardened into a sad determination to aid Great Britain if the latter decided to do something to stop the rot. The United States, in spite of Roosevelt's persistent efforts to educate his people internationally, embarked on a legislative orgy designed to make neutrality, a policy as old as their nation, absolutely certain at an unimaginable (and impossible) cost. Great Britain descended from the shame of the Hoare-Laval Pact, through the odious farce of non-intervention in Spain, to the indecencies of Munich. In spite of the fact that in 1936 and 1938 Roosevelt had pointedly offered to extend the protective mantle of the United States over Canada, the available evidence indicates that the Canadian Cabinet was ready to accept the arbitrament of war had Great Britain chosen it in September, 1938. The political leaders of French Canada, of course, were in a difficult position because of the patent hostility of the vast majority of their people to any positive implication in events beyond Canada's borders, but they knew that, while Canada possessed the right of neutrality, a policy of neutrality had become impossible.

On March 30, 1939, Prime Minister Mackenzie King summed up Canada's agonized acceptance of the impossibility of isolation in a sentence which already seems to have become the classical statement: "The idea that every twenty years this country should automatically and as a matter of course take part in a war overseas for democracy or self-determination of other small nations, that a country which has all it can do to run itself should feel called upon to save, periodically, a continent that cannot run itself, and to these ends risk the lives of its people, risk bankruptcy and political disunion, seems to many a nightmare and sheer madness."

After war came to Great Britain on September 3, the Canadian Parliament met and on September 10, with virtual unanimity, empowered the Crown to declare war in behalf of Canada. A prophetic quatrain by Charles Mair, written seventy years before the event, had come true with remarkable precision.

First feel throughout the throbbing land
  A nation's pulse, a nation's pride—
The independent life—then stand
  Erect, unbound, at Britain's side.

Simultaneously, although President Roosevelt invoked American neutrality with all its legislative trappings, his administration and the Congress began their inevitable, long, and furious retreat from neutrality, which stretched from the Pittman Act of November 4, 1939, legalizing "cash-and-carry" sales of munitions, to the disaster at Pearl Harbor in December, 1941. Isolationist sentiment might be real enough in Great Britain, Canada, and the United States, and the United States might be strong enough in its own right to persist in isolationism longer than its principal associates, but the national lives of all three depended on positive action to preserve their interests in an integrated world.

Soon after the United States had war thrust upon it as the consequence of its extraordinary interpretations of neutrality, A. L. Burt summed up Canada's position in the North Atlantic Triangle as never more than "a limited independence." Of this she preserved more than she lost when, "with sound instinct, she rejected American neutrality for British belligerency in September, 1939," and so avoided the "doubly humiliating course" of first deserting Great Britain and then tagging back to the rescue "at the heels of the United States." In brief, Burt concluded, "the tragic events that have made us all see the vital dependence of Canada upon the United States" at the same time revealed not only "the vital dependence of Britain upon the United States, but also of the United States upon Britain."[15]

The interplay among Canada, the United States, and Great Britain since September, 1939, cannot be described or interpreted with assurance. An immense amount seems to be known; certain large patterns of development appear obvious; and yet it is clear from the Canadian point of view that some crucial events are still shrouded in secrecy and that both Great Britain and the United States are capable of new policies, or of shifts in old policies, which may be of secondary importance to the major partners and yet by their direct, or even incidental, impact may necessitate rapid, far-reaching adjustments in Canada's course.

The coöperation of the three states in war was probably unique in history and it has probably remained so since the war ended. The great precipitant was the fear which descended upon North America as German armies swept over Europe in the summer of 1940, barred only by an unconquerable Britain, with Canada as her most substantial ally. After Dunkirk, the United States instantly rearmed the almost unarmed troops in Great Britain. In July the United States, Argentina, and Great Britain contrived understandings which enabled the American republics at the Havana Conference to combine as never before, politically and economically. In August Canada and the United States created the Permanent Joint Board on Defence to "consider in the broad sense the defence of the north half of the Western Hemisphere."

And in September Great Britain gave to the United States leases for bases in Newfoundland and Bermuda and leased six others in the West Indies in exchange for fifty much-needed destroyers, promising that she would never scuttle or surrender her navy. Meanwhile Canada had taken Newfoundland and Labrador under her wing and was embarking on the extraordinary development of her armed services which gradually awarded her the chief responsibility for North Atlantic convoys by sea and air; saw her troops distinguish themselves greatly in China, Alaska, Italy, and western Europe; and contributed at least a quarter of the combined British air effort against Europe.

By December, 1940, Roosevelt had outlined to the public the remarkable instrument known as Lend-Lease which may have had British precedents reaching back centuries, and contemporary examples in Canadian arrangements for supplying Great Britain, but which surpassed both in its outright, explicit character. On March 11, 1941, it became law and was operating within five minutes, after having been furiously debated in and out of Congress. A month later, Canada, who had refused Lend-Lease for herself and was in a number of ways, both absolutely and relative to her economic dimensions, contributing more to the cause than the United States was as yet equipped to do, negotiated an agreement at Hyde Park to get around her shortage of American dollars by selling more to the United States and by working up materials in Canada on the Anglo-American Lend-Lease account. In May, while Crete was being conquered, the first American merchantman, the *Robin Moor,* was sunk, and Roosevelt declared an unlimited national emergency. June saw Hitler's attack on Russia. In July the United States began to take over from Great Britain and Canada the defence of Iceland, to which it had already begun convoying American supplies. In August Churchill and Roosevelt issued the Atlantic Charter. In September a fight took place between an American destroyer and a German submarine in Icelandic waters. In October one American destroyer was damaged in battle there and another was sunk. In November Congress repealed the Neutrality Act, and on December 7 Japan attacked the American fleet at Pearl Harbor, initiating the formal state of war to which Germany and Italy subscribed four days later.

Accompanying and following these events was an almost unreserved pooling of American, British, and Canadian energies and capacities in men, money, production, transportation, economic warfare, technology, and research, which was conducted by a great variety of joint committees towards the single end of supreme efficiency, with little more than book-keeping attention to individual national shares. The Alaska Highway, air-routes, and oil pipe-lines were built across Canada, and Canadian uranium entered the dark secrecy of the triangular enterprise which culminated in awful fashion at Hiroshima and Nagasaki in August, 1945. Before the war ended, the three partners had committed themselves to the United Nations organizations which embraced their virtually unanimous ideas and hopes for a more peaceful world. The United States and Canada had emerged from war more powerful than ever before. Great Britain was so weakened and dependent that her North American offspring, independently and together, set about relieving her by unparalleled cancellations of indebtedness, refunding, and new loans.

Out of this welter of circumstances, certain broad Canadian problems emerged—the political status, the economic situation, and the strategic considerations which would determine her potential in the North Atlantic Triangle.

It seemed significant that Canada had little or no trouble with the United States about her political status, but a good deal with Great Britain. Roosevelt and his administrations revealed a sure but delicate touch in dealing with Canada, and Canada more than lived up to American expectations by scrupulously careful procedures, including repurchases of American installations, which absolved her from material obligations to the United States.

Understandably enough, Churchill and his lieutenants were much less deft. On the whole, the embarrassment of dependence seemed to strengthen British assumptions of superiority over Canada. Churchill had been very blunt with Canada as long before as Meighen's campaign of 1921 against the Anglo-Japanese alliance, but had been overridden by Lloyd George. When Churchill became Prime Minister in 1940, he subordinated everything, Canada included, to securing the alliance of the United States. He announced that he preferred the term "Empire" to "Commonwealth," and when he negotiated the Destroyer-Bases Agreement he conspicuously ignored Canada, in spite of the responsibilities which she had assumed in Newfoundland. In his great speeches of report to Parliament and the world, Canadians seldom found what seemed to them their due, or found it inextricably wrapped up in the British package. Canadian airmen, for instance, struggled in vain throughout the war to reveal anything like the true proportions of their activities, for the records of these were not separated from those of the British.[16]

Then, in January, 1944, Field Marshal Smuts and Lord Halifax opened a bold campaign to consolidate the British Commonwealth and Empire into "the fourth power in that group upon which, under Providence, the peace of the world will henceforth depend."[17] Within a week Mr. Mackenzie King had flatly declined the proposal: "With what is implied in the argument employed by both these eminent public men, I am unable to agree. . . . We look forward . . . to close collaboration in the interests of peace not only inside the British Commonwealth, but also with all friendly nations, small as well as great."[18] There was no Imperial War Cabinet, as in 1917–1918, and the Imperial War Conference of May, 1944, tacitly rejected any move towards consolidation. Thus Canada was completely successful in preserving her formal independence of action unimpaired, but the threats to it had been almost exclusively British (except for some natural stupidities by Americans outside or below the administration), and this was not likely to be forgotten, particularly by the French Canadians.

Canada's post-war economic position speedily announced itself. Thanks primarily to enormous American purchases of Canadian securities and other forms of investment during the war, the immediate relationship seemed secure, but Canadian production was perhaps more than ever tied to the British market, while Canadian consumption was tied to American production through the natural determination of Canadians to enjoy the North American standard of living. Within two years this triangle of forces had made it necessary for Canada to curb purchases from the United States very widely by law. The situation was neatly summarized in *The Economist*:[19] "Canada must, for the foreseeable future, come to depend much more heavily on exports to the United States. . . . The American market has proved unstable in the past; it *may* prove so again. But the British market, and other traditional markets abroad, *must* prove unstable. They cannot afford to pay the amount and the kind of money that Canadians will, in the long run, insist on getting." The United States, by the Geneva Agreements of 1947 and other actions, was showing distinct signs of willingness to accommodate Canada, but no one knew how shifts in party policies might delay or alter this natural and mutually advantageous development in American policy.

Unquestionably, Canada's strategic position, in an age when the armed power of the United States was conceived in terms of the shortest air- and sea-routes across the North Atlantic, the North Pacific, and the North Pole, had much to do with increased American awareness of, and considerateness towards, Canada. The fact that the world's best deposits of uranium were at Great Bear Lake heightened that interest. Canada's response took the form (so far as the public knew) of cordial military, naval, and air co-operation, combined with thorough formal protection of her sovereignty. At the diplomatic level the United States treated Canada circumspectly, but elsewhere the situation was confused because, while Americans found it unnatural to think of Canadians as foreigners and were astoundingly hospitable to them in the United States, Canadians were much more sensitive about Americans in Canada and were determined not to be taken for granted by Americans anywhere.

Reduced to their extreme terms, Dominion problems of status, economics, and strategy seemed to pose the question whether or not Canada was becoming a quasi-protectorate of the United States, primarily because of the decline of Great Britain. Naturally, therefore, Canada made strenuous efforts to avoid being left with only one string to her bow. During the war she was conspicuous in her exertions to cultivate friendly relations with the Latin American countries, exchanging diplomatic representatives with them and even flirting with the Pan American Union. To French Canadians in particular, there was considerable appeal in the idea of getting moral support from fellow-Latins and Roman Catholics instead of from Great Britain in resisting engulfment by the

United States.[20] Yet, as other chapters of this volume indicate, Pan-Americanism, even as a device for offsetting the United States, was not strong enough in Canada to produce results in practical politics. Moreover, the American administration had made it tolerably clear that it would be happier if Canada remained outside the Pan American Union.

The United Nations Organization, therefore, afforded a distinctly more attractive arena, and by September, 1947, Canada had progressed from her rather diffident beginnings at San Francisco to the point of deciding to put her active energies and aspirations into that body. Mr. Louis St. Laurent, Minister of External Affairs, in effect gave public notice that Canada had decided against Pan-Americanism, would embark on positive peace-making rather than on merely passive or critical policy in the United Nations, and would seek election to the Security Council. On receiving that election, Canada at once began to assume its onerous responsibilities, in spite of the obvious inclination of the major powers to unload disproportionate duties on the smaller powers because of their own inability to agree. If Canada persisted in this course, it was believed, she could avoid the loss of the habit of initiative which is usually the concomitant of subordination, and could gain an international prestige which would serve her well in relations with the United States.

Yet it would be a mistake to conclude that the North Atlantic Triangle has ceased to operate for Canada. In spite of the ethnic dualism that makes her a nation-state rather than a nation, she is very strongly tied by bonds of tradition, gratitude, and interest to Great Britain, and she will continue to make sacrifices towards British survival and revival. Imponderable though the consideration may seem to outsiders, it is from the mere existence of Great Britain that a large and powerful proportion of the Canadian peoples extract the essence of their cherished conviction that they are British, not United States, Americans.

CHAPTER XXIII

Trade and the World Economy

BY FRANK A. KNOX

THE HIGH LIVING STANDARD of Canadians is the result of their practice of large-scale methods in exploiting the rich natural resources of the country.[1] The products of Canadian farms, forests, and mines are marketed abroad in such large amounts that before the war Canada supplied 40 per cent of the world's wheat exports, two-thirds of its news-print, and 40 per cent of its non-ferrous metals.[2] On the other hand (see chap. ii, "The Geography," pp. 47 ff.), the country imports coal, oil, and iron and steel products in unusually large amounts to maintain the variety in consumption which high living standards imply. For the high export income which makes such heavy importing possible, Canada depends upon a healthy world economy. In the past she has also relied on other countries for much of the capital which has made possible the large-scale production that is needed for the economical development of her natural resources.

The relatively heavy dependence upon foreign trade in a few raw-material and food products brings with it a greater degree of fluctuation in national income than is common to countries whose natural resources are more diverse. Movements in the prices of the principal exports and imports may cause sharp changes in barter terms of trade. At times Canadians may be able to buy large amounts of imports with their exports, at others much less. Exporting countries are usually the first to suffer when world prosperity turns into depression; if they have borrowed heavily

[1] For notes to chapter xxiii see pages 584–585.

in the past and therefore have regular and relatively invariable interest and dividend payments to make to other countries, declines in export income are bound to reduce drastically the residue of foreign exchange which is available to pay for imports. Imports must thus fall with exports, and very soon bring to the whole economy a sharp recession in income and employment.

These difficulties Canada shares with all colonial economies. Usually, however, such countries are intimately related to but one industrial nation for markets and for capital, and thus escape a source of instability which has greatly afflicted Canada, especially in the period between the First and Second World Wars. Canada trades heavily with both the United States and the United Kingdom. It is true that much of the trade with each is complementary. With Britain, wheat is exchanged for textiles; and with the United States, news-print and non-ferrous metals for coal and iron. If trade with sterling and dollar countries came near to balancing, Canada might count herself more fortunate than those who must depend upon either alone. The fact is, however, that, while Canada buys much more than half of her imports from the United States, she sells to them much less than half of her exports. Most of Canada's exports go to the United Kingdom and other overseas countries which provide, in return, but a small part of Canada's imports. Thus Canada lives at one apex of the North Atlantic Triangle. Her economic fortunes are influenced not only by the direct currents of trade which pass between her and the other two points of that triangle, but also by the state of the traffic along the third side. Canada depends upon the sale in New York of her surplus sterling, gained from exports, to pay for the excess of imports from the United States. That the economic relationships between the sterling and the dollar areas should be such as to keep the value of sterling high in New York is, therefore, a vital matter for Canada.

The importance of this relationship is heightened by the fact that the whole trading economy of the Western world depends for its prosperity upon the power of these two great countries, Great Britain and the United States, to buy the goods produced by smaller nations and lend them the capital for economic development. To place exports more widely upon the markets of other countries would not, therefore, substantially lessen Canada's dependence upon them.

In the course of the nineteenth century the growing political and economic power of the United Kingdom made her the most important of the Great Powers. The application of the steam-engine to production and transportation transformed the basic conditions of economic life. But it was the world-wide imitation of the commercial and financial policies of the United Kingdom—private enterprise, freer trade, and an international gold standard, managed by the London money-market—which released the full productive potentialities of the new methods. In that release it was of critical importance that the expanding markets of the British Isles should be open to the exports of the new areas which British capital was developing. Even when, in the nineteenth century, the choice had to be made between free trade and the preservation of British agriculture in the form which it had had for centuries, the British people did not falter. They committed their fortunes unreservedly to trade with the group of nations which their commercial and financial skill had brought into existence and was maintaining successfully. They had attained not only the economic power and skills, but also the national attitudes required for world leadership.

To Britain as world centre the countries overseas were linked by ties of obvious mutual interest. They had perforce to accept the harsh discipline which free trade and the international gold standard sometimes imposed upon them. There was no other country to which they might turn for markets and capital for development. Few of them had much prospect of a decent standard of living otherwise than by foreign trade. Only to the United States, the most considerable partner in this international system, did this prospect of escape eventually open. For the first half of the nineteenth century the Americans bought and borrowed in Britain, sold their exports in British markets, and kept to a low-tariff policy as did other colonials. The Civil War not only stimulated the growth of manufacturing industry, but caused the erection of an enormous tariff wall behind which American manufacturing was to grow into one of the wonders of the age.

When the railways created an internal market so large that specialized production for it alone could bring the economies which British factories found only in production for a world market, a sure foundation was laid, for the first time in any country overseas, for an economy which might become largely independent of the world trading system which the British had built up. In the diverse and extended agricultural regions of their country Americans found most of the raw materials and food products which the British trader had to assemble from the ends of the earth. This area, occupied by one people, was so huge and so rich that the advantages which other countries might get only by means of an extensive commerce were here to be obtained from domestic trade alone. Thus it came about that, in the last quarter of the nineteenth century, when the British people were demonstrating their capacity for world leadership by committing their economic fortunes to the working of the international trading system which they had brought into being, there was growing up in the largest overseas partner in that economy not only the plain possibility of becoming independent of it, but also of eventually assuming by sheer economic weight the role of world leader. Into that position the United States was suddenly catapulted by the First World War; a Second World War has made its industry and financial power overwhelming.

Thus, in the leadership of the Western trading world, there has been substituted, for a country long experienced and adapted to that role by natural situation and the decisions of her people, a country with almost no qualifying experience, whose natural situation seems bound to give primacy to domestic rather than international considerations, and whose commercial policy has therefore been the very reverse of that required of the key country in a world trading system. In the inter-war period, while this transformation was in course, the world suffered from divided leadership. The ability and the desire to give guidance were divorced from the economic power which alone could have made it effective. It is perhaps not too much to say that this situation has dominated the trend of Canada's economic transactions abroad. The purpose of this chapter is to analyse briefly the changing trends of Canada's merchandise trade and in particular to relate them to this great change in the conditions under which international trade has been conducted since the beginning of the twentieth century.

The great boom in wheat which ushered in Canada's twentieth-century economic history was a typical nineteenth-century episode in colonial development, delayed until the farming areas to the south had been filled and reduction in transportation rates made it possible to export wheat profitably from the Canadian prairies. As the British market was the factor which induced this development, so from Britain came the capital which made it possible. In 1914 about three-fourths of the foreign capital invested in Canada was British. In the first decade of the century, from 50 to 60 per cent of Canada's exports were going to the British market.

TABLE 1

CANADA'S MERCHANDISE EXPORTS, 1900–1947
(Millions of dollars)

Year	To the United Kingdom	To the United States	To other countries	Total
1900 *	97	58	14	169
1914 †	215	163	53	432
1918	845	417	277	1,540
1920	489	464	286	1,239
1922	299	293	148	740
1926	508	480	332	1,321
1926 ‡	315	476	481	1,272
1929	224	519	435	1,178
1932	149	169	177	495
1937	385	391	265	1,041
1944	1,796	1,444	350	3,590
1945	1,422	1,134	918	3,474
1946	626	948	819	2,393
1947	750	1,059	914	2,723

SOURCES: See note 1, pp. 584–585. All amounts expressed to the nearest million.
* Fiscal year ending June 30.
† For the years 1914 through 1926, the data are based on the fiscal year ending March 31.
‡ For the years 1926 through 1947, the data are based on the calendar year.

Already, however, the growing industrialism of the United States was making itself felt. Apart from this alternative source of imports, most of Canada's purchases would have been made in Great Britain. Actually, only about 25 per cent were being made there, against 60 per cent in the United States. Indeed, the rising prosperity in the United States was tending to attract more of Canada's exports. By 1910 the downward trend in the percentage of exports going to the United Kingdom, which was to continue until 1930, was already under way. Though the unbalanced state of trade with the centre of the world economy was thus already evident, its future significance for Canada was obscured by Brittain's successful leadership of the world economy and in particular by the stability in the rates of exchange between the pound and the dollar which the gold standard and London's financial skill had maintained for decades.

TABLE 2

CANADA'S MERCHANDISE IMPORTS, 1900–1947
(Millions of dollars)

Year	From the United Kingdom	From the United States	From other countries	Total
1900	44	102	26	173
1914	132	396	91	619
1918	81	793	89	964
1920	126	801	137	1,065
1922	117	516	115	748
1926	164	609	155	927
1926	148	652	173	973
1929	188	875	209	1,272
1932	61	246	91	398
1937	148	463	165	776
1944	94	1,113	191	1,398
1945	100	1,119	223	1,442
1946	138	1,378	306	1,822
1947	182	1,951	402	2,535

SOURCES: See table 1.

During the First World War, European shortages, increased wartime demands, and the price inflation which accompanied them nearly quadrupled the value of Canada's exports, and arrested the trend away from the United Kingdom, which in 1917 received 64.5 per cent of the total—a level not attained again even in the Second World War. While the bulk of these exports consisted of foods and raw materials for the production of which the previous period of economic development had made preparation, a surprising proportion consisted of shells and explosives. Imports, mostly from the United States, made no such growth, though they reflected mainly consumer needs, since the relatively simple munitions and explosives industry did not make heavy demands for American parts and components.[3]

These temporary shifts in the proportions of Canadian trade with the centre of the world economy and its rising rival, the United States, were accompanied by a permanent change of great importance. Since war had closed the British market as a source of capital, Canada was forced to turn to the United States. Though contemporaries probably thought this change temporary, it proved to be permanent; never again did Canada resort to the British capital market on a large scale. In this very important particular,

TABLE 3

TOTAL BRITISH AND FOREIGN CAPITAL INVESTED IN CANADA, 1900–1946
(Millions of dollars)

Year	By Great Britain	By the United States	By all other countries	Total
1900	1,050.1	167.9	13.7	1,231.7
1907	1,345.5	345.4	49.8	1,740.7
1913	2,793.1	779.8	172.7	3,745.6
1914	2,778.5	880.7	177.7	3,836.9
1918	2,729.0	1,630.0	176.6	4,535.6
1921	2,493.5	2,260.3	152.2	4,906.0
1926	2,354.7	3,464.5	146.3	5,965.5
1930	2,766.3	4,659.5	188.0	7,613.8
1933	2,682.8	4,491.7	190.0	7,364.5
1939	2,475.9	4,151.4	286.0	6,913.3
1945	1,766.0	4,982.0	347.0	7,095.0
1946	1,645.0	5,135.0	350.0	7,130.0

SOURCES: The estimates for 1900–1913 are from Jacob Viner, *Canada's Balance of International Indebtedness, 1900–1913* (Harvard Univ. Press, 1924), as tabulated, along with the writer's estimates for 1914–1926, by F. A. Knox, "Canadian Capital Movements and the Canadian Balance of International Payments, 1900–1934," in Herbert Marshall *et al.*, *Canadian-American Industry: A Study in International Investment* (Toronto, 1936), Table A, p. 299.

The estimates for 1930–1946 are from the Dominion Bureau of Statistics. *The Canadian Balance of International Payments, Preliminary Statement, 1947* (Ottawa, 1948), p. 37.

Being made by different methods, the three estimates here used are not comparable, but they give an indication of trends.

Canada thus early shifted her connexions from the declining to the rising world centre. As she did not immediately turn the larger part of her export and other current transactions to countries which would pay in United States dollars, her dollar problem, temporarily relieved by borrowing, was accentuated when the time came to repay.

In 1918 Canadians were given a preview of some of the problems they were to meet after the war and an indication of the importance to them of the new financial power of the United States. The entry of the United States into the war in 1917 had shifted the burden of financing British war purchases in North America mainly to the shoulders of the American Government. As the latter needed the full lending-power of the local money-market to finance its own war loans, Canadian borrowing there fell away sharply from a net of $138,000,000 in 1917 to zero in 1918. The British Government, having exhausted its power to acquire dollars otherwise than from the American Government, was unable to maintain the previous level of its purchases in Canada. The Canadian Government and the banks both made additional loans to the British Government in 1918, and the United States made sizable purchases of munitions in Canada. Nevertheless, in 1918 the value of Canada's exports decreased by about one-fifth of their 1917 amount, and the total balance of payments on both current and capital account by almost one-quarter.[4]

The early reconversion to peace-time production which this slackening of war demand permitted Canadian industry, together with the high level of money income, was sufficient to maintain consumer demand and cause an actual expansion of money income to 12 per cent above the level of 1917, the peak year for war production. Imports actually fell somewhat, but total current and capital payments shrank by only a little over 1 per cent. Canada's balance of payments in fact lacked an export surplus sufficient to finance the Canadian Expeditionary Force overseas and the advances to the United Kingdom. Despite the fact that the value of the pound sterling was pegged in terms of the American dollar, the Canadian dollar began to fall on the foreign exchanges before the war was over.

The inability or unwillingness of Canada to finance a larger part of her own overseas trade, which, together with short crops, cut exports in 1918, also prevented the country from sharing in the post-war boom. While the exports of the United States increased greatly in 1919 and 1920, Canada's were practically stable despite the world-wide price rise, the physical volume being well below the 1917 peak.[5] The fall in the value of the pound in New York after the war symbolized Britain's lack of power to buy in North America, and Britain's share in Canadian exports suffered a collapse. Prosperity in the United States attracted more Canadian exports. Canada's national income rose despite the stability of export income, as did imports, still about 70 per cent from the United States. To the adverse balance of trade, other current transactions added net debits to make a total current account deficit of $323,000,000. Though United States capital had begun its post-war movement into Canada, the $143,000,000 net credits thus obtained failed to balance the accounts at current exchange rates and the Canadian dollar sank on the exchanges to its lowest post-war value. In Montreal, in 1920, the average premium on the United States dollar was 12.4 per cent.

The short but severe depression following the collapse of the post-war boom cut Canada's exports by about one-third in value. This was mainly due to the fall in prices, though physical volume also shrank.[6] A fall of almost one-quarter in the national income, a rise in the value of the pound sterling, and the continued high premium on the United States dollar decreased Canada's imports and sharply reduced the United States proportion. These drastic changes in merchandise trade brought approximate equality in the value of exports and imports in 1921, and halved the current account deficit. As the deficit was almost offset by the net capital inflow, no further depreciation of the Canadian dollar occurred; in fact, the premium on New York funds fell slightly.

The speed and extent of the economic recovery in the United States in 1922 and 1923, while other countries of the world trading system remained relatively depressed by the low level of economic activity in the former centre of the world economy, Great Britain, and by the disturbed currency situation on the continent of Europe, may be thought of as a declaration of independence by the United States from the world system. For the first time the course of the American economy was different from that of the system to which it had hitherto belonged; the weight of the domestic sector had grown so great as to be the predominant element in determining the course of business. From this point on, the world had two economic centres. The extent of the revival brought such an expansion in the United States in national income and savings that a bond market of unprecedented size was created. American investors put money into foreign assets not only in the late 1920's but in the early 1920's as well.[7] In this investing abroad the United States began to perform one of the primary functions of a world centre. What was still lacking to other nations was free access to a large and unfailing market for their exports.

The long delay in the recovery of European agriculture after the war, the low European tariffs on food imports during the period of food scarcity, the rising European dollar purchasing power from American investments in Europe, and the recovery of the pound sterling in New York, all stimulated Canada's exports to the United Kingdom and other countries in the early 1920's. At the same time, the rise of news-print and non-ferrous metal exports to the United States was added to the other exports which American prosperity always attracts. Thus, despite the increased American tariffs of 1921–1922, Canada's sales to the United States and the United Kingdom grew at about the same rate. Their relative shares in Canadian trade were not much altered. To this export expansion Canada's national income and merchandise imports showed almost no response. Surpluses replaced deficits and, as capital was still coming into the country on balance, the Canadian dollar returned to par with the United States dollar and the gold standard was resumed on July 1, 1926.

In the last three years of the 1920's the delayed effects of this favourable balance of international payments, together with a developing domestic investment boom, produced a sharp reversal in Canada's economic condition. The national income reached a new high, and increased consumer buying power, along with the heavy imports from the United States which always accompany an investment boom in Canada, brought about a great increase in imports, mainly from the United States, while the recent steady increase in exports petered out.

Canada's balance on current account turned adverse in 1927 and a gold drain set in. Because of the Finance Act, which was passed during the First World War to provide necessary additional cash reserves, the chartered banks were now able to enlarge their cash reserves, continue their domestic expansion, and shift the consequent gold drain to the Department of Finance. When the Government's stock of gold was threatened with exhaustion, an informal embargo was placed on the redemption of Dominion notes in gold, and the United States dollar stood at a premium much above the gold-export point through much of 1929.

Depressions test Great Powers severely; and economic policies which may be adopted become very important factors in determining their length and severity. During the nineteenth century Britain perfected financial procedures by which the foreign-exchange needs of overseas countries in difficulties upon the onset of depression might be supplied, and the stability of exchange rates within the world trading system might be maintained to the general advantage. Her acceptance of the full implications of free trade not only kept British markets open to the goods of other countries, but so increased her dependence upon food imports that her purchases from others were bound to continue heavy even when business declined. Thus the situation of the overseas trading partners in the trading system which Britain had built up was alleviated, levels of foreign trade were kept high, and general collapse was avoided.

In the early 1930's the United States failed dismally to perform either of these essential tasks of a world economic centre. Its merchandise imports from other countries fell from $4,400,000,000 in 1929 to $3,100,000,000 in 1930, to $2,100,000,000 in 1931, and to $1,300,000,000 in 1932. In the world financial crisis of 1931, United States banking balances abroad were actually reduced by over $600,000,000. For this failure there are many reasons. As a continent in itself, the United States is quite able to supply the essential needs of its people for food, raw products, and manufactured goods. Its imports are for the most part non-essentials which expand greatly in good times and shrink disastrously when booms fade. Tariff changes have certainly accentuated the rate of decline; but it is not clear that either much lower tariffs or stable tariffs would alone assure to other countries the relatively large and stable market for their products in the United States which the United Kingdom has hitherto afforded the dependent countries of the world economy, including in the past the United States itself. Stability of income and employment at high levels would alone be adequate to that end. Successful functioning as a great importer and stabilizer of world trade will make much greater demands upon the economic policy of the United States than it did upon that of Britain.

Continentalism largely explains the failure in the financial field also. New York has been a national rather than an international money-market; its bankers have been concerned mainly with domestic rather than international finance. Even the effort of the Federal Reserve Bank of New York in the late 1920's to play the role appropriate to a central bank in a world money-market was frustrated by its inability to control domestic finance. In the United Kingdom, on the contrary, the charge was frequently made during the 1920's that the Bank of England was sacrificing domestic to international interests. But the fate of the whole British economy was then so obviously dependent upon foreign trade that such a clash of interests could hardly become very serious. In the United States, however, the dominance of domestic factors is bound to cause a deep division of interests which will make it difficult indeed for New York or Washington to play the role in world finance which London has played.

The economic policy to which the United States resorted in 1930 was the traditional one of raising tariffs. To raise tariffs in a small country of a world trading group may contribute to stability by restricting imports and helping balance the country's international payments. Applied in a large country where domestic factors control the movements of business, the policy has little point even as a stimulus to employment. But, when applied in a country whose market is of prime importance to neighbouring smaller countries, such a policy can be a disrupting factor of prime importance to the whole world economy.

In Canada, hard hit once more by this favourite American device, the reaction was strong. Not only did Canadian tariffs rise in retaliation, but the Canadian Government, fresh from an appeal to the people, took the lead in pushing for an imperial preference system which would exclude a country ill-adapted both by economic situation and inclination to give the world the economic lead required. London was to be restored as the effective centre of a new system, smaller than the old, it is true, but still having within it the possibility of developing a stable and mutually advantageous trade between its members. Scorned in 1930 as fantastic by a British Labour Government, the suggestion was embraced at Ottawa in 1932 by a British coalition government faced with the task of rebuilding some sort of international system out of the wreck of the old in the financial storms of 1931. However natural the Hawley-Smoot Tariff and the Ottawa Agreements may have been in the circumstances of the time, it is difficult to avoid the conclusion that the trade disruptions which they helped to bring about lengthened the depression and made it more severe.

The magnitude of the depression which overtook Canadians in the 1930's is shown plainly by all the familiar indications. From the 1928 peak to the 1932 trough, exports fell from $1,341,000,000 to $495,000,000; national income shrank from $5,200,000,000 to $2,800,000,000; and imports decreased from $1,272,000,000 in 1929 to $368,000,000 in 1933. The boom in domestic development expired; the creation of gross domestic capital shrank from $1,312,000,000 in 1928 to $145,000,000 in 1933.[8] Heavy borrowing in New York in 1930 alone maintained the value of the Canadian dollar there in the face of a deficit on current transactions of $337,000,000. In 1931, however, net borrowing ceased; the pound sterling fell in New York to an average discount of 6.81 per cent, and the Canadian dollar to an average discount of 3.67 per cent. Though an export surplus of almost $100,000,000 appeared in 1932 because of the more drastic decline of imports than of exports, Canada's current transactions were still heavily adverse. The pound having declined to an average discount of 27.96 per cent in New York, the Canadian dollar therefore stood on the average for the year at 11.91 per cent discount. By 1933 the heavy premium on the United States dollar had further cut imports and enlarged the favourable balance of trade; declining costs of production brought the export of non-monetary gold for the first time into a significant position in the Canadian balance of payments at $82,000,000; net interest and dividend payments were lower; and the current transactions balanced at an average discount on the Canadian dollar of 8.04 per cent in New York.

The changes in the geographical distribution of Canadian merchandise trade, which this transition from prosperity to deep depression brought about, revealed the familiar pattern by which Canada's trade with the United States varies more over the business cycle than does trade with the United Kingdom and other countries. As imports from the United States consist mostly of consumers' goods of a luxury type, or of fuel, raw materials, and parts required by a high level of domestic production and capital creation, they fall off, with the ending of a boom, relatively more than imports from the United Kingdom. Since Canadian exports to the United States are very responsive to high levels of production and consumption there, they fall more than exports to the United Kingdom. American tariff increases accentuated this decline both in 1921–1922 and in the early 1930's.

In 1931–1932 British tariff action appears for the first time as a significant influence on Canadian trade. The protection given to Empire products in the British market in 1931 by the Import Duties Act and its increase by the Ottawa Agreements of 1932 probably account in part for the up-turn in Canada's exports to the United Kingdom in 1932, whereas exports to the United States and to other countries did not turn upwards till 1933 and 1934, respectively. The fact that, while British business was stabilized after the abandonment of the gold standard in 1931, depression deepened in the United States worked in the same direction, however. In 1933 Canadian imports from the United States stood at only 23 per cent of their 1929 value, whereas those coming from the United Kingdom stood at 42 per cent, and from other countries at 39 per cent. The distribution of Canada's import trade therefore changed against the United States. There were similar changes in the distribution of Canadian exports, and the pattern of recovery in 1922–1925 is substantially repeated in 1932–1935. A striking variation appeared, however, in the last two years of the American up-swing. Whereas, in 1926–1929, Canada's total exports stopped growing and those to the United Kingdom actually declined, in 1936 and 1937 exports to both countries continued to grow and the British percentage actually increased slightly.

For the relative growth of Canadian exports to the United Kingdom after 1932 a relatively prosperous Britain, tariff changes, and the spectacular recovery in the foreign-exchange value of the pound sterling were largely responsible. American tariffs hit Canada's trade hard in 1930. Of exports of animal products, for instance, 53 per cent went to the United States in the fiscal year 1929; in 1934 the percentage was 24; and in 1937, 34. Of that smaller percentage, fish, live animals, and furs made up the bulk; meats and dairy products had all but disappeared. British exports in this group rose from 30 per cent in the fiscal year 1929 to 54 per cent in 1937, mainly bacon and hams and cheese.[9] Empire preferences and the British building-boom also encouraged Canadian exports of wood products and non-ferrous metals, especially copper. The important reductions in the Trade Agreements of 1935 in the American tariffs against Canada, together with American business recovery, once more attracted a proportion of Canada's total exports almost as high as in 1926–1929. The sharp rise in the British share compared with the late 1920's was almost entirely at the expense of Canada's trade with other countries.

Exchange-rate movements also played a prominent part. The culmination of the American banking and economic crisis in 1933, and the United States Government's policy in 1933 and 1934 of raising the price of gold depreciated the United States dollar and raised the value of the pound sterling in New York from an average discount of 12.90 per cent in 1933 to an average premium of 3.55 per cent in 1934. In Montreal the United States dollar sank from a premium of 8.74 per cent in 1933 to a discount of 1.00 per cent in 1934, remaining near par until September, 1939. This disappearance in Canada of a premium on the United States dollar and the appearance of an actual premium on the pound must have been a powerful reinforcement of the other factors tending to turn a larger share of Canadian exports to the United Kingdom.

In the recovery of 1933–1937 Canada's national income lagged behind the rise of exports, as it had done in the early 1920's. Imports rose even more rapidly than exports or national income, and the American percentage grew, as it always does when production of consumer and capital goods rises in Canada. In total value, however, imports remained so much below exports that the Canadian balance of trade became ever more favourable, reaching an export excess of $342,000,000 in 1936. The rise of the price of gold in the United States so stimulated gold production in Canada that a new export amounting in 1937 to $145,000,000 was added to other current credits. As net interest and dividend payments had not risen above their 1933 level, the upshot was a current-account surplus of sizable dimensions. This surplus was used up, however, in financing a relatively new phenomenon in the Canadian balance of payments, a persistent net export of capital. Earlier Canadian borrowings in the United States were now maturing or were being refunded in Canada. With the return of the Canadian dollar to par with the United States dollar in 1934, profits on American direct investments in Canada might now be returned to the United States without loss.

Clearly, the changes which took place in the distribution of Canada's trade in the Second World War were much the same as those which occurred in the First. Canada became a main supplier for the United Kingdom, whose share in exports therefore rose greatly at the expense of trade with other countries overseas. The hazards of war-time ocean trade concentrated Canadian buying of imports on the United States market; the shares of Britain and other countries fell much as they had in the First World War.

The diversion early in the war of Canada's exports from the United States dollar area to the United Kingdom and to other sterling-area countries raised an acute problem for Canada. In the First World War, sterling received for Canadian exports could be freely converted into American dollars at a high rate, which was maintained through the whole struggle at $4.76 in New York. On the outbreak of the Second World War, Britain ended the convertibility of sterling into dollars; thereafter the dollar yield of Canada's exports to the sterling area became a matter to be decided by negotiation. In Canada foreign-exchange control was begun on September 16, 1939, as a disrupting fall of the Canadian dollar in New York would probably have resulted from free export of capital at that time. Thereafter, foreign exchange resulting from the sale of goods and services to other countries had to be sold to the newly-constituted Foreign Exchange Control Board and exchange for current transactions obtained from it. The Canadian dollar was devalued at the same time by setting $1.10 and $1.11 as the Board's buying and selling prices, respectively, for the American dollar.

After the fall of western Europe to Hitler in the summer of 1940 had stepped up Canada's plans for war production, it became clear that, because of the dependence of Canadian industry on United States raw materials and parts, Canada's need for

American dollars would rise with her war production. There was therefore great danger that lack of dollars might limit it. To prevent this, additional restrictions were placed on non-essential uses of United States dollars by Canadians, notably by the War Exchange Conservation Act of 1940. Further, by the Hyde Park Agreement of April, 1941, between the Canadian and the American governments, it was arranged that the United States would purchase from Canada some types of munitions and ships being made in Canada and certain strategic materials for the use of its armed forces and to a lesser degree for transfer to the United Kingdom under the Lend-Lease Act. In these ways Canada was provided with the dollars needed to employ her war production resources most effectively and to reduce continental duplication of munitions production capacity. It is for this reason that, as the war went on, Canada's exports to the United States grew as a proportion of the total. Britain's payments shrank relatively, both for this reason and because, after the initiation of Mutual Aid to the Allied Powers by the Canadian Government, some goods of a type previously paid for by the United Kingdom were now paid for directly by the purchasing countries.[10]

In the years 1945–1947 the war pattern and trends in Canada's trade continued. The fact that the United States remained the main source of imports left Canada with a United States dollar problem much like that of the early years of the war. Similar methods were adopted to deal with it: the restriction of non-essential imports from, and the encouragement of exports to, the United States. The restriction on imports was regarded as temporary, but problems of longer range arose in the redirection of exports. After the war the proportion of exports going to the United States was not much changed, but the share of other countries rose sharply at the expense of the United Kingdom. But for Canadian and United States loans and credits to Great Britain, the fall in the latter's share would have been much greater. The question was whether the proportion of exports to the United Kingdom and other countries would now rise as it did in the 1920's; whether, in other words, Canada might again use large export surpluses with countries overseas to meet the debits in the net balance of payments in United States dollars.

It is idle to look for the restoration of Britain's dominance in a world economy like that of the nineteenth century. A more reasonable hope is that the United States may become the centre of a new world economy with objectives and methods appropriate to the twentieth century. American sponsorship of the Bretton Woods institutions and the International Trade Organization, the scale of United States post-war relief and loan programmes, and especially the extensive aid to European recovery under the Marshall Plan indicate a growing realization that the recovery of other countries and a high level of international trade are vital to American prosperity, an attitude which may well inspire conduct appropriate to world economic leadership.

Any failure of the United States to achieve reasonable economic stability or to adapt its tariff and other international economic policies to its new position as a world centre might, however, result in the grouping of countries more closely around the United Kingdom in an attempt to obtain the advantages of a stable world economy, even though on a smaller scale than that of the nineteenth century. As such a trend would involve relatively less trade with dollar countries, it would be serious for Canada. That the Canadian Government was assiduous in its efforts to promote the recovery both of the United Kingdom and of western Europe and to further the creation of institutions and policies appropriate to a twentieth-century world economy is not surprising. Lack of success in such plans would certainly lead to a drastic redirection of Canada's export trade towards United States dollar countries. Trade with each of the sterling and dollar groups which would then emerge would have to be more nearly balanced than hitherto.

But even success in creating a multi-lateral trading world would not relieve Canada completely of the need to redirect her export trade; it would but moderate the speed and the extent of the movement. It was a condition of the success of the nineteenth-century economy that goods and capital moved mainly over the same routes. Countries usually borrowed where they sold their exports. Since 1914 Canada has shifted her external borrowing from London to New York. It is true that the proportion which Britain takes of Canada's exports has also declined since 1900. But the shift has not been to the United States but to other countries. Some of these do pay in dollars. But it would seem necessary, if a more secure basis for the Canadian economy is to be found, that a larger share of Canadian goods be sold in Canada's natural dollar market, the United States itself. It is likely, therefore, that the effort which began in 1947 to sell more goods there will outlast the restrictions on imports from the United States, which was then the main reliance of the programme of dollar conservation.

The difficulties in the way of the United States becoming as satisfactory a world economic centre as Britain proved to be in the nineteenth century are immense. The United States is a continent, not an island; and continentalism not only magnifies the necessary adjustments but diminishes the will to try them. American movement in this direction may well be slow and, for a long time, incomplete. Canadians may be consoled by the reflection that their chances of a viable adjustment to the situation are at least as favourable as those of any other country which, of necessity, must remain in the American orbit. The record of successful negotiation and accommodation between the two countries is already a notable one. Canada's trade and industry are closely interwoven with those of the United States. Capital moves perhaps more readily into Canada than into any other country. Nor can the United States be unaware of the diplomatic and strategic necessity of a strong economy on its northern border. If Canada patiently persists in the course which her history suggests, there should be no insuperable difficulty in making the rest of the adaptation required by the rise of the United States to the dominant position in the world economy.[11]

CHAPTER XXIV

International Organization

BY F. H. SOWARD

Addressing a meeting in Ottawa under the auspices of the the United Nations Association of Canada in September, 1947, on the eve of the second session of the United Nations Assembly, Mr. St. Laurent, then Canadian Secretary of State for External Affairs, announced that Canada would be a candidate for election to the Security Council. Such a step, he said, would confront the country with "new and onerous responsibilities." "We shall be forced," he warned, "as never before in Canada in time of peace to make decisions on major questions of policy arising from situations which exist far from our shores and which some may feel do not directly affect us." In justification of this course the Secretary of State for External Affairs argued that, disappointing as the record of the United Nations had been to date, it still represented the best hope for mankind and for Canada, whose survival lay in the development of machinery for international coöperation. If Canada wished to enjoy the benefit of such a development she must be willing to accept the resulting responsibilities at a time "when the going is hard and when the future is by no means certain."

With this frank and realistic assessment of the position and, equally important, with the general approval with which the country greeted Mr. St. Laurent's declaration, Canada may be said to have reached maturity in international affairs. In the hard school of adversity, politicians and people alike had learned that status without responsibility and security without commitments were impossible.

The initial Canadian approach to problems of international organization had been almost fortuitous and unplanned. The First World War had seen a colony, which had pioneered in the development of responsible government at home, and had successfully opposed the creation of a centralized system of imperial control in London, committed to war by the action of the United Kingdom. The war effort of a country of eight million people was impressive and costly, the toll of human lives equalling that of the United States, which was of course in the war for a much shorter period. The conviction steadily grew in the mind of the war-time Prime Minister, Sir Robert Borden, that the sacrifices of Canadian troops on the blood-soaked plains of France and Flanders had earned for their country "a new conception of the status of the Dominions in their relation to the governance of the Empire." Out of this conception stemmed the assertion by Sir Robert of the right of the Dominions to "an adequate voice in foreign policy and foreign relations," which was approved at the Imperial War Conference of 1917.

The transition from this claim to insistence upon separate representation from Great Britain at the Peace Conference was logical and inevitable. Again it was based upon the war effort of the Dominions and as such had a particular appeal to Clemenceau. When Wilson's Committee drafted the Covenant of the League of Nations at the Peace Conference, it was equally to be expected that the Dominions and India should press for individual membership in the League, a claim which was recognized, except for Newfoundland. At all times Borden was a leader in this insistence on Dominion status in international affairs. It was he who secured public declaration from the Big Four (drafted by himself) that they did not consider the permanent membership of the British Empire in the League Council a barrier to the election of a Dominion to temporary membership.[1]

Similarly, in the International Labour Commission meetings, when an American expert endorsed a proposal to bar the Dominions from the right of election to the Governing Body of the International Labour Organization, the Canadian Prime Minister took up the matter with President Wilson. He also informed Lloyd

---

[1] For notes to chapter xxiv see pages 586–587.

George that, unless the offending clause were modified, Canada, after ratifying the peace treaties, would immediately withdraw from the League of Nations.[2] The protest was successful.

In September, 1919, when the Canadian Parliament debated a resolution approving the peace treaties, Sir Robert emphasized in his speech the recognition that the Dominions had received and the importance of their entry into the family of nations. The subsequent debate became in large part a wrangle as to whether or not a real constitutional advance had been made. In the words of Professor Glazebrook, "A casual visitor to Parliament in these weeks might well have come away wondering what had been the topic before the house; but a reader of Hansard of earlier decades would have recognized a traditional theme that might be started off by anything related to external affairs."[3] Only a few M.P.'s[4] were concerned with the new international responsibilities Canada had undertaken in her search for status, and they were mainly dubious of the implications of the commitments to the support of collective security outlined in the Covenant. "In military matters," said Rodolphe Lemieux, "we are governed also by and from London; and we do not want to be governed by and from Geneva."

In the twenty years between world wars, Canadian policies in Geneva were those which might be expected of a North American state confident of its own security and uneasily aware of the embarrassing absence of the United States from the League of Nations. "Close your eyes and you might easily think that the voice of America were speaking," wrote an acute French observer after listening to a Canadian delegate.[5] "In this association of mutual insurance against fire, the risks assumed by the different states are not equal," said Senator Dandurand at the famous debate on the Protocol of Geneva in 1924. "We live in a fire-proof house, far from inflammable materials. A vast ocean separates us from Europe." And again in 1936, "It is unreasonable to expect a North American state to have the same international outlook, the same conception of interest or of duty as a European state facing widely differing conditions," warned Prime Minister King.

Well in advance of Senator Borah, Sir Robert Borden had objected to the sweeping character of Article X. After failing to secure the deletion of the offending article from the Covenant,

Canadian spokesmen attempted to secure adoption by the Assembly of an interpretative resolution which bound the League Council in recommending the application of military measures against an aggressor state "to take account more particularly of the geographical position and of the special conditions of each state," and underlined the right of the constitutional authorities of each state "to decide . . . to what degree the member is bound to assure the execution of this obligation by employment of its military forces." Although the adoption of the resolution was blocked in 1923 by the single vote of Persia, its political importance was substantial in shaping policy in Geneva. In keeping with this cautious attitude, the Canadian Government also opposed the Protocol of Geneva.

Five years later, in welcoming the Kellogg Pact, the Canadian Government epitomized its attitude when it described the League "with its limitations as an indispensable and continuing agency of international understanding." The League was praised for bringing together in periodic conference the representatives of fifty states, thereby building up barriers against war "by developing a spirit of conciliation, an acceptance of publicity in international affairs, a habit of coöperation in common ends, and permanently available machinery for the adjustment of differences." At the same time, in viewing the League performance of this task, the Canadian Government reaffirmed its opposition to the application of sanctions "automatically or by the decisions of other states."

This distrust of automatic sanctions was paralleled by an emphasis upon the usefulness of developing in Geneva techniques of arbitration, conciliation, and judicial settlement. Had it not been for its willingness to respect the British request for a united Commonwealth front, the Canadian Government would have accepted the compulsory jurisdiction of the Permanent Court of International Justice well before 1929. During her term on the League Council, election to which in 1927 had been welcomed as another proof of international recognition, Canada became *ex officio* a member of the Preparation Commission for the Disarmament Conference and there steadily advocated an extensive reduction of armaments.

In contrast with the arguments of a French delegate who suggested that disarmament is the effect, not the cause, of security, "Our experience has taught us that the reduction of armaments can itself be a source of security," said Sir George Perley at the opening sessions of the Conference in 1932. What became known as the great Canadian speech in this period was a homily upon the success of the United States and Canada in maintaining between them an undefended frontier—with the implication that European states should go and do likewise.

In the timid 'thirties, when the authority of the League was challenged by Japan and Italy, Canadian policy in Geneva was uncertain and reticent, a not-uncommon attitude among League members. During the development of the Sino-Japanese "incident," Canada was prompt to endorse the Stimson doctrine of non-recognition, but cautioned against "premature action" and continued to regard public opinion as "the final and effective sanction for the maintenance of the integrity of international agreements." Dr. Carter has assessed the Canadian position as half-way between that of Britain, Australia, and New Zealand, "whose strategic interests were involved in areas in which they felt incapable of defending them, and whose economic ties with Japan were strong," and that of the Irish Free State and South Africa, "neither of whom was influenced by these considerations."[6]

In the Italo-Ethiopian dispute Canada began well in a vigorous advocacy of League principles, but soon retreated from too conspicuous a role in the organization of punitive measures. In October, 1935, at the first meeting of the Committee of Eighteen, which had been established by the Assembly to coördinate sanctions against Italy, the Canadian representative urged the delegates to "show the world that the League was no longer to be scoffed or laughed at but that it meant business." Soon afterwards the general election in Canada brought defeat to the Conservative Government, and the new Liberal administration had to decide what course of action it should pursue. In a carefully worded statement issued almost immediately after taking office, the King Government stressed "the difficulty of making general commitments in advance to apply either economic or military sanctions," and made clear that it did not recognize "any commitment binding Canada to adopt military sanctions," but agreed to coöperate in applying the economic sanctions already proposed, with the proviso that this decision was "not to be regarded as necessarily establishing a precedent for future action."

Meanwhile Dr. W. A. Riddell, the Canadian Advisory Officer in Geneva, assumed the duties of his Conservative predecessor on the Committee of Eighteen and was faced with the problem of deciding whether he should pursue the same firm course that had already aroused much interest in Geneva. Dr. Riddell asked for instructions, but, before they were received, sponsored a proposal for the extension of the embargo on key commodities to Italy to include oil, coal, iron, and steel. Although his instructions, which arrived too late to prevent his action, had told Dr. Riddell "to do nothing in the matter of extending sanctions," the Canadian Government decided at first not to disavow him in order to avoid embarrassment. Subsequently, when it became clear that Italy vigorously resented the oil embargo, which was looked upon as being essentially a Canadian policy, and when feeling in Quebec was hostile, the Government issued a press statement in December, explaining that the Government had not intended and did not intend to take the initiative in the extension of the embargo, and that the views of Dr. Riddell "represented only his own personal opinion." Canada, it was announced, would be prepared to consider proposals for revision of economic sanctions, but would limit its participation "to coöperation in purely financial and economic measures of a pacific character which are accepted by substantially all the participating countries."[7]

The Government's action was sharply criticized in most of the English-language press, which was only partly mollified by a second press release explaining that the Canadian Government was not necessarily opposed to the embargo being extended, but did not feel that Canada should take the initiative.[8] Further criticism was diverted by the disclosure of the Hoare-Laval proposals, which discomfited League supporters in Canada who had been urging that Canada should align herself with Great Britain in a strong stand.

As disillusionment increased about collective security, the Canadian Government became increasingly chary of commitments. In March, 1936, at the time of the German occupation of the

Rhineland, the Prime Minister told the House of Commons that Canada's first duty, both to the Empire and to the League, "with respect to all the great issues that come, is, if possible, to keep this country united." In June the Government favoured the lifting of sanctions against Italy after that country's military success in Abyssinia. "Collective bluffing cannot bring collective security," said Mr. King, "and most countries have shown they are not prepared to make firm commitments beyond their immediate interests." In future it would be clearly impossible for Canada to make binding commitments to use either economic or military force.

At the League Assembly in September, the Canadian Prime Minister made a powerful plea for a League which would confine its efforts to conciliation, a speech which Lord Beaverbrook's *Daily Express* gleefully summarized in a head-line as "Canada shows the way out." The speech did not rule out Canadian coöperation in resistance to any aggressor, but it did mean that "any decision on the part of Canada to participate in war will have to be taken by the Parliament or people of Canada in the light of all existing circumstances; circumstances of the day as they exist in Canada as well as in the areas involved." In the words of J. W. Dafoe, the leading Liberal editor in Canada and the most consistent champion of a strong League policy, "The League of Nations, with assurances of most distinguished consideration, was ushered out into the darkness by Mr. Mackenzie King."[9]

In the three years that followed the Prime Minister's speech at Geneva, the Canadian Government did not depart from its policy of opposition to automatic commitments in support of collective security. Thus in May, 1938, the Prime Minister told the House of Commons, "So far as the Canadian Government is concerned, the sanctions articles have ceased to have effect by general practice and consent and cannot be revived by any state or group of states at will." On the other hand, there was no attempt to secure neutrality by legislation such as preoccupied the American Congress during the same period. Repeatedly Mr. King reaffirmed the Government's intention of making no advance commitments, but of taking whatever action it thought most appropriate in the nation's interest. He once described Canadian foreign policy as being best summarized in the words of St. Paul: "If it be possible, as much as lieth in you, live peaceably with all men." But on another occasion Mr. King reminded his listeners that "forces of evil were present in the New World fighting against the forces of good. As long as there was this conflict, those who wished to see the good triumph must take every possible means to prevent evil from gaining ground." The most positive action taken by the Prime Minister remained secret for seven years. In the summer of 1937 he visited Hitler in Berlin and warned him that "if there was a war of aggression, nothing in the world would keep the Canadian people from being at the side of Britain."

Like most Englishmen and Americans, Canadians rejoiced at the initial triumph of appeasement at Munich, but this "success" did not deter the Government from almost doubling the defence estimates for 1939. In March of that year, following the German occupation of Prague, the Prime Minister indicated his surprise and disapproval of this action and made a forecast of first-rate importance in keeping with his previous statement to Hitler. "If there were a prospect of an aggressor launching an attack on Britain, with bombers raining death on London, I have no doubt what the decision of the Canadian people and Parliament would be. We would regard it as an act of aggression menacing freedom in all parts of the British Commonwealth." In that statement, which went uncriticized by the Opposition parties, was foreshadowed Canadian policy when the Nazis invaded Poland. Like President Roosevelt, the Prime Minister pleaded with Hitler and Mussolini to explore every effort at peaceful settlement of the differences with Poland, but when such appeals went unheeded there was no hesitation.

Parliament was summoned in special session on September 7, 1939, and without a division approved a declaration of war on Germany. As the Prime Minister was to say later with pride, "Ours was not an automatic response to some mechanical organization of Empire. Canada's entry into the war was the deliberate decision of free people by their own representatives in a free Parliament."[10]

In the twenty years between wars the position of Canada in the International Labour Organization was complicated by her federal system of government. As in Australia and the United States, federal jurisdiction over labour problems was decidedly limited, the provinces having jurisdiction over wages, hours, and conditions in industry. Consequently, of the sixty-seven draft conventions forwarded to member states by the I.L.O. for ratification between 1919 and 1939, only nine had been ratified by Canada; six of these pertained to maritime questions where the jurisdiction of the federal government was unquestioned.[11]

The following episode illustrates the difficulties of the divided jurisdiction. When the first director of the I.L.O. visited Canada in 1923, he found the Canadian Government very sympathetic; the Prime Minister gave him an opportunity of meeting the Cabinet and "explaining to them his hopes and desires as regards Canadian collaboration." But when the I.L.O. director visited the capital of the Province of Quebec, a key province for labour legislation, "all the members of the Provincial government were by a curious coincidence suddenly and simultaneously called out of town."[12] Subsequently, relations with Quebec ministers and officers were far more cordial.

In the closing period of the Bennett administration (1930–1935), during what has been called its "New Deal" phase, four I.L.O. conventions were ratified by federal action in the hope that recent decisions of the Judicial Committee of the Privy Council pointed to a more liberal interpretation of federal powers by that body. Unfortunately, this did not prove to be so, and the action of the Government was declared *ultra vires* in January, 1937.

In commenting on this difficulty in its report on Dominion-provincial relations, the Rowell-Sirois Royal Commission observed: "The situation is entirely unsatisfactory and we recommend that the Dominion and the provinces together should decide how international labour conventions should be implemented. It seems that the best method would be for the provinces to give the Parliament of Canada power to implement such international labour conventions as the Government of Canada has ratified or may ratify in future."[13]

The absence of the United States from membership in the I.L.O. until 1934 gave unexpected significance to Canadian membership. It made the Canadian Government anxious to have the I.L.O. proceed cautiously in its formative period, in the hope that the United States might reconsider its position. This attitude was reflected in the views of N. W. Rowell, the chief Canadian delegate to the first conference of the I.L.O., which met in Washington in 1919. When an Italian workers' delegate proposed a motion calling for the Council of the League of Nations to undertake "to examine and solve the problem" of distribution of raw materials and means of maritime transport of raw materials, Mr. Rowell forcibly and clearly indicated Canada's opposition. "It might just as well be clearly understood," he said, "that the nations which have raw materials will deal with them as they believe fair and in the national interest; but they will deal with them by their own parliaments, their own legislatures; and they will not accept international regulations with reference to the control of their own property." In making this statement Mr. Rowell was not only voicing the sentiments of a "Have" state but was also, as he said years afterwards, seeking to prevent putting a weapon "in the hands of the opponents of the League in the United States which might destroy the chance of the United States entering the League."

Canadian membership made particularly timely the role of workers' delegates from Canada to the I.L.O., since most of them came from trade unions which were affiliated with the American Federation of Labor. Workers' delegates from other countries were well aware of the situation and its implications. They were prompt to elect Tom Moore, president of the Trades and Labour Congress of Canada, as a workers' delegate to the Governing Body of the I.L.O. Mr. Moore held the post for fifteen years and proved to be a very useful member of the Governing Body.

In the I.L.O., as in the League, Canada did not relax her interest in questions of status so long as any doubts remained. Since the Canadian Advisory Officer in Geneva, Dr. W. A. Riddell, had been an officer of the I.L.O. before his appointment, he was particularly interested in I.L.O. matters. As the normal representative of Canada on the Governing Body of the I.L.O. by virtue of Canada being ranked as one of the eight chief industrial powers, he was zealous in asserting the rights and interests of Canada and other overseas countries in I.L.O. questions and in decrying what he regarded as excessive European dominance in the I.L.O. on most questions. Similarly, when the United States and the U.S.S.R.

both entered the I.L.O. in 1934 and threatened to displace Canada and Belgium among the eight chief industrial powers, Dr. Riddell fought a delaying action to protect Canada's position, which showed perhaps a greater zeal for his country's interest than appreciation of the importance of securing American and Soviet coöperation. The withdrawal of Germany from the I.L.O. soon afterwards cleared up an awkward situation.

From a tepid interest in the I.L.O., Canada gradually shifted to a policy of friendly coöperation of a limited character. Canadians were gratified when Senator Robertson was chosen to preside at the I.L.O. conference in 1932. Canadian Labour was well informed about the work of the I.L.O. through representation in its administration. Its spokesman at the New York conference in 1941 described the I.L.O. as "our instrument of international planning for the future." The invitation to the I.L.O. to take shelter in Montreal in the gloomy days of 1940 was a friendly and popular gesture.

As the Second World War increased in intensity and magnitude, the Canadian people found themselves playing a part of far greater dimensions than anyone had anticipated in 1939. For a year after the fall of France, Canada was Britain's principal ally in a world almost hypnotized by the success of the Nazi war machine. Before the war ended, Canada was third in naval power and fourth in air power among the Allies, while the Canadian army played a significant role in the march to the Rhine.

In the economic sphere the contribution of Canada was of such proportions that the London *Economist* wrote on May 29, 1943, "In absolute terms the distance that separates Canada from the Great Powers is less than that between her own achievement and that of any other of the smaller Powers." A gift of $1,000,000,000 to Britain in 1942 was followed by the institution of Mutual Aid to Canada's allies, which in proportion to Canada's resources was as great as American Lend-Lease. Alone among the combatant Allies, Canada chose not to receive Lend-Lease assistance from the United States. Partnership with that country had rapidly increased in intimacy, following the establishment by the two governments of the Permanent Joint Board on Defence in August, 1940.

After Pearl Harbor the two countries worked successfully and harmoniously in a number of joint committees to combine their economies, as far as was practicable, into a single unit for war purposes. Tangible appreciation of Canadian achievement in the economic sphere came in the form of membership with the United States and the United Kingdom on the Combined Production and Resources Board, the Combined Raw Materials Board, and the Combined Food Board. In closest secrecy, Canada also became associated with these countries in research on atomic energy and made available large quantities of uranium, necessary for the manufacture of the atomic bomb. Public recognition of Canada's role came in November, 1945, when the three governments issued a joint statement recommending the creation of an Atomic Energy Commission under the jurisdiction of the United Nations.

In the war-time conferences that proceeded to develop plans for what were later described as Specialized Agencies, Canada was effectively represented by her statesmen, diplomats, and experts. After the Food Conference at Hot Springs in 1943, a Canadian, Mr. L. B. Pearson (who later became Under-Secretary, and in 1948 Secretary, of State for External Affairs), was chosen chairman of the Interim Food Commission and subsequently presided at the meeting in Quebec which drafted the constitution for the Food and Agriculture Organization. Mr. Pearson also acted as chairman of the Committee on Supplies, which was established after the initial meetings of the United Nations Relief and Rehabilitation Administration. In that organization Canada became the third largest contributor and the second largest source of supplies. To the competence and reliability of Canadian experts in the work of the U.N.R.R.A. the late Fiorello La Guardia paid warm tribute during the United Nations Assembly meetings in New York in 1946. In differing with his government's decision to wind up the U.N.R.R.A., and seeking an alternative policy, La Guardia declared, "I would be willing to designate Canada as a committee of one to draw up a plan and I would take it sight unseen."

In 1944 at Chicago, in the discussions on international civil aviation, Canadians played a useful role in attempting to find a middle ground between British and American policies, and their efforts were praised by the American chairman of the Conference. Canada was elected to the Interim Council of the P.I.C.A.O. and Montreal became its headquarters. At Bretton Woods the detailed plans of the Canadian financial experts on currency stabilization likewise represented a compromise between British and American proposals, and the New York *Times* reported that the plan finally agreed upon bore the closest resemblance to the Canadian one. These experiences in international administration increased both Canadian appreciation of the value of international agencies and self-confidence in the nation's capacity to make a useful contribution. Service became of greater concern than status.

"Canada's part in the last war raised her to the status of a nation," declared a prominent Liberal Member of Parliament and future Cabinet Minister in May, 1944.[14] "Canada's part in this war has given her opportunities and responsibilities of world-wide interest. Today Canada stands in the shadow of no other land. Our unique position gives us a unique opportunity to serve other peoples as well as our own."

A few months later a leading Canadian historian stated: "We have outlived the era when a perverse sensitiveness concerning status drove us into national ineffectiveness. We have outlived it partly because there is no longer a question of status to be settled. . . . But we have also reached an era when we must think not only of what larger recognition we can ask from others, but also of what we can accomplish ourselves."[15]

In official statements of policy on international administration a shift in attitude from the pre-war position of cautious detachment early became discernible. In his speech preceding the declaration of war, Prime Minister King warned European neutrals of their danger if Britain and France should go down in the struggle, and asked, "And if this conqueror . . . is able to crush the peoples of the continent of Europe, what is going to become of the isolation of the North American continent?" Three times during 1941, in both Canada and Britain, he urged action in war-time for the creation of the new order that must be "on its way" when the war was over. In February, 1942, in a national radio broadcast on the eve of the Second Victory Loan, Mr. King said, "The fortunes of battle since the outbreak of war; the fate of nations that lie today prostrate beneath the heel of the aggressor; the terrific tasks which face the nations still battling for their freedom—all these go to show that neutrality has become a snare and isolation an illusion."[16]

The Canadian Minister to the United States repeated this last phrase in a speech in New York describing Canadian policy and added: "No American country is in a better position to appreciate the truth of this than Canada. Four years of the last war and three years of this have taught us that there can be no security in a world half-slave and half-free; and no peace in this hemisphere if aggression is permitted to run rampant elsewhere throughout the world. Peace is indivisible."[17]

A Gallup Poll released on November 20, 1943, revealed that 78 per cent of the Canadian people were in favour of the Dominion's taking an active part in the maintenance of world peace even if it meant sending Canadian forces to keep peace in other parts of the world. Two months later, at the opening of Parliament, the Speech from the Throne stated: "The time has come when all the nations now united in the common purpose of winning the war should seek unitedly to ensure an enduring peace. . . . You will accordingly be invited to approve of Canadian participation in the establishment of an international organization to further national security through international coöperation."

At the Conference of Commonwealth Prime Ministers in May, 1944, Mr. King opposed any advocacy of a reorganized centralized Commonwealth, but readily joined with the other Commonwealth leaders in endorsing "a world organization to maintain peace and security . . . endowed with the necessary power and authority to prevent aggression and violence." A definite statement of the extent to which Canada was prepared to contribute to international security came in the Prime Minister's statement to the House of Commons on August 11, 1944. "We have made it clear," said Mr. King, "that Canada will do its full part in carrying out agreed security schemes whether they involve the creation of an international police force or alternatively of measures for seeing that there will always be an overwhelming preponderance of power available to protect the peace."

Paralleling this willingness to have Canada participate in guaranteeing security in the post-war world, on which all the major parties agreed, was an advocacy of functionalism in international affairs which may be attributed to the lessons of wartime experience. The first reference to the use of this principle in determining representation in international bodies appeared in a speech by the Prime Minister on July 9, 1943. After describing the chief agencies which had been established for the direction of the war, and referring discreetly to the informal and exploratory talks that had been proceeding in Washington and London about the peace settlement in which Canadian officials and exports had taken part, Mr. King expressed his conviction that the time was approaching, even before victory had been won, for the united nations to be embodied in some form of international organization.

Then came an interesting and suggestive comment on the application of the functional principle to representation in the new international bodies, which, Mr. King maintained, was the position he had taken "right along." Authority in international affairs should not, he felt, be concentrated exclusively in the Great Powers. On the other hand, it could not be divided equally among all the thirty or more united nations, and certainly not among the world's more than sixty sovereign states, or all effective authority would disappear. In the new international institutions likely to be set up after the war, effective representation could not be restricted to the largest states nor could it be extended to all. It must be determined on a "functional basis," admitting to full membership "those countries, large or small, which have the greatest contribution to make to the particular object in question." This would provide a compromise between the theoretical equality of states and the practical necessity of limiting representation to a workable number.

The fact that this statement coincided with the invasion of Sicily prevented it from receiving the attention it deserved at home and abroad, but the general comment was distinctly favourable. So consistent a critic of the Government's policy as the Montreal *Gazette* saw in the principle of functionalism "a new and wholly Canadian concept" which might contain the solution to a major post-war problem and make Canada the spokesman of those smaller countries whose importance was greater than their numerical size would indicate.

During the Dumbarton Oaks conversations, which began in August, 1944, and were confined to representatives of the United States, the U.S.S.R., China, and the United Kingdom, Mr. King made it clear to the Canadian Parliament that Canada had not been invited to take part in these discussions and was, of course, not directly represented. But he added that Canada had been kept fully informed of the topics which would come under discussion, and the Commonwealth prime ministers had examined the problem at their meeting in May and were in general agreement on the attitude which the United Kingdom would adopt in Washington.[18] "We know the line," said Mr. King, "which will be presented, for example at Washington, in regard to world organization by the officials who are discussing it there."

The Prime Minister did not complain of the restricted conversations, since, in his view, it was "a correct application of the functional idea of world organization" for the greatest states to take the lead in the organization of power. However, he was careful to point out that unless the smaller countries played their due part in the new system there might be ever present in their minds the fear, with Munich as a reminder, that the Great Powers might settle their differences at the expense of others. For that reason, although he unhesitatingly endorsed the principle of the Great Powers being permanent members of the new world Council, he felt that it was essential that the smaller powers should also be represented there. Here again the functional idea should necessarily be applied. He suggested that "those countries which have the most to contribute to the maintenance of the peace of the world should be most frequently selected. The military contribution actually made during this war by the members of the united nations provided one good working basis for a selective principle of choice."

Following the release of the text of the Dumbarton Oaks Proposals on October 9, in which provision was made for six states to hold non-permanent membership in the proposed Security Council, but in which no reference was made to any principle of selection, the Prime Minister issued a carefully worded press statement. The Proposals were commended to the earnest study of the Canadian people, but the Government reserved its judgement upon them until there was time for their examination. An indication of Canadian opinion was afforded at the ninth conference of the Institute of Pacific Relations in January, 1945. The Canadian delegation, which was almost equally divided between government officials and specialists in Canadian affairs, was reported, in a pamphlet summarizing the discussions of the conference, as pressing Canada's claim to membership on the Security Council "on the dual basis of power and responsibility."[19]

In the period between the publication of the Dumbarton Oaks Proposals and the opening of the San Francisco Conference, the Canadian Government made thorough preparations for the international debate on the new charter. Through its diplomatic representatives, informal exchanges of views took place with the foreign offices of the Great Powers and of the leading secondary powers, such as Brazil and Belgium. On January 12, 1945, a formal memorandum was submitted to the sponsoring powers outlining certain proposals for strengthening the effectiveness of the proposed international organization, and during a visit to Washington, D.C., in March, Prime Minister King discussed these suggestions with President Roosevelt.

Representatives of the Commonwealth governments met in London, and in April outlined the attitudes of their respective governments towards the proposals. By a formal vote of 200 to 5, the Canadian House of Commons approved Canada's participation in the San Francisco meeting, agreeing that "the establishment of an effective international organization for the maintenance of international peace and security is of vital importance to Canada and, indeed, to the future well-being of mankind; and that it is in the interests of Canada that Canada should become a member of such an organization." Parliament and Government went no farther, however, than to accept the principles set forth in the Dumbarton Oaks Proposals as "a satisfactory general basis for a discussion of the Charter of the proposed international organization."

The choice of delegates for San Francisco was also significant of the anxiety of the Government to place the international issue above party politics and to provide a delegation as representative as possible so that Canada should speak "with a clear, strong, and united voice." Besides the Prime Minister, the Minister of Justice, Mr. St. Laurent (who was subsequently to become the first Cabinet Minister charged exclusively with the administration of External Affairs), and the Liberal leader in the Senate, the delegation included Mr. Gordon Graydon, leader of the Progressive Conservative party in the House of Commons; Mr. M. J. Coldwell, national and parliamentary leader of the C.C.F. party; a leading French-Canadian Progressive Conservative Senator; and the only Liberal woman member of the House of Commons. Among the alternate delegates and senior advisers were the three senior members of the Department of External Affairs, Messrs. Robertson, Wrong, and Pearson, and the Canadian ambassadors to the U.S.S.R., Brazil, and Chile. Because of the general election in June, the parliamentary delegates were unable to be present for the entire Conference, but the effect of their participation was noticed in subsequent debates on the approval of the Charter.

The key-note for Canadian policy at San Francisco was struck by Mr. King in his address at the second plenary session on April 27. He declared that the delegation came to the Conference "with one central purpose in view . . . to coöperate as completely as we can with the delegations of other nations in bringing into being as soon as possible a Charter of world security." He thought it advisable to reserve for the committee stage any specific suggestions for amendments to the Proposals, but he indicated Canada's desire to see the smaller powers assigned a greater part in the new organization than that proposed for them at Dumbarton Oaks. Mr. King recognized that power and responsibility must go hand in hand, but he bluntly added, "Power, however, is not exclusively concentrated in the hands of any four or five powers and the Conference should not act on the assumption that it is." To do so would tend, he argued, to foster "a new type of isolationism, a feeling that the task of preserving the peace should be left exclusively to the Great Powers."

In the committee stage of the Conference, where the basic work was done, Canada was given special representation as one of the fourteen states elected to the Executive Committee. Her representatives also served on the Coördination Committee, which examined the paragraphs of the Charter as drafted by the appropriate technical committees to see that they were consistent in form and substance. It was probably in these committees that the Canadian delegates did their most useful work, out of the lime-light of publicity, but in such a way that two of them were among those strongly considered as possible choices for Secretary General of the United Nations.

Like delegates from other smaller countries, the Canadians disliked the range and force of the veto power in the Security Council which the Great Powers had arrogated to themselves at Dumbarton Oaks and Yalta. Their dislike was indicated in the heated discussions at San Francisco, though not with the vehemence and persistence that made the Australian spokesman, Dr. Evatt, a conspicuous figure. The Canadian delegation supported the latter in his original motion to exclude the peaceful-settlement chapter of the Charter from the veto power of the Great Powers. But when it became clear that the Great Powers would not consent to this diminution of their authority, and when they issued a statement promising that they would exercise their veto powers with responsibility and restraint, the Canadians abstained from voting on the revised Australian amendment.

On two other questions involving the Security Council the Canadian delegation was more successful. It will be remembered that the Dumbarton Oaks Proposals had not specified the qualifications which made non-permanent members eligible for election to the Security Council. At San Francisco the delegates pressed vigorously for election rules which would ensure the possibility of electing a large number of those states which could make substantial contributions to the work of the Council. This policy was in line with the functional approach that had been expounded by the Prime Minister. These efforts were largely successful and are reflected in Article 23 of the Charter dealing with the election of non-permanent members to the Security Council.

Canada also endeavoured to secure for smaller powers some voice in proceedings of the Security Council which affected their interests. In this, success was limited but significant. The proposal to give voting rights as well as temporary membership in the Security Council for any state whose interests were affected by a question under discussion was withdrawn on the objection of the Great Powers that it could not be reconciled with the voting principles worked out at Yalta, although such a right had been conceded in the League Covenant.

The Canadians then returned to the charge with a second proposal stipulating that "Any Member of the United Nations not represented on the Security Council shall be invited to send a representative to sit as a member at any meeting of the Security Council which is discussing, under paragraph 4 above [Article 42], the use of the forces which it has undertaken to make available to the Security Council in accordance with special agreement or agreements provided for in paragraph 5 above [Article 43]." Mr. King pointed out the anomaly of the Great Powers' being protected by their veto from any use of their forces or economic resources without their consent, while, under the existing proposals, all other states could be so bound if all the Great Powers and two other states on the Security Council agreed upon the sanctions proposed. The Canadian amendment commanded wide-spread support, and its substance was incorporated into Article 44 of the Charter, a wholly-new article which the chairman of the United States delegation commended as "a significant and constructive change."

The last major achievement of the Canadian delegation was the reorganization, expansion, and clarification of the chapter in the Dumbarton Oaks Proposals which had to do with international economic and social coöperation, a subject of special concern to Canada because of the nature of her economy and international contacts. As compared to the chapters on the Assembly and the Security Council, the description in chapter ix of the proposed new Economic and Social Council was vague, inconclusive, and almost makeshift in outline. The intent of the Canadian amendments, which revised chapter ix completely, was to strengthen the new body and expand its fact-finding functions so that they might have what a Canadian called "the antiseptic quality of light." Five proposals were adopted, which appear in

Articles 55, 56, 62, 64, and 66 of the Charter. Five other amendments, to Articles 57, 59, 63, 64, and 70, were inserted to clarify the relationship between the United Nations and the various specialized agencies.

Canada also attempted to insert a clause in the Charter to the effect that in the election of the eighteen members of the Economic and Social Council "due regard" should be paid "to the necessity of arranging for the adequate representation of states of major economic importance." This suggestion—another application of functionalism—was later withdrawn when the new Council was given wider powers in the social and cultural fields. But the result was achieved largely by the inclusion of a provision that retiring members should be eligible for immediate reëlection, a concession which is not allowed in Security Council elections.

In the debates on other sections of the Charter, it may generally be maintained that the Canadians have supported the principles of effective internationalism. They opposed the veto of the Great Powers on the admission of new members to the United Nations Organization. While disagreeing with those delegates from smaller countries who seemed to aim at subjecting the Security Council "to a sort of inquisition," they secured the inclusion in the Charter (Article 24:3) of a provision obliging the Security Council to make annual and, when necessary, special reports to the General Assembly. The Canadians were opposed to the principle that permanent members of the Security Council should automatically be members of the Trusteeship Council. The substance of their three recommendations on the nature of the Secretariat appears in Articles 100, 101, and 105 of the Charter. In them the emphasis is on the international character of the Secretariat, in the hope of freeing it as much as possible from national pressures such as the League of Nations had unfortunately experienced. The Canadians joined with delegations from many other states in seeking a flexible procedure for amendment of the Charter, but they were defeated by the rigid attitude of the Great Powers.

Parliament, when it assembled in the autumn of 1945, was called upon to approve the Charter of the United Nations and did so unanimously. The House of Commons debate, in which every party was represented, including Social Credit and Labour Progressive, was marked by general approval of Canada's role at the Conference, repeated reminders that isolationism was no longer feasible, and sober conjectures on the progress towards world peace that had been achieved at San Francisco. Mr. St. Laurent, the Acting Secretary of State for External Affairs, described the Charter as a "great improvement" on the Dumbarton Oaks Proposals, and declared that it was "a first step in the direction of that coöperation between the nations which appears to be essential to the survival of civilization." Even Mr. Maxime Raymond, the leader of the *Bloc Populaire,* the most isolationist party in the House, accepted the Charter with resignation as a "lesser evil," but thought it valuable for its emphasis on economic and social coöperation. General approval was modified by the doubts of the Social Credit leader, Mr. Solon Low, who detected sinister international financial influences behind some of its provisions, while conceding the need of some form of international organization for mutual protection.

In the brief but stormy period of history following the Conference at San Francisco, Canada, like other peace-loving nations, has endeavoured to make the United Nations an effective agency of international coöperation. From past experience Canadians had learned, as their Minister of External Affairs stated, that "security for this country lies in the development of a firm structure of international organization."[20] In keeping with this belief the Government has been meticulous in its efforts to send strong delegations to all United Nations meetings. Besides ambassadors, government officials, and Cabinet ministers, delegations to the Assembly have included Opposition as well as government parliamentarians, either as delegates or as advisers, a practice which has undoubtedly helped to raise the level of debate on external affairs in Parliament. As was done after the San Francisco Conference, a full report has been prepared on problems discussed at each Assembly and the attitude of the Canadian delegation. Such reports have been described as "the fullest, the frankest, and the most explanatory of any government."[21]

The Government was prompt in securing Canada's adherence to the various specialized agencies created by the United Nations, with the result that this country was among the few which could be listed in 1947 by the United Nations Secretariat as a member of all eight. In keeping with its policy of scrupulous respect for its obligations under the Charter, the Canadian Government obtained authority from Parliament in 1947 which would enable it to implement promptly any decision of the Security Council calling for the application of the economic sanctions required under Article 41 of the Charter. The Government is equally prepared to negotiate the special agreement or agreements on the employment of armed forces with the Security Council, also called for by Article 43 in the Charter. But the initiative in this matter must come from the Security Council, and action in that body has been delayed by the lack of agreement in its Military Staff Committee on the terms of such agreements. In the opening debate of the 1946 Assembly in New York, the chairman of the Canadian delegation expressed the anxiety of the Canadian people and government to know "what armed forces, in common with other members of the United Nations, Canada should maintain as our share of the burden of putting world force behind world law," and urged "all possible speed" on the part of the Security Council and the Military Staff Committee in organizing the enforcement measures.

No international organization can function effectively without efficient techniques as well as progressive policies. Canadian delegates to United Nations meetings have devoted special attention to this practical problem, but, it must be confessed, with only moderate success. They first raised the question in the meetings of the Executive Committee in London during August and September, 1945, when preparations were being made for the first meeting of the General Assembly and for the inauguration of other United Nations bodies. The Canadians suggested that if carefully drawn rules of procedure were approved before the Assembly, the Security Council, or the Economic and Social Council began their deliberations, much time would be saved in arguing rules of order and other questions of procedure in which international conferences can so easily become entangled.

Canadian efforts in behalf of such rules were reasonably successful, except for the Security Council, for which the United States and the U.S.S.R. were unwilling to accept regulations as detailed as those the Canadians favoured. A second effort was made a year later at the General Assembly meeting in New York, following the disappointing debates of the Security Council in the first half of the year. The Canadian delegation submitted an eight-point memorandum[22] to the Political Committee on "Pacific Settlement by the Security Council," which the United Kingdom and Australian delegations generally supported. This document was among the proposals for reform in procedure which the Security Council was asked to consider.

In comparable problems of efficiency, such as the selection of committee chairmen on a basis of competence rather than of regional eligibility, the use of more precise and less pedantic phraseology in United Nations resolutions and conventions, and the study of methods for economizing on the time of the Assembly, the Canadians have steadily and persistently aimed at furthering improvements in technique.

It should not be thought that Canada, because of her concern with these practical matters, has been reticent in expressing her views on major problems of policy. Here again the emphasis has been on a realistic approach rather than on a display of oratorical pyrotechnics for the advancement of unrealizable causes. As Mr. St. Laurent once remarked, "In a country of our stature there is little point in recommending international action if those who must carry the major burden of whatever action is taken are not in sympathy." For that reason Canadians have not been active in denouncing the veto power by presenting spectacular resolutions which stand no chance of being adopted. On the other hand, they have not hesitated to deplore the position of the Security Council, which, because of the misuse of the veto, has become "frozen in futility and divided in dissension."

On several occasions the suggestions and draft resolutions of Canadian delegates have helped to crystallize policy in the United Nations meetings or to find a middle way between the sharply-opposing views of the United States and the U.S.S.R. This has been demonstrated in the work of General McNaughton on the Atomic Energy Commission, in the debates on relief after the American decision to oppose the continuance of the U.N.R.R.A., in the framing of the resolution on disarmament in the 1946 Assembly, and in the adoption of the resolution on war-mongering in the Second General Assembly. A Canadian, L. B. Pearson, was the skilful chairman of the Political Committee at the special Assembly meeting on Palestine in the spring of 1947, and played a conspicuous part in the attainment of agreement between the U.S.S.R. and the United States on the resolution concerning the partition of Palestine which had had so stormy a passage in the autumn of 1946. Possibly because of this record, "informed quarters" at Lake Success told an Associated Press correspondent[23] that Canada, after her election to the Security Council, might be expected to play a conciliatory role in a new Security Council line-up for 1948.

During 1948 Canada was the only state, other than the Great Powers, serving simultaneously on the Security Council, the Economic and Social Council, and the Atomic Energy Commission. To be in this key position at a time of acute political and economic disquiet offered both a challenge to statesmanship and a recognition of Canada's stature as a middle power. That their nation held this position was a cause for sober gratification to the Canadian people.

But membership in the Security Council came at a time when the gulf between the bloc of states dominated by the U.S.S.R. and the West was still widening. The Soviet refusal to coöperate in the European Recovery Programme, the activities of the Cominform, the Communist seizure of power and destruction of democracy in Czechoslovakia, and the pressure upon Finland to sign an alliance gave impetus, in the spring of 1948, for attempts to organize security on a regional basis. As Mr. Bevin, the British Foreign Secretary, put it, "The free nations of western Europe must now draw closely together."

Even before these nations did draw together in the Treaty of Brussels, March 17, 1948, the Canadian Government had indicated that it was thinking on similar lines. In the General Assembly debate of September, 1947, Mr. St. Laurent told the delegates, "Two or more apartments in the structure of peace are undoubtedly less desirable than one family of nations dwelling together in amity undivided by curtains or even more substantial pieces of political furniture. They are, however, to be preferred to the alternative of wholly separate structures." Consequently,

Prime Minister King warmly endorsed the Brussels Treaty as a partial realization of the ideal of collective security, and added, "The peoples of all free countries may be assured that Canada will play her full part in every movement to give substance to the conception of an effective system of collective security by the development of regional pacts under the Charter of the United Nations."

Three months later, when the American Senate endorsed the Vandenberg resolution, which recommended the association of the United States with regional and other collective arrangements that affected its national security, the way was clear for what became the North Atlantic Pact. By the time the Treaty was published (March 18, 1949), the Canadian public had been repeatedly warned by Prime Minister King, Mr. St. Laurent, his successor as Prime Minister in November, 1948, and Mr. Pearson, the new Secretary of State for External Affairs, that the United Nations under present conditions could not guarantee security to its members, that clear-cut agreements to resist aggression jointly were the best deterrent to an aggressor, and that communism was a dangerous and disruptive force internally and internationally. The three major political parties had all endorsed the negotiation of a regional pact in their national conventions. The solidarity of public opinion in endorsing the Government's position was indicated in the debate in the House of Commons on March 28, 1949, when only two members opposed adherence to the proposed Treaty. It was therefore possible for Canada to have the honour of being the first signatory to deposit its ratification at Washington.

This impressive demonstration of unity in national policy reflects the grim and costly lessons which Canada has had in two world wars and a period of "cold war." To enter into a commitment to maintain the security of the North Atlantic area, as embodied in Article 5 of the North Atlantic Treaty, is a far cry from the attitude of "no commitments" in the 'thirties, even though the Treaty carefully respects the right of each signatory state to decide what action should be taken, and thereby permits the Government to respect its pledge to consult Parliament in so grave an emergency. It also gives Canada, under Article 9, a voice in continuous consultation with the Great Powers before grave decisions are made, which was not true a decade ago.[24]

Then again, the Treaty is favoured by Canada because it contains clauses pledging the signatories to mutual aid and coöperation in the economic and social spheres which make it more than a mere armed alliance. Article 2, which pledges the parties to "contribute toward the further development of peaceful and friendly international relations by strengthening their free institutions, by bringing about a better understanding of the principles upon which these institutions are founded, and by promoting conditions of stability and well-being," to "seek to eliminate conflict in their international economic policies," and to "encourage economic collaboration between any or all of them," has been termed the "Canadian" article.

In view of the manner in which the Treaty is carefully drawn so as to harmonize with the Charter of the United Nations, it is regarded by Canadians as a buttress supporting the general security structure. Or, to vary the metaphor, it may be compared, as Mr. Pearson has done in a speech to the American Academy of Political Science, to a "smaller, lower-geared machine," able "to give the United Nations a starting push and help it to 'get rolling' in the way we originally intended."[25] Finally, it pledges Canada to armed conflict in the area most congenial to it geographically, politically, and economically. For Canadians, the North Atlantic area is familiar territory with whose fortunes their destinies have long been linked. That will help to explain their general acceptance of the North Atlantic Treaty and the lack of corresponding interest in the Pact of Rio de Janeiro, to which Canada is eligible to adhere.

Since the Treaty came into force, Canadian ministers of External Affairs and National Defence have shared in the preliminary organizational meetings of the North Atlantic Council and the Defence Committee. Canada has also accepted membership in the Regional Planning Groups for North America and the North Atlantic Ocean and has agreed to share in the defence planning for western Europe "as appropriate." It still remains to evolve a satisfactory basis for the Canadian contribution to the stock-pile of munitions which is needed to defend the West. During the

Second World War the Hyde Park Agreement of 1941 made North America a single economic unit for war production. Some such measure is required today if Canada is to finance the import of strategic materials and contribute to the common defence pool. If the United States were free today to purchase defence material in Canada, as it was between 1941 and 1945, the financial aspect of the problem would be greatly simplified. As Prime Minister St. Laurent described the situation to an American audience, "Without some arrangement for reciprocal defence purchasings with the United States, Canada cannot make the most effective contribution to the security of this area and the North Atlantic area. And our aim in Canada is the greatest possible coöperation for our common security consistent with the maintenance of our independence as a nation."[26]

Canada's general policy on international organization was well expressed by her Secretary of State in his address to the General Assembly of the United Nations on September 26, 1949:

> So far as the Canadian Government is concerned, we have tried to make practicability the touchstone of our attitude towards the United Nations. Where we consider there is any real promise that a proposed course of action will contribute effectively to the solution of any particular problem, we are prepared to give it our full support. On the other hand, we wish to avoid giving to the United Nations, tasks which in the light of the limitations under which it now suffers, and which must some day be removed, it is clearly unable to perform. We wish to be certain that before any course of action is initiated there is a reasonable expectation that it can be carried through to a good conclusion, and that the members of the United Nations will support the organization in this process.

Having examined some of the difficulties confronting the United Nations, Mr. Pearson concluded:

> We must, however, in spite of all obstacles keep everlastingly at the task. Only by so doing can we maintain in the minds and hearts of all people, faith in the United Nations as the best, possibly the only, hope for the prevention of a war which, if we allowed it to occur, would engulf and destroy us all.

NOTES AND REFERENCES

Notes and References

NOTES TO CHAPTER I

The People

[1] For a useful sketch of early settlement, see Vol. V, Part III, *Canada . . . Geographical* (1911), by J. D. Rogers, in Sir Charles Lucas (ed.), *A Historical Geography of the British Colonies* (7 vols. in 11, Oxford Univ. Press, 1888–1923).

[2] *Canada Year Book, 1945,* p. 122. See also V. C. Fowke, "Canadian Agriculture in the Postwar World," *Annals of the American Academy of Political and Social Science,* Vol. CCLIII (September, 1947).

[3] For a brief introduction to this topic see Mason Wade, *The French-Canadian Outlook* (New York, 1946).

[4] E. C. Hughes, *French Canada in Transition* (Chicago, 1943), p. 151.

[5] E. C. Hughes and M. L. McDonald, "French and English in the Economic Structure of Montreal," *Canadian Journal of Economics and Political Science,* Vol. VII (November, 1941).

[6] For a study of the situation in Montreal see E. R. Younge, "Population and the Assimilation of Alien Groups in Canada," *ibid.,* Vol. X (August, 1944).

[7] *Canada Year Book, 1945,* p. 107.

[8] Younge, *op. cit.*

[9] Hughes, *op. cit.*

[10] The standard work on this topic is by M. L. Hansen and J. B. Brebner, *The Mingling of the Canadian and American Peoples* (New Haven, Conn., and Toronto, 1940).

NOTES TO CHAPTER II

The Geography

[1] J. W. Watson, "Canada—Power Vacuum or Pivot Area," in *New Compass of the World* (ed. by H. W. Weigert *et al.;* New York, 1949).

[2] For a more detailed comparison see chap. xvi, "The Canadian Community," pp. 375 ff.

[3] J. W. Watson and W. R. Mead, "Canada in the American Balance," *Culture* (Quebec), Vol. V (1944).

[4] See also chap. ix, "Western Canada," pp. 192 ff.

[5] *Canada Year Book, 1946,* p. 274. Naturally, these conditions vary with the price and quantities of production.

[6] *Ibid.,* pp. 259–260.

[7] See chap. iii, "The Founding of French Canada," pp. 57, 59, 61–62, 66, 67, 71, and chap. iv, "The British North American Colonies," pp. 84, 90, for references to the part played in early Canadian history by English and French fur-traders.

[8] W. J. Waines, *Prairie Population Possibilities,* Royal Commission on Dominion-Provincial Relations (Ottawa, 1939).

[9] A. W. Currie, *Economic Geography of Canada* (Toronto, 1945), p. 229.

[10] J. R. Randall, "Agriculture in the Great Clay Belt of Canada," *Scottish Geographical Magazine,* Vol. LVI (January, 1940).

[11] R. F. Grant, *The Canadian Atlantic Fishery* (Toronto, 1934), p. 3.

[12] E. S. Moore, *The Mineral Resources of Canada* (Toronto, 1933), p. 23.

[13] Dominion Bureau of Statistics. *Canada, 1947* (Ottawa, 1947), p. 116.

[14] Dominion Bureau of Statistics. *Census of Canada, 1941,* Vol. VIII, Agriculture, Part I, p. 423; Part II, p. 853.

[15] See chap. xxiii, "Trade and the World Economy," pp. 537 ff., for a full analysis of the trade situation after the Second World War and the effect of internal trade movements on Canadian conditions.

[16] *Canada, 1947,* p. 151.

[17] Dominion Bureau of Statistics, Department of Trade and Commerce. *The Future Population of Canada,* Bulletin No. F-4 (Ottawa, 1946), p. 5.

NOTES TO CHAPTER III

The Founding of French Canada

[1] James Mooney, *The Aboriginal Population of America North of Mexico,* Smithsonian Miscellaneous Collections (Washington, D.C.), Vol. LXXX, No. 7 (1928), gives the figures for 1600 (in editorial summary) as about 221,000 in British America. The only Iroquois included in this would be a few in Quebec Province south of the St. Lawrence. The Micmacs are estimated at 3,500; the Algonquin and Ottawa bands, 6,000; the Huron confederates and Tionontati, 18,000; the Neutrals, 10,000; the Crees, 15,000; various British Columbia tribes, 85,800; Eskimoes, about 26,000.

[2] A Pole, sent by the Danish King Christian I. Henry Harrisse, *The Discovery of North America* (London and Paris, 1892), pp. 657–658.

[3] Thomas Lloyd, "the most expert seaman in England" (Harrisse, *ibid.*), took out ships belonging to John Jay, Jr., on July 15, 1480, but returned without having found the island of Brasylle, and two, three, or four caravels were sent yearly for seven years before 1498.

[4] In *Encyclopedia of Canada* (ed. by W. S. Wallace; 6 vols., Toronto, 1940), H. H. Langton, *s.v.* "Cartography," omits reference to this map, originally drawn on a piece of (birch?) bark sent from Canada, wrapped in a piece of satin, and "very carefully kept in a box" in the geographical collections of the War Department in Paris, France. Harrisse (*op. cit.*) could find no trace of it and considers it apocryphal, though he admits that Denys visited these coasts. A facsimile exists in the Canadian Archives.

[5] Hakluyt, *Divers Voyages Touching the Discovery of America and the Islands Adjacent* (Hakluyt Society, London, 1850), p. 71.

[6] *Purchas, His Pilgrimes,* Part III, p. 809, cit. in H. P. Biggar (ed.), *The Precursors of Jacques Cartier, 1497–1534* (Ottawa, 1911), p. xxix, n. 5.

[7] J. B. Brebner, *The Explorers of North America, 1492–1806* (London, 1933), p. 117.

[8] Roughly co-extensive with the present Maritime Provinces (New Brunswick, Nova Scotia, and Prince Edward Island).

[9] The first fishing-crews doubtless wintered in Newfoundland early in the sixteenth century. "Sabine (L.?) states that in 1522 there were forty or fifty houses in Newfoundland." D. W. Prowse, *A History of Newfoundland* (London, 1895), p. 59.

[10] Stock-holders included Radisson and Groseilliers, who had gone to England in 1665 and led an English expedition to the Bay in 1668–1669.

[11] Seigneury granted to La Salle by the Sulpicians. The name Lachine is said to refer to his dreams of finding a passage to China. It was from here that he set off in 1669, and it was subsequently a starting-point for the west-bound fur "brigades."

[12] Fourteen was a more mature age then than now, however. When Champlain married twelve-year-old Helene Boullé, the contract stipulated that she should return to her parents for two years, the implication being that the marriage might then be consummated, and it was at about this same age that Anne Cecil, formerly (at the age of twelve) engaged to Philip Sidney, married the Earl of Oxford.

[13] For a scholarly account of these events, including responsibility for the expulsion, which was not ordered by the British Government, see J. B. Brebner, *New England's Outpost: Acadia before the Conquest of Canada* (Columbia Univ. Press, 1927). Longfellow's *Evangeline* gives a highly romanticized version.

[14] The *arpent* is an old French measure, varying from district to district. The *arpent de Paris,* in general use in Canada, comprised about five-sixths of an acre; and a linear *arpent,* comprising about 192 English feet, was also in use.

NOTES TO CHAPTER IV

The British North American Colonies

[1] J. B. Brebner, *The Neutral Yankees of Nova Scotia . . .* (Columbia Univ. Press, 1937).

[2] The position on American fishing-rights in Canadian territorial waters has been altered many times. See *Encyclopedia of Canada* (ed. by W. S. Wallace; 6 vols., Toronto, 1940), *s.v.* "Fisheries."

[3] On the border, tension was prolonged by American sympathizers who arranged demonstrations and incited border incidents on the mistaken assumption that the majority of Canadians wanted to break the British connexion.

[4] Newfoundland received responsible government in 1854.

NOTES TO CHAPTER V

The Dominion: Genesis and Integration

[1] There was general sympathy in Canada for the North, and a considerable number of Canadian volunteers fought in the Union Army, but, as the war continued, irritating incidents along the border caused friction, owing chiefly to Confederate attempts to use the Canadas as a base for the operation of a spy system and even for direct military action.

[2] For several years the threats of Fenian invasions at points along the border as far west as Manitoba created a tremendous impression on the popular mind in Canada, and the efforts to repel the invasions which were actually attempted were a strong stimulus to the growth of national feeling in the young Dominion.

NOTES TO CHAPTER VI

The Twentieth Century

[1] *Canada Year Book, 1914,* p. 251. This invaluable official annual is the source of virtually all the statistics incorporated in this chapter.

[2] G. P. de T. Glazebrook, *A History of Transportation in Canada* (Toronto and New Haven, Conn., 1938).

[3] The standard life of Laurier is O. D. Skelton, *Life and Letters of Sir Wilfrid Laurier* (2 vols., Toronto, 1921).

[4] The action taken is briefly summarized in C. P. Stacey, *The Military Problems of Canada* (Toronto, 1940), pp. 67–68.

[5] *Ibid.,* pp. 70–74.

[6] E. H. Armstrong, *The Crisis of Quebec, 1914–18* (Columbia Univ. Press, 1937).

[7] *Canada Year Book, 1938,* p. 404.

[8] Sir Charles Lucas (ed.), *The Empire at War* (5 vols., Oxford Univ. Press, 1921–1926), II, 294.

[9] For a more detailed study of constitutional developments, see chap. xi, "The Federal Constitution," pp. 281–296, and chap. xii, "The Machinery of Government," pp. 297–313.

[10] Department of External Affairs, Information Division. *Radio in Canada,* Reference Paper No. 28 (Ottawa, 1948).

[11] The effectiveness of an organization like the C.B.C. must always be a matter of personal opinion. The Corporation has been much criticized—and it is certainly desirable that it should be subject to constant public scrutiny and review. The present writer's own opinion is that, on balance, it has done well for Canada and that a return to completely private broadcasting would be a national disaster.

[12] *Canada Year Book, 1938,* p. 769.

[13] J. B. Brebner, *North Atlantic Triangle: The Interplay of Canada, the United States and Great Britain* (New Haven, Conn., and Toronto, 1945), p. 309.

[14] The report of the Rowell-Sirois Commission is briefly summarized in *Canada Year Book, 1940*, pp. 1157–1163.

[15] A. R. M. Lower, *Colony to Nation: A History of Canada* (Toronto, 1946), p. 524.

[16] For full discussion of external policy see chaps. xxi–xxiv.

[17] The delegate Walter Alexander Riddell has described the incident in *World Security by Conference* (Toronto, 1947).

[18] Stacey, *op. cit.*, pp. 146, 180.

[19] Stacey, *The Canadian Army, 1939–1945: An Official Historical Summary* (Ottawa, 1948), pp. 308–309.

[20] For a discussion of these matters see Terence Sheard, "The B.C.A.T.P. and Defence Policy," *International Journal*, Vol. II (Winter, 1946–1947), pp. 37–46.

[21] *Canada Year Book, 1947*, p. 509.

NOTE TO CHAPTER VII

Fundamental and Historic Elements

[1] Potash, extracted from wood-ashes, was especially useful to the new settler since it was a by-product of his land-clearing operations and he had little if anything else to sell.

NOTE TO CHAPTER VIII

Eastern Canada

[1] These and similar figures do not include Gaspé, which is a part of Quebec and for which separate statistics are not available; nor do they include Newfoundland, which was not in the Dominion in 1941.

NOTES TO CHAPTER IX

Western Canada

[1] This point is analysed at some length in. U.S. Congress. *The Future of the Great Plains—Message from the President of the United States Transmitting the Report of the Great Plains Committee*, 75th Cong., 1st sess., S. Doc. 144 (1938).

[2] Except for a comparatively small part of the Peace River area which lies within the province of British Columbia.

[3] Paul F. Sharp, "The American Farmer and the Last Best West," *Agricultural History*, April, 1947, pp. 65–75.

[4] Dominion Bureau of Statistics. *Census of the Prairie Provinces, 1946*, Preliminary Bulletin, Agriculture, 7-400-0, October 31, 1947.

[5] Summer-fallow fields were formerly ploughed with mould-board ploughs which turned under all stubble and other "trash." As weeds began to grow, the ploughed surface was cultivated from time to time during the summer with the result that the soil was reduced to a fine mulch or, when dry, to a near-

powder. The one-way disk breaks the soil surface without pulverizing it and without burying stubble and straw.

[6] By *Statutes of Canada,* 25–26 Geo. V. c.23 (1935).

[7] This is in addition to some 650,000 acres already under irrigation in the Prairie Provinces.

[8] *Statutes of Canada,* 3 Geo. VI. c.50 (1939).

[9] Population estimates for 1946 are: Winnipeg, 231,200; Edmonton, 111,750; Calgary, 97,250; Regina, 56,520. By way of further example, in Saskatchewan there are 8 cities, 82 towns, 385 villages, and approximately 675 hamlets. Regina is by an appreciable margin the largest city in the province, and only a dozen places, inclusive of the cities, have populations in excess of 2,000.

[10] Though geologically in the Shield, the development of this area has been associated with that of the Mackenzie Valley.

[11] The Yukon gold discoveries had comparatively little lasting effect upon the regional economy, owing to the early exhaustion of the deposits which could be exploited by methods then available, and the limited range of alternative resources in the area. The succeeding analysis in the chapter refers particularly to British Columbia.

[12] *Report of the Royal Commission on Dominion-Provincial Relations* (Ottawa, 1940), Book I, "Canada, 1867–1939," pp. 122–123.

[13] Ocean freight-rates on lumber from Vancouver to New York fell from $27.30 per thousand board feet in 1920 to $10.11 in 1929. The mill cost of lumber in British Columbia was $22.50 per thousand board feet in 1929. See *ibid.*

NOTES TO CHAPTER X

Trends and Structure of the Economy

[1] D. G. Creighton, "British North America at Confederation," Appx. 2, p. 47, in *Report of the Royal Commission on Dominion-Provincial Relations* (Ottawa, 1939).

[2] *Canada Year Book, 1913,* pp. 227–228.

[3] O. J. McDiarmid, *Commercial Policy in the Canadian Economy* (Harvard Univ. Press, 1946), pp. 145–146.

[4] Jacob Viner, *Canada's Balance of International Indebtedness, 1900–1913* . . . (Harvard Univ. Press, 1924).

[5] *Canada and Its Provinces,* Vol. IX, pp. 198–199.

[6] H. A. Logan, *Trade Unions in Canada* (Toronto, 1948), p. 19.

[7] These estimates are based mainly on figures presented by J. J. Deutsch, "War Finance and the Canadian Economy, 1914–1920," *Canadian Journal of Economics and Political Science,* Vol. VI (November, 1940); also F. H. Brown, "The History of Canadian War Finance, 1914–20," in *War Finance in Canada,* by F. H. Brown, J. D. Gibson, and A. F. W. Plumptre (Toronto, 1940).

[8] Economic historians seem to be agreed on this point. See Deutsch, *op. cit.,* pp. 525–526; Brown, *op. cit.,* pp. 1–5; Royal Commission on Dominion-Provincial Relations, *The Rowell-Sirois Report,* Vol. I, p. iv; Adam Shortt,

"Early Economic Effects of the War upon Canada," *Preliminary Economic Studies,* Carnegie Endowment for International Peace, Division of Economics and History (New York, 1918), Vol. I.

[9] These figures are from Deutsch, *op. cit.*

[10] *The Rowell-Sirois Report,* Vol. I, p. 100.

[11] Annual data do show some minor shifts of occupational distribution after the war. There is some evidence of a "back-to-the-farm" movement during the 1921–1922 depression, after which the share of agriculture in total employment resumed its downward trend. Manufacturing suffered a decline in both absolute and relative terms, and, while the total number of manufacturing employees rose again in 1923, manufacturing did not regain its 1920 share of total employment. Other industries, however, show remarkable stability, with the share of the construction industry increasing during the depression years. Figures of national income produced tell essentially the same story. Thus the annual data give little support to the "readjustment" thesis.

[12] R. B. Bryce, "The Effects on Canada of Industrial Fluctuations in the United States," *Canadian Journal of Economics and Political Science,* Vol. V (August, 1939).

[13] An important deduction which Mr. Bryce makes from this close relationship of Canadian investment with economic conditions in the United States is that with the approach of that country to economic maturity, "if Canadian opportunities are to be realized, investment in this country may have to become more independent of American conditions and sentiment than heretofore."

[14] For figures see *The Rowell-Sirois Report* and *Comparative Statistics of Public Finance.*

[15] K. W. Taylor, "Canadian War Time Price Controls, 1941–6," *Canadian Journal of Economics and Political Science,* Vol. XIII (February, 1947)

[16] Cash requirements include such items as maturing Canadian National Railway bonds, other C.N.R. outlays, and Central Mortgage and Housing Corporation loans.

[17] Department of Reconstruction, Directorate of Economic Research. *Location and Effects of Wartime Industrial Expansion in Canada, 1933–44* (Ottawa, 1945), p. 1.

[18] H. S. Fox, "Canada's Economy in 1945," *Foreign Commerce Weekly,* January 19, 1946.

[19] Department of Reconstruction. *Op. cit.,* p. 35.

[20] Minister of Reconstruction. *Employment and Income* (*with Special Reference to the Initial Period of Reconstruction*), (Ottawa, 1945), pp. 5–7.

NOTES TO CHAPTER XI

The Federal Constitution

[1] But in Quebec the civil law is of French origin and is based not on the common law of England but on the Roman law.

[2] At the moment of writing, the federal government has made proposals with the purpose of finding an acceptable amending process.

[3] The position of the Senate in Canada is not unlike that of the House of Lords in the United Kingdom. Legislation of general importance is now rarely initiated in the Senate. Its chief function at present is to delay legislation which it considers extreme, ill-advised, or prejudicial to local interests, until there has been opportunity for the full weight of public opinion to make itself felt. As appointments are for life, a new government will find itself at first, and perhaps for some time, without a Senate majority. An abrupt break with the past is thus exceedingly unlikely under the Canadian system.

[4] The same situation exists in the relations of the provincial Premier and his Cabinet with the Lieutenant-Governor and the legislature.

[5] Senate representation is on a regional rather than a provincial or numerical basis. By the British North America Act, Canada was "deemed to consist of Three Divisions," to which a fourth was added by subsequent legislation crystallized in the Amending Act of 1915. Each of the four divisions, the Maritime Provinces, Quebec, Ontario, and the Western Provinces, represents an economically or culturally distinct section, the interests of which may be considered to need protection on some basis other than numerical. The entrance of Newfoundland in 1949 disturbed this balance in some degree by giving this fourth Maritime Province additional senators.

[6] For example, of the five provinces which entered Confederation with second chambers, four have since abolished them: Prince Edward Island, 1873; Manitoba, 1876; New Brunswick, 1892; Nova Scotia, 1926. Quebec retains the bicameral organization.

[7] The expansion in these fields is treated more fully in chap. xix, "Education," pp. 436–456, and chap. xvii, "The Social Services," pp. 390–407.

NOTES TO CHAPTER XII

The Machinery of Government

[1] The system described in detail in this chapter is that of the federal government, but the same general relationship exists in the provinces among Lieutenant-Governor, Premier, Cabinet, and legislature.

[2] This statement must be qualified in two respects. First, a technical exception is to be found in the procedure of constitutional amendment. Then it is the Canadian Parliament that addresses His Majesty with a petition for British legislation amending the British North America Act. Needless to say, the Cabinet bears the responsibility for initiating this parliamentary request. A more important exception, however, is to be found in appeals from decisions of Canadian courts. In these appeals the judgements of the Judicial Committee of the British Privy Council take the form of advice to the Crown. The Canadian Cabinet has no more responsibility for this advice than has the British Cabinet; the Judicial Committee is in effect an independent court of law. These points

will be modified if the amending process is changed (see chap. xi, note 2) and if appeals to the Judicial Committee are ended. (See p. 312.)

3 The British North America Act lays down several occasions on which the Governor General is to refer to British authorities. But the Governor has now no connexion with British ministers and has no reason to consult the King, who would necessarily have to rely upon the very same Canadian ministers at the Governor's side. An informative example of legislative recognition of this situation was provided in 1947, when the provision for certified statutes to be sent by the Governor to London was deleted from the Canadian law governing publication. The royal veto (exercised originally on British ministerial advice) has long since fallen into the same disuse that prevails in Britain—and for the same reason, namely, its incompatibility with Cabinet responsibility in Parliament.

4 The accession of Newfoundland added six more senators and seven more members of the House of Commons.

5 See note 4.

6 Exceptions are most apt to occur when a seat must be found for a party leader or Cabinet Minister who has been defeated or who is entering the House for the first time.

7 Besides the ministries named, there were, in 1949, Secretary of State, Trade and Commerce, Mines and Resources, Transport, National Revenue, Fisheries, Post-Office, and Public Works. The *Canada Year Book* gives the particulars for any year.

8 Provincial sessions are shorter than those of the House of Commons; and cabinets are usually smaller, comprising, besides the Premier and the Attorney General, a provincial secretary and treasurer, and ministers of departments dealing with such subjects as Health and Welfare, Education, Forests, Mines and Fisheries, Municipal Affairs, Planning and Development, Public Works, Reform Institutions, and Travel and Publicity.

9 The Exchequer Court of Canada, a purely Dominion court, is not unlike an American court in that its jurisdiction is determined by the nature of the cases or the parties to the controversy.

NOTES TO CHAPTER XIV

Political Parties and Ideas

1 Grandfather of the Canadian Prime Minister who retired in 1948.

2 A term taken from the stone-masons of the time, who wanted clear grit in the sand for their mortar.

NOTES TO CHAPTER XV

The State and Economic Life

1 This typically Canadian constitutional expression means during the pleasure of the provincial Premier and the Cabinet; the part played by the Lieu-

tenant-Governor in the transaction is purely nominal (cf. chap. xi, "The Federal Constitution," p. 288).

2 The organization of municipal commissions is dealt with in chap. xiii, "Local Government," pp. 314 ff.

3 See chap. iv, "The British North American Colonies," pp. 78 ff., and chap. xi, "The Federal Constitution," p. 577, n. 1.

4 In the years 1930–1941 the federal government contributed about 40 per cent of the monies expended on public relief in Canada.

5 D. C. MacGregor, "The Problems of Price Level in Canada," *Canadian Journal of Economics and Political Science,* Vol. XIII (May, 1947), p. 180. As Professor MacGregor points out, precision in the income-tax ratio is difficult to achieve.

NOTE TO CHAPTER XVII

The Social Services

1 For a fuller statement see chap. xi, "The Federal Constitution," pp. 291 ff., in regard to residual power.

NOTES TO CHAPTER XVIII

The Cultural Pattern

1 *Canadian Life* (Toronto), April, 1949.

2 Cf. Robert Ayre, "A Country in Search of Itself," *Culture,* Autumn, 1948, p. 375: "In the course of time, attacking prejudice and stale tradition, battling bravely for a Canadian way of looking at Canada, the Group became an accepted tradition itself and a powerful influence. But the country it exploited, celebrated with such joyous patriotism, was not all Canada. It was the wilderness, and since the wilderness had little content and subtlety, the painting, while exciting in its immediate impact, was lacking in the qualities that make for the greatest art. Canada was slowly maturing and it began to realize (as most of the Group did, for that matter) that the wilderness was empty. Painters were growing up who reacted violently against the Group or simply ignored it. Some, 'socially conscious,' resented it because there was no humanity in its landscape; others, 'art conscious,' sought values that they could find in the studios rather than in the northern woods."

3 *Ibid.,* p. 371.

4 E.g., Vancouver, Calgary, Edmonton, Saskatoon, Winnipeg, London, Ottawa, Quebec, Kingston, Sackville, Halifax.

NOTES TO CHAPTER XIX

Education

1 In Newfoundland the denominational "public" schools, the interdenominational common schools, and the collegiate institutes which take the form of denominational "colleges" give a course of eleven or twelve grades roughly

corresponding to the junior and senior matriculation and second- and first-class certificate work in other provinces. Memorial University College in St. John's offers two-year courses in arts, sciences, pre-medical work, and domestic science, one-year courses in teacher-training, and three-year courses in engineering, which are accepted for credits at Canadian universities. There are also courses in adult education and an important and well-attended course in navigation.

[2] The organization in Newfoundland has followed lines somewhat similar to those in Quebec, in that education has been similarly involved with denominational life. In 1946, under commission government, prior to the decision to join Canada, the Council of Education consisted of the Commissioner for Home Affairs and Education, the Secretary of Education, and representatives of Roman Catholics, the Church of England, the United Church of Canada, and the Salvation Army, the denominational representatives being the executive officers of the set-up.

[3] The dates given are those claimed by the foundations themselves. Some institutions have celebrated various dates, such as the date of the charter, the date of the actual beginning of classes, and so on.

[4] The struggle for secularization of government-sponsored education was a part of the general struggle against establishment. See also chap. xx, "Religion and Religious Institutions," pp. 457–483.

[5] Federation, affiliation, and association represent varying degrees of connexion and coöperation.

[6] Statistics in this and similar lists throughout the chapter are as of 1947.

NOTES TO CHAPTER XX

Religion and Religious Institutions

[1] In Newfoundland, which in 1948 voted to join Canada, the division of portfolios has been on a generally tripartite basis, with representation for Roman Catholics, the Church of England, and the United Church of Canada (formerly chiefly Methodist). The Salvation Army also has been represented on the Council of Education.

[2] A dispatch to the Toronto *Globe and Mail,* December 17, 1947, reported Premier Duplessis of Quebec as expressing himself strongly in favour of strict observance of Sunday.

[3] In 1941, more than 90 per cent of Canadian Roman Catholics were native-born. About 40 per cent of these were classed as rural. Of non-native, non-French Roman Catholics, about 45 per cent appeared to be rural.

[4] Their most prominent poet of the day, Professor E. J. Pratt, confines himself almost exclusively to sober epics of heroic accomplishment with a strong scientific and mechanical flavour.

[5] Owing to their system of voting themselves into or out of the Union by congregations, a privilege not accorded to the Methodists, a considerable minority of the Presbyterians remained outside.

[6] As one of their distinguished representatives, the Abbé Arthur Maheux, has done: see *Ton Histoire est une épopée* (Quebec, 1941).

[7] C. W. Robinson, *Life of Sir John Beverley Robinson . . . Chief-Justice of Upper Canada* (Toronto, 1904), p. 178.

[8] The problem of Dominion-provincial relations was involved; cf. chap. v, "The Dominion," pp. 112, 119 ff.

[9] The province was 86.6 per cent Roman Catholic in 1941. Ontario was 76.8 per cent Protestant.

NOTES TO CHAPTER XXI

Historic Factors

[1] Emigration elsewhere than to the United States was negligible.

[2] M. L. Hansen and J. B. Brebner, *The Mingling of the Canadian and American Peoples* (New Haven, Conn., and Toronto, 1940). Population figures may be found in *Seventh Census of Canada, 1931,* Vol. I.

[3] The most authoritative account of the naval question is by G. N. Tucker, "The Naval Policy of Sir Robert Borden, 1912–14," *Canadian Historical Review,* Vol. XXVIII (March, 1947), pp. 1–30.

[4] Quoted in R. A. MacKay and E. B. Rogers, *Canada Looks Abroad* (Oxford Univ. Press, 1938), p. 332.

[5] Louis S. St. Laurent, *The Foundations of Canadian Policy in World Affairs,* Duncan and John Gray Memorial Lecture (Univ. of Toronto Press, 1947).

[6] Department of External Affairs. *Report on the United Nations Conference on International Organization* (Ottawa, 1945), pp. 37–38.

[7] The text of the submission will be found in G. de T. Glazebrook, "The Settlement of Germany," *International Journal,* Vol. XI (Spring, 1947), pp. 132–143.

NOTES TO CHAPTER XXII

The North Atlantic Triangle

[1] Library of Congress, Manuscripts Division. John Watson Foster Papers, a.l.s., Confidential, London, December 27, 1897: John Hay to John Watson Foster.

[2] Among the achievements of this group was the transformation of the good lyric poet, Wilfred Campbell, into a bad imperialistic bard. See C. F. Klinck, *Wilfred Campbell: A Study in Late Provincial Victorianism* (Toronto, 1942), pp. 103–112 and chaps. iii, v, and vi, *passim.*

[3] G. N. Tucker, "The Naval Policy of Sir Robert Borden, 1912–14," *Canadian Historical Review,* Vol. XXVIII (March, 1947), pp. 1–30; and E. A. Forsey and G. N. Tucker, "Correspondence," *ibid.* (June, 1947), pp. 241–242, are more revealing of British pressure (Winston Churchill) and of Borden's embarrassment after his badly-calculated responses to it than of the adverse complex of political forces in Canada and of the lack of candour in the British Cabinet as

to Canada's share in the policy-making Committee of Imperial Defence which made him give up his attempt.

[4] Borden was his own historian: in the Marfleet Lectures at Toronto in 1921, *Canadian Constitutional Studies* (Toronto, 1922); in the Rhodes Memorial Lectures at Oxford in 1927, *Canada in the Commonwealth* (Oxford, 1929); and in *Robert Laird Borden: His Memoirs* (ed. by Henry Borden; 2 vols., Toronto, 1938). While this was historically advantageous in many ways, the *Memoirs,* in particular, invited the more impersonal views which Canadian historians have been providing since about 1938.

[5] The Duke of Connaught shared Queen Victoria's views of the prerogatives of the Royal Family in matters military: *ibid.,* Vol. II, pp. 601–604. Mr. Law assumed that Canada would turn over her large armies to British direction without being informed as to their intended use: *ibid.,* pp. 620–626; see also pp. 773–775 and 809–818.

[6] Note especially *Report of the Conference on the Operation of Dominion Legislation and Merchant Shipping Legislation, 1929* (Ottawa, 1930).

[7] *Canadian Constitutional Studies,* pp. 121–122.

[8] *Canada in the Commonwealth,* pp. 96–99; *Memoirs,* Vol. II, pp. 760–761, 767–768, 1002–1007.

[9] *Memoirs,* pp. 841, 907.

[10] This question receives tantalizingly scant references in Borden's *Memoirs,* but see the fragmentary evidences of the crisis early in 1918: *ibid.,* pp. 766–773; and, for an over-all view, J. J. Deutsch, "War Finance and the Canadian Economy, 1914–1920," *Canadian Journal of Economics and Political Science,* Vol. VI (November, 1940), pp. 525–542.

[11] Achieved by Canada in 1927.

[12] Edgar McInnis, *Canada: A Political and Social History* (New York, 1947), pp. vii–viii.

[13] Meighen succeeded Borden as Prime Minister in 1920, but lost the election of 1921 to W. L. Mackenzie King and the Liberals. He also lost in 1926 and was succeeded in his own party by R. B. Bennett, whose prime-ministership of 1930–1935 was the only subsequent interruption in the sway of Mr. King and the Liberals.

[14] A. B. Corey, R. G. Trotter, and W. W. MacLaren (eds.), *Conference on Canadian-American Affairs, 1939* (Boston, 1939), p. 17.

[15] A. L. Burt, "The American Key," *Revue de l'Université d'Ottawa,* Vol. XII (April–June, 1942), p. 3.

[16] Compare W. A. Mackintosh, "Keynes as a Public Servant," *Canadian Journal of Economics and Political Science,* Vol. XIII (August, 1947), p. 382: "The Canadian insistence on dealing direct with Washington rather than as a part of the Commonwealth he comprehended intellectually. He respected it—he was even patient with it. He never really understood it." Recall also the resignation of General A. G. L. McNaughton, Commander of the Canadian Army, because of similar difficulties with General Sir Bernard Montgomery.

[17] Halifax at Toronto, January 24, 1944.

[18] Canadian House of Commons, January 31, 1944.

[19] *The Economist,* Vol. CLIV (January 10, 1948), p. 46.

[20] This was vividly illustrated in Maxime Raymond's speech of April 3, 1939, against Canadian implication in British wars: *Commons Debates,* Vol. III (1939), pp. 2542 ff. See also Iris S. Podea, "Pan American Sentiment in French Canada," *International Journal,* Vol. III (Autumn, 1948), pp. 334–348.

NOTES TO CHAPTER XXIII

Trade and the World Economy

[1] The following notes with regard to the sources of information for this chapter may be useful.

For the fiscal years ending June 30, 1900–1906, for 1907 (nine months only, from June 30, 1906, to March 31, 1907), and for the fiscal years ending March 31, 1908–1926, the figures for merchandise trade in tables 1 and 2 are from the Dominion Bureau of Statistics. *Canada Year Book, 1940,* pp. 530 f.

For the calendar years 1926–1947 the figures for merchandise trade in tables 1 and 2 are from the Dominion Bureau of Statistics. *The Canadian Balance of International Payments, Preliminary Statement, 1947* (Ottawa, 1948), pp. 22 ff. The percentages for these years were calculated by the writer from the balance of payments data.

For use in a discussion of changes in Canadian trade it is important to have Customs data adjusted to reflect the actual payments and receipts arising from imports and exports. Unfortunately, the balance of payments estimates which make this adjustment for the years 1900–1926 show only total trade. The adjusted total has not been broken down into the three groups used in the Bureau's estimates. Customs data as given in the *Canada Year Book* have therefore had to be used for the years before 1926. The two figures given for 1926 indicate the difference made by the balance of payments adjustment. See the Dominion Bureau of Statistics. *The Canadian Balance of International Payments, 1926–1944* (Ottawa, 1945), pp. 12 f.

All references in the text to balance of payments items for the years 1900–1925, including calendar-year totals for merchandise trade, are taken from F. A. Knox, *Dominion Monetary Policy, 1929–1934: A Study Prepared for the Royal Commission on Dominion-Provincial Relations* (Ottawa, 1939), pp. 89 ff. The estimates there included for the years 1900–1913 are from Jacob Viner, *Canada's Balance of International Indebtedness, 1900–1913 . . .* (Harvard Univ. Press, 1924). For the years since 1926 the estimates of the Dominion Bureau of Statistics are used. Estimates on United States balance of payments are from U.S. Bureau of Foreign and Domestic Commerce. *The United States in the World Economy: The International Transactions of the United States during the Interwar Period,* by H. B. Larry and associates, Economic Series, No. 23 (1943).

Exchange-rate data cited for the years 1914–1926 are either calculations made by the writer from daily exchange-rate data supplied by Canadian banks or from the Federal Reserve *Bulletin.* For 1928–1945 see Bank of Canada. *Statistical Summary, 1946 Supplement,* pp. 126 ff.

Canadian national-income data are taken from the following:

1914–1920 J. J. Deutsch, "War Finance and the Canadian Economy, 1914–1920," *Canadian Journal of Economics and Political Science,* Vol. VI (November, 1940), p. 538.

1919–1937 *Canada Year Book, 1945,* p. 909.

1938–1947 Dominion Bureau of Statistics. *National Accounts, Income and Expenditure, 1938–1946* (Ottawa, 1947); *National Accounts, Income and Expenditure, Preliminary, 1947* (Ottawa, 1948).

United States national-income data from U.S. Department of Commerce, Office of Business Economics. *National Income, Supplement to Survey of Current Business.*

2 *Canada Year Book, 1947,* p. 872.

3 *Ibid., 1920,* pp. 344 ff., 348.

4 F. A. Knox, "Canadian War Finance and the Balance of Payments, 1914–1918," *Canadian Journal of Economics and Political Science,* Vol. VI, No. 2 (May, 1940), pp. 226 ff.

5 K. W. Taylor, "Post-War Fluctuations in Canadian Foreign Trade," *Journal of the Canadian Bankers' Association,* Vol. XXXIV, No. 3 (April, 1927), p. 303.

6 *Ibid.*

7 Larry, *op. cit.,* pp. 93 ff.

8 Dominion-Provincial Conference on Reconstruction. *Public Investment and Capital Formation: A Study of Public and Private Investment Outlay, Canada, 1926–1941* (Ottawa, 1945), pp. 30 f.

9 *Canada Year Book, 1931,* p. 520; *1936,* p. 532; *1939,* p. 510.

10 "Canada did not receive any United States dollars under the Lend-Lease system. Aid extended by Canada to other countries in the years 1942–1948 under the Mutual Aid procedure, the contributions of 1942 to Great Britain and in later years to U.N.R.R.A., and through Military and other official relief amounts to $3,492,000,000." Dominion Bureau of Statistics. *The Canadian Balance of International Payments, 1926–1948* (Ottawa, 1949), p. 168.

11 The recent devaluation of the pound sterling and many other currencies in terms of the United States dollar should be a prime factor promoting that greater importing by Americans which is so essential to the restoration of a world trading system centred on the United States. As the American dollar has again gone to premium in Canada and sterling currencies to sharp discounts, the tendency of Canada's exports to flow in increasing amounts to dollar markets is strengthened. The effect of this change in diverting Canada's imports from the now dearer American market to the cheaper overseas markets is a welcome aid in countering what may even so prove to be a very drastic decline in Canada's trade with non-dollar countries. Thus, currency readjustments have increased rather than diminished Canada's economic dependence upon the United States market.

NOTES TO CHAPTER XXIV

International Organization

[1] Henry Borden (ed.), *Robert Laird Borden: His Memoirs* (Toronto, 1938), Vol. II, p. 961.

[2] *Ibid.*, p. 951.

[3] G. P. de T. Glazebrook, *Canada at the Paris Peace Conference* (Canadian Institute of International Affairs, London and Toronto, 1942), p. 11.

[4] Members of the federal Parliament and of the provincial legislatures, respectively, are often spoken of as M.P.'s and M.P.P.'s, from the abbreviations appended to their names, in the latter erroneously, as the correct abbreviation was originally M.L.A.

[5] André Siegfried, *Canada* (London, 1937), p. 290.

[6] G. M. Carter, *The British Commonwealth and International Security, 1919–1939* (Toronto, 1947).

[7] Later it was revealed that on two occasions after the Riddell disavowal, the Government approved the inclusion of oil in the embargo.

[8] Parallel speeches were made by delegates from Scandinavia, Holland, and Switzerland.

[9] J. W. Dafoe, "Canada's Foreign Policy," *Proceedings*, Conference on Canadian-American Affairs, 1937 (Montreal, 1937), p. 225. Cf. A. R. M. Lower's comment: "Thereafter Canada had no foreign policy except a correct neutrality. Her voice was not raised in international affairs and she left it to the great powers to wreck the world as they deemed best." *Colony to Nation: A History of Canada* (Toronto, 1946), p. 548.

[10] Speech at the Mansion House in London (September, 1941), p. 7.

[11] Between 1934 and 1939 the United States ratified only five conventions, all of them dealing with maritime questions.

[12] This episode is described by the present director of the I.L.O., Mr. Edward J. Phelan, who accompanied Albert Thomas on this mission, in his memoir *Yes and Albert Thomas* (London, 1936), pp. 168, 172–173.

[13] *Report of the Royal Commission on Dominion-Provincial Relations* (Ottawa, 1940), Book II, p. 48.

[14] Brooke Claxton, "The Place of Canada in Post War Organisation," *Canadian Journal of Economics and Political Science*, Vol. X (November, 1944), p. 421.

[15] R. G. Trotter, "Canada and World Organisation," *Canadian Historical Review*, Vol. XXVI (December, 1945), p. 145.

[16] *The Inauguration of the Second Victory Loan*, p. 2.

[17] Quoted in Grant Dexter, *Canada and the Building of Peace* (Canadian Institute of International Affairs, Toronto, 1944), pp. 142–143.

[18] During the Dumbarton Oaks conversations the British delegation met every day with representatives of the diplomatic missions of Canada, Australia, New Zealand, South Africa, and India.

[19] C. C. Lingard and R. G. Trotter, *Peace with Progress* (Toronto, 1945), p. 21.

[20] Louis S. St. Laurent, *The Foundations of Canadian Policy in World Affairs* (Univ. of Toronto Press, 1947), p. 6.

[21] Escott Reid, *Canada's Role in the United Nations* (Ottawa, 1947), p. 2.

[22] *The United Nations, 1946: Report on the Second Part of the First Session of the General Assembly* (Ottawa, 1947), pp. 204–206.

[23] Associated Press dispatch, December 15, 1947.

[24] Cf. L. B. Pearson, "Canada and the North Atlantic Alliance," *Foreign Affairs,* April, 1949, p. 377.

[25] L. B. Pearson, *Canada and the North Atlantic Treaty* (Ottawa, 1949, mimeographed).

[26] Address at Rensselaer Polytechnic Institute, Troy, New York, on October 14, 1949 (Ottawa, 1949, mimeographed).

A SELECTED BIBLIOGRAPHY

A Selected Bibliography

WHILE as comprehensive a choice as possible has been made within the limits of space available, many useful titles have of necessity been omitted, and frequently selections have had to be arbitrary, particularly for books of specialized interest. A number of bibliographical works and other sources of further information have, however, been included. In general, articles, despite their value for many topics, have been omitted. When books have been reprinted or issued in more than one edition, the most recent date of publication has usually been given.

For general reference, (1) *Canada Year Book,* published annually by the Dominion Bureau of Statistics, contains statistical information and special articles on trade, population, resources, and many other matters of public interest, and is especially useful. Also published annually by the Bureau for more popular distribution is the smaller, well-illustrated (2) *Canada: The Official Handbook of Present Conditions and Recent Progress.* The very great range of government publications, Dominion and provincial, provides a mine of material; information is available from the King's Printers in Ottawa and in the provincial capitals, or from the appropriate departments. The Information Division of the Department of External Affairs, Ottawa, besides furnishing an information service, publishes the monthly (3) *External Affairs* and issues other bulletins. (4) *Labour Gazette,* and (5) *Canadian Statistical Review,* which lists the recent statistical publications, are issued by the Department of Trade and Commerce. (6) *Canadian Almanac and Directory,* published annually in Toronto since 1848, lists post-offices, banks, newspapers, societies, personnel of Civil Service, academic institutions, and the legal profession, and gives information regarding federal tax rates, population, government departments, and legal matters. Current information is also provided in successive editions of (7) *Canadian Parliamentary Guide;* (8) *Canadian Who's Who;* (9) *5,000 Facts about Canada;* and (10) *Quick Canadian Facts.*

Interesting as general descriptions and interpretations are (11) Alexander Brady, *Canada* (London, 1931); (12) B. K. Sandwell, *The Canadian Peoples* (Toronto, 1941); and, by a keen foreign observer, (13) André Siegfried, *Canada, An International Power* (New York, 1949).

Historical, geographical, and biographical material is given in (14) W. S. Wallace (ed.), *Encyclopedia of Canada* (6 vols., Toronto, 1940), and (15) *Dictionary of Canadian Biography* (2 vols., 2d ed., Toronto, 1945); and in (16) L. J. Burpee (ed.), *The Oxford Encyclopædia of Canadian History,* which is Vol. XII of the series (17) Makers of Canada (ed. by W. L. Grant; London and Toronto,

1926). Still very useful for the years of its publication is (18) *Canadian Annual Review of Public Affairs* (Toronto, 1902–1938). The Canadian Institute of International Affairs, with its national office in Toronto, publishes numerous pamphlets and offers an information service.

Bibliographical information may be obtained from (19) *Canadian Index: A Guide to Canadian Periodicals and Films* (successor to *Canadian Periodical Index*), published monthly at Ottawa by the Canadian Library Association; also from (20) *The Canadian Catalogue,* comprising titles published in or about Canada or by Canadian authors, issued annually by the Toronto Public Libraries, which also published (21) *A Bibliography of Canadiana* (ed. by F. M. Staton and Marie Tremaine; 1934). A complete bibliography covering history, the social sciences, and literature is provided in the lists and cumulative indices of the Toronto quarterlies (22) *Canadian Historical Review,* and (23) *Canadian Journal of Economics and Political Science,* together with the annual survey of "Letters in Canada" published by (24) *University of Toronto Quarterly.*

Among other journals which print articles and reviews on a variety of subjects are (25) *Queen's Quarterly,* Queen's University, Kingston, Ontario; (26) *Dalhousie Review,* quarterly, Dalhousie University, Halifax, N.S.; (27) *Culture,* bilingual quarterly, Quebec; (28) *Revue de l'Université Laval,* monthly, Quebec; (29) *Canadian Review of Music and Art,* monthly, Toronto; (30) *Revue de l'Université d'Ottawa,* quarterly, Ottawa; (31) *International Journal,* quarterly, Canadian Institute of International Affairs, Toronto; (32) *Canadian Bar Review,* monthly, Ottawa; (33) *University of Toronto Law Journal,* yearly, including survey of Canadian legislation; (34) *Canadian Forum,* monthly, Toronto; (35) *Public Affairs,* Institute of Public Affairs, Dalhousie University; (36) *Saturday Night,* weekly, Toronto; (37) *Canadian Geographical Journal,* monthly, Canadian Geographical Society, Ottawa; (38) *Beaver,* illustrated quarterly, dealing especially with the North, Hudson's Bay Company, Winnipeg. The principal financial papers are (39) *Financial Post,* weekly, Toronto; (40) *Financial Times,* weekly, Montreal.

PART ONE: THE SETTING

Chapter I: The People

On the Canadian people, basic information on origins, distribution, activities, and so on may be found in (41) decennial censuses and in (42) publications of the Bureau of Statistics, Ottawa. The Census of 1941 was the eighth since Confederation. (43) A full chronological list of censuses was published in the Census of 1931, Vol. I. In the period of provincial governments before 1867, census material varies in quality and quantity. It is very good for the French régime.

Useful references on demographic trends and ethnic groups include (44) R. H. Coats (ed.), "Features of Present-Day Canada," in *Annals,* American Academy of Political and Social Science (Philadelphia), Vol. CCLIII (1947); (45) D. C. Harvey, *The Colonization of Canada* (Toronto, 1936); (46) Georges Langlois,

Histoire de la population canadienne-française (Montreal, 1935); (47) Raoul Blanchard, *L'Est du Canada français, "province de Québec"* (Montreal, 1935), and (48) *Le Centre du Canada français* (Montreal, 1947); (49) J. M. Gibbon, *Canadian Mosaic: The Making of a Northern Nation* (Toronto, 1938), a popular treatment; (50) Robert England, *The Central European Immigrant in Canada* (Toronto, 1929), and (51) *The Colonization of Western Canada* (London, 1936); (52) Marcel Giraud, *Le Métis canadien: son rôle dans l'histoire des provinces de l'ouest* (Paris, 1945); (53) M. L. Hansen and J. B. Brebner, *The Mingling of the Canadian and American Peoples* (New Haven, Conn., and Toronto, 1940); (54) R. H. Coats and M. C. MacLean, *The American-Born in Canada: A Statistical Interpretation* (Toronto, 1943); (55) W. A. Carrothers, *Emigration from the British Isles* (London, 1929); (56) Diamond Jenness (ed.), *The American Aborigines, Their Origin and Antiquity* (Toronto, 1933), and (57) *The Indians of Canada* (Ottawa, 1934).

CHAPTER II: THE GEOGRAPHY

On geography and natural resources much information may be found in the publications of the Canadian Geographical Society, including (37) and the pamphlet series (58) Geographical Aspects, on the individual provinces; in (59) publications of the Geographical Survey of Canada; and in the statistics and special articles in (1).

Individual volumes include (60) Griffith Taylor, *Canada: A Study of Cool Continental Environments and Their Effect on British and French Settlement* (London, 1947); (61) Benoît Brouillette, *Le Canada par l'image* (Montreal, 1935); (62) Geological Survey of Canada, *Geology and Economic Minerals of Canada* (Ottawa, 1947); (63) A. W. Currie, *Economic Geography of Canada* (Toronto, 1945); (64) E. S. Moore, *Elementary Geology for Canada* (Toronto, 1944); (65) C. F. Koeppe, *The Canadian Climate* (Bloomington, Ill., 1931); (66) *Atlas of Canada* (Ottawa, 1915).

The development of the Canadian North and Arctic in recent years has given rise to a rapidly increasing literature which may be followed in such journals as (67) *Polar Record,* (68) *Arctic Institute Journal,* and in bibliographies and reviews of (22), (23), (31), (38).

Only a few of many books may be listed: (69) C. A. Dawson (ed.), *The New North-West* (Toronto, 1947), includes a bibliography; (70) *Canada's New Northwest: A Study of the Present and Future Development of Mackenzie District of the Northwest Territories, Yukon Territory, and the Northern Parts of Alberta and British Columbia* (North Pacific Planning Project, Ottawa, 1948); (71) Vilhjalmur Stefansson, *Arctic Manual* (New York, 1945), and (72) *The Friendly Arctic* (new ed., New York, 1943); (73) Richard Finnie, *Canada Moves North* (Toronto, 1948); (74) Peter Freuchen, *Arctic Adventure: My Life in the Frozen North* (New York, 1935); (75) W. E. Gilbert, *Arctic Pilot: Life and Work on North Canadian Air Routes* (London and New York, 1940); (76) P. H. Godsell, *Arctic Trader: The Account of Twenty Years with the Hudson's Bay*

Company (Toronto, 1943); (77) Burnet Hershey, *The Air Future: A Primer of Aeropolitics* (New York, 1943); (78) Mrs. Tom Manning, *Igloo for the Night* (London, 1943; Toronto, 1946); (79) Jeannette Mirsky, *To the North! The Story of Arctic Exploration from Earliest Times to the Present* (New York, 1934); (80) W. P. Morrell, *The Gold Rushes* (London, 1940); (81) L. J. Burpee, *The Search for the Western Sea* (Toronto, 1935).

PART TWO: HISTORICAL BACKGROUND

On the general history of Canada there are a number of surveys, among which the most recent are: (82) D. G. Creighton, *Dominion of the North* (Boston, 1944); (83) A. R. M. Lower, *Colony to Nation* (Toronto, 1946); (84) Edgar McInnis, *Canada: A Political and Social History* (New York, 1947); (85) Jean Bruchési, *Histoire du Canada pour tous* (2 vols., Montreal, 1940–1946), and his shorter interpretation, (86) *Canada, Réalités d'hier et d'aujourd'hui* (Montreal, 1948). Narrative and less analytical is (87) G. W. Brown, *Building the Canadian Nation* (5th ed., Toronto, 1948). (88) Carl Wittke, *A History of Canada* (3d ed., New York, 1941), is by an American scholar. (89) G. M. Wrong, *The Canadians: The Story of a People* (New York, 1938), is particularly good on the French period. (90) A. L. Burt, *A Short History of Canada for Americans* (Minneapolis, 1944), was specially written for the purpose indicated by the title. The large coöperative work (91) Adam Shortt and A. G. Doughty (eds.), *Canada and Its Provinces* (23 vols., Toronto, 1914–1917), is still valuable for reference, as is also (92) *Canada and Newfoundland,* Vol. VI (1930) of *Cambridge History of the British Empire.* Readable, brief, and for the most part still authoritative is the series (93) Chronicles of Canada (ed. by G. M. Wrong and H. H. Langton; 32 vols., Toronto, 1914–1916). (94) F. X. Garneau, *Histoire du Canada* (8th ed., 1944–1946), republished in several editions since it first appeared in 1845–1848, has had a powerful influence on the development of French-Canadian national thought.

A few of the many books on special themes but covering broad periods are (95) W. P. M. Kennedy, *The Constitution of Canada: An Introduction to Its Development and Law* (Oxford, 1938); (96) Chester Martin, *Empire and Commonwealth: Studies in Governance and Self-Government in Canada* (Oxford, 1929); (97) M. Q. Innis, *An Economic History of Canada* (Toronto, 1945); (98) G. P. de T. Glazebrook, *A History of Transportation in Canada* (Toronto and New Haven, Conn., 1938), and (99) *Canadian External Relations: An Historical Study to 1914* (London and Toronto, 1942); (100) Edgar McInnis, *The Unguarded Frontier* (New York, 1942), and (101) H. L. Keenleyside, *Canada and the United States* (New York, 1929), are surveys of the relations of Canada and the United States; (102) Ralph Flenley (ed.), *Essays in Canadian History* (Toronto, 1939); (103) J. B. Brebner, *The Explorers of North America, 1492–1806* (London, 1933), and (104) *North Atlantic Triangle* (New Haven, Conn., and Toronto, 1945); (105) William Smith, *The History of the Post Office in British North America, 1639–1870* (Cambridge, Eng., and Toronto, 1920); (106) H. M.

Tory (ed.), *A History of Science in Canada* (Toronto, 1939); (107) C. W. Jefferys, *The Picture Gallery of Canadian History* (Toronto, 1942, 1945), Vol. I, to 1763, Vol. II, 1763–1830, with original drawings and reproductions which are a mine of varied and accurate information based on extensive research; (108) H. A. Logan, *Trade Unions in Canada: Their Development and Functioning* (Toronto, 1948).

Chapter III: The Founding of French Canada

On French Canada and the relations of French- and English-speaking Canada (109) Mason Wade's small volume, *The French-Canadian Outlook* (New York, 1946), the forerunner of a larger work, is specially recommended; also valuable are (110) E. C. Hughes, *French Canada in Transition* (Chicago, 1943); (111) Léon Gérin, *Le Type économique et social des Canadiens* (Montreal, 1938); (112) Edmond Turcotte, *Réflexions sur l'avenir des Canadiens français* (Montreal, 1942); (113) Benoît Brouillette, *La Pénétration du continent américain par les Canadiens français* (Montreal, 1939); (114) J.-C. Bonenfant and J.-C. Falardeau, "Cultural and Political Implications of French-Canadian Nationalism," in *Canadian Historical Association Report* (1946). Popular in tone is (115) Wilfrid Bovey, *The French Canadians Today* (Toronto, 1938). An older study by a European is (116) André Siegfried, *The Race Question in Canada* (London, 1907). (117) Gustave Lanctot (ed.), *Les Canadiens français et leur voisins du sud* (Montreal, 1941), deals with French Canada's relations with the United States. (118) Arthur Maheux's *Canadian Unity: What Keeps Us Apart?* (Quebec, 1944), and (119) *Problems of Canadian Unity* (Quebec, 1944), make a strong French-Canadian plea for common understanding between English- and French-speaking Canadians. Sharply critical of this view is the pamphlet by (120) L. A. Groulx, *Why We Are Divided* (Montreal, 1944).

On the French régime there is a large literature in both French and English. Still of outstanding importance are (121) Francis Parkman's volumes (well known by their individual titles) on France and England in North America. Later authoritative surveys include (122) G. M. Wrong, *The Rise and Fall of New France* (2 vols., Toronto, 1928); (123) W. B. Munro, *Crusaders of New France* (1918), and (124) G. M. Wrong, *The Conquest of New France* (1918), in Chronicles of America series (ed. by Allen Johnson; New Haven, Conn.); (125) M. H. Long, *A History of the Canadian People* (Toronto, 1942–), Vol. I.

Special studies, which are numerous, include the earlier volumes of (91) and (93); (126) W. B. Munro, *The Seigniorial System in Canada* (New York, 1907); (127) Emile Salone, *La Colonisation de la Nouvelle-France* (Paris, 1905); (128) Mack Eastman, *Church and State in Early Canada* (Edinburgh, 1915); (129) J.-N. Fauteux, *Essai sur l'industrie au Canada sous le régime français* (2 vols., Quebec, 1927); (130) J. B. Brebner, *New England's Outpost: Acadia before the Conquest of Canada* (New York and London, 1927); (131) D. C. Harvey, *The French Régime in Prince Edward Island* (New Haven, Conn., 1926); (132) M. I. Newbigin, *Canada: The Great River, the Lands and the Men* (London, 1927); (133) Antoine Roy, *Les Lettres, les sciences et les arts au Canada sous le régime français* (Paris, 1930); (134) Gérard Filteau, *La Naissance d'une nation* (2 vols., Montreal, 1937); (135) Gustave Lanctot, *L'Administration de la Nouvelle-France* (Paris, 1939); (136) Guy Frégault, *La Civilisation de la Nouvelle-France, 1713–1744* (Montreal, 1944).

Extensive collections of source material are available in print: (137) R. G. Thwaites (ed.), *The Jesuit Relations and Allied Documents* (73 vols., Cleveland, 1894–1907); (138) H. P. Biggar (ed.), *The Works of Samuel de Champlain* (6 vols., Champlain Society, Toronto, 1922–1936); and many others.

Chapter IV: The British North American Colonies

On the period of the American Revolution the following special studies will be found useful: (139) A. L. Burt, *The Old Province of Quebec* (Toronto and Minneapolis, 1933); (140) J. B. Brebner, *The Neutral Yankees of Nova Scotia: A Marginal Colony during the Revolutionary Years* (New York, 1937); (141) W. B. Kerr, *The Maritime Provinces of British North America and the American Revolution* (Sackville, N.B., 1941); (142) W. S. Wallace, *The United Empire Loyalists*, Vol. XIII, in (93); (143) J. J. Talman (ed.), *Loyalist Narratives from Upper Canada* (Champlain Society, Toronto, 1946). (144) G. M. Wrong, *Canada and the American Revolution: The Disruption of the First British Empire* (New York, 1935), is interestingly written, but badly balanced and inadequate on some points.

A very critical attitude on British policy towards the French Canadians after the capture of Quebec is found in (145) L. A. Groulx, *Lendemains de conquête* (Montreal, 1920). An opposing view is given in (146) Arthur Maheux, *Ton Histoire est une épopée*, Vol. I: *Nos Débuts sous le régime anglais* (Quebec, 1941), translated into English by (147) R. M. Saunders and published under the title *French Canada and Britain* (Toronto, 1942). (148) Thomas Chapais, *Cours d'histoire du Canada* (8 vols., Quebec, 1919–1923 and 1932–1934), is an intensive and scholarly work covering the period 1760 to 1867.

General political and economic developments from the Conquest to the middle of the nineteenth century are variously illustrated by (149) D. G. Creighton, *The Commercial Empire of the St. Lawrence, 1760–1850* (Toronto and New Haven, Conn., 1937); (150) H. I. Cowan, *British Emigration to British North America, 1783–1837* (Univ. of Toronto Studies, Toronto, 1928); (151) G. S. Graham, *Sea Power and British North America, 1783–1820* (Harvard Historical Studies, Harvard Univ. Press and Oxford Univ. Press, 1941); (152) A. L. Burt, *The United States, Great Britain and British North America from the Revolution to the Establishment of Peace after the War of 1812* (New Haven, Conn., and Toronto, 1940); (153) Fred Landon, *Western Ontario and the American Frontier* (Toronto, 1941); (154) D. C. Masters, *The Reciprocity Treaty of 1854: Its History, Its Relation to British Colonial and Foreign Policy and to the Development of Canadian Fiscal Autonomy* (London, 1937); (155) E. C. Guillet, *Early Life in Upper Canada* (Toronto, 1933), and (156) *The Great*

Migration: The Atlantic Crossing by Sailing-Ship since 1770 (Toronto, 1937). (157) F. L. Babcock, *Spanning the Atlantic* (New York, 1931), includes an account of Cunard's career in Nova Scotia.

Vivid, original accounts of pioneer life, published in readily available editions, are found in (158) Anna Jameson, *Winter Studies and Summer Rambles in Canada* (3 vols., London, 1838); (159) Susannah Moodie, *Roughing It in the Bush; or, Life in Canada* (2 vols., New York, 1852); (160) Catherine P. Traill, *The Backwoods of Canada, Being Letters from the Wife of an Emigrant Officer* (London, 1836).

Biographical works include (161) C. W. New, *Lord Durham* (Oxford, 1929); (162) C. B. Sissons, *Egerton Ryerson, His Life and Letters* (2 vols., Toronto, 1937–1947); (163) V. L. O. Chittick, *Thomas Chandler Haliburton ("Sam Slick"): A Study in Provincial Toryism* (New York, 1924); (164) W. L. Grant, *The Tribune of Nova Scotia: A Chronicle of Joseph Howe,* in (93); (165) William Smith, *Political Leaders in Upper Canada* (Toronto, 1931).

Dealing particularly with the rebellions of 1837 are (166) Gérard Filteau, *Histoire des patriotes* (3 vols., Montreal, 1938–1942); and (167) E. C. Guillet, *The Lives and Times of the Patriots: An Account of the Rebellion in Upper Canada, 1837–1838, and the Patriot Agitation in the United States, 1837–1842* (Toronto and New York, 1938).

Valuable on the West are (168) H. A. Innis, *The Fur Trade in Canada: An Introduction to Canadian Economic History* (New Haven, Conn., 1930); (169) A. S. Morton, *A History of the Canadian West to 1870–71* (London [1938]), and (170) *Sir George Simpson, Overseas Governor of the Hudson's Bay Company* (Toronto, 1944); (171) Douglas MacKay, *The Honourable Company: A History of the Hudson's Bay Company* (Indianapolis and New York, 1936). Popular in tone but reliable are (172) Margaret McWilliams, *Manitoba Milestones* (Toronto and London, 1928); and (173) A. S. Morton, *Under Western Skies* (Toronto, 1937).

There is a wealth of original material in the accounts of explorers and fur-traders: (174) Sir Alexander Mackenzie, *Voyages from Montreal, on the River St. Lawrence, through the Continent of North America, to the Frozen and Pacific Oceans, in the Years 1789 and 1793* (London, 1801); (175) George Vancouver, *Voyages of Discovery to the Pacific Ocean and Round the World in the Years 1790–1795* (3 vols., London, 1798); (176) Alexander Henry, *Travels and Adventures in Canada and the Indian Territories between the Years 1760 and 1776* (New York, 1809); (177) J. B. Tyrrell (ed.), *David Thompson's Narrative of His Explorations in Western America, 1784–1812* (Champlain Society, Toronto, 1916); (178) M. A. MacLeod (ed.), *The Letters of Letitia Hargrave* (Toronto, 1947), also a Champlain Society publication and of interest as containing a woman's impressions of the fur-trading West.

Chapter V: The Dominion

The Confederation period is well described generally in (82), (83), (84). Special aspects and points of view are treated in (179) D. G. Creighton, "British

North America at Confederation," Appx. 2 of (180) *Report of the Royal Commission on Dominion-Provincial Relations* (Ottawa, 1939); (181) R. G. Trotter, *Canadian Federation: Its Origins and Achievement* (Toronto, 1924); (182) L. A. Groulx, *La Confédération canadienne* (Montreal, 1918); (183) C. P. Stacey, *Canada and the British Army, 1846–1871: A Study in the Practice of Responsible Government* (London, 1936), which has a much broader significance than its title indicates; (184) W. M. Whitelaw, *The Maritimes and Canada before Confederation* (Toronto, 1934); (185) L. B. Shippee, *Canadian-American Relations, 1849–74* (New Haven, Conn., 1939). (186) Sir Joseph Pope, *Memoirs of the Right Honourable Sir John Alexander Macdonald* (2 vols., London, 1894; rev. ed., Toronto, 1930), is the authoritative work on the chief architect of Confederation. A full-length biography is in preparation by D. G. Creighton.

Railways, extremely important in this period for both political and economic development, are briefly described in (187) O. D. Skelton, *The Railway Builders,* in (93), and more fully in (98). The Canadian Pacific Railway is treated at length in (188) H. A. Innis, *A History of the Canadian Pacific Railway* (London and Toronto, 1923); and more popularly in (189) J. M. Gibbon, *Steel of Empire* (Indianapolis and New York, 1935).

For the West, besides (169) and (172), the following may be recommended as scholarly and readable: (190) F. W. Howay, *British Columbia* (Toronto, 1928); (191) C. M. MacInnes, *In the Shadow of the Rockies* (London, 1930); and, in particular, (192) G. F. G. Stanley, *The Birth of Western Canada: A History of the Riel Rebellions* (London and New York, 1936).

Valuable special studies on settlement are (193) A. S. Morton, *History of Prairie Settlement,* and (194) Chester Martin, *"Dominion Lands" Policy,* both in Canadian Frontiers of Settlement (Toronto, 1938), Vol. II; and (195) J. B. Hedges, *Building the Canadian West: The Land and Colonization Policies of the Canadian Pacific Railway* (New York, 1939).

The establishment and early history of the Royal North West (later Royal Canadian) Mounted Police are described in (196) R. C. Fetherstonhaugh, *The Royal Canadian Mounted Police* (New York, 1938); and (197) Sir Cecil E. Denny, *The Law Marches West* (Toronto, 1939).

Chapter VI: The Twentieth Century

The emergence of Canada as a nation is treated with special reference to constitutional background in (95), (96), and (198) R. M. Dawson, *The Development of Dominion Status, 1900–1936* (Oxford, 1937). The life and work of Sir Wilfrid Laurier are described in biographies by (199) O. D. Skelton (2 vols., Toronto, 1921); (200) J. W. Dafoe (Toronto, 1922); and (201) J. S. Willison (Toronto, 1926), Vol. XI of (17). (202) J. W. Dafoe, *Clifford Sifton in Relation to His Times* (Toronto, 1931), is an important study of one of Laurier's colleagues especially connected with the West. Of value as a source is (203) Henry Borden (ed.), *Robert Laird Borden: His Memoirs* (2 vols., Toronto, 1938). (204) Robert Rumilly, *Histoire de la province de Québec* (23 vols., Montreal

[1940–1948?]), is chronological and anecdotal but useful in the absence of better works. A detailed analysis of the important election of 1911 is given in (205) L. E. Ellis, *Reciprocity, 1911: A Study in Canadian-American Relations* (New Haven, Conn., and Toronto, 1939).

Canada's military effort in the First World War is described by (206) F. H. Underhill in *The Empire at War* (ed. by Sir Charles Lucas; 5 vols., London, 1921–1926), Vol. II. A popular contemporary account still useful is (207) J. C. Hopkins, *Canada at War: A Record of Heroism and Achievement, 1914–18* (Toronto, 1919); (208) A. F. Duguid, *Official History of the Canadian Forces in the Great War, 1914–19* (one vol. pub.; Ottawa, 1938), is detailed and authoritative. Excellent on the conscription issue is (209) E. H. Armstrong, *The Crisis of Quebec, 1914–18* (New York, 1937).

Useful on the inter-war period, besides the general works cited, are (210) Chester Martin (ed.), *Canada in Peace and War* (Toronto, 1941); (211) H. S. Patton, *Grain Growers' Coöperation in Western Canada* (Cambridge, Mass., 1928); (212) H. A. Innis and A. F. W. Plumptre (eds.), *The Canadian Economy and Its Problems* (Toronto, 1934). (213) F. R. Scott, *Canada Today* (Toronto, 1939); (214) Herbert Marshall *et al., Canadian-American Industry: A Study in International Investment* (New Haven, Conn., and Toronto, 1936); and in particular the following two parts of (180): (215) Book I, "Canada, 1867–1939," and (216) W. A. Mackintosh, "The Economic Background of Dominion-Provincial Relations," Appx. 3.

The Second World War is still too close for definitive studies to be available. (217) C. P. Stacey, *The Canadian Army, 1939–1945: An Official Historical Summary* (Ottawa, 1948), is an excellent single volume. Less satisfactory, though vividly written, are (218) *The R.C.A.F. Overseas: The First Four Years* (Toronto, 1944), and (219) *The Fifth Year* (Toronto, 1945); a third volume is in preparation. Volumes on the Canadian navy by G. C. Tucker and Joseph Schull are in preparation.

PART THREE: THE ECONOMY

CHAPTER VII: FUNDAMENTAL AND HISTORIC ELEMENTS

CHAPTER X: TRENDS AND STRUCTURE OF THE ECONOMY

Economic trends and the development of the national economy are illustrated in (63), (97), (98), (168), (180), and in special volumes: (220) H. A. Innis, *The Cod Fisheries: The History of an International Economy* (New Haven, Conn., 1940), and (221) *Problems of Staple Production in Canada* (Toronto, 1933); (222) A. W. Currie, *Canadian Economic Development* (Toronto, 1942); (223) W. J. A. Donald, *The Canadian Iron and Steel Industry* (Boston and New York, 1915); (224) A. R. M. Lower, *The North American Assault on the Canadian Forest: A History of the Lumber Trade between Canada and the United States* (Toronto, 1938); (225) J. D. B. Harrison, *Economic Aspects of the Forests and Forest Industry in Canada* (Ottawa, 1938); (226) A. R. M. Lower, *Settle-*

ment and the Forest Frontier in Eastern Canada, and H. A. Innis, *Settlement and the Mining Frontier* (1936), Vol. IX of (245); (227) D. A. MacGibbon, *The Canadian Grain Trade* (Toronto, 1932); (228) A. F. W. Plumptre, *Central Banking in the British Dominions* (Toronto, 1940); (229) B. F. Townsley, *Mine-Finders: The History and Romance of Canadian Mineral Discoveries* (Toronto, 1935); (230) V. C. Fowke, *Canadian Agricultural Policy: The Historical Pattern* (Toronto, 1946); (231) B. H. Beckhart, *The Banking System of Canada* (New York, 1929); (232) W. T. Easterbrook, *Farm Credit in Canada* (Toronto, 1938); (233) L. G. Reynolds, *The Control of Competition in Canada* (Cambridge, Mass., 1940); (234) Herbert Heaton, *A History of Trade and Commerce, with Special Reference to Canada* (Toronto, 1939); (235) O. J. McDiarmid, *Commercial Policy in the Canadian Economy* (Cambridge, Mass., 1946).

Chapter VIII: Eastern Canada

Chapter IX: Western Canada

Regional economic interests are referred to in items (1), (60), (62), (63), and (97). Other special references of importance are (236) S. E. Saunders, *Studies in the Economy of the Maritime Provinces* (Toronto, 1939); (237) Nova Scotia, *Report by the Royal Commission, Provincial Economic Inquiry* (Halifax, 1934); (238) *Newfoundland Royal Commission, 1933, Report* (London, 1933); (239) R. F. Grant, *The Canadian Atlantic Fishery* (Toronto, 1934); (240) G. V. Haythorne and L. C. Marsh, *Land and Labour: A Social Survey of Agriculture and the Farm Labour Market in Central Canada* (Oxford, 1941); (241) Esdras Minville, *Notre milieu: aperçu général sur la province de Québec* (Montreal [1942]); (242) G. E. Britnell, *The Wheat Economy* (Toronto, 1939); (243) W. A. Carrothers, *The British Columbia Fisheries* (Toronto, 1941); (244) F. D. Mulholland, *The Forest Resources of British Columbia* (Victoria, B.C., 1937).

Among the volumes of the excellent series (245) Canadian Frontiers of Settlement (ed. by W. A. Mackintosh and W. L. G. Joerg; Toronto) are (246) W. A. Mackintosh, *Economic Problems of the Prairie Provinces* (1935), Vol. IV; (247) C. A. Dawson and R. W. Murchie, *The Settlement of the Peace River Country* (1934), Vol. VI; (248) A. R. M. Lower, *Settlement and the Forest Frontier in Eastern Canada,* and H. A. Innis, *Settlement and the Mining Frontier* (1936), Vol. IX.

Newfoundland is authoritatively described in (249) R. A. MacKay (ed.), *Newfoundland: Economic, Diplomatic and Strategic Studies* (Toronto, 1946). Other references are (250) T. G. Taylor, *Newfoundland: A Study of Settlement* (Toronto, 1946); (251) R. H. Tait, *Newfoundland* (New York, 1939); (252) A. O. Shelton, *Newfoundland, Our North Door Neighbor* (New York, 1941); (253) Thomas Lodge, *Dictatorship in Newfoundland* (London, 1939); (254) J. R. Smallwood (ed.), *The Book of Newfoundland* (2 vols., St. John's, 1937).

PART FOUR: THE POLITICAL AND CONSTITUTIONAL SCENE

CHAPTER XI: THE FEDERAL CONSTITUTION

CHAPTER XII: THE MACHINERY OF GOVERNMENT

The Canadian system of government in general is described in (255) R. M. Dawson, *The Government of Canada* (Toronto, 1947); (256) H. M. Clokie, *Canadian Government and Politics* (Toronto, 1944); (257) J. A. Corry, *Democratic Government and Politics* (Toronto, 1946); and comparatively in (258) Alexander Brady, *Democracy in the Dominions* (Toronto, 1948). (259) George W. Brown, *Canadian Democracy in Action* (Toronto, 1945), is a brief outline. Current bibliographies and valuable articles appear in (23) and (33). Proceedings in the Dominion Parliament are reported in the printed (260) Debates of the Senate and House of Commons, commonly known as *Hansard.*

Special constitutional developments and problems are treated in (261) W. F. O'Connor, *Report on the British North America Act,* Senate of Canada (Ottawa, 1939), a criticism of the judicial interpretation of the Canadian constitution; (262) W. P. M. Kennedy, *Some Aspects of the Theories and Workings of Constitutional Law* (New York, 1931); (263) R. A. MacKay, *The Unreformed Senate of Canada* (Oxford, 1926); (264) E. A. Forsey, *The Royal Power of Dissolution of Parliament in the British Commonwealth* (Oxford, 1943); (265) R. M. Dawson, *The Civil Service of Canada* (London, 1939). A useful study of federalism which includes Canada is (266) K. C. Wheare, *Federal Government* (London, 1946). Constitutional decisions of the Privy Council are brought together in (267) E. R. Cameron, *The Canadian Constitution as Interpreted by the Judicial Committee of the Privy Council* (2 vols., Winnipeg, 1915; Toronto, 1930); and (268) C. P. Plaxton, *Canadian Constitutional Decisions* (Ottawa, 1939). The standard works on parliamentary practice and procedure are (269) Sir John G. Bourinot, *Parliamentary Procedure and Practice in the Dominion of Canada* (4th ed., Toronto, 1916); and (270) Arthur Beauchesne, *Rules and Forms of the House of Commons of Canada* (3d ed., Toronto, 1943).

Numerous references are available on Dominion-provincial relations, the central problem of Canadian federalism. Extremely valuable is (180), with its appended studies, commonly known as *The Rowell-Sirois Report.* A useful general survey is (271) Wilfrid Eggleston, *The Road to Nationhood: A Chronicle of Dominion-Provincial Relations* (Oxford, 1946). See also (272) Maurice Ollivier, *Problems of Canadian Sovereignty: From the British North America Act, 1867, to the Statute of Westminster, 1931* (Toronto, 1945); (273) J. A. Maxwell, *Federal Subsidies to the Provincial Governments in Canada* (Cambridge, Mass., 1937); (274) Luella Gettys, *The Administration of Canadian Constitutional Grants* (Chicago, 1938).

Chapter XIII: Local Government

The literature is scattered and inadequate. Chapters on local government are included in (256), (257), (258), (259), and (275) W. B. Munro, *American Influences on Canadian Government* (Toronto, 1929). Basic statistical information and occasional articles are found in (1). The chief journals published on local affairs are (276) *Municipal Review of Canada,* monthly, Lachute, Quebec; and (277) *Municipal World* (organ of Ontario Municipal Association since 1894), monthly, St. Thomas.

Chapter XIV: Political Parties and Ideas

Party organization and related topics are well treated in (255), (256), (257), and (258). (278) James Bryce, in *Modern Democracies* (2 vols., New York, 1921), took Canada as one of his examples and has some interesting discussion based mainly upon observations before 1914. A brief analysis of the Canadian political picture on the eve of the Second World War is given in (213), while (279) W. H. Chamberlin, *Canada, Today and Tomorrow* (Boston, 1942), gives the impressions of a shrewd journalist during the war. Useful in throwing light on groups and parties are (108); (280) L. A. Wood, *A History of Farmers' Movements in Canada* (Toronto, 1924); (281) S. D. Clark, *The Canadian Manufacturers' Association* (Toronto, 1939); (282) N. J. Ware and H. A. Logan, *Labor in Canadian-American Relations* (ed. by H. A. Innis; Toronto and New Haven, Conn., 1937); (283) P. F. Sharp, *The Agrarian Revolt in Western Canada: A Survey Showing American Parallels* (Minneapolis, 1948); (284) W. L. Morton, *The Progressive Party in Canada* (Toronto, 1949). The annual volumes of (7) give full lists of members of Parliament, Dominion and provincial, with biographical notes and statistics on elections.

Chapter XV: The State and Economic Life

On the state and economic life, (98) is useful for railways. (180) has excellent material, and in particular (285) J. A. Corry, *The Growth of Government Activities since Confederation* (Ottawa, 1939), which is No. 2 of its appended mimeographed studies. (286) W. R. Plewman, *Adam Beck and the Ontario Hydro* (Toronto, 1947), tells the story of an outstanding experiment in government ownership. See also (287) John Willis, *Canadian Boards at Work* (Toronto, 1941); (288) W. L. M. King, *Industry and Humanity* (Toronto, 1935). Information on combines is contained in (289) *Reports,* Commissioner of the Combines Investigation Act, issued by the Department of Justice.

PART FIVE: SOCIAL AND CULTURAL INSTITUTIONS

Chapter XVII: The Social Services

See (290) H. M. Cassidy, *Social Security and Reconstruction in Canada* (Toronto, 1943), and (291) *Public Health and Welfare Reorganization* (Toronto,

1945); (292) R. D. Defries (ed.), *The Development of Public Health in Canada* (Toronto, 1940); (293) M. K. Strong, *Public Welfare Administration in Canada* (Chicago, 1930); (294) Esdras Minville, "Labour Legislation and Social Services in the Province of Quebec"; (295) A. E. Grauer, "Public Assistance and Social Insurance." The last two are appendices 5 and 6 of (180). Current information is given in (296) *Canadian Welfare* (Ottawa), published eight times a year by the Canadian Welfare Council.

Chapter XVIII: The Cultural Pattern

Cultural development and activity is too large a topic to permit of more than a narrow selection among the materials available. Vol. XII of (91) is a useful survey up to 1912. (297) Vincent Massey, *On Being Canadian* (Toronto, 1948); and (298) Bruce Hutchison, *The Unknown Country: Canada and Her People* (Toronto, 1948), are efforts by well-known Canadians to catch the spirit of the country. (299) J. D. Robins (ed.), *A Pocketful of Canada* (Toronto, 1946), attempts the same thing in a collection of excerpts. (300) L. A. Pierce, *A Canadian People* (Toronto, 1945), is provocative but stimulating and sincere. (301) *French-Canadian Backgrounds* (Toronto, 1940), is a symposium by four well-known authorities: Olivier Maurault, Henri Saint-Denis, Marius Barbeau, L.-M. Gouin.

Canadian Literature

Among the general works are (302) R. P. Baker, *A History of English-Canadian Literature to the Confederation: Its Relation to the Literature of Great Britain and the United States* (Cambridge, Mass., 1920), excellent for the period covered; (303) Pelham Edgar, "English-Canadian Literature," in *Cambridge History of English Literature* (London and Cambridge, 1916), Vol. XIV; (304) L. A. Pierce, *An Outline of Canadian Literature (French and English)* (Toronto, 1927); (305) Camille Roy, *Essais sur la littérature canadienne* (Montreal, 1925), and (306) *Histoire de la littérature canadienne* (Quebec, 1930); (307) I. F. Fraser, *The Spirit of French Canada: A Study of the Literature* (New York, 1939), including bibliography. (308) Séraphin Marion, *Les Lettres canadiennes d'autrefois* (5 vols., Ottawa, 1939–1947), brings out some neglected historic trends; (309) J. D. Logan and D. G. French, *Highways of Canadian Literature: A Synoptic Introduction to the Literary History of Canada (English) from 1760 to 1924* (Toronto, 1924), is ambitious in scope but uncritical. (310) Archibald MacMechan, *Head-Waters of Canadian Literature* (Toronto, 1924), is interesting and well written. The stimulating and at times provocative collection of essays, (311) W. A. Deacon, *Poteen* (Ottawa, 1930), includes a large section on Canadian literature.

Useful for French-Canadian poetry are (312) J. M. Turnbull, *Essential Traits of French-Canadian Poetry* (Toronto, 1938); (313) Jules Fournier and Olivar Asselin (comps.), *Anthologie des poètes canadiens* (3d ed., Montreal, 1933); (314) Guy Sylvestre, *Anthologie de la poésie canadienne d'expression fran-*

çaise (Montreal, 1942). Excellent on English-Canadian poetry is the anthology (315) A. J. M. Smith, *The Book of Canadian Poetry* (Chicago, 1948), which contains a very valuable introduction and an annotated bibliography. (316) E. K. Brown, *On Canadian Poetry* (Toronto, 1944), is the work of an able academic critic.

Very useful small volumes on individual authors are found in the series (317) Makers of Canadian Literature (ed. by L. A. Pierce and Victor Morin; Toronto). Indispensable for recent developments is the annual survey of "Letters in Canada" in (24), which includes a full bibliography and critical essays.

Of the many literary works based on Canadian history or contemporary life only a few can be mentioned. (In general only one title is given for each author, with the most recent date of publication, though for some the date of a first edition has been given as well.) Two works which may now fairly be termed classics have appeared in numerous editions since they were first published: (318) Stephen Leacock's gentle and humorous satire of small-town Ontario, *Sunshine Sketches of a Little Town* (London, 1912); and (319) Louis Hémon's story of French-Canadian habitant life, *Maria Chapdelaine* (Montreal, 1916). The following have a setting in the French régime: (320) Willa Cather, *Shadows on the Rock* (New York, 1946); (321) F. D. McDowell, *The Champlain Road* (Toronto, 1949); (322) Philip Child, *The Village of Souls* (Toronto, 1948); (323) William Kirby, *The Golden Dog* (New York, 1878; Toronto, 1946), a classic which some will find dull reading. Notable also for this period is (324) E. J. Pratt, *Brébeuf and His Brethren* (Toronto, 1940; Detroit, 1942), a poem on the Jesuit martyrs.

For the period of the eighteenth century are (325) K. L. Roberts, *Northwest Passage* (Garden City, N.Y., 1937), a vivid story of action in the Seven Years' War; (326) T. H. Raddall, *His Majesty's Yankees* (Garden City, N.Y., 1942), on Nova Scotia; (327) M. B. Dunham, *The Trail of the Conestoga* (Toronto, 1942), an episode in the migration to Canada after the American Revolution.

For the nineteenth century (328) T. C. Haliburton, *The Clockmaker; or, The Sayings and Doings of Samuel Slick, of Slickville,* not only throws light on the Nova Scotia of a century ago, but is a landmark in the history of humorous writing. It appeared serially in the *Novascotian,* 1835–1836 (first series); London, 1838 (second series); London, 1840 (third series). For the same period in Upper Canada (329) Patrick Slater (John Mitchell), *The Yellow Briar: A Story of the Irish on the Canadian Countryside* (Toronto, 1945), is charmingly written and authentic in tone.

For the twentieth century, selection is made even more difficult by the increasing number of titles. (330) F. P. Grove, *Over Prairie Trails* (Toronto, 1929), and (331) *Fruits of the Earth* (Toronto, 1933), have a western setting; as have also (332) W. O. Mitchell, *Who Has Seen the Wind?* (Boston, 1947); (333) L. G. Salverson, *The Viking Heart* (Toronto, 1947), based on the story of Icelandic settlement in Manitoba; and (334) Irene Baird, *Waste Heritage* (New York, 1939), which has the depression of the 'thirties as a background. (335) Hugh MacLennan, *Barometer Rising* (Toronto, 1942), centres around the Halifax explosion in the First World War. (336) W. R. Bird, *Here Stays Good Yorkshire* (Toronto, 1945), is set in Nova Scotia; (337) Ringuet (pseud.), *Trente Arpents* (Paris, 1939), in rural Quebec; (338) Gabrielle Roy, *Bonheur d'occasion* (Montreal, 1945); trans. (339) *The Tin Flute* (New York, 1947), in Montreal.

Among the French-Canadian writers who have attempted with distinction to catch the spirit and characteristics of French Canada are (340) F. A. Savard, *Menaud, maître-draveur* (Montreal, 1944); trans. (341) *Boss of the River* (Toronto, 1947); (342) Robert Charbonneau, *Ils posséderont la terre* (Montreal, 1941); and (343) Germaine Guèvremont, *Marie-Didace* (Montreal, 1947); (344) Roger Lemelin, *Les Plouffe* (Quebec, 1948), the story of a French-Canadian family in the Second World War. (345) Ralph Allen, *Home Made Banners* (Toronto, 1946); and (346) Hugh Garner, *Storm Below* (Toronto, 1949), deal with the army and navy, respectively, in the Second World War.

Autobiographical rather than fictional are (347) L. G. Salverson, *Confessions of an Immigrant's Daughter* (Montreal, 1949); (348) N. L. McClung, *Clearing in the West* (Toronto, 1935), and (349) *The Stream Runs Fast* (Toronto, 1945); (350) E. M. Richardson, *We Keep a Light* (Toronto, 1945), describes the life of a lighthouse-keeper on the Atlantic Coast.

CANADIAN ART

The most useful general books are (351) *The Development of Painting in Canada, 1665–1945* (National Gallery of Canada, Toronto, 1945), with bibliography and biographical notes; (352) William Colgate, *Canadian Art: Its Origin and Development* (foreword by C. W. Jefferys; Toronto, 1943); (353) Graham McInnes, *A Short History of Canadian Art* (Toronto, 1939); (354) Maurice Gagnon, *Peinture canadienne* (Montreal, 1945); (355) D. W. Buchanan (ed.), *Canadian Painters*. Vol. I, *From Paul Kane to the Group of Seven* (Oxford, 1945).

(356) A. H. Robson, *Canadian Landscape Painters* (Toronto, 1932), has a number of illustrations. (357) F. B. Housser, *A Canadian Art Movement* (Toronto, 1926), is on the Group of Seven. A number of small brochures have appeared in (358) Canadian Art Series (Toronto). (359) *Growing Pains: The Autobiography of Emily Carr* (foreword by Ira Dilworth; Toronto, 1946), is an illuminating book on a Canadian artist of much originality. Reproductions of a number of outstanding and typical Canadian paintings may be obtained through the National Gallery of Canada, Ottawa, or the Toronto Art Gallery.

A few miscellaneous titles may also be included: (360) Ramsay Traquair, *The Old Silver of Quebec* (Toronto, 1940), and (361) *The Old Architecture of Quebec: A Study of the Buildings Created in New France from the Earliest Explorers to the Middle of the Nineteenth Century* (Toronto, 1947); (362) Harry Piers and D. C. MacKay, *Master Goldsmiths and Silversmiths of Nova Scotia* (Halifax, 1948); (363) Helen Creighton (ed.), *Songs and Ballads from Nova Scotia* (Bungay, Eng., 1932). A popular and appreciative account of French-Canadian arts and crafts is included in (115). The numerous writings of Marius Barbeau have touched almost every aspect of French-Canadian culture. See also (364) *Canada from Sea to Sea* (Canadian Information Service, Ottawa, 1947); (365) *The Arts in Canada and the Film* (National Film Board, Ottawa, 1945); (366) *Catalogue of Canadian Composers* (Canadian Broadcasting Corp., 1947). The journals (29), (34), and (36) are useful for contemporary developments.

Chapter XIX: Education

The volumes on the individual provinces in (91) are very useful; also chap. xxiii in (92). An authoritative life of the founder of the Ontario school system, which influenced other provinces, especially in the West, is found in (162); and (1), (6), and (14) give miscellaneous factual information. Special references include (367) *Trends in Education, 1944: A Survey of Current Educational Developments* (Toronto, 1944), prepared by the Educational Policies Committee of the Canada and Newfoundland Education Association; (368) J. C. Miller, *National Government and Education in Federated Democracies, Dominion of Canada* (Philadelphia, 1940); (369) G. M. Weir, *The Separate School Question in Canada* (Toronto, 1934); (370) C. B. Sissons, *Bi-lingual Schools in Canada* (London, 1917); (371) J. B. Brebner, *Scholarship for Canada: The Function of Graduate Studies* (Ottawa, 1945); (372) Watson Kirkconnell and A. S. P. Woodhouse (eds.), *The Humanities in Canada* (Humanities Research Council of Canada, 1947). There are a number of histories of individual universities, colleges, and schools. Current information is given in (373) *Canadian Education,* published quarterly by the Canadian Education Association; and (374) *Canada Educational Directory and Year Book,* Toronto. Publications issued or sponsored by the Canadian Association for Adult Education should also be consulted.

Chapter XX: Religion

Religion and the churches in Canada have not received adequate scholarly treatment, in spite of the importance of the subject. Vol. XIII of (91) has a partial survey up to 1912, but it is not well balanced or interpretative. (153), (162), the last section of (102), and a number of references for chap. iii are useful. (375) S. D. Clark, *Church and Sect in Canada* (Toronto, 1948), is a thorough work of research on the Protestant churches from a sociological point of view. See also (376) C. E. Silcox, *Church Union in Canada* (New York, 1933).

Only a few titles may be chosen on individual churches and areas: (377) I. F. Mackinnon, *Settlements and Churches in Nova Scotia, 1749–1776* (Montreal, 1930); (378) C. W. Vernon, *The Old Church in the New Dominion* (London, 1929), on the Church of England in Canada; (379) W. S. Reid, *The Church of Scotland in Lower Canada* (Toronto, 1936); (380) J. E. Sanderson, *The First Century of Methodism in Canada* (2 vols., Toronto, 1910); (381) A. H. Gosselin, *L'Église du Canada* (4 vols., Quebec, 1911–1917); (382) A. G. Morice, *History of the Catholic Church in Western Canada* (2 vols., Toronto, 1910); (383) J. H.

Riddell, *Methodism in the Middle West* (Toronto, 1946); (384) L. A. Pierce, *The Chronicle of a Century, 1829–1929: The Record of One Hundred Years of Progress in the Publishing Concerns of the Methodist, Presbyterian, and Congregational Churches in Canada* (Toronto, 1929).

PART SIX: EXTERNAL RELATIONS

Chapter XXI: Historic Factors

The general histories and other titles already cited are useful: (99), (100), (152), (154), (185), (203), (205). The journals (3) and (31) are indispensable for current developments, as is also the quarterly (385) *Round Table,* London. Two volumes in the important series (386) Canada in World Affairs (Toronto) have been published: (387) F. H. Soward *et al., The Pre-War Years* (1941), and (388) R. M. Dawson (ed.), *Two Years of War, 1939–41* (1943); others are in preparation.

British Commonwealth relations in general up to 1939 are treated in (389) W. K. Hancock, *Survey of British Commonwealth Affairs.* Vol. I, *Problems of Nationality, 1918–1936* (Oxford, 1937); Vol. II, *Problems of Economic Policy, 1918–1939* (London, 1940–1942); (390) H. V. Hodson (ed.), *The British Commonwealth and the Future* (London, 1939); (391) G. M. Carter, *The British Commonwealth and International Security, 1919–1939* (Toronto, 1947); (392) H. G. Skilling, *Canadian Representation Abroad, from Agency to Embassy* (Toronto, 1945), traces the rise of the diplomatic service. No adequate study of the effects of the recent war and post-war period on Commonwealth relations has yet been made, but information of interest is found in (393) W. Y. Elliott and H. D. Hall (eds.), *The British Commonwealth at War* (New York, 1943); and (394) J. G. Allen, *Editorial Opinion in the Contemporary British Commonwealth and Empire* (Boulder, Colo., 1946).

Chapter XXII: The North American Triangle

The historic relations of Canada and the United States are treated on an extensive scale in the 25-volume series (395) Relations of Canada and the United States, published under the direction of the Carnegie Endowment for International Peace, J. T. Shotwell, director. Volumes already cited include: (104), which ends the series and presents a synthesis and interpretation, (53), (54), (117), (152), (153). See also (396) P. E. Corbett, *The Settlement of Canadian-American Disputes* (New Haven, Conn., 1937). On the International Joint Commission see (397) C. J. Chacko, *The International Joint Commission between the United States of America and the Dominion of Canada* (New York, 1932); and (398) R. A. MacKay, "The International Joint Commission between the United States and Canada," *American Journal of International Law,* Vol. XXII (1928). (399) George W. Brown, *The Growth of Peaceful Settlement between Canada and the United States;* and (400) F. H. Soward and A. M. Macaulay, *Canada and the Pan American System* (Toronto, 1948), are published in the Contemporary Affairs Series of the Canadian Institute of International Affairs.

Canada's relations in the Pacific are treated in (401) C. J. Woodsworth, *Canada and the Orient* (Toronto, 1941); (402) A. R. M. Lower, *Canada and the Far East, 1940* (1940), in the series, Institute of Pacific Relations Inquiry (New York).

Still of interest, though outmoded in places by events, are (403) A. B. Corey, R. G. Trotter, and W. W. MacLaren (eds.), *Conferences on Canadian-American Affairs, 1935–1941* (4 vols., Boston, 1936–1941); (404) R. A. MacKay and E. B. Rogers, *Canada Looks Abroad* (Oxford, 1938); (405) C. P. Stacey, *The Military Problems of Canada* (Toronto, 1940). An important special topic is dealt with in (406) M. E. Nichols, *CP—The Story of the Canadian Press* (Toronto, 1948), and (407) Carlton McNaught, *Canada Gets the News* (Toronto, 1940).

Chapter XXIII: Trade and the World Economy

The economic aspects of Canada's external relations are dealt with in many of the references already cited for chapters vii–x, and also in scattered articles and documents not brought together in readily accessible form, such as the publications of the Bank of Canada and other organizations, public and private. Authoritative and valuable is (408) C. D. Blyth, *The Canadian Balance of International Payments, 1926–1948* (Ottawa, 1949). (409) J. D. Gibson (ed.), *Canada's Economy in a Changing World* (Toronto, 1948), is a symposium sponsored by the Canadian Institute of International Affairs. Early war-time developments are described in (410) J. F. Parkinson (ed.), *Canadian War Economics* (Toronto, 1941); and (411) A. F. W. Plumptre, *Mobilizing Canada's Resources for War* (Toronto, 1941). See also (412) D. R. Annett, *British Imperial Preference in Canadian Commercial Policy* (Toronto, 1948).

Chapter XXIV: International Organization

For the period before 1939 see (413) G. P. de T. Glazebrook, *Canada at the Paris Peace Conference* (London and Toronto, 1942); (414) F. H. Soward, *Canada and the League of Nations,* International Conciliation Series, No. 238 (New York, 1932); (415) W. E. Armstrong, *Canada and the League of Nations: The Problem of Peace* (Geneva, 1930); and critically in (416) S. M. Eastman, *Canada at Geneva: An Historical Survey and Its Lessons,* Canadian Institute of International Affairs, Contemporary Affairs Series, No. 20 (Toronto, 1946). See also (417) W. A. Riddell, *World Security by Conference* (Toronto, 1947); and (418) J.-P. Després, *Le Canada et l'Organisation Internationale du Travail* (Montreal, 1947).

Canada's participation in international affairs during the 1940's and especially in the United Nations Organization can be followed adequately only in the publications of the Department of External Affairs and in articles and books currently listed in the quarterly bibliographies (22) and (31). See in particular (3); and the annual volumes (419) on Canada and the United Nations published by the Department of External Affairs.

INDEX

Index

ACKNOWLEDGEMENT

THE GENERAL EDITOR *desires to record his sincere appreciation of the splendid coöperation he has received from the staff of the University of California Press in the editing of the manuscript and the making of this book. In particular he is indebted to Mr. Harold A. Small, the Editor of the Press; to Mr Amadeo R. Tommasini, Designer and Production Manager; and to Miss Genevieve Rogers for editorial assistance.*